Contemporary Corrections

G. Larry Mays
New Mexico State University

L. Thomas Winfree
New Mexico State University

Wadsworth Publishing Company

I⊤P® An International Thomson Publishing Company

Belmont, CA · Albany, NY · Bonn · Boston · Cincinnati · Detroit · Johannesburg · London
Madrid · Melbourne · Mexico City · New York · Paris · Singapore · Tokyo · Toronto · Washington

MAY 1 4 1996

Criminal Justice Editor: Sabra Horne
Development Editor: Dan Alpert
Project Development Editor: Claire Masson
Marketing Manager: Mike Dew
Project Manager: Debby Kramer
Print Buyer: Karen Hunt
Permissions Editor: Veronica Oliva
Production: Melanie Field, Strawberry Field Publishing

Designer: Harry Voigt
Photo Research: Linda Rill
Copy Editor: Erin Milnes
Illustrator: Joan Carol
Cover: Stephen Rapley
Compositor: TBH Typecast, Inc.
Printer: R. R. Donnelley & Sons, Inc./Crawfordsville
Cover Printer: Phoenix Color Corp.

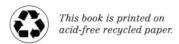

*This book is printed on
acid-free recycled paper.*

Printed in the United States of America
1   2   3   4   5   6   7   8   9   10

For more information, contact Wadsworth Publishing Company, 10 Davis Drive, Belmont, CA 94002, or
electronically at http://www. thomson.com/wadsworth.html

International Thomson Publishing Europe
Berkshire House 168–173
High Holborn
London, WC1V 7AA, England

Thomas Nelson Australia
102 Dodds Street
South Melbourne 3205
Victoria, Australia

Nelson Canada
1120 Birchmount Road
Scarborough, Ontario
Canada M1K 5G4

International Thomson Publishing GmbH
Königswinterer Strasse 418
53227 Bonn, Germany

International Thomson Editores
Campos Eliseos 385, Piso 7
Col. Polanco
11560 México D.F. México

International Thomson Publishing Asia
221 Henderson Road
#05–10 Henderson Building
Singapore 0315

International Thomson Publishing Japan
Hirakawacho Kyowa Building, 3F
2–2–1 Hirakawacho
Chiyoda-ku, Tokyo 102, Japan

International Thomson Publishing Southern Africa
Building 18, Constantia Park
240 Old Pretoria Road
Halfway House, 1685 South Africa

Library of Congress Cataloging-in-Publication Data
Mays, G. Larry.
    Contemporary corrections / G. Larry Mays, L. Thomas Winfree.
        p.   cm.
    Includes bibliographical references and index.
    ISBN 0-534-54216-6
    1. Corrections.   2. Corrections—United States.   I. Winfree,
Latham T. (Latham Thomas).   II. Title.
HV8665.M39   1997
365—dc21   97-44689

Brief Contents

Preface xvii

1 Introduction 1
2 A Brief History of Punishments and Corrections 31
3 Sentencing and Criminal Sanctions 64
4 Jails and Local Detention Facilities 102
5 Prison Systems 142
6 Inmates 187
7 Probation and Parole 230
8 Community Corrections 273
9 Administration of Corrections Programs 311
10 Correctional Law and Inmate Litigation 343
11 Unresolved Issues and the Future of Corrections 373

Glossary 411
References 430
Credits 453
Index 454

Contents

Preface   xvii

1   Introduction   1

What Is "Corrections"?   1
Philosophies of Punishment   2
  Retribution   3
  Deterrence   5
  Rehabilitation   5
  Isolation   7
  Incapacitation   7
  Reintegration   8
  Restitution   9
  Restoration   9
Attitudes Toward Corrections   10
The Role of Criminological Theory   12
  From Free Will to Determinism   13
  Crime, Criminals, and Deterministic Forces   14
  Behavior Modification   16
  Crime, Criminals, and Social Forces   18
  Reviewing Criminological Theory   22
Corrections Programs   25
Conclusion   27
Critical Review Questions   28
Recommended Readings   28
Key Terms   29
Notes   29

2 A Brief History of Punishments and Corrections   31

Introduction   31
Early History   32
Crime and Punishment in Prehistoric Context   32
Babylonian and Judaic Views on Punishment   34
Greek and Roman Laws   35
The Law of Europe in the Middle Ages   38
European Law in the Fifteenth Through Seventeenth Centuries   40
The Age of Enlightenment, the State, and Criminal Sanctions   42
   Montesquieu   42
   Cesare Beccaria   43
Prison Reform and Penitentiaries   43
The Pennsylvania System versus the New York System   44
   Eastern Penitentiary and the Pennsylvania System   45
   The Auburn System   47
Penitentiary Reform in the Nineteenth Century   50
   Alternatives to Prison   50
   Foreign Opponents and Proponents   52
   The Cincinnati Meeting of the National Prison Association   53
   Enoch Wines   53
   Zebulon Brockway   54
From the Rehabilitative Ideal to the Justice Model   56
   From the Medical Model to Rehabilitation   57
   The "Just Deserts" or Justice Model of Punishment   57
   Implications for Contemporary Corrections   59
Conclusion   60
Critical Review Questions   61
Recommended Readings   61
Key Terms   62
Notes   62

3 Sentencing and Criminal Sanctions   64

Introduction   64
Sentencing: Who Decides?   65
   The Legislative Role   65
   The Role of Juries   70
   The Role of Judges   70

Sentencing: What Are the Choices?   71
  Probation   71
  Fines and Forfeitures   74
  Misdemeanor Sentences   75
  Felony Sentences   76
  The Death Penalty   77
Sentencing: How Are Decisions Made?   83
  Concurrent Sentences   84
  Consecutive Sentences   84
  Plea Bargaining   84
Sentencing Strategies   86
  Indeterminate Sentences   86
  Determinate Sentences   86
  "Guided" Sentences   87
  Mandatory Sentences   88
After the Verdict   91
Appeals of Convictions   92
Special Sentencing Considerations for Juveniles   96
Conclusion   99
Critical Review Questions   99
Recommended Readings   100
Key Terms   101
Cases Cited   101

4   Jails and Local Detention Facilities   102

Introduction   102
A Brief History of Jails   103
Contemporary Jails and Detention Facilities   103
  What Is a Jail?   104
  How Many Jails?   105
  How Many Inmates?   106
  Jail Inmates and Gender   107
  Variations in Jail Use   107
The Physical Plant of Jails   109
The Administration of Jails   113
Jail Employees   114
  The Number of Employees   115
  Employee Assignments and Quality   115

Major Jail Issues   116
  Local Politics   116
  Local Funding   117
  Location Issues   117
  Makeshift Structures   118
  Privatization   120
  Jail Standards   122
  Removing Juveniles from Adult Jails   123
  Inmate Programming   124
Other Local Detention Facilities   127
  Alternative Forms of Incarceration   127
  Police Lockups   130
  County Workhouses, Penal Farms, Etc.   131
  State-Run Jails   131
Conclusion   138
Critical Review Questions   139
Recommended Readings   140
Key Terms   141

5 Prison Systems   142

Introduction   142
Prisons as Total Institutions   143
Prisoner Management and Related Issues   144
  Institutional Goals   144
  Inmate Classification   147
Prison Types and Functions   149
  Building Design and Inmate Supervision   152
  Prison Security Levels   155
Prisons for Women   158
Prison Labor   159
  From the Auburn Prison Factory to the Great Depression   159
  Contemporary Prison Industries   161
  Joint Venture Programs   162
Federal Prison System   163
  Facilities Profile   164
  Programs Profile   166
State Prison Systems   168
  Facilities Profile   170
  Programs Profile   173

Juvenile Corrections   178
   Facilities Profile   179
   Programs Profile   180
Conclusion   182
Critical Review Questions   183
Recommended Readings   184
Key Terms   185
Cases Cited   185
Notes   185

6 Inmates   187

Introduction   187
Prison Inmate Characteristics   188
   Federal Prisoners   188
   State Prisoners   190
   Female Prisoners   193
Jail Inmate Characteristics   194
   Gender and Jail Inmates   196
   Federal Jail Inmates   196
   Juvenile Jail Inmates   197
Prison and Jail Culture   197
   Characteristics of the Inmate Subculture   197
   The Inmate Code   198
   Inmate Role Types and Prison-Adaptive Behavior Modes   198
   Origins of Inmate Social Organization   201
   Men's versus Women's Prison Culture   203
   Prison Culture in the 1990s and Beyond   205
Violence in Correctional Institutions   205
   Inmate-Initiated Victimization   205
   Riots and Other Disturbances   210
Juvenile Inmates   212
   Characteristics of Juvenile Inmates   213
   Offenses of Juvenile Inmates   215
   The Culture of Juvenile Correctional Facilities   216
   Conditions of Confinement for Juvenile Offenders   216
Inmate-Centered Issues   218
   Problem Inmates and Inmate Problems   218
   Gangs in Correctional Settings   220
   Jailhouse Suicide   222

Conclusion   224
Critical Review Questions   225
Recommended Readings   226
Key Terms   226
Cases Cited   227
Notes   227

7   Probation and Parole   230

Introduction   230
The History of Probation   230
    Forerunners of Modern Probation   231
    John Augustus: Father of Probation   232
    The Growth of Probation Services   233
Administration of Probation   234
    Eligibility for Probation   234
    Granting Probation and the Pre-Sentence Investigation   234
    Conditions of Probation   236
    Length of Supervision   238
Violation of Probation   238
    Preliminary Hearing   239
    Revocation Hearing   240
    Sentencing   241
Origins of Parole   241
    Parole and the Great Depression   242
    Parole Today   242
Administration of Parole   242
    Parole Eligibility   243
    Granting Parole and the Parole Board   243
    Conditions of Parole   245
    Length of Supervision   245
Violation of Parole   247
    Preliminary Hearing   248
    Revocation Hearing   248
Probation and Parole Officers   249
Probation and Parole Services Today   255
    Profiles of Probationers and Parolees   257
    Trends in Probation and Parole   259

Probation and Aftercare for Juvenile Offenders   261
   Juvenile Probation and Aftercare   262
   Trends in Juvenile Probation   265
Conclusion   266
Critical Review Questions   270
Recommended Readings   270
Key Terms   271
Cases Cited   271
Notes   272

8 Community Corrections   273

Introduction   273
Defining Community Corrections and Intermediate Punishments   275
   Supporters   275
   Detractors   276
   What Is Reintegration?   277
   Government and Private Sponsorship   278
   Administering Community-Based Programs   279
   Measuring Success and Failure in Community Corrections   280
Reentry Programs as "Community-Based Corrections"   282
   Work Release   284
   Educational Release   284
   Furloughs   285
Diversion   285
   Origins of Diversion   285
   Can We Divert? Should We Divert?   286
   Types of Diversion Programs   287
   Success and Failure   287
Fines, Forfeitures, and Restitution   288
   Objectives of Economic Sanctions   288
   Types of Programs   289
   Success and Failure   291
Community Service   292
   Objectives of Community Service   292
   Types of Programs   292
   Issues in Community Service   292
   Success and Failure   293

House Arrest and Electronic Monitoring   294
  Objectives of House Arrest and Electronic Monitoring   295
  Success and Failure   296
Community Alternatives for Juveniles   297
  Changing Definitions of Juvenile Offenders   297
  Transferring Juveniles to the Adult System   298
  Diversion Programs   299
  Restitution Programs   299
  Wilderness, Survival, and Self-Reliance Programs   300
  Success and Failure   301
Issues in Community Corrections   303
  The Role of the Victim in Punishment   303
  The Role of Community Stakeholders in Punishment   304
  Merging Treatment and Punishment   305
  Gender and Community Corrections   305
Conclusion   308
Critical Review Questions   308
Recommended Readings   309
Key Terms   310
Cases Cited   310
Notes   310

9   Administration of Corrections Programs   311

Introduction   311
Administration and Management   312
  Why Study Administration or Management?   313
  Managing Inmates and Managing Staff   314
An Overview of Bureaucracy   314
Leadership Styles   316
Issues Facing Corrections Managers   321
  Who Manages? The Characteristics of Corrections Managers   321
  Corrections Administrators' Backgrounds   329
  Centralization versus Decentralization   329
Modern Management Tasks   330
  Recruitment and Retention of Staff   330
  Dealing with Employee Unions   331
  Building Facilities   332
  Managing Inmate Populations   332

Cost Containment   332
  Dealing with the Courts   332
Inmate Management   333
Conclusion   334
Critical Review Questions   340
Recommended Readings   341
Key Terms   341
Notes   342

10   Correctional Law and Inmate Litigation   343

Introduction   343
The History of Correctional Litigation   345
Correctional Litigation and Post-Conviction Relief   347
  Access to the Courts   347
  Legal Assistance and Legal Access   350
  Inmate Advocates and Advocacy Groups   351
Laws and Litigation Dealing with Probation and Parole   353
Issues Raised by Correctional Lawsuits   355
Recent Trends in Litigation by Prison and Jail Inmates   358
  Expanding Litigation to Jails   358
  New Areas of Litigation   358
  The Impact of Litigation   361
Capital Punishment and Prisoner Litigation   363
Conclusion   367
Critical Review Questions   369
Recommended Readings   370
Key Terms   371
Cases Cited   371

11   Unresolved Issues and the Future of Corrections   373

Introduction   373
Future Correctional Philosophies   374
Future Correctional Practices   377
  Intermediate Sanctions   377
  Parole Supervision   379
  Boot Camps   379

New Kinds of Institutions and Architecture   381
Prison (and Jail) Industries   382
Banishment   383
Technological Applications   384
The Future of the Death Penalty   386
Future Correctional Populations   388
Race and Prisoners   388
Women in the Correctional System   392
The Young and the Restless, the Old and the Infirm   393
Infectious Diseases and Crowded Facilities   395
Correcting Juvenile Offenders   398
Dealing with Institutional Violence and Inmate Uprisings   401
Future Correctional Problems   403
Women in the Correctional Workplace   403
Legislative Trends   404
Reform Movements   404
Controlling Correctional Costs   405
Dealing with Crowding   406
Conclusion   407
Critical Review Questions   407
Recommended Readings   408
Key Terms   409
Notes   409

Glossary   411
References   430
Credits   453
Index   454

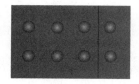

Preface

To the Student

This book is about a topic as old as human history and as current as the daily newspaper. It deals with one of the most fascinating and frustrating parts of the modern criminal justice system: the punishment or correction of law violating. As you read through the chapters you will see something of the dilemma facing us today as we decide who will be punished (or "corrected"), how, and for how long. You will soon come to realize the extent of the public's disenchantment with the corrections enterprise in the United States today. People of all political persuasions, races, genders, religious backgrounds, and economic statuses are unhappy with the current state of U.S. corrections. However, there is very little consensus about other approaches we might take.

Much has been written about the field of corrections. This book will expose you to the tip of the iceberg. Certainly there is more information available to you. However, we have approached our book from the standpoint of providing the baseline information essential for an introductory course. Many schools offer higher-level courses in correction studies. In fact, a course could be (and at some institutions is) taught on the subject matter covered in each chapter of this book. However, we decided early in the process of preparing the manuscript that not all the research and data on corrections could or should be presented in one book. Nevertheless, we have devoted a substantial amount of coverage to all major topics.

We have tried to incorporate chapters into the book that will be useful not only today, but also as references for you in the future. This means that we have included some fairly "standard" chapters covering jails, prisons, inmates, probation and parole, and community corrections. In addition, we offer some unique chapters on administration and inmates' rights and litigation. The careers in corrections features will interest many of you. Students are always curious about what they can do with a particular college degree and what is waiting for them out there in the "real world." Our final chapter does not simply summarize the book. It focuses on a number of the most enduring problems facing corrections agencies and personnel. We wanted to end the book with a bang, and we hope you feel inspired to begin forming your own conclusions.

For some of you, this may be the beginning of a life-long adventure. After taking the course for which you will use this book you might decide to seek work in the field of corrections. Some of you may decide to devote your lives to the study of corrections or punishments ("penology" as it traditionally has been called), and this could be the beginning of a research career. Wherever you find yourself, we want this course and this book to provide you with a firm foundation.

To the Instructor

This text is primarily intended for undergraduate students taking their first, survey course in corrections. In the process of creating this book a number of principles have guided our efforts, and we feel that these are particular strengths of this book. The following list will outline these principles or features for you.

We wanted to provide some historical background, but to deal primarily with the present reality of corrections in the United States. In doing so, we were committed to addressing not only what does not work with the system, but also what does work. We believe that we have achieved a text that is both objective and unbiased.

We have made every effort to present a book that is thorough in its background research and coverage, without overwhelming students with too much detail. Therefore, we have made every effort to include what we consider to be the essential elements necessary for this course, without straying into interesting, but ancillary areas. The result—the first "core" corrections book—is designed to be accessible to all college undergraduate students, and is priced to be affordable.

We have utilized a format that will make this book usable at institutions on both quarter and semester academic calendars. In most instances, unless the instructor decides to do otherwise, all of the material can be covered in one academic term. A quick scan of the table of contents shows that we begin with a brief history and coverage of some of the theories relating to crime causation. As we show later, these theories have clear implications for correctional programs and treatment approaches. We deal with the issue of sentencing and criminal sanctions to show how cases arrive at the doorstep of the correctional system. We also address correctional institutions such as jails and prisons, as well as the numerous alternatives to incarceration incorporated in probation, parole, and community corrections.

We have tried not to divide the material into too many discrete units. Therefore, rather than offer catchall chapters on juveniles or female offenders, we have integrated this information at relevant points throughout the text. Although this material may not be presented in one lump, we have devoted as much space to these topics as most other textbooks, but in a more fluid manner.

We have attempted to maintain a practical focus throughout the text. For example, one element of particular interest to your students, and one designed to help you in advising, is the careers in corrections feature. This material should be especially helpful for students deciding whether a correctional position is in their future or not.

We have also touched on some of the hot button issues currently facing corrections. These topics appear in the two chapters on administration and litigation, and they should not only spark student interest but vigorous classroom debate as well. Additionally, the sections on corrections in the twenty-first century will provide students with a preview of the kinds of issues potentially facing them in the future.

We have provided boxed material covering some of the key theoretical elements in corrections, a number of the major historical figures in the field, and some of the most current statistics available on the state of corrections in the U.S. today.

Each chapter includes a list of key terms, a list of recommended readings, and critical review questions. The glossary presents brief definitions of all the important terms used in the book. We have also provided a thorough set of teaching supplements including an instructors manual with detailed chapter outlines, learning objectives, and a wide range of possible test questions from which to choose (these are available in both hard copy and in a computerized format as well). There is also a student study guide that includes much of this information to assist students in mastering the course material. Additionally, there will be a CD-ROM providing an overview of the criminal justice system, and the flow of cases through the system.

Finally, we see this as a work in progress. Both of the authors fully recognize that the last word has not been written or spoken on corrections, and the situation is changing very rapidly (as we discovered when we were trying to get the most up-to-date information into the book). New information and supplements are coming out almost daily from the Justice Department's Bureau of Justice Statistics and other federal and state agencies. We hope we have addressed some of the questions you might have, and some we have raised ourselves. If not, and you wish to contact us with questions or provide us with feedback, our e-mail addresses are *glmays@nmsu.edu* and *twinfree@nmsu.edu*. Feel free to write us.

Acknowledgments

A book such as this one is the product of the efforts of many people. We would like to mention as many as possible, and we hope not to inadvertently leave any out. First, our families were infinitely patient with us as we often worked double-time to complete the manuscript. We have dedicated this book to them and their names are mentioned individually in the dedication. Second, we sincerely appreciate our editor Sabra Horne, development editor Dan Alpert, and Melanie Field for their occasional nagging and frequent encouragement. The manuscript reviewers also proved to be extremely helpful in this process: Mary Brewster, West Chester University; Kevin Courtright, Hilbert College; Stephen Gibbons, Western Oregon State University; Philip Holley, Southwestern Oklahoma State University; Devereaux Kennedy, State University of New York College at Cortland; Lucien Lombardo, Old Dominion University; James Marquart, Sam Houston State University; Dale Mooso, San Antonio College; Gary Perlstein, Portland State University; Jerry Phillips, Linn-Benton Community College; and Harry Spiller, John A. Logan College. Finally, three of our graduate students—Conan Becknell, Dana Lynskey, and Brandi Woods—were instrumental in the production of this book. Two of our undergraduate students, Stephanie Hansen and Rachel Mangas, provided very capable research assistance in the final months of this project. They all served as researchers, gofers, and sounding boards for ideas (and for some of our complaints).

G. Larry Mays
L. Thomas Winfree

1

Introduction

Chapter Outline

- What Is "Corrections"?
- Philosophies of Punishment
- Attitudes Toward Corrections
- The Role of Criminological Theory
- Corrections Programs
- Conclusion

- Critical Review Questions
- Recommended Readings
- Key Terms
- Cases Cited
- Notes

 What Is "Corrections"?

What comes to your mind when you hear the word *corrections*? Do you think about prisons with massive stone walls in movies such as *Escape from Alcatraz* or *The Shawshank Redemption*? Or, perhaps you think about inmates working on a chain gang or prisoners in white uniforms working on a "hoe line" in the fields. Are these images a true and accurate reflection of contemporary corrections?

The answer is yes, but as we stand on the threshold of the twenty-first century, corrections encompasses so much more. For example, the U.S. Department of Justice estimates that nationwide 5.3 million adults, nearly three of every 100 adults, were under some type of correctional supervision in 1996 (Department of Justice 1996b). Of this total more than 3 million adults were on probation and another 700,000 were on parole. The remaining one-third—roughly 1.6 million adults—were confined in prisons and jails (Gilliard and Beck 1997b). In 1997, the odds of a Black male going to a federal or state prison sometime in his life were one in four; among Hispanics these odds were one in six; and among White males the odds of serving time were 1 in 23 (Bonczar and Beck 1997). These numbers do not include the juvenile population we also have under correctional supervision, but they do demonstrate that corrections is a large (and growing) component of the criminal justice process in the United States.

The film *The Shawshank Redemption* is based in one of the nation's
old fortress-like prisons. This motion picture, though a fictional
account, shows something of the daily routine for inmates in these
prisons. Andy (Tim Robbins) and Red (Morgan Freeman) spend much
time "on the yard" discussing prison life.

In this chapter we explore the philosophical and practical underpinnings of
contemporary corrections. First, to understand better the form and nature of
our nation's formal response to criminals, we examine the philosophies that
provide the foundation for "correcting" convicted offenders. Second, we review public and political attitudes that are shaping contemporary corrections
policy. Third, we explore the many explanations that criminologists developed
over the past one hundred years or so that help us understand crime and
criminals. These theories will be especially useful when we start to consider
the methods designed to treat convicted criminals in the many correctional
programs and agencies we will review. Finally, we conclude with a brief
overview of the nation's corrections programs.

We begin our investigation of the philosophy underlying contemporary corrections with eight ways to think about punishments.

Philosophies of Punishment

As we progress through this book, we look at many different correctional programs, agencies, and institutions. Whatever the institutional or organizational
arrangement we examine, it is important to remember that different philosophies guide these programs. In fact, throughout the history of corrections dif-

While often thought of as a by-gone era, inmates can still be seen in some prison settings working in agricultural pursuits. The inmates shown here are working a "hoe line" at the Ferguson Prison in Texas.

ferent philosophies have dominated the field at different times. The dilemma in contemporary corrections is to decide which philosophy seems to be driving our policy choices at any one point in time. In order for students to understand contemporary corrections, we need to explore the historical origins of these different and sometimes contradictory philosophies.

Retribution

One of the oldest correctional philosophies is **retribution.** In simplest terms, retribution refers to revenge or retaliation for a harm or wrong done to another individual. Archaeologists have unearthed written codes dating back more than 3,500 years that clearly spell out a retributionist approach. For example, both the Code of Hammurabi, King of Babylon, and the Law of Moses recorded in the biblical books of Exodus, Leviticus, and Deuteronomy spelled out the way individuals (or society as a whole) were to exact revenge on offenders. From these laws, and similar ones historically, we have what has come to be called the *lex talionis,* or the law of retaliation (Abadinsky and Winfree 1992). Box 1.1 provides several examples of the law of retaliation.

The idea that criminals deserve or have earned punishment for the sake of punishment has developed a new following among both liberals and conservatives since the 1970s. In the mid-1970s, the ability of the criminal justice system, but particularly the corrections component, to affect prosocial

Some modern correctional facilities look more like college campuses
rather than prisons. One such example is the Illinois State Penitentiary
at Vienna. Inmates at this facility are housed in dormitory-like units
each with a radio, desk, and twin bed.

changes in criminals came under severe criticism (see "Rehabilitation,"
page 5). Simultaneously, a derivative of the *lex talionis* emerged. This new
rationale for punishment, called just deserts or retributive justice, suggests
that criminals have earned society's wrath and deserve to be punished for the
sake of punishment (Fogel 1975). Whether they "learn" to change (rehabilitation) or are frightened away from their prior illegal ways of behaving (deterrence) is irrelevant. They simply deserve punishment, much as the criminals
and law violators of the days of the *lex talionis* deserved their punishments.
Only the forms of punishments in the *lex talionis* are different, not the reasons for employing them.

In the 1990s, critics of the current system suggest that what has emerged is
a philosophy of **penal harm.** Punishments, especially prison, were nearly
always meant to be uncomfortable. Since the 1980s, however, the prison population in the U.S. has increased at a far greater rate than the prison system's
ability to deal with it. The chief mechanisms of change were mandatory sentencing laws and restrictions on the use of parole or its abolition. Consider
what Richard Wright (1996, 135) observes are the consequences of the penal
harm movement: "By promoting prison overcrowding and its related evils,
the penal harm movement has clearly extended degradation, provocation,
and deprivation well beyond the act of imprisonment to the daily *conditions*
of confinement" (emphasis in the original).

Box 1.1

Ancient Examples of the *Lex Talionis*

From the Code of Hammurabi:

> If a man destroy the eye of another man, they shall destroy his eye.
>
> If he break a man's bone, they shall break his bone.
>
> If a man knock out a tooth of a man of his own rank, they shall knock out his tooth.

From Exodus 21:23–25:

> And if any mischief follows, then thou shalt give life for life, eye for eye, tooth for tooth, hand for hand, foot for foot, burning for burning, wound for wound, stripe for stripe.

Deterrence

The **deterrence** philosophy assumes that punishing an individual—that is, "correcting" that person's behavior—can prevent future criminal behavior. One definition says that deterrence is designed to demonstrate "the certainty and severity of punishment to discourage future crime by the offender and by others" (Department of Justice 1988, 90). This definition owes much to the writing of Beccaria and other eighteenth-century philosophers, including Jeremy Bentham. Moreover, deterrence consists of two separate but equally important dimensions. The first form is **specific deterrence.** This approach presumes that if a criminal offender is punished in some fashion, that particular individual will be dissuaded from committing a future infraction. The ultimate form of specific deterrence is the death penalty. We can be assured that those people executed for their crimes will not reoffend in the future.

While specific deterrence may be very important in the scheme of contemporary corrections, perhaps the second dimension—**general deterrence**—seems as important, if not more so. As noted, specific deterrence assumes that we punish the individual offender for the benefit of the individual. By contrast, general deterrence assumes that we punish the individual offender for the benefit of society. In other words, particular criminals are punished—for example, by sending them to prison or even executing them—to prevent others in society from committing the same or similar crimes. This philosophy is educative in its approach. It assumes that those punished for their misdeeds serve as "object lessons" for the rest of us. As the famous saying goes, uttered at the scene of a public execution by a witness, "There but for the grace of God go I."

Rehabilitation

The most prominent correctional philosophy in this country for many years was **rehabilitation.** Rehabilitation includes "providing psychological or educational assistance or job training to offenders to make them less likely to engage in future criminality" (Department of Justice 1988, 90). Since the mid-1970s rehabilitation has fallen into some disfavor, but between the 1950s and the 1970s it was the philosophy most frequently espoused by those associated with what is often called **penology,** the systematic study of punishments.

Rehabilitation is based on the notion that human beings—no matter what their ages or what their crimes—are amenable to change. Rehabilitation is virtually synonymous with reformation, and this philosophy assumes that if offenders are given the opportunity and they are subjected to various treatment programs—such as individual and group counseling, drug and alcohol treatment, remedial education, and vocational education—their behavior can change and they can eventually lead crime-free lives.

A 1970s assessment of correctional program evaluation (Lipton, Martinson, and Wilks 1975; Martinson 1974) brought the efficacy of rehabilitation programs into question. Some critics said rehabilitation does not work, and some critics went even further and said "nothing works." However, further reflections on the topic of rehabilitation (for example, Cullen and Gilbert 1982) have caused many to reconsider the state of rehabilitation as a viable correction philosophy. In fact, the reality of the situation is that rehabilitation may work after all. Why was such a gloomy picture painted in the 1970s, then? We have several possible answers to this question.

First, correctional treatment programs have often been created with little attention to program evaluation. In other words, no evaluation component was included in the program when it was first created, and only after a few years of operation did someone (often a funding agency) decide that it might be a good idea to find out how successful the program was. Therefore, some programs were assumed to work or not work based on anecdotal evidence, intuition, or "gut feelings." Because of inadequate or nonexistent evaluation any number of treatment programs were assumed not to work.

Second, of the treatment programs that were evaluated during the 1960s and 1970s many were reviewed with inadequate statistical techniques. The result was that some of these programs initially appeared not to work but upon reexamination fared better.

Third, some correctional treatment programs were almost designed to fail. Some treatment approaches had no theoretical underpinnings, and program designers and implementers only had vague notions about what the programs should achieve. A variety of the diversion programs developed for the juvenile justice system fit this category (Decker 1985). Programs were created with the stated purpose of diverting certain juvenile offenders from the formal process of adjudication, But such a statement begs the questions "Diverted from what?" "Diverted to what?"

In summarizing rehabilitation as a correctional philosophy, a few key points should be made (Rogers and Mays 1987, 519–20, with apologies to Abraham Lincoln):

- No treatment program will work with every possible offender.
- Some programs may not work with any offenders.

- Some programs have a high degree of efficacy; that is, they work with a broad range of offenders.
- Unfortunately, some offenders cannot be helped.

We have come to realize that in corrections, much as in drug and alcohol treatment programs, people get "better" when they want to get better.

Isolation

In some ways, **isolation** is a very old correctional philosophy that really has served two purposes throughout recorded history. The first is the simple incarceration of people in dungeons or towers to separate them from most human contact, that is, isolation as punishment. The second is what we might call the "rotten apple" response to criminal offenders. According to one age-old saying, "One rotten apple spoils the whole barrel," and, therefore, isolating offenders protects the rest of society from "spoiling." For these reasons, some penologists view this function of punishment as providing a measure of social sanitation. Prisons and jails, then, become the dumping ground for society's unwanted elements, considered dangerous by some and simply unpleasant by others (see Welch 1996a). Finally, we should not lose sight of the fact that jail and prison inmates have low visibility: they are out of sight, out of mind. If they are in society, running around free, not only are they a threat to law-abiding citizens, they also serve to remind us of the failure of the law to protect us and deter them.

Incapacitation

The contemporary version of isolation is incapacitation, sometimes called **selective incapacitation.** Incapacitation involves "separating offenders from the community to reduce the opportunity for further crime while they are incarcerated" (Department of Justice 1988, 90). Much of the contemporary emphasis on incapacitation was founded on the work of Marvin Wolfgang and his colleagues at the University of Pennsylvania. Their so-called Philadelphia Birth Cohort Studies identified a group of high-risk and high-rate offenders (Wolfgang, Figlio, and Sellin 1972), who were later labeled "career criminals." An assortment of policies, of which selective incapacitation was primary, were developed to address the problems created by these persistent law violators (Walker 1994, 56–62).

At the heart of selective incapacitation lies the assumption that career criminals can be identified early in their careers, perhaps as young as their preteens or teenage years and that once these career criminals are identified, the full force of the criminal prosecution apparatus will be brought to bear on them. Selective incapacitation reflects a desire by policy makers to ensure that career criminals are caught, convicted, and sentenced to a significant period of incarceration. The presumed outcome of this approach is a substantial reduction in the total crime rate based on having the most persistent

Career criminals may come in a number of different varieties. Lawrence Ohlin, pictured here, is a heroin addict convicted under the California law that provides for long prison terms after conviction of a third felony (the so-called "three strikes legislation"). Ohlin's third offense? Stealing a pair of blue jeans.

offenders behind bars and, thus, incapacitated for much if not all of their most crime-prone years.

As some critical observers pointed out, the concept of the career criminal and the selective incapacitation approach to dealing with career criminals are based on assumptions that are open to challenge and different interpretations (Greenwood 1982; Walker 1994). The issue of early identification of these individuals has been problematic. Also, selective incapacitation assumes that there is a finite number of high-rate criminals, and that if we catch the most persistent ones, there will be no more to take their place. Both the states and the federal government have pursued this expensive policy option that is of unknown value at this point. Nevertheless, the image of the career criminal is one that is both frightening to the public and politically powerful for many politicians. This means that we are likely to continue to see references to career criminals and programs designed to deal with such offenders for years to come.

Reintegration

Beginning in the late 1970s and moving into the early 1980s, most corrections professionals began to emphasize the value of **reintegration** as a correctional philosophy (Rogers and Mays 1987). Reintegration recognizes the fact that a very high percentage of the people in prison (probably more than 90%) eventually will get out. Once they get out, many of these offenders have a very difficult time making any kind of transition (smooth or not) back into society. They must readjust to their families, to work, and to the general notion that now they are "ex-cons" and that this is a designation not warmly received by most members of the public. Therefore, something must be done to help in the transition from institutional life back into free society.

The process of reintegration is important for several reasons. First, most offenders who "fail" (that is, recidivate) do so in the first few months out of prison. Second, the longer we incarcerate an individual the more difficult the transition process becomes. Thus, the corrections system must help offenders in making the transition from institutional life to the free world. Otherwise, many of them will return to crime and eventually return to prison.

Restitution

Some people would question whether **restitution** is a correctional philosophy. Restitution entails "having the offender repay the victim or the community in money or services" (Department of Justice 1988, 90). As originally envisioned by many, restitution was designed to be an alternative to incarceration (Cromwell and Killinger 1994, 279–80). In many jurisdictions judges now incorporate restitution orders into the conditions of probation. Critics of this system of punishments question whether it is truly an alternative to incarceration. They suggest that those offenders ordered to make restitution would normally have received a probated sentence and possibly a fine (Tonry 1995). In those instances, restitution becomes a probation add-on, or a way of making probation seem more punitive. Therefore, rather than being a correctional philosophy in-and-of itself, restitution is part of the general trend toward requiring greater accountability from offenders.

Restoration

The most recent philosophy to gain followers in the field of corrections is that of **restoration.** Restorative justice, or the "balanced approach," as it is sometimes called, has recently been applied to juvenile and adult offenders (Armstrong, Maloney, and Romig 1990; Maloney, Romig, and Armstrong 1988). This approach to corrections is based on three key elements: accountability, community protection, and competency development. Gordon Bazemore (1992) says that accountability requires offenders to repay or restore victims' losses resulting from their crimes, much like reparation or restitution. Community protection supports the notion of public safety in concert with the least costly, least restrictive correctional alternative. Competency development emphasizes remediation for the social, educational, or other deficiencies the offender possesses when coming into the correctional system. As Bazemore emphasizes, however, the key is "balance," that is, each of the three elements should pay an equal role in correcting deviant behavior.

After briefly reviewing these correctional philosophies, what are we to make of the state of contemporary corrections? Do any of these philosophies appear in current correctional programs? The answer certainly is that all of them do, in one form or another. Is any one of them the dominant philosophy in contemporary corrections? The answer to this question is probably that no one philosophy dominates the field and that all of them may be vying for superiority at different times. Much like the field of mental health 20 or 30 years ago, contemporary corrections can be characterized as caught in a "model muddle" (Siegler and Osmond 1974). In other words, we often try to make corrections programs be all things to all people, and some programs end up employing conflicting or competing elements. How have we come to find ourselves in this muddle? Actually, this single question has several possible answers. No doubt political realities and public pressure have played a major role, and we will explore the role of the public and policy makers in the next section of this chapter.

 ## Attitudes Toward Corrections

Ask anyone in the field of criminal justice today what the current mood is toward crime and punishment, and you will get the same answer: punishment, punishment, and more punishment. Bernard (1992, 3–6) has described this phenomenon regarding the juvenile justice system, but it applies to adult criminal justice and corrections as well. He says that in juvenile justice society goes through a cycle of response to juvenile offenders. Another way to understand this concept is to envision policy change as a pendulum that swings back and forth from leniency to harsh punishment.

People perceive, at some point, that the correctional treatment programs in existence are too soft on criminals, and there are calls for more punitive responses. The public and policy makers today generally feel that leniency contributes to more criminality and that the only proper response to this increased criminality is tougher punishment. Therefore, we find ourselves in the midst of a get-tough part of the cycle for both juvenile and adult offenders.

One idea that drives the cycle of juvenile delinquency is the notion that we are currently in the midst of a crime wave (Bernard 1992; see also Rogers and Mays 1987; Walker 1994). The reality is that crime rates have largely been stable for a decade, and that most categories have shown declines. Therefore, the idea that a crime wave is sweeping the nation is for the most part a myth, at worst, or a misconception, at best.

However, if the public believes the political rhetoric about a crime wave, they are more susceptible to the politicians' suggestions of solutions to the crime wave. One key strategy proposed by politicians was to implement

---

Box 1.2

**The Mass Media, Politics, and Public Perceptions
of Crime and Justice in the United States**

In the United States do the media simply report the news, or do they create the news? This question is hotly debated today. Many involved in the news industry would stoutly defend their record as objective reporters of the news "as it happened." However, as observers such as Gregg Barak have noted, the large public audience for violent and crime-related news, especially the most sensational stories or any story involving celebrities, has resulted in a disproportionate amount of newspaper space and radio and television air-time devoted to these stories. The TV news producer's cliché "If it bleeds it leads" bears witness to this trend. Such reporting distorts the reality of crime, in terms of the amount of crime committed, the seriousness of the crime, and the nature of both victims and perpetrators. In the end the public and policy makers perceive that a crime wave is sweeping the nation and that current responses are insufficient and more drastic measures should—must—be taken. This outlook frequently translates into more, and more punitive, crime control policies. *Sources:* Barak (1995); Chernak (1995).

---

mandatory stiff sentencing for drug-related offenses and other crimes. The next step was to build more jails and prisons to house all of the additional individuals incarcerated as a result of the new laws. The outcome of these efforts in most jurisdictions has been counterintuitive. We have made more laws, made the punishments more stringent, put more people behind bars, and have seen very little change in the crime rate around the country.

What we have seen change are the rates of incarceration in the United States. As Figure 1.1 and Table 1.1 show, the United States has experienced dramatic increases in the rates of imprisonment, particularly since 1980. Our nation leads the world with an incarceration rate of 650 prisoners per 100,000 population (Gilliard and Beck 1997).

We are in a prison and jail crowding crisis nationwide. Local, state, and federal governments all have increased their capacities to incarcerate over the past decade. Unfortunately, as some have warned us, and as we now are starting to acknowledge, we cannot build ourselves out of our crowding crisis (Thompson and Mays 1991). In fact, it has been suggested that jail and prison capacity might drive the prisoner population numbers (Klofas 1991b). It is what some have called the *Field of Dreams* notion in corrections: If you build it (a jail or prison), they (inmates) will come. At $20,000 to $50,000 per bed space to build and at $20,000 to $30,000 per year per inmate to house people in jails and prisons, we will very quickly reach the absolute limit of what we can afford in terms of persons behind bars.

If we were using private sector terminology we would say that corrections is a growth industry, and the truth is it really is a growth industry (Mays and Gray 1996). In fact, it is so much so that private sector corrections companies are getting into the market, and those already in are expanding. The crucial

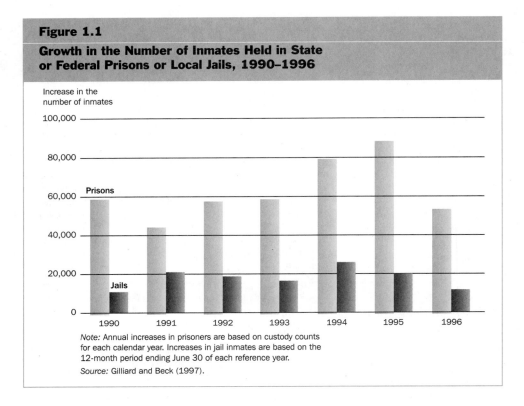

Figure 1.1

Growth in the Number of Inmates Held in State or Federal Prisons or Local Jails, 1990–1996

Increase in the number of inmates

Note: Annual increases in prisoners are based on custody counts for each calendar year. Increases in jail inmates are based on the 12-month period ending June 30 of each reference year.

Source: Gilliard and Beck (1997).

point is that while the end of the "get-tough" movement is not in sight, such an approach to crime and punishment is incompatible with governmental downsizing and cutbacks. The reality is that a clash in these two forces looms on the horizon.

As we will see in the following section, the pendulum of shifting public policy has its parallel in the evolution of criminological theories. To some degree, our attitudes about corrections are impacted by our understanding—or mis-understanding—of the "causes" of criminal activity.

The Role of Criminological Theory

When some students read—or even hear—the word *theory,* minds snap shut, learning stops. To sneak theory into their work, textbook writers, professors, and the few others who find theory interesting, resort to trickery. They use terms such as *frameworks, concepts, philosophies,* and the like. You may have observed that we used several of these strategies already in this chapter. For example, we described the underlying philosophies associated with punishment. Deterrence, for one, is also a theory, as are most of the other punishment philosophies we described.

Table 1.1

Number of Persons Held in State or Federal Prisons or Local Jails, 1985, 1990–1996

	Total inmates in custody	Prisoners in custody		Inmates held in local jails	Incarceration rate*
		Federal	State		
1985	744,208	35,781	451,812	256,615	313
1990	1,148,702	58,838	684,544	405,320	461
1991	1,219,014	63,930	728,605	426,479	483
1992	1,295,150	72,071	778,495	444,584	508
1993	1,369,185	80,815	828,566	459,804	531
1994	1,476,621	85,500	904,647	486,474	567
1995					
June 30	1,561,836	89,334	965,458	507,044	594
December 31	—	89,538	989,007	—	—
1996					
June 30	1,630,940	93,167	1,019,281	518,492	615
Percent change,					
6/30/95–6/30/96	4.4%	4.3%	5.6%	2.3%	
Annual average increase					
12/31/85–6/30/96	7.8%	9.5%	8.1%	6.9%	
12/31/90–6/30/96	6.6%	8.7%	7.5%	4.6%	

Note: Jail counts are for midyear (June 30). Counts for 1994–96 exclude persons who were supervised outside of a jail facility. State and federal prisoner counts for 1985 and 1990–94 are for December 31.

*Total of persons in custody per 100,000 residents on July 1 of each reference year.

Source: Gilliard and Beck (1997b, 2).

Our current task—to help you understand why people commit crimes—is best achieved by describing both the theories and their practical aspects, particularly as they shape the nation's punitive responses to crime.[1] The details of these theories, and the research that either supports or attacks their causal arguments, are adequately described elsewhere (Akers 1996; Curran and Renzetti 1994; Winfree and Abadinsky 1996). Instead, we present a brief sampling of crime theories, with an emphasis on those with correctional implications. We start with the origins of criminological theory.

From Free Will to Determinism

Criminologists have spent more than 200 years applying philosophy and science to the study of crime.[2] "Modern" criminology is often dated from Cesare Beccaria's late eighteenth-century attempts to apply what we now call deterrence theory to crime. Beccaria believed that humans, as rational beings endowed by their creator with **free will,** are responsible for their own actions. Without certain and swift punishments that accord the unwanted act the required amount of severity, some people simply choose crime. The idea that criminals willfully choose to be law violators largely directed the study of crime for nearly a century.

In the 1870s, Cesare Lombroso reported a criminological application for Charles Darwin's evolutionary theory. Criminals, according to what became known as the Lombrosian or Italian School of criminology, have few choices to make since their criminal tendencies reflect inborn atavistic tendencies. In this context, criminal behavior is a result of **biological determinism.** Criminals, as atavists, are what we might today call genetic misfits or biological "throwbacks" to an earlier, primitive and more violent being.

Lombroso's ideas, first published as *The Criminal Man,* in 1876, spawned a generation of deterministic anthropologists, psychologists, and economists. As **positivists,** these social scientists looked for answers in measurable aspects of the human condition. And as determinists, they also believed that external or internal forces beyond the individual's control were at work turning that person into the criminal so despised and feared by society. Criminal anthropologists carried on the work of early biological determinists as they grappled with the external, measurable signs of an inner, crime-inducing characteristic. Psychological determinists looked at forces within the human mind that could explain criminal conduct. Economic determinists, and later social determinists, believed that the distribution of wealth, and the treatment of certain segments of society based on economic stratification created conditions ripe for crime.

The implications of determinism for correctional practice are intriguing. If criminals are born, then society can do little to change them. Therefore, the purpose of prisons is to warehouse this dangerous segment of society. However, if economic or social forces precondition some people to become criminals, then changing these forces could alter an individual's pathway to crime. During the late nineteenth century, advocates of social change spoke out for "social engineering" that, in effect, would rescue those placed by accident of birth in poor economic conditions. However, some sociologists such as Herbert Spencer railed against tinkering with society. Spencer, a social Darwinist, believed that government should not attempt to alter the lives of society's less fortunate in any substantial way. "The quality of society," wrote Spencer (1864, 313), "is physically lowered by the artificial preservation of its feeblest members [and] the quality of a society is lowered morally and intellectually by the artificial preservation of those who are least able to take care of themselves."

Crime, Criminals, and Deterministic Forces

Biological determinism did not disappear in the wake of conflicting evidence in the early twentieth century. In the late nineteenth century, it was widely believed that feeblemindedness was related to crime. The late–twentieth-century version of this idea alleges a link between IQ and crime: low IQ correlates with crime-proneness. Other more complex causal sequences link IQ and crime, some of which include the influences of school performance, socioeconomic status, and race. One contemporary perspective suggests that certain racial groups have lower IQ scores than others. Because of the lower IQ scores, these minority-group individuals are found disproportionately living in poverty and involved in crime (see, for example, Gordon 1987; Hernnstein and Murray 1994; Wilson and Herrnstein 1985). Most credible criminologists reject the race-IQ-crime equation as unsupported by research (Winfree and Abadinsky 1996, 51–52). However, some members of U.S. society welcome race-based explanations no matter how weak the evidence.

According to another position, labeled as neopositivism because of its ties to nineteenth-century positivism, school performance mediates between IQ and crime-proneness (Hindelang 1973). Youngsters with low IQs who later fail in school have higher delinquency rates and are more likely to commit a crime than those individuals with equally low IQs who manage to complete their schooling.

The correctional implications of IQ are built into the system. Nearly every convicted offender is subjected to some form of IQ testing. These scores are used to decide mental functioning and amenability for various correctional treatment plans, as well as inmate classification (that is, a low-functioning individual may need special housing to avoid exploitation by other inmates). Although we are not sure what is being measured by IQ tests (Bartol 1991, 132), they continue to shape correctional practice and criminological discussions on the causes of individual criminality (Bartollas and Conrad 1992; Champion 1990a).

Several other forms of modern biological determinism have their origins in biochemical imbalances. For example, the crimes committed by drug addicts, including alcoholics, may be symptoms of other biochemical problems, including, perhaps, a biological tendency for addictive disorders (Gold, Washton, and Dackis 1985; Goleman 1990). Other biological determinists have attempted, with limited success, to link crime and low levels of certain chemicals, including, in women, the hormone estrogen, and high levels of others, including, in men, the hormone testosterone. In one of the more interesting arguments about the role of biochemical imbalances, Lee Ellis (1991) asserts that criminals' blood exhibits low levels of a naturally occurring enzyme, monoamine oxidase. MAO, as the enzyme is also known, helps to regulate several key neurotransmitters, including those in the brain. Ellis also observes that MAO is generally lower in three groups: males, youths and young adults (individuals in their second and third decades of life), and African-Americans, three groups that are overrepresented in the criminal population.

Before we rush to order regular doses of MAO for members of these groups, it is important to note that the association between MAO and undesired social behavior is modest at best. Moreover, the idea that we can "treat" criminals with chemicals is not new. Chemical therapies for criminals have been around for decades (Berman 1938; see also Hippchen 1982). In prisons and mental hospitals, some "inmates" could not be managed without their use. Certain parolees and probationers may have chemical therapies included as a condition of their release. Many sex offenders are given hormonal treatments in the belief that these measures will "control" their sexual obsessions and subsequent law-violating conduct.

Besides very real questions about the ability of these chemical therapies to control the undesired behavior, numerous moral and ethical dilemmas surround forced treatment or proactive treatment of possible offenders (that is, members of certain "at-risk" groups). Can we subject people to intrusive and disruptive biochemical treatments based on a statistical probability that they might offend? Are we punishing people for what they *might* do? What are the limits to the extent to which our collective need to feel safe outweighs individual liberties? Even if we can do these things, should we do them?

Finally, **psychological determinists** view defects of the mind as the cause of all misbehavior, crime being but one form. Freudian psychoanalysts link such human misbehavior to problems with the **id** (primitive urges that are hedonistic), the **ego** (that part of the individual influenced by parental training and the like), and the **superego** (the social aspect of the individual formed as the child integrates itself into the larger community). According to August Aichhorn (1925), the superego takes its form and content from the child's efforts to emulate the parents or parental figures. Sometimes, however, the superego fails to develop properly and, as a result, leaves only the ego to control the id impulses. Conflicts arise because of the individual's abnormal relationship with parents or parental figures. Excessive control during the child's formative years results in a superego that is too rigid and inflexible. Thinking bad and doing bad are often confused. The individual with the excessively controlling superego seeks punishment as a way of dealing with unconscious guilt. The person with the weak superego is unable to control aggressive, hostile, or antisocial urges. Crime, given this set of psychological factors, is nearly inevitable.

In either case, the treatment is the same: Through dream analysis and "free association" (that is, talking about the first thing to come into your mind), the person with a poorly developed superego is made aware of the problem. With the help and guidance of a trained therapist, who becomes a parental figure, the "patient" eventually develops an appropriate superego and, as important, the inappropriate behavior ceases.

Behavior Modification

An offshoot of behaviorism, behavior modification has perhaps the broadest practical implications of any psychological explanation. Behaviorism begins with the premise that all behavior is the result of learning responses to various stimuli (Skinner 1974). From this perspective, deviant and criminal behavior are inappropriate learned responses. Behavior is shaped by the presence or absence of various reinforcers, which stimulate behavior, and punishers, which retard or extinguish behavior. Since most crime involves a great deal of risk and very little reward, the role of behaviorism in crime causation mystifies some people. The psychologist Hans Eysenck has an explanation: "An action followed by a small but immediate gratification will tend to be repeated, even though it is followed by a large but delayed painful consequence" (quoted in Taylor, Walton, and Young 1973, 47).

What is the practical role of behaviorism in corrections? Two forms have dominated the field of corrections over the past 30 years. First, **reality therapy (RT)** holds the offender accountable for his or her actions. In practice, RT is paternalistic and even authoritarian, which may explain its popularity with correctional workers. The moral standards of the therapist must become the moral standards of the client (Bersani 1989, 88). The therapist develops a close relationship with the client and uses praise and concern as the reinforcers and punishers. Through a lengthy interactive process, the clients come to see the error of their ways and, to gain favor with the therapist, change their behavior.

Second, behavior modification programs, built around "token economies," have long been a feature of prisons and even community-based correctional programs (Wexler 1975). On the one hand, good behavior earns the client rewards. Among the more critical of these are early parole from prison, temporary work or educational release into the community, and increased institutional privileges (including access to exercise or entertainment activities and better work conditions). On the other hand, bad behavior yields punishments such as the loss of the previous rewards and additional negative stimuli, including temporary residence in an isolation facility or undesired housing unit and lower paying and less rewarding work situation.

Finally, psychology also provides unique insights into one of the most intriguing puzzles observed by correctional workers. Frequently, the most acquiescent and pliable inmates make horrible candidates for release back into the community. Why? One answer may lie in a variant of psychopathology called **arousal theory.** Part of psychology, psychopathology recognizes that some criminals have no conscience. **Psychopaths** commit crimes without conventional concerns for morality or any thought of the consequences of the crime. Psychopaths are different from (healthy) people, at least in a biopsychological way. According to Lee Ellis (1990), because of a genetic defect, the brain functioning of psychopathic criminals quickly becomes habituated to incoming stimuli. Low arousal psychopaths regard ordinary activities as boring. They seek to maximize their sensory stimulation, perhaps through risk taking or criminal activity (or, occasionally, both). People with this brain functioning disorder may be literally immune to efforts designed to alter their behavior. Low arousal criminals receive little benefit from learning or punishing in most institutional environments, as the existing stimulation barely keeps them awake (Bartol 1991; Chesno and Kilmann 1975). The world outside the prison, by contrast, presents these people with too many stimuli, far more than they can manage without resorting to inappropriate behavior.

Crime, Criminals, and Social Forces

In the early twentieth century, sociologists emerged as major players in the ongoing quest to understand crime and criminals. As sociologists, they completely disavowed biological and psychological determinism as too narrow and individualistic in orientation. Crime was a far broader and societal problem, not, as the psychologists suggested, solely or largely an individual problem.[3]

In many theories crime is viewed as a consequence of social forces. Consider, for example, the contributions of the Chicago School of sociology to the study of crime. Looking at the relationship between greater Chicago and its inhabitants, social ecologists at the University of Chicago in the 1920s and 1930s believed it was the geographic area and not the people who inhabited it that held the answer to understanding crime. They said crime emerged in certain segments of the community owing to disturbed, distressed, or incomplete social connectedness in certain parts of the community (Shaw and McKay 1942). These areas exhibited high mobility, as various ethnic groups replaced each other in conditions of extreme poverty. City government largely ignored the schools, parks, and other public services in these areas to the point that they were falling apart. The social ecologists claimed that these geographic areas suffered from **social disorganization.**

The significance of the Chicago School for corrections is found in two general themes. First, social ecology helped shape an entire group of theories that emphasized the cultural transmission of criminal (and other deviant) values from one generation to the next. Edwin H. Sutherland, an early proponent of this approach, summarized his ideas about the **cultural transmission thesis** and the learning of criminal values, orientations, and actions in **differential association theory** (Sutherland and Cressey 1974). According to Sutherland's theory, criminal behavior, like all social behavior, is learned. For crime, he proposed that those who became criminals were exposed to more definitions favorable to breaking the law than definitions favorable to complying with the law. The sources of definitions, which included motives, drives, rationalizations, and the mechanics of committing crime, varied in four key ways. Some sources, such as parents and youthful friends, came early in one's social development. They had high **priority.** Some definitional sources were encountered with greater **frequency** than others. Often, exposure to the sources of certain definitions lasted longer than others, in which case they were described as having greater **duration.** Finally, some definitional sources enjoyed greater **intensity** than others, meaning that such sources were high in prestige and the emotional ties to the sources were considerable.

Social disorganization theorists tell us that there are delinquent areas, not just delinquent people. At times neighborhoods deteriorate so badly that prosocial forces decline and disorder and crime prevail.

Because learning is central to the advocacy of criminal values, definitions, and the like, perhaps it could be used to learn alternative, noncriminal ways. Donald Cressey, Sutherland's student and coauthor, believed in the ability of differential association to guide change. Cressey (1955) advocated that offenders be exposed to prosocial definitions in a group context within a correctional setting. Inmates could then help to change their peers for the better. Unfortunately, Sutherland left unexplored how the learning would occur, except to say that it would occur as does all learning. How and why are some definitions selected over others, when we are all exposed to great masses of information throughout our lives? This missing element made the application of Sutherland's principles to a correctional setting difficult.

Robert Burgess and Ronald Akers (1966) proposed that the missing element was operant conditioning. Some definitions were continued because of reward mechanisms, while others were extinguished by punishers, concepts borrowed wholesale from behaviorism. In later refinements of Akers' (1985, 1992) **social learning theory,** he articulated the two central ideas. First, learning occurs by two mechanisms: **imitation,** which as the term suggests involves modeling behavior after that observed in others, and **differential reinforcement.** The latter term refers to the operant conditioning principle that rewarded behavior is retained and repeated, and punished behavior is extinguished. Further, Akers addressed the learning of motivating definitions (**discriminative stimuli**). The first type of definition puts the behavior, in this case crime, in a positive light; the second form helps to counter or neutralize the "undesirableness" of the criminal behavior in question (Akers 1985, 50).

As a result, a criminal adopts those definitions that view the crime in question, say burglary, as an accepted and honorable vocation. Moreover, they also buy into those neutralizing definitions that define victims as unworthy of pity, because of, perhaps, their high socioeconomic status or the fact that their property is insured anyway.

Victim-offender confrontation programs, which may be part of a nontraditional settlement of violent and property crimes, have links to social learning theory. Besides jail or prison time, probation, fines, and other forms of punishment, the offender may be required to meet the victim, assuming this is acceptable to the latter. Seeing the victim as a human being and understanding that person's suffering is meant to break down the discriminative stimuli. Offenders find this process very stress-inducing and few leave these meetings without being affected in some way.

Other correctional applications of social learning theory include therapeutic communities. Select groups of offenders work on the attitudes and behavior of every member of the community. Reinforcers and punishers come from one's peers, other offenders engaged in the same reform process. The theory (and practice) of therapeutic communities is straightforward. Drug-using offenders, for example, find a supportive community of reform-minded peers toward whom they can express their best human emotions rather than their worst. These programs have enjoyed considerable success with both prison-confined and community-based felons (Yablonsky 1989; Wexler, Lipton, and Johnson 1988).

In the style of the cultural transmission thesis, some crime and deviance researchers adopted a **subcultural hypothesis.** Many such theories employ the notion that much crime emerges from delinquent or deviant subcultures. For example, delinquent youths may band together in gangs and reject both society and its values, thus reducing the impact of society's rejection of them (Cohen 1955). Or it might be that members of the lower class share similar **focal concerns,** including getting into trouble and thrill-seeking behavior, some of which is illegal (Miller 1958). Still other subculturalists note the existence of violent subcultures in society (Wolfgang 1958; Wolfgang and Ferracuti 1967). Violence becomes an accepted and expected way of dealing with all sorts of problems among members of these subcultures, but especially resolving questions of honor and "manhood" (Wolfgang and Ferracuti 1967).

The application of the subculturalist arguments to corrections is perhaps best visualized in a prison or jail setting. In Chapter 5 we discuss **prisonization,** a process by which inmates take on the culture and values of an inmate social system, essentially an inmate subculture. Whether inmates bring the culture of the street into the prison or whether prison culture is a product of the **pains of imprisonment** is much debated. Whatever its source, there seems to be little doubt that within the prison there exists a powerful subculture, complete with rules and regulations, values and prejudices. The cultural transmission thesis tells us much about a multigenerational inmate subculture, a phenomenon not unlike the situation in crime-prone inner cities described by Shaw and McKay (1942).

The cultural transmission theorists, particularly Sutherland and Akers, based their explanations of crime and deviance on a single assumption about social beings. That is, we have to learn to be deviant, just as we have to learn to be normal. Conversely, the social control theorists say that society provides the "social glue" that binds us together. Without this glue there is a tendency for people to engage in individual hedonistic activities, many of which are law-violating. Before we discuss this perspective we must explore its philosophical roots.

Emile Durkheim (1897), a turn-of-the-century French sociologist, believed that many of society's ills, including crime, derived from times when the social fabric of society, and the glue that held the individual members to it, were weakened. Wars and economic changes were among the preeminent causes of this weakened state, which he labeled **anomie,** or a generalized sense of normlessness. The norms, including laws, did not seem to apply during these chaotic times of economic and social change. Crime, suicide, and other socially disturbing behavior peaked during anomic times.

Durkheim viewed anomie as a societal-level condition, not something that could be observed in the individual. Two criminologists took different aspects of Durkheim's work and applied it to individual human behavior. First, Robert K. Merton (1957) saw anomie as creating a rift or break between the culturally espoused success goals (that is, status and financial security and the luxuries they provide, such as fancy cars, nice clothes, and the newest electronic gadgets) and the institutionally limited means to attain the goals (such as education, thrift, and hard work). More important, he believed that this was a condition felt directly by the individual. Merton developed several categories of adaptation to describe people's behavior. Conformists try legitimate means, including hard work and discipline, to attain such worthwhile and culturally valued goals as financial stability, status, and the like. When conformists meet with barriers, as in limited access to the legitimate means, they stand face-to-face with the **anomic trap:** They can either accept their fate and work hard but achieve little or turn to one of Merton's other adaptations.[4] Innovators, unlike conformists, avoid legitimate means and use illegitimate ones to achieve success. Although Merton identified other adaptations as well, it is the innovator who poses the most direct problems for the criminal justice system.[5]

The implications of Merton's theory for corrections are straightforward, but difficult to implement. Giving an offender the means to confront a life in which the deck may be stacked against him or her has direct ties to Merton's anomie theory. That is, people facing the anomic trap must be offered legitimate alternatives not normally made available to them. Increased educational opportunities or job training, both of which are found in correctional settings, are good examples. At the community level, the 1960s War on Poverty also had ties to a form of anomie theory called **differential opportunity theory** (Cloward and Ohlin 1960). One advocate of that theory, Lloyd Ohlin, worked briefly and unsuccessfully as a government bureaucrat in an attempt to carry out the practical aspects of anomie theory.[6]

Travis Hirschi (1969), a social control theorist, was influenced by Durkheim's discussion of the forces that hold society together. He believed that the **social bond** was the sum of the forces in a person's social and physical environment that connect him or her to society and its moral constituents. The latter include social institutions such as family, school, and the law. Hirschi identified four types of ties that an individual has with social institutions. **Attachment** is the affection for and sensitivity to members of social groups. Without attachments the individual is free to deviate. **Commitment** refers to the stake the individual has in conformity. How devoted is she or he to conventionality? The third element is **involvement:** To what extent does the person engage in conventional activities? **Belief,** the final element, explores the idea that the correctness of norms is variable; that is, the norms (and laws) may not hold the same significance for all people in society. The greater the belief in those norms, the lower the chance of delinquency. Indeed, Hirschi believed that the probability of law-violating behavior is directly proportional to the extent to which any of these elements of the social bond are weakened.

As for correctional practice, prison inmates and other convicted criminals may be among the most "de-bonded" individuals in society. If the social bond can be reestablished, and that is not a given, then re-bonding would have to occur across all four dimensions. Consider, by way of example, our brief discussions of reintegration, restoration, and restitution. These philosophies and social bonding theory all imply that offenders must be made a part of the society from which they came and that the links between offenders and the community must be reestablished (some would argue established for the first time). Social bonding theory's central warning is that any treatment or rehabilitation program must address all aspects of the offender's relationship to the community. Moreover, conditions of release, whether probation or parole, must necessarily limit an offender's contacts with "known criminals" and "prior criminal associates."[7] The minimization of these negative distractions enhances the probability of conventional bonding.

Reviewing Criminological Theory

We have tried to accomplish three goals with this abbreviated look at crime theory. First, we suggested a wide range of possible answers to questions that most people find difficult to answer. That is, we suspect that nearly everyone who contacts law violators, including staff members in the correctional system, engages in speculation about what brings offenders to crime. Why did they do it? Why do some stop? Why do others continue to do it even after they

Box 1.3

Power and Crime: A Missing Dimension?

The late 1960s and early 1970s witnessed the emergence of several important criminological theories, all of which attacked the dominant social structural, biological, and psychological theories as supporting the status quo. Instead, said a growing and vocal group of criminologists, the study of crime should include the dimension of power: Who has it? Who lacks it? Who uses it to what ends?

Some of these critics, including labeling theorists Howard Becker and Edwin Schur, suggested that the state's power to affix a negative stigma to those accused of crimes is perhaps the greatest evil. The truth in the label is irrelevant, but is taken as proof of the power of the state to engage in evil if an innocent person is arrested, tried, convicted, and sentenced as a law breaker. Importantly, labeling theorists warn us that even the "falsely accused" can succumb to the power of a negative label and become what we call them. The other important element is the power of the label to change a person's life and to resist any attempts to alter it. A criminal label has the potential to become, for the person labeled, a *master status,* the designation (as in murderer, sexoffender, burglar, etc.) by which that person will forever be known and remembered, along with the associated negative behavioral characteristics.

Other power-based crime theories include Marxist critiques of the criminal justice system. Marxists view the police, courts, and corrections as serving the interests of the wealthy (the capitalists), those who own the means of production and feed off the labor of the workers (the proletariat). Criminals, according to Marxists such as Richard Quinney, are either victims of the system or freedom fighters, fighting back against an unjust system. Later Marxists, including William Chamb-liss and Robert Seidman, tempered this view with more sophisticated images of the relationships between capitalism, law, and crime. State authority emerged as not simply an instrument of oppression, but an instrument for insuring the long-term dominance of capitalism as a way of life.

Many policy implications may be derived from theories emphasizing state power; however, carrying out any policy changes may be difficult, especially if the Marxists are correct. Indeed, the strategies suggested by Marxist theories are demystification of the existing system, which is supposed to occur before revolution, and revolutionary changes in the balance of power. Given the general failure of Marxism in the world as a political force, neither has occurred. Labeling presents a different policy picture. First, labeling theory helps us understand why assuming a normal life is so difficult for ex-offenders, since the negative label "ex-con" has been added to those they already possess. Second, a reduction in the formal reactions to those accused of crimes is viewed as one way to reduce future criminality. One approach has been called "radical noninterventionism" by Schur, meaning that society and its agents of social control may have to overlook some forms of juvenile delinquency to avoid more serious adult criminality. Third, deinstitutionalization, a process by which prisons and other institutional places of confinement are abandoned as methods of punishment, has been tried on a limited scale with juveniles. These responses to crime, while they make sense if we believe labeling theory, do not seem to fit well with the nation's obsession with punishment for its own sake. (See punishment philosophies.)

Sources: Becker (1963); Chambliss and Seidman (1982); Quinney (1970); Schur (1973).

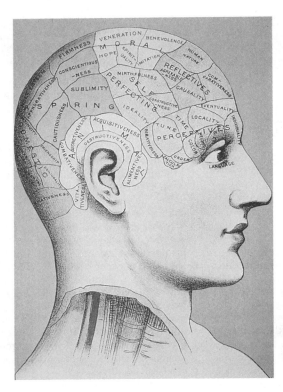

Phrenologists believed that the brain controlled human behavior through various localities that represented higher and lower propensities. Before you scratch your ear, check out the behaviors controlled by that region.

are punished? These theories—individually and collectively—provide answers to these questions. But what do we do with these answers? This question leads to a second purpose of this review of theories. At a minimum, the answers provided by criminologists allow us to understand the responses of law violators to the correctional system, their values, attitudes, outlooks, perspectives, rationalizations, and the like. These theories also have the potential to inform correctional workers about what to expect from offenders placed in their charge by the courts. Certainly, experience can also give insights, but theories yield far more systematic and broadly applied insights into the lives of criminals in general and convicted offenders specifically.[8] That is, they have the potential to make the career transition from civilian to correctional worker a bit smoother for all concerned, the keepers and the kept.

Finally, punishment philosophies and theories of crime causation allow penologists to design better methods for treating the offenders' problems, as with the prison-based therapeutic community or restricted conditions of probation and parole. If society cannot change their extrainstitutional behavior (that is, if rehabilitation or deterrence is not possible or not practical), then, at a minimum, the goal of corrections should be the proper, adequate, and humane treatment of offenders while they are under the control of correctional authorities. Before you dismiss these views as the ramblings of do-gooders, consider that if you treat human beings as wild animals, abusing them at every turn, they often will respond as wild animals. Nearly all convicted offenders, as a practical matter, must be released into the community at some point.

Saying that crime theory is impractical is a little like saying that disease etiology theories (the ideas that tell us how diseases evolve and kill or sicken people) are impractical. Disease epidemiologists—those people who must investigate the spread of diseases and direct efforts to eradicate them—would find their work nearly impossible without such theories. Unless the theories can give the epidemiologists some clues as to how diseases work, we have little hope of tracking, slowing, or eventually stopping their spread. The same is true of the relationship between criminology and corrections.[9]

Corrections Programs

The United States has 51 correctional systems, one for each state and one for the federal government. If we add the District of Columbia and some large local governments, such as Los Angeles County and New York City, that operate their own correctional "systems," the number is even higher.

The corrections component of the criminal justice system can be dissected in many different ways, but for the sake of simplicity dividing corrections programs into three categories is easiest: (1) community-based programs and treatment, (2) intermediate sanction programs, and (3) institutional placement programs. In this section we briefly outline some types of programs and agencies that can be found in each of these categories. This summary treatment introduces much of the materials with which we will deal in the remainder of the text.

Community-based programs and treatment efforts include many agencies and philosophies, some related and some not. For instance, the traditional programs of probation and parole are really community-based corrections efforts. The whole notion behind probation and parole is that the offender is treated in the community, under supervision, and is guided by restrictions, as opposed to being treated in the artificial environment of an institution. Some penologists suggest that it is more effective to treat the offender in a natural environment where day-to-day problems of family, acquaintances, and peers must be confronted and that probation and parole officers can help establish the support systems that will allow probationers and parolees to adjust to crime-free lives. As we will see later in this book, such assumptions are not always borne out for an assortment of reasons.

Community-based programs may also include residential placements such as group homes or halfway houses. Two types of halfway houses are employed: halfway-in for probationers, and halfway-out for parolees. In either instance, the idea is that the offender's original living arrangement is neither acceptable nor desirable. Arrangements must be made for an alternative housing placement. Nonsecure residential placements provide shelter, structure, and more constant surveillance than do traditional probation or parole alone, and the residents have a built-in support system and accountability group.

Intermediate sanction programs are among the fastest growing in contemporary corrections. We will briefly mention some types of programs that properly can be labeled intermediate sanctions, and discuss some reasons for their popularity. To begin with, universal agreement is lacking on what is an intermediate sanction, and arriving at a precise definition is difficult. However, the simplest way to describe intermediate sanctions is to say that they include any type of program existing on the corrections continuum between traditional probation and incarceration (Cromwell and Killinger 1994, 366). Some intermediate sanctions, such as split sentences and intermittent confinement, require that the convicted person serve brief periods of confinement in a local, state, or federal facility, followed by a period of community supervision. Thus, intermediate sanctions are both alternatives to incarceration and alternative forms of incarceration.

Not everyone agrees that court orders for community service and victim-offender restitution programs should be included in the list. More commonly, practices such as intensive probation supervision, house arrest, electronic monitoring, and shock probation/incarceration programs (all discussed in Chapter 8) are listed when the topic of intermediate sanctions arises (Castle 1991; Gowdy 1993).

Finally, the area most closely associated with the corrections subsystem is secure institutional confinement. Even in this area, noting the variety of institutional placements is important (Department of Justice 1988, 58, 96). For example, institutionalization can include jails, workhouses, or penal farms for misdemeanants confined at the local level. State and federal institutions cover a wide spectrum from the lowest security level "camps" and farm or ranch programs (often for juveniles or youthful offenders) up to the most secure prisons.

Prisons in the United States typically fit into one of three security classifications: minimum (the least restrictive form of residential confinement), medium (a bit more restrictive, but some freedom of movement within the institution exists), and maximum (the most restrictive form of residential living for prisoners with few opportunities for movement even within the institution). Variations on these traditional categories exist. For instance, some states have added "close security" or "minimum restrictive security" as types of classifications, but more on those concepts in Chapter 5. Prisons differ in security levels based on the types of inmates they house (that is, the crimes the offenders have committed) and the escape threats posed by the inmates. In fact, having a range of inmate security classifications within a given prison is also possible.

This brief overview is a reminder that "corrections" does not mean just one thing, it is really a vast array of different programs and agencies reaching from the community into the most secure institutions. We will examine all of the various facets of corrections as we progress through the book, beginning with an overview of the history of corrections in the following chapter.

 ## Conclusion

How are we dealing with individuals convicted of violating the criminal laws in this country? The following chapters outline the programs that exist for dealing with criminal offenders. Each chapter presents something of where we have come from, where we are now, and where we are going. The final chapter in the book particularly looks at what the future holds for employment prospects, program growth and development, persistent problems, and what the next century may hold for us in terms of the corrections component of the criminal justice system.

Several "realities" become apparent when we begin a systematic study of corrections. For one thing, there may not be universal agreement on what "corrections" really is. Some people believe that corrections and punishment are synonymous: To correct is to punish and to punish is to correct. However, as we have already seen there are a number of different approaches or philosophies related to contemporary corrections. As you read through the book examine the various programs and agencies we discuss and ask yourself: "What correctional philosophy is behind this program?"

We have also examined many of the criminological theories developed over nearly two centuries. Each of these theories makes certain assumptions about human behavior, and many contemporary corrections programs are explicitly or implicitly based on some of these theories. Again, as you read the following chapters ask yourself: "What theory helps me understand why people behave the way they do, and what can we do about that behavior?"

Additionally, the corrections subsystem is part of the more complex network of agencies we call the criminal justice system. As you progress through the book ask yourself: "How do the other parts of the criminal justice system help, or impede, the efforts of correctional agencies?"

Finally, keep in mind the substantial role played by the attitudes and opinions of the general public and policy makers. There is a series of questions we must all ask ourselves about our feelings toward corrections:

What shapes these attitudes?

Are the attitudes based on facts or assumptions?

What must we do to stay informed (and keep others informed) about the nature of the correctional process?

As you read the following chapters you may want to come back periodically and review these questions and those below. The effort will pay off. Questions such as these (and the ones at the end of each subsequent chapter) will help hone your critical thinking skills and enhance the learning process. If any current problem confronting society deserves critical thinking, it is contemporary corrections.

Critical Review Questions

1. What is being "corrected" in corrections, or is this term itself being misapplied?

2. How do you personally respond to the idea of retribution? Can you think of any modern-day applications? How do you feel about a murder victim's next-of-kin requesting to view the execution, pull the switch, or activate the syringes?

3. What kinds of personal motivations work for an individual's rehabilitation? Can we change people against their will?

4. What is the difference between isolation and incapacitation? Is one more important than the other? Why? To whom is it more important?

5. Are there real limits to restitution? To whom is restitution most unfair and why?

6. What terms would you use to describe most nineteenth-century criminological theories? Be sure to justify the use of these terms.

7. Are there any forms of determinism that you find personally offensive? Identify the forms and tell why they offend you.

8. Are we victims of our biology? Are we the victims of our minds?

9. Have twentieth-century sociologists helped us to understand the social forces behind crimes and criminals? Distinguish between those that explain the emergence of criminals and those that explain the crime rate.

10. Why is it important that we understand the forces shaping our images of crime, justice, and corrections?

Recommended Readings

Currie, Elliott. 1992. *Reckoning: Drugs, the cities and the American future.* New York: Hill and Wang. Any book on crime and justice by Currie is worth reading. This one is no exception. Currie brings his considerable skills as a social analyst to bear on the great burden the major cities must carry with the double dose of evil of crime and drugs. He poses several no-nonsense solutions for these problems.

Newman, Graeme. 1978. *The punishment response.* Philadelphia: Lippincott. This book is one of the best available sources of information about the history of punishment. It traces the philosophical and practical origins of punishments from sacred forms to contemporary methods.

Reiman, Jeffrey. 1990. *The rich get richer and the poor get prison: Ideology, class, and criminal justice.* 3rd ed. New York: Macmillan. A great book in both title and content. Reiman answers many questions about the stratification of crime in contemporary society. Also he has an interesting perspective on criminal justice, that is, is it criminal *justice* or *criminal* justice?

Walker, Samuel. 1994. *Sense and nonsense about crime and drugs: A policy guide.* 3rd ed. Belmont, CA: Wadsworth. A balanced treatment of a wide range of policies and other responses to both crime and drugs. It shows the problems and prospects associated with each side of the coin for liberal and conservative answers to the nation's often interrelated crime and drug problems.

Winfree, L. Thomas, Jr., and Howard Abadinsky. 1996. *Understanding crime: Theory and practice.* Chicago: Nelson-Hall. A different kind of criminology book. The authors explore a wide range of theories about crime and criminals and then proceed to demonstrate the pragmatic implications of those theories for criminal justice practitioners.

Key Terms

anomic trap	duration	prisonization
anomie	ego	psychological determinists
arousal theory	focal concerns	psychopaths
attachment	free will	reality therapy
behavior modification	frequency	rehabilitation
belief	general deterrence	reintegration
biological determinism	id	restitution
commitment	imitation	restoration
cultural transmission	intensity	retention elections
thesis	involvement	retribution
deterrence	isolation	selective incapacitation
differential association	*lex talionis*	social bond
theory	pains of imprisonment	social disorganization
differential opportunity	penal harm	social learning theory
theory	penology	specific deterrence
differential reinforcement	positivists	subcultural hypothesis
discriminative stimuli	priority	superego

Notes

1. This information is often treated in considerable detail in a course, entitled Criminology, on the nature and extent of crime. Our task is to compress the relevant parts of that course into part of a chapter without the usual numbing effect of study after study in support of or against this or that theory. We believe that we have been faithful to the central assumptions, concepts, strengths, and weaknesses of each theory included in this discussion.

2. We are aware of a long tradition of crime "theories" going back to original sin and other Judeo-Christian accounts of crime and criminals, including Cain and Abel (for example, the "mark of Cain" as a sign of evil.) There are also numerous medieval and Age of Enlightenment attempts to explain criminal

conduct as possession by the devil or other evil spirits, including some interesting but inconclusive ideas about evil faces reflecting evil minds (that is, *physiognomy,* a fancy term for the idea that you can tell a criminal by looking at him or her). Equally interesting and discredited are the phrenologist's ideas about bumps on the head telling us about a person's criminal proclivities. Our concern in this chapter is largely the past 100 years of "scientific" criminology and competing explanations.

3. Some early sociologists who studied crime and other forms of socially unacceptable misbehavior saw in their work a way of discrediting psychological or biological explanations and proselytizing their own sociological theories, including Emile Durkheim's anomie theory and Edwin H. Sutherland's differential association theory.

4. Whether people consciously or unconsciously turn to other adaptations is not clear. The consensus view seems to be that it is not a conscious decision-making process.

5. One could argue that retreatists, those who abandon both the legitimate means to success and the cultural goals of success for their own usually more hedonistic means and goals, are also a source of trouble for the criminal justice system. Also, rebels, who actively challenge all rules, including goals and means, are potentially thorns in the side of authority and hence problems for the justice system. We stick to innovators to facilitate this discussion.

6. Ohlin's "failure" was unrelated to the utility of the theory, but rather to the political threat it seemed to pose for some in government at the time. See Winfree and Abadinsky (1996, 235–37) for more on this abandoned attempt to implement criminological theory.

7. In point of fact, this condition could be linked to either social learning or social bonding. From a social learning perspective, old criminal cronies are potential sources of pro-criminal definitions. From a bonding perspective, such ties could weaken the bond to conventional society.

8. Once you have finished this book, or perhaps as you are reading it, we challenge you to read one of the several very good books written by ex-prisoners about their experiences with the correctional system. You will recognize the aforementioned theories—or concepts derived from them—in their vivid and raw descriptions of life as a convicted felon. Included among these titles are Greg Newbold's *The Big Huey,* Jack Abbott's *In the Belly of the Beast,* and Victor Hassine's *Life Without Parole.*

9. We selected the disease model to emphasize the significance of theory. In later chapters, you will notice that a disease model of crime gained a foothold in correctional philosophy and practice in the 1950s. The medical model was the source of contentious debate among criminologists and penologists (Bartollas and Dinitz 1989). Is crime a disease? Is a crime-ridden society a diseased or sick society? Can we find a "cure" for crime? Does the disease model inject a false sense of scientific certainty into the crime debate? Ask your instructors for answers to these questions. They love these kinds of questions!

A Brief History of Punishments and Corrections

Chapter Outline

- Introduction
- Early History
- The Age of Enlightenment, the State, and Criminal Sanctions
- Prison Reform and Penitentiaries
- The Pennsylvania System versus the New York System
- Penitentiary Reform in the Nineteenth Century
- From the Rehabilitative Ideal to the Justice Model
- Conclusion
- Critical Review Questions
- Recommended Readings
- Key Terms
- Notes

Introduction

To fully appreciate the contemporary correctional system one must examine the historical and philosophical roots of all punishments. Fiction provides one way of looking at the evolution of punishments. Consider, for example, the punishments represented in the following accounts (some are fictional, others based on fact):

- In *Ben Hur,* a Roman court sentences the title character (played by Charlton Heston in the film), a wealthy Jew in the Roman province of Judea, to life as a galley slave, to row until he dies. In characteristic Heston fashion Ben Hur saves the life of a powerful Roman general and earns both his freedom and Roman citizenship. Most galley slaves died chained to their oars in battle or from old age, illness, or injuries suffered at their masters' hands.

- The hero of Charles Dickens's *A Tale of Two Cities* literally loses his head for crimes allegedly committed against French revolutionary forces. Sidney Carton goes to his death uttering the famous lines: "It is a far, far better thing I do, than I have ever done; it is a far, far better rest that I go to, than I have ever known" (Dickens 1859, 15). Carton died for unrequited love, sacrificing his life so that his rival, Charles Darnay, could live, a rare act of altruism when it comes to capital punishment.

- In the film version of *Papillon,* Steve McQueen, cast as an uncommon thief, meets Dustin Hoffman's character, a white-collar criminal, at a penal colony in French Guiana. Penal colony inmates spent their sentences building roads and other capital improvements in support of France's colonial goals in Central America. If they violated major rules, penal colony officials sent inmates to the even more repressive and brutal facility on Devil's Island. McQueen's character escapes, but the fate suffered by Hoffman's character was more common: death or life as a colonist, even after he had served his sentence.

- The film *Brubaker* begins with a fictionalized account of how real-life prison reformer Tom Murton, played by Robert Redford, first encountered Arkansas's brutal prison farm system. Brubaker finds grotesque forms of punishment commonplace, including the "Tucker Telephone," that consisted of attaching the output lines from an old-fashioned crank telephone to a man's genitals and "dialing home." In the end, Redford/Murton unearths the prison's secrets, quite literally, and suffers the fate of many prison reformers: His boss fires him. Nonetheless, as the movie ends, the Arkansas prison system changes for the better.

These fictional accounts portray a wide range of sanctions for law violators over the past 2,000 or more years: life at hard labor as a slave of the state, the death penalty, transportation to a distant penal colony, and incarceration in an inhumane prison. Like most works of fiction, they have mostly happy endings. The long history of punishment records few such happy endings.

Early History

Providing a truly comprehensive history of punishments is beyond the scope of this chapter. However, clear benchmark events, laws, and penal systems exist that shaped the community's responses to crime and criminals. Most of these penal developments occurred during the past 3,000 to 4,000 years, paralleling the development of Western Civilization. A key to understanding current punishments lies in the development of **legal systems.**

Crime and Punishment in Prehistoric Context

The resolution of crime and punishment issues in clans and tribes relied heavily upon rituals of reconciliation and, to a lesser extent, rituals of exclusion (Pfohl 1981; see also Gargarin 1986, 19–50, and Vinogradoff 1920,

During the reign of the Emperor Justinian, twelve scholars prepared
the Corpus Juris Civilis, or Justinian Code, a legal system that lasted
nearly 1,000 years.

299–389).[1] Tribal rules governed in the **pre-legal** stage, rules passed orally
from generation to generation, describing inappropriate acts and appropriate
sanctions. For example, if someone violated one of the community's minor
rules, the accompanying punishment was usually mild and carried out immediately by the entire community. By contrast, if the norm in question was
more important and the sanction equivalently more severe, elders in the community might be called upon to judge the transgressor (Gargarin 1986, 21–22;
Pfohl 1981, 83). Both parties—the victim and the perpetrator—had to agree
on the "justness" of the "settlement" recommended by the elders. Settlements
were less about deciding guilt or innocence and more about ending strife in a
homogenous community, therefore, reconciliation was emphasized (Gargarin
1986, 23; Pfohl 1981, 84; see also *restorative justice* in Chapter 1).

Among the reconciliation rituals was **restitution,** an act that required the
offender or the offender's kin to repay the loss in a roughly equivalent harm.
Reconciliation emphasizes the restoration of a sense of balance between the
victim and the perpetrator. Both parties usually agreed in advance to a symbolic act, absent any serious injury or loss of life (Pfohl 1981, 81–83). Tribal
groups typically reserved **blood revenge,** in which the emphasis was on killing the offender (and perhaps all of the offender's kin), for intergroup offenses

---

Box 2.1

Origins of the Blood Feud

The blood revenge is a ritual of reconciliation? Get real! Given our ethnocentric position, viewing the blood revenge as a ritual of reconciliation is difficult, but, says Stephen Pfohl, that is precisely its intent. In pre-legal societies, not even homicide was viewed as an individualistic wrong. Homicide was a crime against the entire clan. Therefore, "If one member kills another then the kin of the victim are believed to have the right to exact an equal toll from the kin of the killer" (p. 81). Recall too that this form of reconciliation occurs largely between clans and tribes. Loss of life repays the debt. "The offending and victimized groups are able to return to the rituals of cooperation" (p. 82).

Blood feuds occur when one of the parties feels that attempts at reconciliation lack equity: either the person whose death was to have paid the debt was too valued by his or her kin or, from the other clan's perspective, unworthy of the debt. In this situation, each side feels wronged by the other; no one is happy; and, a case of blood revenge becomes a blood feud.

Source: Pfohl (1981).

(Pfohl 1981). Given the strong blood relationships in most tribes, the worst intragroup punishment was **banishment,** a ritual of exclusion. Anthropologists tell us that when faced with banishment, a transgressor in such a **proto-legal system** would often commit suicide rather than leave (Edgerton 1976).

Babylonian and Judaic Views on Punishment

Historians often call Mesopotamia, the area between the Tigris and Euphrates Rivers, "the cradle of civilization." Beginning around 5000 B.C.E., proto-legal systems arose in the city-states of the fertile southern plain between the two rivers. In the eighteenth century B.C.E., the Babylonians became the dominant proto-state in the region. Historians credit the great Babylonian king Hammurabi with codifying the region's many formal and informal rules. Among the **Code of Hammurabi**'s 282 clauses, about 50 reveal Babylonian responses to crimes and punishments. Death penalties and fines were common; however, the principle of "an eye for an eye, and a tooth for a tooth," or the *lex talionis,* appears at regular intervals. The *lex talionis* is an act of retaliation against the offender. However, according to Hammurabi's code, punishment was inflicted in the name of the city-state, not the victim or the victim's relatives.

Roughly 800 kilometers to the west of Mesopotamia was Canaan. Here Judaism flourished as a religion, a culture, and a system of laws. In this region of the world, the exchange of laws, like trade and commerce, was common. Consequently, the inclusion of the *lex talionis* in the **Law of Moses,** as summarized in the book of Deuteronomy, is not surprising.[2] Deuteronomy 19:21 contains the following statement: "Your eye shall not pity; it shall be life for life, eye for eye, tooth for tooth, hand for hand, foot for foot!" Penalties for other misdeeds were equally harsh. For example, the penalty for idolatry was death by the sword, and could be the fate of an entire city, if all were led astray (Deut. 13:13–19); and death by public stoning was the fate of the incorrigible son, one who is "stubborn and unruly" (Deut. 21:18–21). As harsh as some Judaic penalties were, their imposition could not shock the conscience of the community: "If a man guilty of a capital offense is put to death and his corpse hung on a tree, it shall not remain on the tree overnight. You shall bury it the same day" (Deut. 21:22–23).

Greek and Roman Laws

Even after the establishment of the Greek city-states around 1000 B.C.E., disputing parties either employed the pre-legal tribal normative systems or consulted the oracles.[3] Nearly all disputes in ancient Greece, including most forms of homicide, were private matters. Their resolution was left to the injured party's family. Draco, a seventh-century B.C.E. Athenian politician and **archon** (*chief magistrate*), altered the traditional method of dispute resolution.

Perhaps it is no accident that Draco's name derives from the Greek word **drakon,** meaning serpent or dragon, or that his reputation is found in the word *draconian,* meaning severe or harsh. According to the Greek historian Plutarch, Draco's approach to jurisprudence was to make nearly all offenses capital crimes in 621 B.C.E.[4] Like many lawgivers before him, Draco codified existing views on the punishment of homicide and established an application procedure (Gargarin 1986, 88). That is, those accused of homicide escaped punishment by going into exile, which act Athenians viewed as an admission of guilt. Ancient Athenian execution methods were especially brutal: The fortunate criminals died by being thrown from a high place or by ingesting poison, while those less fortunate died by starvation or exposure to the elements while staked out in a public place.

In 594 B.C.E., after years of dissent and unrest, the Athenian elite elected the Archon Solon (c. 639–c. 559 B.C.E.), a respected poet and merchant. He ordered sweeping social and economic reforms that, along with those made by Cleisthenes (c. 506 B.C.E.), culminated in the creation of the Athenian democracy of freemen. Among Solon's first acts was the repeal of Draco's criminal penalties for all offenses except homicide. He substituted fines, public humiliation, and banishment for the death penalty wherever possible. For example, the archon could order a "convicted" thief to give back the stolen property or its value and to pay a fine of an equal amount to the public coffers (Gargarin 1986, 9). Solon also distinguished between two kinds of wrongs: the private suit, brought only by the injured party, and the public suit, that anyone could bring. Aristotle called the public suit one of Solon's most democratic reforms (Gargarin 1986, 69).

The Romans were famous for "borrowing" from the Greeks, from food and fashion to architecture. An exception seems to have been the creation of

The great reformer, Archon Solon, may have filled the public coffers with his use of fines instead of executions for public crimes.

Rome's first major civil and criminal code, the **Twelve Tables** (Lewis and Reinhold 1990, 107). For the nearly 300 years following the founding of Rome, that city's residents relied upon unwritten customs for legal guidance and the good will of Roman patricians—nobility—to enforce them justly. As often happens when the powerful have all of the cards, "blind justice" was rare—especially justice for plebeians or lower-class citizens of Rome. In the fifth-century B.C.E., with Rome lurching forward from a kingdom to a republic, ten nobles codified the existing customs. The result was the Twelve Tables (Cary and Scullard 1975, 66–68).

The Twelve Tables essentially remained in force from 450 B.C.E. to the fall of Constantinople and the Eastern Roman Empire in 1453. Legal scholars and historians regard the civil elements of the Twelve Tables, and subsequent revisions dealing with property and contracts, to be among ancient Rome's finest achievements (Gibbon 1932; Jolowicz 1954). Twenty-seven sections of Table VIII dealt with criminal law violations and appropriate sanctions. Nine of the 27 sections required imposition of the death penalty, including crimes as diverse as parricide (killing a parent), libel, arson, nocturnal meetings for any purpose, and treason. Those who bribed judges—as well as the judges

---

Box 2.2

Table VIII: Torts or Delicts

The following four sections deal only with the crime of theft:

If theft has been done by night, if the owner kills the thief, the thief shall be held lawfully killed.

It is forbidden that a thief be killed by day . . . unless he defends himself with a weapon. Even though he has come with a weapon, unless he uses his weapon and fights back, you shall not kill him. And even if he resists, first call out.

In the case of all other thieves caught in the act, if they are freemen, they should be flogged and adjudged to the person against whom the theft has been committed, provided that the malefactors have committed it by day and have not defended themselves with a weapon. Slaves caught in the act of theft should be flogged and thrown from the [Tarpeian] Rock [on the Capitoline Hill of Rome]. Boys under the age of puberty should, at the praetor's discretion, be flogged, and the damage done by them should be repaired.

If a person pleads on a case of theft in which the thief has not been caught in the act, the thief must compound for the loss by paying double damages.

Sources: Cary and Scullard (1975); Gibbon (1932).

---

themselves—were subject to capital punishment. In nearly all cases, the method of execution was as brutal as those practiced in ancient Greece, including scourging, a practice of whipping until the flesh is laid bare, followed by crucifixion. Others were bound hand and foot, placed in a sack with wild animals, or hurled into the sea.

Roman law did not end with the Twelve Tables, becoming instead an evolving system of laws. Changes often took centuries. For example, Roman law evolved to the point where, in the late third century B.C.E., two systems existed: *jus civile,* dealing exclusively with relations between Romans, and *jus gentium,* laws for foreigners. Romans, of course, retained more rights than noncitizens (hence the importance of Roman citizenship for Ben Hur). After 100 B.C.E., Roman legislators enacted the *jus honorarium,* a method of magisterial law meant to supplement, aid, and correct existing law. This move essentially created **case law.** With the Roman Empire's establishment in 27 B.C.E., the Roman Senate lost to the Roman emperor the power to create laws.

At the start of the sixth century, all that remained of ancient Rome's glory was the Byzantine or Eastern Empire, headquartered in Constantinople. Justinian I became emperor in 527 and took control of an empire embroiled in trouble (Norwich 1988, 181–90). His generals returned Africa and Italy to the Eastern Empire but at great cost. Justinian found help in his quest to centralize control over the Empire in a re-codification of the old Roman laws. He assigned the task to twelve scholars, who completed their work on the **Corpus Juris Civilis** in 535. Justinian's legal experts provided few changes to the old Roman law. The punishments are those of old Rome; the penal sections were very brief. Rather, the importance of the *Corpus Juris Civilis,* or Justinian's Code, is its durability (Gibbon 1932). This legal system survived the Middle

Ages and the fall of the Eastern Empire in 1453. Justinian's Code became modern Germanic law and **canon law,** the sacred laws of the Roman Catholic church.

The Law of Europe in the Middle Ages

In 476 the Goths, one of the primary groups of ancient Germans, deposed Romulus Augustulus, the last Roman emperor. The fall of Rome signified the beginning of the Middle Ages, which ended only in the late fifteenth century with the reunification of Spain, the discovery of the Americas, and the European Renaissance. During the Middle Ages, law derived from two sources: the Roman Catholic church's canon law and tribal laws, such as the Germanic *lex salica.* Most legal principles during medieval times were a mixture of canon law, tribal law, and even the old Roman codes (Friedman 1977, 41).

The *lex salica* was the customary law of the ancient Germanic tribes. After the Ostrogoths and Visigoths invaded the Roman Empire, they learned the value of formal laws and codified the *lex salica* between the fifth and ninth centuries (Dopsch 1969, ch. 7). Germanic law dealt primarily with penal sanctions and procedures, although it included property rights (LeGoff 1989, 27, 30–33). Because the Germanic tribes considered law to be a personal matter, they allowed those they ruled, including Romans, to use their own system of laws (LeGoff 1989, 30). The people of Europe, but especially the Anglo-Saxons in the British Isles, tended to merge the *lex salica* with their own cultural norms, the latter strongly rooted in blood ties and kinship.

Germanic tribal law allowed for blood revenge. However, the Goths quickly learned that blood revenge eventually leads to blood feuds. Under the *lex salica,* and other medieval laws that followed it, judges could order **botes** (compensations for wrongdoings). For example, a murderer or a murderer's family could make the **wergild** (a price paid by a killer's family to the victim's family to atone for the murder and avoid reprisals) as restitution for a death, accidental or intentional, and in so doing avoid the blood feud. The *lex salica* contained the following passages concerning mutilations: "For tearing off someone else's hand, or a foot, an eye, the nose, 100 **solidi,**[5] but only 63 if the hand remains attached; for tearing off the thumb 50 solidi, but only 30 if it remains attached; for tearing off the index finger (the finger used to pull the bow with) 35 solidi; any other finger 30 solidi; two fingers together 35 solidi; three fingers together 50 solidi" (Le Goff 1989, 33; see also Dopsch 1969, 364–65). Obviously, the *lex salica* is not the *lex talionis:* Nearly every offense had a monetary value.

With the establishment of **feudalism** in ninth-century Britain, a system of **wites** (punishments) allowed the local lord or king to collect and keep the *botes.* This change is significant. No longer were *all wrongs* capable of correction by direct compensation to the victim or the victim's family. The "victim" was the state, and the state benefited from a feudal compensation system:

This is a sample page of William the Conqueror's Domesday Book—
the first catalog of English Common Law.

slaves were worth one amount, freemen another, minor nobility still more, and at the top was the king. For example, violations of the **king's peace** often resulted in fines 10 times the normal amount or the offender's death (Johnson and Wolfe 1996, 38–39; Newman 1978, 106–7).

Royal proclamations called **dooms** recorded these laws and *wites*. The importance of the dooms in the regulation of life in Britain grew throughout the seventh and eighth centuries as they increasingly regulated commerce and trade, "restricting trade to given ports or market towns and by requiring witnesses to sales transactions" (Johnson and Wolfe 1996, 39). After his conquest of Britain in 1066, William I ordered a survey of all English traditions, geography, and dooms. The result was the Domesday Book, the source of English common law.

During the Middle Ages, corporal and capital punishments, while rare, were horrific in execution. Fines and banishment were the more common punishments (Newman 1978, 103–8, 113). Many celebrated felons, especially those who threatened the king's peace, and many religious offenders[6] received either capital or corporal punishments, or a creative combination of both. Medieval punishments, like those in ancient Greece and Rome, often served a religious or sacred function (Newman 1978). For example, crucifixion, breaking on the wheel, and death by disembowelment, all of which combined torture and eventual death, allowed criminals the opportunity to confess before dying. (For a graphic portrayal of this punishment, see the death of Mel Gibson's character, William Wallace, in the film *Braveheart*.) Owing to their often horrific nature, medieval punishments also dispensed individual and collective vengeance. Finally, medieval codes, following feudalistic principles, reserved many of the worst forms of capital punishment—for

---

Box 2.3

**Corporal Punishment in Tudor England
and the American Colonies**

Several forms of corporal punishment mentioned by Newman are familiar to most
Americans.

- The *stocks* consisted of heavy wooden
  timbers with holes cut for feet and
  hands. The person held in the stocks was
  seated on the ground or a small stool.
  Stocks were found at every English jail
  by the fourteenth century and served
  chiefly as a means of detaining people
  until trial. By the seventeenth and eighteenth centuries public drunkenness
  could earn a person a turn in the stocks,
  making them instruments of punishment
  and public embarrassment.
- Designed for punishment and public
  ridicule, the *pillory* consisted of heavy
  wooden timbers set on a post; restraining holes for the victim's head and hands
  were cut in the timbers. "It was not
  uncommon for those sentenced to the
  pillory to be killed at the hands of angry
  spectators" (p. 117).
- *Public whipping* may be the oldest and
  most widely used form of corporal pun-

ishment. Again, like pillorying, death
was a likely outcome, particularly when
the strokes were administered in an
excessively harsh fashion or the victim's
health was poor. Also, the quality of
medical treatment was primitive in
Tudor England and colonial America,
increasing the likelihood of serious
injuries or even death. As we will see
later in this chapter, whipping played a
major role in discipline maintenance
among prisoners during the early days
of the American prison movement.

- Finally, *pressing* was a particularly
  gruesome form of corporal punishment
  in which the accused person who
  refused to enter a plea was placed on a
  hard surface beneath a board. Weights
  were then added to the top of the board
  and, at regular intervals, more weights
  added. The accused was then offered
  every opportunity to enter a plea.
  Source: Newman (1978).

---

example, drawing and quartering, disembowelment, and beheading—for
important political criminals, such as Wallace (Newman 1978, 47). Common-
ers, when executed, were quickly hanged or possibly impaled on a stake.

European Law in the Fifteenth
Through Seventeenth Centuries

Punishments took several interesting twists and turns with the rise of the
English Tudor (1485–1603) and Stuart (1603–1689) dynasties. By the seventeenth century, nearly all felonies—some 200 or more crimes—warranted the
death penalty upon a conviction at trial. Graeme Newman (1978, 114–23)
notes that common offenders, particularly those convicted of lesser crimes,
often received a physical or corporal punishment such as the stocks, the pillory, the whipping post, or pressing. These forms of physical punishment
were commonplace in the American colonies long after hanging had replaced
them in England.

Vagrants, idlers, debtors, and common prostitutes received different treatment from late Tudor and early Stuart kings: The courts removed them from

When the United States declared its independence, the English continued to send prisoners to Australia. This 1903 drawing shows inspection of convict settlers by the British army commander.

society. For example, English courts in the late sixteenth and early seventeenth centuries began sentencing minor offenders to work on public and private projects. Forced to reside in places of short-term imprisonment called houses of corrections and workhouses, inmates became an easily exploited labor source. One of the most notorious English workhouses, St. Bridget's Well, or **Bridewell,** opened in 1557. Bridewell became a national model, and in 1576 Parliament ordered every county in England and Wales to establish Bridewell-style workhouses. The guiding principle was that by forcing people to work at difficult and unpleasant tasks, they would be reformed.

Transportation, an updated and highly structured version of exile or banishment, was a second method for removing offenders from society, including those sentenced to death. Two factors influenced the movement toward transportation. First, the "new" workhouses and houses of corrections quickly filled. Second, English colonization efforts required vast amounts of cheap labor. One way to encourage people to emigrate to the colonies and discourage their return to England was to banish them in lieu of far more horrible fates. Parliament's passage of the Vagrancy Act of 1597 allowed for the legal deportation of criminals deemed incorrigible. A royal Order of Council in 1617 allowed judges to issue a reprieve in the execution of any punishment if the offender sought employment in an overseas colony. Parliament modified this law in 1718 to allow the transportation as indentured servants—a form of slavery—of all persons sentenced to three or more years imprisonment. Former indentured servants or penal colonists could never return to England.

Box 2.4

**Transportation to Australia:
The Rest of the Story**

Robert Hughes contends that beginning in 1787 and continuing until 1857, 160,000 Welsh, English, and Irish convicts, male and female, were shipped to penal colonies in Australia. Not wishing to repeat their experiences in Georgia and other American colonies, the English government controlled the prisoners in the Australian penal colonies. Todd Clear and George Cole observe that an 1837 commission found that rather than reforming criminals, the quality of life in the penal colonies was abysmal: "It created societies that were most thoroughly depraved." Acting on this report, Parliament adopted a policy of penitentiaries for the sentencing of felons to hard labor in 1840. However, it was only when Australians threatened to revolt in 1857 that transportation formally ended. *Sources:* Clear and Cole (1986, 63); Hughes (1987,162).

By these means, the British courts ordered an estimated 2,000 convicts a year transported to the American colonies from 1597 to 1776 (Sellin 1976, 73).

The Age of Enlightenment, the State, and Criminal Sanctions

In the seventeenth century, Isaac Newton, Francis Bacon, John Locke, René Descartes, and Baruch Spinoza made enormous scientific and intellectual advances. In the next century, a group of intellectuals and social critics emerged who shared a belief in **natural law.** As a philosophy, natural law stresses that some rules are fundamental to human nature and discoverable by human reason without knowledge of, or reference to, the artificial laws of society. Science, they believed, held the answers to all of society's challenges, social and political. The state was, from this position, a rational instrument for human progress. These latter philosophers formed a rationalist, humanitarian, and scientific movement known as the **Age of Enlightenment.** The works of two men in particular are central to the Age of Enlightenment's impact on punishment: Montesquieu and Cesare Beccaria.

Montesquieu

Charles-Louis de Secondat, Baron de La Brède et de Montesquieu (1689–1755) may seem an unlikely revolutionary, especially given his birthright. At the time in Europe, the highborn and well-educated noblemen enjoyed criticizing the very caste system that produced them. A jurist and political philosopher, Montesquieu was a prolific author; his greatest work, *On the Spirit of Laws* (1748), compared republican, despotic, and monarchical forms of government. He advocated the separation and balancing of powers into the judicial, executive, and legislative branches. This separation, Montesquieu believed, guaranteed the individual's freedom.

Montesquieu wrote about more than freedoms. He also argued passionately about proportionality in punishment (Nugent 1977). Only despotic governments full of terror, he wrote, supported severity in the punishment of criminals. Montesquieu characterized monarchies and republics as more moderate forms of government. As such, they relied on honor and virtue, turning to higher goals, such as preventing crime and correcting the law violator. "Leniency reigns in moderate governments" (Nugent 1977, 158). These ideas came to the attention of people outside the Enlightenment movement.

Cesare Beccaria

Any list of Age of Enlightenment philosophers would be incomplete without Cesare Bonesana, Marchese de Beccaria (1738–94), known to history as Cesare Beccaria. His crowning work, *On Crimes and Punishments* (1764), influenced generations of legal and penal reformers. On the legal front, Beccaria believed that punishments could deter crime, but only if they were certain, swift, and severe. (See Chapter 1.) Beccaria also espoused many ideas related to crimes and punishments. For example, he endorsed the segregation of inmates by age, gender, and offense—radical ideas for the day. Perhaps one measure of the radical nature of his suggestions is that, although a member of a well-respected aristocratic family, Beccaria initially published his work under an alias. Proposing humane and just treatment for prisoners, convicted or otherwise, was as unpopular—and as potentially dangerous to those making the suggestion—in the eighteenth century as it has been at times in the twentieth. (Recall Tom Murton's fate.)

Prison Reform and Penitentiaries

Two men, one English and one Colonial American, translated the Age of Enlightenment's emphasis on humanism and rationalism into punitive philosophies that would profoundly influence their respective nation's responses to crime and punishment for generations. John Howard (1726–90) was a squire (member of the landed gentry) when, at the age of 47, he assumed the duties of the sheriff of Bedfordshire. In this position, he inspected the gaols (jails) in his jurisdiction. He was appalled at the conditions he found. Traveling to the European continent, Howard found that not all prisoners existed in conditions of squalor or were regularly exploited by gaolers. He unfavorably compared English and Welsh prisons and gaols with those found, for example, in the Ghent House of Enforcement. Howard lobbied the English House of Commons, providing a detailed and convincing document in *The State of Prisons in England and Wales* in 1774 (Johnson and Wolfe 1996, 129–30).

Howard's efforts to convince the English Parliament that conditions in gaols must change resulted in passage of the Penitentiary Act in 1779.[7] This act led to the creation of a new class of institution, largely incorporating Howard's main concerns about humane treatment, productive labor, and sanitary living conditions. As with many later efforts at prison reform, passing a legislative act—and even building penitentiaries—was not the same as changing the way prisons were operated. Later generations of inspectors met with resistance from those charged with funding and implementing the necessary changes in the conditions of confinement. The criticisms offered by those opposed to increased spending for prison inmates in the late eighteenth century and early nineteenth century are not all that different from those voiced today: Operating a humane prison costs too much money, and the prisoners deserve the lowest standard of living capable of sustaining life.

Benjamin Rush (1747–1813) was a highly regarded physician before he began his somewhat brief career as a penal reformer. Rush, a signer of the Declaration of Independence, was a friend of many influential Colonial and early American figures, such as Thomas Jefferson and John Adams. In 1786, Rush spoke out *against* a series of changes in Pennsylvania's penal law. He voiced two concerns: punishments should not be public events and reformation of offenders could be achieved through punishment that encouraged penance (Hawke 1971; McKelvey 1936).

The Friends' Society, or Quakers of Pennsylvania, formed the Philadelphia Society for Alleviating the Miseries of Public Prisons in 1787. Rush, a Presbyterian, attended the first meeting of the society, and he forever became associated with its goals—goals similar to those earlier espoused by Howard. In 1789, the society, with Rush as a prime spokesperson, attempted to improve the lot of inmates incarcerated at Philadelphia's **Walnut Street Jail,** a facility originally commissioned in 1773. The General Assembly of Pennsylvania agreed and directed that this facility be designated a penitentiary house. A year later, the General Assembly authorized the construction of a special cell block in the yard of the Walnut Street Jail. Based on Rush's belief that the only purpose of temporarily removing offenders from society was to reform them, this solitary confinement area imprisoned offenders *for* punishment, but not *as* punishment.

The Pennsylvania System versus the New York System

Historians agree that throughout most of the first half of the nineteenth century, two prison systems vied for the attention of penal reformers in the nation and the world, the Pennsylvania and the Auburn Systems. While the two philosophies emerged at about the same time—the first quarter of the nineteenth century—we begin with the Pennsylvania System.

Box 2.5

Jeremy Bentham and the Panopticon: Who's Watching Whom?

Jeremy Bentham (1748–1832) was a penal reformer and philosopher often mentioned in the same context as Beccaria, Howard, and Rush. A Scottish moralist, Bentham dabbled in penal reforms. He believed that order and discipline could be achieved if inmates were under the constant supervision of a central inspector. Competing for a contract to build a central prison for England, Bentham proposed the Panopticon, or inspection house. At the central hub of a multi-tiered circular building was a glass inspection house. A series of louvered windows, consisting of movable slats that when opened, allowed supervisory guards to keep watch over the prison's inmates. Bentham believed that the power of the inspection house model lay in its unpredictability: Inmates never knew when they were being watched.

The Panopticon was never fully implemented. It was viewed as too commercial, prone to corruption by profit-seeking contractors for the factory Bentham proposed to operate at the prison. The Panopticon design was also critiqued for failing to incorporate sufficient religious contemplation, in spite of the fact that the design called for a prison chaplain who would deliver sermons from the central hub to a captive audience. The physical design did have its good points and was adopted in two English prisons at Milbank on Thames (1817) and Pentonville (1842), and in the United States at Pittsburgh's Western Penitentiary (1826) and Illinois's Stateville (1924).

Sources: Barnes and Teeters (1959); Schafer (1969,106–8).

Eastern Penitentiary and the Pennsylvania System

Among the first truly new prisons, built from the ground up as state penitentiaries and guided by a penal philosophy other than prison-as-punishment, were two constructed in Pennsylvania. These facilities, the first opened in 1826 in Pittsburgh as Western State Penitentiary and the other in 1829 in Cherry Hill as Eastern State Penitentiary, followed what penologists call the **Pennsylvania System.** To prevent fraternization among prisoners observed at the Walnut Street Jail, officials extended solitary confinement to the new Pennsylvania prisons. These massive structures resembled gigantic stone wheels laid on their side with wings of cells branched out like spokes from a hub that was the central rotunda. The cells at Eastern, as portrayed in Figure 2.1, measured about 8 by 12 feet. Each cell had a locked door that led to a high-walled, unroofed yard in which the inmates engaged in solitary exercise and contemplative thought.

We have little indisputable evidence that the Pennsylvania System accomplished its goals. Likewise, only anecdotal evidence exists that it drove inmates insane or created a hardened class of criminals (Gibbons 1996, 352). Few states adopted the Pennsylvania System's philosophy of solitary confinement by architectural design. Even Pennsylvania abandoned this system in 1913. Curiously, many European prisons constructed in the 1800s followed

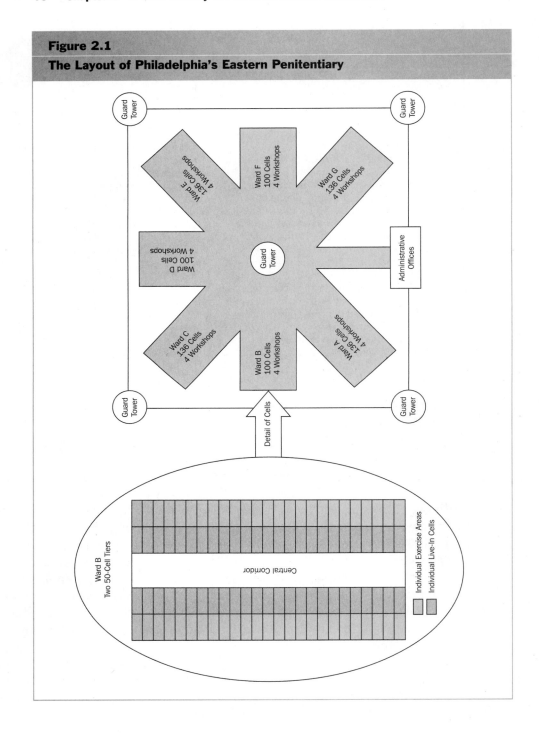

Figure 2.1

The Layout of Philadelphia's Eastern Penitentiary

the solitary confinement system. In the United States, however, the Pennsylvania System contained the seeds of its own demise in its basic philosophical element: solitary confinement. First, building and supervising individual cells for hundreds of prisoners were very costly undertakings. Second, the separation and isolation of inmates did not allow for the profitable exploitation of inmate labor (McKelvey 1936). The Auburn (New York) system corrected both of these design shortcomings.

The Auburn System

Following the American Revolution, a series of events in New York State led to the creation of the **Auburn System,** which would compete with and eventually replace the Pennsylvania System. The New York State legislature, following the lead of Pennsylvania, abolished capital punishment in 1796 for all but first-degree murder and treason. As a result, the state experienced a growing need for space to house convicted felons. The legislature authorized a prison to be constructed in the Greenwich Village section of New York City. New York's **Newgate Prison,** opened in 1797, soon became overcrowded and experienced a series of riots and uprisings in 1799 and 1800. By the early 1820s, Newgate Prison had nearly twice the number of inmates as called for in its original design. The prison housed adults and juveniles, men and women, many convicted of relatively minor offenses. Only the use of generous "good time" credits for early release of inmates and the implementation of fines and jail sentences for minor property offenders kept Newgate's population from the bursting point.

In 1816, the New York State legislature authorized construction of a new prison in the upstate town of Auburn. The initial design of the Auburn prison, as shown in Figure 2.2, was similar to Philadelphia's Walnut Street Jail and New York's Newgate Prison: The prison's south wing had both two-man and congregate cells. Several years later, William Brittin (?–1821), the prison's first warden, built the north wing with solitary cells, each of which was 7 feet long, 3 feet wide, and 7 feet high. The center of the north wing consisted of five tiers of 20 cells each, set back to back. Besides the building itself, each wing had a fully enclosing wall. First occupied in 1821, the north wing represented more than a change in prison architecture. Inmates followed a strict regimen of isolation, both physical and social, that was intended to subdue the inmates' depraved hearts and stubborn spirits. Prison administrators abandoned this regimen in 1825. Inmates worked as groups during the day at light manufacturing in congregate shops. They ate in congregate dining halls. Outside of working and eating, inmates remained in their one-person cells for the remainder of the day. Reading, except the Bible, was strongly discouraged.

Regimentation was a key to maintaining discipline at Auburn, but it was not the only tool utilized by the custodial staff. Guards strictly enforced a

Figure 2.2

The Layout of New York State's Auburn Prison

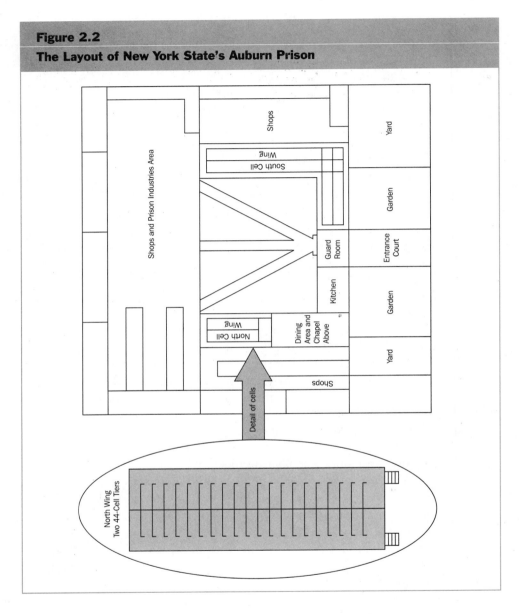

rigid **silent system:** That is, inmates marched, ate, and worked in complete silence. Auburn prison officials also "invented" a number of other prison innovations, many of which were used well into the twentieth century, including the infamous **lockstep shuffle,** in which an inmate stood in line with the right foot slightly behind the left and the right arm outstretched with the hand on the right shoulder of the man in front of him. The column of men moved forward together in an undulating shuffle. The black-and-white striped uni-

This 1878 wood engraving shows convicts in their striped uniforms marching with the lockstep shuffle into the dining hall at New York's "Sing Sing" Prison. Regimentation and harsh discipline were often parts of the everyday life in such prisons.

form and caps also originated at Auburn, a dress code that survived to the 1950s in some state prisons.

A threefold classification system for inmates was also adopted in 1817. The north wing, with its solitary cells, held the hardened criminals. Somewhat less dangerous inmates received a mix of three days a week in solitary and congregate work for the rest of the week. The least dangerous inmates worked in prison shops six days a week. Finally, those inmates who violated the rules came up against a punishment system that emphasized the whip. Elam Lynds (1784–1855), Brittin's replacement and the man who was "credited" by many as creating the punitive excesses of the Auburn System, said of flogging:

> I consider the chastisement by whip the most efficient and, at the same time, the most humane which exists; it never injures health, and obliges the prisoner to lead a life essentially healthy . . . I consider it impossible to govern a large prison without a whip (Beaumont and Tocqueville 1832, 163).

Hard work. Social isolation. Strict regimentation. The silent system. Corporal punishment. These are the characteristics of a correctional philosophy that, along with its unique architectural design, we know as the Auburn System. Was it a success? If success means imitation, then the answer is yes. Auburn was the most emulated prison system of its day in the United States, spreading to 11 states and the District of Columbia in only a decade. New

York built another maximum-security Auburn-style prison at Ossining ("Sing Sing"), employing prison labor almost exclusively. Another measure of success is longevity, and here, too, the Auburn System scores high marks. Some critics suggest that by the middle of the eighteenth century the model was largely compromised by overpopulation of existing prisons. Nonetheless, elements of the Auburn System survived well into the twentieth century. Finally, the Auburn System received mixed economic marks. Although cheaper to build and operate than Pennsylvania-style prisons, Auburn-type prisons rarely returned a profit. Contractors found the labor unreliable and the goods manufactured shoddy. As a source of cheap workers, prison contractors often got what they paid for: poorly performed labor.

One lasting "legacy" of the Auburn System is, for many penologists, the heavy reliance on severity as the key method by which contemporary security staff maintain control in a prison environment (Bartollas and Conrad 1992, 75; Johnson 1996, 48). Other penologists view the architectural design of one- and two-person cells stacked in tiers surrounded by high stone walls and guard towers—the **big-house prison**—as another legacy of the Auburn-style prison (see Irwin 1980; Irwin and Austin 1994). Still others point to the stratification of inmates into security risk levels as an important part of the Auburn System (Champion 1990a, 197).

Penitentiary Reform in the Nineteenth Century

Critics and supporters of the penitentiary movement created a cottage industry of imitative prisons and alternatives to incarceration. Nearly as soon as prisons such as Newgate, Auburn, and Cherry Hill opened to inmates, foreign visitors arrived and reported on what they saw. Some were complimentary; others were not. The end result was the creation of an alternative correctional philosophy, one that emphasized reformation and reintegration into society. It began, oddly enough, in the British penal colony at Van Diemen's Land, now known as Tasmania, off the coast of Australia.

Alternatives to Prison

In 1840, Captain Alexander Maconochie (1787–1860), a retired naval officer, arrived in Australia. He assumed the superintendency of the **penal colony** at Van Diemen's Land. Shocked by the conditions he found, Maconochie set about to humanize the penal colony. Maconochie proposed a plan to ready the offender for life in the free society, a plan that would enable penal colonists to avoid returning to a life of crime (Barry 1958, 72). Unfortunately, Maconochie, like other penal reformers before and since, incurred the wrath of his superior, Sir John Franklin, the lieutenant governor of Van Diemen's Land and a close personal friend. Franklin fired Maconochie before full implementation of the treatment plan.

Maconochie's next stop was the superintendency of the penal colony at Norfolk Island (an island near Australia). The Colonial Office in London, which ran all of the Australian penal colonies, saw merit in Maconochie's ideas. By the early 1840s the Colonial Office was under increasing pressure to rid itself of the penal colonies. Maconochie created a system of "marks of commendation" given to inmates for good behavior. An inmate with a fixed number of marks—all in the experiment were men—could earn his **ticket-of-leave,** or the right to move about freely in the colony. Misbehavior earned the offending party not the whip but a loss of marks.

Conditions for the experiment at Norfolk Island were less than ideal. New and so-called "doubly convicted" offenders[8] lived on the island, making implementation of the mark system difficult. Maconochie, an independent and headstrong individual, insisted that all inmates be treated the same. Public doubts about the experiment resulted in the recall of Maconochie to England in 1844. The Norfolk Island experiment was abandoned shortly thereafter, and the colony returned to a more punitive system of control.

In 1853, Parliament passed the **Penal Servitude Act** as part of the English penal system reorganization. This act allowed prisoners to be released—paroled—on a ticket-of-leave and supervised by local law enforcement. That same year, the Home Office commissioned Walter Crofton (1817–97) to investigate living conditions in Irish prisons. In 1854, Crofton became director of the Irish prison system. Crofton, an admirer of Maconochie's effort at Norfolk Island, created what has come to be called the **Irish Ticket-of-Leave System.** Crofton's system consisted of four stages:

1. During the first three months inmates were placed in solitary confinement and fed reduced rations. They did not work. Crofton believed that after three months of enforced idleness even the most shiftless and lazy inmate would be anxious for something to do. Their first real jobs were agricultural in nature, requiring little skill and providing few rewards; however, inmates were provided full rations at this point.

2. Working with other inmates in a special closed prison on an island off the coast of Ireland, the industrious prisoner could earn marks, like those detailed by Maconochie, for transfer to the third stage. This stage consisted of four levels and typically required at least 12 months to achieve; the inmate could spend several years, depending on the original sentence and prison behavior.

3. Inmates in this stage worked in an open prison with few restrictions and only a handful of unarmed guards. The purpose of this facility was to show the inmates trust. Those inmates who, in turn, showed genuine signs of reformation could earn their promised ticket-of-leave.

4. Parolees, called ticket-of-leave men, were given a conditional release from prison. Those residing outside Dublin were supervised by local police. A civilian employee, called the inspector of released prisoners, supervised those living in Dublin.

Only inmates serving terms of three years or more were eligible for the Irish System. While there was considerable debate over the use of police as supervisors and other more political infighting among prison officials, the Home Office adopted Crofton's system for all of England in 1877.

Foreign Opponents and Proponents

Among the foreign dignitaries who visited prisons in the United States before the mid-nineteenth century were four particularly illustrious ones. Two such visitors, Gustave de Beaumont (1802–66) and Alexis de Tocqueville (1805–59), were lawyers, magistrates, and widely traveled social critics. For nine months in the early 1830s, the pair toured prisons throughout the new nation. They observed inmate living conditions and talked with staff, including wardens such as Auburn's infamous Captain Elam Lynds. Upon returning to France, De Beaumont and De Tocqueville prepared *On the Penitentiary System in the United States and Its Application to France* (1832), a generally favorable, but candid, look at U.S. prisons. The French Revolution of 1848 interrupted plans to build a Pennsylvania-style prison system. Following an aborted building effort in 1853, France adopted a massive program of transportation to penal colonies. (The most infamous French penal colony, part of which was Devil's Island, mentioned at the beginning of the chapter, was located in French Guiana.)

Also in early 1930s, the British Home Office commissioned William Crawford (1788–1847), a London wine merchant and philanthropist, to investigate the suitability of U.S. prisons for Britain. Crawford traveled extensively, visiting penitentiaries in 14 states and the District of Columbia; he also stopped at a number of jails along the way. Upon returning to England, he prepared a massive document, *Report on the Penitentiaries of the United States* (1834), that included detailed descriptions of all the facilities he visited.

By the late 1830s, the Home Office approved plans for a model prison based on Pennsylvania's Eastern Penitentiary. This prison, later known as Pentonville, opened in 1842 and was followed two years later by Reading Prison. (Remember the problems the British were having with their penal colonies by the late 1830s and early 1840s.) The Pennsylvania approach alone quickly proved ineffective. After the Penal Servitude Acts of 1853 and 1857, the Home Office assigned every inmate to Pennsylvania-type solitary confinement for nine months, followed by placement in an Auburn-type regimen (Johnston 1969, xvi).

The fourth critic of the U.S. prison systems was far less complimentary than De Beaumont, De Tocqueville, or Crawford. Charles Dickens (1812–70) made several trips to the United States, the first in 1842. Not yet 30 years of age and already a great celebrity, Dickens had by that time published five novels, including *Oliver Twist* (1839) and *Nicholas Nickleby* (1839). He was no stranger to questions of law, justice, and punishment, having served as a court stenographer and parliamentary reporter. He took a general disliking to American ways, reserving his most biting comments for the American penal system. Describing his visit to Eastern Penitentiary, Dickens (1842, 238) wrote:

> In the outskirts, stands a great prison, called the Eastern Penitentiary: conducted on a plan peculiar to the state of Pennsylvania. The system here, is rigid, strict, and hopeless solitary confinement. I believe it, in its effects, to be cruel and wrong. . . . I believe that very few men are capable of estimating the immense amount of torture and agony that this dreadful punishment, prolonged for many years, inflicts upon the sufferer. . . . I hold this slow and daily tampering with the mysteries of the brain, to be immeasurably worse than any torture of the body.

Dickens saw a prison system different from that visited by his contemporaries, but then Dickens was a master of detail.

The Cincinnati Meeting of the National Prison Association

In 1870, the National Prison Association (later the American Correctional Association), under the leadership of its first president, Rutherford B. Hayes, held its first National Congress on Penitentiary and Reformatory Discipline in Cincinnati. More than 130 delegates from 24 states, Canada, and South America attended the congress. The graduated release systems developed by Maconochie and Crofton stood as centerpieces for discussion at this conference. The congress and the National Prison Association initiated the modern penal reform movement in America. Two names are synonymous with its implementation, Enoch Wines and Zebulon Brockway.

Enoch Wines

Enoch Cobb Wines (1806–79) was a scholar, possessing three college degrees, including a doctor of law. During his adult life, Wines was a secondary school and college educator, a Christian minister, and, over the course of the last 17 years of his life, a penal reformer. He published his first book on crime and punishment in 1864, and this work, *The True Penitent Portrayed: A Doctrine of Repentance,* reflected Wines the scholar and Christian. He, like many of his reform-minded contemporaries, believed in the power of religious training and hard work to alter the course of human lives. Wines opposed the imposition of severe and regular punishments for their own sake. Wines advocated instead that those who would reform or change criminals should first demonstrate their concern for and interest in offenders by rewarding positive steps toward reformation and restricting the use of harsh punishment for those who failed. To this end, he supported an approach built upon the Irish Ticket-

The Elmira Reformatory began as the flagship institution of the "progressive movement." It included vocational training for its youthful offenders. In this 1898 photo, inmates learn the craft of sign painting.

of-Leave System as a means of identifying progress and the indeterminate sentence.

Enoch Wines died less than a decade after the Cincinnati conference. Thanks to his written works, Wines's influence on corrections in the United States continued well into the twentieth century. He was, however, largely an outsider, a theoretician and academician. An organizer whose skills were legendary among his contemporaries, he served as secretary of the New York Prison Association and first president of the National Prison Association, later serving as that organization's secretary. However, it remained for others to implement his reform ideas, to translate theory into practice. Zebulon Brockway was one of the most prominent of these practitioners.

Zebulon Brockway

In the last quarter of the nineteenth century Zebulon Reed Brockway (1827–1920) brought attention to the practical issues associated with the corrections reform movement. Brockway's career began at age 21 when he assumed the positions of guard and, in short order, clerk at Connecticut's Wethersfield Prison. Over the next 28 years he served as superintendent of three different facilities, earning a national reputation as a penal reformer and innovator. For example, as superintendent of the Monroe County Penitentiary in upstate New York, he created programs intended to reform youthful offenders, a

---

Box 2.6

England's Borstal System

In 1897, toward the end of Brockway's reign at Elmira, Sir Evelyn Ruggles-Brise (1857–1935) visited the reformatory. Ruggles-Brise convinced the British Prison Commission to create a similar system for his nation's youthful offenders. England's Borstal System, restricted to youths between 16 and 21, treated convicted youths not as criminals or delinquents, but as "lads" in need of reform. The Borstal System emphasized that each youth had unique problems that the individual, with the help of caring staff, must solve. These goals were also to be achieved in a less militaristic and structured environment than that found at Elmira, superficially resembling an English public school. As a former

Borstal staffer and member of the Prison Commission, Alexander Paterson (1884–1947) observed: "You cannot train a man for freedom in conditions of captivity."

As an interesting postscript to the Reformatory movement, California and a handful of other states adopted the American Law Institute's revised Borstal plan in the early 1940s, called the Youth Correction Authority Act. Thus, Brockway's reformatory model, largely discredited by researchers and investigatory state commissions, continued to impact U.S. correctional policy for youthful offenders in the guise of the "newly discovered" Borstal plan.

Sources: Bartollas and Conrad (1992, 93); Ruggles-Brise (1921).

---

group for which he developed a special interest. In Brockway's autobiography, *Fifty Years of Prison Service* (1912), he claimed that at the Michigan House of Correction, a facility for young men, he allowed inmates a measure of self-governance. The passage of an indeterminate sentence by the Michigan legislature in 1867 was largely due to Brockway's lobbying. Brockway's most important contributions to corrections occurred in a small, upstate New York town called Elmira.

Shortly after the American Civil War, the New York State legislature authorized construction of a "reformatory" to be built in the town of Elmira, a 500-bed facility that would house first-time offenders between the ages of 16 and 30. When Elmira opened its doors to the first transfer inmates from Auburn in July 1876, Brockway was its superintendent. After a somewhat inauspicious transition period of about four years, when escapes and even staff murders occurred, Brockway implemented his famous three-step program for inmates, with progression through the steps based on a system of marks similar to those proposed by Maconochie and Crofton a generation before.

The first stage in the reformation process consisted of information gathering, an interview process often conducted by Brockway personally. Today this stage is called **intake.** New inmates began Brockway's program in the second grade (of a three-grade classification system), where they were the objects of treatment by Elmira's staff. In what must have been one of the earliest prison-based internship programs, students and lecturers from nearby Elmira College provided the reformatory with a strong educational foundation. Other "medicine" in Brockway's treatment program included farm work, institutional maintenance, and even labor in an iron foundry. When prison-based industries were temporarily outlawed in the 1880s, the young men of Elmira reformatory daily practiced close-order drills with wooden rifles. Earning three marks each for education, labor, and behavior every month for six months moved a youth to the first grade or top inmate level. Poor behavior and indolence resulted in the loss of points and even assignment to the third grade, or discipline group. A full year of cumulative monthly marks of nine could earn a youth a parole hearing and release, the final stage in Brockway's program.

Brockway tightly controlled both the institution and reports of its success and, far less often, chronicled its failures. A tireless self-promoter, his early glowing reports of successes led to widespread emulation of the reformatory model. Within a quarter century 12 states had adopted the reformatory model. By the early 1930s, nearly one-half of the states had adopted reformatory plans for youthful offenders and even young adults based on the Elmira model.

From the Rehabilitative Ideal to the Justice Model

The late 1800s were exciting times in the emerging disciplines of criminology, the scientific study of crime and criminals, and penology. In point of fact, these disciplines merged in the work of Cesare Lombroso, the Italian physician whose work we described in Chapter 1. Over the course of his extensive medical career, Lombroso identified four main types of criminals and four subtypes within one of the main ones. Heredity, he surmised, was the principal cause of criminal tendencies in all of them. As a consequence, there was essentially no way to change or to alter the behavior of the criminal. Unlike Classical criminology, which emphasized the ability of laws and punishments to deter criminals, the fixed and immutable nature of criminals was at the heart of the Lombrosian or Positivistic School of criminology. Moreover, this approach to crime and criminals was also at odds with the reformation ideals of Rush and Wines that found expression in the work of Crofton and Brockway.

Lombroso's theories had little direct influence on Anglo-American penology, although they influenced several generations of criminologists. Continental European penology, however, abandoned rehabilitation for confirmed criminals (Johnson and Wolfe 1996, 203). When U.S. prison officials learned of Lombroso's ideas at the 1894 meeting of the National Prison Association, they rejected them "based on strong feeling that all men were responsible for their acts and, if sane, reformable by penological methods" (Johnson and Wolfe 1996, 204). By the late 1800s, reform ideals held sway in penological theory and practice. U.S. penologists during this era believed that the key to understanding crime was not unchangeable biological conditions, heredity, or even deterrence. Science held the key to understanding the criminal mind; medicine provided the model for its cure.

From the Medical Model to Rehabilitation

After the pronouncements of the 1870 Cincinnati conference, penal system administrators placed greater emphasis on reforming or changing offenders.[9] The most common approach was to develop an individualized treatment plan for each offender. Steeped in nineteenth-century positivism and progressivism, treatment equated crime to an "illness" and reform to "the cure." A careful reading of Rush's writings reveals that diet and physical well-being were part of the good doctor's overall plan for a successful prison. Increasingly in the late nineteenth and early twentieth centuries, prison officials turned to the emerging social and behavioral sciences for answers to a vexing question: How can we change the criminal?

The **medical model** of corrections was the dominant approach to prisoner management in the early twentieth century. The specific treatment changed, according to the best social and behavioral science of the day. Eventually group therapy and behavior modification became the preferred treatments for many prisons. Prison administrators added education and vocational training in the hopes of offering the offender skills useful in free society.

A turning point in the treatment of offenders was the 1929 adoption of a scientific treatment regimen by the Federal Bureau of Prisons. Within a decade, nearly every state had adopted the reality or the rhetoric of rehabilitation, a term popularized after World War II. **Rehabilitation,** or the process of returning an offender to an orderly or acceptable manner of behaving, became a primary goal of the nation's corrections system.[10] Between the 1870s and the 1950s, the locus of this rehabilitation process moved from the prison and reformatory to the community. **Reintegration,** a concept popularized in the 1970s, provided a bridge between the prison and the community. Advocates of reintegration understood the importance of minimizing the problems inmates encountered as they moved from the restrictive prison lifestyle to the free society. However, a series of events in the mid-1970s cast doubt on rehabilitation's future.

The "Just Deserts" or Justice Model of Punishment

Over a 20-year period following the end of World War II, U.S. prisons experienced a rash of inmate uprisings and riots. By the late 1960s, prison officials began to question the efficacy of prison-based rehabilitation (Clear and Cole 1997). Also, after a decade of legal and social liberalism in the 1960s, a wave of conservative ideas flooded the nation beginning in the mid-1970s and crested with the election of Ronald Reagan in 1980. As an answer to a conservative's dream, Robert Martinson (1974) wrote a very negative report of correctional and adjudication programs, questioning whether rehabilitation was possible within the current correctional system.

A series of vocal critics also questioned the current system's ability to "get the job done." For example, as the American Friends Service Committee (1971, 20) noted in *Struggle for Justice,* their report on punishment in the United States: "Retribution and revenge necessarily imply punishment, but it does not necessarily follow that punishment is eliminated under rehabilitative regimes." In the early 1970s, they called for a moratorium on new prison construction.

Norval Morris (1974) responded to calls to abandon the prison system in *The Future of Imprisonment.* Prisons, he speculated, would outlive him and all of his contemporaries. The challenge, according to Morris, was to eliminate what he saw as a destructive linkage between the time to be served (a judicial decision) and any treatment or rehabilitative goals (an executive decision). Indeed, Morris expressed little faith in the ability of the 1970s prison system to rehabilitate inmates. Prison is necessary to control the dangerous (Morris 1974, 58). Prison administrators should provide programs to assist those who want to change. For the rest, wrote Morris (1974, xi), prison's sole function is "**just deserts.**" To this end, Morris called for a new prison solely for repetitively violent offenders: If people do not want to change, we should not expend our resources to make them change, even if we could.[11]

As these attacks on rehabilitation and incarceration raged, David Fogel (1975) articulated a "new" model of justice in ". . . *We are the Living Proof . . ." The Justice Model for Corrections.* Like Morris, Fogel (1975, 192) criticized the level of discretion exercised by correctional officials charged with administering the medical model: "The justice perspective demands accountability from all processors, even the 'pure of heart.' *Properly understood, the justice perspective is not so much concerned with administration of justice as it is with the justice of administration"* (emphasis in the original).

Fogel espoused a punishment model whereby offenders took responsibility for their own actions (see too, von Hirsch 1976). The **justice model** rests on the assumption that the individual has free will to choose to violate the criminal law, and in choosing crime deserves to be punished. Both treatment and rehabilitation, by the terms of this model, are rejected as primary goals for corrections. Punishment, or just deserts, is enough.

Just deserts and the justice model are mixtures of liberal thinking on crime and criminals (the concern for due process, monitoring the excesses of an all-powerful criminal justice system, and reining in an insulated correctional system) and conservative thinking (an emphasis on punishment for its own sake and the attainment of retribution as embodied in the *lex talionis*). Also, there seems to be little doubt that the justice perspective is a recasting of the classical views of humanity and crime: all rational human beings should be accountable for their own actions. As Andrew von Hirsch (1976, 49) characterizes this behavior: "Someone who infringes on the rights of others does wrong and deserves blame for his conduct. It is because he deserves blame that the sanctioning authority is entitled to choose a response that expresses moral disapproval; namely, punishment." A key question left unanswered by the proponents of this model is, What will be the effect of a justice model on the corrections system of the United States?

Implications for Contemporary Corrections

By the mid-1980s, incapacitation joined just deserts to create one of the most punitive and prison-oriented penal philosophies witnessed in human history. **Incapacitation** is a strategy for limiting an adjudicated criminal's ability to commit new crimes. **Selective incapacitation** is a refinement of this idea and, as a penal philosophy, owes much to criminologist Marvin Wolfgang's **longitudinal study** (a study involving repeated observation over a long period of time) of a youth cohort in Philadelphia. Wolfgang, Figlio, and Sellin (1972) observed that about 6 percent of the youths in their sample accounted for about one-half of the law-violating behavior. Later social scientists, studying repeat offenders, reinforced the idea that a few "career criminals" accounted for most of the nation's crime (Blumstein et al. 1988; Greenwood and Abramse 1982). By the mid- to late 1980s, a simple solution began to take shape: selectively incarcerate career criminals. But how do we identify them? Here again, the answer was simple: **Career criminals** are repeat offenders. Therefore, those who continue to appear in the judicial and correctional systems are the career criminals. In response, state and federal legislators began to limit the early release of offenders from prison, and, by **habitual offender statutes,** send others to prison for life.

Beginning in the 1980s, a national obsession with the fear of crime provided a popular groundswell of support for building more prisons to incarcerate more offenders, but especially repeat offenders (Irwin and Austin 1994, 5–7). The nation added "getting tough on criminals" to its political and social agenda. Politicians and citizens alike ignored the dire predictions of social scientists about the consequences of an "imprisonment binge" (Clear 1994a; Gottfredson and McConville 1987; Irwin and Austin 1994). Neither group seemed particularly interested in learning exactly who was in prison and for what crimes.[12] The imprisonment rhetoric was far more important than its reality. As a consequence, nearly every state began a prison-building boom in the 1980s. When we entered the 1980s, less than 20 years ago, the nation's prison population was less than 350,000. As we end the 1990s, our prison population is significantly more than 1 million and growing at an annual rate that exceeds the increases in both the crime rate and the population rate.

The United States is in the midst of an imprisonment binge. Nation-wide prisons and jails are faced with crowding. Here 400 inmates are shown crowded into a dormitory facility at the Limestone Facility in Alabama.

Conclusion

If, at the outset of this chapter, you assumed that only "primitive" societies resorted to brutalizing forms of punishment, and that only the "civilized" nations of the twentieth century advocated more humane forms, then you were wrong on both counts. Put aside for the moment, if you can, the death camps of Nazi Germany and Bosnia. Anthropologists have revealed that even contemporary "pre-legal" communities continue to practice rituals of reconciliation. Little of what passes for the United States' penal philosophy could be called conciliatory. Most current forms of punishment are, instead, exclusionary forms of punishment. For example, Irwin and Austin (1994, 12), in describing the nation's current strategy of imprisonment, harken back to an earlier epoch:

> In many ways, our current situation is that of Eighteenth-Century England, which was passing through even more unsettling changes than we are today and was faced with unprecedented crime waves in its new, crowded, filthy, polluted, slum encircled, rabble-ridden cities. After experimenting with extraordinary punishments, particularly wholesale hanging and the use of prison barges, England turned to banishment as its primary penal measure. . . . America has had to construct its locations of banishment within its borders. This it is doing at a feverish pace. . . . Although we lack

an Australia where we can set up prison colonies, we are increasingly building huge megaprison settlements in isolated rural locations where land is cheap and recession-starved communities are anxious for economic benefits that a major prison will bring.

We will see in later chapters whether Irwin and Austin are accurate or are guilty of resorting to hyperbole in their descriptions. You are the judge.

Critical Review Questions

1. What we refer to as "primitive" cultures practiced restitution and restoration in prehistoric times. There is, in the descriptions of these practices, restorative justice. Explain how they achieved this balance. (Be sure to address the issues of blood revenge and banishment in your answer.) Would it work today?

2. The Babylonian Code of Hammurabi and the Judaic Law of Moses have both been described as examples of *lex talionis*. How are they similar and how do they differ?

3. Would you characterize either the ancient Greek or Roman law as concerned about the value of human life? How do they differ from earlier tribal and proto-state laws?

4. "Feudal law favored the rich and powerful." Elaborate on the accuracy of this statement.

5. In a 100-word paragraph, summarize the contributions of the various members of the Age of Enlightenment to our modern ideas of crime and punishment.

6. Compare and contrast the Pennsylvania and Auburn Systems. Why was the Pennsylvania System doomed from the start?

7. Who are the De Beaumonts and Dickens of today? That is, who are the great social commentators of our day who shape society's response to issues of crime and punishment?

8. Who, in your opinion, was the greater reformer, Enoch Wines or Zebulon Brockway? What is the basis of your judgment?

9. What is the conflict between the medical model and the just deserts model?

10. How do you feel about the current "punishment binge?"

Recommended Readings

Fogel, David. 1975. *". . . We are the living proof . . ." The justice model for corrections.* Cincinnati: Anderson. The book that defines the justice model; a clear articulation of what is meant by just deserts and how to accomplish it.

Johnson, Herbert A., and Nancy Travis Wolfe. 1996. *History of criminal justice.* 2nd ed. Cincinnati: Anderson. This book provides a thoroughly readable and interesting examination of the history of crime and punishment. It contains details missing from our necessarily abbreviated treatment. If you like good history books, this one is for you.

McKelvey, Blake. 1936. *American prisons: A study in American social history prior to 1915.* Chicago: University of Chicago Press. McKelvey's work is perhaps the finest summary of the social history of this nation's prisons, although it is lim-ited in that it covers only the period from the first prisons to 1915.

Murton, Thomas O. 1976. *The dilemma of prison reform.* New York: Praeger. This book provides an excellent examination of prisons and prison reform from the founding of penology in the United States to the era of Attica in the 1970s.

Key Terms

Age of Enlightenment	incapacitation	Newgate Prison
archon	intake	penal colony
Auburn System	Irish Ticket-of-Leave	Penal Servitude Act
banishment	System	Pennsylvania System
big-house prison	*jus civile*	pre-legal systems
blood revenge	*jus gentium*	proto-legal systems
botes	*jus honorarium*	rehabilitation
Bridewell	just deserts	reintegration
canon law	justice model	selective incapacitation
career criminals	king's peace	silent system
case law	Law of Moses	ticket-of-leave
Code of Hammurabi	legal systems	transportation
Corpus Juris Civilis	*lex salica*	Twelve Tables
dooms	lockstep shuffle	Walnut Street jail
drakon	longitudinal study	*wergild*
feudalism	medical model	*wites*
habitual offender statutes	natural law	

Notes

1. Distinctions between clans and tribes are often arbitrary or imposed by an-thropologists (Hunt and Walker 1974, 264; Vinogradoff 1920, 306, 344). Clan members typically descend from a com-mon ancestor. Members of the same clan may not marry one another. Tribes are groups of clans that also share a legendary common ancestor, as in a tribe formed by brothers or sisters in the distant past. However, the common ancestor is usually far enough removed to allow marriage between tribal mem-bers. For simplicity's sake we use the term *tribe* to refer to both.

2. Deuteronomy means "second law." In reality, what this book contains is not a new law, but rather a partial repetition, completion, and explanation of the law Moses brought down from Mount Sinai.

3. Among both ancient Greeks and Ro-mans, the oracle, such as the Oracle of Delphi, was the place where mediums contacted the gods for help in making decisions.

4. In all likelihood, this account is an ex-aggeration, perhaps a case of "dirty tricks" by an unflattering historian hun-dreds of years removed from Draco. The myth became the reality.

5. The solidus was a common gold coin of the late Roman Empire. In medieval times, a solidus was worth between 12 and 40 silver denarii with the denarii being a common unit of payment, depending on the weight in silver of the denarii. The *lex salica* fixed the exchange rates. (Today, the denarii symbol (d) is used for the British pence.)

6. By the term "religious offenders" we refer to the victims of the Holy Inquisition. Pope Gregory IX established the papal Inquisition in 1233 as a means of combating heresy. Papal inquisitors often resorted to torture to secure confessions. Burning at the stake was rarely used, imprisonment was common. The independent Spanish Inquisition, chartered by Ferdinand and Isabella in 1478 and not abolished until 1834, was far harsher—and deadlier—than the Holy Inquisition of Rome.

7. Howard's belief in the reformative power of hard yet productive work led to the coining of a new term: *penitentiary.* The word *penitentiary* derives from the Latin word *poenitentiae,* meaning regret. Thus, the penitentiary was conceived as a place where those who violate society's laws are sent to think about their misdeeds and express their regret for them, all the while performing hard labor that results in products with real value.

8. The term *doubly convicted* denoted any inmate convicted of a new crime upon his or her arrival in the penal colony.

9. We are describing the philosophies and policies of prison reform and not necessarily what was actually happening in the prisons and jails. These topics are addressed in later chapters.

10. In 1972, at an American Society of Criminology meeting, one of the authors shared the podium with an ex-offender who railed against the prevailing rehabilitation practices in U.S. prisons. He asked the assembled audience a straightforward question: "I was never habilitated, so how can I be *re*habilitated?"

11. Over the past few years, Morris and his co-author Michael Tonry (1990) have become passionate proponents of the development of intermediate sanctions: those punishments that lie between imprisonment and release into the community.

12. Irwin and Austin (1994, 20–64) maintain that few parole violators return to prison for new offenses. Moreover, most people sentenced to prison go there for relatively minor offenses. Very few offenders sentenced to prison, perhaps as few as one in five, have committed a truly serious crime. Increasingly, state and federal courts sentence these less serious offenders to life in prison under habitual offender laws, hardly the intent of the legislators.

3

Sentencing and Criminal Sanctions

Chapter Outline

- Introduction
- Sentencing: Who Decides?
- Sentencing: What Are the Choices?
- Sentencing: How Are Decisions Made?
- Sentencing Strategies
- After the Verdict
- Appeals of Convictions
- Special Sentencing Considerations for Juveniles
- Conclusion
- Critical Review Questions
- Recommended Readings
- Key Terms
- Cases Cited

Introduction

The judge bangs down the gavel and pronounces the sentence on the newly convicted offender: "I sentence you to spend not less than 5, nor more than 20 years in the state penitentiary." Most people would say that the court process has now ended, and corrections can begin, but is that really an accurate statement? In this chapter we will examine how cases arrive at correctional agencies and the legal constraints placed on corrections by legislatures and the courts.

It is important to note at the beginning of any discussion of criminal sanctions that a variety of social goals go into the sentencing process. These may correspond to the punishment (philosophies) discussed in the opening chapter. For instance, the Department of Justice (1988, 90) lists and defines the following sentencing goals:

1. **Retribution.** This involves giving offenders what they deserve ("just deserts") in relation to the offenses for which they have been convicted; retribution is an expression of society's disapproval for the criminal act.

2. **Incapacitation.** By removing offenders from the community through incarceration, their opportunities for criminal conduct are diminished.

3. **Deterrence.** The goal of deterrence is to prevent future law-violating behavior; it has two dimensions—prevention of violations by the person being punished (specific deterrence) and prevention of violations by others in society (general deterrence).

4. **Rehabilitation.** This goal focuses on providing assistance to the offender (through counseling, educational programs, or job training) to reduce the likelihood of future criminal behavior.

5. **Restitution.** The aim of restitution is to have the offender repay either the victim or the community (or potentially both) for losses or harm suffered.

Sentencing also reflects other factors considered important by judges, legislators, and the general public (Department of Justice 1988, 90). For example, most individuals advocate that punishment should be as severe as the crime was serious. This is called **proportionality.** Also, most criminal justice system personnel and members of the general public feel that similar offenders and similar offenses should be treated the same. This is the principle of **equity.** Finally, the sentence should incorporate some recognition of the offender's criminal history. This is the notion of **social debt.**

Sentencing of convicted offenders is accomplished by the courts and, though this process goes on outside of the corrections system, correctional agencies receive those individuals sentenced by the courts, and must work with these convicted offenders. This chapter will examine the sentencing process for those convicted of law violations and also will explore the options open to judges and juries in disposing of criminal cases.

Sentencing: Who Decides?

The sentencing process for those convicted of a crime is somewhat mysterious to most people. Even if a trial has been fairly public, sentencing often occurs some time after the adjudication and after the public's fascination with the trial has likely faded. In fact, once the press reports that an individual has been convicted, media attention typically is focused elsewhere. Therefore, in this section we must consider one of the basic questions relative to sentencing: Who decides?

The Legislative Role

In terms of sentencing, legislatures establish the basic rules of the game. The United States Congress and the 50 state legislatures each have the power to decide what is against the law and to define the elements of criminal offenses in the jurisdictions under their control. Several important factors relating to the criminal law must be described in order to understand legislative authority in establishing laws.

We often think that the judge plays a major role in sentencing criminal defendants. However, judges, prosecuting attorneys, defense attorneys, and probation officers all can play a part in developing the most appropriate sentence for an offender. Quite often the courtroom work group has a sense of what Samuel Walker calls the "going rate," or the most likely sentence, given the circumstances.

First, we need to recognize that there are different degrees of seriousness in relation to criminal events. At the most basic level we can divide all crimes into **misdemeanors** and **felonies.** Additionally, finer distinctions may be made within these two categories.

All states do not use the same definitions and distinctions for crimes. However, misdemeanors are always the least serious and felonies are the most serious offenses. The Department of Justice (1981, 132) says that a misdemeanor is "an offense punishable by incarceration, usually in a local confinement facility, for a period of which the upper limit is prescribed by statute in a given jurisdiction, typically limited to a year or less."

By contrast, felonies may prescribe sentences of one year or more, including life in prison or the death penalty, possibly combined with substantial fines. A few states begin the felony category at two years of incarceration (Department of Justice 1981, 92). Offenders incarcerated for felonies will serve their sentences in state or federal prisons.

As previously mentioned, states may further differentiate degrees of seriousness for felonies and misdemeanors (Abadinsky and Winfree 1992, 17–18). For instance, some jurisdictions have a classification for **petty misdemeanors.** These are the least serious crimes, and when they involve violations of municipal ordinances they simply may be called **infractions** (Department of Justice 1981, 93). The least serious misdemeanors may call for penalties only involving fines.

Felonies also may include subcategories. In some states felony offenses are divided into degrees (first, second, third, etc.). Other states use designations such as Class A or Class B, or Class I or Class II (Abadinsky and Winfree 1992, 18).

Second, we should note that the criminal law is composed of two parts: **substantive law** and **procedural law.** The substantive law is enacted by legislatures and defines what behaviors constitute crimes. Legislatures also provide by statute, and courts add by case law, the law of criminal procedure. Unlike the substantive law, which defines criminal behavior, procedural law tells us how we must conduct the arrest and prosecution of criminal offenders. These laws have been called the "rules of the game."

It is also important to emphasize that the prosecution bears the burden of proof in criminal cases. Under our Anglo-American system of law we frequently hear the phrase that the defendant is "innocent until proven guilty." This means that the state must prove guilt and that the defendant need not prove innocence. This distinguishes our system of justice—called an **adversarial system**—from that of many European countries that employ accusatorial systems of justice. In an **accusatorial system** the defendant is presumed guilty unless he or she can prove innocence, a much more difficult task to accomplish!

Along with the prosecution bearing the burden of proof, comes the level of proof sufficient to result in a conviction. In civil cases in the United States, juries are instructed to base their verdicts on the **preponderance of the evidence.** While this term does not have a precise meaning, generally it is understood to mean that a verdict is based on the amount of evidence necessary to tip the decision-making scales in favor of one party or the other. To complicate matters, in civil cases such as traffic accidents both parties may be partially at fault.

By contrast, in criminal cases a verdict must be based on evidence sufficient to prove the defendant **guilty beyond a reasonable doubt.** Again, this does not have a precise definition, but normally we say that a reasonable doubt is "the state of mind of jurors in which, after the comparison and consideration of all the evidence, they cannot say that they feel an abiding conviction, a moral certainty, of the truth of a criminal charge against the defendant" (Rush 1994, 114). Scheb and Scheb (1989, 667) add that reasonable doubt is "the doubt that a reasonable person might entertain in regard to the veracity [truth] of a proposition after hearing the evidence."

Another concern in criminal law is the **corpus delicti,** or "body" of the crime. Unlike what most people would assume, the corpus delicti does not necessarily refer to a dead body, but to the elements that must be proved in order to establish that a crime has been committed. One of the elements of a crime is the **actus reus,** or guilty act. The guilty act can take several forms, and at times a crime does not have to be *completed* in order for a crime to exist.

For instance, if an individual enters a convenience store, flashes a handgun, and demands money, the crime of armed robbery would have been committed in most states. What if the potential robber never made it into the store? What if he was intercepted in the parking lot by a security guard or an off-duty police officer? Or, what if an accomplice reported the crime to the police after it was planned, but before it could be committed? In these cases **attempts** or **conspiracies** have taken place, and these may be treated as less serious forms of armed robbery, but as crimes in-and-of themselves nevertheless. It is interesting to note that while attempts, solicitations, and conspiracies were treated as misdemeanors under the **common law** (unwritten law developed in England primarily from judicial decisions based on custom and precedent that constituted the basis of the English legal system and the legal system of the U.S. except for Louisiana), most jurisdictions now classify them as felonies (Scheb and Scheb 1989, 65). Attempted crimes, conspiracies, and other efforts that fall short of the completed act are called **inchoate offenses** in criminal law (Department of Justice 1988; Rush 1994; Scheb and Scheb 1989).

A second consideration in crime classification is the degree of involvement. Under English common law, a distinction was made between **principals** and **accessories before the fact.** Principals included those people who actually committed a crime and accessories were individuals who contributed in some way to the crime's commission. In contemporary U.S. criminal law, the federal government and most of the states have eliminated the distinctions between principals and accessories before the fact, although they still may treat accessories after the fact differently (Scheb and Scheb 1989, 61).

The third element of the criminal law of concern to us is **mens rea,** or the guilty mind. The presence of a guilty mind is often expressed in terms of forming **criminal intent.** Criminal intent can be expressed or implied, and different crimes will require that different amounts of intent must be proven. For example, in a crime such as armed robbery the state has very little to prove in relation to intent if the person entered the convenience store, produced a handgun, and demanded money. In this case, the intent is fairly self-evident. However, in a case in which the charge is embezzlement, the state may have to establish that the offender took money with the intention of converting it to his or her own use.

Unlike the guilty act, the guilty mind may be difficult for the state to prove because of **affirmative defenses.** Affirmative defenses arise when an accused individual alleges that criminal intent was not present because of mitigating factors. An important consideration in an alleged affirmative defense is that the burden of proof shifts to the party raising the issue: the defendant.

Many possible affirmative defenses exist, but we will consider a few of the most common, and occasionally most controversial. One such defense is **infancy,** and while this defense is not utilized often, it still occurs periodically. The infancy defense rests on the common law notion that children under the age of seven are incapable of forming criminal intent (Champion 1992; Rogers and Mays 1987). At times this defense is raised in offenses committed by children, but it also may be used based on an offender's "mental age."

Another affirmative defense, and one of the most controversial, is **insanity.** The insanity defense is a legal concept and, contrary to what most people assume, not a medical concept (Abadinsky and Winfree 1992, 26). The issue is not whether the person committed the offense, but whether he or she had sufficient mental capacity at the time of the offense to have mens rea. Several different tests have been applied over the years in regard to the insanity defense and the most common have included the **M'Naughton rule** and the **irresistible impulse test.** The M'Naughton rule asks whether at the time of the offense the defendant knew the difference between right and wrong. The irresistible impulse test is based on the notion that defendants may know the difference between right and wrong but suffer from a mental defect that prevents them from controlling their behavior (Abadinsky and Winfree 1992, 26–27).

It is important to note several factors concerning the insanity defense. First, it is not used very often in criminal trials. Samuel Walker (1994, 151) says that insanity is used in only about 2% of all cases that go to trial, that insanity is typically only alleged in cases involving homicides or attempted homicides, and even then not very frequently. Second, even when insanity is alleged, it is often not a successful defense. Again, Walker (1994, 151) states that insanity is successful in less than 5% of the cases in which it is asserted. In the end the jury has to believe that the offender was insane at the time of the offense and, thus, incapable of forming criminal intent. Third, the defense is used so little and with so little success that it determines the outcome of only a tiny fraction of cases and thus is only symbolically important to the criminal law (see, for example, Walker 1994). Fourth, because of the controversy surrounding it, 12 states—Alaska, Delaware, Georgia, Illinois, Indiana, Kentucky, Michigan, New Mexico, Pennsylvania, South Carolina, South Dakota, and Utah—have eliminated the insanity defense altogether or have added the option of a verdict of "guilty, but mentally ill" (Department of Justice 1988, 87).

A third affirmative defense is **alibi.** Many students believe that an alibi is simply an excuse, as in the case of "The dog ate my homework." However, alibi comes from the Latin word meaning (elsewhere.) Therefore, in this defense the accused individual is saying "I could not have committed this crime because I was somewhere else at the time."

Finally, one of the most frequently occurring affirmative defenses is **entrapment.** Entrapment is alleged to have occurred in cases in which the police have initiated proactive investigations, particularly into vice-related activities such as drug dealing, gambling, and prostitution. The courts have routinely ruled that entrapment does not exist if the police provide an opportunity for a person to do what he or she is already inclined to do [see, for example, *United States v. Russell* (1973)]. However, the essential question facing the judge and jury is, Where did the idea for the crime originate? If the police concocted the idea for the crime and then orchestrated events so the alleged offender could commit the act, they are guilty of entrapment.

Again, except for affirmative defenses, the prosecuting attorney bears the burden of proving the elements of the offense, and it is at the point where the guilty mind and guilty act come together that a crime exists. Some people call this the **point of convergence** or the **nexus.**

Beyond the statutory law, judges and juries also enter into the sentencing picture. The following sections will explore the roles played first by juries and then by judges in arriving at a conviction and determining the appropriate sentence.

The Role of Juries

The primary role played by the jury is as the "trier of facts." This means that juries have the responsibility to decide who is telling the truth, what evidence means, and eventually whether the defendant is guilty. Kassin (1995, 145) reminds us that in the deliberation process "Jurors are expected to base their opinions on an accurate appraisal of evidence to the exclusion of nonevidentiary sources of information." Given the presumption of innocence, the jury decides whether that presumption has been sustained or whether the state has produced sufficient evidence to prove guilt beyond a reasonable doubt.

Interestingly, some states explicitly instruct jurors on their right to ignore the law and base a decision on their collective sense of "moral justice" (Scheflin and Van Dyke 1995, 154). This is called **jury nullification** and while it has long been a recognized principle in the criminal law, it remains controversial.

In most criminal cases, once the jury has decided that the defendant is guilty or innocent, its responsibilities have been discharged. However, as we shall see later in this chapter, there are certain circumstances—particularly in death penalty cases—in which the jury, and not the judge, decides the sentence.

The Role of Judges

Judges perform several responsibilities before and during the trial, and though the jury is the "trier of facts," the judge is the "trier of the law." This means that the judge decides during the trial what the proper procedures are and, at the time of jury deliberations, what instructions will be given to the jury.

In most criminal cases, after the verdict is reached, the judge will request a pre-sentence investigation report and will set a date for sentencing. (The pre-sentence investigation will be discussed in detail in Chapter 7.) In many states, for criminal cases, the judge is ultimately responsible for imposing the

Jury trials are guaranteed to criminal defendants under the U.S. Constitution's Sixth Amendment. Jurors are the ultimate triers of the facts of a case, and in most jurisdictions, their verdicts must be unanimous. In some cases, especially those involving the death penalty, the jury decides what the punishment will be.

sentence on convicted offenders. As we will see in the next section, the judges decide whether incarceration is appropriate and whether the defendant should be extended any type of leniency.

Sentencing: What Are the Choices?

Before we consider the choices available as criminal sentences, it is important to reemphasize a point made initially in this chapter: Legislatures decide what is against the law and in the process decide what the appropriate penalties are. Judges impose sentences, but legislatures decide the sentences that can be imposed.

Probation

The most common criminal disposition in the United States is **probation,** and this is true for juveniles as well as adults. For example, at the end of 1985 almost two-thirds of the nation's offenders were on probation. And, while that percentage has decreased somewhat, at the end of 1990 still more than 60% of the people supervised by correctional agencies were on probation.

Probation can be defined as "the conditional freedom granted by a judicial officer to an alleged or adjudged adult or juvenile offender, as long as the person meets certain conditions of behavior" (Department of Justice 1981, 170).

There are several factors about probation that are very important to remember in the broader sentencing context.

First, probation is a *sentence.* Although the definition provided above allows for probation to be imposed on alleged violators (the idea of "informal probation" is often used with individuals such as minor juvenile offenders and will be discussed below) virtually everyone upon whom probation is imposed has pleaded guilty or been found guilty. The fact that probation is a sentence means that the court has continuing jurisdiction over the probationer.

Second, probation is a *judicial function.* Probation is imposed by and supervised under the auspices of a judge. At times the probation department is operated by the court itself (especially for juvenile probationers), but in many instances probation is a state-level executive function. Even with probation operating outside of the judicial branch of government, probation officers must work in close cooperation with the sentencing judges. This is especially true in the preparation and presentation of pre-sentence investigation reports.

Third, probation is imposed *in lieu of incarceration.* Instead of sending the convicted offender to jail or prison, probation offers the person another chance to remain free in the community instead of serving a sentence behind bars.

Finally, probation is *conditional.* This means that the person's continued freedom is contingent upon meeting the terms of probation. As we will discuss in Chapter 7, the terms of probation can be classified into several categories. Conditions can be general (applied to all offenders) or specific (applied to the specific offender). They may also be *criminal*—that is prohibiting future criminal behavior—or *technical,* meaning they have no basis in law but merely require or prohibit certain behaviors. (We will give a more detailed treatment of these topics in Chapter 7.)

In relation to probation conditions, there is a clear trend in contemporary sentencing: the imposition of more, and more severe, conditions. Because jail and prison capacity are scarce commodities and because we are sending more people to these institutions for longer periods of time, we do not have sufficient bed space to house all of the country's convicted offenders. Therefore, probation becomes an alternative and even a preferred sentencing option for many offenders. The trend in the United States has been not only to put more people on probation, but to sentence increasingly severe offenders to probation sentences (see, for example, Champion 1988, 1990).

To make probation more meaningful or "tougher" for an increasingly serious caseload, additional conditions have been added. For instance, several states have experimented with house arrest, including the use of electronic monitoring, to keep closer surveillance on probationers (see Ford and Schmidt 1985; Renzema and Skelton 1990). House arrest, with or without electronic monitoring, is designed to keep offenders at home and off the street. It is based on the assumption that they will have fewer opportunities to offend and that this type of confinement, though less restrictive than prison, still removes some of the temptations that might face the probationer. The use of electronic monitoring makes probation more punitive, as offenders often must return directly home after work and remain in the home, except for certifiable emergencies, until time for work the next morning. Although the purposes served by electronic monitoring and its effectiveness as a correctional program are still being debated, it is quite obvious that judges are turning to home confinement, perhaps supplemented with electronic monitoring, with increasing frequency. For many this approach has become a probation "add-on" instead of an alternative to incarceration (Clear 1988).

Another condition imposed on probationers is **restitution.** Restitution is "a court requirement that an alleged or convicted offender pay money or provide services to the victim of the crime or provide services to the community" (Department of Justice 1981, 185). Judges may order restitution to be paid to property crime victims, although it could be employed in personal crimes as well, and restitution becomes one of the probation conditions. Before going further, there are several problems associated with the use of restitution that need to be examined.

First, it is easy for a judge to order restitution to be paid as part of the probated sentence. Collecting the amount ordered, however, still remains problematic. In fact, in most courts the responsibility for collecting restitution orders falls to largely overburdened probation officers.

Second, restitution presumes some ability to pay. The dilemma here often is that the offenders are unemployed to begin with. The lack of ability to pay may be a particular problem for juvenile offenders.

Third, there is still some question about the purposes being served by restitution. Although it is clear that proponents of restitution assume that this action increases the accountability of the offender and the satisfaction of the victim, the connections are not always obvious. Therefore, we find that restitution programs may not be able to deliver on some of their early promises and that they may provide another probation "add-on."

A community service requirement may suffer from many of the same deficiencies as restitution. In fact, the Bureau of Justice Statistics (an agency of the Department of Justice) includes community service in its definition of restitution (given above). These issues will be treated at greater length in Chapter 8, but for our purposes it is sufficient to note that probation can be standard or it can be enhanced (intensive); it can be treated as a stand alone program or as one incorporating a number of other components such as home confinement, electronic monitoring, restitution, and community service. In the end, however, the essential points concerning probation are that whatever form it takes it is the primary sentence imposed in this country and that it is a sentencing alternative to incarceration.

Fines and Forfeitures

Fines and forfeitures of property or assets are very old sanctions that seemed to have been rediscovered in recent years. The history of penal sanctions shows that fines and forfeitures have long been used with individuals who have broken the law. For instance, the Anglo-Saxons in Britain had systems of monetary payments called *botes* and *wergilds* almost 1,500 years ago (see Chapter 2).

The most common application of fines is traffic offenses. In most states persons charged with motor vehicle violations are subject to a fine and "court costs." But the use of fines has been expanded in recent years. Probably the most conspicuous use of fines in major criminal cases has come under the federal Racketeering Influenced Corrupt Organizations (RICO) statutes. These laws were designed to deal with individuals traditionally associated with organized crime groups. However, they have been applied to a variety of criminal enterprises. Thus, individuals convicted of federal RICO violations, or their state-level equivalents, may find themselves facing very hefty fines ranging from hundreds of thousands of dollars to several million dollars as well as the forfeiture of assets associated with their criminal enterprise.

Another recent innovation is the imposition of **day fines** (Winterfield and Hillsman 1993). Day fines have been employed for some time in Europe and South America, but the use of such fines in the United States did not occur until the Richmond County (New York) Criminal Court implemented a program in the time period from 1987 to 1989. Box 3.1 outlines the essential elements of a day fine program, but at this point two very critical factors are worth additional attention.

In most courts in the United States fines have always been based on the nature of the crime. This means that legislatures have prescribed what the range of fines would be for a specific offense and that presiding judges have imposed the appropriate amount if a conviction occurred. The problem with such an approach is that imposition of a fine based on the offense does not take into account the individual offender's ability to pay. This takes us to the next factor. The day fine principle is tied to a person's earnings. Therefore, whereas the fines may vary from individual to individual for the same offense (equity), they proportionately sanction all individuals.

Winterfield and Hillsman (1993) in their evaluation of the Staten Island Day-Fine Project note that as of 1993 this sentencing option had only been tried in a limited number of jurisdictions: Maricopa County, Arizona; Richmond County, New York; four courts in Oregon; and one court each in Connecticut and Iowa. However, based on the Staten Island experience, several conclusions already can be drawn:

1. Day fines can be used in most courts of limited (misdemeanor) jurisdiction in the U.S.

Box 3.1

How Day Fines Work

The concept behind day fines is simple: Once the amount of punishment to be administered to an offender is separated from a consideration of how much money that offender must pay, judges determine how much punishment an offender deserves— a quantity denominated in a nonmonetary unit. These *punishment units* are translated into monetary terms based on how much money the offender makes per day.

Practically speaking, the day fine approach consists of a simple, two-step process. First, the court uses a *unit scale* or *benchmark* to sentence the offender to a certain number of day fine units (for example, 15, 60, or 120 units) according to the gravity of the offense and without regard to income. To guide the court's choices, benchmarks or unit scales are typically developed by a planning group of judges, prosecuting attorneys, and defense counselors familiar with disposition patterns in a court. Second, the value of each unit is then set at a percentage of the offender's daily income, and the total fine amount is determined by simple multiplication.

Source: Winterfield and Hillsman (1993).

---

2. Day fines can replace traditional, fixed fines.

3. Fines are higher for wealthier offenders.

4. On average, fines increase 25% when day fines are imposed.

5. The total fines imposed increases 14% when a day fine system is used.

6. Despite the higher level of fines, a higher rate of collection results when day fines are imposed.

Day fines constitute an additional variation on a long-used criminal sanction. These **means-based penalties** provide "fairer punishments . . . without making the process of imposing fines too difficult or time-consuming for judges" (Winterfield and Hillsman 1993, 6).

Fines traditionally have been a revenue source used to support court or general governmental operations. Recently, however, fines have been designated to support certain programs, especially those involving victims' assistance (Department of Justice 1988, 96). In some ways the use of fines in the criminal justice system proves the old adage that "everything old is new again." That is, while fines have been around for centuries, at the end of the twentieth century legislatures and the courts seem to have rediscovered their use.

Misdemeanor Sentences

It is important to note in this section that legislative bodies decide which offenses will be misdemeanors and which will be felonies. The distinction is important for more than just academic purposes because classification of a crime as a felony or misdemeanor indicates where a sentenced offender will be housed and for how long.

Misdemeanor sentences can take a variety of forms. For instance, traffic cases, the most common misdemeanor offenses, typically involve the assessment of fines. Misdemeanors also may result in probation. However, for misdemeanor probation to be meaningful, it may require the existence of a county-level probation agency. As we will see in Chapter 7 much of the probation work in the United States is carried on by state-level agencies. Therefore, probation in misdemeanor cases may only involve an admonition by the judge to "stay out of trouble" and little else.

When people think about misdemeanor sentences, county jail time is the most common image that comes to mind, and, indeed, county jails do play a significant role in sanctioning misdemeanants. There are other local institutions such as work camps, county penal farms, and other local detention facilities designed to hold sentenced misdemeanants. These facilities will be explored in Chapter 4, but for the time being it is sufficient to note that counties often have one or more facilities to house those convicted of misdemeanors.

Felony Sentences

For decades in this country felony sentences meant prison. Today that is no longer true. For example, as previously mentioned, fines are increasingly being used, especially in crimes of an economic nature (that is, crimes in which large sums of money change hands) such as drug trafficking and other organized criminal activities. Also, as a result of state prison crowding, courts frequently are turning to probation for felony offenders (see, for example, Champion 1988). This means that probation is no longer simply the preferred sentence for first, minor, and property offenders, but is now becoming a common sentence for more serious and repetitive offenders. As we will see in Chapter 7, this may mean significant differences in the way probation services are structured and delivered.

Short of prison, convicted felons are subjected to a variety of **intermediate sanctions.** These sentences involve any punishment more severe than standard probation, but less severe than imprisonment (Gowdy 1993). Intermediate sanctions can involve a variety of different programs. Day fines, intensive probation supervision, and electronic monitoring and house arrest are some of the most common. Additionally, not to overlook the possibility of a combination of probation and confinement, some offenders may receive **shock incarceration,** a short period of confinement followed by community supervision, or other alternative forms of incarceration. All of these will be discussed at length in Chapter 8.

The use of intermediate sanctions has spread nationwide and at all levels of government. However, as Delaware Governor Michael Castle (1991, 1) warned a group of National Institute of Justice conference attendees, "People too often assume that public protection means prison, and that anything less than complete incarceration for all criminals will endanger public safety." He added: "Successful intermediate sanctions programs have been adopted in many communities, despite the burden of public resistance. But accomplishing change means putting an end to the old-fashioned and inaccurate concept that criminal justice means prisons and *only* prisons."

Finally, convicted felons always face the possibility of imprisonment. The length of the potential sentence—one year or more—and the place of incarceration—a prison instead of a county jail or other local correctional facility—distinguish felonies from misdemeanors. Convicted felons increase their chances of imprisonment if they are **recidivists** (repeat offenders), convicted of multiple property offenses, or if they have committed one very serious personal crime, particularly one of a heinous or notorious nature (Department of Justice 1988; Beck et al. 1993). In the extreme case, convicted felons might receive the death penalty. Because of this possibility, particularly for individuals convicted of first-degree murder, we will turn our attention briefly to the issue of the death penalty.

The Death Penalty

In some ways a discussion of the death penalty does not belong in a corrections book, since it has nothing to do with "correcting" law-violating behavior. However, because we are considering sentencing, and because the death penalty is a sentence the courts can impose under a fairly limited range of circumstances, it seems appropriate to deal with capital punishment here.

The death penalty has been in existence since our nation's colonial period. In fact, we inherited our legal framework for capital punishment from England, where at one point virtually all felonies called for the death penalty. While the English have abandoned capital punishment, the United States remains one of a small group of nations to employ it.

Perhaps the best way to begin a discussion of the death penalty is to say that there are probably three groups into which we can classify people's opinions. One group is opposed to the death penalty under any and all circumstances. A second group could be described as enthusiastic death penalty advocates, and they support its use for all first-degree murders and, in some instances, for other crimes as well. Both of these groups constitute small but vocal minorities. The majority of citizens could be described as favorable toward the death penalty for first-degree murder—or at least not opposed to it—but more ambivalent than the vocal advocates. It is also important to note that people support or oppose the death penalty for a variety of reasons. And, as we will see, sometimes both groups choose the same grounds for either opposing or supporting capital punishment.

At the most basic level, proponents and opponents may take their respective positions based on religious or moral grounds. For instance, opponents may invoke the admonition from the Ten Commandments that "thou shalt not

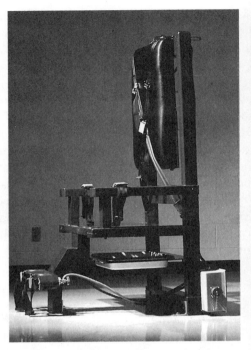 

The death penalty is very much a part of the criminal justice system in the United States. Over 3,000 inmates are on death row throughout the nation, and in recent years we have witnessed an increasing amount of executions. The electric chair, such as this one at the Florida State Prison at Starke, has been replaced by more "humane" forms of execution in most states.

A few states have retained lethal gas as a means of execution. One of the nation's most famous (or some would say infamous) gas chambers is the one at California's San Quentin Prison.

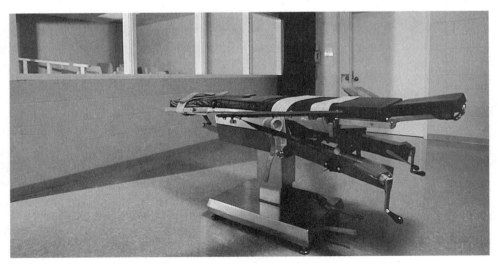

The preferred method of execution by many states is death by lethal injection. Pictured here is Virginia's "death house."

Timothy McVeigh was convicted of killing eight federal agents in the bombing of the federal building in Oklahoma City. His case may involve an execution.

kill." Proponents may counter with citations from the biblical book of Deuteronomy that provide, under certain circumstances (for example, adultery, murder, and bestiality to name a few), that citizens should take up stones and stone the offending parties to death. Therefore, people of similar religious backgrounds may disagree on the death penalty.

Another area of dispute is the question of "justice." As Ernst Van den Haag (1975; Van den Haag and Conrad 1983) notes, the fact that some people receive the death penalty and others who are equally deserving do not, does not make capital punishment any less just. He reminds us that justice is giving people what they deserve and that states that permit capital punishment designate it for cases in which the life of another has been taken, especially if the death involved premeditation. The debate whether capital punishment provides justice or not is largely philosophical, although that does not decrease its importance, particularly for those whose execution is ordered by the court. Other positions in the death penalty discussion, however, are much more practical in nature.

For instance, the capital punishment debate sometimes centers on economics or expedience. Opponents argue that it is just as costly to execute a person, especially after numerous lengthy and expensive appeals, as it is to keep the person in prison for life without the possibility of parole. Proponents argue just the opposite: executions are much less costly. Both groups agree on one point, however: the death penalty is final. Once the person has been executed, all appeals are exhausted and there is no opportunity to correct any mistakes that might have been made. The possibility of executing an innocent person is troubling to death penalty opponents; proponents say that appeals take care of virtually every correctable error and that few undeserving people are executed.

The final issue in the death penalty debate is legal and constitutional in nature. The framers of the Constitution presumed the existence of the death penalty. They provided in the Fifth Amendment that "No person shall be held to answer for a *capital,* or otherwise infamous crime, unless on a present-ment or indictment of a grand jury . . . nor be deprived of *life,* liberty, or prop-erty, without due process of law" [emphasis added].

The other provision raised in regard to the death penalty is the Eighth Amendment provision prohibiting the imposition of cruel and unusual pun-ishments. It is this proscription that has served as the basis for many recent Supreme Court appeals directed at capital punishment. For instance, in the case of *Furman v. Georgia* (1972) the U.S. Supreme Court struck down the death penalty as it was being administered in more than 30 states. The Court gave numerous reasons, but the argument essentially focused on two factors: (1) juries had virtually unbridled discretion in deciding on the death penalty (not only for first-degree murder but, in some states, a variety of other of-fenses such as rape and armed robbery as well) and (2) most states did not provide for instructions concerning **mitigating** and **aggravating circum-stances.** This meant that although executions were not "cruel" they were "unusual" because they were capriciously and arbitrarily imposed. It is im-portant to note that the Supreme Court did not say in *Furman v. Georgia* or in any subsequent case, that the death penalty is unconstitutional in and of itself.

Four years after *Furman,* in the case of *Gregg v. Georgia* (1976), the Supreme Court upheld the newly reimposed death penalties of Georgia and several other states. The new laws departed from what had existed before *Furman* in two major ways. First, the range of crimes was severely narrowed. As a result of *Gregg* only first-degree murder qualifies for capital punishment in most states that permit this penalty. Second, death penalty states began to use **bifurcated hearings,** a system in which a trial is conducted to determine the defendant's guilt or innocence and then, for guilty defendants, a sentenc-ing hearing is held to determine whether the death penalty should be im-posed. In both the original trial and in the sentencing hearing the jury's verdict must be unanimous. When the jury's decision is not unanimous about a death sentence, the court will impose life imprisonment (in some states without the possibility of parole).

As of the end of 1995, 38 states and the federal government had the death penalty, and as Table 3.1 shows, certain states dominate the statistics (Snell 1996). Since Gary Gilmore's 1977 execution, in the wake of the *Gregg* deci-sion, five states have led the nation in the number of people sentenced to die and in the number of executions. Texas leads with more than 100 executions

Table 3.1

Status of the Death Penalty, December 31, 1995

Executions during 1995		Number of prisoners under sentence of death		Jurisdictions without a death penalty
Texas	19	California	420	Alaska
Missouri	6	Texas	404	District of Columbia
Illinois	5	Florida	362	Hawaii
Virginia	5	Pennsylvania	196	Iowa
Florida	3	Ohio	155	Maine
Oklahoma	3	Illinois	154	Massachusetts
Alabama	2	Alabama	143	Michigan
Arkansas	2	North Carolina	139	Minnesota
Georgia	2	Oklahoma	129	North Dakota
North Carolina	2	Arizona	117	Rhode Island
Pennsylvania	2	Georgia	98	Vermont
Arizona	1	Tennessee	96	West Virginia
Delaware	1	Missouri	92	Wisconsin
Louisiana	1	22 other jurisdictions	549	
Montana	1			
South Carolina	1			
Total	56	Total	3,054	

Source: Snell (1996).

since it resumed capital punishment in 1982 ("Cashier Killer Marks . . ."
1995). In fact, Texas executed 19 inmates in 1995 alone. The four states following Texas in the number of executions between 1977 and 1995 include Florida (36 executions), Virginia (29 executions), Louisiana (22 executions), and Georgia (20 executions).

While five states have dominated the death penalty statistics in terms of the number of executions, Table 3.1 shows that several states have quite a few death row inmates. Three states—California, Texas, and Florida—house more than one-third of the nation's death row population. As we can see in the table, Texas tops the chart with 19 executions, but Florida's and California's low numbers of executions in 1995 (3 and zero, respectively) indicate that the rate of sentencing and rate of execution of the sentence are not necessarily commensurate. Table 3.2 shows that the most common method for capital punishment currently is lethal injection, followed by electrocution and lethal gas.

From the available data several important points should be made. First, the average length of stay on death row is more than nine years. In many cases, this means special housing for all or part of the inmate's sentence and the likelihood that most inmates will pursue many legal mechanisms to have their convictions overturned. Second, the number of death row inmates continues to grow every year. In fact, during 1995, 310 inmates were added to the death row population while only 56 were executed. Between 1977 and 1995, 4,857 federal and state inmates entered prisons under death

Table 3.2

Method of Execution, by State, 1995

Lethal injection	Electrocution	Lethal gas	Hanging	Firing squad
Arizona[a,b]	Alabama	Arizona[a,b]	Delaware[a,c]	Idaho[a]
Arkansas[a,d]	Arkansas[a,d]	California[a,c]	Montana[a]	Oklahoma[f]
California[a,e]	Florida	Maryland[g]	New Hampshire[a,h]	Utah[a]
Colorado	Georgia	Mississippi[a,i]	Washington[a]	
Connecticut	Kentucky	Missouri[a]		
Delaware[a,c]	Nebraska	North Carolina[a]		
Idaho[a]	Ohio[a]	Wyoming[a,j]		
Illinois	Oklahoma[f]			
Indiana	South Carolina[a]			
Kansas	Tennessee			
Louisiana	Virginia			
Maryland[g]				
Mississippi[a,i]				
Missouri[a]				
Montana				
Nevada				
New Hampshire[a]				
New Jersey				
New Mexico				
New York				
North Carolina[a]				
Ohio[a]				
Oklahoma				
Oregon				
Pennsylvania				
South Carolina[a]				
South Dakota				
Texas				
Utah[a]				
Virginia[a]				
Washington[a]				
Wyoming[a]				

Note: The method of execution of federal prisoners is lethal injection, pursuant to 28 CFR, Part 26. For offenses under the Violent Crime Control and Law Enforcement Act of 1994, the method is that of the state in which the conviction took place, pursuant to 18 USC 3596.

[a] Authorizes two methods of execution.

[b] Arizona authorizes lethal injection for persons sentenced after 11/15/92; those sentenced before that date may select lethal injection or lethal gas.

[c] Delaware authorizes lethal injection for those whose capital offense occurred after 6/13/86; those who committed the offense before that date may select lethal injection or hanging.

[d] Arkansas authorizes lethal injection for persons committing a capital offense after 7/4/83; those who committed the offense before that date may select lethal injection or electrocution.

[e] Use of lethal gas is currently prohibited in California pending a legal challenge in federal court.

[f] Oklahoma authorizes electrocution if lethal injection is ever held to be unconstitutional and firing squad if both lethal injection and electrocution are held unconstitutional.

[g] Maryland authorizes lethal injection for all inmates, as of 3/25/94. One inmate, convicted prior to that date, has selected lethal gas for method of execution.

[h] New Hampshire authorizes hanging only if lethal injection cannot be given.

[i] Mississippi authorizes lethal injection for those convicted after 7/1/84 and lethal gas for those convicted earlier.

[j] Wyoming authorizes lethal gas if lethal injection is ever held to be unconstitutional.

Source: Snell (1996).

sentences, and during this period 313 inmates were executed. Another 1,870 prisoners were removed from death sentences in ways other than execution (Snell 1996, 2).

Third, virtually all of the 3,054 inmates on death row in 1995 had been convicted of murder. Roughly two-thirds had prior felony convictions, and about 1 in 12 had a prior homicide conviction (Snell 1996).

Fourth, some death row inmates are fairly young. Table 3.3 shows the age at which jurisdictions allow the death penalty to be imposed. However, about

Table 3.3

Minimum Age Authorized for Capital Punishment, 1995

Age 16 or less	Age 17	Age 18	Age 19	None specified
Alabama (16)	Georgia	California	New York	Arizona
Arkansas (14)[a]	New Hampshire	Colorado		Idaho
Delaware (16)	North Carolina[b]	Connecticut[c]		Montana
Indiana (16)	Texas	Federal system		Louisiana
Kentucky (16)		Illinois		Pennsylvania
Mississippi (16)[d]		Kansas		South Carolina
Missouri (16)		Maryland		South Dakota[e]
Nevada (16)		Nebraska		Utah
Oklahoma (16)		New Jersey		
Virginia (14)[f]		New Mexico		
Wyoming (16)		Ohio		
Florida (16)		Oregon		
		Tennessee		
		Washington		

Note: Reporting by states reflects interpretations by state attorney general offices and may differ from previously reported ages.
[a] See Arkansas Code Ann.9-27-318(b)(1)(Repl. 1991).
[b] The age required is 17 unless the murderer was incarcerated for murder when a subsequent murder occurred; then the age may be 14.
[c] See Conn. Gen. Stat. 53a-46a(g)(1).
[d] The minimum age defined by statute is 13, but the effective age is 16 based on interpretation of a U.S. Supreme Court decision by the state attorney general's office.

[e] Juveniles may be transferred to adult court. Age can be a mitigating factor.
[f] The minimum age for transfer to adult court is 14 by statute, but the effective age for a capital sentence is 16 based on interpretation of a U.S. Supreme Court decision by the state attorney general's office.
Source: Snell (1996).

half of those sentenced to die were 29 years of age or older at the time of sentencing.

Finally, questions of race and ethnicity are prominent in the capital punishment debate. It is not correct to say that most of the inmates awaiting execution are racial or ethnic minorities, since in 1995, 1,730 (56.6%) were White. Minorities, African-Americans particularly, were, however, disproportionately represented in the nation's death row population: 1,275 (41.7%) were African-American. Hispanics—because they are an ethnic group—could be classified in more than one racial category, and they accounted for 237 death row inmates among those for whom ethnicity was known (Snell 1996).

Sentencing: How Are Decisions Made?

It would seem to be a fairly easy proposition to figure out how much time an offender should get and then how much time that person would have to serve, but as we shall see in this section the numbers may add up different ways. Often sentencing is complicated by the presence of multiple charges. In fact, sometimes prosecuting attorneys have been accused of overcharging in order to gain tactical advantages. The two most prevalent types of overcharging are horizontal and vertical (see Holten and Lamar 1991; Neubauer 1992; Rubin 1984). **Horizontal overcharging** is the practice of charging a defendant with every possible criminal charge related to the event. It is sometimes called bed-sheeting. This allows the prosecutor to go forward with the most serious offense and to dismiss the others as part of a plea bargain.

Vertical overcharging is charging a suspect with more serious charges than can be proven in court. For example, the police may believe that an individual unlawfully killed another person, that second-degree murder would be the most appropriate charge. However, the prosecuting attorney might charge first-degree murder in order to have leverage over the defendant and to have room for negotiation in an attempt to plea bargain. Such a tactic raises ethical questions in regard to the prosecutor's conduct (see Gershman 1995), but it increases the likelihood that the accused will enter into a plea agreement. Plea bargaining will be discussed in the following paragraphs and in a later section of the chapter as well. However, before dealing directly with plea bargaining, we need to explain **concurrent sentences** and **consecutive sentences.**

Concurrent Sentences

The Department of Justice (1981, 46) defines a concurrent sentence as "a sentence that is one of two or more sentences imposed at the same time after conviction for more than one offense and to be served at the same time." Thus, while a person might be charged with and convicted of six counts of residential burglary, the judge can impose concurrent sentences and this would have the effect of no more time to serve than on a single sentence. As mentioned previously, multiple charges give the prosecuting attorney leverage in trying to reach a plea agreement with a defendant. It makes prosecutors look like they are giving something up, but as a practical matter, multiple charges with concurrent sentences mean that the defendant will not serve more time, no matter how many counts there are.

Consecutive Sentences

Consecutive sentences provide a way for the judge to "stack" time against a convicted defendant. The Department of Justice (1981, 46) defines a consecutive sentence as "a sentence that is one of two or more sentences imposed at the same time, after conviction for more than one offense, and which is served in sequence with the other sentences." Some people have suggested that this is one way judges can retaliate against defendants who refuse to take the "low and go," that is, those defendants who refuse to plea bargain and insist on their right to trial. This "jury trial penalty" in effect says to the defendant "you take some of my time, I take some of yours" (Neubauer 1992, 289).

Plea Bargaining

Now that we have discussed concurrent and consecutive sentences a discussion of plea bargaining should make more sense. However, it is important to note that plea bargaining is not simply bargaining over the plea (that is, a discussion of what plea the defendant will enter). The negotiations that go on between the defense attorney and the prosecutor are not over whether the defendant will plead guilty; they concern some aspect of leniency. In reality, the negotiations deal with three distinct but related factors: sentences, counts, and charges.

The average person believes that plea bargaining is all about the sentence and nothing else, and though the sentence is important, it is not the only matter of concern. For example, the defendant may want to reduce the number of counts in order to receive a shorter sentence, but with concurrent sentencing the time served for one count or ten counts might actually be the same. Why negotiate over counts, then? In some states the number of counts may influence whether a defendant is charged as a habitual offender. This could be critical because most habitual offender laws provide very long prison terms or sentences with no opportunity for parole.

The particular charge may be of concern also. The charge may be important because of its impact on shortening the sentence, but a change in charges may also foreclose the opportunity for certain kinds of sentences as well. Take the example of homicide. In most states a conviction for first-degree murder carries a potential death sentence or life in prison without parole. Therefore, a person who pleads guilty to second-degree murder cannot be sentenced to the death penalty, but still might have to serve a very long prison term.

The bottom line about plea bargaining is this: leniency of some type is being sought. The leniency that results may or may not impact the sentence whatsoever. The actual impact may depend on the prosecutor's attitude toward the defendant and the crime(s) with which he or she is charged, and the judge's attitude toward the prosecutor's sentencing recommendations. With the possibility of charge, count, and sentence bargaining combined with concurrent or consecutive sentences, it is a little difficult to speculate on what the final sentence may be. If so, how does anyone know what to expect? The answer is fairly simple: all of the parties involved in the courtroom work group—judges, prosecutors, and defense attorneys—have a sense of what is reasonable and fair in a particular case, given the cases that have gone on before (see, for example, Eisenstein and Jacob 1977; Neubauer 1992). Walker (1994) and others have called this the **going rate.** All of the regular parties in the trial and sentencing process know, from their past experiences, what a case is "worth." Therefore, given a particular set of facts the courtroom work group will most likely agree on the appropriate sentence. This includes whether the defendant should receive probation and, if not, what a reasonable incarceration period should be. In most jurisdictions the courtroom work group is relatively free to craft a sentence based on their perceptions of the going rate. However, as we shall see in the next section, some states have provided guidance on the discretion that can be exercised by the courtroom work group members, particularly the judge.

Sentencing Strategies

If the sentencing process did not seem complex enough with concurrent and consecutive sentences, in this section we shall explore a number of sentencing strategies. Each is reasonably easy to understand, but each complicates the sentencing picture. What should be an easy question to answer—how much time will the defendant be sentenced to and serve?—often is one of the hardest to answer.

Indeterminate Sentences

For most of our recent history, the dominate sentencing system has been **indeterminate sentencing.** An indeterminate sentence is "a type of sentence to imprisonment where the commitment, instead of being for a specified single time quantity, such as three years, is for a range of time, such as two to five years, or five years maximum and zero minimum" (Department of Justice 1981, 107).

To fully understand indeterminate sentences, we need to return to a point made at the beginning of this chapter: legislatures decide the sentences to be imposed. Therefore, the legislative branch is responsible for determining that a sentence should be indeterminate and then for setting the minimum and maximum terms allowable. This means that an indeterminate sentence is easy to recognize because it involves a minimum and maximum term of imprisonment. Furthermore, although the legislature establishes the sentencing range, and the judge imposes the sentence prescribed, the time served is determined by the parole board. It is at this point that the numbers become confusing once again.

In most states using indeterminate sentencing, inmates first become eligible for parole based on some fraction of the minimum sentence served, for example one-third or one-half. Let us assume, for purposes of illustration, that an offender was sentenced to serve one to five years in a state that required one-half of the minimum sentence be served before parole eligibility. This means that this prisoner would be eligible for parole (although not guaranteed of receiving it) after serving only six months in prison. As a result of the discrepancies between the sentence imposed and the sentence served, many groups have called for changes in state and federal laws and a move toward more "truth in sentencing" (see, for example, Walker 1994).

Determinate Sentences

The trend toward determinate sentencing in the United States began in the 1970s. A **determinate sentence** exists when "a single time quantity is set and this is in effect the maximum" (Department of Justice 1981, 107). Whereas an indeterminate sentence provides a sentence range with a minimum and maximum term, determinate sentences specify a particular number of years or months to be served.

Most of the states that have changed from indeterminate to determinate sentencing have also limited or eliminated parole. In its place these states use some type of **good time credits.** With good time, inmates are able to reduce their sentences by a certain number of days or months. The "discount rate" for good time credits differs from state to state, but in some states the maximum rate at which good time credits may be accumulated is one day for each day served, or a 50% discount rate. When the federal government changed to determinate sentencing in 1987, Congress set the maximum allowable good time rate for federal prisoners at 54 days per year, or a 15% discount rate (see Mays 1989).

One of the interesting features of determinate sentencing is that this reform effort was supported by liberals and conservatives alike (Walker 1994). Conservatives felt that indeterminate sentences did not truly reflect the amount of time that an inmate would have to serve: there was no truth in the sentencing process. They also felt that judges had too much discretion in sentencing. By contrast, liberals argued that parole boards had too much discretion and that they often based their decisions on factors unrelated to the likelihood of the offender's success on parole. Therefore, determinate sentencing was designed to constrain the discretion of judges and parole boards.

However, within the criminal justice system discretion is never eliminated, it simply passes to someone else. With greater reliance on determinate sentences the chief beneficiaries of this displaced discretion have been the prosecuting attorneys, who already enjoyed a great deal of discretion anyway. As the following section illustrates, determinate sentencing can be taken one step further. Legislatures can also provide for "guided" sentences.

"Guided" Sentences

Perhaps the prototype for guided sentences is the sentencing guidelines developed by the State of Minnesota (Knapp 1984). Much has been written and said about the Minnesota sentencing guidelines (see, for example, Knapp 1982, 1986; Lagoy, Hussey, and Kramer 1978), but several factors related to "guided" sentences need to be repeated here.

First, the premise behind sentencing guidelines is that sentencing is a difficult process and that judges need all the help they can get in carrying out this task. Related to this notion is the idea that judges typically have too much discretion and that this results in excessive sentencing disparities. Therefore, sentencing guidelines should promote more uniform sentences and limit the possibility that judges would inappropriately exercise their sentencing powers (Department of Justice 1988, 90–92).

Second, sentencing guidelines often are established by looking at a limited number of factors related to the sentencing process. For example, Minnesota's sentencing guidelines are based on a two-dimensional matrix (Knapp 1982, 1986; Neubauer 1992). Therefore, the sentencing process only considers the present offense and the defendant's criminal history. Missing are factors such as race/ethnicity, financial status, drug or alcohol dependence, and employment history. Although judges might consider all of these relevant to their sentencing decisions, the Minnesota Sentencing Guidelines Commission felt that they were irrelevant.

Third, although sentencing guidelines do promote sentencing consistency, they typically allow for departures from the mandated sentences. In order to do this, in most states, the sentencing judge must provide written justification for departures above or below the prescribed sentence.

Finally, the use of sentencing guidelines has been taken one step further through the implementation of **presumptive sentences.** California and other states have developed presumptive sentencing (Department of Justice 1988, 91). Under this scheme, conviction for a specified crime, given a particular defendant's criminal history, results in a presumptive or "normal" sentence to which the defendant is ordered, unless there are clear reasons for departures above or below the presumptive number. This would be the ultimate example of sentencing consistency because the presumptive sentencing system would prescribe for the judge the sentence that should be imposed in most cases. As always, the judge could depart from the presumptive number but to do so would require a written statement detailing the reasons for departure. Box 3.2 presents a comparison of the sentencing regimes used by different states.

Mandatory Sentences

One measure of increasing sentencing severity in many states is the development of mandatory sentences. **Mandatory sentences** actually can take a couple of forms. One of the most common is mandatory incarceration. For example, in 1979 the State of Tennessee developed what were called Class X crimes, and throughout the state there were signs proclaiming that "Class X Protects." This get-tough approach to serious crime, proposed by then-governor Lamar Alexander, prohibited the dismissal of Class X charges or reduction to a lesser charge unless the trial judge approved. It also prohibited bail during an appeal and the use of suspended sentences or probation (Thomas and Edelman 1988).

Under classification schemes like Tennessee's Class X Felony Act, conviction for a crime such as armed robbery called for a mandatory prison term. In effect, mandatory sentencing removes some sentencing discretion from trial judges. As is true in most cases, when judges lose discretion someone else gains that discretion, and in most instances the prosecuting attorney is the big winner.

An additional form of mandatory sentencing involves **mandatory minimums.** For instance, some states provide that individuals convicted of armed

Box 3.2

Comparison of Sentencing Regimes and the States That Use Them (as of 1986)

Mandatory sentencing: Law requires the judge to impose a sentence of incarceration, often of specified length, for certain crimes or certain categories of offenders. There is no option of probation or a suspended sentence.

Mandatory sentencing laws were in force in 46 states (all except Maine, Minnesota, Nebraska, and Rhode Island) and the District of Columbia as of 1986. In 25 states imprisonment was mandatory for certain repeat offenders. In 30 states imprisonment was mandatory if a firearm was involved in the commission of a crime. In 45 states conviction for certain offenses or classes of offenses lead to mandatory imprisonment; most such offenses were serious, violent crimes, and drug trafficking was included in 18 of the states. Many states made drunk driving an offense for which incarceration is mandated (usually for relatively short periods in a local jail rather than a state prison).

Presumptive sentencing: The discretion of a judge who imposes a prison sentence is constrained by a specific sentence length set by law for each offense or class of offense. That sentence must be imposed in all unexceptional cases. In response to mitigating or aggravating circumstances, the judge may shorten or lengthen the sentence within specified boundaries, usually with written justification required.

Presumptive sentencing was used, at least to some degree, in about 12 states.

Sentencing guidelines: Explicit policies of procedures are specified for deciding on individual sentences. The decision is usually based on the nature of the offense and the offender's criminal record. For example, the prescribed sentence for a certain offense might be probation if the offender has no previous felony convictions, a short term of incarceration if the offender has one prior conviction, and progressively longer prison terms if the offender's criminal history is more extensive.

Sentencing guidelines came into use in the late 1970s. As of 1986 they were

- used in 13 states and the federal criminal justice system
- written into statute in the federal system and in Florida, Louisiana, Maryland, Minnesota, New Jersey, Ohio, Pennsylvania, and Tennessee
- used system-wide, but not mandated by law, in Utah
- applied selectively in Massachusetts, Michigan, Rhode Island, and Wisconsin
- being considered for adoption in other states and the District of Columbia

(continued)

Box 3.2 *(continued)*

**Comparison of Sentencing Regimes
and the States That Use Them (as of 1986)**

Sentence enhancements: In nearly all states, the judge may lengthen the prison term for an offender with prior felony convictions. The lengths of such enhancements and the criteria for imposing them vary among the states.

Sentencing enhancements: In some states that grouped felonies according to their seriousness, the repeat offender may be given a sentence ordinarily imposed for a higher seriousness category. Some states prescribed lengthening the sentences of habitual offenders by specified amounts or imposing a mandatory minimum term that must be served before parole can be considered. In other states the guidelines provided for sentences that reflect the offender's criminal history as well as the seriousness of the offense. Many states prescribed conditions under which parole eligibility was limited or eliminated. For example, a person with three or more prior felony convictions, if convicted of a serious violent offense, might be sentenced to life imprisonment without parole (the "three strikes and you're out" policy).

Source: Department of Justice (1988).

robbery or any crime involving a firearm are required to serve a mandatory minimum prison term. Individuals convicted of armed robbery not only are required to serve a prison sentence (mandatory imprisonment), but also they are required to serve a mandatory minimum prison term. This approach also has been used by Massachusetts in its famous Fox-Bartley handgun law (see Walker 1994).

Perhaps the most notable form of mandatory sentencing involves the so-called "three strikes and you're out" legislation enacted by a number of states and the federal government. Peter Benekos and Alida Merlo (1995) call this legislation a "politicized crime control policy" that moves beyond "getting tough" to "getting even tougher."

As of 1995, 37 jurisdictions had proposed and 15 jurisdictions had adopted such sanctions. The motivation behind the "three strikes" legislation seems to have been a small number of what Samuel Walker (1994) calls "celebrated" cases. Recent research on "three strikes" sentencing noted that "The intent of this campaign has primarily been to target dangerous offenders who habitually prey on innocent victims. The nature of this approach has involved an effort by both state and Federal legislators to enact policies that identify, and incapacitate for life, violent and/or nonviolent habitual offenders" (Turner et al. 1995, 16).

Box 3.3

"Baseball Sentencing" Meets Corrections

Nationwide, liberal and conservative politicians alike have rushed to demonstrate their outrage at certain particularly heinous crimes such as the killing of Polly Klass. One response has been the introduction of so-called "three strikes and you're out" laws in many states and by the federal government. While the intention of these laws has been to more severely sanction habitual offenders, there are several unintended consequences as well.

For example, Peter Benekos and Alida Merlo suggest that harsher penalties remove the incentives for plea bargaining and cause the already crowded criminal courts to deal with more trials, which necessitates more judges, courtrooms, juries, prosecutors, and public defenders. They also maintain that "there is little doubt that an immediate effect of the legis-

lation will be to increase the already enormous prison population in the United States" (p. 6).

These additional costs might be justifiable, if public safety is enhanced. However, as Turner and associates note, many states include a variety of nonviolent crimes in their habitual offender statutes. This means that repeat property offenders, more often than violent personal offenders, are likely to be the "strike out" victims. In the end we may substantially increase our prison populations with inmates sentenced to life terms for multiple property or nonviolent drug offenses.

Ask yourself: is the "value" worth the "price"?

Sources: Benekos and Merlo (1995); Turner et al. (1995).

However, as Box 3.3 shows, both the public and politicians may get less than they bargained for, and at higher prices, with three strikes sentencing. This approach to sanctioning "serious" offenders may once again demonstrate that the policy enacted may not perform as originally envisioned.

In this section we have attempted to describe and discuss the main sentencing variations in use throughout the United States today. The major systems have been mentioned here, but states are free to develop alternatives or hybrids to the forms now in use. With this foundation in place it is appropriate to turn to two final topics in regard to the world of courts and criminal sentences: (1) once a sentence has been imposed, where does the prisoner go? and (2) after a sentence has been ordered, where does that leave the convicted defendant in regard to possible appeals?

After the Verdict

Once the defendant has been found guilty, the judge typically will delay sentence imposition until a pre-sentence investigation report can be completed. Pre-sentence investigation will be discussed at length in Chapter 7, but it is important to note that at this time the probation department will undertake a thorough examination of the defendant's life history including the family, employment, personal, and legal status.

If the defendant is to be placed on probation a probation plan will be drawn up by the probation officer and approved by the judge regarding the

conditions the probationer must meet. If the convicted offender is going to be incarcerated a whole new set of actors come into play.

In most states, if a convicted felon is imprisoned, the first place he/she will be sent is a correctional reception and diagnostic center. At this facility the correction department's staff will determine where the offender will be sent initially. In some states judges have the authority to sentence individuals to specific correctional facilities, but in most jurisdictions this authority is reserved for the corrections department. Once the initial process has been completed, the new inmate will be transported to the appropriate correctional institution. Upon arrival at the starting point in the correctional journey, the inmate typically will face additional screening to determine whether a general population assignment is appropriate and which housing unit seems best suited to the offender's needs, risk assessment, and escape potential. Therefore, not only will correctional personnel make classification decisions concerning prison placement, they will make classification decisions for placement within a given prison. After these decisions have been made, the inmate will be assigned housing for the duration of the sentence or until additional classification decisions have to be made.

We have already discussed in this chapter and we will discuss further in Chapter 7 the various ways prison sentences can be shortened. However, as we will see in the following section, many inmates spend a considerable amount of their imprisonment seeking ways to legally challenge their convictions. Therefore, we will now turn our attention to the methods for challenging a criminal conviction and the potential for having a conviction overturned.

Appeals of Convictions

Prison inmates are stripped of many of their rights and practically all of their possessions, but they have an abundance of time. Some of this time is not spent constructively; some inmates scheme to escape, to create havoc within the institution, to smuggle in contraband, and to carry on criminal enterprises from within the prison walls. Some inmates spend their time in more positive pursuits: enrolling in an educational program, learning a skill or trade, participating in bodybuilding, or using the prison's legal resources to challenge convictions. This last point is one that might be considered constructive or not constructive depending on one's perspective, but it is an activity that consumes the attention of what often are called "jailhouse lawyers" (see, for example, Thomas 1988).

Jailhouse lawyers have come to occupy a prominent role in the inmate social world. These individuals are typically not bar-approved attorneys, but really "writ writers." Jailhouse lawyers are inmates who have developed a specialized expertise in challenging their convictions and those of other inmates as well.

Box 3.4

Johnson v. Avery, 393 U.S. 483 (1969)

The Tennessee Department of Corrections had a regulation that stated:

> No inmate will advise, assist or otherwise contract to aid another, either with or without a fee, to prepare Writs or other legal matters. It is not intended that an innocent man be punished. When a man believes that he is unlawfully held or illegally convicted, he should prepare a brief or state his complaint in letter form and address it to his lawyer or a judge. A formal Writ is not necessary to receive a hearing. False charges or untrue complaints may be punished. Inmates are forbidden to set themselves up as practitioners for the purpose of promoting a business of writing Writs.

Johnson was serving life in the Tennessee State Penitentiary when in February 1965 he was transferred to the prison's maximum security unit for violation of the policy concerning preparing writs for other inmates. Johnson appealed to the District Court of the Middle District of Tennessee for "law books and a typewriter." The district court held that the disciplinary confinement was unlawful and ordered him returned to his previous security classification.

The State of Tennessee appealed the district court's order, and the U.S. Sixth Circuit Court of Appeals found in the state's favor. The court of appeals ruled that the state had an "interest . . . in preserving prison discipline and in limiting the practice of law to licensed attorneys" and that this interest "justified whatever burden the regulation might place on access to federal habeas corpus."

Justice Fortas, in writing for the U.S. Supreme Court majority, held that "in the absence of some provision by the State of Tennessee for a reasonable alternative to assist illiterate or poorly educated inmates in preparing petitions for post-conviction relief, the State may not validly enforce a regulation which absolutely bars inmates from furnishing such assistance to other prisoners." This meant that if the anti–jailhouse lawyer regulation was to stand, the state had to provide a *reasonable* alternative to the legal assistance provided by other inmates. Otherwise, the policy was constitutionally invalid.

Because of the potential power derived from skills such as those possessed by jailhouse lawyers, some states have attempted to prohibit inmates from providing legal assistance to other inmates. Tennessee was one such state, and the policies of the Tennessee Department of Corrections prohibiting the activities of jailhouse lawyers were challenged before the U.S. Supreme Court in the case of *Johnson v. Avery* (1969). In that case the Supreme Court held that inmates might be restricted, but could not be prohibited from assisting other inmates in filing appeals of their convictions or other legal documents.

In addition to *Johnson v. Avery,* the case of *Bounds v. Smith* (1977) provided for expanded legal access by prisoners. As a result of these and other cases inmates now enjoy less restricted access to the courts. However, access to the courts is virtually meaningless unless the courts to which inmates appeal their causes are sympathetic to their plight. For almost 30 years state prison inmates have found courts, especially federal district courts, willing to hear their cases. Therefore, the remainder of this section will provide a brief overview of some of the mechanisms by which inmates appeal their causes and a few of the issues they have raised on appeal.

Generally, inmates have used two legal mechanisms for appealing their convictions or the conditions under which they are confined. For much of our history the primary means of appeal has been the **writ of habeas corpus** (Mays 1981, 1984). This mechanism has been available to federal prisoners since the creation of Article III of the United States Constitution. Congress also extended the right of federal court review of state prisoners' cases in 1867 (Department of Justice 1984).

Under a writ of habeas corpus prisoners assert that they are being held unjustly, and they ask the courts to require the state to justify their conviction and incarceration. Thus, habeas corpus petitions challenge the very fact of incarceration, and a successful challenge means the conviction could be overturned and the prisoner retried or set free (Mays and Olszta 1989). For most inmates who are successful in their habeas corpus claims a retrial is more likely than release.

Whereas habeas corpus petitions dominated inmate appeals from 1961 to 1976, beginning in 1977 civil rights claims began to play a more significant role. Unlike habeas corpus appeals, civil rights actions challenge not the fact of incarceration, but the conditions under which the inmate is incarcerated. Civil rights appeals have increased tremendously over the past three decades, and their scope and significance will be explored further in Chapter 10.

As previously mentioned, one of the primary issues raised by inmates on appeal is access to the courts. Often this is the most fundamental issue in the appeals process, because it alleges that the inmate has been deprived of legal reference materials or legally trained assistants in order to facilitate whatever the substantive challenge may be. In many instances, access to the courts is really a catchall phrase for lack of counsel or ineffective representation by counsel. The appeal's substance indicates the appropriate remedy. For instance, if the inmate alleges inadequate representation by counsel at trial, and the court finds that the attorney did not adequately discharge his or her responsibilities, the appropriate remedy would be a retrial. If the allegation is that the inmate is not receiving adequate legal assistance within the prison, the remedy would be to provide the necessary materials or assistance.

Inmates also may challenge other trial procedures that might have resulted in their convictions. For instance, inmates may claim that physical evidence or an admission was improperly admitted at trial (see, for example, *Mapp v. Ohio* [1961]; *Wong Sun v. United States* [1963]; *Chimel v. California* [1969]). They may also assert that they were denied the right to a jury trial or that the jury was improperly constituted. For example, the appeal in the Supreme Court case of *Batson v. Kentucky,* 476 U.S. 79 (1986) alleged that racial minorities were systematically excluded from trial juries. Another trial problem is lack of a speedy trial. The Supreme Court has defined in very broad terms what constitutes a speedy trial (see, for example, *Klopfer v. North Carolina* [1967]; *United States v. Marion* [1971]; *Barker v. Wingo* [1972]), and all states and the federal government now have laws defining the time limits within

Table 3.4

Speedy Trial Requirements, by State

States that restrict time from arrest to trial	Time limit	States that restrict time from indictment to trial	Time limit	States that restrict "unreasonable delay"
California	75 days	Minnesota	60 days	Delaware
Nevada	75	Wisconsin	90	District of Columbia
Alaska	120	Washington	104	Kentucky
North Carolina	120	Wyoming	120	Maine
Texas	120	Colorado	180	New Jersey
Iowa	135	Maryland	180	North Dakota
Arizona	150	Montana	180	Oregon
Illinois	160	Nebraska	180	Rhode Island
Florida	180	Kansas	190	South Dakota
Hawaii	180	Missouri	190	Tennessee
New Mexico	180	Mississippi	270	Vermont
New York	180	Virginia	270	
Pennsylvania	180	Georgia	2 terms of court	
Ohio	270	West Virginia	3 terms of court	
Idaho	360			
Louisiana	360			
Indiana	365			
Massachusetts	365			
Arkansas	3 terms of court			
Oklahoma	4 terms of court			
Utah	4 terms of court			

Note: States without restrictions include Alabama, Connecticut, Michigan, New Hampshire, and South Carolina.

Source: Bureau of Justice Statistics (1988).

which a suspect must be brought to trial. Failure to do so in a timely manner may result in the dismissal of the charges in many jurisdictions.

Speedy trial considerations are critical, but one of the most common bases of appeal is inadequate jury instruction by the judge. Typical errors here include what the judge says or does not say. For instance, it may be an appealable error if the judge makes a misstatement of what the law actually provides. In order to prevent this most judges will simply read the law's relevant portions to the jury. An error of omission might be a judge's failure to instruct the jury on the general meaning of probable cause or failure to give instructions on lesser inclusive offenses with which the jury might find the defendant guilty (for example, in a first-degree murder trial the judge normally will give instructions on second-degree murder, voluntary manslaughter, and involuntary manslaughter).

In regard to appeals of criminal convictions, the basic question is this: Is the error harmless or not? If the appellate courts hold that an error was harmless, the conviction usually is allowed to stand. If the error was not harmless, the appellate court may order the conviction overturned and the defendant immediately released, or order a retrial with special attention given to correcting the original error.

In concluding this section, it is important to note a few very important points. First, in order to have the basis for an appeal in general an error in law must have occurred (see Rush 1994, 125). That is, the judge must have erred in some manner prior to or during the trial process. Second, though there are lots of federal and state criminal convictions every year, the percentage of cases actually appealed is fairly small. Third, of the convictions appealed, only a small percentage result in relief: research from the late 1970s found that only about 3% of the state appeals in federal courts were successful (Department of Justice 1988, 88). Finally, of the successful appeals most result in rehearings on specific issues or retrials of the case and not outright dismissals of the charges. Therefore, inmates are not leaving prisons in large numbers as a result of overturned convictions.

The issue of inmate litigation will be explored in greater depth in Chapter 10, but for the time being we will turn our attention to the sentencing of juvenile offenders. As the next section shows, there are special considerations when it comes to sanctioning juveniles.

Special Sentencing Considerations for Juveniles

Since 1967 the juvenile justice system in the United States has undergone massive changes in both philosophy and practice. For instance, under the original juvenile court, procedures were to be private, informal, and nonadversarial. This meant that hearings were closed to the public, that they did not adhere to strict criminal procedure standards, and in most cases neither prosecuting nor defense attorneys were present. With the case of *In re Gault* (1967) a due process revolution swept over the U.S. juvenile court. *Gault* particularly changed the juvenile court's nonadversarial nature and now, routinely, attorneys appear for both sides.

Not only was the original juvenile court nonadversarial, but the procedures applied to adjudications and dispositions generally were civil and not criminal in nature. This meant that while guilt beyond a reasonable doubt was required for adult criminal cases, in juvenile court youngsters could be found delinquent on the preponderance of the evidence, a much lower standard of proof. The U.S. Supreme Court case of *In re Winship* (1970) changed the requirement on the standard of proof for delinquency from the civil standard to the criminal standard of "beyond a reasonable doubt."

Another special sanctioning consideration for juvenile offenders is the range and types of dispositional options available to the judge. For example, **informal probation** is often available to juvenile courts (Rogers and Mays 1987). This disposition distinguishes juvenile proceedings from adult proceedings in that for adults probation is only assigned after conviction. However, for juveniles, informal probation is a diversionary mechanism employed *prior* to adjudication.

Box 3.5

"Cut Me a Hickory Switch"

In 1995, State Representative Doug E. Gunnels, from Greenback, Tennessee, introduced a bill in the Tennessee legislature that provided for public caning for individuals convicted of vandalism, burglary, and burning the U.S. flag.

An article in *Corrections Digest* quoted Gunnels as saying: "I'm not an expert on crime, but people who are involved in more serious crime usually start out with crimes like this." The inspiration for this bill was reported to be the Michael Fay case, where an American youngster was publicly caned by Singapore authorities after his vandalism conviction.

Source: Corrections Digest (1995, 3).

When adults are convicted of crimes, the court has sentences ranging from fines to probation to imprisonment or even execution, where appropriate. With juveniles the options are somewhat different, and the range is much narrower. For instance, fines might be levied against juveniles in traffic cases, but such cases may not be within the juvenile court's jurisdiction. They may be heard, instead, in limited jurisdiction courts (such as municipal courts) where the traffic cases of adults are heard as well. For the juvenile court, incarceration typically comes as a last resort after probation and other community-based sanctions have been exhausted. In most states, even when incarceration is ordered, the length of secure confinement sentences is much more limited for juveniles than for adults.

Therefore, for juveniles to receive more severe sanctions, they must be tried as adults. Every state grants authority to the juvenile courts to transfer offenders to adult courts for trial if the juveniles meet certain conditions relating to age and the offense they are alleged to have committed (Champion and Mays 1991). However, two facts are essential to note. First, the U.S. Supreme Court in the case of *Kent v. United States* (1966) provided that before juveniles can be tried as adults they must be given a probable cause hearing to determine the merits of the transfer petition. Second, while it would appear that juveniles who are tried as adults would receive more severe sanctions, this is not always the case. Champion and Mays (1991) in reviewing the literature on juvenile transfers found that when these youngsters arrive in adult court they are often treated as first or relatively minor offenders and are given probation instead of incarceration (see also, Feld 1981; Sagatun, McCollum, and Edwards 1985). The transfer process, then, often is symbolic in nature, providing the promise of more severe treatment without ever delivering on it.

The final feature of juvenile sanctions is the narrower range of sentencing alternatives. U.S. juvenile courts are not permitted to impose the death penalty on juvenile offenders. In order for a juvenile to be executed, the youngster must be tried as an adult—typically for first-degree murder—and must be at least 16 years of age at the time of the offense (see, for example,

Sentencing in the Twenty-First Century

The sanctioning of criminal offenders in the U.S. has gone in two different directions. First, there has been a movement to make sentences less severe for minor offenders, both adults and juveniles. We have moved in the direction of diverting minor offenders from the formal adjudication system and of providing an expanded menu of sentences available to judges. Such individuals are being sent to first-offender programs and DWI schools and are being ordered to perform community service in lieu of fines or incarceration.

Second, sanctions have gotten more severe for juveniles and adults accused of committing more serious crimes. As a result of changes in the laws and as a result of responses to a perceived nationwide crime wave, more offenders are being sentenced to prison for longer periods of time. Currently the United States is in the midst of an "imprisonment binge" (Irwin and Austin 1994).

Although these two trends could continue into the twenty-first century, for the remainder of this section we want to explore what might be awaiting us in terms of criminal sanctions. Admittedly, some of the sanctions proposed are far-fetched, but things that seemed far-fetched 50 years ago no longer seem so exotic.

For instance, as a result of the example set in many Islamic and Asian countries, some people in the United States have called for use of corporal punishment (Newman 1983). This could mean that instead of sending people to prison—once looked upon as a humane alternative to corporal or capital punishment—the state could subject them to caning (as is done in Singapore) and then release them. (See Box 3.5.) Although different U.S. jurisdictions probably will never cut off hands the way some Islamic countries do, the use of public stocks again may not be so unrealistic.

The most unusual punishment proposals concern genetic engineering, the use of electrodes implanted into the offender's brain, the application of certain types of medication, or various surgical procedures. In dealing with certain sexual offenders, for example, both surgical and chemical castration have been proposed and practiced. Other types of mood- and behavior-altering medications already are available and conceivably could be employed in dealing with criminal offenders.

Finally, the most exotic punishment proposals involve vaporization or atomization much like *Star Trek*'s transporter beam or the use of cryogenics to deep-freeze offenders until some future date when their behavior can be modified by some yet-to-be invented method. It is also possible, given our current and future space travel technology that society will return to banishment or transportation of prisoners to distant worlds where penal colonies will be established. Does this sound too fantastic to be possible? Don't count on its being that far out. (See Box 3.6 for a high-tech strategy that's being talked about today.)

Box 3.6

Sentencing Goes "High Tech"

At least one person is speculating on where sentencing options might take us in the twenty-first century. New Mexico Governor Gary Johnson recently said in a news conference that the possibility exists that microchips could be implanted into the heads of convicted offenders as one way to monitor their whereabouts. The governor suggested that though the state was not seriously considering such an option at the present time, the possibility always exists that technology would be applied in situations to help the state control its prisoner population overflow. The use of the microchips would replace—or supplement—the current technology available in electronic monitoring programs. New Mexico was the first state to employ contemporary electronic monitoring technology, and the presence of major federal laboratories in the state increase the likelihood that futuristic technologies will be developed and applied in the criminal justice system.

Source: "Felons May Get Microchip Implants" (1995).

Stanford v. Kentucky [1989]). Therefore, the most severe sanction typically available to the juvenile court is a two- to three-year incarceration period in secure custody.

Conclusion

In order for cases to reach correctional agencies and institutions, they have taken some time to work their way through a complex maze of procedures developed by legislatures and implemented by the courts. By the time the judge's gavel sounds and the sentence is imposed, the accused offender has made several stops along the way. However, even after the sentence is imposed, the case may not be finished. As we have seen in this chapter, inmates may continue their legal battles for years, if not for decades.

It is important to remember as we conclude this chapter on sentencing and correctional sanctions that a variety of actors shape the political and legal environment in which corrections professionals must work. It is a world into which they may have some input, but clearly they do not possess total control.

Critical Review Questions

1. Which of the five goals of sentencing listed at the beginning of the chapter seem to be most influential today?

2. Are some of the goals of sentencing associated with the "liberal" approach to crime control? Are some associated with the "conservative" approach?

3. How do affirmative defenses differ from other parts of a criminal trial? How do they differ from other forms of defense?

4. What are the different *types* of sentences that may be imposed on convicted offenders? Who decides which offenders get which sentences?

5. Some people have said that sentencing is the most complex and time-consuming function performed by the courtroom work group. What are some of the factors that add to this complexity?

6. What, if any, corrective purposes does the death penalty serve?

7. What kinds of cases are likely to bring about calls for "three strikes and you're out" legislation? Have any of these types of cases been in the news lately?

8. Inmates may file a variety of different appeals while they are incarcerated. What might be some of the motivations for inmate "writ writers"?

9. Where would a "jailhouse lawyer" fit into the inmate social system and why? What happens if the "jailhouse lawyer" really has been a lawyer? Can you think of any cases in which attorneys have been incarcerated?

Recommended Readings

Abadinsky, Howard. 1995. *Law and justice: An introduction to the American legal system.* 3rd ed. Chicago: Nelson-Hall. This book provides the reader with a general overview of the nature of law and the history and structure of the contemporary legal system in the United States. It is useful for providing readers with information on the general processing of criminal cases.

Champion, Dean J., ed. 1989. *The U.S. sentencing guidelines.* New York: Praeger. This edited volume, published two years after implementation of the federal sentencing guidelines, provides an excellent historical review of guided sentencing. It also examines the various ways guided sentencing practices can impact the criminal justice system.

Eisenstein, James, and Herbert Jacob. 1977. *Felony justice: An organizational analysis of criminal courts.* Boston: Little, Brown. This is another classic work on the dynamics of courthouse politics. It examines the operation of criminal courts in Baltimore, Chicago, and Detroit and develops the notion of the courtroom work group.

Holten, N. Gary, and Lawson L. Lamar. 1991. *The criminal courts: Structures, personnel, and processes.* New York: McGraw-Hill. This is a "no frills" approach to describing and explaining the criminal court system in the United

States. The two authors (one of whom is a state attorney) particularly deal with the politics of the courts and provide a finely detailed look at many of the actors in the judicial process. An entire chapter is devoted to the process of sentencing.

Katzman, Gary S. 1991. *Inside the criminal process.* New York: Norton. This book provides a detailed analysis of criminal cases. It is written from the perspective of an attorney who also is a law school lecturer.

Rosett, Arthur, and Donald R. Cressey. 1976. *Justice by consent: Plea bargains in the American courthouse.* Philadelphia: Lippincott. Although somewhat dated, this books remains a classic piece of research on the nature and processes of plea bargaining. Students interested in courts and particularly those planning on going to law school would be especially well served in reading this volume.

Walker, Samuel. 1994. *Sense and nonsense about crime and drugs: A policy guide.* 3rd ed. Belmont, CA: Wadsworth. One of the most frequently cited recent books dealing with criminal justice policy (such as sentencing) in the United States. Walker takes on both liberals and conservatives and argues that most crime control policies are based on largely unsubstantiated beliefs, what he calls crime control "theology."

Key Terms

accessories
accusatorial system
actus reus
adversarial system
affirmative defenses
aggravating
  circumstances
alibi
attempts
bifurcated hearings
common law
concurrent sentences
consecutive sentences
conspiracies
corpus delicti
criminal intent
day fines
determinate sentence
deterrence
entrapment
equity

felonies
going rate
good time credits
guilt beyond a reasonable
  doubt
horizontal overcharging
incapacitation
inchoate offenses
indeterminate sentencing
infancy
informal probation
infractions
insanity
intermediate sanctions
irresistible impulse test
jury nullification
M'Naughton rule
mandatory minimums
mandatory sentences
means-based penalties
mens rea

misdemeanors
mitigating circumstances
nexus
petty misdemeanors
points of convergence
preponderance of the
  evidence
presumptive sentences
principals
probation
procedural law
proportionality
recidivist
rehabilitation
restitution
retribution
shock incarceration
social debt
substantive law
vertical overcharging
writ of habeas corpus

Cases Cited

Barker v. Wingo, 407 U.S. 514 (1972)
Batson v. Kentucky, 476 U.S. 79 (1986)
Bounds v. Smith, 430 U.S. 817 (1977)
Chimel v. California, 395 U.S. 752 (1969)
Furman v. Georgia, 408 U.S. 238 (1972)
Gregg v. Georgia, 428 U.S. 153 (1976)
In re Gault, 387 U.S. 1 (1967)
In re Winship, 397 U.S. 358 (1970)
Johnson v. Avery, 393 U.S. 483 (1969)
Kent v. United States, 383 U.S. 541 (1966)

Klopfer v. North Carolina, 386 U.S. 213 (1967)
Mapp v. Ohio, 367 U.S. 643 (1961)
Stanford v. Kentucky, 492 U.S. 361 (1989)
United States v. Marion, 404 U.S. 307 (1971)
United States v. Russell, 411 U.S. 423 (1973)
Wong Sun v. United States, 371 U.S. 471 (1963)

4

Jails and Local Detention Facilities

Chapter Outline

- Introduction
- A Brief History of Jails
- Contemporary Jails and Detention Facilities
- Variations in Jail Use
- The Physical Plant of Jails
- The Administration of Jails
- Jail Employees
- Major Jail Issues
- Other Local Detention Facilities
- Conclusion
- Critical Review Questions
- Recommended Readings
- Key Terms

Introduction

The college student looks into his rearview mirror and sees the flashing lights and the dark figure of a uniformed police officer approaching. The officer nears the driver's door of the small pickup truck and asks the driver to step out. After a brief conversation, the officer senses that based on his erratic driving the 20-year old young man not only has been drinking, but probably is impaired. She administers a series of field sobriety tests and decides to place the student under arrest. A quick inventory of the pickup's cab turns up several recently emptied beer cans.

After processing the necessary paperwork, the officer transports the student to the county jail for booking. There he is administered a breath test to determine his blood alcohol level, and he "blows" a 0.12 BAL on the meter.

Once the booking process has been completed, the student is allowed to make a phone call, and reluctantly he calls his parents to bail him out. In the meantime he is placed in the jail's "drunk tank." As his eyes focus in the dim light, and he begins to look around, one image flashes into his mind: the bar scene from *Star Wars*. He cannot ever remember seeing a group of people who looked like those with whom he was now incarcerated, unless it was from a movie.

A Brief History of Jails

One of the interesting things about jails is that we find their existence very early in the history of the U.S. In fact, jails existed during our country's colonial period and by the time of the Revolutionary War many villages and towns had what was often called the "common jail." Like many other features of the American criminal justice system, the jail finds its origins in England. As English settlers came to the American colonies they brought the institution of the jail with them. In fact, as early as Virginia's Jamestown Colony, jails played an important role in community life. The Advisory Commission on Intergovernmental Relations (ACIR) in its 1984 report entitled *Jails: Intergovernmental Dimensions of a Local Problem* noted that when jails came to the American colonies from England along with them came "county responsibility, sheriff administration, and fee-type compensation" (ACIR 1984, 3). However, the early English jails did not look or operate as our modern local detention facilities do.

Jails today fulfill several functions, but early English jails primarily existed to hold prisoners until they could be tried or sentenced. Like their English counterparts, early American colonial jails primarily held people awaiting trial or punishment and did not exist as places of punishment. In some instances in which fines had been imposed, individuals were confined in jail until the fine could be paid, either by the offender or the offender's family (Moynahan and Stewart 1980, 13–15). However, the use of the jail as a place of punishment was an American break from the English tradition, and eventually jails in this country came to house three types of inmates: those awaiting trial, those convicted but awaiting sentencing, and those sentenced to serve jail time (ACIR 1984, 3–4).

Even from the earliest American colonies, jails were locally built, financed, and operated facilities. This meant that the buildings were simply but sturdily built and that they seldom had the capacity to separate various groups of inmates, thus the designation "common jail." Males and females, adults and children, hardened criminals and "undesirables" all typically were accommodated in a single room or a small number of cells.

Contemporary Jails and Detention Facilities

It is readily apparent from this brief review that this country's jails have had less than a distinguished history. Some people have questioned whether jails today have progressed very far from the conditions of colonial jails and, in fact, the National Advisory Commission on Criminal Justice Standards and Goals (1973, 273) said in its report that "the jail has evolved more by default than by plan. Perpetuated without change from the days of Alfred the Great, it has been a disgrace to every generation." Many jails have improved, particularly in the past two decades, but to understand them more fully we need to examine what constitutes a jail and the various functions performed by contemporary jails.

What Is a Jail?

We need to recognize that jails are separate and distinct from a number of other institutions designed to incarcerate people. The National Advisory Commission (1973, 274) says that "Local control, multiple functions, and a transient, heterogeneous population have shaped the major organizational characteristics of jails."

The Department of Justice (1991a, xiv) reports that for purposes of the National Jail Census, jails are "locally administered [facilities] that [hold] inmates beyond arraignment (usually more than 48 hours) and that [are] staffed by municipal or county employees." This definition does not include "physically separate drunk tanks, lockups" and other facilities that do not hold people after they have been formally charged. Box 4.1 shows something of the range of contemporary jail responsibilities.

The jail occupies a unique place in contemporary society and within the criminal justice system. The jail is the gateway to the criminal justice system, but all too often jails are confused with prisons and vice versa. For example, the news media often report that an offender faces a long "jail term" for a crime when, in reality, the individual is facing a prison sentence. As an extension of the characteristics listed by the National Advisory Commission, three elements help distinguish contemporary jails from prisons.

First, jails are distinctive because of the *various populations* they house. Unlike prisons—which tend to be single-gender institutions operated by state and federal governments, and which house convicted felons—jails are local institutions that have very heterogeneous populations. Jails house pretrial detainees (often up to one-half of their average daily population [ADP]) who have not yet been convicted of a crime, but who are unable to make bail, even in relatively modest amounts. They also contain convicted misdemeanants serving sentences up to one year and convicted felons awaiting transportation to state or federal prisons. Probation and parole violators also may be detained for short time periods in jail while they await judicial or administrative hearings. To further complicate the picture, jails are called upon to incarcerate males and females, adults and occasionally juveniles, and an assortment of people with social problems such as mental illness, communicable diseases, and substance abuse (Judiscak 1995). John Irwin (1985) has characterized the modern jail as the institution used to incarcerate the "rabble." He

---

Box 4.1

Functions Served by Jails

Among the functions served by jails:

- Receive individuals pending arraignment and hold them awaiting trial, conviction, or sentencing
- Readmit probation, parole, and bail-bond violators and absconders
- Temporarily detain juveniles pending transfer to juvenile authorities
- Hold mentally ill persons pending their movement to appropriate health facilities
- Hold individuals for the military, for protective custody, for contempt, and for the courts as witnesses

- Release convicted inmates to the community upon completion of sentence
- Transfer inmates to federal, state, or other authorities
- House inmates for federal, state, or other authorities because of crowding of their facilities
- Relinquish custody of temporary detainees to juvenile and medical authorities
- Sometimes operate community-based programs with electronic monitoring or other types of supervision

Source: Department of Justice (1995).

---

includes society's disorderly or unruly segments as part of the rabble, along with members of the permanent urban underclass.

Second, the jail is unique because of its *location*. Jails traditionally have been located in the central business districts of most cities, often in the same building as, or immediately adjacent to, the town or county courthouse. This is unlike prisons, which frequently are situated in relatively remote locations.

Third, the jail is unique because of the *way it is administered*. Roughly 70% of the U.S. jails are administered by elected sheriffs (Kerle and Ford 1982). These officials typically come from law enforcement backgrounds and relatively few are even marginally interested in the jail's operation. Jail management for most sheriffs is a responsibility that is incidentally inherited when they take office, because of statutory or constitutional mandates.

For most sheriffs this means that jail operations are both financially and operationally subordinate to their law enforcement duties. It must be remembered that although jails are administered by law enforcement officials, they are not really law enforcement entities. By the same token, although jails are incarceration facilities, they are not fully a part of the criminal justice system's corrections component.

How Many Jails?

A quick review shows that another factor that distinguishes jails from prisons is that jails are much more numerous. In 1990 in the United States there were 1,207 state and 80 federal prisons (Department of Justice 1992b); in 1991 the number of federal prisons had grown to 95 (Department of Justice 1994b). By contrast, the 1993 National Jail Census identified 3,304 facilities that met the definition of a jail used by the Bureau of Justice Statistics. Previous censuses were conducted in 1970, 1972, 1978, 1983, and 1988, and in each of these reports the number of jails decreased. For example, in 1970 there were 4,037 jails, in 1972 there were 3,921, in 1978 this number had declined to 3,493, by 1983 the number was down to 3,338, and in 1988 it was 3,316.

It is difficult to know for certain why the number of jails has declined over time; however, in all likelihood the jails that have disappeared have been small jails that have been combined with larger jails in a county jail system or those that have merged with jails in other cities or adjacent counties through regional jail arrangements.

How Many Inmates?

On June 29, 1990, the Annual Survey of Jails found that there were 405,320 inmates detained in local jails in the United States; the "average" jail housed roughly 122 inmates. This is deceiving, however, since it is somewhat difficult to talk about the "average" jail in the United States: not only are jails unique facilities within the criminal justice system, but also each is a unique entity unto itself. An illustration of this point is the most recent accounting of the size distribution of various jails (Department of Justice 1995):

Rated capacity	Number of jails
Fewer than 50 inmates	1,874
50–249 inmates	1,016
250–499 inmates	209
500–999 inmates	129
1,000 or more inmates	76

As is readily apparent, more than one-half (56.7%) of the U.S. jails have a rated capacity of 50 or fewer inmates, yet these jails contain only 34,332 inmates—or roughly 7.5% of the nation's jail inmate population. The 1988 National Jail Census indicated that about half of the small jails are located in the South (see also Mays and Thompson 1988). This is generally the case for all jails: 1,591 of the 3,304 jails are in the South. The clear trend, however, is toward fewer small jails and more medium-to-large jails.

Most incarceration facilities have had steady population increases over the past two decades, and this is true for jails. In the 1978 National Jail Census, 158,394 jail inmates were incarcerated on February 15. On June 30, 1983, the number was 223,551, and on June 30, 1988, it was 343,569. The 1989 and 1990 Annual Surveys of Jails indicated jail populations of 395,553 and 405,320, respectively. At that time the nation's jails were housing inmates at 104% of their rated capacities (Department of Justice 1992c, 10). The most recent figures (June 30, 1994) from the U.S. Department of Justice show a record number of 490,442 inmates in city and county jails in the United States (Department of Justice 1995, 1), but because of additional construction the percentage of capacity occupied is down to 97%.

By any measure utilized, U.S. jails are faced with burgeoning inmate populations. In spite of a 93% increase in the number of inmate beds from 1983 to 1994, the number of inmates increased by 106%. While the one-day population numbers say something about jail capacity in relation to size, and by implication the degree of crowding, they do not represent the full picture of the number of inmates passing through jails in a given year. For example, in 1989 there were 9,774,096 jail admissions and 9,494,814 releases in the United States. By 1990 these totals had grown to 10,064,927 admissions and 9,870,546 releases. It is important to remember that these numbers result from total bookings and do not reflect the *individuals* brought into and released from jails. Although most detainees are only booked into jail once in a year, others might enter the jail many times during a given year. Therefore, in all likelihood, the number of individuals passing through the nation's jails in 1990 was somewhere between 5 and 8 million.

Jail Inmates and Gender

The inmate world will be discussed more fully in Chapter 6 but, for the time being, it is important to note something of the gender distributions of jail inmates. Two features will be addressed in this section: (1) the numbers, percentages, and increases in female jail inmates and (2) the types of facilities in which they are incarcerated.

First, U.S. jail inmate populations traditionally have been overwhelmingly male. In fact, males constituted 90% of the jail population on June 30, 1994 (Department of Justice 1995). However, it is important to note that the percentage of females has increased from 7% in 1983 to 10% in 1994 and, as Table 4.1 shows, their numbers have more than tripled during the same period—from 15,652 to 48,879.

Second, while virtually all of the women inmates are held in mixed population jails, some are incarcerated in jails that house women only. These single-sex jails are among the most uncommon of all facilities for incarceration. In 1992, with more than 3,300 jails nationwide, there were only 18 jails exclusively for women (Stohr and Mays 1993).

Recent research on the inmates of women-only jails shows that while they may fare no better than in mixed population jails, they certainly fare no worse (Gray, Mays, and Stohr 1995). All jail inmates exhibit a variety of personal deficiencies and programming needs, and this is true of female as well as male inmates (Department of Justice 1992c). However, as we will see in one of the sections to follow, in general jails do not do a very good job of dealing with most inmate needs during periods of incarceration.

Variations in Jail Use

As was stated earlier, jails can differ greatly from county to county, even within the same state. Two individuals—Patrick Jackson and John Klofas—have

Table 4.1

Number and Average Daily Population of Men, Women, and Juveniles in Local Jails, Midyear 1985, 1990–1996

	1985	1990	1991	1992
Average daily population[a]	265,010	408,075	422,609	441,889
Number of inmates, midyear[b]	256,615	405,320	426,479	444,584
Adults	254,986	403,019	424,129	441,780
Male	235,909	365,821	384,628	401,106
Female	19,077	37,198	39,501	40,674
Juveniles[c]	1,629	2,301	2,350	2,804
Held as adults[d]	—	—	—	—
Held as juveniles	1,629	2,301	2,350	2,804

	1993	1994	1995	1996
Average daily population[a]	466,155	479,757	509,828	515,432
Number of inmates, midyear[b]	459,804	486,474	507,044	518,492
Adults	455,500	479,800	499,300	510,400
Male	411,500	431,300	448,000	454,700
Female	44,100	48,500	51,300	55,700
Juveniles[c]	4,300	6,700	7,800	8,100
Held as adults[d]	3,300	5,100	5,900	5,700
Held as juveniles	1,000	1,600	1,800	2,400

Notes: Data are for June 30 in 1985 and 1992–95; for June 29, 1990; and for June 28 in 1991 and 1996. Detailed data for 1993–96 were estimated and rounded to the nearest 100.
[a] The average daily population is the sum of the number of inmates in a jail each day for a year, divided by 365.
[b] Inmate counts for 1985 and 1990–93 include an unknown number of persons who were under jail supervision but not confined. Detailed counts for 1994–96 were estimated based on number of inmates held in jail facilities.

[c] Juveniles are persons defined by state statute as being under a certain age, usually 18, and subject initially to juvenile court authority even if tried as adults in criminal court. In 1994 the definition was changed to include all persons under age 18.
[d] Includes juveniles who were tried or awaiting trial as adults.

Source: Bureau of Justice Statistics (1997c).

contributed greatly to our understanding of jail differences through their research.

Jackson (1988) examined jail use in three California jails: the Los Angeles Central Jail, the San Francisco Jail, and the Yolo County Jail. These jails differed not only in the population size served, but also in how they were utilized by local authorities. For example, on average, the Los Angeles Central Jail inmates had been charged with more serious offenses than those in the other two jails. This may be a reflection of this jail's use as a post-arraignment facility. By contrast, many of the inmates booked into the San Francisco Jail were charged with nonserious, public order offenses (such as drunkenness and vagrancy) and most spent relatively short time periods in jail. Jackson attributes this to the San Francisco Police Department's policy of picking up disreputable persons in order to keep them off the street and encourage the city's tourist business. Whatever the characteristics of the counties and their jails,

Riker's Island in New York City is home to a number of the city's jails. Many of these facilities reflect the architecture, such as tiers of cells, of a past era. Almost irrespective of the abuse they suffer, jails seem to be particularly enduring facilities.

Jackson found that most of the people booked into all three of these facilities resembled Irwin's "rabble."

Klofas also has added to our understanding of jails and has expanded on Jackson's concepts by developing a jail use typology (Klofas 1987, 1988, 1991a). Klofas' typology involves four types of jails based on two different factors: booking rates and holding rates. For instance, **holding jails** book inmates at a low rate, but detain them for some time. This type of jail would be consistent with Jackson's (1988, 1991) assessment of the Los Angeles County Central Jail. The second type of jail Klofas calls a **processing jail.** These jails book persons at a high rate, but hold them for relatively short time periods. The third group includes **low-use jails.** These facilities both book and hold inmates at very low rates. Low-use jails are most often found in rural counties or small towns. The final category is called a **high-use jail.** These jails both book and hold at high rates and would be exemplified by major urban institutions such as Chicago's Cook County Jail.

The Physical Plant of Jails

A great deal of wear and tear results from the number of jail admissions and releases every year. In fact, jails are regularly and routinely vandalized.

The Cook County Jail in Chicago is similar to many big-city jails today—crowded. At times, inmates must be housed in areas not designed to hold them such as the dining or recreation facilities.

Nevertheless, jails still seem to be particularly enduring buildings. This means that counties must choose wisely when they select the jail's design, location, and building materials. In a later section we will explore site selection for jails, but now we turn our focus to the varieties of jail configurations. These designs have gone through at least three different developmental phases.

The most traditional jail design is very similar to that of prisons. This is often called the **linear design,** in that most are composed of long straight hallways with right angle corners, and cells located along these hallways (Nelson 1988). One of the characteristics of linear design facilities is that custody personnel are located outside of the inmate cells and surveillance takes place by officers looking into the individual cell. This pattern of inmate management is called **intermittent supervision.** With this type of surveillance, officers can only know what is going on in the cells when they directly observe inmate activity. Figure 4.1 illustrates the layout of a linear design facility.

Second-generation jails frequently employ the use of closed-circuit television cameras or other types of devices to enhance officers' observations of inmate activity. These jails are called **remote supervision** facilities, in that officers rely on mechanical apparatuses to aid in observing inmates at times other than when they make their rounds. Remote surveillance is used in some jails where closed-circuit television can give constant, if indirect, observation to inmate and staff activities. Remote surveillance is especially prevalent at

Figure 4.1

Linear Design Jail

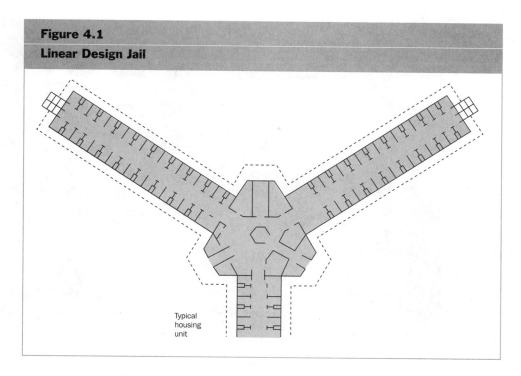

Typical
housing
unit

jail entrances (sally ports), booking areas, drunk tanks, and corridors along which inmates may pass. Closed-circuit televisions typically are not used to monitor the activity in inmate housing areas.

Third-generation designs commonly are called **new generation jails.** These facilities provide one of the most promising answers to better jails (and not just bigger ones). Sometimes these structures are also called **podular design** or **direct supervision jails** (Nelson 1988; Zupan 1991; Zupan and Menke 1988; Zupan and Stohr-Gillmore 1988). The new generation jail is different in organizational management, design, and inmate management philosophy than traditional, linear jails. In design it departs from traditional jails by confining inmates in housing pods of 16 to 46 (Zupan and Menke 1991). Occasionally, the housing pods are slightly larger, but the key idea is that each inmate within a pod has a small sleeping room and the center of the pod is an open day room or programs area. Ideally, inmates feel safer under this arrangement since they can retreat to their own sleeping quarters and shut, and perhaps lock, the door at certain times (Zupan and Stohr-Gillmore 1988).

New generation jails also differ from traditional jails in their approach to inmate management (Davis 1987). As previously mentioned, inmate supervision in a conventional, linear jail can be characterized as intermittent or remote. Custody officers periodically make rounds past or through the housing units to see whether any prohibited activity is taking place. After the officer

New generation or direct supervision jails involve not only a change in architecture, but also a change in inmate management style. The Santa Rita Jail in Alameda County, California, opened in 1989 as a modified direct supervision jail. Living pods house inmates in groups of 30. Sheriff's deputies monitor inmate activity from above in control booths and court appearances are conducted through a video system between the jail and the courts.

wanders by, inmates are free to return to whatever they were doing for another 30 or 45 minutes.

New generation jails are "direct supervision" facilities in that a custody officer is on duty in each housing pod 24 hours per day. The officer has direct contact with the inmates, and this approach requires interpersonal communication and human relations skills not traditionally called for by custody personnel. It also requires a more open or participative management style by facility administrators. Figure 4.2 shows the podular design of a new generation jail.

While new generation jails are not *the* solution to contemporary jail problems, they do offer hope on a number of fronts (Conroy, Smith, and Zupan 1991; Wallenstein 1987; for a more cautious view, see Wells 1987). First, evidence indicates that direct supervision will allow jails to be built to commercial construction standards without necessarily having to use expensive security construction and protection devices (Nelson 1988). This results in some cost savings. Second, research indicates that inmates may not only feel safer, they actually may be safer in new generation jails (Sechrest 1989a; Zupan and Menke 1991; Zupan and Stohr-Gillmore 1988). Third, after the

Figure 4.2

Podular Design: "New Generation" Jail

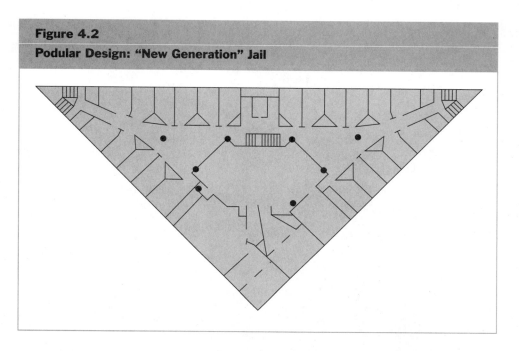

initial apprehension of moving from a traditional design to a direct supervision jail, staff job satisfaction increases and remains relatively high (Stohr, Self, and Lovrich 1992). The implication for jail administrators is that new generation jails require more training and more sophisticated human relations skills by staff than before. This means that most direct supervision jails will have to hire more and better qualified employees and, in all likelihood, pay them more (McCampbell 1990).

The Administration of Jails

Jails fit into one of a small number of administrative patterns. As mentioned previously, about 70% of U.S. jails are operated by a sheriff's department (Kerle and Ford 1982). A second common administrative pattern is for the jail administrator to be appointed by the county government as the head of a county department. Under this arrangement the jail administrator reports to the county manager, county judge, board of supervisors, or some similar body. A third arrangement places control of the jail under a chief of police. This pattern is most common in counties with unified law enforcement operations or in large municipalities that operate their own jails. Fourth, in some very large urban areas (Dade County, Florida; Los Angeles; and New York City, for instance), the jail is part of a countywide corrections department (Haque 1989). In these cases each facility may be designated as a special use entity—one jail

The Metropolitan Correctional Center in San Diego is an example of a federal high-rise jail. This facility and others like it were designed to provide short-term incarceration for federal detainees. The Metropolitan Correctional Centers/Metropolitan Detention Centers are built around the podular design or direct supervision approach to inmate management.

may be for female inmates, another may be for pretrial detainees, and another may be for those inmates actually sentenced to serve time.

Perhaps the most unique form of jail administration in the United States is that found in Kentucky. Kentucky is the only state to elect the local jailer. Box 4.2 describes some of the historical and contemporary features of Kentucky's distinctive jail administrative system.

The administrative arrangement may imply something of how significant the jail's operating budget is. Additionally, the type of jail administration may indicate the pay, status, and deployment patterns of personnel, and it is to the personnel issue that we now turn our attention.

Jail Employees

The physical plant problems of jails are substantial. However, no matter what the jail's age or configuration, the greatest influence on day-to-day jail operations will be the quality of the personnel employed. In a survey of problems facing jail managers, Guynes (1988) found that personnel concerns were second in importance only to crowding. The personnel issues facing jail administrators are easy to enumerate: the number of employees, employee assignments and quality, training, and compensation.

Box 4.2

The Kentucky "System" of Jail Administration

The Commonwealth of Kentucky provides an interesting case study on jail administration, and a look back to our past as well. Kentucky is the only one of the states to have popularly elected local jailers. Some people trace this approach to filling local offices to the era of Andrew Jackson and the advent of the "long ballot," where every public office—from governor of the state to local dog catcher, and even jailer—was elected and not appointed.

Kentucky holds another distinction as well: in 1983 it became the last state to eliminate the English fee system for providing jail funding. [The last state, before Kentucky, to eliminate the use of inmate fees was Maryland in 1906.] Prior to elimination of the fee system, the county provided the jailer a per diem amount, established by state law, for each inmate housed. From this amount inmates were to be fed,

supplies were to be purchased, and personnel were to be paid. Anything left over, in effect, became the jailer's salary.

Because the fee amount was meager, and subject to change so infrequently, many of the small, rural jails in the state operated on shoe-string budgets. Historically jailers in the mountain counties held other jobs and ran the jail with the help of their families, particularly their wives, who often were the cooks and de facto jail managers. In some of these counties the wages for the jailers were so modest that most citizens would not think of running for office. As a result, the position almost became hereditary: as a jailer would retire or die his wife or one of his sons would run for office, and in virtually every case would be elected.

Sources: Bain (1988a, 1988b).

The Number of Employees

Most jails are understaffed (Mays and Thompson 1991). This is particularly true for small jails, rural jails, and for many jails during the night shift. In some counties it is not uncommon to have the night shift jail personnel serve as sheriff's department dispatchers or to fulfill a variety of other functions (Kerle and Ford 1982). In traditionally designed jails this may mean that inmates are unsupervised for long periods of time, and when this happens assaults and suicides may occur with little possibility of timely intervention by the staff.

Employee Assignments and Quality

Employee assignments and employee quality are virtually impossible issues to separate. Employee quality/assignment is related to the two dominant administrative patterns used in jails.

In the most traditional staffing approach, custodial personnel are simply sheriff's deputies assigned to work in the jail. These employees often are (1) newly hired personnel awaiting the beginning of a training academy class, (2) newly trained deputies awaiting assignment to road patrol, (3) deputies who request jail assignments (occasionally older deputies who have grown tired of the rigors of patrol), and (4) deputies placed in the jail as a form of limited duty assignment (because of accidents or injuries) or as punishment (Ford 1993; Rowan 1993; Struckhoff 1989). For the latter punishment duty group, sheriffs view jail assignments as most appropriate because here deputies can do less harm, or at least they are out of the public eye.

In the second deployment pattern, sheriffs or jail administrators develop two separate career tracks: one for patrol deputies and one for detention facility personnel. For jails using this approach, these are distinct and not interchangeable career options. Therefore, personnel cannot simply transfer from one function to the other. The problem posed by this procedure is that detention officers frequently are paid less than patrol personnel and hold real or imagined second-class citizenship in relation to uniformed deputies who have law enforcement responsibilities (Rowan 1993).

Two keys to improved employee quality are improved training and better compensation. In most states jail training has been marginal, at best, or totally absent, at worst. Most jail training involves the "technical" aspects of facility operations (for example, the use of physical restraints, report writing, and inmate disciplinary practices) and "human relations" (for example, interpersonal communications skills, dispute resolution, etc.). Jail training experts emphasize that it is not law enforcement training—although it involves elements of law enforcement training—and it is not corrections or prison training either. In the end, *jail* training is unique and distinctive unto itself.

The nature of jail training is one reason some sheriff departments have decided to separate the law enforcement and custody career paths. Law enforcement officers carry weapons and generally receive training ranging from 10 to 20 weeks (400 to 800 hours) in length. By contrast, custody officers are not armed and may only receive 2 to 4 weeks of training. This is the justification for lower pay and one of the reasons for a perceived second-class status.

Major Jail Issues

Almost by design jails deal with society's problems and exhibit many problems themselves. This section will address jail problems, particularly those that seem the most resistant to change or reform.

Local Politics

One of the major problems facing contemporary jails is that they are products of their local political environment (Advisory Commission on Intergovernmental Relations 1984; National Advisory Commission 1973; Thompson 1986). Not only are most jails administered by the sheriff but also they are subject to the policy directives and funding control of the city council or county commission or board of supervisors (Ricci 1986). In the worst of all possible situations, a sheriff of one political party confronts a dominant coalition of county commissioners of the other political party and a policy stalemate results.

The jail's local political nature becomes acutely apparent in the budgetary process. Jails must compete in budget negotiations with schools, roads, health care, solid waste disposal, and parks and recreation. All of these are programs and agencies that are more politically popular with voters than jails.

Local Funding

A second problem for jails is also related to local politics: the local financing of jails. Jails are the victims of low county funding priorities and they suffer additionally because counties have relatively inflexible revenue bases (National Advisory Commission 1973). Most of the counties in the United States rely heavily, if not exclusively, on property taxes for funding, and students of local government have long recognized that property taxes are the least responsive revenue sources in terms of growth in the local economy.

When we combine political conservatism ("Lock 'em up and throw away the key") with fiscal conservatism ("Public money shouldn't be wasted on bad people and the jails that house them"), we find jails suffering from what could easily be called the "double whammy" (Clear and Cole 1990, 210; Mays and Thompson 1991, 11–12).

In the 1980s, in an effort to deal with persistent financial problems in regard to prison construction, Ohio moved from reliance on general obligation revenue bonds to the use of lease-purchase agreements (DeWitt 1986d). This approach—which was extended to cover jail construction in 1986—offers several advantages over traditional capital construction methods. For instance, a lease does not obligate governments to an ongoing debt. Additionally, lease agreements may be negotiated in relatively short time periods, sometimes as quickly as 45 days. And, perhaps most critically, unlike the issuance of general obligation bonds, lease agreements seldom require voter approval (DeWitt 1986d).

California also takes a different approach to funding jail construction and improvement (Lammers and Morris 1990). Because of voter initiatives such as Proposition 13, establishing property tax limitations, California has created the County Jail Capital Expenditure Fund to provide a statewide general obligation bond pool of money accessible to counties. As a result, from 1980 to 1988 $1.455 billion became available to counties struggling to deal with jail "litigation, deterioration, and crowding" (Lammers and Morris 1990, 2). Innovative approaches to construction financing—like those undertaken by Ohio and California—help jurisdictions cope with the shortcomings inherent in local financing of jails.

Location Issues

Some of the problems associated with jails can only be solved through expansion, construction, or relocation. Expansion of existing facilities frequently is the least costly and the most desirable option when the issue is simply one of needing additional space. However, expansion may not be feasible in the jail's present location. Also, it may not be possible to expand a building that is 50 to 100 years old.

For some counties the real decision is not over building a bigger jail, but over building a more suitable jail (Hall 1987). The preferred site for most jurisdictions is at or near the jail's present location. Often related agencies, businesses, and services—the courthouse, lawyers' offices, and bail bonding businesses—have built up near the jail and have a vested interest in keeping the jail in its present location. If additional land must be purchased, the county will face a funding dilemma: jails are often located on prime commercial real estate (Orrick 1989). Therefore, to acquire additional property for the building and perhaps parking, even under the government's right of imminent domain, will involve a lengthy and expensive process.

Most counties faced with a major jail expansion or relocation project will be forced to look for property away from the traditional central business district sites. Remote locations are more feasible now because of improved prisoner transportation systems, but especially because of **video arraignments,** which allow judges and lawyers to be in one place while the prisoners are in another. The chief disadvantage associated with these nontraditional jail sites is that they may be far from established utility connections. They also may be near land set aside for industrial or agricultural purposes, or near suburban housing developments. County authorities frequently will experience opposition from neighboring landowners who express a vocal **NIMBY** (not in my back yard) sentiment (Mays and Czerniak 1992/93; Welsh et al. 1991). In the face of organized opposition, politicians may back down from a jail relocation decision, once again illustrating the jail's political nature.

Makeshift Structures

For some counties the problem of jail crowding is chronic, but for others it is acute. One of the most common occurrences of acute jail crowding is the situation faced by many counties in regard to their weekend jail populations. Weekend jail populations frequently swell because of three factors (Department of Justice 1983). First, law enforcement activity during the weekend period can put additional prisoners—especially those charged with crimes such as driving while intoxicated (DWI)—into the inmate population. Second, in some jurisdictions judges may not be available on the weekends to conduct bail hearings with the same frequency as they are during normal weekday business hours. This causes some prisoners to languish in jail over the weekend simply because they cannot make an initial appearance before a judicial officer. Third, some judges increasingly have turned to weekend sentences, again particularly for cases such as those involving DWI offenders (May 1978).

Jail crowding in some counties, particularly the large urban ones, has long gone beyond the point of being acute. For these counties crowding is a

Box 4.3

This is Not a Camp Out

Sheriff Joseph Arpaio is called by many the "meanest sheriff in the country." And guess what, he likes the title. He has been featured in news stories on television, in news magazines, and in newspapers with national circulations. He has fed inmates baloney sandwiches and has purchased inexpensive bulk food products such as corndogs. He has also prohibited cigarettes and coffee in the jail.

So when the Maricopa County, Arizona, Jail was faced with crowding problems Sheriff Arpaio had a simple solution: buy surplus military tents in which to house the inmate overflow. No air conditioning in the Arizona desert in the summer time? No problem. Sheriff Arpaio's advice? If you don't like it here, don't come back to my jail.

Source: "Taking No Prisoners" (1995).

Inmates in the Texas prison system have been housed in tents to alleviate the crowding facing many of the state's prisons. Tents have also been used in jail systems such as the one in Maricopa County, Arizona, to house inmates either on a short-term or on a long-term basis.

chronic problem requiring long-term solutions. These counties may be faced with the options of adding other facilities or expanding their current facilities.

Perhaps one of the most promising approaches to dealing with jail crowding is through the use of alternative jail structures. These structures may be converted schools, warehouses, or similar structures and they are variously known as **jail annexes** or **satellite jails.** New York City has gone so far as to employ two former British troop ships as jail barges that are moored in the East River (Haque 1989; Welch 1991). Some of the alternative structures are high-tech and they employ some of the most current construction technologies. Others are decidedly low-tech. Box 4.3 describes a practice criticized by many jail observers, but which has been used extensively by the sheriff of Maricopa (Phoenix) County, Arizona.

These alternative structures enjoy several advantages. First, they already exist in some form and therefore only need modification. Second, most can be renovated or modified to less costly minimum-security standards, unlike many central jails. Third, they are very useful for work release or similar types of inmates who need less security than the jail's general population. Finally, these facilities give counties overflow capacity for weekend populations, which may increase by as much as 20% over weekday rates in some jurisdictions.

Opposition to the use of makeshift facilities can be grouped into two categories. Welch (1991) argues that the use of alternative structures expands our capacity to punish. The second problem of such structures is that they are often touted as "temporary solutions." In reality, they tend to be fairly enduring because the crowding situation they are designed to address is a chronic problem for many jurisdictions. Therefore, the use of alternative structures keeps criminal justice decision makers from ever having to address the root of the problem: the patterns of jail use (see especially Klofas 1987, 1991a).

Privatization

One of the most hotly debated concepts in corrections has been **privatization** (see, for example, Logan 1990; Mays and Gray 1996; Robbins 1988), and although this issue will be explored in greater depth elsewhere in this book, we will examine its application to jails here (see, especially, Collins 1987a, 1987b).

Privatization provides several advantages for counties looking for ways to deal with many of their jail problems (McCullough and Maguigan 1990; Ward 1990). For instance, the private sector may be able to help a county finance jail renovation or construction when the taxpayers have refused to approve a capital bond issue. The private sector also can furnish construction services by providing a "turn-key" option on a lease-purchase provision. In either situation the private contractor completes construction for the governmental body and then turns the operation over to a public sector agency (Bowen and Kelly 1987). Experience in many counties has demonstrated that private sector organizations are able to obtain land and build jails more quickly and at less cost than are governments (Hackett et al. 1987).

The private sector also may be able to save counties money through contracting for specific services. Among the most commonly provided private options are food services, medical care, counseling, and education/job training. In the case of private provision of particular services, we have what some have characterized as a **public-private partnership** (Cox and Osterhoff 1991).

Table 4.2
Privately Operated Jails and Detention Centers, 1993

Facility	Contractor
Tuscaloosa Metro Detention Facility (AL)	Concept, Inc.
San Diego City Jail (CA)	Wackenhut Corrections Corporation
Seal Beach City Jail (CA)	Corrections Services, Inc.
Hernando County Jail (FL)	Corrections Corp. of America
Bay County Jail and Jail Annex (FL)	Corrections Corp. of America
River City Correctional Center (Louisville, KY)	U.S. Corrections Corp.
Union Parish Detention Facility (LA)	Capital Correctional Resources, Inc.
Santa Fe Detention Center (NM)	Corrections Corp. of America
Torrance County Detention Facility (NM)	Corrections Corp. of America
Silverdale Facilities (Chattanooga, TN)	Corrections Corp. of America
Metro-Davidson County Detention Center (TN)	Corrections Corp. of America
Lockhart Work Program Facility (TX)	Wackenhut Corrections Corp.
Permian Basin Regional Jail (Midland, TX)	GRW Corp.
Odessa Detention Center (TX)	GRW Corp.
Tarrant County Community Correction Facility (TX)	Esmore Correctional Services, Inc.

Source: Bureau of Justice Statistics (1994).

In its most complete form, the private sector can operate jails. Corrections Corporation of America, one of the nation's largest private contractors, runs county jails for Santa Fe and Torrance Counties in New Mexico. Table 4.2 provides a list of the privately run jails and detention centers, along with the contractor's name as of December 1993. This list does not include facilities operated for state corrections departments or those holding special categories of inmates for federal agencies such as the Immigration and Naturalization Service.

The private approach to total facility management has been relatively controversial for several reasons. For example, some people believe that the private sector has little or no business in the operation of detention facilities, prisons, or jails (see, for example, Feeley 1991; Gilbert 1996; Logan 1987; Mullen 1984; Robbins 1988). For these authorities, operating institutions of confinement is inherently a governmental function, and one in which the private sector should not be involved. However, a quick review of U.S. corrections history shows that the private sector has been involved in various ways throughout the entire development of corrections (Durham 1989). Nevertheless, jail privatization presents some unresolved dilemmas.

It is important to remember in any discussion of privatization that the governmental entity is not removing its obligation to pay for incarcerated individuals. What happens is that rather than the government being obligated for line-item costs, everything is included in an inmate per diem charge. Critics argue that such a pricing arrangement provides an incentive for the private contractor to minimize inmate expenditures and to keep the beds as full as possible in order to maximize profits.

One argument for privatization, however, is that private contractors can provide certain goods and services at much reduced costs. For example, if a county needs to buy sheets and towels for jail inmates to use, the purchase must be advertised for bids. This may take some time, and there is no guarantee that the county will receive the lowest possible cost. By contrast, private jail operators are free to purchase whatever they need from suppliers willing to give them the lowest possible cost, perhaps even lower than normal because of quantity discounts or long-term contracts. This holds true particularly for cleaning and janitorial supplies and food purchases. For most counties, private sector companies *may* be able to operate a jail at a lower cost than government employees can, but there is no automatic guarantee of this (Hackett et al. 1987).

One of the most attractive features of private jail operations is the potential reduction of legal liability. This issue is significant for two reasons. First, many private contractors specify that any jail they build and operate will conform to American Correctional Association (ACA) standards. This means that new jails will be eligible for accreditation and, thus, will have a lower risk for successful inmate lawsuits. Second, however, local policy makers must be aware that contracting for jail operations does not completely exempt them from legal liability. It may mean that such liability is reduced or that it is shared with the private operator, but it does not mean that the local governing body is off the hook when it comes to going to court (see Chaires and Lentz 1996).

In the end, the private sector may contribute most substantially to jail operations in the following ways:

1. Private industry can build more quickly and, potentially, less expensively than many local governments can.

2. The private sector may be able to provide some functions at either reduced cost or better quality at the same cost than a local government is able to provide.

3. The private sector may be able to provide expansion space—such as satellite jails or other low-security facilities—to lessen the population crunches faced by many U.S. jails.

Jail Standards

The development of jail standards has been going on for almost two decades. The American Correctional Association issued its first edition of *Standards for Adult Local Detention Facilities* in 1977. The third edition was published in 1991.

The ACA standards cover areas such as training and staff development, building and safety codes, security and control, safety and emergency procedures, inmate rights, food service, sanitation and hygiene, health care, and work and industries programs (American Correctional Association 1991b).

Additionally, some states have expanded upon the minimum standards and have further requirements dealing with construction and operations.

Research within the past decade (see, for example, Thompson and Mays 1988a, 1988b) has uncovered several points about state jail standards. First, states are increasingly adopting jail standards in one form or another. Second, as of 1983, 25 states had enacted mandatory standards, typically combined with periodic inspections, and enforcement procedures. An additional 6 states had voluntary standards, and 6 states had combined state prison–jail systems. This leaves 13 states without jail standards (American Jail Association 1994).

Third, jails in those states with mandatory standards, regular inspections, and enforcement mechanisms have more effective programs and operating procedures (Thompson and Mays 1988a). More to the point, jails in these states are more likely to provide inmate medical care within the jail itself and to have inmate medical, suicide, and alcohol screening. They also keep inmates confined to their cells for fewer hours per day and rely less often on emergency room services for medical care. Most importantly, states with mandatory standards and inspections have substantially fewer inmate deaths—by natural causes or suicide—than their nonstandard, noninspected counterparts (Thompson and Mays 1988a, 1988b).

Given the amount of litigation and the poor record of success counties have enjoyed in inmate lawsuits, the trend for the future likely will be more states with standards, more states with mandatory standards, standards concerning a wider variety of issues, and more vigorous inspections and enforcement. As many jail administrators have learned, having jail standards will not keep a jail from being sued. However, having standards and adhering to those standards may greatly diminish the mishandling of inmates and the likelihood of a *successful* suit.

Removing Juveniles from Adult Jails

An ongoing controversy for at least two decades involves incarcerating juvenile offenders in adult jails (see Schwartz 1989, 1991). One of the major provisions in the Juvenile Justice and Delinquency Prevention Act of 1974 was the removal of juvenile detainees from adult jails, but as Ira Schwartz (1991) notes, this has become an "unfinished agenda."

Juveniles in adult jails present numerous problems, but a few are particularly worthy of mention. For instance, the average daily population of juvenile detainees in adult jails increased from about 1,700 in 1983 to more than 3,400 in 1993 and 6,700 in 1994 (Department of Justice 1995, 3). While many (76% in 1994) of these youths are to be tried as adults, on any given day a significant number of accused juvenile offenders are still housed in adult facilities. Most people assume that these are the worst of the worst juvenile offenders, but this is a shaky assumption at best. In many small, rural counties, there is no juvenile detention center, and so the options often are adult jail or nothing.

Most jail administrators are reluctant to house juveniles in their facilities under any circumstances. Juvenile detainees present inordinately high suicide risks, and they must be housed with sight and sound separation from adult offenders (Dale 1988). The result is that juvenile detainees may end up in the jail's most remote parts, in order to separate them from adults, but in the locations where assault and suicide risks are the greatest.

For most counties, the solution has been relatively simple: build a separate juvenile detention center to house these youngsters. If a county does not have a sufficient population or the economic resources to support its own juvenile detention facility, it might join with adjacent cities or counties to create a regional facility.

Whatever solution local governments settle on, two things remain clear. The juvenile jail removal initiative has not been successful, and the number of juvenile detainees, which had leveled off at around 1,700, recently has started to rise dramatically. Where economically feasible, many counties have moved toward removing juveniles from adult jails in order to provide a safer environment for the detainees, and to lessen liability potential.

Inmate Programming

Not all of the problems facing the contemporary jail are the result of the physical plant or the staff. Many problems result from the types of people housed in the jail. As mentioned previously, Irwin (1985) characterizes much of the jail inmate population as "rabble," or society's permanent underclass (see also Welch 1989). Many jail inmates are living at society's margins even when they are not incarcerated. They tend to be drawn disproportionately from racial and ethnic minorities and, in general, come from the lowest socio-economic strata. They often are unemployed, and they tend to suffer from a variety of physical and psychological difficulties. In other words, they have problems outside of the jail, and when they come to jail they bring these problems with them.

Although not everyone in jail goes to prison, virtually everyone in prison has done time in jail. Therefore, it is safe to assume that what is true for prison inmates is equally true for jail inmates. Therefore, jail administrators need to consider constructive ways to use inmate time during their incarceration, since for some inmates this may involve a considerable amount of time—either all at once or over many periods of incarceration. One jail administrator attending a national conference on creating a jail research agenda commented that he had inmates "serving life on the installment plan" (Saxton 1991).

The essential question then is what kinds of programs are most appropriate considering the jail's physical space and budget? Many jail inmates are unemployed at the time of their arrest. This is often the case because of a lack of educational achievement (in 1989 53.8% of them did not possess a high school diploma or GED) and lack of marketable job skills. For some, long criminal histories have rendered them virtually unemployable (see, especially, Department of Justice 1991b).

Lack of sufficient employment will mean that many jail inmates cannot post even a modest bail and up to 60% of them cannot afford an attorney (Neubauer 1992). Frequently, these inmates go to court on relatively minor charges without an attorney and simply plead guilty to the charges. For them the "process is the punishment" (Feeley 1979). In addition to financial impediments, most inmates bring a host of medical problems to jail with them. A large percentage of jail inmates report significant preincarceration drug and/or alcohol usage patterns (Mays, Fields, and Thompson 1991). Many inmates are dependent on several substances.

These inmates suffer from withdrawal symptoms and some are conspicuously malnourished. They need medical treatment as well as counseling in order to stabilize their physical and emotional conditions. Drug- and alcohol-dependent inmates may bring serious psychological problems into the jail environment as well. In fact, these inmates may be prime candidates for suicide in jail (Kennedy and Homant 1988; Winfree 1988; Winfree and Wooldredge 1991; Wooldredge and Winfree 1992). Therefore, jails need to carefully screen incoming inmates for signs of substance abuse, provide them with immediate care and treatment, and promote some type of long-term solution to the causes of chemical dependency. This means that jails need to provide detoxification facilities and treatment programs such as Alcoholics Anonymous or Narcotics Anonymous. These programs may be provided by staff members or they may be available through the assistance of community groups and organizations.

In the end it is important to remember that for many regular detainees, substance abuse and criminality should not be considered in terms of cause and effect relationships. Instead all of these factors are part of a larger deviant lifestyle (Mays, Fields, and Thompson 1991).

Medical considerations and programming may take a variety of forms in jail. For instance, mental health problems may extend beyond substance abusing inmates. Jerrell and Komisaruk (1991) and Kalinich, Embert, and Senese (1988, 1991; also Senese, Kalinich, and Embert, 1989) have characterized the jail as contemporary society's mental health clinic. As a result of the movement to deinstitutionalize many of those individuals formerly committed to state psychiatric hospitals, some people who need mental health care are left to live on the streets of most large cities (Judiscak 1995). Supposedly, care was to be provided for these people through community mental health programs. However, because most of these programs are overworked and underfunded, a host of potential clients do not receive the services they need. After these people wander the streets long enough, their often bizarre

Table 4.3

Local Jail Inmates Known to be Positive for HIV, by Size of Jurisdiction, June 30, 1993

| Size of jurisdiction[a] | Number of jail inmates | | Type of HIV infection/AIDS case | | | | HIV/AIDS cases as a percentage of jail population |
	In all jurisdictions	In reporting jurisdictions[b]	Total[c]	Asymp-tomatic	Symp-tomatic	Confirmed AIDS	
Total	459,804	371,509	6,711	2,800	1,200	1,888	1.8%
50 largest[d]	184,416	136,308	3,926	1,638	775	929	2.9
500 or more[e]	103,893	87,816	1,374	625	143	487	1.6
250–499	51,297	41,760	490	246	83	146	1.2
100–249	55,099	49,168	470	149	109	144	1.0
Fewer than 100	65,099	56,457	451	142	90	182	.8

Notes: [a] Based on the average daily population between July 1, 1992, and June 30, 1993.
[b] Excludes inmates in facilities that did not report data on HIV/AIDS cases.
[c] Detail does not add to total because not all jurisdictions reported data on the type of HIV infection or confirmed AIDS.
[d] Jurisdictions were ranked by their average daily population between July 1, 1992, and June 30, 1993.
[e] Excludes the 50 largest jurisdictions.
Source: Bureau of Justice Statistics (1995b).

appearance and behavior will bring them into contact with local law enforcement officers who put them in jail to appease citizen complaints or as a "mercy booking" (Jerrell and Komisaruk 1991). Thus, we have deinstitutionalized but criminalized mental health treatment in this country (Haddad 1993; Hecht and Smithhart 1987). Ironically, many jail inmates receive no better mental health treatment in jail than they did when they roamed the streets.

One of the most dramatic health-care issues facing contemporary jails involves the presence of inmates with the human immunodeficiency virus (HIV) or those whose cases have progressed to the full development of acquired immunodeficiency syndrome (AIDS) (see Hammett and Moini 1990; Marchese 1989; Messing 1993; Perkins, Stephan, and Beck 1995). Jail inmates seem particularly susceptible to AIDS since many of them have histories of intravenous drug use and may engage in activities, such as needle sharing, that place them at risk.

Since 1981 more than 5,000 cases of AIDS have been reported in prisons and jails in the United States. A 1989 study by the National Institute of Justice found 1,750 cases of AIDS in "30 large city and county jail systems" (Hammett and Moini 1990, 2) and Perkins, Stephan, and Beck (1995) indicated that on June 30, 1993, there were 6,711 jail inmates reported as HIV-infected. Of these 6,711 individuals, 1,888 had AIDS and another 1,200 had some of the symptoms associated with AIDS. Table 4.3 shows something of the prevalence of HIV/AIDS in U.S. jails.

Although there have been no documented cases of job-related HIV infection of correctional officers (Hammett and Moini 1990; Takas and Hammett 1989), inmates who are HIV-positive pose an assortment of problems for contemporary jails. First, uninformed and untrained staff members may suffer from panic over the prospect of working with inmates who are carrying the AIDS virus. The thought of *possible* contamination is always present. Second, a panic can be caused among other inmates when a known HIV-positive inmate is housed in the jail's general population. Third, there may be negative legal repercussions from administratively segregating HIV-positive inmates from the general population, especially if such segregation takes on a punitive dimension. Finally, jails assume medical responsibility for those inmates they house (Lawrence and Zwisohn 1991; Welch 1989). Therefore, as part of each jail's programming structure there must be ongoing AIDS awareness education for both staff members and inmates.

The final group of programs for jail inmates can be classified under the general heading of rehabilitative services. These programs can include religious activities provided by local churches or jail chaplains, recreation, sessions on coping skills, anger management, and improved parenting techniques (for both male and female inmates). These efforts do two things for the inmate: they teach skills and abilities that should be useful in the outside world and they promote constructive use of time within the jail. Unfortunately, recent research involving a group of women-only jails found that although such programs are administratively desirable and clearly sought by the inmates, few jails provide programs that actually meet inmates' needs (Gray, Mays, and Stohr 1995).

 Other Local Detention Facilities

Before considering what may happen to jails in the twenty-first century, it is important to note that there are other local detention facilities. In this section we will briefly consider the other types of facilities used for short-term incarceration.

Alternative Forms of Incarceration

Although the future may witness an expansion of alternatives to incarceration, the current public mood to increase the amounts and forms of incarceration may override the alternatives movement. What we may see instead of alternatives to incarceration is different structures or alternative forms of incarceration. In this section we will briefly discuss two such alternatives: minimum-security facilities for low-risk or no-risk offenders and shock incarceration or boot camp programs.

In terms of jail security levels, one point is very apparent: virtually all jails are built to maximum-security specifications. This is a very inefficient system since maximum-security space is the most expensive to construct and not all jail inmates warrant maximum-security confinement. In fact, most inmates in practically all jails can be housed in something much less than maximum-security detention. Therefore, a number of local jurisdictions are constructing parts of their new jails or completely separate facilities to house lower-risk inmates.

This approach seems particularly appropriate for certain inmates. For example, individuals charged with minor property crimes such as shoplifting seldom warrant anything above minimum-security custody. The same is probably true for most of the individuals charged with DWI, especially those sentenced to serve weekend terms. For these inmates all that is needed is a place to report to and a set of walls, perhaps enclosed within a fence, to contain them for their 48-hour-or-so stays. Therefore, satellite jails and jail annexes often serve the jurisdiction's purposes just as well as a high-rise, high-security central jail facility, and at a much lower cost. Because jail bed space is both an expensive commodity and a scarce one, jurisdictions are increasingly likely to turn to alternative and less costly facilities to house their low-security inmates.

A growing trend in alternatives to prison incarceration has been the use of shock incarceration programs such as boot camps. To date, most boot camp programs have been operated by state prison systems, but as Table 4.4 shows several of the nation's jail systems are operating boot camp programs as well. The programs already in existence are probably indications of the future for many local jail systems. In fact, a recent report by the National Institute of Justice noted that "for a number of reasons, a jail-operated boot camp could be of strategic value to the criminal justice system. Although the average length of stay for defendants and offenders admitted to jail is relatively short (15–16 days) compared to State prisoners (16–18 months), jails increasingly house inmates who can spend many months in confinement" (Austin, Jones, and Bolyard 1993, 1).

As of 1992, 10 localities were operating boot camp programs and another 13 indicated that they would open such a program in either 1992 or 1993. Although doubts remain about the long-term effectiveness of boot camp programs (see, for example, MacKenzie 1990; MacKenzie and Shaw 1990; Sechrest 1989b), there is no doubt about their popularity, especially among politicians. Therefore, we must ask: What are the goals of a boot camp program? Three objectives have been most commonly mentioned.

First, boot camp programs may aid jail administrators in reducing crowding. As the National Institute of Justice report on jail boot camps notes, however, "given the relatively short stay for most jail inmates, this objective will not be met unless the program carefully targets inmates who will spend at least 90 days or more in custody" (Austin, Jones, and Bolyard 1993, 5).

Second, one of the benefits of boot camps that has been touted since these programs first appeared is their rehabilitative merits. Again, the National Institute of Justice report warns:

Table 4.4

Jail Boot Camps: Organizational Attributes in Selected Counties

	Travis, TX	New York City—Men	New York City—Women	Santa Clara, CA	Nassau, NY	Orleans, LA	Harris, TX	Ontario, NY	Brazos, TX	Oakland, MI
Startup date	9/88	10/90	10/91	4/91	4/92	8/86	5/91	3/92	2/92	7/90
Bed capacity	76	300	100	44	38	126	384	18	12	60
ADP[a]—County jail system	2,222	21,449	21,449	4,026	1,940	4,600	14,512	120	352	1,550
ADP—Boot camp	57	210	84	26	14	80	348	15	12	47
Percentage of capacity	75%	70%	84%	59%	37%	63%	91%	83%	100%	78%
Annual admissions	266	1,059	210	124	—	177	814	106	36	119
Program length in days	90–120	60	70	63–70	90 days	250–300	90–120[b]	5	120	56
Average length of stay	120	60	70	65	—	275	120	5	120	56
Number of staff	20	119	24.5	8.5	21	24	119	19	7	10
Administrative	5	3	4	0.5	5	1	4	3	0	1
Custody	3	101	17	8	14	23	65	6	4	8
Program	12	15	3.5	0	2	0	50	10[d]	3	1
Total annual budget	$1.1 million	$367,119[c]	$858,174	$507,000	$600,000	$879,175	$3.5 million	no separate budget	—	$403,423
Staff-to-inmate ratio	1:3	1:2	1:4	1:3	1.5:1	1:4	1:3	1:2[d]	1:2	1:5
Cost per inmate/day	$53	$5[c]	$28	$53	$117	$30	$26	—	—	$24
Funding source(s)	county	city	city	county	federal, state, and county	county	state and county	—	county and inmate commissary	county

Notes: [a] ADP = average daily population.
[b] Length of stay is extended beyond 120 days for inmates with disciplinary problems.
[c] Staff salary only, does not include maintenance costs.
[d] Part-time volunteer personnel; not included in staff-to-inmate ratio.

Source: Austin, Jones, and Bolyard (1993).

Box 4.4

The Courts Regimented Intensive Probation Program of Harris County, Texas

An example of a county-level boot camp operation is the Courts Regimented Intensive Probation Program (CRIPP) operated by Harris County, Texas (see Burton et al. 1993). Unlike most boot camp programs, which are operated by state prison systems, the CRIPP program is county-run. Burton and his colleagues (1993) examined the operation of the Harris County program and found that several features were prominent.

First, potential participants were given thorough medical examinations prior to reporting to the program. Second, the participants were given the opportunity to participate in vocational training. Third, physical training (a key element in virtually all boot camp programs) was the primary activity for most program participants. Finally, drug and alcohol counseling were made available to address participants' chemical dependency problems.

The evaluation of the CRIPP effort found that there were substantial and statistically significant changes in participants' attitudes in a variety of areas. In fact, Burton et al. (1993, 51) concluded that the "CRIPP boot camp experience did positively change probationers' attitudes in crucial areas, which may potentially shape the likelihood of future criminality." However, as their evaluation of CRIPP also noted, the missing ingredient in many programs may be high-quality and thorough aftercare programs. As Burton et al. (1993, 51) emphasize, "in the absence of 'intensive' quality 'aftercare' programs, boot camp participation alone will likely fail—as have similar correctional treatment programs—as a solution to reforming offenders."

Source: Burton et al. (1993).

Reversing the cumulative negative experiences of youthful offenders within a 90-day period is, at best, an extremely difficult objective. A boot camp program can help initiate the process by improving an offender's ability to read, developing work skills, making job referrals, and dealing with long-term drug abuse histories. . . . But these gains do not necessarily translate into reductions in crime rates (Austin Jones, and Bolyard 1993, 5).

The third benefit associated with correctional boot camps is the improvement in community relations. If a jail can be operated more efficiently as a result of the boot camp, this efficiency should translate into improved standing within the community. Particularly of interest are work projects completed by the boot camp inmates and a safer jail environment. These two elements send the message to the community that inmates are being appropriately punished and that the administrators, not the inmates, run the facility. Therefore, whether boot camps can live up to all of their promises or not, in all likelihood they will become part of many contemporary jail systems.

Police Lockups

One of the most pervasive detention facilities in the United States is the **police lockup.** There are so many, in fact, that we do not have an exact count. However, estimates are that there are somewhere between 13,000 and 15,000 such facilities around the country (Abadinsky and Winfree 1992; Clear and Cole 1990). A number of features distinguish lockups from other types of detention facilities.

First, most lockups are located in a police building. In some cities renovated structures such as old service stations have been pressed into service as lockups (see, for example, Welch 1991). Second, lockups are for the temporary detention of suspects until they can be interrogated or fully processed by the police prior to being transferred to the county jail. Finally, as recent research has indicated, lockups are very dangerous places to be (see Winfree 1988). Because they serve as temporary holding structures, inmate activities may not be monitored as closely as they would in a county jail. This often results in higher levels of inmate-on-inmate assaults, and particularly higher numbers of inmate deaths than would be found in jails or prisons.

County Workhouses, Penal Farms, Etc.

In many U.S. counties, separate facilities are maintained for misdemeanants serving terms longer than 90 days. Rather than retaining inmates serving 6- to 12-month sentences in the main jail, the county may operate a workhouse or penal farm. These facilities tend to be located away from the courthouse and the central business district, where the jail is traditionally found. Inmates serving time in these long-term facilities have a variety of work responsibilities. For instance, they might perform parks and recreation maintenance or work in farming or agricultural pursuits. They also might be responsible for assisting in the maintenance and care of government vehicles. Inmates in these institutions tend to be low-security inmates, and expanded programming opportunities may be available in these settings that are not traditionally available at the central jail. While long-term misdemeanor institutions like workhouses and penal farms may be more common in rural settings, even urban counties such as Los Angeles and San Diego may operate facilities for long-term inmates outside of the central jail setting.

State-Run Jails

We have emphasized throughout this chapter that jails are locally operated and funded facilities, and this is one feature that distinguishes them from prisons. However, we also must give consideration to state-assisted and **state-run jails.**

In the area of state assistance there are numerous examples. One that merits note is the movement by the Commonwealth of Virginia to establish regional detention centers (Leibowitz 1991). There, as a result of state initiative, 12 regional jails, involving 24 counties and 11 cities, have been established. This provides an intermediate step toward state creation and operation of jails. However, some states have gone even further.

Jails in the Twenty-First Century

Given the demands for local space for incarceration, and the increasingly complex missions they find themselves fulfilling, there is no doubt that jails will continue to play a major role in local criminal justice processes into the next century. However, as long as the jail continues to be with us, at least two issues are likely to remain concerns: (1) alternatives to incarceration, and (2) innovative architectural styles (new generation jails).

Alternatives to Incarceration

It has often been said of contemporary jails and prisons that we cannot build ourselves out of the crowding crisis (see, for example, Klofas 1991b; Welsh et al. 1991). Many jurisdictions have discovered that once a new jail is completed, it may be filled within a few short months. The "building binge" seems never ending, and though every year additional bed space is added in U.S. facilities, crowding is still a problem.

However, some jurisdictions have chosen to go the route of expanding alternatives to incarceration instead of trying to catch up with the unmet demand for jail space. These counties have reached the conclusion that not everyone convicted of a crime deserves jail time. Policy makers in these counties have decided that jail space is a very precious commodity and it must be used wisely (see Jackson 1988; Klofas 1991a).

A variety of alternatives to incarceration exist. Most of them will be discussed in other chapters in this book, but here we will briefly detail them and relate them to the question of jail space. The basic assumption about alternatives to incarceration is that every jail bed space saved or emptied, is one less bed space that has to be built. Therefore, programs such as house arrest and electronic monitoring may provide us with alternatives to incarceration (Ford and Schmidt 1985; Renzema and Skelton 1990).

The key to evaluating these programs can be stated as a very simple question: would the person placed on house arrest and/or electronic monitoring actually go to jail if these programs were not available? Advocates believe that electronic monitoring provides one solution to the jail crowding dilemma (see, for example, Hipschman 1987). Unfortunately, evidence indicates that these programs end up being *add-ons* and may not save much jail bed space (however, see Hatrack 1987). Todd Clear (1988), in an examination of the use of electronic monitoring as an alternative to jail incarceration, finds this approach not to be a true alternative program. In fact, when examined in light of traditional goals, he characterizes electronic monitoring as a program in search of a correctional philosophy.

Part of this seems to result from the types of programs and the offenders selected for these programs. Because of public opinion (or politicians' perceptions of public opinion) electronic monitoring and house

Jails in the Twenty-First Century (continued)

arrest programs tend to choose low-risk offenders. These individuals are not likely to cause a major disaster or a public outcry if they "fail." However, in most instances, these offenders would not be placed in jail, even if the electronic monitoring–house arrest approach was not available. Therefore, if these people are not likely candidates for jail in the first place, putting them into an alternative program does not save jail space.

One of the chief criticisms of these programs remains that they monitor an individual's location, but not behavior. This may be an important function for offenders such as drunk drivers, but it may not be effective for individuals convicted of selling drugs or child pornography.

As previously mentioned, some of the same criticisms that have been leveled at electronic monitoring also may be applied to community service and restitution. That is, instead of being true alternatives to incarceration, these programs may simply be probation add-ons. If indeed this turns out to be the case, then community service and restitution will not fulfill their promises of being alternatives to incarceration either.

New Generation Jails and Beyond

One component of jail theory and practice that has seen a great amount of change in the past two decades is architecture. Jail architecture has been a particularly troubling problem: (1) most local

jurisdictions build new jails very infrequently—typically, once every 20 to 30 years; and (2) most architects have very little training and experience in detention facility design. Both of these factors mean that jails can be designed that repeat past structural mistakes (such as blind spots), or that a new jail can be very attractive but not especially functional. In fact, there is a danger that a jail design can be "too attractive" and that public criticism will arise from the construction of a "motel" instead of a jail.

If we look at the jail architectural changes that have occurred in the past two decades, we see that jail design and construction in the future will likely be based on five elements: lower operating costs, lower construction costs, speed of construction, flexibility of space, and expandability. All of these elements are related in some way to the inescapable conclusion about jails in the twenty-first century: we cannot continue to build and operate jails in this nation the same way we have for the past two centuries. Therefore, we will consider the impact each of these five factors will have on jail architecture in the next century.

Jail design is inevitably related to jail operating costs. As private sector companies have learned, a properly designed facility may allow for the elimination of staff posts throughout the jail. A **post** is any position that must be staffed 24 hours

(continued on next page)

Jails in the Twenty-First Century (continued)

Many counties have been faced with building new and bigger jails to house their growing inmate populations. One example of an urban jail, employing a podular or direct supervision design, is the Twin Towers Correctional Facility built by Los Angeles County. This high-rise, high-tech jail is designed to hold up to 4,000 inmates.

per day. The elimination of a post is a cost-saving measure far beyond what initial appearances would indicate. In fact, the personnel numbers are astounding: in order to staff one post a jail must employ about five people. Therefore, through certain designs the jail might be able to eliminate two or three posts and save on the personnel costs of 10 to 15 employees.

Lower construction costs have been addressed briefly already in this chapter. This jail issue is fairly simple: construction costs are high because most housing units are built to maximum-security standards and the construction materials must be of the highest security grade possible. Two factors have recently appeared that seem to indicate that jails can be built in less costly ways. First, in the design and construction of new generation jails commercial grade materials, such as solid core wooden doors instead of steel doors, have been used with some success (see Nelson 1988). Direct inmate su-

Jails in the Twenty-First Century (continued)

pervision allows jails to dispense with some of the high-security materials they have relied on in the past and still be assured that inmates are safe, are not escaping, and are not vandalizing the facility. The second, cost-saving innovation for jail construction has been the introduction of precast concrete materials. The use of these materials has allowed the motel industry to reduce the construction costs on many projects. The same technology can be applied to jail construction as well.

Many of the construction innovations in corrections have come about as a result of prison construction or expansion (see, for example, DeWitt 1986a). However, some of the new construction approaches have been tested in jails as well. For instance, one of the pioneers in the use of prefabricated concrete cell modules was Pinellas County, Florida (DeWitt 1986b). The Pinellas County Jail was built with three connected octagonal units (see Figure 4.3). One of the units contains the jail's support functions and control center. The two housing units were designed to hold 192 inmates in eight 24-inmate pods. The precast concrete elements were cast off-site and then brought together during construction. The final building figures showed the cost to Pinellas County to be $14,500 per inmate, or $29,000 for each two-person cell (DeWitt 1986b, 1986c).

The question of construction speed is related to construction costs as well. The use of prefabricated materials is one way to save time

and money in the construction process, but construction speed is related to two factors—site selection and the bidding process—associated with government construction projects. Site selection continues to be a problem for new jail construction (see Mays and Czerniak 1992/93). Many jurisdictions have gone through painful and protracted site selection processes only to have the community rally behind the NIMBY cry ("not in my back yard"). Even when the site is chosen and the design is selected, the bidding process for goods and services is often cumbersome and extended.

It is at this point that the private sector enters the picture again. Private sector corporations have gotten into the jail construction and operations business promising governments time savings through private procurement of land for construction and more streamlined goods and services bidding procedures. If the private sector is able to deliver on its promises to save time, in the process money will be saved as well.

One of the continuing dilemmas for most contemporary jails is not necessarily the lack of space, but the lack of flexibility in using available space (National Advisory Commission 1973, 275). Most jails are constructed to be operated one way over the entire life cycle of the building. Unfortunately, jail needs change and jail administrators have a difficult time adjusting to needs for more recreation space, more housing

(continued on next page)

Jails in the Twenty-First Century (continued)

space, more space for female inmates and less for males, and so on. Therefore, one area in which jail designers and architects can assist administrators and staffs is in creating jail space that rapidly can be converted to other uses. Some of this is already being done in the "new generation" or podular design facilities, which allow housing pods to be redesignated for different inmate population needs. Nevertheless, even in these jails space can be relabeled but is not designed to be functionally reconfigured. This flexibility may be a difficult proposition, given the purposes jails serve, but it does not seem impossible to achieve.

Additionally, twenty-first century jails must be expandable, a feature most contemporary jails are sadly lacking. Historically, jails have been built in the central business districts of most communities as part of, or adjacent to, the county courthouse. These locations are marked by three very distinct characteristics: small parcels of land, very expensive real estate costs, and, in most instances, limited parking.

When today's jails need to be expanded the choices are frequently not very appealing. The present facility can be expanded by continuing to place additional stories onto the existing building. This is often a very expensive proposition and may not be possible, depending on the building's structural soundness. The jurisdiction also may choose to look for another site in the central business district and face the high real estate

costs for the land chosen. The final option is to move the jail away from the downtown area even if it means separating the jail and the courthouse. This option may reduce costs for the purchase of the site, allow for increased and free parking for employees and jail visitors, and allow for future expansion.

Jail expansion can take a variety of different forms. It might involve the addition of housing units (pods) onto the jail's central structural core. Expansion might provide for separate minimum-security and work-release housing as well. These types of inmates and this type of space will have very different requirements from the rest of the jail. Therefore, allowing for separate housing units minimizes the likelihood that these inmates will introduce contraband into the more secure jail environment.

Finally, although many jurisdictions have moved toward closer contacts between custodial staff members and inmates through architectural designs such as podular jails, other jurisdictions seem to be headed in the opposite direction. That is, in order to minimize personnel costs and operating costs in general, some jurisdictions have constructed jails that rely very heavily on technology and reduce the face-to-face contact between inmates and staff. This may be a cost-saving measure in the short run, but time will tell if this is indeed the safest and most humane way to build and operate local detention facilities.

Figure 4.3
Floor Plan of the Pinellas County (Florida) Jail

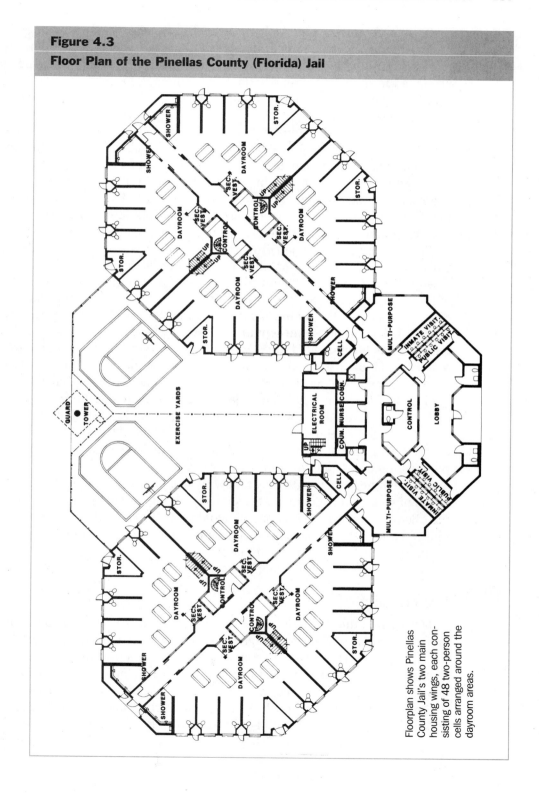

Floorplan shows Pinellas County Jail's two main housing wings, each consisting of 48 two-person cells arranged around the dayroom areas.

Six states—Alaska, Connecticut, Delaware, Hawaii, Rhode Island, and Vermont—already have state-operated jails (Thompson and Mays 1988b). In most instances, geographical features (such as state size) and low population promote the state operation of jails. For example, Delaware has only three counties. Therefore, the operation of state prisons and county jails has been combined.

Nevertheless, what traditionally has been the case for the six states mentioned, may also be the future for other states as well. Let us take the most recent and ambitious case: the state of Texas. The 254 county jails in Texas have had to deal with persistent crowding for more than a decade. Since the state prisons operated by the Texas Department of Criminal Justice (originally the Texas Department of Corrections) were placed under court order to reduce crowding, sentenced felons have been backing up in county jails (Taft 1979). The result of local jail crowding has been a search for housing alternatives including jail expansion and new jail construction.

Additionally, Texas has stepped in to offer counties relief from a dilemma of the state's making. In 1992 the Texas legislature created a new category of offenders to be designated "state jail felons" (Harris-George, Jarrett, and Shigley 1994). To house these inmates and provide relief for prison crowding the state has been divided into 13 regions; each region is to contain either a Mode 1 or Mode 2 state jail. The Mode 1 jails eventually will have 17,000 bed spaces and will be operated by the Texas Department of Criminal Justice, Institutional Division. The Mode 2 jails will provide an additional 7,000 beds and will be operated by the Community Supervision Department, the county probation agency (Harris-George, Jarrett, and Shigley 1994). This movement, coupled with the construction of additional prison space has dramatically reduced inmate populations in some areas.

Although not every state may follow the leads of Virginia and Texas in terms of state involvement, states should play a greater role in dealing with the dilemmas facing jails (Thompson and Mays 1991). The creation of state-assisted and state-run jails is one possible solution to some of the persistent problems faced by contemporary jails.

Conclusion

Jails present a dilemma for students of corrections. They are primarily operated by local law enforcement agencies, yet they serve more than law enforcement purposes. They are not truly correctional facilities, but they hold inmates for up to one year for misdemeanor convictions. Also, some of the people who are in jail at any one time may eventually end up in prison.

Unlike state and federal prisons, local jails house largely undifferentiated populations. Some house both adults and juveniles, and the vast majority contain both males and females. They incarcerate pretrial detainees and convicted offenders also. The convicted inmates include misdemeanants who may serve terms of up to one year and convicted and sentenced felons who are awaiting transportation to prison.

Jails also are confronted with inmates who have a variety of medical, emotional, personal, and psychological problems. The mentally ill and individuals with communicable diseases increasingly are found in local jails, as are a substantial number of inmates who have substance abuse problems. This means that jails house quite a cross-section of society's ills. John Irwin has called this chronic jail population the "rabble," or those people living on the margins of society. Others have likened the contemporary jail to a sewer, periodically flushing out human waste.

Whatever we think about the current state of jails, a few conclusions seem inescapable. First, jails are not going away; they are here for the long-term. They have been one of the criminal justice system's most enduring facilities, and their demise is nowhere on the horizon. Second, given their sheer numbers and the size of the population that passes through them each year, we cannot afford to continue to ignore jails. Third, the nature of the inmate populations in contemporary jails makes them exceedingly dangerous places in which to be incarcerated, which means that they are not likely to be out of sight or mind in the future, as ugly incidents are reported by the media. Finally, the nature of jails and those who work or are housed in them means that many of them are litigation "time bombs." As prisons systems found themselves in court during the 1970s and 1980s, so are jails finding themselves in court during the 1990s, and in all likelihood, far beyond.

Critical Review Questions

1. Briefly describe the range of functions served by local jails, including the types of inmates they house. How do these compare with prisons (discussed in this chapter and Chapter 5)?

2. John Irwin talks about jails managing the "rabble" or society's underclass. What kinds of people might law enforcement officers encounter that could be classified as "rabble"?

3. What kinds of features or characteristics distinguish jails from prisons? [You may want to refer back to this question after you have read Chapter 5.]

4. In most state and local detention or correctional facilities we talk about the average daily population (ADP) of inmates. Are there problems with determining the ADP for some jails in the United States? What are some of the problems?

5. What has happened to the number of jails in the U.S. since the 1970s? What might have caused this change?

6. Are there "special" problems created by incarcerating women in jails? Are these problems lessened if women are incarcerated in women-only jails?

7. What are the different types of jail designs currently found in the United States? What do the different designs imply in terms of staff-inmate interaction?

8. Who is primarily responsible for administering jails in the United States and why? What are some other possibilities for jail administrative organization?

9. What status do jail employees enjoy in the criminal justice system? What influences their status, and what could improve their status?

10. Think about the possible justifications for privatizing local jails. What might motivate a county commission (or similar group) to want to privatize the local jail?

11. Should jail inmates receive treatment programs similar to those used with prison inmates? Why or why not? Do jails benefit from inmate programming? If so, how?

12. What are the major mental and physical problems facing inmates in local jails?

13. Can we distinguish jails from police lockups? What types of features are associated with each of these facilities?

Recommended Readings

Advisory Commission on Intergovernmental Relations. 1984. *Jails: Intergovernmental dimensions of a local problem.* Washington, DC. A careful analysis of the varieties of problems facing jails up until the mid-1980s. This report especially focuses on the political dimensions of local jail problems.

Irwin, John. 1985. *The jail: Managing the underclass in American society.* Berkeley: University of California Press. This book provides a *critical* look at contemporary jails—both analytically and philosophically. Irwin looks at the way jails are used in various places, especially cities such as San Francisco. Whatever your political persuasion, this is a must-read book on jails.

Kerle, Kenneth E., and Francis R. Ford. 1982. *The state of our nation's jails.* Washington, DC: National Sheriffs' Association. This report, commissioned by the National Sheriffs' Association, has to

be considered a landmark in terms of current thinking on jails. Kerle and Ford carefully examine, in a concerned but neutral way, the deficiencies facing jails in the United States. The report may be hard to locate in some libraries, but it is an essential reference work on jails.

Moynahan, J. M., and Earle K. Stewart. 1980. *The American jail: Its development and growth.* Chicago: Nelson-Hall. Although somewhat dated, and slightly abbreviated, this book nevertheless provides a good history of jails in the United States from the colonial period through the 1970s. It contains data from one of the first modern jail censuses as well.

Thompson, Joel A., and G. Larry Mays, eds. 1991. *American jails: Public policy issues.* Chicago: Nelson-Hall. This edited book was prepared in conjunction with the Policy Studies Organization. It contains a number of chapters written by some of the major jail researchers in the

United States. Although it is largely a scholarly reference work, it is readable by and useful to students and practitioners as well.

Zupan, Linda L. 1991. *Jails: Reform and the new generation philosophy.* Cincinnati: Anderson. This book is one of the most thorough treatments of the "new generation" or direct supervision approach to inmate management available. Zupan explores the history, architectural design, and staff issues relating to podular/direct supervision jails.

Key Terms

direct supervision	low-use jails	processing jails
high-use jails	new generation jails	public-private partnership
holding jails	NIMBY	remote supervision
intermittent supervision	podular design jails	satellite jails
jail annexes	police lockups	state-run jails
jails	post	video arraignments
linear design	privatization	

5

Prison Systems

Chapter Outline

- Introduction
- Prisons as Total Institutions
- Prisoner Management and Related Issues
- Prison Types and Functions
- Prisons for Women
- Prison Labor
- Federal Prison System
- State Prison Systems
- Juvenile Corrections
- Conclusion
- Critical Review Questions
- Recommended Readings
- Key Terms
- Cases Cited
- Notes

Introduction

Driving home for the weekend with a friend, you pass a cluster of massive buildings. It is nighttime, yet the buildings are bathed in high-intensity, sodium-vapor lights, giving the entire area—you estimate that it encompasses at least 100 acres—the eerie appearance of high noon. Tall towers punctuate long stretches of chain-link fence, the latter topped with vicious-looking spirals of spiked wire. Signs on the highway have already warned you not to stop your vehicle for hitchhikers as a state prison is in the area. Your friend, knowing that you have taken several criminal justice classes, turns to you and asks, "What kind of prison is that?"

As you consider the question, you realize that most of your answer must be based on aspects of the prison that lie beyond your limited view from the highway. All you saw were some of the more visible parts of the prison's main buildings. You did notice that it was surrounded by a substantial, secure, and well-guarded series of fences. A complete answer to your friend's question would require information about the design of the facility and the security-level classification of inmates. An even more comprehensive answer would depend upon still more information, for example, the gender of the inmate and whether the facility was operated as a public prison or, more rarely, a private-sector prison. Before you can address the issues in the first question, your friend turns and asks, "So what's it like to live in a fish bowl like that?" Since you are many miles from home, you decide to start your "lecture" with an overview of prisons as total institutions.

Prisons as Total Institutions

Prisons are institutions for the confinement of convicted felons remanded to the custody of a state or federal agency for punishment. In most jurisdictions, prisons, also called penitentiaries or correctional facilities, house convicts for sentences ranging from one year to life. In those states that authorize capital punishment, a state penitentiary is often the place of execution for capital criminals.

Few terms capture the essence of contemporary prisons as does *total institutions*. Social anthropologist Erving Goffman (1961) defined **total institutions** as physical and social environments in which others control nearly every aspect of the resident's daily life. As Goffman (1961, 4) wrote about total institutions, "Their encompassing or total character is symbolized by the barriers to social intercourse with the outside and to departure that is often built right into the physical plant, such as locked doors, high walls, barbed wire, cliffs, water, forests, or moors." "Inmates" of all total institutions make few choices for themselves. They are told when to wake up, when to eat, when to work, and when to go to sleep. They are also furnished with few choices when it comes to the basic needs: food, clothing, and shelter. In the most extreme—and totally controlled—form of total institutions, those in control restrict freedom of movement. The greater control, the more total the institution. Few institutions in U.S. society at the close of the twentieth century exhibit higher levels of control over participants than prisons.

Are the characteristics of total institutions necessarily bad? Is it wrong that religious orders are isolated from the surrounding world and require high levels of commitment and obedience from members? Would we want members of the armed forces to be individualistic, living where they wanted, with each individual making his or her own decisions about decorum, dress, and discipline? No is the obvious answer to these questions. In fact, in this chapter we provide examples of the positive and the negative effects of prisons as total institutions. If prisons did not adequately control inmates' freedom, they would be considered failures. As we will see, some prisons have no walls or fences, and the inmates generally remain within the control of the prison authorities. Other prisons, such as Alcatraz, are famous for both their anti-escape measures and their escape attempts. Some critics of contemporary prisons raise the following question: What are the costs to prisoners and

glums, Goffman described prisons
along society's total institutions. Prisons,
he observed, protect society from those
who pose an intentional threat, whose welfare is secondary to security. Goffman further observed that the inmates of total
institutions undergo rites of passage, especially when they enter the institution. **Rites
of passage** are rituals that reinforce the
idea that the newly admitted inmates are
no longer free individuals but "the property" of the institution. A key element in
rites of passage, practiced to a great or
lesser extent in all total institutions, is
dehumanization. For example, nearly all
total institutions take away the newly admitted inmates' clothing and personal be-

longings, after which they are screened
for medical or psychological problems,
checked for contagious diseases, and issued institutional clothing. The inmates
reach the depths of dehumanization when
they achieve **nonperson status.** Goffman
defines this as the point in a person's institutional career when the keepers no longer
consider the kept to be human beings. In
prisons (and jails), this transformation often begins before entrance to the facility.
Prisoners generally have prior experiences
as suspects, defendants, and jail detainees.
The idea of institutional dehumanization
upon admission to prison is a well established fact.
Source: Goffman (1961).

society of essentially caging human beings? This question leads to others.
How do the prisoners in these different types of total institutions differ from
one another? Is it possible to effect positive changes in convicted felons serving time in a prison environment? How does the treatment of women in
prison differ from that received by men? We begin looking for answers with
the topic of prisoner management.

Prisoner Management and Related Issues

Because prisons are total institutions, those who operate the prisons must
assume responsibility for all phases of inmate life. This is the theory of prisons as total institutions. Prison operations depend heavily on how effectively
and efficiently prison officials manage the daily affairs of a group of individuals who may resist all such efforts. Indeed, we can summarize these lessons
in two themes: institutional goals and inmate classification.

Institutional Goals

Prisons have two widely acknowledged goals: custody and treatment. Often
these goals are viewed by practitioners and penologists alike as conflicting.
Custody is the legal or physical control of a person. Prison authorities are
responsible for the legal *and* physical control of inmates. As such, they have
an obligation to provide minimal comforts and needs. However, these obligations are secondary to restricting the inmates' liberty to protect the public.

Treatment is a term borrowed from medicine by early positivistic penal reformers and used to refer to a particular method of therapy based on a diag-
nosis: A person is sick, he or she is examined by a physician, and a regimen
of therapy is recommended. Prisons historically have offered a wide range
of "treatment programs," including primary and secondary education, vocational training, counseling on both the individual and group level, and therapy based on psychological and psychiatric testing. To understand the
often-conflicting relationship between custody and treatment goals, we turn
next to a brief look at who in the prison is responsible for achieving each set
of goals.

Custody is the chief responsibility of correctional officers (prison guards).
They are guided by an overarching philosophy that stresses the safety and
security of the institution, its staff, and lastly its inmates. Authority, regimentation, and architecture are the correctional officers' chief weapons (Farmer
1977; Lombardo 1984). The mix of these three elements defines the security
level of any given prison, a topic examined in detail later in this chapter.
Custodial staff members are, by the demands of the job, "prison police." Correctional officers (COs) rarely have more than a high school education. Consequently, they have low job marketability and equally low career mobility,
unless it is within the prison system. The guards' position in the prison management structure mandates that they must be suspicious of any unusual
exchanges, verbal or physical, that occur between inmates and, in some situations, inmates and staff members. Guards must be on the lookout for illegal
drug and home-brew liquor stashes, weapons, and other contraband. Overt
misbehavior directed at guards and even inmate riots pose a constant threat,
even if the probabilities of such events occurring are low. More often they
must intervene between assaultive individual inmates and groups of inmates,
still another risk factor.

Distinct from COs, prison-based treatment staff include but are not limited
to counselors, caseworkers, case managers, psychologists and psychiatrists,
social workers, recreational workers, chaplains, educators, nurses, and physi-
cians. Volunteers from the community often work in service-delivery positions
within the prison. For example, programs intended to establish and maintain links between inmates and families may be operated by local volunteer
groups. They may sponsor "socials" on visiting days or operate a day-care
center on the prison grounds. Similarly, religious groups may establish regular contact with inmates, sometimes building and maintaining prison-based
chapels or meeting rooms at private expense. Volunteers are also essential to
specific groups, ranging from formal organizations, such as Rotary Clubs and
Toastmasters, to informal groups, such as craft and literary clubs.

Most treatment staff and many volunteers have attended college. Many
treatment jobs require postbaccalaureate degrees. Few staff members, except
case workers, case managers, and recreational workers, typically have prior
work experience as correctional officers. Although their salaries may be low

Careers in Contemporary Corrections
Corrections Officer

The entry-level position in institutional corrections is the **correctional officer.** Students with college degrees often resist the suggestion that they begin their careers as correctional officers. However, higher levels of educational attainment are increasingly common. The title correctional officer is common in institutional corrections, but we need to recognize that for jails and other local detention facilities the designation may be jail deputy, detention officer, custody officer, or even the traditional title of guard.

The Bureau of Justice Statistics reported that on June 30, 1994, there were 205,453 correctional officers employed in state and federal prisons housing adults. Juvenile institutions employ an additional 39,376 personnel, and if the percentages are equivalent for these institutions, between one-half and two-thirds of these employees are correctional officers. In most institutions, COs wear a uniform similar to that of a police officer, although in recent years some jails and prisons have made an effort to get away from the traditional, military-style uniforms.

Correctional officers may perform a variety of tasks, but their basic function is to make sure that the institution, its staff, and the inmates are safe. Above all else, safety and security are the primary concerns for correctional officers, regardless of the type of institution in which they work.

Correctional officers will have the most direct and immediate contact with inmates of any institutional employees. They will be responsible for head counts or "bed checks," and they will often escort inmates as they move from one part of the facility to another. Correctional officers will make "rounds" to check on inmate activities, and they have the primary responsibility for issuing disciplinary reports for rules infractions.

One of the most challenging aspects of the corrections officer's position is the direct contact with inmates. In prisons COs always have been locked in with the inmates, and as a result of the movement to-

ward direct supervision in many new jails, officers are located in the housing pods with inmates as well.

Face-to-face contacts can give the correctional officer a sense of accomplishing something in the lives of convicted offenders. It can also result in a high level of anxiety, a very cynical attitude toward life, and feelings of despair and hopelessness. The correctional officer stands to have the greatest impact on inmates' lives, therefore work attitudes of COs are important.

Another common feature of the work world of correctional officers is shift work. More than any other job in corrections, COs are required to staff posts within their facilities on a 24-hour-per-day basis. This means that beginning correctional officers can expect to work on a variety of shifts, as well as being expected to work weekends and holidays.

Most correctional officers will be required to work a 40-hour-week assignment, but the distribution of hours may vary. For example, some institutions are organized around something other than traditional eight hours per day, five days per week shifts for COs. Some prisons and jails assign the custody staff to 10- or 12-hour shifts, but for fewer days per week. Opinions differ on the desirability of such shifts and the effects longer shifts have on officer morale, fatigue, and work performance.

In terms of expected pay, the range will vary widely depending on the type of facility and the level of government. People typically assume that federal jobs pay better than state jobs and that state employees make more than local employees. Although this is generally true, it is not always the case. In 1994, 3 states (Kentucky, Louisiana, and Tennessee) had starting salaries for COs from $13,000 to 14,999. Starting salaries in 14 states (Alabama, Arizona, Florida, Missouri, Montana, New Mexico, North Dakota, Oklahoma, South Carolina, South Dakota, Texas, Virginia, West Virginia, and Wyoming) ranged from $15,000 to $16,999. Another 4 states (Idaho, Mary-

---

Careers in Contemporary Corrections (continued)

Corrections Officer

land, New Hampshire, and Pennsylvania) started COs from $19,000 to $20,999. The remaining 17 states had starting salaries above $21,000. During the same year, the U.S. Bureau of Prisons hired correctional officers in the range of $24,585 to $31,932. For the most complete pay information consult your local detention facility's personnel office, the department of corrections in your state and in neighboring states (virtually all of them have a homepage on the World Wide Web), and the U.S. Bureau of Prisons (they also have a Web site).

One area of consideration for many students is the employment (and promotion) prospects in a given field. As should be fairly obvious, the employment prospects in corrections are excellent. We are adding new facilities and expanding existing ones all around the nation. Therefore, there

should be a heavy demand for entry-level corrections officers. One projection indicates that the number of additional correctional officers needed between 1990 and 2005 is expected to be 197,224, or a projected growth of nearly 70%. This compares with an average growth in all jobs in the United States of 25%.

It is fairly simple to translate these numbers into promotion prospects. As facilities need additional correctional officers, they will also need additional supervisors and managers. In fact, in the world of institutional corrections the likelihood exists today for greater promotion prospects and at a more rapid pace than at perhaps any time in our nation's history.

Sources: DeLucia and Doyle (1994); Maguire and Pastore (1995); Stinchcomb (1992); Williamson (1990).

---

in comparison to similarly educated individuals in the public sector, treatment staff members often receive higher salaries than all but the highest ranks among custodial or security staff.

Besides education and income, other factors distinguish treatment staff from custodial staff. For example, treatment personnel may work in less "prison-like" parts of the institution, often in private or semiprivate offices. Treatment staff members rarely wear uniforms, while, in most prisons, custodial personnel are easily distinguished by their uniforms. Perhaps the greatest point of divergence between custodial prison staff and treatment staff is a philosophical one. To do their job effectively, treatment staff must nurture mutual trust between them and inmates. As important, they must involve inmates actively in their own "treatment." The coercion used by treatment staff, therefore, must be low and the trust expressed toward inmates must be high. It is on these points that treatment and custody staff may part company (Street, Vinter and Perrow 1966; Zald 1968).

Inmate Classification

By the middle of the nineteenth century, prison reformers had set up policies calling for the separation of inmates into broad categories. Prison administrators separated men from women, adults from children, those with communicable diseases from the reasonably healthy, and even debtors from murders, thieves, and other dangerous criminals. Brockway's "moral interviews" eventually gave way to criminal and social histories, supplemented by psychological testing. Psychological and personality testing, popularized during World War I, became the staple of prison systems during the first three decades of the twentieth century. Individual treatment models, fueled by twentieth-century positivism, translated into the adoption of many screening, testing, and diagnostic techniques all intended to assist prison officials in the segregation of inmates. The result was a primitive form of **inmate classification.** By the 1930s classification schemes focused on so-called psychiatric diagnoses, which often had little to do with the services available in prisons.

Inmate classification systems developed after World War II addressed the dangerousness of the offender to the public, largely based on his or her criminal record and personality inventories. These "diagnoses" determined the proper "security level" for a given inmate. Subsequently, these same personality inventories and other psychological tests provided insights into an inmate's treatment needs. **Classification officers** made recommendations based on psychometric testing, interviews, and criminal records, tempered by their own "clinical" and often cynical experiences dealing with prison inmates. After the classification officer made a recommendation and the prison's classification committee agreed or disagreed, the actual placement of any given inmate was often shaped more by space availability than their recommendations.

Prisoner classification systems changed in two ways during the 1970s. First, a series of appellate cases stressed that classification systems can resolve many unconstitutional conditions of confinement found in several of the nation's prison systems, including Arkansas, Rhode Island, and Alabama. In the wake of these court decisions, prison policy makers learned that to avoid litigation they should employ classification systems that met three goals: (1) classify inmates to the least restrictive security level needed to provide for public safety, both of the community at large, the staff, and other inmates; (2) assess inmate needs on a regular and recurring basis, while not excusing the inmate from responsibility for his or her own behavior; and (3) encourage prosocial changes in prison inmates by extending positive incentives to those inmates who exhibit control over their own welfare (Craddock 1996, 90).

A second development was an increase in criticism of existing inmate treatment programs. The medical model, as we related in Chapter 2, evolved from the reform era. This positivistic approach emphasizes the ability of science to provide the tools to change human beings. In the late 1960s and early 1970s the medical model came under attack on two fronts. Liberals viewed it as a form of mind control and the misapplication of science to social ills. Conservatives viewed it as pampering rather than punishing criminals. Throughout the 1970s, what passed for treatment plans were scaled back or phased out in entire prison systems. By the late 1970s and early 1980s, the courts required rational classification of inmates. However, prisons had few programs in which to place inmates "diagnosed" as needing special treatment. By default, classification became more of a custody weapon than a treatment tool.

Contemporary prisoner classification schemes typically combine two or more of the following models: (1) correctional personnel views of risk prediction (that is, whatever the correctional personnel view as problematic characteristics in inmates becomes part of the classification scheme) are central to **consensus models;** (2) **equity-based models** attempt to treat all inmates the same, including only those factors related to the current offense; and (3) **prediction models** base inmate classifications on a variety of legal, psychological, social, and even medical information about the offender, the goal being to predict and control intraprison behavior (Craddock 1996, 91).

Current classification schemes are far more objective and rational than those employed even 20 years ago. About one-quarter of the states use their own system or one rooted in selected elements of psychometric tests such as the Minnesota Multiphasic Personality Inventory (**MMPI**) or the Quay Adult Internal Management System (Buchanan and Whitlow 1987). Roughly one-quarter of the states have adopted the National Institute of Corrections' (NIC) **Custody Determination Model.** This model bases custody and security assignments on such factors as the offender's expression of violence before and since incarceration, alcohol and drug abuse involvement, and severity of the current offense. Another one-quarter of the states use a system originally developed by the Federal Bureau of Prisons (BOP). The BOP system focuses on six factors: (1) type of detainer, (2) severity of current offenses, (3) expected length of incarceration, (4) prior prison commitments, (5) history of escapes, and (6) history of violence. Roughly equal shares of the remaining 20% of the states use either a combination of the NIC and BOP systems or one created by the Correctional Services Group. This latter system, the **Correctional Classification Profile** (Buchanan and Whitlow 1987), assesses inmate needs because of the risk posed to both the institution and public at large in eight dimensions. These dimensions include medical and health-care needs, mental health-care needs, security and public risk needs, custody and institutional risk needs, educational needs, vocational training needs, work skills, and proximity to residence of release and family ties. Ultimately, inmate placement in a specific program, prison unit, or institution remains subject to resource availability. Where there is no space or where space is limited, an inmate may receive a far different and perhaps less scientific or more subjective prison placement.

Prison Types and Functions

Facility design refers to the general plan for the entire prison complex. Prison designers must incorporate a wide range of inmate and staff activities, ranging from feeding inmates and doing their laundry to providing for simple creature comforts such as toilets, showers, and recreational areas. These wide-ranging institutional functions, some of which are unpopular with the public, give prison planners many of their greatest challenges. Some designs are cheaper to build than others. Some more expensive designs are more easily maintained than those with lower "front-end" costs. However, construction costs and upkeep are not the only issues considered by prison planners and architects. The facility's ability to keep inmates in one location may be a very important practical matter: prisons with walls and secure internal zones tend to have fewer wandering inmates than correctional facilities that have no walls, fences or, for that matter, many locked doors.

Four main facility design models, illustrated in Figure 5.1, have enjoyed popularity over the past two hundred years. For example, Pennsylvania's Eastern Penitentiary (see also Figure 2.1), which when viewed from above looks like the cross-section of a spoked wheel, is called a **radial-design prison.** New York's Auburn Prison (see also Figure 2.2) was a modification of this design; its aerial view resembles the rays of a setting sun. The spokes, or rays, which contain cells and the various elements of institutional support (for example, prison laundry, kitchen and dining area, gymnasiums, work areas) spread out from a central hub. One spoke moves out from the hub to the administrative offices of the facility and its main entrance. The hub is, in effect, the "**Times Square**" for the facility: All people moving from spoke to spoke about the facility must pass through this area. This basic idea has strengths and weaknesses. For securing the facility and facilitating physical searches of inmates, it has few peers. In case of inmate disturbance or riot, whoever controls Times Square controls the facility. The radial-design prison has never been popular in the United States. Only a few active facilities exist, including the main facility at the United States Penitentiary at Leavenworth (Kansas) and New Jersey's Rahway and Trenton state prison facilities.

The **telephone-pole design prison** has a central corridor (the pole) for easy movement around the facility. The cross members of the telephone pole contain the living areas, work assignments, institutional support facilities, and administrative functions. Prisons of this design are, like the radial design, typically stacked floor upon floor. They allow inmates of differing classifications to be housed in the same facility and yet have limited contact with each other. On the negative side of the ledger is the fact that the central corridor is easily barricaded by inmates during riots and similar disturbances. Wrestling back control of the central corridor from entrenched inmates is often easier said than done.

The **courtyard-design prison,** with its reliance upon the walls of the institution to provide security, is considered one of the more modern and progressive of prison plans. Similarly constructed fortresses and castles with central courtyards have served as prisons for centuries. Examples include the Bastille of Paris and Peter the Great's Fortress in Moscow. In the modern courtyard-design prison all institutional units, including housing, education, medical,

Figure 5.1

Overhead Views of Prison Designs

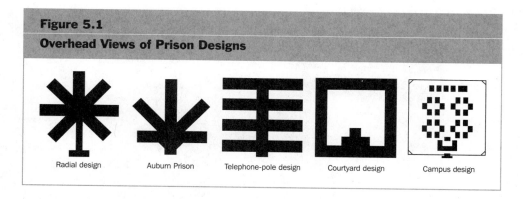

Radial design   Auburn Prison   Telephone-pole design   Courtyard design   Campus design

prison industry, and dining, face a central and often expansive courtyard. All doors, except those providing entrance to administrative areas, open to the courtyard. Nearly all movement throughout the facility is shunted through the central courtyard. Therefore, this feature has become the defining element for this type of prison. The courtyards may contain recreational areas or landscaped park-like areas. Often courtyards are joined to create "daisy-chain" facilities consisting of as many as four or more similar structures, each a nearly self-contained unit. This design is especially important to jurisdictions anticipating growth in prison construction, because the daisy-chains can be connected one to the other. They can still share certain finite resources such as central dining services and other support units (for example, medical, dental, and laundry services). Again, as with several previous designs, the courtyard design is especially useful when inmates of varying classification levels must be housed at the same location: All inmates at the same classification level share the same courtyard unit. One shortcoming, however, is that all individuals in a given courtyard unit must share the same common area, no matter how high the units are stacked.

At times prison designs favor form over function. That is, prison designers and state or federal planners may feel that impressing critics of the nation's prison system is an important concern, more important than creating the reality of a walled prison unit or an ultra-secure correctional facility. Occasionally, prisons contain inmates who are viewed as low security risks, either to themselves, their peers in the prison, or the community at large. In addition, most prisons for female offenders contain inmates of varying security risks and at many classification levels, but the image of a walled prison unit is deemed by policy makers and others as inappropriate. These prisons often resort to the **campus-design prison,** which by any objective standard more closely resembles a small- to moderate-sized college than a prison. Living units, built to resemble private homes but having large dormitory wings, are scattered throughout large, well-maintained grounds. Work assignments and institutional support buildings may look like classroom buildings and

In 1971, New York State experienced one of the nation's bloodiest prison riots in Attica. On September 11, inmates and negotiators met inside the prison yard to try and resolve the takeover of the prison.

libraries. In campus-design prisons, evidence of perimeter security and patrol is typically downplayed. Casual visitors may have trouble spotting guards or distinguishing the inmates from the staff. In medium-security, campus-design prisons, perimeter security may be maintained by several chain-link fences, topped by concertina razor wire, and several secure gates.

Building Design and Inmate Supervision

Simply looking at the outside of a prison building rarely yields insights into the physical layout of the living units. It is here that inmates may spend between 16 and 23 hours per day. A little knowledge, and a walk through the living unit, can quickly reveal the physical layout, and along with it many features about the prison and its approach to managing the facility. For example, **linear-design living units** are among the oldest designs currently in use. As in jail construction, linear-design prison living units have a hallway leading to individual cells, two-person (or more) cells, or dormitories. A central control area at one end of the hallway controls movement in and out of the cell area. Normally, movement is through a sally-port area consisting of a set of two steel or barred doors with mesh-screen or "unbreakable" glass inserts. The sally-port doors may be electronically controlled and both cannot be opened together to prevent quick movement of inmates through the security area.

In the traditional linear-design living unit, the cells are off the central hall-way. This design allows secure movement through the area by correctional officers or other inmates in transit to and from their cells. Linear-design prisons based on the Auburn model include back-to-back cells, in which inmates looked out of their cells and walls or windows. Prisons based on the Pennsylvania model include face-to-face cells. In this latter model, inmates typically had an exterior window, while their cell door faced others across the hallway.

The linear-design living area also reveals much about the prison's approach to supervision and inmate management. For example, unless the correctional officer is literally standing in front of a given cell or is somehow in direct line of sight with the cell, maintaining visual contact with cell occupants is nearly impossible. Consequently, this method of supervision is called **intermittent supervision.** Guards and other correctional workers have only sporadic contact with inmates while they are in the living areas, which, again, ranges from a minimum of 16 hours per day in most cases to as many as 23 hours per day. Some linear-design prisons (and jails) rely upon listening devices imbedded in the walls of the cells or scanning television cameras to provide **remote** or **indirect supervision.** Most currently available electronic monitoring methods are easily overcome by prison inmates who have 24 hours per day for many years to think of ways to defeat them.

Modified linear-design living units typically have a security area surrounded by sally-ports that control access to clusters of individual cells, which in some designs share a common or "day area." Individual cells hold one, two, or more inmates and are normally secured (that is, locked) only during the sleeping hours. In still others, the modified design includes a dormitory arrangement with dozens of beds, some configured as bunk-beds serving two inmates. In its most extreme (and security-conscious) form, the modified linear design differs from the linear design only in that the cells are not arranged in a straight line. Facilities with a common or shared living area differ from podular-design facilities (discussed next) mainly in terms of their physical makeup (for example, fixtures and doors are far more "target hardened" against inmate vandalism) and security arrangements (for example, movement around the living area is far more controlled than it is in podular-design living areas). In either case, groups of cells may be stacked one upon the other to form a large open area of cells and, in some designs, one common living area on the first floor of the cluster.

Surveillance in the modified linear design living area is also remote, since correctional officers rely heavily upon electronic monitoring, two-way mirrors that look into each cell from a secured gallery area behind the individual cells, and glass viewing windows. Correctional officers rarely enter the common area.

Podular-design living units represent a break with both traditional living-area design and staff supervision of inmates. Pods consist of individual cells

Box 5.2

Philosophical and Practical Implications of Direct Supervision

Intermittent supervision allows guards to observe the inmate behavior on an irregular basis, but only when guards try to look into the cell or dormitory area, normally while protected by a steel or barred door. This method provides for the protection of correctional officers, but also tells the inmates that the guards fear, hate, or distrust them. Inmates also easily defeat the security provided by intermittent supervision through the coordinated use of lookouts and patterned, regular behavior by guards.

Indirect supervision, usually accomplished by television cameras, listening devices, or other electronic sensing means, also has severe shortcomings. It can be defeated by inmates who have lots of time on their hands. This method, like intermittent supervision, also dehumanizes the prison (and jail) experience. It gives the impres-

sion that guards fear or hate inmates. Both intermittent and indirect supervision also leave certain areas of confinement totally or occasionally unprotected.

In contrast, **direct supervision** places the correctional officer in direct physical contact with inmates, usually in a dormitory or living area, as is found in many podular-design prisons. The fear-hate syndrome is reduced, as is the unprotected space created by architecture and the lax or incomplete supervisory practices of intermittent and indirect supervision. Inmates feel less isolated and negative when guards roam the common area of the cellblock, dormitory, or pod. Perhaps some institutions have adopted a policy of using both direct and intermittent supervision, employing roving and stationary COs.
Source: Zupan and Menke (1988).

or living areas, often arranged in a triangle, which share a central common or day area. Unlike the modified linear design, the cell doors are less secure, often consisting of standard "solid-core" doors with locks controlled by inmates. Steel security doors control entry to the pods. Sally-ports may be used at the points of entry to the pod. Also like the modified linear-design facilities, pods may be stacked, with two floors of living areas opening onto a single common or day area. Stacks of two or more floors of pods may extend upward dozens of floors, a design used in many of the BOP's Metropolitan Detention or Correctional Centers and large urban jails using the podular design. Pods look less institutional than either the linear- or modified linear-design living areas.

A defining criterion for modern podular design, versus the modified linear-design living area, is the supervision strategy: Podular-design prisons employ **direct supervision,** meaning correctional officers spend most of their workdays in the common or day area, among the inmates. Correctional officers provide far higher levels of supervision for inmates. Although they may appear more vulnerable to inmate assaults, the events rarely occur. The practice of "management by walking about," often used in business and education, provides a far more personal view than either intermittent or remote surveillance. Direct supervision also provides a far more humane work environment for correctional officers and a more humane living environment for inmates (Zupan 1991).

Prison Security Levels

Earlier we learned that some inmates could reside free in the community and no one would be in any greater danger than before. At the other extreme are inmates who must be locked up for nearly 24 hours per day because they are escape risks or pose another serious threat to institutional operations. In very important ways, the prison's physical appearance and security provisions mirror the inmates' characteristics. These factors define the **security level** imposed on an entire institution or part of an institution. The range of security facilities is from maximum-security facilities, which typically imprison the most dangerous prisoners, to, in most states, minimum-security facilities, which house far less dangerous individuals. Each type of facility is unique and merits special consideration.

Vintage **maximum-security prisons** typically have high stone or concrete walls that completely encircle the facility. Many appear castle-like to first-time visitors. In newer maximum-security prisons concentric chain-link fences topped with barbed or razor wire provide external security. Strategically placed in the corners or in central locations stand even taller gun towers. COs, armed with a broad assortment of firearms, have an unobstructed view into virtually every corner of the facility, including the outside perimeter. High security fences and gates partition off maximum-security cellblocks from one another and other parts of the prison. Frequently prisons at this security level have one centralized control zone, Times Square, through which all inmates moving about the prison must pass.

Inmates have virtually no privacy in a maximum-security prison. Unarmed COs patrol the corridors. They view each inmate behind the bars of a cage-like cell that, depending on court orders and current capacity, the inmates may share with two or three others. Guards conduct frequent and often unannounced **inmate counts,** during which a staff member must physically view each inmate. Some jails and prisons use a system resembling grocery store bar codes for quick inmate counts. Every time an inmate moves about the facility, this system records his or her whereabouts. Cell areas and inmates are subject to unannounced **shakedowns** (that is, searches for weapons, drugs, and other contraband) by COs. Sometimes inmates are subjected to unpleasant and thorough **body cavity searches.**[1] These searches usually occur when an inmate is moving from an unsecured area of the facility to a more secure one or after an inconclusive shakedown caused by information provided by a "snitch" or inmate informant.

Rules control literally all inmate behavior. Visits, except those with an attorney, are closely monitored. Physical contact may be prohibited. Prisoners and their visitors may be required to talk through screen-mesh barriers or via telephones and speaker systems, both of which are subject to monitoring. Even telephone calls to the outside may be monitored, to prevent escape plans, smuggling attempts, and even the commission of crimes by

The U.S. Bureau of Prisons is currently building a complex of prisons at Florence, Colorado. One of these prisons is a maximum security facility designed to replace the U.S. Penitentiary at Marion, Illinois. High security is of utmost importance at this facility.

incarcerated inmates (for example, coordinating ongoing criminal activities, blackmail, or "con" jobs involving people in the outside world). Control of all aspects of inmate life is as close to total as is humanly possible. Security and custody are the primary goals of such institutions.

Medium-security prison facilities are less restrictive and regimented than maximum-security prisons. They may not even be called a prison, called instead correctional facility or institution. Unless they are converted maximum-security "big houses," most medium-security prisons do not have encompassing masonry walls. They may be enclosed by a double chain-link fence, again topped by barbed or razor wire. The area between the fences may contain electronic anti-intrusion devices—infrared or motion sensors—that warn of escape attempts. Strategically located gun towers are another characteristic of most medium-security prisons. Guards on foot or in vehicles provide "roving security" around the perimeter of medium-security prisons.

Medium-security prisons often use congregate-housing, or dormitory-style living arrangements. If a podular design is employed, inmates may have small individual cells for sleeping, but a congregate living area for the rest of the time. At the other extreme, inmates may have to share huge open bay areas with 50 or more inmates. In either case, inmates share a common and readily accessible toilet and showering area.

Box 5.3

Super-Max Prisons: Beyond Maximum Security

The **super-max prison** exceeds even the maximum-security prison's coercive and custodial elements. This type of facility is reserved for the "baddest of the bad," those inmates who pose such a threat to society, both freed and confined, that they must be totally isolated. Inmates are locked down for 23 hours per day in single-person cells. Meals are delivered to the cells and inmates have few opportunities to mix with each other. The nation's prison systems operate few such separate facilities, although many maximum-security prisons maintain a super-max area called the *administrative segregation unit*. These areas are reserved for very troublesome inmates and usually for short periods of incarceration.

The modern model for the super-max correctional facility is the federal penitentiary at Marion (Illinois). The entire Marion facility was "locked-down" for a decade,

following the death of two correctional officers in a 1983 inmate riot. Inmates were allowed one hour per day for exercise and personal hygiene. The rest of the day they were required to remain in their cells. Lockdowns became a significant management feature at Marion and at its successor, the maxi-max prison at the Federal Correctional Complex in Florence, Colorado. This 575-bed facility, called administrative maximum security, is a stand-alone facility but administratively part of the United States Penitentiary-Florence. The facility has six levels of security. Based on the inmates' security classification, they may have access to such support facilities as visitation, administration, health service, education program areas, chapel, a gymnasium, and personal services found in the commissary.

Sources: Bureau of Prisons (1994); Maurer (1985).

Medium-security prisons have fewer rules than maximum-security facilities. Inmates may be required to wear institutional clothing only when working at their assigned tasks or on other prison business. Otherwise, they may be allowed to wear "civilian clothes" when engaged in recreational activities or "free time." Inmate movement about the prison is also less restricted. Except a central control area, movement throughout the rest of the institution may be controlled by less sophisticated and less expensive gates and doors. Searches and counts, unless warranted by breaches in security, occur with less regularity.

The inmates in medium-security prisons pose far lower escape or behavioral risks than do those residing in maximum-security prisons. Inmate transfers between these types of facilities, however, may be a response to either good or bad behavior. Medium-security facilities may actually adjoin maximum-security facilities, thus allowing for quick and inexpensive inmate transfers. Creating correctional complexes with varying **security levels** also saves on expensive security components.

Minimum-security prison facilities may also be called open-campus correctional institutions or camps. They are rarely called prisons or penitentiaries. Some are ranches or farms whose inmates raise crops or livestock, or they may be forestry camps whose inmates maintain public park lands and fight forest fires. For minimum security risk women, states often employ cottage-design facilities. This often gender-specific response to female offenders is based on a decades-old philosophy that women are better served in a "homelike" environment (see the next section). The inmate in a minimum-security facility poses no security risk. He or she is often a nonviolent offender (for example, a white-collar or professional criminal), has a short sentence (unless an old inmate), has displayed otherwise exemplary pre-institutional behavior, or faces imminent release from state custody.

You might assume from the descriptions of the minimum-security facility compared to the others that the inmates there have an easy life. The former is far less oppressive and restrictive than the latter. However, inmates still are not free to come and go as they please. They must follow certain institutional rules and regimentations. They are still the objects of physical and psychological abuse from other inmates and guards. What also might amaze some is the fact that many inmates prefer higher security facilities: Maximum- and medium-security prisons pose fewer opportunities for victimization at the hands of dangerous fellow inmates.

Prisons for Women

In 1873, nearly a century after Beccaria called for the segregation of prison inmates according to gender, Indianapolis opened the first U.S. prison for women run by women, followed by similar facilities in Massachusetts (1877) and New York (1887). The first such women-only prisons employed the cottage-system design. These facilities more closely resembled Brockway-style reformatories than Auburn-style prisons, which is not surprising since Brockway operated the Detroit House of Shelter for Women as a reformatory in the 1870s. In the cottage-style reformatory for women, female staff supervised inmates and taught appropriate domestic skills. More often than not prison officials treated the women as children gone astray (Freedman 1981; Rafter 1985).

By 1940, 23 states had separate women's prison facilities, a number that increased to 34 by 1975. The remaining states contracted with other states or the private sector to house female offenders sentenced to prison terms. The first federal prison for women was in rural Alderson, West Virginia, now FCI-Alderson; it was a cottage-style reformatory and opened in 1927. The reformatory model was abandoned in the mid-1930s, to be replaced by a campus model that took its lead from the vocational training programs in men's correctional facilities. In women's prisons the programs emphasized marketable and gender-specific skills (Rafter 1985).

Unlike male convicts, most of whom reside in either medium- or maximum-security prisons, eight of ten female inmates live in minimum- or medium-security facilities (Maguire and Pastore 1995, 550). Carol Smart (1976a) observes that this phenomenon is a function of the sexist view that women are more passive. However, women's prisons have more rules than comparably classified men's prisons and are fewer. As a result, these classification statistics may be misleading.

Of the 45 states that contain women's prisons, 9—New York, Michigan, Florida, North Carolina, Oklahoma, Tennessee, Texas, California, and Oregon—have more than one such facility. As Helen Gibson (1976, 99) observes, even if a state's only women's prison looks like a low-security facility, it cannot be: "Because all women sentenced to prison must be housed in one institution, all must live by rules that are established for the control of the very few." The practice of incarcerating such a broad range of offenders in a single institution must undermine that institution's classification system. However, even if there were sufficient prisons of differing security ratings or if a single institution had sufficient separate units, the situation might not improve. "Classification systems that result in risk-factor scores are developed with males and may not be useful for a female population" (Pollock-Byrne 1990, 85–86).

Prison Labor

The history of punishment is closely related to the use of work as punishment. Many inmate-laborers, available to work free or nearly free, congregated in one place or mobile enough to move from job site to job site has been an attractive idea to many labor contractors, including prison wardens. Before the creation of the "modern" penitentiary, many prisons were mines, farms, or public-works projects requiring large pools of surplus labor. As the idea of the penitentiary gained a foothold in England and the United States, so did the concept of prison industries: Penal reformers believed that, in addition to their economic value, prison industries, whether the inmates manufactured brooms, shoes, or metal craft, prevented the idleness that plagued early houses of detention.

From the Auburn Prison Factory to the Great Depression

In the first 100 years after Auburn Prison and its imitators opened their doors in the early 1800s, three systems of prison industries evolved:

- The **contract system** sold inmate labor to private vendors who provided the necessary machinery, tools, raw materials, and even supervisory staff. Ideally, the factory was found near or even in the prison, as the vendor essentially rented space from the prison. When this form of prison labor came under attack, prison administrators took over production of the finished products, which were subsequently provided to wholesalers (Schaller 1982).

- The **lease system** was a modification of the contract system used after the Civil War. Private vendors used prison labor for a fixed fee. Unlike the contract system, the inmates typically went to the work, often in agriculture or mining. Closely resembling indentured servitude or the system of slavery outlawed by the Thirteenth Amendment to the U.S. Constitution, the lease system largely affected African-American and poor white males in the "Old South" (Sellin 1976, 145).

- In the late 1800s, the **state-use system** evolved as a response to objections about unfair competition from prison labor. This system, a form of sheltered market in which prison labor does not directly compete with private industry, allowed prison systems to use inmate labor for the production of goods consumed either within the prison system or by state government (Schaller 1982). In some states, this system was limited to license plate production or construction of new prison facilities, while in other states, most notably Texas, prison labor manufactured literally everything consumed by inmates, from food to soap to clothes.

The early sellers or purveyors of prison labor learned a hard truth: Free labor is worth every penny you pay for it. For example, Auburn Prison, which was literally a factory within the prison walls, took more than 10 years to show a modest profit (Durham 1989).

Not all of the problems associated with the use of prison labor were related to its profitability. In the 1890s, prison industries and cheap prison labor came under attack on three fronts (McKelvey 1936, 93–118). First, competitors in the free market sector complained that those using prison labor could undersell them on labor costs alone. Organized as the National Anti-Contract Association, this group of manufacturers campaigned against the use of prison labor. Second, the emerging labor union movement targeted prison labor as unfairly competing with workers in the free market sector. Finally, scandals involving exploitation of prison workers occurred in the late 1800s, including charges brought against the Elmira Reformatory and Zebulon Brockway. Legislatures in eastern states, including Massachusetts, New York, and Pennsylvania, were among the first to use prison labor, and to create laws curbing its use (McKelvey 1936, 126–44). Congress enacted legislation in 1887 that outlawed the contracting of federal prisoners (McKelvey 1936, 201).

In spite of a strong antiprison labor movement with broad public support, the widespread use of prison labor continued until the Great Depression. Ten months before the stock market crash that caused the Depression, President Herbert Hoover signed the **Hawes-Cooper Act** into law on January 19, 1929. Hawes-Cooper made all inmate-manufactured goods transported through a state subject to that state's laws. By the late 1920s and early 1930s, dozens of states had laws restricting the manufacture, transportation, and sale of prison-made goods. If a manufacturer or wholesaler wanted to get prison-made goods across that state for sale in a third, unrestricted state, Hawes-Cooper made their transportation theoretically more expensive, if not practically impossible. By the mid-1930s millions of laborers were out of

Box 5.4

**Guidelines for Contemporary
Prison Industries**

The Private Sector/Prison Industry Enhancement Certification Program authorizes correctional agencies to engage in the
interstate shipment of prison-made goods
for private businesses if

- Inmates working in private-sector prison
  industries are paid at a rate not less than
  the rate paid for work of a similar nature
  in the locality in which the work takes
  place.

- Prior to the initiation of a project, local
  unions are consulted.
- The employment of inmates does not
  result in the displacement of employed
  workers outside the prison, does not
  occur in occupations in which there is
  a surplus of labor in the locality, and
  does not impair existing contracts for
  services.

work. In 1935 Congress passed the **Ashurst-Sumners Act** to encourage those
states that still permitted the sale of prison-manufactured goods to enact
more restrictive state legislation. This act made it a crime for any interstate
transportation company to ship prison-made goods into a state whose laws
restricted their sale. Every state in the Union enacted laws restricting the sale
of inmate-manufactured goods by 1940. The state-use system and other
forms of sheltered-market prison labor projects, such as public lands and
parks projects, continued over the next 30 years. In the face of federal control
of interstate commerce, prison industries effectively ceased to exist for nearly
40 years.

Contemporary Prison Industries

The 1970s, notes David Duffee (1989, 350), provided a climate of change for
prison industries in the United States.

- Labor unions no longer exerted the political clout they had between
  the 1930s and 1950s.
- State and federal legislators encouraged prison managers to become
  more efficient and cost effective.
- Prisoners' rights activists successfully attacked postincarceration barriers to employment for convicted felons, increasing the value of
  prison-based vocational training.
- Rehabilitation was out; work, and the security it brought the institution, was in.
- The Free Ventures Project, a seven-state experiment in private enterprise, gave inmates real jobs and real skills with postinstitutional
  marketability.

In 1979 the U.S. Congress enacted Public Law 96-157 (codified as 18 U.S.C.
1761 and 41 U.S.C. 35), which created the Private Sector/Prison Industries

Enhancement Certification Program (PS/PIEC). The **PS/PIEC** program removed many but not all of the interstate restrictions placed on inmate-manufactured goods by Hawes-Cooper and Ashurst-Sumners. Box 5.4 contains a summary of the strict guidelines set in this law. Between 1970 and 1985, legislatures in nearly half the states repealed state-use-only statutes. The new laws allowed for the limited sale of prisoner-manufactured goods to the private sector (American Correctional Association 1986; Flanagan and Maguire 1993). The net effect of both legal trends was a resurgence of interest in prison industries.

Joint Venture Programs

As of 1993, the U.S. Department of Justice, which administers the PS/PIEC program, reported certifying 32 correctional agencies with approximately 1,000 inmate-workers to operate private-sector prison industries. For example, Jostens, Inc., the nation's largest manufacturer of graduation gowns, operated a manufacturing plant in a South Carolina prison; Trans World Airlines had a reservation center at the California Youth Authority's Ventura Training School for youthful offenders; the Chesapeake Cap Company, a subsidiary of the nation's largest manufacturer of embroidered emblems, placed a plant at Connecticut's Somers' Correctional Institution (Sexton 1995).

Between 1979 and 1992, inmates employed in prison-based **joint venture programs** earned more than $28 million, nearly 20% of which, or $5 million, went back to the institution to offset the costs of incarceration. Due to federal and state taxes, victim compensation programs, and support for inmate families, 41 cents on the dollar went back to society (Sexton 1995, 13). Although such programs are interesting and could serve as models for other collaborative efforts between prison administrators and the private sector, the fact remains that fewer than 1 inmate in 1,000, or less than $\frac{1}{10}$ of 1 percent of all prisoners in the U.S., participate in certified joint venture programs.

The impact of joint venture programs on prison populations is small in comparison to prison industries that make goods only for consumption within the prison or for sale only to other public agencies. Seeing prisoner-made products for sale in the free market outside the state-use system is rare. About 30,000 state inmates work in all forms of prison-based goods production. Nearly 14,000 federal inmates work in its ambitious **UNICOR** (Federal Prison Industries, Inc.) program (Harlow 1994, 20). Nevertheless, fewer than 50,000 of the nation's more than 1 million state and federal inmates are kept busy making things. (We return to these inmate work programs later in this chapter.) The essence is this: Although many changes occurred in prison-labor philosophy and practices in the last quarter of the twentieth century, most inmates continue to work at jobs related to the prison operations and maintenance, with a small but growing fraction employed in goods production for general distribution and sale.

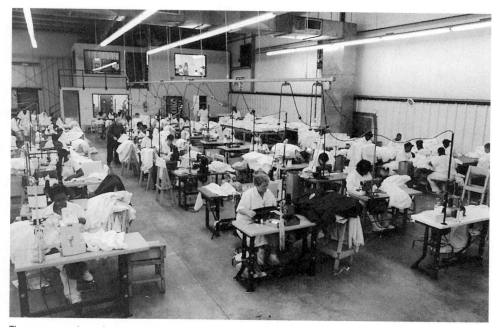

There are a variety of prison industries programs today. Here, female inmates make prison uniforms in a garment factory at the Tutwiler Prison in Elmore, Alabama. These programs keep inmates active and give them opportunities to earn money.

Federal Prison System

The U.S. Congress authorized the construction of three United States penitentiaries in 1891. Until passage of this legislation, federal prisoners were housed in state prisons and local jails. It took more than a decade to build and open these large prisons. While construction of new facilities was underway, the former military prison at Leavenworth, Kansas, housed federal prisoners. The first "new" federal penitentiary opened in 1902 in Atlanta, Georgia, followed four years later by the inmate-constructed federal penitentiary at Leavenworth. In the 1920s, the federal prison system added a women's prison, a youth facility, and a detention center, operated by the Justice Department and supervised by the superintendent of prisons and prisoners (Bureau of Prisons 1994). The Volstead Act (alcohol prohibition) and a series of new federal laws against controlled substances such as heroin, cocaine, and marijuana were also features of the 1920s. These federal law-enforcement initiatives, and new federal laws protecting banks and criminalizing interstate theft of automobiles, brought thousands of new felons into the federal prison system.

On May 14, 1930, President Herbert Hoover signed legislation creating the Federal Bureau of Prisons (**BOP**).[2] The BOP's goals were to ensure consistent, centralized administration of the federal prison system, professionalize the prison service, and provide more humane care for federal prisoners. Over the next few years, the BOP opened several new federal correctional facilities, including the Federal Penitentiary at Lewisburg (Pennsylvania), and other prisons at El Reno (Oklahoma), La Tuna (Texas), and Milan (Michigan). In 1933, the Medical Center for Federal Prisoners opened in Springfield (Missouri). In 1934, the BOP formed the Federal Prison Industries, Inc., known today by its trade name UNICOR.

The number of inmates housed by the BOP between 1940 and 1980 grew slowly from 20,000 to nearly 25,000.[3] Changes in federal antidrug policies, parole policies, and sentencing mandates created a huge increase in the number of federal prisoners beginning in the 1980s. For example, in 1986 the federal prison population stood at more than 40,000 sentenced and unsentenced inmates, itself an increase of 16,000 inmates in only five years. The federal prison system held roughly 90,000 inmates in 1995. In ten years the system had more than doubled its inmate population. By 1997, the BOP's 26,000-plus staff, including nearly 11,000 correctional officers, supervised nearly 98,000 inmates in 90 institutions. Another 11,000 inmates were contracted out to nonfederal facilities.[4]

Facilities Profile

The BOP operates four types of facilities: The United States penitentiary (**USP**), the federal correctional institution (**FCI**), the federal prison camp (**FPC**) and satellite FPCs, and Metropolitan Correctional/Detention Centers (**MCC/MDC**).[5] The federal transfer center (**FTC**), the facility that coordinates the movement of federal prisoners, is in Oklahoma City. The BOP classifies institutions according to five security levels: high, medium, low, minimum, and administrative. Bureau staff arrived at security designations by weighing, in order of importance, the impact of seven features on facility security. These security features include the presence of external patrols, gun towers, external security barriers, external detection devices, type of housing, internal security features, and staff-to-inmate ratios. Staff-to-inmate ratios are critical. They range from averages of 1:2 in maximum-security penitentiaries to a low of 1:10 in minimum-security facilities. Administrative- and medium-security facilities average one staff member for every three inmates, whereas the low-security facilities average a 1:4 ratio.

The BOP's high-, medium-, and minimum-security levels relate well to maximum, medium, and minimum security. Two security levels are new: low and administrative security. In essence, **low security** gives the BOP a means of distinguishing between those facilities with more custody needs than an open campus, but less than that provided by a double chain-link fence topped with concertina razor-wire. The inmates incarcerated in these facilities are a greater risk and enjoy fewer privileges and freedoms than minimum-security inmates, but are less threatening than medium-security inmates. Inmates living in low-security units are mostly housed in dormitory units. **Administrative security** is for special-use facilities that must provide a reasonably high security program for all inmates within the facility, with some inmates enjoying greater privileges and freedoms than others, depending on their location within that facility. The key to recognizing administrative security is that the facilities resemble jails: They house inmates at literally all risk levels.

Metropolitan Correctional Centers and Metropolitan Detention Centers are all at the administrative security level. These institutions did not exist until the mid-1970s, when the BOP opened 5 of the 10 existing MCC/MDC facilities. In many ways, these MCC/MDC facilities resemble large jails, since they house between 500 and 2,000 inmates of virtually every possible legal designation: convicted, accused, and in-transit federal felons and misdemeanants. Two MCC/MDC facilities, Springfield (Missouri) and Rochester (Minnesota), are medical centers and detention facilities. The former is for men only, while the latter houses both men and women. One metropolitan center, in Lexington (Kentucky), houses nearly 2,000 women and a federal medical center for women. Three of the remaining MCC/MDC facilities house only men, with the rest having segregated bed spaces for men and women.

The BOP's 13 federal prison camps (FPC) are minimum security. FPC-Alderson (West Virginia), which is the oldest continually functioning federal women's facility, and FPC-Bryan (Texas) house only women. The remaining 11 prison camps house only men. Thirty-four "satellite camps" are physically next to a federal penitentiary, federal correctional institution, or federal MCC/MDC. Four of these satellite facilities incarcerate only women. Three are found next to larger facilities for women, while one, FPC-Phoenix (Arizona) Satellite Camp, is next to a federal correctional institution for men only. **"Campers"** are the lowest risk of all federal prisoners. Most campers are white-collar criminals or other nonviolent offenders. Except FPC-Alderson and FPC-Maxwell (Alabama), which house nearly 1,000 inmates each, most federal prison camps are small facilities, ranging from fewer than 50 at FPC-Florence (Colorado) to nearly 700 at FPC-Duluth (Minnesota). Most, particularly the satellite FPC facilities, average 300 to 400 inmates.

Federal correctional institutions hold inmates at security levels ranging from low to high. Four FCI facilities have multilevel security ratings. For example, FCI-Butner (North Carolina) houses male inmates at low, medium, and administrative levels. Butner also has a minimum-security FPC satellite camp, making it a four security level facility. Sixteen FCIs are exclusively low security. The security level of more than half the nation's 42 FCI facilities is medium-level security, or, rarely, medium plus high or administrative level. FCI-Danbury (Connecticut) and FCI-Dublin (California) are the only two all-female FCI facilities, one for each coast and both at the low security level. A mixed-gender facility, FCI-Mariana (Florida), provides bed spaces for women at medium and high security.

A United States penitentiary (USP) houses the nation's maximum-security inmates. USP-Atlanta and USP-Leavenworth are more than 90 years old. USP-Lewisburg (Pennsylvania) came into the system in 1932, followed by USP-Terre Haute (Indiana) in 1940. No new federal penitentiaries were built for nearly 20 years until USP-Lompoc (California) opened in 1959, followed by USP-Marion (Illinois) in 1963. It would be another 30 years before the opening of USP-Allenwood in 1993. USP-Florence, part of the new Federal Correctional Complex in Colorado, should be fully functioning before the end of the 1990s. As this construction pattern clearly shows, in spite of the rapid growth of federal prison inmates, the construction of expensive, maximum-security facilities has taken lower priority than the creation of a system of FCI, FPC, and MCC/MDC facilities. The two newest federal penitentiaries, USP-Allenwood and USP-Florence, each have fewer than 650 bed spaces, when compared with the other federal penitentiaries that, excepting USP-Marion, house between 1,400 and 2,000 inmates each. USP-Marion is a small penitentiary, built to house only about 400 inmates. After the close of Alcatraz in the 1960s, the BOP transferred most high-risk federal inmates to USP-Atlanta. However, by the 1980s, USP-Marion housed these inmates, a function now assumed by the administrative-maximum unit at USP-Florence.

Programs Profile

The federal government operates many programs at its nearly 100 secure facilities. Three emphases are clear: (1) work, (2) education and vocational training, and (3) drug treatment. Work is important for at least three reasons. First, work keeps the inmates busy for extended periods. All able-bodied federal inmates have a job. Second, well-developed work habits, combined with vocational training, can lead to a successful post-release job placement. Third, inmates provide a ready labor pool in the prison for institutional jobs.

Federal facilities operate two main work programs (Bureau of Prisons 1994). The Federal Prison Industries, Inc., known widely as UNICOR, provides work assignments for roughly 21% of all federal prisoners. Inmates manufacture and refinish furniture, produce textiles and paint brushes, refurbish vehicle components, assemble electrical cable and radio mounts for military applications, and produce signs and other metal products. The U.S. government purchases all of the items produced by inmate labor. General maintenance of the BOP facility is the second work program. About three of every four federal inmates work at institutional jobs, including health services, food services, educational and recreational services, law library, business office, and general institutional maintenance. The typical inmate works between 35 and 44 hours per week. The best paying jobs are typically in UNICOR, where inmates average 85 cents per hour. Federal correctional facility jobs average 46 cents per hour, and range from 17 cents per hour for

---

Box 5.5

**Pilot Programs: A Joint BOP
and NIDA Project**

The BOP, in cooperation with the National Institute of Drug Abuse (NIDA), operates three even more intensive and lengthier residential programs under the **pilot programs** at FCI-Butner, FCI-Lexington, and FCI-Tallahassee. This program, under evaluation and review at these three primarily medium-security institutions, consists of five main elements. First, inmates select themselves into the program, but must have at least 18 months left on their sentence before they leave federal custody. Second, while in the pilot program they participate in a wide range of treatment and therapeutic programs similar to those administered under the comprehensive program. The third and fourth elements set this program apart from the others. Upon release from the FCI, inmates enter a halfway house, where they live under severe restrictions, including drug testing. At the end of six months, they leave federal supervision. However, they may continue in voluntary aftercare for an additional six months.

Sources: Bureau of Prisons 1994; National Task Force on Correctional Substance Abuse Strategies 1991.

---

farming, forestry, and ranching to 76 cents for non-UNICOR goods production (Harlow 1994, 20).

Educational and vocational training programs at federal facilities are extensive in breadth and depth. Tens of thousands of inmates participate in the education and literacy programs, with upwards of 5,000 or more each year graduating the general education development program. In fact, inmates without a high school diploma or GED certification must enroll for 120 days in the educational and literacy program. At the end of the 120 days, inmates can opt out of the program, but if they do so are placed in and limited to entry-level (and low paying) institutional jobs. The 12th-grade literacy level has been standard for all inmates since 1991. Besides basic education, the BOP provides training in 40 different vocations. Inmates also have access to courses offered by a broad range of technical schools, community colleges, and four-year colleges and universities.

Besides work and education, federal facilities also emphasize drug treatment, a logical response to the large number of drug-involved inmates in the federal system. The BOP operates three primary drug treatment programs (Bureau of Prisons 1994). **Drug education,** a nonresidential, information-oriented program, has by far the widest application, with nearly 10% of all federal prisoners participants. It is also mandatory for all drug-involved inmates. At the next level is **centralized counseling services,** an outpatient program consisting of group and individual counseling, self-help groups, and speciality seminars. The **comprehensive program** is a residential approach to drug treatment. Participants, all of whom are volunteers, must enter a nine-month, unit-based program of intensive individual and group counseling. Box 5.5 describes more intensive drug programs offered by the BOP.

Table 5.1

Number and Rate (per 100,000 Resident U.S. Population for Each Sex) of Sentenced Prisoners in State and Federal Institutions, 1925–95

| | | | (Rate per 100,000 resident population in each group) | | | |
| | | | Male | | Female | |
	Total	Rate	Number	Rate	Number	Rate
1925	91,669	79	88,231	149	3,438	6
1926	97,991	83	94,287	157	3,704	6
1927	109,983	91	104,983	173	4,363	7
1928	116,390	96	111,836	182	4,554	8
1929	120,496	98	115,876	187	4,620	8
1930	129,453	104	124,785	200	4,668	8
1931	137,082	110	132,638	211	4,444	7
1932	137,997	110	133,573	211	4,424	7
1933	136,810	109	132,520	209	4,290	7
1934	138,316	109	133,769	209	4,547	7
1935	144,180	113	139,278	217	4,902	8
1936	145,038	113	139,990	217	5,048	8
1937	152,741	118	147,375	227	5,366	8
1938	160,285	123	154,826	236	5,459	8
1939	179,818	137	173,143	263	6,675	10
1940	173,706	131	167,345	252	6,361	10
1941	165,439	124	159,228	239	6,211	9
1942	150,384	112	144,167	217	6,217	9
1943	137,220	103	131,054	202	6,166	9
1944	132,456	100	126,350	200	6,106	9
1945	133,649	98	127,609	193	6,040	9
1946	140,079	99	134,075	191	6,004	8
1947	151,304	105	144,961	202	6,343	9
1948	155,977	106	149,739	205	6,238	8
1949	163,749	109	157,663	211	6,086	8
1950	166,123	109	160,309	211	5,814	8
1951	165,680	107	159,610	208	6,070	8
1952	168,233	107	161,994	208	6,239	8
1953	173,579	108	166,909	211	6,670	8
1954	182,901	112	175,907	218	6,994	8
1955	185,780	112	178,655	217	7,125	8
1956	189,565	112	182,190	218	7,375	9
1957	195,414	113	188,113	221	7,301	8
1958	205,643	117	198,208	229	7,435	8
1959	208,105	117	200,469	228	7,636	8
1960	212,953	117	205,265	230	7,688	8
1961	220,149	119	212,268	234	7,881	8
1962	218,830	117	210,823	229	8,007	8
1963	217,283	114	209,538	225	7,745	8

State Prison Systems

State prisons represent a unique national growth industry, especially in the last quarter of the twentieth century. Table 5.1 contains a summary of the number and rate of prisoners incarcerated in state and federal institutions between 1925 and 1995, broken down by offenders' sex. Early prisoner statistics are notoriously unreliable. Nonetheless, during the first 40 years the

Table 5.1 *(continued)*

Number and Rate (per 100,000 Resident U.S. Population for Each Sex) of Sentenced Prisoners in State and Federal Institutions, 1925–95

		(Rate per 100,000 resident population in each group)				
				Male		Female
	Total	Rate	Number	Rate	Number	Rate
1964	214,336	111	206,632	219	7,704	8
1965	210,895	108	203,327	213	7,568	8
1966	199,654	102	192,703	201	6,951	7
1967	194,896	98	188,661	195	6,235	6
1968	187,914	94	182,102	187	5,812	6
1969	196,007	97	189,413	192	6,594	6
1970	196,429	96	190,794	191	5,635	5
1971	198,061	95	191,732	189	6,329	6
1972	196,092	93	189,823	185	6,269	6
1973	204,211	96	197,523	191	6,004	6
1974	218,466	102	211,077	202	7,389	7
1975	240,593	111	231,918	220	8,675	8
1976	262,833	120	252,794	238	10,039	9
1977[a]	278,141	126	267,097	249	11,044	10
1977[b]	285,456	129	274,244	255	11,212	10
1978	294,396	132	282,813	261	11,583	10
1979	301,470	133	289,465	264	12,005	10
1980	315,974	139	303,643	275	12,331	11
1981	353,167	154	338,940	304	14,227	12
1982	394,374	171	378,045	337	16,329	14
1983	419,820	179	402,391	354	17,429	15
1984	443,398	188	424,193	370	19,205	16
1985	480,568	202	458,972	397	21,296	17
1986	522,084	217	497,540	426	24,544	20
1987	560,812	231	533,990	453	26,822	22
1988	603,732	247	573,587	482	30,145	24
1989	680,907	276	643,643	535	37,264	29
1990	739,980	297	699,416	575	40,564	32
1991	789,610	313	745,808	606	43,802	34
1992	846,277	332	799,776	642	46,501	36
1993	932,074	359	878,037	698	54,037	41
1994	1,016,760	389	956,691	753	60,069	45
1995	1,085,363	411	1,021,463	796	63,900	48

Note: See Notes, figures 6.1 and 6.4. These data represent prisoners sentenced to more than one year. Both custody and jurisdiction figures are shown for 1977 to facilitate year to year comparison.
[a] Custody counts.
[b] Jurisdiction counts.

Source: Maguire and Pastore (1996, 556); Bureau of Justice Statistics (1997a, 8, 86–89). Table adapted by Mays and Winfree.

overall rates typically rose slowly to a plateau, remained there a few years, and then dropped down: The rates in 1967 were identical with those recorded in 1929 and 1945. In 1976 the incarceration rate per 100,000 resident population in the U.S. was 120. This rate rose steadily throughout the 1980s and 1990s, and stood at 411 in 1995, an increase of 243% in a little less than 20 years. Never before in the 70-plus years of recorded national prisoner statistics had there been an increase of 100% in a similar period.

The patterns observed for male and female inmates are also instructive. In 1976, the rate for male inmates was 238 per 100,000 resident population. The prisons held 252,794 male inmates. In 1995 the per-capita rate was 796 with more than 1 million inmates. The rate for women in 1976 was 9 per 100,000 and only 10,039 inmates. By 1995 the nation's prisons held more than 60,000 female inmates. For females, the per-capita rate stood at more than 48.

Clearly, prisons as a type of total institution are male "sanctuaries," although female offenders are closing the gap. For example, beginning in 1976, men took 14 years to double their incarceration rate. The rate for women doubled in 10 years, and doubled again in only 7 years. The rate for men has increased by "only" about 40% since their 1990 doubling. Unless the processing of women through the criminal justice system experiences never-before-seen increases, women may never achieve full "parity" with men in their imprisonment rates. If we assume a doubling of the female per-capita rate each 7 years and a similar doubling for males every 14 years, by 2023 the rate for men would stand at 3,000, whereas the rate for women would be 960. The real question embedded in these projections is whether the nation can literally and socially afford to have nearly 2,000 people out of every 100,000—1 person in 50—in prison? Can the nation afford the more than 400 prison inmates per 100,000 population currently incarcerated?

Facilities Profile

Four facility-based prison statistics help us to appreciate the extent of the "prison business" in the nation's more than 1,200 correctional facilities: the number of prisons, the number of inmates, the incarceration rate, and the population housed as a percentage of capacity. First, the number of prisons translates directly into capital expenditures. Review the statistics summarized in Tables 5.2 and 5.3. In 1995 two states, California and Florida, had roughly 100 prison facilities each, followed closely by mega-prison system states such as North Carolina (93), Texas (92), and Michigan (73). At the other extreme are 16 states, including Wyoming, Hawaii, New Mexico, and Montana, that had fewer than 10 facilities in 1995. In 1995 approximately three-fifths of the states operated between 10 and 50 adult correctional facilities. However, the number of prisons in a state alone is sometimes a deceiving statistic. For example, in 1995, Montana's eight prisons incarcerated nearly 1,683 inmates. New Mexico's eight prisons held only slightly fewer than 4,000 inmates. California's 102 prisons incarcerated more than 126,000 inmates, making it the largest prison system in the nation, a distinction it still holds. Florida's 98 prisons, by contrast, housed about 62,000 inmates. Prison population density—and a correctional policy governing the number and size of facilities in the state—accounts for the differences. New Mexico and Florida, two states with very different state and prison populations, have prison systems with

Table 5.2

Number of State and Federal Correctional Facilities, Midyear 1990 and 1995

Region and jurisdiction	Number of facilities[a]		Region and jurisdiction	Number of facilities[a]	
	1990	1995		1990	1995
U.S. total	**1,287**	**1,500**	**South**	**534**	**629**
Federal	80	125	Alabama	28	31
State	1,207	1,375	Arkansas	13	15
			Delaware	8	8
Northeast	**182**	**204**	District of Columbia	11	15
Connecticut[a]	20	23	Florida	100	98
Maine	7	9	Georgia	32	43
Massachusetts	20	21	Kentucky	15	23
New Hampshire	5	6	Louisiana	20	17
New Jersey	25	25	Maryland	21	27
New York	62	68	Mississippi	24	22
Pennsylvania	30	37	North Carolina	91	93
Rhode Island	7	7	Oklahoma	23	40
Vermont	6	8	South Carolina	32	32
			Tennessee	18	20
Midwest	**255**	**275**	Texas	43	92
Illinois	39	43	Virginia	48	44
Indiana	23	23	West Virginia	7	9
Iowa	24	29			
Kansas	16	9	**West**	**236**	**267**
Michigan	67	73	Alaska	13	20
Minnesota	9	8	Arizona	20	19
Missouri	17	22	California	100	102
Nebraska	7	9	Colorado	14	20
North Dakota	2	1	Hawaii	10	8
Ohio	22	28	Idaho	7	10
South Dakota	2	2	Montana	5	8
Wisconsin	27	28	Nevada	17	18
			New Mexico	11	8
			Oregon	11	12
			Utah	8	9
			Washington	16	29
			Wyoming	4	4

Note: Prison census midyear data were reported as of June 29, 1990, and June 30, 1995.

[a] The prison census counts state, federal, and private facilities that have custody over adults sentenced to confinement. It includes prisons, penitentiaries, boot camps, prison farms, reception, diagnostic, and classification centers, road camps, forestry and conservation camps, youthful offender facilities except in California, vocational training facilities, prison hospitals, drug and alcohol treatment facilities, and state-operated local detention facilities in Alaska, Connecticut, Delaware, Hawaii, Rhode Island, and Vermont. The census excludes privately operated facilities that are not predominantly for state or federal inmates, military facilities, Immigration and Naturalization Service facilities, Bureau of Indian Affairs facilities, U.S. Marshals Service facilities, and public hospital wings and wards reserved for state prisoners.

Source: Bureau of Justice Statistics (1997a, 52).

similar policies on prison population density. California and Montana average nearly twice the number of inmates at each facility as are found in New Mexico and Florida.

Looking at the geographical region of the country provides an illuminating way to examine per-capita incarceration rates. The South incarcerates the most people and has the nation's highest per-capita incarceration rate,

Table 5.3

Prisoners Under Control of State or Federal Correctional Authorities, by Region and Jurisdiction, Midyear 1995 and 1996

Region and Jurisdiction	Total 6/30/96	Total 6/30/95	Percent change from 6/30/95 to 6/30/96	Prison Incarceration Rate 6/30/96
U.S. total	**1,164,356**	**1,105,551**	**5.3%**	**420**
Federal	103,722	99,466	4.3%	33
State	1,060,634	1,006,085	5.4	388
Northeast	**165,224**	**158,184**	**4.5%**	**306**
Connecticut[b]	14,975	15,005	(0.2)	319
Maine	1,468	1,459	0.6	112
Massachusetts	11,996	11,469	4.6	178
New Hampshire	2,050	2,065	(0.7)	177
New Jersey	27,753	25,626	8.3	347
New York	68,721	68,526	0.3	379
Pennsylvania	33,939	29,844	13.7	281
Rhode Island[b]	3,226	3,132	3.0	198
Vermont[b,c]	1,096	1,058	3.6	143
Midwest	**199,414**	**190,573**	**4.6%**	**318**
Illinois[c,d]	38,373	37,790	1.5	322
Indiana	16,582	15,699	5.6	281
Iowa[c]	6,176	5,692	8.5	216
Kansas	7,462	6,927	7.7	289
Michigan[c]	41,884	41,377	1.2	436
Minnesota	5,040	4,764	5.8	108
Missouri	20,541	18,940	8.5	383
Nebraska	3,248	2,801	16.0	193
North Dakota	640	610	4.9	90
Ohio[d]	45,314	43,521	4.1	405
South Dakota	2,049	1,820	12.6	279
Wisconsin	12,105	10,632	13.9	209
South	**467,900**	**446,755**	**4.7%**	**487**
Alabama	21,495	20,082	7.0	487
Arkansas	9,430	9,081	3.8	358
Delaware[b]	5,148	4,651	10.7	425
District of Columbia[b]	9,763	10,484	(6.9)	1,444
Florida[c]	64,332	61,992	3.8	448

followed by the West, the Midwest, and the Northeast. Disaggregated incarceration rates range from a high of 1,566 for the District of Columbia to a low of 101 for Minnesota. The rate for the Federal Bureau of Prisons, which encompasses the entire nation, is only 31 per 100,000 population, while the aggregate rate for all states is 358.

The fourth and final prison-based statistic is population housed as a percentage of capacity, commonly called the "prison crowding rate." (See Table 5.4.) The highest capacity is the highest number of inmates that can be admitted and allow the prison to stay within some recognized limits.[6] For example, in 1995, the federal BOP was at 125% of its highest rated capacity.

Table 5.3 (continued)

Prisoners Under Control of State or Federal Correctional Authorities, by Region and Jurisdiction, Midyear 1995 and 1996

Region and Jurisdiction	Total 6/30/96	Total 6/30/95	Percent change from 6/30/95 to 6/30/96	Prison Incarceration Rate 6/30/96
South (continued)	**467,900**	**446,755**	**4.7%**	**487**
Georgia[c]	34,808	34,111	2.0	468
Kentucky	12,652	11,949	5.9	325
Louisiana	26,673	24,840	7.4	611
Maryland	22,118	21,441	3.2	413
Mississippi	13,785	12,446	10.8	486
North Carolina	30,671	26,818	14.4	397
Oklahoma[d]	19,134	17,605	8.7	580
South Carolina	20,814	19,482	6.8	540
Tennessee	15,634	14,933	4.7	293
Texas	129,937	127,092	2.2	659
Virginia	28,827	27,310	5.6	421
West Virginia	2,679	2,438	9.9	144
West	**228,096**	**210,573**	**8.3%**	**375**
Alaska[b]	3,583	3,237	10.7	355
Arizona[c]	22,143	20,907	5.9	481
California	142,814	131,860	8.3	438
Colorado[d]	11,742	10,757	9.2	306
Hawaii[b]	3,693	3,583	3.1	225
Idaho	3,623	3,240	11.8	304
Montana	2,182	1,894	15.2	247
Nevada	8,064	7,487	7.7	493
New Mexico	4,528	4,121	9.9	253
Oregon	8,564	7,505	14.1	221
Utah	3,643	3,272	11.3	182
Washington	12,059	11,402	5.8	218
Wyoming	1,458	1,308	11.5	301

Notes: ( )Indicates a negative percent change.
[a] The number of prisoners with a sentence of more than one year per 100,000 in the resident population.
[b] Prison and jails form one integrated system. Data include total jail and prison population.
[c] Population figures are based on custody counts.
[d] Population counts for inmates sentenced to "more than one year" include an undetermined number of inmates sentenced to "one year or less."

Source: Gilliard and Beck (1997, 3).

The aggregate rate for the nation's prison system was 103% of the highest rated capacity. Nineteen states and the District of Columbia reported year-end capacities at or below 100% of the highest rated capacity. According to the design capacity rates, which are often more than 25% lower than the rated capacities, crowding in the nation's prisons is even greater.

Programs Profile

Nine out of ten state inmates participate in training, some program, activities, or work assignment, as compared to nearly all federal prisoners. Education and vocational training programs are widespread in state prison systems.

Table 5.4

Design and Rates Capacities of State Correctional Facilities, Midyear 1990 and 1995

Region and jurisdiction	Design capacity		Percentage of design capacity occupied		Rated capacity		Percentage of rated capacity occupied	
	1990	1995	1990	1995	1990	1995	1990	1995
U.S. total	**541,568**	**585,051**	**122%**	**133%**	**650,600**	**909,906**	**101%**	**103%**
Northeast	**92,700**	**119,379**	**127%**	**126%**	**109,448**	**141,157**	**106%**	**107%**
Connecticut	7,158	12,788	134	115	9,275	15,466	103	95
Maine	1,287	1,528	117	96	1,311	1,452	115	101
Massachusetts	5,454	7,334	152	147	6,299	9,173	132	117
New Hampshire	897	1,757	161	125	1,049	1,769	137	124
New Jersey	14,867	14,056	113	138	16,189	14,244	103	136
New York	46,955	52,885	120	130	56,406	66,815	100	103
Pennsylvania	13,706	24,485	152	121	16,353	27,587	127	106
Rhode Island	1,790	3,561	137	86	1,790	3,599	137	85
Vermont	586	965	138	105	776	1,052	104	98
Midwest	**114,846**	**115,513**	**123%**	**149%**	**134,106**	**154,320**	**106%**	**122%**
Illinois	20,949	22,243	128	166	23,409	26,424	114	140
Indiana	12,871	—	96	—	13,701	12,512	92	116
Iowa	3,674	4,499	123	150	4,520	6,341	100	106
Kansas	5,312	6,835	104	100	5,312	6,835	104	100
Michigan	26,885	30,986	118	130	30,979	41,326	103	98
Minnesota	2,840	4,319	114	106	3,299	4,319	96	106
Missouri	11,304	11,992	129	153	15,033	18,650	97	98
Nebraska	1,661	2,119	144	136	1,819	2,334	131	123
North Dakota	575	637	97	106	575	637	97	106
Ohio	22,489	24,780	141	177	28,766	24,780	111	177
South Dakota	1,109	—	112	—	1,252	1,516	100	124
Wisconsin	5,177	7,103	130	147	5,441	8,646	124	120
South	**229,126**	**205,793**	**111%**	**124%**	**262,286**	**416,591**	**97%**	**96%**
Alabama	12,825	14,236	97	126	12,825	18,248	97	96
Arkansas	6,530	8,044	99	103	6,530	8,044	99	103
Delaware	2,968	3,279	116	141	3,526	4,561	96	101
District of Columbia	5,633	7,362	129	118	7,411	8,751	96	99
Florida	32,668	51,696	130	120	47,069	67,879	90	91

Table 5.4 (continued)

Design and Rates Capacities of State Correctional Facilities, Midyear 1990 and 1995

Region and jurisdiction	Design capacity		Percentage of design capacity occupied		Rated capacity		Percentage of rated capacity occupied	
	1990	1995	1990	1995	1990	1995	1990	1995
Georgia	17,399	—	107	—	19,676	29,677	94	101
Kentucky	6,559	9,374	105	106	7,280	10,374	95	96
Louisiana	13,917	13,250	100	122	14,142	16,861	99	96
Maryland	10,877	14,163	157	148	15,640	19,670	109	106
Mississippi	7,363	8,263	93	116	7,363	9,982	93	96
North Carolina	17,125	22,985	107	111	18,996	27,488	97	93
Oklahoma	6,123	10,791	171	137	9,439	14,684	111	101
South Carolina	12,538	14,323	120	128	15,669	17,717	96	104
Tennessee	7,616	11,006	109	118	9,229	13,223	90	98
Texas	53,465	—	93	—	51,971	124,657	96	94
Virginia	13,898	14,882	105	152	13,898	22,497	105	101
West Virginia	1,622	2,119	96	103	1,622	2,278	96	96
West	**104,896**	**144,386**	**139%**	**140%**	**144,760**	**197,840**	**101%**	**102%**
Alaska	2,473	3,128	98	100	2,580	3,325	94	94
Arizona	13,889	19,800	100	107	14,641	21,249	95	100
California	56,323	78,389	164	161	92,075	123,559	101	102
Colorado	4,526	6,633	124	122	4,992	8,464	112	96
Hawaii	2,178	1,750	118	189	2,552	2,646	101	125
Idaho	1,531	2,118	115	137	1,781	2,626	99	110
Montana	888	1,278	143	132	898	1,274	142	132
Nevada	5,126	5,338	110	137	5,934	7,080	95	103
New Mexico	3,025	3,854	103	104	3,179	4,137	98	97
Oregon	5,339	6,011	112	124	5,339	7,728	112	96
Utah	3,036	3,710	92	102	3,029	3,695	92	103
Washington	5,766	11,374	122	100	6,712	11,080	105	103
Wyoming	797	1,003	137	115	1,048	977	104	118

Note: A variety of capacity measures is used by correctional reporting authorities to reflect both available space to house inmates and the ability to staff and operate an institution. Design capacity is the number of inmates that planners or architects intended for the facility. Rated capacity is the number of beds or inmates assigned by a rating official. Percentage of design capacity occupied is determined by dividing the number of inmates housed on the day of the census by the reported capacity. Percentage of capacity occupied is based on the midyear populations from facilities which reported capacity levels.

Source: Bureau of Justice Statistics (1997a, 58).

Box 5.6

Shock Incarceration: A Multi-Program Approach to First Offenders

In 1983, the Georgia Department of Corrections opened its first **shock incarceration** unit (SIU) at the Dodge Correctional Institution. Like nearly all shock incarceration programs that followed, the Georgia SIU included a military-style "boot camp" training phase, followed by a supervised release from custody. The idea of drill instructor staff ordering recently shorn inmates to do 100 pushups or straighten up the line appealed to many politicians and prison officials. In a sense, shock incarceration represented a total institution within a total institution, military basic training within a prison compound.

Shock incarceration programs typically confine first-time, nonviolent offenders for between three and six months. During this time, they expose them to military-style drill and ceremony, and a strict regimen of physical exercise and labor. Over the past 10 years many shock incarceration programs have added two important elements missing from early boot camps. First, a combination of individual and group counseling address the treatment goals. Depending on the age of the participants, they participate in basic adult education or secondary-school education. The counseling is often drug-related. Second, most new programs include an intensive aftercare supervision program.

By 1993, 32 states operated 52 shock incarceration programs, many involving juvenile and youthful offenders. Since 1993, the federal government has operated boot camps as intensive confinement centers at ICC-Bryan (Texas) and ICC-Lewisburg (Pennsylvania). Do they work? Were the high expectations for this public-relations winner too high? For answers to these and other questions about shock incarceration, you must wait until Chapter 12.

Sources: Bourque, Han, and Hill (1996); Cowles, Castellano, and Gransky (1995); Peterson (1996).

Nearly all states provide at least adult basic education (ABE) or general education development (GED) (Maguire and Pastore 1995, 560). They also offer vocational technical, prerelease, or job readiness training. Most allow inmates access to two-year college or community college level coursework. At the higher educational levels, state participation dropped off sharply: about one state in three offered courses for the baccalaureate degree. Only Maryland, New York, Oklahoma, and Texas reported graduate degree programs.

Jobs are important in the state prison systems, but less uniformly so than in the federal system. Whereas more than 90% of all federal prisoners work, only about 7 in 10 state prisoners have any work assignments (Harlow 1994, 19). The most common jobs in state prisons are the same ones found in the federal system outside UNICOR. More than half the state inmates work in janitorial services, food preparation, maintenance, repair or construction, grounds and road maintenance, and other services. Only about 4% produce something besides food. The manufactured goods tend to be ones consumed by the prison or state, including furniture, vehicle refurbishment, and plates, and signs of all descriptions and materials. State-prison inmates average 56 cents per hour, or about 10 cents per hour more than in the federal system. Most inmates work between 20 and 44 hours per week (Harlow 1994, 20).

Box 5.7
Private Prisons

As much of the decade of the 1990s has already passed, we have come to realize that private prisons are a reality in corrections. No longer are we asking *whether* we will have private facilities but *when*. We recognize that a number of states have already added private facilities to their correctional mix. In examining private prisons we need to carefully analyze the types of services that might be provided, then we must turn briefly to the issues still facing private prisons.

The services provided by private contractors span quite a continuum. At one end, the private sector can provide financing and construction management for what will be a state-run facility. At the other end of the continuum, are completely privately operated facilities under the control of companies such as Corrections Corp. of America, Wackenhut Corrections Corp., and U.S. Corrections Corp. The presence of these companies in the private prison market demonstrates that there is interest in providing the full range of correctional services. Between these two extremes there are private contractors providing food service, medical and dental treatment, and educational programs in state-run prisons from coast to coast.

However, it is important to acknowledge that lingering problems are associated with private prisons. The following list provides a brief overview:

- At the most basic level is the issue of *propriety*. In other words, is it appropriate for the private sector to be in the business of incarcerating people?
- The focal issue for most debates is finances. Does the private sector *always*

provide lower operating costs? The answer is "It depends." A state may negotiate a contract for lower costs for the same level of services now being provided publicly, or it may negotiate for a higher level of services based on the cost currently being paid to publicly operated prisons. Expenditures are always tied to the contract specifications.

- Legal issues also emerge in the discussion of privatization. At the most basic level we can say that states cannot contract away their liability. Private contractors may reduce the state's exposure to risk, they might share that exposure, but, ultimately, the state bears financial responsibility for inmate treatment, including harm.
- Most states will continue to deal with personnel issues even if private prisons are built. Will state employees lose their jobs? Will the private contractor pick them up as employees? What will happen to their benefits and protections as civil servants?
- Finally, an ongoing issue is contract monitoring. Once a state privatizes some or all of its facilities, it must have a mechanism in place to make sure the contractor complies with all provisions of the contract.

What is the future of private prisons? Undoubtedly, we will see more in the next decade. Will these facilities solve our problems, including institutional crowding? Probably not. Crowding depends on policy choices, not simply a function of too few prison bed spaces.
Source: Mays (1996).

A few states, such as Texas, pay their inmates nothing for the work performed. As in the federal system, the lowest paid prisoners work in farming, forestry, or ranching, averaging 31 cents per hour. The best paid state prisoners work in maintenance, repair, or construction (94 cents per hour) and goods production (84 cents per hour).

Drug, mental health, and sex-offender programs receive varying degrees of attention—and resources—in state prison systems. For example, a 1993 survey of 40 states and the District of Columbia found that about half allocated health-care funds to alcohol and drug treatment beyond those funds allocated to mental health treatment. Another 16 provided funds for mental health treatment but no funds specifically for alcohol and drug treatment (Maguire and Pastore 1995, 16). The treatment of sex offenders presents another interesting set of responses from the various jurisdictions. There are security and logistic reasons for congregating sex offenders in one location: these inmates are often resource-intensive, requiring specialized treatment, and they often present a security risk in the general population. Among 48 states and the District of Columbia, only the District, Maine, and Maryland reported that they had no separate programming for sex offenders; all of the other states offered at least individual and group counseling for sex offenders (Maguire and Pastore 1995, 561–63). Alaska, Colorado, Illinois, and Iowa congregate their sex offenders in single-purpose institutions, as does the federal government. Minnesota, Missouri, Nebraska, New Hampshire, Oklahoma, Oregon, South Dakota, Tennessee, Utah, Virginia, and West Virginia segregate sex offenders in separate wings in all or some institutions. The rest of the state prison systems and the District of Columbia house sex offenders within the general population.

Juvenile Corrections

Until the nineteenth century, the history of adult corrections was the history of juvenile corrections. One notable exception to this generalization was the creation of the Vatican's *Silentium* in 1703, a facility in which youthful offenders were expected to show remorse for their misdeeds. As a rule, however, there were few organized attempts to segregate juvenile prisoners from their adult counterparts until the classification schemes of reformers such as Beccaria, Howard, and Rush. The creation of the **house of refuge** in the 1820s is widely accepted as the beginning of the juvenile corrections movement in the United States (Krisberg and Austin 1993, 15–16). In 1825, the New York House of Refuge, the nation's first such facility, began providing shelter and care for delinquent and dependent children. Within three years, houses of refuge opened in Boston and Philadelphia. Under the ***parens patriae*** principle, the state replaced parents as the party responsible for correcting the misbehavior of children.

After the Civil War, reformer Charles Loring Brace and the "Child Savers," sent delinquent and dependent children by train across the country to be adopted—or indentured—by "caring" families on the American frontier (Schlossman 1977). Many of these children were the wayward offspring of recently arrived immigrants. Juvenile farms, forest camps, and ranches "inspired" many of these same immigrant children with basic American values, including the work ethic. Most of these youths toiled at jobs that had few applications in the work world to which they eventually would return.

By the end of the nineteenth century, the efforts of reform-minded groups concerned about the "urban masses" and "racially inferior immigrants" and other like-minded Child Savers culminated in the creation of the juvenile court (Platt 1969; Schlossman 1977). The juvenile court's goals were reformation and rehabilitation. Beginning in 1899, the states and the federal government created an entirely separate system of justice for juveniles. The various reformation and rehabilitation programs met with little resistance since youthful offenders, tried and sentenced by civil-law juvenile courts with lower standards of proof, enjoyed fewer constitutional protections than adults.

In the 1960s, both adult and juvenile corrections experienced many legal challenges. This was the era of civil rights. Cases contesting the juvenile court's exclusively civil proceedings and subsequent sanctions flowed through the appeals courts. Some decisions actually extended certain rights to children. Moreover, the **Juvenile Justice and Delinquency Prevention Act** was a key piece of juvenile corrections legislation enacted by Congress in 1974. This act called for the deinstitutionalization of status offenders. Later federal legislation mandated that juveniles be removed from jails or isolated by sight and sound from adult inmates, although, as we will see, the states have been slow to respond to this mandate.

Also, in 1974, the juveniles' right to treatment initially was upheld by two federal district court decisions. In *Nelson v. Heyne* (1974), an appeals court cited the origins of the juvenile court in the social reform movement of the nineteenth century as a reason for guaranteeing a juvenile's right to treatment. Also in 1974, another federal court ruled in *Morales v. Turman* that juveniles did not enjoy a "universally accepted right to treatment." By the end of the 1970s, confusion reigned in the federal courts over the question of a juvenile's right to treatment, leaving the issue for the individual states to decide. Amid judicial indecision, the National Advisory Committee for Juvenile Justice and Delinquency Prevention (1980, 487) wrote that "juveniles in residential facilities should have a right to maximum level of treatment services, such as individual and group counseling, and psychiatric, psychological, and casework services."

Juveniles, like adults, have experienced punitive crime control measures, characterized as the retributive justice era, beginning in the 1980s (Bernard 1992; Binder, Geis, and Bruce 1988; Fogel 1975). With the appellate courts fuzzy on whether juveniles enjoyed a right to treatment, funding for such programs declined. By the 1990s the focus was on removal of certain violent juvenile offenders from the juvenile justice system and their trial and punishment at the hands of the adult justice system.

Facilities Profile

There are two juvenile correctional systems, one public and the other private. At the time of the last comprehensive survey in 1989, the nation's 1,100 public-sector juvenile correctional institutions incarcerated approximately

57,000 youthful offenders of both sexes. Nearly 700 of these institutions were secure facilities. More than half kept the inmates at strict (maximum) or medium security (Krisberg, DeComo, and Herrera 1992, 22). More than 600,000 juveniles passed through all of the public facilities in a given year, staying an average of one month (Krisberg, DeComo, and Herrera 1992, 7).

The private sector has more than 2,000 juvenile-detention and shelter facilities. They house roughly 40,000 juveniles for an average three-month stay. The fact that fewer than 150,000 juveniles move through these private facilities in a given year is attributable to the longer stays. Also, private juvenile correctional facilities are less crowded than those in the public sector. Only about 300 of the private-sector institutions were secure facilities; only about one in five was a strict- or medium-security level facility (Krisberg, DeComo, and Herrera 1992, 36).

Programs Profile

States operate six basic forms of juvenile corrections. Two forms, including group homes and halfway houses and shelters, are discussed in Chapter 8. The rest have total-institutional, secure-facility features and, as such, resemble prisons for adults, including the following:

- **Reception and diagnostic units** provide the assessment and classification of youthful offenders coming into the state juvenile correctional system. A judge may order a 60- to 90-day diagnostic commitment to decide the youth's suitability for incarceration or community placement. However, judges sometimes use these commitments as punishment. For example, Lozano, Mays, and Winfree (1990) found youths assigned to New Mexico's Youth Diagnostic and Development Center with three or four previous commitments to the same facility. Most were never sent to the state's secure facilities. Apparently some judges in New Mexico viewed commitment to the diagnostic unit as a chance to shock the youth into behaving. Winfree and Zingraff (1973), in a study of a southeastern school for boys, reported that the youths' stay in the reception unit also provided them a chance to ease into institutional life without the same level of anxiety and danger that awaited them in the residential cottages. By the time they arrived in their residential unit, the boys "knew the ropes" and could better function in the school.

- **Detention facilities** provide temporary secure custody for juveniles. These facilities guarantee a child's appearance in court, house children who cannot return to their homes, and protect children from themselves or others. Most juvenile admissions in the public sector, perhaps 80% or more, involve detention centers, making them the most common form of youthful detention (Krisberg, DeComo, and Herrera 1992, 16). These facilities provide few amenities beyond basic educational courses.

Prisons in the Twenty-First Century

Projecting into the future of prisons, one needs only look first at the present and next at the past. Prisons change at a rate exceeded only by a terrestrial gastropod mollusk, or slug. Atomic-level chemical "sniffers," developed to secure the national borders against drugs, will find their way into prisons. New internal- and external-perimeter security technologies will be applied to the prison of the future, making escape nearly impossible and prison life no doubt less interesting, if you overlook those inmates trying to defeat the new technologies as they come online. Computers will make the monitoring of inmates far less labor-intensive. Finally, as the architectural designs employed by the BOP in its newest facilities clearly show, new institutions, including maximum-security penitentiaries, will be less forbidding and far more esthetically appealing to the casual visitor in the future.

Inside the prison of the future, several far less technical features are potentially far more important than the impact of technology. First, as we will see in the next chapter, health care, especially as related to infectious diseases such as AIDS/HIV, tuberculosis, and hepatitis could create a very costly drain on limited prison resources. As even a brief review of Chapter 11 reveals, ignoring these problems and letting the diseases sort out the inmates is not an option.

Second, with current sentencing laws, it is likely that the nation's prisons will become increasingly crowded and the inmate population will grow older in the next century. Given longer sentences, including an increasing reliance on the sentence of life without parole, with less time off for good behavior, the proportion of the prison population older than 55 will grow dramatically by the end of the decade. Providing health care and appropriate nutrition for these "elder inmates" will also prove costly. Again, unless a state's chief executive resorts to extensive use of pardons or clemency provisions of existing or new laws, not many options exist for either the state or federal prison systems.

Third, as more prison systems privatize, we should prepare for a scenario in which privately run prisons use inmate labor to support for-profit enterprises. Work conditions will join confinement conditions as central issues in the private prison of the future. Work slowdowns and work stoppages (strikes), not prison riots, may be among the chief management concerns of the private-sector prison warden. How to deal with prison unions rather than prison gangs may be mandatory training for correctional administrators in the next century.

- **Training schools** are the mainstays of the public-sector juvenile residential institutions: On any given day, one-half of all juveniles in state custody reside in a training school (Krisberg, DeComo, and Herrera 1992, 8). Most states operate at least one secure training facility, and most have one for each sex (Rogers and Mays 1987, 454). As Kenneth Wooden (1976) observed more than 20 years ago, there are two basic types of training schools: one looks like a miniature maximum-security penitentiary, often with masonry walls or chain-link fences. The other type, based on an idea introduced in the 1850s, more closely resembles a small community of houses or cottages. Inmates are expected to work, theoretically at some task related to a free-world vocation, hence the name training school.

- **Outdoor programs,** including farms, ranches, and, more recently, wilderness experience programs, replaced the houses of refuge. The "child saving" principle behind these programs was a simple one: Children cannot be reformed until they are removed from the corrupting influence of city life and exposed to the rewards of hard work and industry. Contemporary youths sent to farms, ranches, and forestry camps, like their counterparts in the training school, spend half a day in school, and the other half-day performing often very strenuous manual labor. The purpose of outdoor and wilderness programs such as VisionQuest and Outward Bound is to instill a sense of accomplishment, while building self-esteem. These programs are also conducted in far less institutional settings than state-run schools, camps, ranches or farms. In 1989, there were roughly 5,000 youths involved in public- and private-sector ranches and camps (Krisberg, DeComo, and Herrera 1992, 8).

Conclusion

As we close this chapter, we think that reflecting on what prisons are and are not might prove useful. Prisons are not meant to serve as resorts or vacation residences for offenders on hiatus from their lives of crime. Prisons are a type of total institution specifically designed for punishment and security. The punishments rendered must be humane and follow specific legal guidelines. This requirement, supported by the U.S. Constitution, state and federal laws, and Supreme Court decisions, has its limits. For example, the rights of the confined are constrained by the security needs of the prison. Moreover, security arrangements—especially those found in maximum-security or super-max prisons—often create bleak living and working conditions for those subjected to them, the keepers and kept alike. Thus, prisons exhibit a dynamic give-and-take relationship between the security needs of the institution and the rights of the confined.

It is also interesting that at the close of the twentieth century, we see communities competing for new prison construction. Prisons mean jobs, jobs that are nonpolluting, renewable and, except for private prisons, protected by civil service regulations. Therefore, prisons and prisoners are powerful economic forces for the communities in which they are found. We find it ironic that at the beginning of this century prisons were viewed as a source of cheap, expendable, and exploitable labor. Inmates were a labor source that prison officials could use with little accountability. As we close the century, the jobs associated with maintaining these facilities have become a major economic commodity. We suspect that as we progress into the next century, prison jobs—those performed by inmates and those associated with the security and maintenance of the facility—will become even more important to the nation's economy.

Except those special cases eligible for the death penalty, prison terms (and, for that matter, jail terms) are what the public demands when criminals are caught and punished. As we will see in Chapters 7 and 8, imprisonment is not always what the offender gets. That is, there are alternatives to imprisonment, options that many policy makers and penologists believe have adequate punishment value and provide some measure of public security. As for imprisonment, we will address in the next chapter what prison does to and for those who are incarcerated and those who must supervise that incarceration.

Critical Review Questions

1. Not to make you feel uncomfortable or anything, but when you were reading Goffman's contributions to our understanding of total institutions, what parallels did you see between prisons and higher education?

2. Summarize briefly the main conflicts between custody and treatment as institutional goals for prisons. Include any divisions between custody and treatment staff in your response. In what other kinds of total institutions might attempts to attain these goals be less troublesome?

3. Why is it essential to the smooth functioning of prisons that administrators classify prisoners? Why not just put all prison inmates in a single prison with no concern for classifying them according to any criteria?

4. We presented much information about prison security levels. In the previous chapter you learned about jail security levels. Compare and contrast life in prisons and jails as defined by security level concerns? How are they similar? How do they differ? Where would you rather spend a year? Why did you make this choice?

5. What do you think about attempts to use classification schemes designed for men in prisons for women?

6. What is your response to concerns about expanding the use of prison labor to the point that it might compete with private enterprises? Would your answer be altered if you knew that a relative could be replaced by a prison laborer? What if we had to pay prison inmates "the prevailing wage." What accommodations would make the use of prison labor less troubling to even those who are pro-labor union? What do you think of making prison

inmates "pay their own way," by taking out a share of their wages to pay for room and board and even child support, if they have children?

7. What do you think are the most impressive aspects of the federal prison system? How likely is it that these characteristics will find their way into the state-level prison system? Give the basis of your optimism or pessimism.

8. What was your response to the information about prison populations in the U.S. today? Short of unrealistic solutions, such as turning Arizona or Alaska into penal colonies, how can we solve the prison crowding problem? What would you be willing to support and why?

9. What prison-based programs do you think hold the most promise for helping inmates "turn their lives around?" Which ones do you think are a waste of time and money? What are prisons not doing for (or to) inmates that they should consider? Be sure to provide the basis for your response to each question.

10. We presented a necessarily brief overview of juvenile corrections. What special protections and programs do juvenile inmates enjoy? How do you feel about these differences?

Recommended Readings

Irwin, John. 1980. *Prisons in turmoil.* Boston: Little, Brown. Long before he wrote *It's About Time* with James Austin and more than 10 years after penning *The Felon* (his doctoral dissertation), Irwin predicted many of today's current prison problems in this important work. Included among the dozens of topics Irwin addresses—as only an ex-convict can—are prison gangs, racial divisions, and prisoner economics. In an especially interesting prediction, Irwin warns against determinate sentencing: Prison populations will boom. He was right. They did.

Jacobs, James B. 1977. *Stateville: The penitentiary in mass society.* Chicago: University of Chicago Press. The most infamous prison in Illinois, Stateville is often mentioned in the same class of prisons as Attica, San Quentin, and Jackson. This book explores the social organization of a unique total institution. Jacobs describes how, with the infusion of legal rights, Stateville, which has been among the most authoritarian of prisons, moved to a more legalistic and bureaucratic model of operation. This book is a fascinating account of a complex social system.

Johnson, Robert. 1987. *Hard time: Understanding and reforming the prison.* Pacific Grove, CA: Brooks/Cole. This book is about maximum-security prisons for adult males. Divided into three main parts, Johnson provides a detailed and thorough history of prisons and describes the patterns of adjustment to life in a maximum-security prison. In the final and briefest section, he suggests reform strategies that he believes will allow inmates to live in maximum-security prisons and not abandon all hope.

Pollock, Joycelyn M., ed. 1997. *Prisons: Today and tomorrow.* Gaithersburg, MD: Aspen. This book is a well-organized and well-written work on prisons. It represents a highly unusual and informative concurrence of area experts. Among the book's strongest elements are the chapters on race and gender, inmate classification, and the revisiting of rehabilitation.

Key Terms

administrative security
Ashurst-Sumners Act
body cavity searches
boot camp
BOP
campers
campus-design prison
centralized counseling
    services
classification officers
comprehensive program
consensus model
contract system
Correctional Classification
    Profile
courtyard-design prison
custody
Custody Determination
    Model
dehumanization
detention facility
direct supervision
drug education
equity-based model
FCI

FPC
FTC
Hawes-Cooper Act
house of refuge
inmate classification
inmate counts
intermittent supervision
joint venture programs
Juvenile Justice and
    Delinquency
    Prevention Act
lease system
linear-design living units
low security
maximum security
MCC/MDC
medium security
minimum security
MMPI
modified linear-design
    living units
nonperson status
outdoor programs
parens patriae
PIEC

pilot programs
podular-design living
    units
prediction model
prison
PS/PIEC
radial-design prison
reception and diagnostic
    unit
remote/indirect
    supervision
rites of passage
security levels
shakedowns
shock incarceration
Silentium
state-use system
super-max security
telephone-pole design
    prison
Times Square
total institutions
training school
treatment
UNICOR

Cases Cited

Morales v. Turman, 364 F.Suppl 166 (Tex., 1973)

Nelson v. Heyne, 491 F.2D 353 (7th Cir. 1974)

Notes

1. The question of inmate privacy is an interesting one with respect to cavity searches: Who should do it? Men working in prisons for women is not unusual. However, it has only been in the past 20 years that female COs have become commonplace in prisons for men. Inmates have sued over who should conduct thorough searches, including cavity searches. The courts have mandated that inmates undergoing a search of this nature should be provided at least a small measure of privacy.

2. Material concerning the BOP's history is taken from Bureau of Prisons (1994).
3. Material concerning the growth of the BOP is taken from Bureau of Prisons (1997b).
4. The BOP contracts with the private sector for more than 300 halfway houses (called community corrections centers) for inmates who are within 30 to 180 days of release.
5. The material on BOP facilities and programs is taken from Bureau of Prisons (1997b).

6. Prison population documents, such as the Bureau of Justice Statistics's annual *Correctional Populations in the United States,* typically report two capacity statistics. The first is the design capacity, or the number of inmates that planners or architects intended for the facility. The rated capacity is the number of beds or inmates assigned by an rating official. The latter statistic, as revealed in Table 5.4, is often far higher than the former.

6

Inmates

Chapter Outline

- Introduction
- Prison Inmate Characteristics
- Jail Inmate Characteristics
- Prison and Jail Culture
- Violence in Correctional Institutions
- Juvenile Inmates
- Inmate-Centered Issues
- Conclusion
- Critical Review Questions
- Recommended Readings
- Key Terms
- Cases Cited
- Notes

Introduction

Who is serving time in the nation's prisons and jails? How many are violent offenders? Does one racial or ethnic group dominate the "inmate class?" How dangerous is institutional life for inmates *and* staff? Do prisons and jails meet the unique needs of female inmates and other "special" inmate groups? What happens to minors upon incarceration? Is the institutionalized life of juveniles different from that experienced by adults? These questions represent only a sampling of what most students typically ask when a class on corrections turns to the subject of prison and jail inmates. You may have thought of more. (We hope that this is the case.)

Twenty years ago the average college student was unlikely to have much experience with either jails or prisons. Given the volume of people run through the jailhouse turnstiles and prison admissions over the past ten years, statistically at least, that probability has increased. If you are between 18 and 25, you are in the prime age group for both crime perpetrators and crime victims. If you are older than 45, your chances of being incarcerated drop substantially. If you are female, you are far more likely than your mother to have a jail or prison experience. If you are Hispanic or African-American, your probability of incarceration has increased dramatically since your parents' day. If you are an African-American male, perhaps one in four of your cohorts will be incarcerated in a prison, let alone a jail, where the odds are even greater.

Confused? Concerned? Enraged? Are you curious about what is going on in the nation's prisons and jails? To help you understand these observations about inmates and answer the questions we posed in this introduction, we begin with the characteristics of prison inmates.

Prison Inmate Characteristics

Three types of prison inmates merit close inspection: federal prisoners, state prisoners, and female prisoners.

Federal Prisoners

At the midpoint of the 1990s, the average federal prisoner was a non-Hispanic, White male in his late 30s.[1] Figure 6.1 highlights the gender, race, and ethnicity breakdowns for federal prisoners. Females accounted for fewer than 1 in 10 federal prison inmates. Nearly two-thirds of the female inmates were White, whereas more than one-third were African-American, proportions very similar to those observed for males. Asian-Americans and Native Americans accounted for most of the rest. In terms of ethnicity, Hispanics accounted for roughly one-quarter of the federal inmates, male and female, a rate that exceeds their proportion in the U.S. population.

The fact that prison populations have grown dramatically since the early 1980s is a well-documented fact. You might wonder who these offenders are. The trends in offense types (**public-order offenses, property offenses,** drug offenses, and violent offenses), summarized in Figure 6.2, reveal an interesting pattern over the last two decades of the twentieth century. Violent offenders account for a far smaller proportion of the federal prison population in 1995 than in 1980. This observation is true in spite of the fact that the number of violent offenders in 1995 is nearly twice that recorded in 1980. In 1995, 6 of every 10 federal criminals was a drug offender. Fifteen years earlier, about 1 in 4 federal criminals had a drug offense as his or her most serious crime. Moreover, the proportion of property offenders, like the proportion of violent offenders, declined between 1980 and 1995 as well. The proportion of public-order offenders, which included illegal immigration, illegal possession of weapons, and escape and flight to avoid prosecution offenses, also roughly doubled over this time. The primary increases were for drug offenders.

Two factors underlie these trends. First, in the wake of the so-called Drug War, federal prisoners grew exponentially. Nearly one federal inmate in four is not a U.S. citizen, a statistic that owes much to the interdiction of illicit

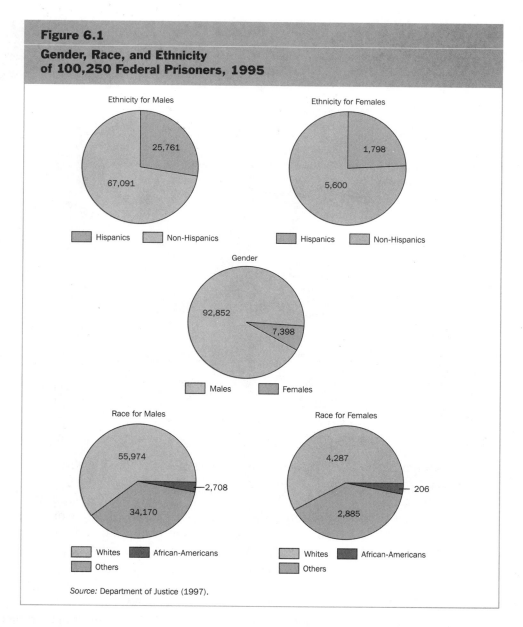

Figure 6.1

Gender, Race, and Ethnicity of 100,250 Federal Prisoners, 1995

Ethnicity for Males

25,761

67,091

Hispanics   Non-Hispanics

Ethnicity for Females

1,798

5,600

Hispanics   Non-Hispanics

Gender

92,852

7,398

Males   Females

Race for Males

55,974

2,708

34,170

Whites   African-Americans
Others

Race for Females

4,287

206

2,885

Whites   African-Americans
Others

Source: Department of Justice (1997).

drugs (Harlow 1994; Inciardi 1992; Walker 1995). Second, the nation's courts began "getting tough" on drug offenders in the 1980s. Congress enacted the **Sentencing Reform Act of 1984,** the so-called truth in sentencing law, that mandated specific sentencing guidelines for federal judges. Under the Sentencing Reform Act, which went into effect in late 1987, federal offenders must serve a minimum of 85% of the actual sentence.

Between 1987 and 1992, two trends emerged for federal prisoners.[2] First, among all federal offenders, the average maximum sentences increased from

Figure 6.2

Federal Prisoners by Most Serious Offense, 1980, 1985, 1990, 1995

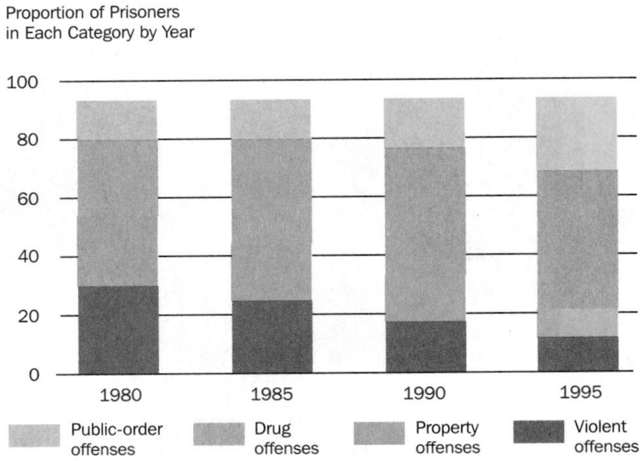

Proportion of Prisoners
in Each Category by Year

	1980	1985	1990	1995
Violent offenses	6,572	7,768	9,557	11,321
Property offenses	4,651	5,289	7,935	7,524
Drug offenses	4,900	9,482	30,470	51,737
Public-order offenses	2,040	2,514	8,585	15,762

Source: Bureau of Justice Statistics (1997a).

53 months to 62 months. However, drug offenders' average sentences increased from 62 months to 82 months. Second, the average time served in prison rose from 15 months to 24. Nearly the entire increase came at the expense of drug offenders, whose average time served rose from 22 months to 33 months, up an average of 50%. Clearly, changes in federal drug-law policies and new sentencing laws contributed to the building boom in federal prison facilities described in Chapter 5.

State Prisoners

Given 51 different reporting systems and nearly 1,400 adult institutions, a completely accurate picture of the nation's nonfederal inmates eludes us. We do have some informative fragments, however. For example, like federal inmates, nearly all state prisoners are male. (See Figure 6.3.) Almost half of all state prisoners are non-Hispanic African-Americans. This latter generalization holds equally true for male and female state prison inmates.

In 1991 the average state prison inmate was a male in his mid-30s.[3] More than 55% had never been married, and about 18% each were divorced or

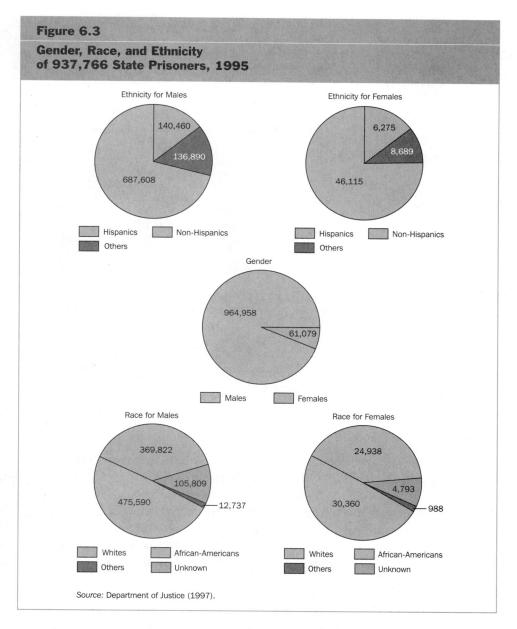

Figure 6.3

Gender, Race, and Ethnicity of 937,766 State Prisoners, 1995

Ethnicity for Males

140,460
136,890
687,608

Hispanics   Non-Hispanics
Others

Ethnicity for Females

6,275
8,689
46,115

Hispanics   Non-Hispanics
Others

Gender

964,958
61,079

Males   Females

Race for Males

369,822
105,809
475,590
12,737

Whites   African-Americans
Others   Unknown

Race for Females

24,938
4,793
30,360
988

Whites   African-Americans
Others   Unknown

Source: Department of Justice (1997).

married. The median educational level was 12 years. About 4% were citizens of another country, a percentage far below that observed for federal inmates. Of the state inmates 50% reported drug use in the month before their current offense; nearly 33% used drugs at the time of his or her arrest for the current offense.

Figure 6.4 summarizes the proportion of state prisoners convicted of the four classes of crimes. The absolute number of offenses in these categories

Figure 6.4

State Prisoners by Most Serious Offense, 1980, 1985, 1990, 1995

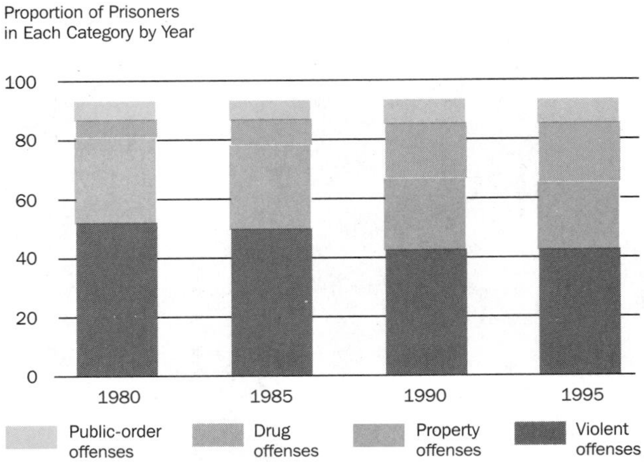

Proportion of Prisoners
in Each Category by Year

	1980	1985	1990	1995
Violent offenses	173,300	246,200	313,600	457,600
Property offenses	89,300	140,100	173,700	237,400
Drug offenses	19,000	38,900	148,600	224,900
Public-order offenses	12,400	23,000	45,500	66,100

Source: Bureau of Justice Statistics (1997a).

rose substantially between 1980 and 1995, increasing from 294,000 to nearly 1 million. In 1980 and 1985, a violent crime was the most serious offense for about one-half of all state prisoners. By 1990 and, again in 1995, drug and property crimes were the most serious, in roughly equal proportions, for nearly one-half of the prison inmates. As with the federal system, the increase for drug offenders was the most dramatic, increasing manyfold. The proportion of prisoners convicted of public-order offenses has changed little since 1980.

The fastest-growing segment of the nation's prison population is Hispanic.[4] Figure 6.5 reveals the per-capita rates for all male inmates, federal and state. In spite of disproportionate increases in Hispanic inmates, their per-capita rate is about one-third that of African-Americans, *but nearly equal to the rate for African-American males in 1980.* The estimated per-capita incarceration rate for African-Americans was seven times that of whites. We return to the question of these disparities in Chapter 11. Write down your speculations or informed guesses and compare them to our answers.

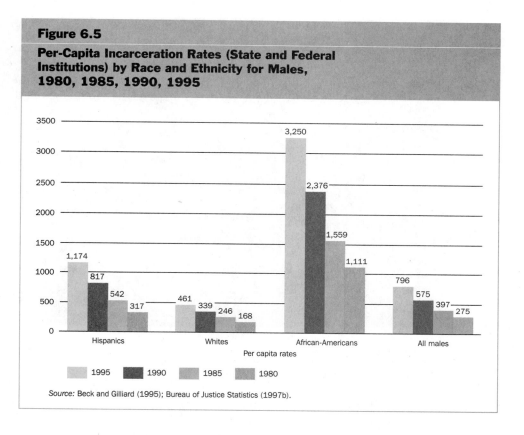

Figure 6.5

Per-Capita Incarceration Rates (State and Federal Institutions) by Race and Ethnicity for Males, 1980, 1985, 1990, 1995

Per capita rates

1995 ▮ 1990 ▮ 1985 ▮ 1980

Source: Beck and Gilliard (1995); Bureau of Justice Statistics (1997b).

Female Prisoners

In 1991 the average female prison inmate was, at 31 years old, slightly younger than her male counterpart.[5] She was typically a never-married, African-American with some high school education. Two-thirds of the women had at least one child less than 18 years of age. More than half of the female prisoners were unemployed at the time of their arrest, as compared to less than one-third of the male inmates.

Substance use played an important role in the lives of female prisoners. Almost half reported that they committed their current offense under the influence of drugs or alcohol. More than half had been using drugs before prison. Nearly 4 female inmates in 10 reported daily drug use in the month before arrest. All these figures are equal to or higher than those for male prisoners.

In general, women's sentences are shorter than men's. For example, 4 in 10 females had a maximum sentence of less than five years, compared to about one-quarter of the male prisoners. About one-quarter faced 15 years or more, including life in prison or the death penalty, compared to more than one-third of the males. These sentencing disparities are at least partly due to differences in offense patterns. "Women were more likely than men to be in

Female inmates are increasingly becoming a part of the nation's prison population. These women are part of a boot camp style program operated at the Federal Intensive Confinement Center for Women in Bryan, Texas.

prison for drug and property offenses, which had shorter average sentences than violent offenses" (Snell 1994, 4).

By the mid-1990s, the rate of increase for females was nearly twice that for males (Mumola and Beck 1997, 5). Women represented a different problem in the 1990s than ever before. In the 1980s, the proportion of women whose most serious crimes were violent offenses decreased by 25%, but drug-offense arrests increased 150%.[6] By the early 1990s, about 6 of 10 females were property or drug offenders, and another one-third violent criminals.

Jail Inmate Characteristics

Jails house men and women, adults and juveniles. Each of these subpopulations must, by law and custom, be segregated from each other by sight and sound. For juveniles, the entrance to their facility should be different from that used by adults, even if the buildings adjoin.[7] In addition, most jails house up to seven different types of inmates: (1) pretrial detainees, awaiting trial on charges ranging from minor misdemeanors to the most serious felonies; (2) convicted misdemeanants, serving their time in the local jail, although some may be incarcerated at the "county farm" rather than the downtown jail; (3) prison-bound felons, residing temporarily in the local jail before trans-

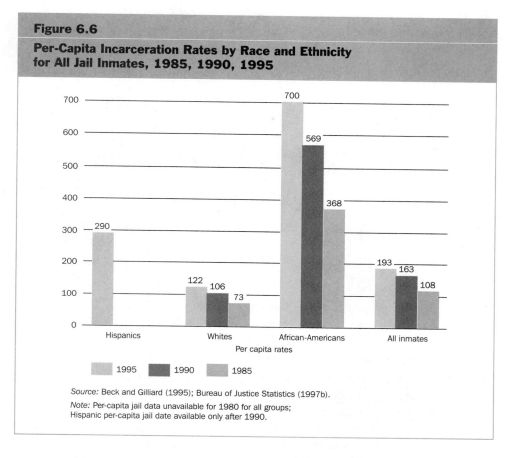

Figure 6.6

Per-Capita Incarceration Rates by Race and Ethnicity for All Jail Inmates, 1985, 1990, 1995

Source: Beck and Gilliard (1995); Bureau of Justice Statistics (1997b).

Note: Per-capita jail data unavailable for 1980 for all groups; Hispanic per-capita jail date available only after 1990.

fer to a prison or penitentiary; (4) appellate-case convicted felons, awaiting their day in court in a jail close to the appellate court; (5) alleged probation or parole violators, pending hearings on the charges; (6) detainees, awaiting a decision to charge on alleged crimes or transfer to other jurisdictions on outstanding warrants but in either case considered flight risks; and (7) material witnesses, being "protected" by the authorities because of threats against their health and well-being (these individuals are not usually kept in the same part of the jail as the "criminal" inmates). About one-half of all jail inmates are unconvicted (which is not necessarily to say innocent) of any crime.[8]

On any given day in 1995 the nation's jails held roughly 500,000 inmates.[9] This figure translates to a per-capita rate of 193 jail inmates for every 100,000 residents, a rate that is nearly twice that reported in 1985. (See Figure 6.6.) About 90% of jail inmates were males. The per-capita incarceration rate for Blacks was six times that for Whites. As reflected in Figure 6.7, non-Hispanic Blacks and Whites each accounted for roughly equal shares of 80% of the jail population. The next largest category of jail inmates was Hispanic, whose per-capita rate was midway between those reported for

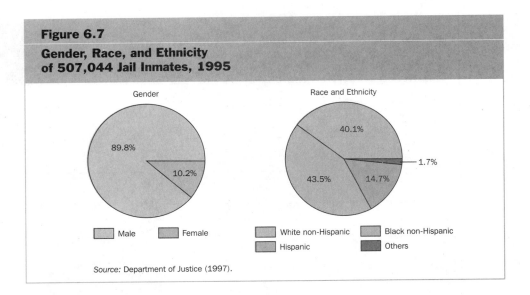

Figure 6.7

Gender, Race, and Ethnicity of 507,044 Jail Inmates, 1995

Gender

89.8%

10.2%

Male   Female

Race and Ethnicity

40.1%

1.7%

43.5%   14.7%

White non-Hispanic   Black non-Hispanic

Hispanic   Others

Source: Department of Justice (1997).

non-Hispanic Blacks and Whites. Other races—mainly Asians, Pacific Islanders, and Alaskan Natives—accounted for the remainder.

Gender and Jail Inmates

In 1995, nearly 56,000 women resided in jail, or more than 10% of the entire adult jail population. We find four distinct differences in the sociolegal characteristics of female and male jail inmates.[10] First, more female jail inmates than males were first-time offenders (33% versus 20%). Second, women prisoners were far more likely than men to report welfare income (30% versus 8%). Third, 66% of the female jail inmates stood accused of either drug offenses or property offenses as the most serious charge. Male jail inmates, by contrast, faced a wider range of offenses. Fourth, drugs and alcohol also played major roles in the women's criminal activities, roles that exceeded those reported for male jail inmates. Not only were the women's overall levels of drug involvement higher, but their reported drug use during the commission of the present offense was also higher.

Federal Jail Inmates

The BOP operates seven facilities that are essentially jails. As of 1994, the Metropolitan Correctional Centers/Detention Centers (MCC/MDC) held 6,000 persons. Nearly twice that number resided in local jails. As with most local jail inmates, roughly one-half of the federal "jail" inmates were awaiting either adjudication or serving sentences of one year or less (Perkins, Stephan, and Beck 1995, 12). As is true in most jails, more than 9 of 10 federal jail detainees were men. Nearly three-quarters of the inmates were White, with

most of the rest (one-fourth) African-American. Asians, Pacific I:
American Indians, and Alaskan Natives together accounted for t

Juvenile Jail Inmates

The nation's jails held almost 7,000 juveniles in 1994 (Perkins, S........, ...
Beck 1995, 3). Besides 1,586 individuals classified as juvenile delinquents,
another 5,139 juveniles held in jails were awaiting trial as adults or had been
convicted as adults (Perkins, Stephan, and Beck 1995, 3).[11] The nation's public and private juvenile detention facilities held another 96,000 inmates.

Prison and Jail Culture

Donald Clemmer (1958) gave penologists a new way of thinking about prison
inmates. The ideas he proposed have general applicability to all total institutions dedicated to the custody and control of society's law violators. Clemmer
was once a correctional officer at Menard, a 2,300-inmate Illinois penitentiary. Based on these experiences and other observations, he described a
prison community in his classic study *The Prison Community*, first published
in 1940. He also identified the process of becoming a member of this community as prisonization. **Prisonization** occurs when prison inmates "take on in
greater or less degree the folkways, mores, customs, and general culture of
the penitentiary" (Clemmer 1958, 299).

The prison community, Clemmer believed, is not one highly integrated
body of men or women (or rarely both men and women). Some prisoners are
more deeply committed and involved than others. According to Clemmer
(1958, 302), prisonization was highest among inmates who possessed certain
characteristics. That is, the most highly prisonized inmates (1) had a long
sentence, (2) exhibited unstable personalities originating in preprison life,
(3) lacked positive relations outside the prison walls, (4) revealed a readiness
and capacity for integration into the inmate subculture, (5) accepted completely an inmate code as a reflection of the inmate subculture's norms and
values, (6) lived in the same cell or in close proximity with others of like persuasion, and (7) participated in gambling and abnormal sexual conduct.

Characteristics of the Inmate Subculture

A subculture is a social group that exhibits unique characteristics, including
norms, rules, regulations, and the like, sufficient to distinguish it from others
within the surrounding society. However, this group differs in some significant
ways from the dominant group. The lifestyle, personal or group goals, norms,
ideals, perspectives, and orientations of subcultural adherents often place
them in conflict with the dominant group.

In the present context, within any given prison (or jail) there exists a parallel society, what Clemmer called the prison community. This community, or

prison subculture, is negativistic, with its social venom directed equally at the prison staff and the free society. Whatever prison authorities or society values, the prison subculture, by definition, devalues.

Inmates new to prison life are **"fish,"** a term that signifies their low and easily exploited status in the subculture. Upon their arrival more experienced inmates may take them aside and explain "the facts of prison life." If the fish are weak or fail to understand the code's lessons, other inmates will exploit them. If they are strong or learn to use the system to their own benefit, they may rise to positions of leadership in the subculture. Most inmates in the prison community simply try to stay out of trouble and do their own time.

The Inmate Code

The **inmate code** is the normative expectations of the prison subculture. Lloyd Ohlin (1956) provided a clear understanding of the inmate code's dos and don'ts:

> The [inmate] code represents an organization of criminal values in clear cut opposition to the values of conventional society, and to prison officials as representatives of that society. The main tenet of this code forbids any type of support or nonexploitative liaison with prison officials. It seeks to confer status and prestige on those inmates who stand in opposition to the administration. . . . These criminal beliefs and attitudes place a high premium on physical violence and strength, on exploitative sex relations, and predatory attitudes toward money and property. They place a strong emphasis on in-group loyalty and solidarity and on aggressive and exploitative relationships with conventionally oriented out-groups.

Box 6.1 presents the basic tenets of the inmate code.

Violators of the code receive swift and severe justice. Proof beyond a reasonable doubt is not a tenet of the inmate justice system. Suspicion may be enough to set the inmate "wheels of justice" in action. The code has few penalty provisions. Most code violations result in corporal punishment or death. The guilty enjoy no appeals process. If an inmate believed that a provision of the inmate code had been violated, then that person was generally free to act as he or she saw fit. As in most tribal-law communities (see Chapter 2), it was always possible that someone associated with the alleged norm violator would seek retribution or retaliation. Given the significance attached to physical prowess by inmates, many prisoners form extensive protective alliances in the interest of self-preservation.

Inmate Role Types and Prison-Adaptive Behavior Modes

What kind of student are you? How do you think other students or your professors describe you to each other? Do you have a life outside the college or university setting? The answers to these questions help define who you are on

Box 6.1

Tenets of the Inmate Code

Don't Interfere with Inmate Interests
- Never rat on a con.
- Don't be nosy.
- Be loyal to your class—the cons.

Don't Lose Your Head
- Play it cool and do your own time.

Don't Exploit Inmates
- Don't break your word.
- Don't steal from the cons.
- Don't sell favors.
- Don't be a racketeer.
- Don't welsh on debts.

Don't Weaken
- Don't whine.
- Don't cop out (cry guilty).
- Don't suck around (looking for special privileges from authorities).
- Be tough, be a man.
- Don't be a sucker.
- Be sharp.

Source: Sykes and Messinger (1960).

and off campus. Similar questions about prison and jail inmates define who they are in their unique social setting. Joseph Fishman (1934) provided an early glimpse into the life of prison inmates. In *Sex in Prison,* Fishman provided a rich tapestry of images about a system of social arrangements he called the prison subculture. The language of the inmates was unique, forming an argot unlike that found outside the prison walls. Much of this language described relationships between inmates, including sexual ones.

In 1944, Clarence Schrag suggested that inmates exhibited at least four different roles:

- **Right guys** are those rare inmates who follow all of the precepts of the inmate code. The basic orientation of this inmate type is antisocial, adding status to the right guys. Right guys are, by definition, the prototype prisoner as defined by the inmate code: They are the most prisonized of all inmates.

- **Con-politicians** are inmates with money and influence, the latter with both guards and other inmates. Moreover, they can obtain, through skill and manipulation, virtually any good or service wanted by those inmates with enough money to pay. These inmates are pseudosocial, pretending to be prosocial, while engaged in antisocial conduct.

- **Outlaws** are inmates whose reliance on force and physical violence allowed them to obtain what they wanted from other, more easily exploited inmates. Given the exploitation found in prisons and jails, some inmates need outlaws. Most inmates avoided them.

- **Square Johns** are inmates who follow the prison's official rules, participate in institutional programming, and generally ignore many essential provisions of the inmate code, except perhaps the prohibition of **"snitching"** on fellow inmates. As such, square Johns are low on the prison subculture status hierarchy. In spite of being convicts, these individuals are basically prosocial; they are the least prisonized of Schrag's role types.

Later studies of inmate roles added several new wrinkles. For example, Sykes and Messinger (1960) divided Schrag's outlaws into the **gorillas,** extremely predatory inmates, bent on exploiting other inmates, and the **toughs,** highly volatile and aggressive inmates who fight for any reason. Schrag's con-politicians are similar to Sykes and Messinger's **merchants (peddlers).** Sykes and Messinger also identified several low-status members of the inmate subculture beyond the square John. **Weaklings (weak sisters)** are inmates who are not tough and are unable to withstand the rigors of prison life. **Rapos (innocents)** maintain their innocence, a source of irritation to many other inmates. Finally, **rats (squealers)** are inmates who betray other inmates to the staff and violate one of the most sacred tenets of the inmate code.

Sykes and Messinger (1960) also identified a series of inmate types based on sex roles adopted by prisoners. **Wolves** were predatory inmates who provided protection for weak inmates in return for sexual favors. **Fags** were homosexual inmates who enjoyed the passive role associated with this lifestyle orientation. Finally, **punks** were otherwise heterosexual inmates coerced into a passive homosexual role, often by wolves. Although this research is nearly 40 years old, these inmate-created terms—or very similar ones—are still used by prisoners. (Box 6.2 presents further information on the sex life of male inmates.)

Besides specific role adaptations within the prison culture, inmates may also engage in three strategies, or adaptive behavior modes, to survive institutional life (Irwin 1970). "Not all inmates can be classified neatly by these adaptive styles. Some vacillate from one to another, and others appear to be following two or three simultaneously" (Irwin 1970, 68). At some time or another, however, nearly all inmates exhibit one or more of three strategies for adapting to prison life. First, there is **"doing time,"** which means that the inmates view the prison experience as a "temporary break in their careers, one which they take in stride" (Irwin 1970, 69). Their main task boils down to keeping busy, passing time, making life as palatable as possible, and keeping out of trouble. Professional criminals, including thieves and other property offenders, commonly practice "doing time."

Second, some inmates fail to view the outside world as home. They are **"jailing,"** meaning that as inmates they seek positions of power and authority, usually as merchants, con-politicians, or possibly as gorillas or toughs (Irwin 1970, 74). Many jailing inmates literally have been raised in an institutional setting since childhood. Prison or jail is where they feel comfortable.[12]

Finally, some inmates "get with a program" and gain as much personal improvement as they can from within the prison; they are said to be **gleaning** (Irwin 1970, 76). Gleaning may start small, such as learning to read. However,

A major concern in any correctional institution is to provide meaningful treatment programs. Many inmates come to prison with educational deficiencies, and prisons must strive to overcome those deficiencies. One of the major thrusts of educational programming is providing GED classes for those inmates.

such activities expand quickly, as they become their own reward, branching into areas such as vocational training, personal growth and enrichment, and advanced educational programs. Even physical activities such as weightlifting and body shaping can be considered as a form of gleaning: the ultimate goal is to improve the individual (Irwin 1970, 78).

Origins of Inmate Social Organization

Clemmer's explanation of the depth of an inmate's movement into the prison subculture provides several clues as to prisonization's origins. He believed that much of what we see in prison represents inmates' responses to incarceration. However, prisoners bring certain ways of acting with them into prison. As other researchers examined prison role types and the general prison social system, two arguments emerged to explain what they found: the prison deprivations and cultural importation hypotheses.

Clemmer (1951, 313, 319), when responding to questions about the origin of the prison social system, observed that "men who come to prison are not greatly different from those already there. . . . Most persons admitted to prison already possess 'criminality' in various degrees." Lloyd McCorkle and Richard Korn (1954) provided an early statement of the internal forces—the deprivations associated with prison life—that shaped the inmate subculture.

They concluded that the inmate subculture is isolated from any socially beneficial contacts with the outside world. Prison prevents inmates from forming relationships with the members of the noncriminal world. Moreover, it also requires that they cope with the general theme of social rejection (McCorkle and Korn 1954, 88). According to this position, called the **deprivation perspective** on prisonization, a major function of the inmate subculture and its normative system is to prevent social rejection from being internalized and converted into self-rejection. The presence of an inmate subculture "permits the inmate to reject his rejector rather than himself" (McCorkle and Korn 1954, 88).

Gresham Sykes (1958) described the **pains of imprisonment** felt by residents of total institutions. These pains or common problems include the deprivation of liberty, goods and services, heterosexual relationships, autonomy or freedom of movement, and security (Sykes 1958, 65–78). However, it was through the work of Sykes and Sheldon Messinger (1960) that the collective inmate response to these pains became known as **solidary opposition.** They proposed that inmates seek to neutralize partially the consequences of imprisonment by a state of mutual solidarity. As the inmates move in "the direction of solidarity, as demanded by the inmate code, the pains of imprisonment become less severe" (Sykes and Messinger 1960, 11).

Clemmer's original observations about the prison community left the door open for an alternative hypothesis. He suggested that inmates did not enter prison completely without values or prior experiences. The idea that inmates bring certain orientations with them into the prison took shape as the **cultural importation hypothesis.** John Irwin and Donald Cressey (1962) observed that the inmate culture has beliefs, attitudes, and lifestyles with obvious parallels to life outside prisons, especially life on the high-crime streets of the nation's inner cities. Research on the prison community generally supports the idea that they import the inmate code and subculture into the prison. For example, Charles Wellford (1967) also suggested that the deprivation hypothesis has overlooked the obvious relationship between prior activities and commitment to the inmate code. Prior involvement in the "criminalistic subculture" was the key to understanding prisonization (Wellford 1967, 203). Hugh Cline (1968), in a study of prisonization in 15 different Scandinavian prisons, failed to find support for the deprivation hypothesis. He reported that the most antisocial climates are present in institutions with inmates who collectively have greater experiences in crime.

So what is more important? Does the negativism of the inmate social system and its code derive from street values? Or are they a response to the rigors of prison life? Charles Thomas (1970) believes that integrating both perspectives into a single model provides a more inclusive way of viewing prisonization. The explanations offered by the deprivation hypothesis cannot adequately explain the inmate subculture. For its part, the importation hypothesis includes more than just what the inmates bring with them.

A thorough model includes more than traditional deprivation and importation factors. It adds such elements as the frequency and quality of inmate contacts with extraprison individuals and groups. Also important is the extent to which the self-perceived stigmatization negatively impacts the inmates' future life outside prison. Lastly, a comprehensive model incorporates the degree to which prison interrupts extraprison networks of supportive relationships with friends and family. The inclusive model describes a social environment in which "imported" aspects of prisonization interact with imprisonment pains. It accents "a broader variety of influences that provide a more sophisticated understanding of why a particular type of subcultural system emerges within so many prisons and why inmates vary in their degree of integration into that system" (Thomas and Petersen 1977, 55).

Men's versus Women's Prison Culture

In Chapter 5, we looked at how the prisons for men and women are different. In this chapter we related how the inmate populations are different. One important question remains unanswered: How are the prison communities in women's prisons different from those found in men's prisons?

The prison communities of women's prisons and those found in prisons for men are very similar. For example, prisonization exists in both. The deprivations of incarceration—the pains of imprisonment—impact women just as intensely as they do men. Women also suffer deprivations not reported for men, including the loss of their children (Baunach 1985; Smart 1976b).[13] Women also display acute needs for emotional support in prison, particularly the need to establish emotional relationships with other women (Giallambardo 1966; Ward and Kassebaum 1965). Female prison inmates are far less "criminalized" than their male counterparts (Bowker 1981, 410). Female offenders have traditionally committed less serious offenses and have far less extensive involvement in criminal subcultures outside of prison. Cut off from families—including their own children—and friends, women far more than men appear to experience feelings of helplessness, powerlessness, dependency, and, ultimately, despair (Mahan 1984, 381; see also Gibson 1976, 99). Not surprisingly, then, researchers report the existence of both an inmate code and role adaptations in women's prisons (Giallambardo 1966; Mahan 1984). The female inmates' roles, like those found in men's prisons, center on the exercise of raw power, the delivery of goods and services, and sexual relationships (Giallambardo 1966; Simmons 1975). (Box 6.2 presents further information on female inmates' sexual lives in prison.) Women's prisons too have their share of snitches and squares (Heffernan 1972), and politicians and outlaws (Simmons 1975).

The social worlds found in men's and women's prisons exhibit at least two key differences. First, the social climate of the average women's prison is, in comparison to even a medium-security men's prison, far less tense; the institutions are far less violent.[14] Most female prisoners come to prison because of

Box 6.2

Sex and Prison Life

In the 1930s, Fishman focused on sex and related its significance to the prison subculture. Subsequent researchers have provided even greater insights into the role sex plays in everyday prison life. For example, sex in men's prisons and jails is a consensual act between parties, an economic exchange identical to prostitution in the free world, or a forced act of violence between an aggressor and a victim, a form of rape. More recently, Daniel Lockwood observed that even a consensual act may involve coercion if one inmate gives another three choices: "fight, flee, or fuck." An inmate may form a sexual liaison as a basic exchange relationship: His sexual partner, in this case usually more physically powerful or at least more prone to the use of violence, protects him from other inmates in exchange for sex. Forced sex may show power and domination. It also helps to establish one's "machismo" or masculinity in relationship to the weaker inmate. Prison prostitutes may "trick" for survival. For example, at Louisiana's Anglo Prison in the late 1970s and early 1980s, a well-developed system of pimps sold the sexual services of feminine-looking inmates called "gal-boys." Inmates may also achieve status from their work as male prostitutes. As a new prostitute at a southeastern boys' training school observed to one of the authors: "Now the other guys pay attention to me. I've got all the smokes (cigarettes) and lighters (an important commodity on the inmate economic system) I want."

In contrast, Rose Giallambardo, Esther Heffernan, and Alice Propper independently report that for the most part homosexual liaisons among women inmates are voluntary, not coerced or forced. A term such as "stud," "butch," or "pimp" defines the masculine roles, whereas "femme," "broad," or "fox" is used for the feminine roles. Prostitution occurs in women's prisons, as "chippies" or "tricks" sell themselves to studs. Giallambardo (1966) observed that role switching, that is, changing from a stud to a femme, is common. Propper noted that these liaisons and extended families give female inmates "security, companionship, affection, attention, status, prestige and acceptance" (p. 155).

Sources: Bowker (1980); Fishman (1934); Giallambardo (1966); Heffernan (1972); Lockwood (1980); Propper (1981); Scacco (1982).

a drug offense or property crime. Far fewer are violent personal offenders. Therefore, women's prisons have a less criminalized inmate population than that found in men's prisons (Welch 1996b, 360). Second, the functions served by the inmate subculture in prisons for men and women are different. For example, the inmate subculture in men's prisons exists largely to protect inmates from each other. The subculture also helps neutralize the rejection associated with incarceration, and provides a buffer between inmates and staff. In prisons for women, the subculture exists for these reasons plus an additional one: The subculture provides female inmates with emotional support (Pollock-Byrne 1990, 59–63; Welch 1996b, 360). One abiding characteristic of women's prison is the existence of extended **"play families"** in women's prisons, including spouses, children, parents, siblings, and grandparents (Giallambardo 1966; Ward and Kassebaum 1965). Female inmates assume the various roles; in some instances, the inmates prepare official-looking adoption, wedding, and even divorce documents. The primary purpose of these families is emotional support.

Prison Culture in the 1990s and Beyond

Does the code operate in contemporary prisons? Does the prison subculture exhibit the same characteristics in the 1990s that it did in the 1940s and 1950s? Prison communities today appear to operate according to the principles of a negativistic code, one very similar to that revealed in the works of Clemmer, Sykes, and others. Whether the code supports a solidary inmate subculture is quite a different matter. Irwin (1980) suggests that the solidary inmate subculture has fragmented into competing groups based largely on race and ethnicity. Leo Carroll's (1974) study of race relations in a Rhode Island maximum-security prison supports this view. Carroll (1974, 160, 162, 169) observed that even after integration inmates resegregated themselves in their living arrangements, in the prison theater, and even in the gym area. James Jacobs (1977) described how African-American street gangs gained a foothold and expanded their power base in Stateville (Illinois) Prison. Eventually, Chicago gangs, including the Blackstone Rangers, Vice Lords, and Devil's Disciples, took over the convict world at Stateville. White and Hispanic gangs extended their reach into Stateville, although, owing to their smaller numbers, they had far less influence than the African-American gangs. In this manner, and at prisons across the nation, loyalty to the "inmate class" changed to loyalty to one's race, ethnic group, clique, or gang.

The changes in the inmate community are not limited to Illinois and Rhode Island. Irwin and Austin (1993, 74) note that "prison populations have become much more racially heterogeneous and divided, and the old prison leaders have lost control over other prisoners." The inmate code may be alive and well, but the object of inmate loyalty has changed. Inmate relationships have become far less predictable. Right guys and older, experienced inmates no longer play a major role in settling inmate disputes. One consequence of these shifting loyalties is an increase in prison violence.

Violence in Correctional Institutions

Violence in the nation's correctional institutions takes many forms. Two major forms are of particular interest to prisoners, staff, and the public at large: inmate-initiated victimizations and riots or related disturbances, each having several subtypes.

Inmate-Initiated Victimizations

The three primary types of inmate-initiated victimizations are physical violence, psychological victimization, and economic victimization. **Physical violence** chiefly translates into deaths, injuries, and other assaults. The number of inmate deaths is a matter of public record. For example, in 1995, the nation's state prisons reported 3,358 inmate deaths.[15] Nearly all were males whose deaths resulted from an unspecified illness or natural causes,

Careers in Contemporary Corrections

Correctional Counselors

In both institutional and community-based correctional agencies some individuals are hired to do diagnostic and counseling work. **Correctional counselors** typically will operate at one of two levels of responsibility within correctional institutions. First, counselors will function within a number of treatment environments in prisons. Some of these counselors will do initial screening and psychological testing of inmates to determine the security classification and the most important treatment programs. Occasionally these positions are considered **psychological technicians or diagnosticians.**

These individuals also may be responsible for conducting group and individual counseling sessions in areas such as substance abuse, sex offending, anger management, and similar areas. For example, in the New Mexico Department of Corrections these people are listed as **classification officers,** and in the U.S. Bureau of Prisons they are called **case managers.**

At a slightly higher level, in many institutions there will be a **clinical psychologist** who is responsible for supervising counselors and for approving all treatment plans. The degree of responsibility and title for these individuals will vary according to the expected levels of education and experience.

Counselors in prisons can expect to make about the same, or slightly more, than probation and parole officers (typically these are in the range of $20,000–$30,000 for initial appointment, up to $30,000–$45,000 for the upper end of the range). Clinical psychologists may be among the highest paid nonadministrative workers in a prison. The demands of the job and the qualifications expected necessitate higher than average salaries.

Workloads for counselors and psychologists will vary depending on their specific assignments and the size of the unit or facility in which they work. In prisons—in contrast to community-based corrections—caseloads may be smaller, but the clients may have more serious treatment needs.

This is especially true for the large number of inmates with long-term substance abuse problems. Counselors in prisons also have to deal with inmates who are diagnosed as HIV-positive and those who have gone on to develop AIDS.

The real challenge to the correctional counselor's job may not be related so much to the volume of work, but rather to dealing with client failure—either real or perceived. Also, much like the emotional intensity experienced by probation and parole officers, correctional counselors also are plagued by stress and job burnout.

When the issue of educational requirements is mentioned in relation to correctional careers, students typically find that positions such as psychologist and counselor require some of the highest educational levels in the corrections field. For example, at a minimum counselors normally will be required to possess a master's degree. Sometimes agencies specify a particular subject area, but typically the choices are among counseling, psychology, social work, and criminal justice. Occasionally these positions also may require either full-time related job or internship experience. Psychologists may be required to possess a Psy.D., Ph.D., or Ed.D. or other appropriate professional degree. After completion of their doctoral work, or as part of the work required toward the degree, these individuals may have to complete a supervised clinical internship often lasting a year or more.

One of the most important aspects of any job is the long-term promotion potential. In the area of counseling of clinical psychology it is difficult to provide a complete picture of promotion possibilities. Many of the positions for psychologists are in the nonheirarchical divisions of prisons. Therefore, there may be additional pay grades for Psychologist II and Psychologist III, but there are not necessarily supervisory or management responsibilities associated with these job titles. In fact, for those individuals who have started their careers as case managers, or some similar title,

---

Careers in Contemporary Corrections *(continued)*

Correctional Counselors

promotion potential may be severely limited unless they are willing to relocate to another facility or move into positions with less direct inmate contact such as chief of classification or associate warden for programming.

Because psychologists typically are considered "professional" personnel—much like doctors, nurses, dentists, and pharmacists—they often are chosen based on an evaluation of their credentials rather than on a written entrance examination. However, in some positions they may be required to hold an appropriate professional license or to complete requirements for state licensing within a specified period of time.

Psychologists and counselors routinely are subjected to background checks and

possibly to polygraph examinations as well, if this is required of corrections employees generally. At this level they may be subjected to the routine investigations conducted on all job applicants to verify the truthfulness of their applications and to detect any glaring problems of a legal or personal nature.

Although treatment and rehabilitation efforts generally have been de-emphasized by some correctional organizations, these issues are far from dead. As long as there are correctional agencies, particularly secure care institutions, there will be a need for correctional psychologists and counselors.

Sources: DeLucia and Doyle (1994); Williamson (1990).

---

complications caused by AIDS, suicides, accidental injuries, and executions. After illness or natural causes, the cause of death for most male inmates was (unspecified) by the agency. Only 67 died of injuries caused by another inmate. Not one of the 73 female prisoners died of injuries suffered at the hands of another inmate. Again, illness or natural causes and AIDS accounted for 5 in 6 of the deaths, with most of the rest classified as "unspecified causes." The total number of prison deaths is about what we would expect in a population of this size (Clear and Cole 1990, 376).

Jail deaths present a different picture.[16] In 1993, locally administered jails reported 647 deaths, roughly one-third the number observed for the prisons.[17] As in prisons, more than one-half of these inmates died of natural causes or AIDS.[18] Jailhouse suicide, however, is the second leading cause of jail deaths, accounting for more than one-third of all jail deaths. In other words, twice as many people commit suicide in jail as in prison, although prisons held twice as many people as jails. Except for suicide, the number of jail deaths is not higher than we would expect given the number of people exposed to the risks of confinement in jails (Winfree 1987, 1988).

Inmates are both the victims of assaults and the perpetrators; inmates also victimize prison and jail guards.[19] Prison-based statistics on both types of assaults exist, but we must interpret them with caution.[20] For example, state prison systems in 42 states and the District of Columbia reported approximately 4,000 assaults on staff in 1991.[21] Five states reported that this information was not available, and another 12 reported between 0 and 9

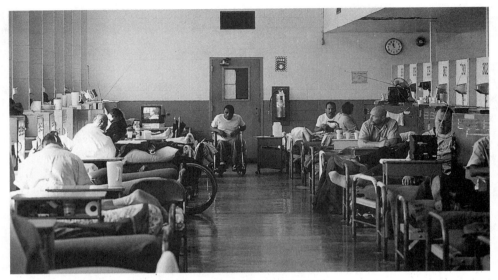

Older and medically infirmed individuals are becoming a larger part of our prison population. This group of inmates is housed in the medical ward at the Chino Prison in California.

inmate-on-guard assaults, figures so low as to lack credibility. Given the wide range, from a low of 0 (Montana and Wyoming) to a high of 995 (New York), an average assault rate would be meaningless. Roughly one-half of the 38 contributing jurisdictions report fewer than 50 assaults a year.

Even when the numbers are high, the assault statistics are suspect. For example, the State of Texas employs more than 20,000 correctional officers and reported 352 staff assaults in 1993.[22] New York State also employs about 20,000 correctional officers and reported 995 staff assaults. The BOP reported 906 assaults among its 11,000 correctional officers. Is the New York State prison system one-third as safe as the Texas system? Is the federal prison system twice as dangerous as the New York State system? In all likelihood, the answer to both questions is no. Rather, assault figures for the nation's prisons are woefully inaccurate and underreported.

Further evidence of the underreporting of violence in prison comes from inmate-on-inmate assaults. In 1993, inmates reported 7,500 such assaults. Generally, those states that failed to keep staff assault statistics also failed to report any inmate assaults. Three states—Connecticut, Florida, and New York—reported more than one-half of all inmate assaults. Yet, these states held only 14% of the nation's total prison population. Rather than being very violent, these three states, compared to most others, may have far better mechanisms for reporting such incidents.[23]

Psychological victimization is the threat of physical harm. Hans Toch (1976) noted that the climate of violence in prisons has no equivalent. According to Toch (1976, 47–8), "Inmates are terrorized by other inmates, and

Box 6.3

The Two Inmate Economies

Most prisons and jails support two inmate economies. The facility's store, commissary, or canteen is at the center of the **legitimate inmate economy.** Inmates have cash deposited in their accounts by friends or relatives or earn credit by their labor. They can then buy brand-name products, rather than rely solely on the prison-issue products available to them free or at nominal cost. Normally, the legitimate economy is credit based: No credit with the canteen means no sale. However, a few correctional systems allow inmates to carry small amounts of cash for purchases at the canteen.

The second economy is a **sub rosa inmate economy,** so named because it exists in secrecy, a black market outside the legitimate inmate economy. In a given year, the volume of goods and services that flow through a large prison's sub rosa economy may reach millions of dollars. After all, the sub rosa economy includes the institutional drug trade, sex trade, gambling trade, and other forms of contraband. Moreover, there is interplay between the sub rosa inmate economy and the legitimate economy of prisons and jails. A pack of cigarettes may cost only a couple of dollars for an inmate with money in his or her canteen account. That same pack of cigarettes can cost several times its retail value when purchased from an inmate merchant. Of course, the facility canteen may not extend credit, whereas the inmate merchant might—at a very high interest rate.

Prison administrators often view the sub rosa economy as a necessary evil. The drugs and other contraband it introduces into the institution may reduce the tensions and frustrations associated with institutional life. Imagine the public relations problems if the correctional administration went into the business of providing what is now contraband.

Source: Kalinich (1980); see also Kalinich (1996); Santos (1996).

spend years in fear of harm. Some inmates request segregation, others lock themselves in, and some are hermits by choice."

Overcrowding alone may not induce victimization (Gaes and McGuire 1985). Inmates are different from laboratory rats confined in an overcrowded cage. The latter will, when the number gets too high, turn cannibal and eat their way to a more manageable number. Nonetheless, the ability of individual inmates to cope with prison or jail is, in Toch's (1985, 66) words, "challenged by every consequence of crowding." For this form of violence, no adequate preventive measures exist. As we observed in our discussion of the prison community, once inmates learn the how and who of "winning through intimidation," preventing the exploitation of a given inmate is very difficult.

Given the complexities of the underground inmate economy detailed in Box 6.3, **economic victimizations** are equally complex. This economy provides goods and services that are in high demand, including drugs and other contraband, sex, weapons, and virtually anything else inmates might want. As in any high-volume illegal business, cash flows through the prison, itself the object of theft, robbery, extortion, and blackmail. The prison economy follows this generalization. Inmates pay exorbitant prices for the illicit goods and services, which is itself another form of victimization. Prison predators victimize them again when other inmates rob, steal, or otherwise deprive them of their possessions. The problem is clear: To whom do inmates complain when other inmates steal something they should not have in the first place?

Riots and Other Disturbances

You may wonder how prisons and jails achieve any measure of peace and civility. Prison riots, work stoppages, sit-down strikes, and similar disturbances are rare events. A **prison riot** is "a collective attempt by inmates to take over part or all of the prison. Riots may be expressive (usually spontaneous) or instrumental (planned with some goal in mind)" (Hawkins and Alpert 1989, 254). In 1993, a total of 21 correctional systems reported 186 incidents; however, only seven warranted the designation of a riot (Lillis 1994).

When prison riots and other disturbances occur they are often deadly. Many famous prison disturbances have become part of modern prison lore. For example, the 1946 Alcatraz prison takeover—called the "**Battle of Alcatraz**" by the warden at the time—was in fact a failed escape attempt. Authorities directed the combined firepower of federal prison guards, marines, and army soldiers at the prison; the Coast Guard and harbor police patrolled the waters around "the Rock" during the uprising (Johnston 1949). Residents of San Francisco watched as antitank rockets and small-arms and machine-gun fire blasted away at inmates trapped in a single cellblock, along with their guard hostages. The prison's construction largely accounts for the fact that only 3 inmates and 2 guards died, along with injuries to 1 inmate and 14 officers.

Except for the massacres of Native Americans in the late nineteenth century, the assault that ended the Attica prison uprising was the bloodiest encounter between Americans since the Civil War (New York Special Commission on Attica 1972). At the end of the four-day **Attica riot** in 1971, precipitated by guard retaliation against two inmates, 10 hostages and 29 inmates had died. Another 3 hostages, 85 inmates, and 1 state police trooper were wounded in the police assault of the prison. One guard and three inmates died at the hands of rioting inmates. One conclusion reached by all official and unofficial investigators of the riot was clear: The inmates failed to realize that to those in charge the lives of the inmate hostages were only slightly more important than the lives of the rioting inmates (Badillo and Haynes 1972; Oswald 1972; Wicker 1975).

Another deadly riot occurred in 1980 at the Penitentiary of New Mexico in Santa Fe. Over a 36-hour period, the prison became a "killing ground" as convicts rampaged through the facility. Most of the 33 dead in the **Santa Fe prison riot** were snitches or inmates against whom other prisoners had "beefs" or grudges (Bingaman 1980; Colvin 1982; Mahan 1982). Inmates also assaulted and sodomized 12 guards. An army of prison guards, state police officers, and National Guardsmen restored order in the facility. The irony of this riot is that several dead snitches warned officials about inmate discontent with the crowded conditions: The facility was at 150% of its rated capacity. Before the riot, a group of inmates initiated a suit against the State of New Mexico, citing administrative incompetence, corruption, and nepotism. After the riot, and the failure of officials to act, New Mexico entered into a consent decree empowering the federal district court to oversee the operation of all medium- and maximum-security prisons.

Social scientists like to classify events, including prison riots. For example, during the 1940s and 1950s dozens of prisons in the nation experienced what we could describe as **frustration riots** between a unified inmate subculture and prison authorities. As Irwin (1980, 63) observed about this period in penal history, "After prisoners were convinced that treatment programs did not work (by the appearance of persons who had participated fully in those treatment programs streaming back into prison for new crimes or violation of parole), hope shaded to cynicism and turned to bitterness." Inmates also responded collectively to the hopeless, brutal, and crowded living conditions found in prisons in the decade after World War II. Between 1950 and 1953, the nation experienced more than 50 prison riots (McCleery 1968, 130).

With the integration of U.S. prisons in the 1960s, race joined frustration as a cause of prison riots, but the prison community had changed. Rising Black consciousness outside the prison took on radical dimensions inside as well. The Nation of Islam (Black Muslims) emerged as a major separatist organization to confront prison officials with demands based on religious freedoms. The traditional inmate social system broke down, and the pace of prison riots picked up. In 1969 and 1970, 98 riots occurred (Reid 1981, 204). Apolitical racial conflict was a crucial factor in many if not most of what were essentially prison-based **race riots** (Garson 1972; Jacobs 1979).

By the late 1960s and early 1970s, prison inmates became increasingly politicized. The inmate "manifesto" or demands submitted to prison officials during the 1970 strike at Folsom (California) Prison merged both inmate racial and political concerns. The **political riot** came of age at Attica in 1971. Richard Hawkins and Geoffrey Alpert (1989, 257) made the following observations about the Attica riot: "The existence of a political ideology and stable inmate factions such as the Black Muslims created a united front among inmates. Inmates, organizing after the riot started, defined the uprising as a political act which bridged diverse inmate interests. The prisoners at Attica used the Folsom manifesto as their model for structuring demands."

The politicization of the prison social system did not survive long in the turbulent prison world of the 1970s. The inmate subculture was far less solidary and far more fragmented. Not surprisingly, the object of violence was less the institution or officials than it was fellow inmates (Colvin 1982). The emergent **rage riots** were spontaneous or expressive in nature, the result of inmate conflicts or efforts by authorities to disrupt inmate conflicts. They were also instrumental, specifically intended to destroy parts of the facility or "pay

Figure 6.8

Fifty Years of Prison Riots

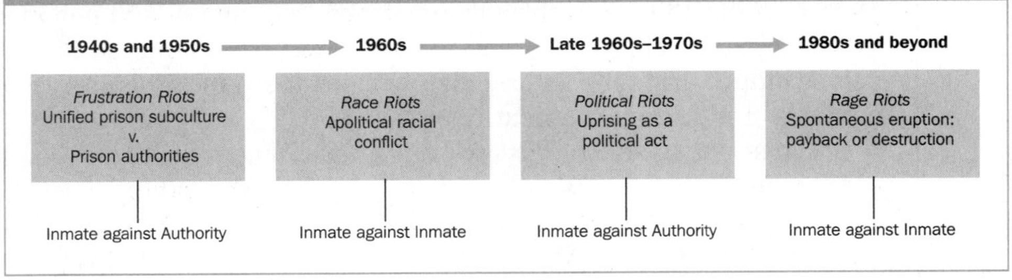

1940s and 1950s	1960s	Late 1960s–1970s	1980s and beyond
Frustration Riots Unified prison subculture v. Prison authorities	*Race Riots* Apolitical racial conflict	*Political Riots* Uprising as a political act	*Rage Riots* Spontaneous eruption: payback or destruction
Inmate against Authority	Inmate against Inmate	Inmate against Authority	Inmate against Inmate

back" or get even with certain individual inmates or groups of inmates. The archetype of the rage riot occurred at the Santa Fe Penitentiary of New Mexico in 1980.

Future prison riots may involve complex inmate motivations. Some may be over living conditions, as the Attica riot was. Others, however, may involve inmate frustrations, fears, or rage, as the Santa Fe and earlier riots did. Still others may involve multiple sets of factors, as did Folsom. Many prisons are very heterogeneous; the solidary inmate subculture is largely a thing of the past. Small groups of inmates may riot for very special and personal reasons (Hawkins and Alpert 1989, 262–65). For example, two riots occurred in 1989 among federal prison inmates at FDC-Oakdale (Louisiana) and USP-Atlanta. The rioters were Cubans facing deportation to their homeland. They rioted not for living conditions, but over legal status. Whereas these riots ended in negotiated settlements, a similar one involving Cuban detainees four years later at FCI-Talladega (Alabama) required an assault by federal authorities. The retaking of FCI-Talladega occurred without serious injuries to either hostages or detainees (Useem et al. 1995). Figure 6.8 presents a brief overview of the history of prison riots in the last half-century.

Juvenile Inmates

As we learned in Chapter 5, the nation operates both public and private correctional systems for juveniles. In order to gain an accurate picture of juvenile inmates, we must compare and contrast the inmate residential populations found in these two.[24] For example, in 1990, detention centers accounted for 82% of the admissions in the public sector, up from 78% in 1982. Training schools, ranches, camps, or farms, which often have similar emphases on security, accounted for 11% of the detainees, down from 15% in 1982. Shelters, reception/diagnostic centers, halfway houses and group homes added about 2% each. If there was a trend during this time, it was from the somewhat less secure training school, ranches, camps, and farms to the higher security detention centers.

The distribution of juvenile admissions to the private correctional system for this same period provides a different story. In 1990, 52% of the private-sector admissions were to shelters, whereas another 27% were in halfway houses or group homes. Eight years earlier, these two facility types accounted for 78% of all youths admitted to private facilities (45% in shelters and 33% in halfway houses or group homes). Detention centers, the facility of choice in the private sector, accounted for 4% of the admissions in 1982 and 8% in 1990. Another 11% of the 1990 private-sector admittees were to training school, ranches, camps, and farms, down from 16% in 1982. The rest of the private sector admissions—about 2%—were to reception and diagnostic centers, a figure that did not change between 1982 and 1990.

Although more private-sector admittees found themselves in detention centers in 1990 than in 1982, overwhelmingly the facilities of choice were less secure than was the case for the public sector. That is, more than one-half of all public-sector detainees resided in maximum-security facilities, whereas the private sector detained more than one-half of its charges at minimum-security facilities. The answers to two questions may help us understand why these two systems were and continue to be so different. First, who are the inmates? Second, what have they done?

Characteristics of Juvenile Inmates

Figure 6.9 contains a summary of the one-day counts for public and private juvenile facilities in 1985 and 1991 by race and gender. This statistic answers the question, How many youths were confined on a specific (census) day? On the census day in 1985, the majority of all public-sector inmates were non-Hispanic Whites (53%), followed by African-Americans (33%) and Hispanics (12%). Others, including Asian-Americans and Native Americans, added another 2%. By 1991, public juvenile facilities were largely minority institutions: Whites accounted for 35% of the inmates, a decrease of more than 33%; the percentage of African-Americans and Others increased by 33% each, and the percentage of Hispanics increased by 50%.

Quite a different picture emerges in Figure 6.9 for the private sector. In 1985, these institutions were largely populated by White youths; little had changed by 1991. Slightly more minority youths, especially African-Americans, resided in private-sector facilities in 1991 as compared to 1985. More than half of the private-sector detainees were White.

The two systems also differed in terms of gender distributions. That is, private facilities housed far more females in 1991 than did public-sector institutions. The proportion of females in the private sector (30%) was 2.5 times greater than that in the public sector (12%). Between 1985 and 1991, the proportion of males to females in each sector did not change.

Figure 6.9

Gender, Race, and Ethnicity of Juvenile Inmates: One-Day Counts for Public and Private Facilities, 1985 and 1991

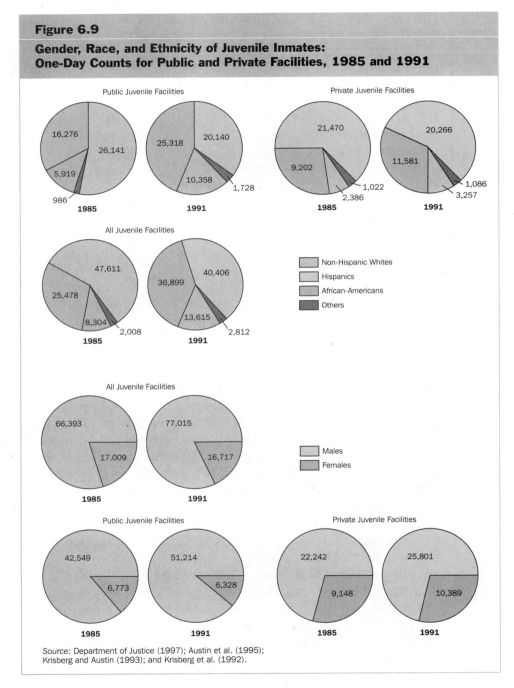

Source: Department of Justice (1997); Austin et al. (1995); Krisberg and Austin (1993); and Krisberg et al. (1992).

In terms of race, ethnicity, and gender, the two systems hold quite different inmate populations. In the public sector, the inmates are overwhelmingly minority males. In the private sector, males account for the majority of the residents, but there are far more females than in the public sector.

Offenses of Juvenile Inmates

In 1991, 95% of the 57,000-plus public-sector residents committed a delinquent offense. The most serious offense for nearly 25% was a serious property offense, including burglary, arson, larceny-theft, and motor vehicle theft. The most serious crime for another 19% was a violent crime, including murder, nonnegligent manslaughter, forcible rape, robbery, and aggravated assault. This means that 43% of the public-sector youths stood convicted of at least one Index Crime, the primary measure of crime in the United States. At the other end of the offense spectrum, only about 3% of the public-sector youthful prisoners were status offenders, having committed an act (such as running away, breaking curfew, or underage drinking) that would not be considered a crime if committed by an adult. Another 1% were nonoffenders, including those who were dependent, neglected, abused, emotionally disturbed, retarded, and other noncriminal/ nonstatus offender states. Another 1% had voluntarily committed themselves to the juvenile facilities.

Among private-sector residents in 1991, 40% of the detainees were truly delinquent youth. Only 13% of those detained in the private sector had committed a serious violent personal or property offense. Another 10% of all private-sector detainees committed a non-index property act, ranging from vandalism to forgery and counterfeiting. Clearly, the commitment offenses for these youths were far less serious than those for detainees in the public sector. This observation receives support from the fact that 27% were nonoffenders, 15% were status offenders, and 18% were voluntary commitments.

As for recent trends, the reasons for custody in the public sector changed little between 1983 and 1991. Most public sector detainees—that is, between 93% and 95%—were delinquent youths. However, in the public sector some subtle changes did occur. For example, the percentage of delinquents increased from 34% in 1983 to 40% in 1991. Along with this increase in delinquent detainees there was a decrease in the proportion of status offenders, down to 15% in 1991 from 20% in 1983. The percentage of nonoffenders and voluntary admissions changed little during this period. Thus, the trend has been toward more delinquent residents in private facilities.[25] Nonetheless, the nation's public-sector juvenile facilities continue to house a far more delinquent clientele and more of them.

These various pieces of the puzzle suggest that the youthful population of public sector detainees is more delinquent—and prone toward more serious "criminal" acts—than are their peers in the private sector. Indeed, we question whether they are true peers at all. Besides differences in offenses, those in the private sector are likely to be White rather than racial or ethnic minorities. Perhaps we should not lose sight of the fact that the private sector is made up of many for-profit institutions, where money is to be made from those who can pay. However, before we are overcome by a wave of cynicism, the private sector also provides—for free and at the public expense—some of the only safe and secure placements for status offenders and nonoffenders. Juvenile corrections in the United States is truly a mixed bag.

The Culture of Juvenile Correctional Facilities

Since Clemmer's pioneering study with adult inmates, researchers have investigated the possibility that juveniles create a similar inmate subculture. The evidence seems to support its existence. For example, juveniles confined in a traditional training school expressed the same collective alienation and isolation as do adults in prison (Thomas, Hyman, and Winfree 1983). These youths also exhibited varying levels of prisonization, as measured by adoption of the tenets of the inmate code. Like their adult prison counterparts, those highly prisonized training-school inmates also expressed both negative attitudes toward the law and delinquent self-identification. Juvenile inmates exhibit role adaptations similar to those found in adult prisons (Zingraff 1975). Lastly, a combination of the importation-deprivation hypotheses also yields the greatest insights into how much prisonization is present among youthful prisoners (Poole and Regoli 1983).

Training-school inmates may be undergoing youthful prisonization. Partial confirmation of this belief comes from research on adult inmates. That is, Irwin (1970) found that **state-raised youths**—individuals who went from "the youth prison" to the adult prison—have a special advantage in the inmate subculture. They are often tougher than inmates without their prior socialization experiences, and they resort more often and more readily to the use of violence (Irwin 1970, 27). State-raised youth inmates start their prisonization experiences early. Through the jailing process they become thoroughly colonized inmates, whose worldview ends at the prison walls (see also Wooden 1976).

Conditions of Confinement for Juvenile Offenders

Kenneth Wooden (1976), in his highly critical book, *Weeping in the Playtime of Others: America's Incarcerated Children,* presents a journalistic account of confinement conditions throughout the nation. The conditions he described as existing in the early 1970s were generally abysmal. Wooden considered juvenile corrections to be a national disgrace. He condemned the universally crowded and miserable living conditions he found in "youth jails," or juvenile detention facilities. This system is the "bastard stepchild of *parens patriae*" (Wooden 1976, 23). Wooden viewed the connection between solitary confinement and suicide (both attempts and successful acts) as one of the most abhorrent aspects of contemporary juvenile correctional institutions. In graphic and personal terms, Wooden described a juvenile correctional system out of control.

An inmate peers through the bars of his cell in the Youth Offenders Unit at the Brazoria Prison in Texas. Juvenile offenders may be housed in separate juvenile units or tried as adults and incarcerated in adult facilities.

In 1991, the Department of Justice's Office of Juvenile Justice and Delinquency Prevention funded a national assessment of the conditions of confinement in juvenile detention and corrections facilities (Parent et al. 1994). The researchers surveyed public and private facilities about specific criteria, including basic needs, order and safety, programming, and juvenile rights. For example, standards for sleeping space, part of inmate basic needs, mandated that each inmate in a single room have 70 square feet or, for three or more occupants, 50 square feet per person. The surveys measured 46 assessment criteria in 12 separate areas.

The authors of the final report prepared from the survey described three major themes.[26] First, they noted widespread and substantial problems in such critical areas as living space, health care, security, and control of suicidal behavior. For example, only 43% of the facilities housing a mere 24% of the total incarcerated youthful inmates provided sufficient living space. Roughly 50% of the facilities, housing 25% of the youthful inmates, have adequate controls in place for preventing inmate suicide attempts.[27]

Second, even when the facilities follow the standards established for such institutions,[28] living conditions in the facility may not improve. "For many important areas of facility operation, practitioners drafting standards did not specify outcomes that should be achieved. Instead, a large portion of existing

standards emphasizes procedural regularity, which is admittedly an important objective. . . . Performance standards can quickly identify problems and
can provide a benchmark against which improvements can be measured"
(Parent et al. 1994, 5). In short, the study recommended the adoption of
performance-based standards, a missing element that the researchers felt
would help administrators in meeting the challenges associated with operating juvenile correctional facilities.

Finally, the answer to solving the confinement problems found in the nation's juvenile institutions is not just to close a few really bad facilities. Rather,
substantial improvements will require that many less seriously deficient facilities improve several operational areas.

In the 1970s, Wooden discussed conditions of juvenile correctional confinement that at best may be described as benign neglect and at worst criminal
negligence. The conditions described in the 1990s continue to raise doubts
about the safety and security of these facilities and the welfare of the children
confined in them. Our knowledge of life in juvenile correctional facilities, like
our insights into prisons and jails for women, is fragmentary. Incarcerated
children and women receive far less attention than do adult male inmates.
The state of our knowledge about juvenile and female inmates is in all likelihood a case of the squeaky wheel getting all the grease. After all, adult male
inmates far outnumber both incarcerated children and women. The result is
that the public who pays and the policy makers who distribute the funds
know very little about inmates and their lives in confinement.

Inmate-Centered Issues

We close our examination of prison and jail inmates with a brief summary of
three key inmate-centered issues. We make no claim that these are the only
remaining inmate-centered issues. Nothing could be further from the truth.
These concerns have plagued prisons and jails since their inception. Moreover, they show no sign of letting up as we approach the twenty-first century.
They, and the racial disparities described earlier, threaten the fragile status
quo of U.S. correctional facilities.

Problem Inmates and Inmate Problems

Prisons and jails have two additional types of living assignments that resemble "prisons within a prison." Both are maximum-security units. They may be
found in a separate wing, floor, or housing unit of the prison or jail.[29] Inmates
live in these structures nearly all day, the fortunate ones leaving their cells
periodically to bath or exercise. No matter how the other prisoners are fed,
inmates in these two types of living assignments have the food brought to
them. They do not work. Residents also may have little access to treatment
programs, educational opportunities, or other amenities available to the general prison population. Here the similarities end.

The inmates housed in these two living arrangements represent opposite ends of the inmate social structure. The first arrangement is the **protective custody unit (PCU).** Inmates living here have been threatened with or have been the victims of physical violence, including sexual violence. Other PCU residents may have reputations among the inmates as snitches or informants. Finally, the PCU is a relatively safe haven for inmates who need to "hide out" from a bad debt. However, one proscriptive norm of many prison inmate codes, even in contemporary prisons and jails, is as follows: "Do not ask for protective custody." According to the code, only very frightened inmates ("weak sisters") or snitches run to the authorities for protection.

Simply seeking protective custody can be viewed as an act of betrayal. Residence in the PCU signifies membership in the lower reaches of the inmate subculture. Once an inmate enters a PCU, return to the general population is rare. If it does occur, assaults, injuries, and even deaths are distinct possibilities. Injuries and deaths within the PCU do occur, since a fellow resident could always exact revenge or carry out a punishment paid for by another.

Given the small number of cells typically available for protective custody[30] and the high demand for their use, protective custody transfers to other facilities are more commonly used to deal with security problems of this nature (Fields 1996, 373). For example, police officers and other public officials, convicted of crimes and sent to prison, may be sent out of state or to the federal prison system. Even this proactive step may not work as the inmate grapevine provides information on nearly every inmate transfer, especially those that seem out of the ordinary.

Correctional authorities reserve the second living arrangement, **administrative segregation,** for unusually disruptive individuals, who, for a variety of reasons, cannot be "mainstreamed" into the facility's general population. Administrative segregation should not be confused with **disciplinary/punitive segregation,** or what used to be called solitary confinement. Court decisions and penal policy strictly control disciplinary segregation, limiting its use to violations of important institutional rules and regulations. The confined inmate's health, welfare, and nutrition must be closely monitored. Stays are subject to maximum limits, usually less than three weeks. *Administrative segregation* is a term used to refer to a cellblock, wing, or separate correctional facility in which disruptive inmates are housed for much if not all of their sentences. Institutional life is different for inmates in administrative segregation, often more difficult than that faced by PCU inmates. Even movement throughout the facility is different for administrative segregation inmates. Given their documented propensity for disruptive and often violent behavior, they are normally shackled, handcuffed, and escorted by one or more officers when moving about the facility. Like inmates in disciplinary segregation, court decisions limit the punitive nature of administrative segregation. The general rule of thumb is that the totality of the conditions they are subjected to while in administrative segregation cannot violate the Eighth Amendment's ban on cruel and unusual punishment. Even being "locked down" in one's cell 23 hours a day does not necessarily violate this amendment (*Bruscino v. Carlson* 1988; see also Chapter 11 for a discussion of general prisoner rights). As these inmates' living conditions derive from their unwillingness to "play by the rules," they enjoy high status among other inmates; however, they may also be much feared if their violence is unpredictable, as is true for outlaws, toughs, and gorillas.

Gangs in Correctional Settings

We should not confuse street gangs with prison gangs, although some experts note that the two cross-fertilize. Earlier in this chapter we cited Jacobs' (1977) study of gang invasion and succession in the Stateville (Illinois) prison. Other state systems experienced similar occurrences. Prison gangs are not part of the traditional inmate subculture. They are cliques and informal groups organized principally or even exclusively on a racial or ethnic basis. The major gangs found in U.S. prisons today include the **Mexican Mafia (EME)**, **La Nuestra Familia (NF)**, **Aryan Brotherhood (AB)**, **Black Guerrilla Family (BGF)**, and **Texas Syndicate (TS)**. Prison gangs require either murder or blood-drawing initiations. All have ties, however tenuous, to gangs outside prison, thus inmates have a supportive social system in and out of the correctional setting. For example, the AB, a White supremacist group, maintains ties with motorcycle gangs outside prison, many of which are involved in the illicit drug trade. Inside prisons these groups "compete" for the lucrative prison drug business. Box 6.4 gives an overview of prison gangs in the United States.

Prison gangs are not just California or New York problems. A recent prison survey found gangs, called **security threat groups** by the American Correctional Association, in 40 state prison systems, the District of Columbia, and in the Federal Bureau of Prisons (American Correctional Association 1994). Indeed, the state systems most affected by gangs were Illinois, with 48.1% of the prison population (14,900) gang members, and New Jersey, with 24.4% (6,000) gang members. The study found a total of 1,153 different security threat groups with 46,190 members. Overall, roughly 6% of the nation's prison population belonged to a prison-based gang.

Besides racial antagonisms and conflicts, several other features of prison gangs make them far more troublesome for prison managers than the solidary inmate social system. First, gangs feud and form alliances, creating security and control problems. Sometimes the problems created by these interracial and inter-cultural feuds often have intraracial or intracultural consequences. For example, the Mexican Mafia and La Nuestra Familia have had an ongoing blood feud since 1968. In its struggle with the EME, the NF allied itself with two very different groups, the White supremacist AB and the BGF. Clearly defining these relationships in a fluid environment is difficult, how-

Box 6.4

Prison Gangs in a Nutshell

The first recorded prison gang was Walla Walla (Washington) State Penitentiary's the Gypsy Jokers Motorcycle Club. For much of the past 25 years, however, the following five groups have been identified as "major players" throughout much of the nation's larger prisons:

- Mexican Mafia (EME). Found in at least nine state prison systems and the federal prison system, the original leadership of the EME modeled the structure and behavior of the Italian Mafia. The EME practices a "blood-in/blood-out" ritual like that practiced by many street gangs. Its original membership was drawn heavily from urban, southern-California Hispanics. Drug sales are the primary activities of the EME, in and out of prison, but it is also known to engage in other criminal activities, including prostitution and illegal gambling enterprises.
- La Nuestra Familia (NF). This gang, composed mainly of rural, northern-California Hispanics, has a "board of directors." The longstanding feud between the EME and the NF often requires that the state agency in charge of prison assignments send members to different institutions. Besides the protection of NF members, the gang engages in the same kinds of prison-based criminal enterprises as the other groups.
- Black Guerrilla Family (BGF). Prison activist George Jackson founded this un-

usual prison gang in the late 1960s. The BGF, in spite of its Maoist orientation, participates in the capitalistic inmate economy. The group is highly dependent on a charismatic leader and central committee. It is also considered highly dangerous by prison officials, as its members routinely assault prison staff. The BGF is believed to have strong ties to extra-institutional gangs, particularly in Chicago.
- Texas Syndicate (TS). Texas residents of Hispanic descent founded this group at California's Folsom prison. In the mid-1970s, this group of Texans found themselves caught between members of the EME and NF. Creating the TS was a means of self-defense. A paramilitary group, members of the TS are legendary for their patience in paying back an insult or other rules violation.
- Aryan Brotherhood (AB). Formed from members of extra-institutional biker gangs and other neo-Nazi groups (similar to late twentieth-century skinhead hate groups), the AB, like ethnic gangs, protects its members and engages in a wide range of criminal activities; however, the prison-based drug trade is their primary focus. Members of the AB are widely recognized as indiscriminately and unpredictably violent.

Source: Pelz (1996).

ever. For instance, members of rival "sets" or cliques from street super-gangs, such as the Bloods and Crips, may unite to provide protection for members. They may also exert control over the sub rosa inmate economy in the prison. Likewise, gangs that may be affiliated outside of the prison may be forced into divided loyalties behind the walls.

Second, riots and other prison disturbances often create a prison power vacuum. New gangs replace the old ones broken up after the riot. For example, following the riot at the New Mexico Penitentiary in 1980, two gangs emerged. One, the Sindicato Nuevo Mexico, is the largest organized prison gang in New Mexico and an offshoot of the Mexican Mafia. In Texas similar evolutionary processes took place after a court decision ending that state's infamous building tender system. **Building tenders** were trusty inmates tacitly acknowledged by prison administrators as agents of informal social control in a given inmate residential area (Stojkovic 1996; Crouch and Marquart 1989). Before *Ruiz v. Estelle* (1980), building tenders maintained economic and social control over their respective buildings in the Texas prison system. In the wake of the power vacuum created by the destruction of the exploitative system of inmate rule, prison gangs replaced the building tenders (Fong 1990).

What can be done about prison gangs? Connecticut's Department of Corrections (DOC) initiated a close custody phase program for members of security risk groups at designated institutions. Inmates identified as members of a security risk group receive a new, higher security classification and a housing assignment in a close custody unit, a form of administrative detention. Here they enter Phase I, which encourages cultural sensitivity and harmonious living, since members of various security risk groups all live together. Once they sign a "letter of intent" to renounce all "gang affiliation," inmates enter Phase II. Prison staff group Phase II inmates into squads of 12 individuals with varying gang affiliations. The squad engages in all daily activities as a group. This phase again emphasizes cultural sensitivity and harmonious living, and a program of understanding and awareness of alternatives to gang membership. Phase II takes approximately 60 days, after which inmates enter Phase III. The final phase adds programming on anger and violence management to the earlier elements. After approximately 90 days, a formal renunciation of the gang allows inmates to return to the general population.

Other states, particularly those with large gang problems, approach security threat groups in a less systematic fashion. The California prison system responded by using classification to break up the gangs and sending members to different prison facilities. However, gang power in California prisons remains high (American Correctional Association 1994). By contrast, throughout most of the 1980s, Texas congregated gang members in separate facilities. This practice created small gang fiefdoms throughout the system (Fong 1990). Another strategy is to create small, semi-autonomous, self-contained "institutions" of approximately 50 to 100 inmates (Levinson and Gerard 1973). The inmates, all of whom have similar classifications and release dates, are supervised by the same team of correctional specialists. This **unit management** approach helps break up existing ties based on race, ethnicity, or gangs. The intended result is that a new form of prosocial group cohesion emerges. Whatever strategy is tried, breaking up the power of gangs is as difficult in prison as it is on the streets.

Jailhouse Suicide

Earlier we observed that **jailhouse suicides** occur at a rate that is far higher than we would expect given the demographics of jails. Even when we factor

Prisoners in the Twenty-First Century

The prisoners of the next century, in all likelihood, will resemble the prisoners of every other century. That is, they will be drawn disproportionately from the most disadvantaged classes in society, what William Julius Wilson (1987) calls the **underclass.** For this group, crime is as institutionalized as poverty. Proportionately, more ethnic and racial group members are also members of the underclass. Therefore, we should not be surprised to see their share of the jail and prison population grow as well.

Several other patterns seem possible, given recent trends. First, the proportion of women in prisons is increasing. In fact, throughout most of the 1990s, the rate for women has outpaced the men's. Parity is a long way off. Nevertheless, this is a group that must receive more attention from policy makers and more money from taxpayers. Second, age will become an even more crucial point of division in prison. The number of young prisoners will increase as states shift juveniles to adult courts for trials and punishments. Moreover, given changes in sentencing laws, many more prison inmates will grow old and die in state custody. This infusion of the very young and the very old into the nation's prison and jail populations will be the source of incredible tensions in the coming decade. Racial tensions, fed by the influx of even larger numbers of young minority group members, many with long juvenile records of violent crime, will rise in the next decade. Concurrent with the influx of younger, more violent criminals, gangs, as mechanism of defense and commerce, will proliferate in the twenty-first century jails and prisons. The fact that prison officials little understand the link between street gangs and prison gangs makes this problem even more urgent.

Short of major changes in public policy and criminal law, prisons in the twenty-first century will house a predominantly drug-related inmate population, most of whom were drug users on the outside. The drug trade in jails and prisons, including alcohol, has traditionally defined much of the sub-rosa inmate economy. The life of an incarcerated person is boring; no matter how busy they are during their working hours, inmates have 18 or more hours to pass before the work cycle begins again. What about inmates—mostly in jails—who have no jobs? They have 24 hours per day, seven days a week to pass. Take away recreational areas, weightlifting equipment, and the like, and the waiting gets worse. Drugs help pass the time. With so many members of the inmate population already with moderate to severe drug problems before incarceration, increasing amounts of the jail and prison operating budgets will go to drug treatment in the next century.

in the millions of people who move through the nation's jails, the suicide rate remains five to six times higher than that of a comparable free-world population (Winfree 1988). This fact is even more startling when we learn that the rates of death by natural causes and homicide in 1978 and 1983 were lower than comparable rates beyond the jailhouse walls (Winfree 1988).

Suicides in the nation's lockups may even exceed the level of those reported for jails. Lockups are places of temporary confinement for periods of 24 hours or less; we know little about their role in the criminal justice system. Perhaps another 1,000 people a year die in these facilities, although this figure is an estimate (Davis and Muscat 1993; see also Charle 1981). The research on jailhouse suicides consistently reports that most suicides occurred within the first 24 hours of arrest, when inmate embarrassment, stress, isolation, and shock are greatest (Smialek and Spitz 1978; Topp 1979). Intoxicated jail inmates pose the greatest risk of committing suicide, especially shortly after arrest, no matter where the place of confinement (Charle 1981; Winfree and Wooldredge 1991).

Can local jail administrators alter the management of their facilities to reduce the rate of death by suicide? A study of suicide in the nation's 180 largest jails provides little hope for jail managers. The researchers concluded that "increased and decreased probabilities of suicide or deaths by natural causes were not impacted in consistent ways by changes in personnel patterns (ratios of full-time staff to inmates), jail clientele (male only, adult only), level of crowding, or turnover rates of the large jails included" (Winfree and Wooldredge 1991, 76). Jails will continue to experience high suicide rates. Jails simply house high concentrations of persons at risk to kill themselves, including drug addicts and alcoholics (Wooldredge and Winfree 1992).

Conclusion

Prisoners today face many of the same pains of imprisonment and deprivations that confronted those confined in prisons and jails 200, 75, or even 50 years ago. A key difference is that prisons and jails today are far less cohesive, more fragmented than they were just 30 years ago. While this is good from an administrative perspective—for example, less organized inmate resistance to prison rules and regulations—there are other, less positive effects as well. Inmate life has become far less predictable. Given the divisiveness that characterizes the inmate social system, the possible causes of violent inmate responses to real or imagined insults have increased dramatically. Larger numbers of inmates and declining resources translate into fewer dollars to spend on anything unrelated to institutional security. The strict enforcement of "chicken-shit rules" that define what inmates can and cannot do to embellish their living spaces has led to a prison environment that is more drab and monotonous than ever (Irwin and Austin 1993, 78). Never a pleasant living environment, current conditions in the nation's prisons and jails may be worse than they were in the 1950s (Irwin and Austin 1993).

Irwin and Austin's (1993) characterization of the United States as in the midst of an **imprisonment binge** is frighteningly accurate. The future of imprisonment is bleak. Alternatives, such as those described in the next two chapters, may offer some relief. Only basic changes in law-enforcement and penal policy will stop the spiral toward a time when more minority group members are alumni of prisons than high schools and we spend more per capita on prisons and punishments than education. Perhaps we have reached that stage already?

Critical Review Questions

1. Assume for a moment that you are a congressional analyst who has been charged with examining the "War on Drugs" and the Federal Sentencing Reform Act. Congress has recognized that we are building—and populating—far too many federal prisons. Your boss tells you that the Judicial Affairs Committee will consider revamping one or the other but not both. Which one will you recommend be changed and why?

2. Which single statistic about federal prisoners did you find most interesting? Explain your selection.

3. Answer Question 2 for state prisoners.

4. Answer Question 2 for female prisoners.

5. What are your thoughts on the differences between male and female inmates? Are these differences the result of (a) discriminatory police and prosecutorial practices or (b) the fact that female offenders are different from male offenders? How did you reach this conclusion?

6. What is your reaction to the populations housed by the nation's public and private juvenile corrections systems?

7. What do you think is the absolutely worst aspect of the inmate code? What would bother you least if you were a member of the inmate subculture? What role would you adopt? Explain your answers to each question using substantive material from this chapter.

8. Is the inmate subculture a product of incarceration or related to the extrainstitutional lives of prisoners?

9. What kinds of violence do you think inmates fear most? How did you reach this conclusion?

10. We concluded this chapter with an examination of three inmate-centered issues. Which issue do you think places the greatest burden on the public coffers? (That is, which one will cost the tax payers the most if they are to remedy it?) Which issue do you think poses the greatest threat to the inmates' quality of life? Even if you select the same issue for both parts of this question, give the basis of your thinking for each.

Recommended Readings

Clemmer, Donald. 1940. *The prison community.* New York: Holt, Rinehart & Winston. Clemmer's work has shaped several generations of prison researchers as they seek to understand the form and structure of the inmate social system. What we know of prison roles, intragroup relations, inmate code adoption, and the like evolved from this seminal work.

Giallambardo, Rose. 1966. *Society of women: A study of a women's prison.* New York: Wiley. This pioneering effort on kinship, marriage, and family groups and other social dynamics found in a prison for women has become a classic since its publication in 1966. The author questions the conventional wisdom on the creation of the inmate social system, a perspective largely derived from studies of prisons for men.

Irwin, John. 1970. *The felon.* Englewood Cliffs, NJ: Prentice-Hall. Another classic by ex-convict and now retired professor Irwin. This book, based on in-depth interviews and two years of participant observation by the author, concentrates on the problems a convicted felon encounters while attempting to reenter society. [In fact, we also recommend this book as essential reading in Chapter 7, "Probation and Parole." Read it now or read it later.] The key to understanding the felon is to understand the prison community, a goal Irwin accomplishes in this informative book.

Sykes, Gresham M. 1958. *The society of captives: A study of a maximum security prison.* Princeton, NJ: Princeton University Press. Sykes clearly outlines the significance of the pains of imprisonment and the inmate role types for the operation of a maximum-security prison. The final chapter, "A Postscript for Reformers," remains interesting in spite of having been written 40 years ago. His four goals remain as critical for prisons at the start of the twenty-first century as they were at the midpoint of the twentieth.

Key Terms

administrative segregation	doing time	physical violence
Aryan Brotherhood (AB)	economic victimization	play families
Attica riot	fags	political riots
Battle of Alcatraz	fish	prison gangs
Black Guerrilla Family (BGF)	frustration riots	prison riots
building tenders	gleaning	prison subculture
case manager	gorillas	prisonization
classification officer	imprisonment binge	property offense
clinical psychologist	inmate code	protective custody unit (PCU)
con-politicians	jailhouse suicides	psychological diagnostician
correctional counselor	jailing	psychological technician
cultural importation hypothesis	La Nuestra Familia (NF)	psychological victimization
deprivation perspective	legitimate inmate economy	public-order offense
disciplinary/punitive segregation	merchants/peddlers	punks
	Mexican Mafia (EME)	race riots
	outlaws	
	pains of imprisonment	

Key Terms *(continued)*

rage riots	snitching	toughs
rapos/innocents	solidary opposition	underclass
rats/squealers	square Johns	unit management
right guys	state-raised youth	weaklings/weak sisters
Santa Fe prison riot	sub rosa inmate economy	wolves
security threat groups	Texas Syndicate (TS)	

Cases Cited

Bruscino v. Carlson, 854 F.2d 162 (7th Cir. 1988)

Ruiz v. Estelle 503 F Supp. 1265 (1980)

Notes

1. The information summarized in this section and Figure 6.1 are derived from Department of Justice (1997) and Bureau of Prisons (1997b).

2. Discussion of changes in sentencing patterns is drawn from Austin et al. (1996).

3. Personal characteristics of state prisoners is taken from Harlow (1994); this information was obtained from the first joint survey of state and federal prisoners and has not been repeated.

4. The Bureau of Justice Statistics, following guidelines developed by demographers at the Bureau of the Census, reports figures for non-Hispanic Blacks and Hispanics. We use slightly different descriptors, African-Americans (or Blacks) and Hispanics. Keep in mind, however, that some states report no data on Hispanic origin, while others report only estimates; moreover, in the past, inmate self-reports tended to produce higher estimates for Hispanics (Beck and Gilliard 1995, 9).

5. The insights on women in prison come largely from Greenfield (1991) and Snell (1994); this information, like that for males, is only occasionally reported by the Bureau of Justice Statistics.

6. Men too exhibited changes in the area of drug crimes (Snell 1994). They were only slightly less likely to be sentenced for the commission of violent crimes; there was about a 20% reduction in those for whom property crimes were the most serious offense.

7. A 1980 amendment to the 1974 Juvenile Justice and Delinquency Prevention Act altered the conditions under which juveniles may be housed in jails. Juveniles may be placed in adult jails for limited periods of time, usually six hours or less. When this occurs, the juveniles, like the women in the jail, must be isolated by sight and sound from the adult male inmates. If, however, the juvenile court transfers authority of the youth to the adult criminal court, then he or she may be incarcerated with adult jail inmates.

8. The Bureau of Justice Statistics researchers warn that convicted inmates may actually account for more than one-half since some jails do not distinguish between inmates who are unconvicted and those who are convicted but not yet sentenced (Perkins, Stephan, and Beck 1995, 5).

9. Information about jail inmates is taken from Gilliard and Beck (1997) and Bureau of Justice (1997a).

10. The following information is largely taken from Snell (1992).

11. This second category is relatively new in federal data collection efforts, as is the increase in the transfer of juveniles to adult courts (Champion and Mays 1991).

12. In Goffman's (1961, 62–63) terms, jailing inmates have been colonized. The total institution is home and the outside world is a strange and scary place.

13. A National Institute of Justice project highlights the special relationship between inmate mothers and their daughters. In 1992, NIJ sponsored an inmate mother-child visitation program under the auspices of the Girl Scouts at the Maryland Correction Institution for Women, a multiclassification adult facility for women serving sentences of six months and a day or more. The project was so successful that other states have joined with the Girl Scouts to form similar partnership efforts to link Girl Scouts with their inmate mothers. For more information, see Moses (1995).

14. Recall that, owing to the far smaller number of female offenders in custody, few states operate more than one women's prison. There are fewer than two dozen female-only jails in the entire nation (Gray, Mays, and Stohr 1995). As a consequence, prisons and jails holding women tend to be multiclassification facilities, holding everything from shoplifters to murderers. Oddly, in the case of women's prisons, this wide variety of inmate offense types does not automatically translate into a more threatening institutional environment.

15. Unless otherwise stated, the information on deaths in the nation's prisons comes from the Department of Justice (1997, 105).

16. While there are more jails than prisons, the former hold on any given day less than one-half of the prison population. Confounding our understanding of conditions of jail deaths is the fact that they processed more than 13 million admissions and releases in 1993. The exposure length to the incarceration risks for jail inmates also varies from only a few days or weeks for most suspects to about six months for one-half of all convicted misdemeanants. As a result, jails expose larger numbers of people to the risks of imprisonment for shorter periods of time than do prisons.

17. Perkins, Stephan, and Beck (1995) is the source of the information on jail deaths.

18. The Federal Metropolitan Correctional and Detention Centers reported only eight deaths in 1993, half of which were due to natural causes, but none to AIDS. Suicide and drug overdoses each claimed two victims.

19. Noticeably absent from this discussion is any mention of staff-on-inmate violence. Any such discussion would be highly speculative and would have to rely exclusively on inmate stories and guard anecdotes. We know it occurs. We lack even the roughest estimates of how often or how serious the assaults are.

20. There are virtually no national statistics for assaults in jails. See Sechrest (1991) for a rare study of assaults in a single jail system.

21. Unless otherwise noted, the source of the information concerning assaults on staff and inmates is Maguire and Pastore (1995, 586).

22. Correctional officer figures were used since these individuals have the highest exposure to inmates, thus the greatest probability of being assaulted. As a consequence, we standardized our discussion in terms of correctional officers.

23. In fact, New York State Department of Correctional Services has a well developed system for reporting "unusual" prison incidents (Zausner, 1985).

24. Material on juvenile correctional populations is taken from Austin et al. (1995). The information for juveniles is at aggregate level, meaning that individual level comparisons are not possible. For example, we do not know how many minority females live in private-sector facilities.

25. As corroboration of this trend, a recent Office of Juvenile Justice and Delinquency Prevention Report (Moone 1997) found in 1995 that 44.8% of the private-sector residents committed a delinquent offense. Comparable 1995 data for the private sector was unavailable.

26. Unless otherwise noted, the following summary comes from Parent et al. (1994).

27. Parent et al. (1994, 10) estimated that in a given year more than 11,000 juveniles engaged in 17,000 separate acts of suicidal behavior (that is, attempted suicide, made suicidal gestures, or engaged in self-mutilation).

28. Parent et al. (1994, 4) relied on standards obtained from three national organizations, including the American Correctional Association, National Commission on Correctional Health Care, an affiliate of the American Medical Association, and the American Bar Association/Institute for Judicial Administration.

29. Jails, particularly the medium- and small-sized jails, often do not have the flexibility of maintaining two separate wings or floors. Inmates with both types of problems often find themselves sharing one-person cells in the same cellblock.

30. Less than 1 percent of the BOP's total inmate population resides in protective custody and segregation (Beck and Gilliard 1995, 23). There are no similar figures for protective custody arrangements in state prisons.

7

Probation and Parole

Chapter Outline

- Introduction
- The History of Probation
- Administration of Probation
- Violation of Probation
- Origins of Parole
- Administration of Parole
- Violation of Parole
- Probation and Parole Officers
- Probation and Parole Services Today
- Probation and Aftercare for Juvenile Offenders
- Conclusion
- Critical Review Questions
- Recommended Readings
- Key Terms
- Cases Cited
- Notes

Introduction

For many of us, one of the greatest "injustices" about our system of criminal justice is that convicted lawbreakers commit new crimes before they pay for the old ones. Stated differently, it seems unfair that so many criminals roam the streets, free to offend repeatedly, rather than locked up safely in prison or jail. Because criminals are free, goes this line of thinking, the rest of us—the lawful rather than the lawbreakers—are the prisoners.

Why do we use other forms of punishment besides prisons and jails? Among the oldest and most widely practiced alternatives—and those with the longest list of objections and attractions—are probation and parole. We begin with probation.

The History of Probation

Probation is a period of testing that proves something.[1] The test is whether the probationer can live in the community without returning to crime. Even before the development of formal probation, legal remedies allowed for the testing of accused criminals and provided a "second chance." These methods—the forerunners of modern probation—included benefit of clergy (defined below), judicial reprieve, release on one's own recognizance, and bail.

Forerunners of Modern Probation

Late in the twelfth century, England's Henry II was embroiled in a major conflict with the Roman Catholic church. Henry, the French usurper of the English crown, tried to secularize England's laws. The pope condemned this encroachment on the church's power. **Benefit of clergy** was the eventual compromise worked out between the English crown and the Roman Catholic church. Any ordained member of the clergy accused of a secular crime could have the case transferred to the bishop's court. This transferal was important because it allowed clerics to escape possible persecution at the hands of the king's ministers of justice. Perhaps as important, the punishments for secular crime imposed in the bishop's court ran more to penance than hanging.

Benefit of clergy was not an alternative means of testing whether the accused could live free in the community. **Judicial reprieve,** by contrast, is directly linked to modern probation. A common practice in early English courts, judicial reprieve was a suspension of the imposition of a penal sanction for a fixed time. This practice became popular since a convicted felon's only chance for mercy lay with the king. Suspending the imposition of a court's sentence, which often meant stopping an impending execution, allowed the offender to petition the crown for a pardon. As originally conceived, judicial reprieve was only a stay of execution. However, later courts used it for delaying the execution of a penal sanction indefinitely.

By the eighteenth century, English courts suspended the imposition of a sentence in return for a specified period of good behavior. After successfully living crime-free, the offender could petition the English Crown for a full or partial pardon. Judicial reprieve was important to the English transportation program. A century later, judicial reprieve became an essential legal element for the various Irish, English, and American alternatives to incarceration. In fact, the importance of judicial reprieve for probation cannot be overstated. To give convicted offenders a "second chance," judges needed a discretionary means to stop the imposition or execution of a sentence. Judicial reprieve was ideally suited for this purpose.

Bail and release on one's own recognizance (**ROR**) are two practices that are often viewed by the public as equally problematic and very similar. For essentially hundreds of years, these practices were the only means by which an accused person could secure his or her freedom from confinement. However, the method by which one achieved that freedom differed. **Bail** gave the court a tangible guarantee that the accused would appear on a given date.

Box 7.1

Literacy, the Death Penalty, and the "Neck Verse"

Literacy was an important part of the benefit of clergy policy. In medieval England, few people outside the clergy could read and write. Literate people were too valuable to subject to the whims of the king's justice. By the fourteenth century, any literate person could seek protection under benefit of clergy. The specific test was a passage from Psalms 51:3, the Misere, **Prayer of Repentance:** "Have mercy on me, O God, in your goodness; in the greatness of your compassion wipe out my offense. Thoroughly wash me from my guilt and of my sin cleanse me." Because many offenders faced death in the king's court,

this psalm became known as the "neck verse."

Over the centuries, the use of the neck verse was so widespread that judges frequently ignored it. Prisoners at the dock were viewed as having simply memorized the passage, which was often the case. The well-to-do and literate accused could still call upon the protection of the Fifty-First Psalm. While benefit of clergy was used in the British American colonies, the practice was abandoned shortly after the American Revolution as undemocratic and arbitrary. *Source:* Bedau (1967, 5–6).

The bailor, or person who paid the bail, assumed some measure of responsibility for ensuring the bailed individual's court appearance, a notion that continues today.

As practiced for centuries in England, **recognizance** involved the posting of a bond or surety deposit with the court, for example, the deed to one's property or something else of value. In 1830, the first case of a person being released on his or her own recognizance occurred in *Commonwealth v. Chase,* a Boston municipal court case. Reserved for minor adult offenses or most offenses committed by juveniles, ROR was another essential legal element for probation.

John Augustus: Father of Probation

John Augustus was a prosperous Boston shoemaker when, in 1841, he began an 18-year association with the Boston courts. In the intervening years until his death in 1859, Augustus "bailed on probation" some 1,152 men and 794 women (Barnes and Teeters 1959, 554). Augustus believed that society's laws were intended to reform criminals and prevent crime. In his view, laws and their accompanying sanctions should not serve to achieve revenge and punishment for their own sake. A member of the Temperance Movement, a religious organization dedicated to combating the evils of alcohol, Augustus was forever changed by a visit to a Boston courtroom. As Augustus observed, "I was in court one morning . . . in which the man was charged with being a common drunkard. He told me that if he could be saved from the House of Corrections, he never again would taste intoxicating liquors: I bailed him, by permission of the Court" (Augustus 1972, 4–5).

After carefully selecting his charges, Augustus helped them secure a job and a residence. He supervised them in the community, giving each individual a set of conditions intended to yield prosocial changes. Augustus warned his charges that a return to the old ways would mean a return to court. At the end of the supervision period, Augustus gave the court an impartial report on the accused's behavior. Besides coining the term *probation* to describe his approach to bailing out and treating offenders, Augustus also initiated the correctional practices of the pre-sentence investigation, the conditions of release, supervision, revocation, and supervisory reports to the court on the conduct of those released. In his memoirs, Augustus claimed that only one of the first 1,100 probationers forfeited bail (Dressler 1962, 18).

The Growth of Probation Services

After Augustus' death in 1859, volunteers continued to provide for the probation needs of Boston's courts until the city hired a professional probation officer in 1878. It would take 50 years for the idea of probationary services to spread across the nation and finally achieve acceptance at the federal level. In fact, it took nearly 20 years for the second state, Missouri, to adopt a law similar to that found in Massachusetts. This law, a "bench parole law," authorized courts to suspend sentences under certain conditions. The Missouri statute also provided for "parole officers" to supervise this misnamed form of probation (Glueck 1933, 231). In short order, Vermont (1898), Rhode Island (1899), New Jersey (1900), and New York (1901) joined Massachusetts and Missouri. Between 1903 and 1923, 20 more states and the District of Columbia added probation services. Two-thirds of the state legislatures legalized probation first for juveniles, sometimes taking 10 to 20 years to enact similar probationary provisions for adults (Johnson 1928, 12–13).

Federal authorities failed to embrace probation with the same enthusiasm as the states. In the nineteenth century, federal judges suspended sentences where imprisonment would have caused unusual hardships; however, this did not go unchallenged. In the 1916 *Killits* case (*Ex parte* U.S.), a first-time embezzler made full restitution and avoided prison. When the federal judge suspended a five-year sentence, he referred to banker Killits's otherwise good reputation and high standing in the community. The Supreme Court ruled unanimously that the trial court did not enjoy the constitutional authority to suspend the sentence. Proponents of probation, rather than viewing *Killits* as killing off probation, saw the decision as a mandate to create the necessary legislation. Groups such as the **National Probation Association** lobbied Congress to pass the enabling legislation. President Calvin Coolidge signed a probation bill into law in 1925, creating what is today the Federal Probation and Pretrial Services System.

Administration of Probation

At the close of the twentieth century, **probation** refers to the trial court practice of conditionally releasing a person into the community. Four models of probation services are found across the nation, according to the traditions and policies of the respective state and local governments (American Correctional Association 1997). Either the judicial or the executive branch of government supervises probationers; however, the administration may be local or state. Table 7.1 summarizes the corresponding patterns for each legal jurisdiction.

Eligibility for Probation

The Supreme Court ruled in *U.S. v. Birnbaum* (1970) that probation is a privilege and not a right. The probationary authority is under no constitutional or statutory obligation to provide for its imposition. State and federal statutes prohibit the extension of probation to certain types of offenders. For example, most states specifically exclude offenders convicted of murder, kidnapping, and rape from receiving probation (Abadinsky 1997, 147). Besides statutory requirements, the key external factor that helps the judge or jury in deciding between sentencing alternatives is the pre-sentence investigation.

Granting Probation and the Pre-Sentence Investigation

Few documents take on greater significance in a convicted felon's life than the **pre-sentence investigation (PSI) report.** This document can contribute to a convicted person's loss of liberty or even loss of life. What is a pre-sentence investigation? Who prepares it? The probation officer traditionally prepares the pre-sentence investigation report. In most jurisdictions, the PSI is a short, standardized document presented to the judge or the jury before sentencing. In the past, PSI reports resembled lengthy personal histories. Probation officers interviewed investigating law enforcement officers, victims or victims' next of kin, and witnesses to the crime. The PSI report often included the observations of the accused's school teachers and high school coaches, religious education instructors, friends and acquaintances, coworkers, and family members.

The fact that judges rarely reviewed the long-form PSI reports eased the move to shorter, more concise reports. Time-management practices supported the use of summaries that informed judges as to the key factors in the officer's recommendation. Moreover, probation officers learn early in their careers what judges view as "pertinent facts" at sentencing. Probation officers' "bottom-line" recommendations may reflect what they have observed at previous sentencing hearings or learned from other probation officers. Whether due to investigative excellence or writing for the audience, the out-

Table 7.1

Adult Probation Authorities in the U.S.

State Administration		Local Administration	
Judicial Branch	Executive Branch	Judicial Branch	Executive Branch
Colorado	Alabama	Nevada	Arizona	New York
Hawaii	Alaska	New Hampshire	California	
Massachusetts	Arkansas	New Mexico	District of Columbia	
Nebraska	Connecticut	North Carolina	Illinois	
New Jersey	Delaware	North Dakota	Indiana	
South Dakota	Florida	Ohio	Kansas	
West Virginia	Georgia	Oklahoma		
	Idaho	Oregon		
	Iowa	Rhode Island		
	Kentucky	South Carolina		
	Louisiana	Texas		
	Maine	Utah		
	Maryland	Vermont		
	Michigan	Virginia		
	Mississippi	West Virginia		
	Missouri	Wisconsin		
	Montana	Wyoming		

Note: Probation officers in Minnesota, Pennsylvania, and Tennessee are state or local agents, depending upon local customs and state laws.

Source: American Correctional Association (1997).

come is often the same: Judges follow PSI recommendations between 70% and 90% of the time (Comptroller General of the United States 1976).

PSI reports traditionally answer three questions. First, what mitigating circumstance suggests a sentence other than prison (or the death penalty)? Second, what aggravating circumstance might lead away from a community-based sentence and toward prison (or the death penalty)? Third, does the defendant—now a convicted criminal—have a special need or problem that can best be met in the free community? If the answer to the first or third questions suggests an alternative other than incarceration, then a follow-up question is normally asked: Will the continued presence of the offender in the community pose a public safety risk? Over the past two decades or so, the **victim impact statement (VIS)** has also found its way into PSI reports. The VIS is an oral or written statement by the victim or victim's next of kin. The VIS is not meant as a way to turn the trial into a lynch mob. Rather, it allows the sentencing authority to hear a clear and personal statement of the loss suffered because of the victimization. In spite of the concerns expressed by the Supreme Court in *Booth v. Maryland* (1987), little evidence exists to support the claim that the VIS automatically results in harsher than normal sentences (Lanier and Miller 1995).

Large parts of the PSI report could legally be defined as hearsay. That is, someone other than the informant either saw or heard the defendant do or say something. Probation officers should cross-check the validity and accuracy of both aggravating and mitigating information before its inclusion in the PSI report. The officer may extend a tentative offer of confidentiality to informants. However, such guarantees have limits as the sentencing authority may wish to confirm the reliability of the confidential informants' information (*Gardner v. Florida* 1977).

Once the report is complete, three additional factors typically intervene between the probation officer's recommendation and the trial court's sentence. First, the American Bar Association (ABA) guidelines and the specific questions addressed by the PSI report hint at the difficult decision faced at sentencing. The needs and rights of the defendant must be weighed against public-safety concerns and, more recently, the victims' rights.

Second, the prosecutor may play a major role in determining the sentence through the plea-bargaining process. What is the role of the PSI report if both the prosecuting and defense attorneys, along with the defendant, agree upon an appropriate sentence? The PSI may serve to validate the plea-bargaining agreement. That is, given the specific crime committed, how appropriate is the proposed sentence? The probation officer essentially consults the same "stakeholders," or people with a personal or professional interest in the outcome of the case. For these reasons, PSI reports are often prepared before the trial or plea agreement.

Third, a jail or prison sentence may not be an option because of the absence of bed spaces. Simply put, if the choice is between incarcerating either a violent offender with a record of **recidivism** or a serious nonviolent offender with no previous criminal record, the court may have to place the latter on probation.

Conditions of Probation

A critical recommendation of the Task Force on Corrections was the need for differential treatment of releasees. Specifically, the Task Force (1967) asked probation authorities to acknowledge the unique characteristics of each offender and each offense by providing tailor-made conditions. This standard was not widely adopted, as most jurisdictions continued to use a set of broad and identical conditions for all releasees. The conditions of probation usually address the following issues:

- The probationer will avoid all conduct violating state and federal statutes; in the event the probationer is arrested or detained by the police, he or she will make a report to the agent within a set period (usually 48 to 72 hours).
- The probationer will report in person to the probation authority upon release from custody and for a stipulated period afterward; subsequently, the probationer will make written reports on a regular, often monthly, basis.

Box 7.2

ABA Recommendations: When to Use Probation? When to Use Prison?

Probation is the preferred punishment when

1. The liberty of the individual is maximized by such a sentence; at the same time, the authority of the laws is vindicated and the public effectively protected from further violations of law.
2. The rehabilitation of the offender is promoted affirmatively by continuing normal community contacts.
3. The negative and frequently stultifying effects of confinement are avoided, thus removing a factor that often complicates the reintegration of the offender into the community.
4. The financial costs of crime control to the public treasury are greatly reduced by reliance on probation as an important part of the correction system.
5. Probation reduces the impact on innocent dependents of the offender.

Prison is the preferred punishment when

1. Confinement is necessary to protect the public from further criminal activity by the defendant.
2. The offender is in need of correctional treatment that can effectively be provided if he or she is confined.
3. The seriousness of the offense would be unduly depreciated if a sentence of probation was imposed.

Source: American Bar Association (1970, 3–4).

- The probationer will not drink alcohol to excess (or at all, if this is a condition of release) and avoid using, purchasing, possessing, giving, selling or administering any controlled substances (that is, illegal drugs).

- The probationer will not possess or have under his or her control any type of weapon.

- The probationer will not change his or her job or place of residence without prior approval; nor will the probationer leave the jurisdiction of the court without obtaining a travel permit in advance.

- The probationer will not associate with persons having criminal records.

- The probationers will cooperate with the agent at all times, which includes providing correct and true information verbally and in writing.

The court may also order special conditions, for example, participating in a drug or alcohol program, an anger management program, and the like. Normally, a court officer signs the agreement along with the probationer. If the judge signs for the court, then the probation officer may also sign to signify that all parties are aware of the conditions of probation.

Length of Supervision

The ABA (1970) recommended that misdemeanant convictions receive a maximum of two years on probation. Felony convictions merited a maximum of five years on probation. These guidelines, however, have yet to receive widespread acceptance. Various jurisdictions give probation sentences ranging from 1 to 10 years (Abadinsky 1997). According to a National Institute of Justice report on probated sentences, the average nationwide is 47 months (Cohen 1995). Only the most serious offenses—murder, rape, robbery, and other violent crimes—meet or exceed the ABA recommendation. In the case of murder and robbery, probated sentences exceed 70 months; otherwise, most average probation sentences range from the low 40s to the mid 50s (Cohen 1995).

The probationary period served may not be the same as the judge's sentence. Apart from any questionable behavior, some states allow the sentencing court to end probation before the expiration date. Should the probationer exhibit good behavior, sentencing statutes may authorize judges to reduce the time remaining or end probation together. Usually, before the court can intervene, a probationer must serve a statutory minimum. The minimums range from one to two years, or one-third to one-half the probation sentence, whichever is less (Abadinsky 1997, 155).

Violation of Probation

Probation has only two possible outcomes. First, the person successfully completes probation, whether early, late, or on schedule. The successful probationer has lived by the conditions of probation or no contrary evidence exists. If the sentencing agreement included a deferred imposition of sentence, the probationer reports to the sentencing court. At this point in the process, the judge may set aside the conviction and expunge—that is, erase—the offender's court record. Probationers, having paid their debts to society, no longer live under the watchful eye of the probation authorities.

A second outcome is less positive. That is, the probationer misbehaves by (1) a new arrest or conviction or (2) a violation of the conditions of probation, the latter called a **technical violation.** Both evidence of a new crime and evidence of a technical violation have the potential to start the **probation revocation process.** While the legal requirements vary, a probationer's arrest for a new offense is normally sufficient to warrant a revocation hearing. A new conviction typically provides a *prima facie* basis—sufficient on the face of it— for the loss of probation.

Technical violations are among the most controversial aspects of the revocation process (Czajkoski 1973). For example, the probationer may have failed to notify the probation officer of a change in job or residence, missed therapy sessions or probation reporting dates, or secured a driver's license or

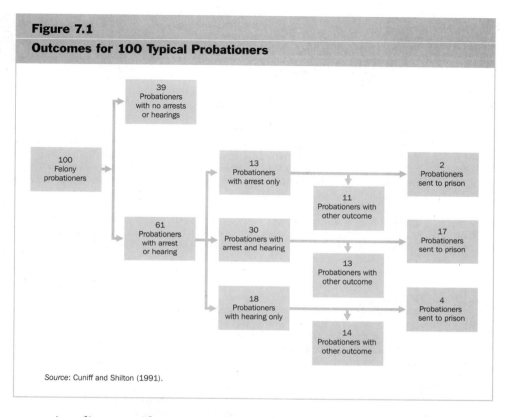

Figure 7.1

Outcomes for 100 Typical Probationers

Source: Cuniff and Shilton (1991).

a marriage license without prior consent. The probationer could be imprisoned for these "crimes." Even an arrest is, in most jurisdictions, a technical violation of probation.

Most probation revocations involve new criminal charges, alleged or proven, rather than technical violations alone. For example, Figure 7.1 summarizes the outcomes for 100 typical probationers in 32 urban and suburban counties (Cuniff and Shilton 1991, 70). One in four probationers made it through supervision with minimal—no officially reported—difficulty. Among the 60 or so probationers in 100 with an arrest or hearing, the researcher found three possible scenarios: (1) probationers were arrested only, (2) probationers were arrested and given a hearing, and (3) probationers were given a hearing only. Most found themselves in the second situation, more than one-half of whom ended in prison. Prison was far less likely when a probationer was only arrested or only given a hearing. Box 7.3 describes who among the probation violators gets prison.

Preliminary Hearing

In the wake of two Supreme Court decisions, *Mempa v. Rhay* (1967) and *Gagnon v. Scarpelli* (1973), the various probationary jurisdictions adopted standardized probation revocation processes. Probationers receive formal

---

Box 7.3

Which Probation Violators Are Sent to Prison?

A 1991 National Institute of Justice (NIJ) study revealed much about the probation violators sent to prison. A total of 162,000 probation violators committed at least 6,400 murders, 7,400 rapes, 10,400 assaults, and 17,000 robberies, all while under community supervision for an average of 17 months. Less than 15% survived three years or more on probation. Nearly one-half failed after serving more than six months but less than two years on probation.

Three-fourths of the former probationers entered prison because of a conviction for a new crime. Among the technical violators, the most common charge—in 87% of the cases—was an arrest for a new offense. More than a third failed to report or **absconded**—left the court's jurisdiction with no intentions of returning. Between 2% and 3% of the technical violators had drug-related charges, including positive tests for alcohol or drug use, failure to report for

drug testing/treatment, and failure to report for alcohol treatment.

Among the NIJ study's 162,000 failed probationers, persons placed on probation for drug and public order offenses found themselves in trouble about six months sooner than most of their more violent peers and several months before most property offenders. This generalization held whether the problem was a new conviction or a technical violation. Violent offenders stayed out of trouble the longest, an average of 21 months for both new crimes and probation violations. If the probationer had a prior probation violation and entered prison for a new conviction, then on average he or she remained free only four months.

Note: The percentages for technical violators exceed 100% since some inmates had more than one type of violation.

Source: Cohen (1995).

---

notice of the specific charges. They must appear at a **preliminary hearing** that serves as a venue for determining the extent of probable cause that a violation of probation occurred. Should the probationer fail to show up, the court normally issues a "failure to appear" warrant. The warrant adds to the accused's problems as this is another charge. Moreover, it is another technical violation. Should the probationer appear and enter a guilty plea, the court has the option of either ordering imprisonment or issuing a reprimand, the latter something like a stern warning. If the accused enters a plea of not guilty or waives the preliminary hearing, the next step is the **revocation hearing.**

Revocation Hearing

The revocation hearing follows the Supreme Court guidelines. Probationers have an opportunity to testify and present witnesses. They also have the opportunity to hear and cross-examine the state's witnesses and challenge any other evidence. Unless a compelling state interest exists, the accused also enjoys the right to counsel at this hearing.

A criminal trial and a revocation hearing differ in at least two important ways. First, as Howard Abadinsky (1997, 166) notes, proof in the revocation hearing need not meet the rigid standard of the criminal case, that is, proof beyond a reasonable doubt. Instead, the lower standard of civil cases, a preponderance of evidence, is required to revoke probation. Evidence that would not normally find its way into a criminal case, including hearsay evidence, is often part of revocation hearings. Any relevant information may be considered by the judge in reaching his or her decision, including work records, therapy or treatment appointments kept and broken, and the accused's relationships with family and friends.

Sentencing

Should the probationer be found "not guilty," he or she returns to probation. Should the court's decision be unfavorable, several options remain open to the judge. If the sustained violations are grave or numerous or both, the court will usually revoke probation and order imprisonment. In situations where the sentencing process was suspended, the judge may, upon revocation of probation, provide whatever specific prison sentence the law allows, up to and including the maximum. If the sentence was formally imposed by the court but its execution was suspended in favor of probation, the judge may only order execution of the original sentence.

Origins of Parole

Ask a French speaker if the use of the term *parole* to describe conditional release from prison is troubling. Most likely he or she would give a resounding affirmative answer. That is, we derive the term *parole* from the French phrase *parole d'honneur*, or word of honor.[2] Perhaps it is no accident that European legal systems, including the French, prefer the term *conditional liberation* to *parole*. The term *parole* entered widespread use only after another Bostonian, Dr. G. S. Howe, wrote an 1846 letter to the Prison Association in New York. Howe wrote that "[prisoners] might be so trained as to be left upon their parole during the last period of their imprisonment with safety" (Klein 1920, 417).

The modern idea of **parole**—conditional release from an executive authority responsible for executing a penal sanction—has its origins in the work of Maconochie, Crofton, and Brockway. Key factors in parole's evolution were good time laws and indeterminate sentences. **Good time laws** began in New York in 1817. These practices allowed officials to shorten an inmate's prison term in exchange for good behavior. Similarly, the indeterminate sentence was an essential part of many early release programs, including Brockway's program at the Elmira Reformatory. However, release and return were nearly automatic since the inmates had few resources once they left the prison gates. Prisoner aid societies turned their attention and resources from incarcerated to released prisoners. Volunteers, in the tradition of John Augustus, worked with paroled offenders in the community. Not until 1845 was the first state-paid employee, again in Massachusetts, employed to help parolees adjust to free-world life.

Parole and the Great Depression

During the Great Depression of the 1930s, parole systems in the U.S. grew as never before. Three sets of forces fed this growth. First, by the late 1930s, only Florida, Mississippi, and Virginia did not use parole as a prison release mechanism; South Carolina did not use existing parole statutes until 1941 (Cahalan 1986, 170). Consequently, the systems for early release were in place.

Second, prison populations in the U.S. grew dramatically between the World Wars. In 1923 the per-capita prison population was 74 per 100,000 population, a rate comparable to that reported in 1890 (Cahalan 1986, 30). By 1940, a year before the entry of the United States into World War II, that per-capita figure had risen to 125, an increase of nearly 70%. In 1931, the National Commission on Law Observance and Law Enforcement delivered a bleak report on the nation's overcrowded prison system. Parole was one answer to the crushing economic burden of prison construction and maintenance during the Depression.

Third, federal laws passed during the Depression severely limited the use of prison labor. Inmates became only an economic drain and not an economic well-spring. Like the nation's prison population, the parole population had been around 20,000 for 20 or more years. Between 1930 and 1940 the number of people on parole increased to more than 40,000 (Cahalan 1986, 50). "Pressing economic conditions, not the press of prison reform, led to the popularity of parole release" (Abadinsky 1997, 212).

Parole Today

According to Newman (1958, 4), parole originated not with a single program or experiment. Parole grew out of many different practices, including transportation of prisoners to America and Australia and both the English and Irish ticket-of-leave systems. Whatever its origins, parole continues to evolve. Today, rather than being released on parole, most state and federal prisoners leave correctional institutions under some system of mandatory early release. Current mandatory release programs do not meet the inmates' rehabilitative and reintegrative needs. Instead, they give overburdened prison systems a way to control inmate populations. As a prison closes in on its legally defined capacity, prison administrators have the option of releasing inmates who are close to their expiration date and have had few disciplinary problems while incarcerated.

Administration of Parole

Unless an inmate dies in prison or jail or, in extraordinary circumstances, receives an executive pardon or commutation of sentence, he or she reenters society by one of three ways, depending on local customs and statutes. First,

expiration release results in the unconditional release of a prisoner from incarceration when the sentence—minus any good time credits—ends. Inmates released in this fashion receive no community supervision. Second, **discretionary release** is the system by which an inmate leaves institutional custody when correctional personnel say that he or she is ready for life on the outside. Another governmental entity, usually the parole board, must concur in this belief and authorize the parole. This system is an outgrowth of the medical model and indeterminate sentencing. Third, inmates leave custody under the **mandatory release,** by which the inmate has a fixed (determinate) sentence and an equally fixed set of parole guidelines. Again, good time credits and other incentives may play a role in early release. Once the bookkeepers tell the paroling authority that an offender has served the statutory minimum, supervised release into the community is automatic. This latter system is used in roughly half the states and the federal prison system.

Parole Eligibility

In many jurisdictions, the key to understanding parole is the **parole eligibility date,** the earliest possible point at which the inmate could leave prison. The calculation of this date varies by jurisdiction and release model. First, the inmate's most serious offense must be eligible for parole. For example, in some jurisdictions, persons convicted of first-degree murder or aggravated homicide must serve "natural life sentences." That is, they will never leave prison alive, unless they are pardoned or their sentences are commuted.

The second criterion depends on whether the jurisdiction employs mandatory release or discretionary release. For mandatory release, the question of time served becomes the deciding factor. If the inmate has served the minimum length required by law, he or she is eligible for a parole hearing. Good time and other credits help compress this important period. The inmate may learn of the parole hearing date soon after entering prison or shortly before the hearing, depending upon institutional policy. Under mandatory release programs, new inmates often have a rough estimate when they are eligible. In many discretionary release systems, an inmate is eligible for a parole hearing upon achieving the minimum sentence, minus any good time credits. In still other discretionary jurisdictions, an inmate is eligible after serving one-third to one-half of the maximum sentence. Finally, eligibility for parole may rest entirely with the parole board. No matter what the system, the parole board decides.

Granting Parole and the Parole Board

There are two basic models for operating parole boards. Many states use an **independent parole board model** that is not under the control of any state agency. The independent board makes all release and revocation decisions for parolees in its jurisdiction. Parole supervision is also part of the independent board's function. Less than one-half the states use the independent model, including some with large parole populations, such as New York, Massachusetts, Florida, and New Jersey (American Correctional Association 1997).

The **consolidated parole board model** is an autonomous panel within the department responsible for administering correctional institutions. The parole board makes all release and revocation decisions. Supervision of parolees is the responsibility of another department, often within the Department of Corrections, Corrections Commission, or similarly named organization. Some states use the same authority—the Department, Board, or Commission of Probation and Parole—to supervise both parolees and probationers. This second model is found in most states and the federal system (American Correctional Association 1997).

Once the decision to consider an inmate for early release has been made, the parole board assesses all relevant information. In states using the indeterminate sentence approach, the board establishes minimum and maximum sentences. Given the emphasis on treatment and suitability for release found in these systems, the board may consider evidence of the inmate's progress toward "rehabilitation." They usually examine the inmate's current and past crimes, along with the following:

- Any indication of repentance for his or her prior criminal acts
- Any indication of prior adjustment in the community
- The inmate's physical, emotional, and mental health
- The adequacy of the parole plan, including questions about jobs, place of residence, and social support systems in the community

The PSI report may find its way into parole board deliberations. Parole boards may also hear from the prosecuting attorney and the offender's victims.

The problems of discretion, arbitrariness, and prediction would seem to be missing from parole decisions in states using mandatory release procedures. Once an offender is statutorily eligible for parole, three criteria alone determine its award. Successful parole candidates

- Must have generally followed the correctional institution's rules and regulations
- Must not pose a significant public safety risk if he or she is released
- Must not have committed crimes by which his or her release will cause citizens to question the validity of the criminal justice system or generate disrespect for the law

Even under this system, however, parole boards enjoy considerable discretion. That is, what is meant by the third requirement? When might a specific criminal's release cause the negative effects the parole board seeks to avoid? Obviously, that is for the parole board—and perhaps other stakeholders who make their positions known to the board—to decide.

Second, the risk posed to the public is, like parole and probation prediction generally, open to speculation. No matter whether they use the discretionary model or mandatory release, about one-half of the states also employ a statistical parole prediction method intended to minimize this risk (Ruanda, Rhine, and Wetter 1994). Colorado's **actuarial risk assessment scale** (see Box 7.4.) asks the inmate's **case manager** to provide responses to 11 questions. Three items (Questions 8, 9, and 10) center on institutional adjustments. Prior criminal record figures in another three items (Questions 1, 3, and 5). Only one item (Question 2) specifically addresses the current offense, while another one (Question 6) asks about current and prior criminal activities. The final three items deal exclusively with the offender's personal life, including employment (Question 4), marital status (Question 7), and current age (Question 11). Based on the summated score, this instrument classifies the inmates as high, medium-high, medium, or low risk for parole. Like many similar instruments, Colorado's scale has been repeatedly validated using inmate records to compare predicted and actual parole outcomes (Patzman and English 1994).

Recommendations may be made by prediction tables or case managers or both, but parole boards decide. Hearings are typically quite short, perhaps no longer than 5 or 10 minutes. Unless statutorily defined, states need not have formal hearings or even inform the prisoner as to the reasons for denying parole. (When inmates receive parole, they rarely want to know why.) In jurisdictions where sufficient discretion remains, parole boards may seek to minimize what statisticians call **false positives**—releasing a convict who looked good, but later committed a crime. Rather than subject the public to danger and themselves to embarrassment, parole boards tend to commit the statistician's other type of error, the **false negative.** That is, they deny parole to people who might otherwise be successes. Where mandatory release practices control the paroling system, unless there are compelling reasons to the contrary, early release is nearly automatic.

Conditions of Parole

The **standard conditions of parole** listed on the parole agreement within a given state are often indistinguishable from those for probationers. Should the inmate have unique needs that require **special conditions of parole,** they become part of the official parole agreement. For example, consider the case of the inmate whose original crime involved a child sex offense. While in custody, the inmate participated in a sex offender program. The soon-to-be parolee receives instructions in the form of special conditions that (1) he or she cannot frequent places where children gather and (2) he or she must participate in a specific therapy program as an outpatient.

Length of Supervision

State and federal laws govern the length of time one spends on parole. Typically, the parolee must spend a minimum amount of time being supervised no

Box 7.4

Colorado's Risk Assessment Scale

COLORADO ACTUARIAL RISK ASSESSMENT SCALE*
To Be Completed by Case Manager / Community Corrections Agent:

Inmate Name_____ DOC #_____

Case Manager_____ Form Date_____ Facility_____

For each item, enter the weight corresponding to the information in the offender's record.

* **This scale does not apply to currently convicted Sex Offenders or Women.**

1. Any prior adult or juvenile felony conviction for burglary, robbery, theft, or auto theft (include deferred judgments):
   - 0 (No)
   - 7 (Yes)
   - 0 (Unknown)   _____

2. Total number of original felony convictions on current prison sentence(s) (Do not count prior convictions):
   - 0 (1)
   - 3 (2-3)
   - 5 (4 +)   _____

3. Total number of prior adult and/or juvenile sentenced incarcerations to prison, jail, or juvenile facility for felony offense: If UNKNOWN, substitute number of prior felony convictions.
   - 0 (None)
   - 3 (One)
   - 5 (Two or more)   _____

4. Employed 50% or more of two consecutive years prior to original arrest date:
   - 0 (Yes)
   - 5 (No)
   - 0 (Unknown)   _____

5. Convicted of a felony or adjudicated a delinquent before age 18:
   - 0 (No)
   - 4 (Yes)
   - 0 (Unknown)   _____

VIOLENT AND GENERAL RISK SCALE

SCORE	RISK LEVEL
34-46	HIGH RISK
28-33	HIGH MEDIUM RISK
15-27	MEDIUM RISK
-3-14	LOW RISK

6. Serious offender classification: Do one or more of the following apply? (check all that apply)
   - ☐ -Current conviction for violent crime (use TABLE A , below).
   - ☐ -Current court conviction for escape (include attempts/ conspiracies);
   - ☐ -Prior conviction for felony against a person in the last 5 years of street time;
   - ☐ -Three or more prior adult or juvenile arrests for: robbery, rape, felony assault, kidnap, or aggravated burglary (weapon or injury);
   - ☐ -Substance abuse history includes one of the following: PCP use, injections of speed, cocaine, or hallucinogens (not heroin), or sniffing volatile substances (glue, paint).
     - 0 (No)
     - 4 (Yes)
     - 0 (Unknown)   _____

7. Ever legally married: (Do not include common law)
   - 0 (Yes)
   - 3 (No)
   - 0 (Unknown)   _____

8. Present incarceration includes administrative action for an escape/walkaway or parole violation in the last 5 years: (technical violation or new crime)
   - 0 (No)
   - 1 (Escape)
   - 2 (Parole Violation)
   - 0 (Unknown)   _____

9. Class I or Class IIA COPD disciplinary infractions during this incarceration:
   - -3 (None)
   - -1 (Yes, but none in last 6 months)
   - 3 (One last 6 months)
   - 5 (2 + last 6 months)   _____

10. Code the most serious disciplinary infraction incurred during the past 6 months:
   - 0 (None)
   - 2 (Class IIA)
   - 3 (Class I)   _____

11. Age at PED or next hearing for governing sentence (whichever applies):
   - 0 (35 +)
   - 1 (25-34)
   - 3 (18-24)

TOTAL SCORE ☐

INSTRUCTIONS FOR COMPLETING RISK SCALE FORM
THIS SCALE DOES NOT APPLY TO WOMEN OR INMATES CURRENTLY CONVICTED OF ONLY SEX OFFENSES.

For items 1-7, if offender is currently in on a TECHNICAL parole, probation, or community corrections revocation use information related to the original commitment offense.

1. File must specifically document adult conviction, juvenile adjudications, or deferred judgements/sentences for burglary, robbery, theft, or auto theft. Do not include theft by fraud and deceit; include theft by receiving and attempts/conspiracies to commit burglary, robbery, theft, or auto theft.
2. Include total number of convictions for this sentence (i.e., two counts of burglary and two counts of robbery total four convictions). Include convictions from other states if the crime would have been a felony if committed in Colorado. If the inmate is currently serving time on a technical parole, probation, or community corrections violation do not count the revocation as a conviction; rather, consider only the original conviction(s).
3. "Incarcerations" include sentences to jail (not pretrial confinement), juvenile commitments to secure facilities (including any commitment to the Department of Institutions), and commitments to prison as an adult. If you can't find incarceration information, substitute the number of prior felony convictions (do not count this one).
4. Consider the last 24 (consecutive) months the inmate was on the street before the original date of arrest. Time spent locked-up or in school is NOT employment. For technical parole, probation, or community corrections violators the 24 month period is the time BEFORE the original prison sentence. YES if file documents full-time or part-time employment which totals at least 12 of the last 24 street months (for example, if the inmate worked halftime for nine months, this totals 4.5 months of employment. NO if inmate was employed less than a total of 12 months. UNKNOWN if file contains inadequate employment information.
5. "Felony" refers to any crime that would be considered a felony if committed by an adult in Colorado.
6. If the offender is presently serving time on a technical parole/probation violation, code this item as if he was serving time on the original sentence.
   -Violent crime: See TABLE A, below.
   -Escape: Do not count escapes handled administratively.
   -Prior conviction: Look for violent felony convictions during the last 60 months the inmate was free (on the street) to commit crimes.
   -Three or more violent arrests: Unlike the other items in the Risk Scale, this requires information on arrests, not convictions.
   -Substance abuse: Note that these are substances that tend to make people behave unpredictably or violently.
7. Do not count common-law relationships.
8. Include county jail escapes and community corrections walkaways. Do not include technical or community corrections violations.
9. Consider only DOC infractions which occurred during this term of incarceration (include time served on technical violations).
10. Consider only DOC infractions which occurred during the past 6 months on the current sentence.
11. Code according to the age the inmate will be at potential parole release date.

TABLE A   SERIOUS OFFENDER CLASSIFICATION: CURRENT CONVICTION FOR VIOLENT CRIME

Murder	Rape/Sex Assault	Kidnapping for Ransom	Aggravated Robbery	1st Degree Burglary
Arson of a Dwelling	Voluntary Manslaughter	Attempted Rape/Sex Assault	Sex Assault on a Child	Kidnapping
Robbery	Felony Assault	Terrorism	Arson	Involuntary Manslaughter
Extortion/blackmail	Escape	Jailbreak	Aggravated Assault	
		Conspiracy/Attempt to Commit a Violent Felony		

Reprinted by permission.

Box 7.5

Which Parolees Return to Prison?

A 1991 NIJ study reported on 155,874 ex-parolees returned to prison for either a new conviction or a technical violation. While on parole, they committed at least 6,800 murders, 5,500 rapes, 8,800 assaults, and 22,500 robberies. They averaged 33 months in prison before release and 13 months on parole before their return. However, these figures varied greatly across offense types. For example, violent offenders averaged 50 months in prison before release. They spent an average of 16 months on parole before committing a new offense. At the other extreme, public-order offenders spent about 20 months in prison before parole. Public-order offenders averaged about 10 months on parole before returning to prison.

The NIJ study revealed that those who spent longer periods in prison—that is, those convicted of homicide, sexual assault, or robbery—also spent more time in the community before violating. Two different sets of forces could explain these figures. First, the really violent offenders may have tried to stay out of trouble because they had tasted prison and did not like it. Unfortunately for them, their victims, and society, they were unsuccessful. It is also possible that drug and property criminals find it even harder to keep out of trouble. Then, too, violent offenders typically face far stricter release conditions and greater levels of supervision than nonviolent ones, factors that seem to hasten revocation. Finally, inmates convicted of "other violent crimes," including kidnapping, served the longest average sentences (75 months); they averaged less than one year before returning to prison. Statistics such as these help punctuate the difficulties in parole prediction.

Source: Cohen (1995).

---

matter how well he or she behaves on parole. Supervision ranges from as little as six months to one year up to as much as four to seven years (Abadinsky 1997, 258). Most states empower the parole authority to discharge a supervisee before the end of the mandated period of supervision. Again, the states exhibit considerable variation in how little time on parole is enough time.

Violation of Parole

Parole, like probation, has two possible outcomes. Success is self-explanatory. Failure involves the same two issues observed for probation: technical violations and new offense violations. (See Box 7.5 for a discussion of which parolees return to prison.) Whatever form the violation takes, the parole officer, having learned of the alleged offense, confers with a supervisor about the appropriate course of action. If the alleged offense is serious, the parole officer asks the court of jurisdiction to issue an arrest warrant. If the officer observed the violation in person, most states allow the officer to take the parolee into immediate custody, an act called a **summary arrest.** Once in custody the parolee's presence at any subsequent hearings is essentially guaranteed. Few states allow parolees bail, adding to the certainty of the parolees' appearance in court. Finally, in some jurisdictions the parole officer, after assessing the

A somewhat apprehensive "client" of the probation and parole system learns about the conditions of his release while still in custody. Pre-release planning is a vital function in determining the time and conditions of release—especially for parolees.

parolee's threat to the community and as a flight risk, may issue a **citation,** a legal document roughly equivalent to a traffic ticket. The citation orders the parolee to appear at a violation hearing.

Preliminary Hearing

In *Morrisey v. Brewer* (1972), the Supreme Court ruled that the parolee, like the probationer, enjoyed limited due process rights. The Court did not mandate that the preliminary hearing take place before the parole board. The only stipulation was that it must be a neutral party. Often a **hearing officer,** typically a supervisory-level or senior member of the parole agency staff, conducts the preliminary (probable cause) hearing. The parolee's case officer presents the government's case. In the event the officer fails to make the case for a violation, the parolee returns to supervision. Should the hearing officer find that probable cause exists for one or more violations, the parolee may be remanded to jail until the revocation hearing.

Revocation Hearing

The hearing board's composition varies from state to state. Often the jurisdiction's parole board decides whether the alleged violator should return to incarceration or to parole. Whoever serves, the tribunal's neutrality is crucial:

Table 7.2

Probation and Parole: Separate or Combined Officers?

Type of Officers	Authority
Separate Officers	Arizona, Arkansas, California, Colorado, Connecticut, Georgia, Hawaii, Illinois, Indiana, Kansas, Massachusetts, Nebraska, New Jersey, New York, North Carolina, Ohio, Rhode Island, South Dakota, Tennessee, Texas, West Virginia, and the District of Columbia
Combined Officers	Alabama, Alaska, Delaware, Florida, Idaho, Iowa, Kentucky, Louisiana, Maine,[a] Maryland, Michigan, Minnesota, Mississippi, Missouri, Montana, Nevada, New Hampshire, New Mexico, North Dakota, Oklahoma, Oregon, Pennsylvania, South Carolina, Utah, Vermont, Virginia, Washington, Wisconsin, Wyoming, and the U.S. Probation and Pretrial Services System[b]

[a] Maine abolished parole in 1976; any state prisoners released under previous parole statutes are supervised by probation officers.

[b] The federal government restructured its sentencing and parole systems in the late 1980s; any federal prisoners released under previous parole statutes are supervised by U.S. probation officers.

Source: American Correctional Association (1997).

they must have no stake in the outcome. While the revocation hearing is more exhaustive and comprehensive than the preliminary hearing, many legal niceties are missing. Again, if the preponderance of evidence supports the alleged violation, the board has several options, including continuation on parole with restricted freedoms or incarcerating the parolee. On those occasions when the hearing board finds in the parolee's favor, supervision continues.

Jurisdictions also vary greatly in their responses to two other key concerns. First, the parole violator may not have to spend the rest of his or her original sentence before a second parole. Unless the violation involved a new offense, eligibility may be statutory and occurs in a relatively short time. Second, paroling authorities also vary in their views on time served under parole supervision. In some states this time does not count toward the original sentence, while in others parolees receive credit for their time in the community.

Probation and Parole Officers

The various jurisdictions in the U.S. take several different approaches to probation and parole work. First, as summarized in Table 7.2, 21 states and the District of Columbia use separate probation and parole officers (American Correctional Association 1997). This model acknowledges that separate governmental entities grant probation and parole. For example, probation officers are officers of the judicial branch of government. In many jurisdictions, judges or court administrators hire, train, evaluate, and fire probation officers. In some jurisdictions, however, probation officers occupy state-level civil service positions. For their part, parole officers receive their powers and authority from the executive branch. Most parole officers, therefore, are state-level civil service employees.

Careers in Contemporary Corrections

Probation and Parole Officers

In probation and parole work, titles are not uniform from jurisdiction to jurisdiction. The most common title is **probation and parole officers,** but in some states they may be known as agents. As we have discussed in this chapter, some jurisdictions separate the supervision of parolees from probationers. For purposes of simplicity, we use the generic title of probation and parole officers (or PPOs), recognizing that both the titles and functions may vary.

One positive aspect of probation and parole work is that PPOs work with one group of offenders—probationers—who have the best prospects for crime-free future lives. Probationers are people with whom we are willing to take a risk and who deserve a second chance. PPOs may be able to provide their clients with drug and alcohol counseling, marriage counseling, and other types of therapies. However, one of the negative aspects of probation and parole work is that most officers have too many clients to provide much individualized attention. Therefore, in many jurisdictions PPOs become service brokers. In this environment (the **broker model**) they will try to match clients to services that are provided by public or private community organizations. In addition to providing services to clients, probation and parole officers also provide surveillance. Surveillance, including both physical and electronic monitoring, is required for both probationers and parolees to verify their adherence to the rules associated with their conditional release.

Parolees are more difficult to work with than probationers, and statistics show lower success rates for paroled offenders than probationers. The biggest challenge in working with parolees is successfully reintegrating them into the community. Such work involves locating housing, finding appropriate jobs or training programs, and trying to smooth the transition back into their family lives.

Among the negative aspects of probation and parole work four seem especially prominent. First, probation and parole work can be emotionally intense. When PPOs get involved in their clients' lives they sometimes find it difficult to leave work at work. For those officers who do not learn to cope with this particular aspect of the job, burnout may result. Sometimes the newest and most idealistic PPOs find it impossible not to get emotionally invested in their clients. Second, some probation and parole agencies do not have especially effective record-keeping systems, and this makes it difficult for some PPOs to have tangible measures of their success. Given the intense criticism periodically leveled at probation and parole agencies, PPOs need regular feedback on how they are doing. Third, as PPOs come to realize, some clients are doomed to failure despite the officer's best intentions. This defeat flies in the face of the high levels of optimism expressed, especially by newly appointed PPOs. Finally, in some jurisdictions probation and parole officers now are issued firearms, and some PPOs consider this a negative aspect of the contemporary work world.

The expected salary levels for PPOs typically are higher than those for correctional officers. It is important to remember, however, that there are fewer PPOs than correctional officers. For instance, in 1994 there were 33,853 individuals working in state and federal probation, parole, or combined probation and parole positions.

In 1994, the lowest average salaries were from about $18,000 to 19,000 (for states such as Arkansas, Maryland, South Carolina, and West Virginia). Most states had average salaries around $20,000–35,000. The highest average salaries were reported by Alaska, California, Michigan, Minnesota, New Hampshire, and Ohio. The salary average for federal probation and parole positions was $47,000. To get the most recent salary information for these positions contact your local probation and parole office or state department of corrections (much of this information is now available through a search of Internet sites).

Educational requirements and prior experience separate PPOs from correctional officers. In virtually all jurisdictions juvenile and adult PPOs are required to have a bachelor's degree. Some of the common preferred majors include counseling, criminal justice/criminology, psychology, social work, and sociology. Furthermore, although agencies require a bachelor's degree, others prefer or require a master's degree in an area related to probation and parole.

As an alternative to the requirement of a bachelor's degree, some jurisdictions may substitute a certain number of years of experience for each year of education required. The important thing to remember about these positions is that given the relatively small number of PPOs—in comparison to correctional officers—the competition is very stiff. Therefore, applicants should enter the process with the greatest amount of education and experience possible.

Finally, because there are fewer PPOs than there are correctional officers, and because probation and parole agencies tend to be less hierarchical than prisons, there are often fewer promotion opportunities for PPOs. Thus, while there will be opportunities for advancement, the number of opportunities may not be as great as in the world of institutional corrections.

Sources: DeLucia and Doyle (1994); Maguire and Pastore (1995); Stinchcomb (1992); Williamson (1990).

The second approach to probation and parole work is a unified system, found in 29 states and the U.S. Probation and Pretrial Services Systems. Combined officers either have a mixed caseload of probationers and parolees or specialize in one type of releasee. Specialization recognizes the unique adjustment problems faced by individuals reentering society after a prison sentence. Maine and the federal government officially no longer offer parole. Since some inmates in these two jurisdictions received parole dates before the law changed, officers provide for their post-release supervision. Other jurisdictions have so few parolees that the probation authority and probation officers supervise their release.

The number of clients assigned to a given probation or parole officer (PPO)—the **caseload**—varies widely across the nation. For example, Figure 7.2 contains a summary of caseloads by state (The supporting data are shown in Table 7.3).[3] Considerable variation exists among these grouped sets of figures. The average monthly caseload for all reporting states was 106. More than one-third of the states and the federal system reported monthly average caseloads of 70 releasees or fewer. At the other extreme, the average caseload for PPOs in a dozen states exceeded 131 releasees. In four states, the PPOs averaged more than 200 cases.

The numbers reported in Figure 7.2, while interesting and important, tell only part of the story. To arrive at these averages, we divided the total number of probationers and parolees in a given jurisdiction by the total number of field officers employed by that jurisdiction. Such statistics can be deceptive. For example, some probationers or parolees are on **intensive supervision.**

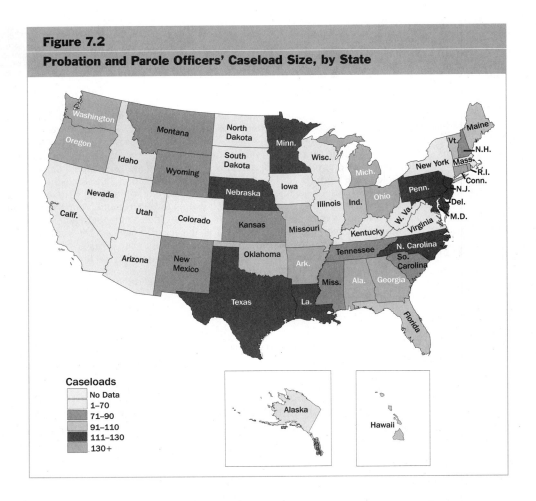

Figure 7.2

Probation and Parole Officers' Caseload Size, by State

Caseloads

- No Data
- 1–70
- 71–90
- 91–110
- 111–130
- 130+

No generic intensive supervision program (ISP) model exists. As the name suggests, officers provide far closer offender supervision. Curfew, multiple *weekly* contacts with PPOs, strict enforcement of probation or parole conditions, unscheduled drug testing, and the requirement to perform community service are common elements (Petersilia and Turner 1990). Because many intensive supervision clients have lengthy drug histories, a zero-tolerance drug-testing policy may be enforced: One "dirty urine" and they go to prison or jail. Typically, intensive supervision involves the assignment of as few as 20 to 25 releasees to each PPO. The significance of this practice for other officers is higher caseloads.

A common practice in parole supervision is to assign far fewer releasees per officer than is the case for probation. Parolees are considered higher risks than probationers. Their release conditions are often more restrictive than those for probationers, requiring more time-intensive field work. Probation

Table 7.3

**Data for Figure 7.2, Probation and
Parole Officers' Caseload Size, by State**

State	Monthly Avg. Caseload	Group	State	Monthly Avg. Caseload	Group
Alabama	175	5	Montana	85	2
Alaska	51	1	Nebraska	113	4
Arizona	60	1	Nevada	51	1
Arkansas	216	5	New Hampshire	82	2
California	63	1	New Jersey	111	4
Colorado	—	0	New Mexico	87	2
Connecticut	175	5	New York	59	1
DC	143	5	North Carolina	115	4
Delaware	161	5	North Dakota	61	1
Florida	104	3	Ohio	140	5
Georgia	193	5	Pennsylvania	116	4
Hawaii	102	3	Oklahoma	100	3
Idaho	52	1	Oregon	283	5
Illinois	57	1	Rhode Island	288	5
Indiana	93	3	South Carolina	75	2
Iowa	67	1	South Dakota	48	1
Kansas	73	2	Tennessee	79	2
Kentucky	51	1	Texas	128	4
Louisiana	114	4	Utah	54	1
Maine	95	3	Vermont	97	3
Maryland	159	5	Virginia	70	1
Massachusetts	47	1	Washington	214	5
Michigan	194	5	West Virginia	45	1
Minnesota	124	4	Wisconsin	62	1
Mississippi	90	2	Wyoming	73	2
Missouri	91	3	Federal	30	1

Source: American Correctional Association (1997); Department
of Justice (1996b); Maguire and Pastore (1996).

officers may also have mixed felony and misdemeanor probationers. If this is
the case, it is very likely that the felony probationers will consume more of
the PPO's time. In jurisdictions in which an officer works exclusively misdemeanor probationers, caseloads of 500, 750, or even 1,000 are common.
These probationers, it is believed, require less supervision. In essence, they
are paperwork probationers. To the extent that the probation officer works a
mixed caseload of felony and misdemeanor probation, the former consumes
more time and gets more attention than the latter.

Rather than simply dividing caseloads into felony or misdemeanor probationers, most probation departments employ a risk-management classification
scheme. PPOs classify releasees into supervision levels using one of an estimated two dozen instruments (Eaglin and Lombard 1982). Most classification
instruments derive from either the National Institute of Corrections Model
Probation Client Classification and Case Management System or the Wisconsin System (Clear and Gallagher 1985). Typically, the instruments recommend

Box 7.6

**Intensive Supervision:
Does It Make a Difference?**

A RAND assessment of ISPs for probationers and parolees at 14 sites around the nation raised as many questions as it answered. The researchers convinced the authorities to assign probationers randomly to either intensive supervision or regular probation or parole. The test and control subjects were followed for one year. The researchers were quick to acknowledge that the time available in the study for failure (that is, one year) was short. Still, the study is acclaimed as the largest experimental study of probationers or parolees ever undertaken.

The findings, however, were problematic for ISP supporters. ISP supervisees reoffended and returned to prison at a higher rate than those on regular probation; they had a technical violation rate twice that of the controls. Apparently, the stricter rules and greater supervision made rules detections—and accompanying revocations— easier for PPOs. According to RAND calculations, ISPs cost more per probation to administer and resulted in somewhat worse results for the nearly identical types of offenders. This finding challenges the utility of intensive supervision. As Petersilia and Turner observed, "Our results suggest that ISP programs, as implemented in this study, are not effective for high-risk offenders *if effectiveness is judged solely by offender recidivism rates*" (1990, xii; emphasis in the original). They also maintained that the most compelling reason for the continued use and even expansion of ISPs is the concept of just deserts, or let the punishment fit the crime. "Routine probation clearly does not constitute just punishment for felons with serious prior records" (1990, xiii).

Sources: Petersilia and Turner (1990, 1993).

assignment to one of the following levels (Bartollas and Conrad 1992, 242; Champion 1988):

- **Minimum supervision** is for those offenders who pose no significant threat to public safety and have no history of serious law violations (that is, the violations are mostly misdemeanors with some property felonies). These low-risk probationers are normally allowed to contact the PPO, by mail or phone, once a month or even less frequently.

- **Medium supervision** is for those offenders who also pose no significant threat to the public but who do have histories of serious law violations (that is, their violations are mostly personal felonies with some misdemeanors). They must physically report to the PPO at least once a month, and the officers may make occasional visits to their place of work or residence.

- **Intensive supervision** is for offenders who have histories of violent behavior or are likely to commit serious crimes in the future (that is, their violations are mostly serious violent felonies). They must be seen by their PPOs several times a month and are subject to even more regular visitations from PPOs than those under medium supervision.

Risk-screening instruments such as these, and similar ones for parolees, help PPOs make time and task allocations for their supervisees. However, according to the research summarized in Box 7.7, these tools are far from perfect.

Box 7.7

Screening Instruments or Screening Officers: Which One Better Predicts Probation Outcomes?

Robert Sigler and Jimmie Williams address the old question of who makes better decisions, a sterile, objective instrument or a human being. They collected information on 520 closed federal probation cases from the Northern District of Alabama. The specific information was identical with that used by four of the major probation screening instruments: Revised Oregon, California BE61A, U.S. Parole Commission's Salient Factor Score, and the U.S. District of Columbia 75 Scale (USDC75A). They also collected the officer's independent classification. Sigler and Williams reported that the officers and the California BE61A were the least conservative, that is, they assigned maximum supervision least often. The Salient Factor Score was the most conservative, assigning 422 (88%) probationers to maximum supervision, as compared with the 25 (6%) assigned by the officers.

How about outcomes? Sigler and Williams reported that officers made better predictions about probationer risks (that is, the correlation between assignment level and failure rate) than the California BE61A and the Salient Factor Score methods made predictions that were about equally as accurate as the USDC75A and made predictions that were less accurate than the Revised Oregon scale. In particular, claimed Sigler and Williams, the use of the U.S. District of Columbia 75 Scale would have helped officers in moving the close calls from lower risk to higher risk categories. Universal application of risk-screening instruments, they warn, may entail its own risk: Success or failure on probation may be dependent to a greater extent on human characteristics than the information considered by such instruments.

Source: Sigler and Williams (1994).

Probation and Parole Services Today

On any given day, more than 5 million adults are under the care or custody of a state or federal correctional agency.[4] Probation is by far the most common form of correctional supervision used in the United States. The probationer figures (for 1995), summarized in Table 7.4, are staggering. State and federal probationers number more than 3 million, with about 98% of that total being supervised by state agencies. Another way of looking at these figures is that we have nearly 1,600 probationers in the United States for every 100,000 adult residents.

Regionally, the South has more people on probation (1,254,817) and more probationers per capita (1,846) than any other region. In fact, the per-capita rates are remarkably similar for the West (1,397), Northeast (1,402) and Midwest (1,485), meaning that the South also places roughly 20% more people on probation than any other region. These figures beg a question: Are southern states as a group more likely to use probation than other states? A few high-performing jurisdictions, including Texas, Delaware, Georgia, and the District of Columbia, have propelled the region to its lead position.

The use of parole also provides some interesting regional and state comparisons.[5] In 1995 the nation's 700,000-plus adults on parole translated into a per-capita rate of 361 for every 100,000 adult residents (see Table 7.5).

Table 7.4

Adults on Probation, 1995

Region and Jurisdiction	Probation population 1/1/95	1995 Entries	1995 Exits	Probation population 12/31/95	Percent change in probation population during 1995	Number on probation on 12/31/95 per 100,000 adult residents
U.S. total	**2,981,022**	**1,578,182**	**1,451,948**	**3,096,529**	**3.9%**	**1,596**
Federal	42,309	18,601	22,404	38,506	—	20
State	2,938,713	1,559,581	1,429,544	3,058,023	4.1	1,576
Northeast	**526,375**	**232,686**	**214,444**	**544,620**	**3.5%**	**1,402**
Connecticut	53,453	37,135	36,081	54,507	2.0	2,201
Maine[a]	8,638	:	:	8,641	—	923
Massachusetts	46,670	34,611	37,601	43,680	−6.4	941
New Hampshire	4,323	3,432	3,408	4,347	.6	509
New Jersey	125,299	59,376	57,552	127,123	1.5	2,125
New York	163,613	45,061	35,175	173,499	6.0	1,276
Pennsylvania[b]	99,524	39,764	32,465	106,823	7.3	1,166
Rhode Island	18,179	9,813	9,314	18,678	2.7	2,483
Vermont	6,676	3,494	2,848	7,322	9.7	1,672
Midwest	**642,546**	**418,160**	**387,163**	**676,997**	**5.4%**	**1,485**
Illinois[a]	104,664	63,862	61,723	109,489	4.6	1,258
Indiana[c]	83,177	76,593	70,312	89,458	7.6	2,073
Iowa	15,902	10,456	9,779	16,579	4.3	783
Kansas[a]	17,256	11,831	7,726	16,547	−4.1	884
Michigan[a,d]	142,640	68,000	62,338	148,337	4.0	2,110
Minnesota[a]	81,972	55,911	57,131	83,778	2.2	2,490
Missouri[a,b,c]	36,295	21,887	18,453	40,595	11.8	1,030
Nebraska[c]	18,639	15,485	14,697	19,427	4.2	1,627
North Dakota	2,036	1,474	1,219	2,291	12.5	486
Ohio[a,d]	90,190	68,077	59,558	99,603	10.4	1,201
South Dakota[e,f]	3,874	4,393	4,643	3,624	−6.5	693
Wisconsin[a]	45,901	20,191	19,584	47,269	3.0	1,254
South	**1,214,375**	**618,343**	**573,402**	**1,254,817**	**3.3%**	**1,846**
Alabama[c,d]	31,284	4,696	4,498	31,416	.4	990
Arkansas	19,606	8,431	5,656	22,381	14.2	1,220
Delaware[c]	15,507	7,395	6,555	16,347	5.4	3,036
District of Col.[a,g]	11,306	4,733	5,777	10,262	−9.2	2,334
Florida[a,d]	247,014	146,989	133,585	255,550	3.5	2,367
Georgia[a,d]	140,694	69,102	67,228	142,453	1.3	2,699

Again, most parolees are under state authority, although the percentage of federal parolees (8%) is higher than that found for federal probation services (2%). Nearly one parolee in six resides in Texas, a state with one of the nation's highest state per-capita rate. In spite of this fact, the Northeast region has the highest per-capita rate. The rate for all southern states is only slightly higher than the national average, followed by the West and Midwest. Except for the Midwest, each region has at least one mega-system of parole. For example, Pennsylvania has 40% of the parolees in the Northeast and that region's highest per-capita rate. Parolees in California account for 70% of that region's total, but, due to its huge population, have a per-capita rate second to Utah's.

A consideration of parole rates reveals that the varying regional rates are also driven mostly by a few "high achieving" states. For example, the North-

Table 7.4 (continued)

Adults on Probation, 1995

Region and Jurisdiction	Probation population 1/1/95	1995 Entries	1995 Exits	Probation population 12/31/95	Percent change in probation population during 1995	Number on probation on 12/31/95 per 100,000 adult residents
Kentucky	11,417	5,582	5,500	11,499	.7	398
Louisiana	33,604	11,431	11,282	33,753	.4	1,088
Maryland	76,940	35,530	41,441	71,029	−7.7	1,884
Mississippi	9,042	3,511	2,958	9,595	6.1	496
North Carolina	90,418	49,804	42,301	97,921	8.3	1,815
Oklahoma[a,d]	26,285	14,195	13,029	27,866	6.0	1,161
South Carolina	40,005	16,643	14,482	42,166	5.4	1,545
Tennessee[d]	34,896	20,431	18,594	36,733	5.3	931
Texas[h]	396,276	200,365	181,144	415,497	4.9	3,119
Virginia[d]	24,089	19,394	19,219	24,264	.7	485
West Virginia[a,d,g,i]	5,992	111	153	6,085	1.6	433
West	**555,417**	**290,392**	**254,535**	**581,589**	**4.7%**	**1,397**
Alaska	2,899	960	1,296	2,563	−12.0	619
Arizona[a,c,d]	34,365	15,514	10,728	32,532	−5.3	1,076
California	277,655	142,560	133,229	286,986	3.4	1,259
Colorado[a,d]	39,065	25,042	21,840	42,010	7.5	1,519
Hawaii	13,088	6,620	6,385	13,323	1.8	1,518
Idaho[c,g]	5,770	6,110	5,711	6,169	6.9	757
Montana	5,656	2,022	1,833	5,845	3.3	922
Nevada	9,410	6,043	5,377	10,076	7.1	890
New Mexico[d]	8,063	7,727	7,514	8,276	2.6	698
Oregon	38,086	13,397	11,758	39,725	4.3	1,695
Utah	7,714	4,136	3,372	8,478	9.9	664
Washington[a,d]	110,279	58,476	43,640	122,306	10.9	3,048
Wyoming	3,367	1,785	1,852	3,300	−2.0	960

Note: — Not calculated.
  : Not Known.
[a] Because of nonresponse or incomplete data, the population on December 31, 1995, does not equal the population on January 1, 1995, plus entries minus exits.
[b] Total exits are estimated.
[c] All data are estimated.
[d] Multiple agencies reporting.

[e] Data are for year ending June 30, 1995.
[f] Data do not include absconders.
[g] January 1, 1995, population count is estimated.
[h] Data are for year ending August 31, 1995.
[i] December 31, 1995, population count is estimated.
Source: Department of Justice (1997:33).

east has five states with per-capita rates ranging from 4 (Maine, which abolished parole in 1976) to 100 (Massachusetts). Two large northeastern states, New Jersey and Pennsylvania, have per-capita rates more than twice the national average. The result is a higher regional per-capita rate for the Northeast than any other region. At the other extreme, the rates for most states in the Midwest—except Illinois, Kansas, and Missouri—are well below 200.

Profiles of Probationers and Parolees

The average probationer is a White male. (See Table 7.6.) Women are proportionately more likely than men to receive a probated sentence (that is, about 10% of arrestees and prison inmates are women). We are uncertain whether this difference is due to sex discrimination or the fact that they commit less serious offenses. While African-Americans account for fewer probationers

Table 7.5

Adults on Parole, 1995

Region and Jurisdiction	Parole population 1/1/95	1995 Entries	1995 Exits	Parole population 12/31/95	Percent change in parole population during 1995	Number on parole on 12/31/95 per 100,000 adult residents
U.S. total	**690,371**	**411,369**	**391,298**	**700,174**	**1.4%**	**361**
Federal[b]	61,430	29,491	22,552	59,136	—	30
State	628,941	381,878	368,746	641,038	1.9	330
Northeast	**173,882**	**77,451**	**67,082**	**184,122**	**5.9%**	**474**
Connecticut	1,146	1,934	1,847	1,233	7.6	50
Maine[a,b]	40	1	2	41	2.5	4
Massachusetts[a,c,d]	4,755	3,727	3,702	4,639	−2.4	100
New Hampshire[a]	835	702	762	785	−6.0	92
New Jersey	41,802	17,198	11,589	47,411	13.4	793
New York	53,832	27,158	25,422	55,568	3.2	409
Pennsylvania	70,355	25,814	22,935	73,234	4.1	799
Rhode Island	525	597	529	593	13.0	79
Vermont	592	320	294	618	4.4	141
Midwest	**82,478**	**62,155**	**56,698**	**87,364**	**5.9%**	**192**
Illinois	26,695	22,706	19,860	29,541	10.7	339
Indiana	3,409	5,310	5,120	3,599	5.6	83
Iowa	3,696	1,665	1,826	3,535	−4.4	167
Kansas[b]	6,291	3,741	3,938	6,094	−3.1	325
Michigan	12,846	9,078	8,062	13,862	7.9	197
Minnesota	1,904	2,581	2,368	2,117	11.2	63
Missouri[a,e]	12,592	5,352	5,278	13,023	3.4	330
Nebraska	771	718	828	661	−14.3	55
North Dakota	94	209	189	114	21.3	24
Ohio	6,453	5,332	5,203	6,582	2.0	79
South Dakota	662	590	564	688	3.9	132
Wisconsin	7,065	4,873	3,462	7,548	6.8	200
South	**253,731**	**101,722**	**111,741**	**243,309**	**−4.1%**	**358**
Alabama[e,f,g]	7,235	1,525	1,525	7,235	.0	228
Arkansas[e]	5,224	4,108	4,477	4,855	−7.1	265
Delaware[e]	1,029	40	259	810	−21.3	150
District of Columbia	6,574	2,702	2,580	6,696	1.9	1,523
Florida[a]	20,573	3,769	9,649	13,746	−33.2	127

than jail or prison inmates, they are still present at a rate that is twice their proportion in the general population. More than half of the probationers committed a felony. About a quarter received a probated sentence because of a misdemeanor conviction. About one in five received probation after a drug- or alcohol-related driving offense. Finally, most probationers are on active status, while roughly the same proportion either are currently inactive, waiting for termination, or have absconded.

Nearly all parolees are males, although this is not surprising given the gender differential in the nation's prison population. White parolees outnumber minority ones (just barely), an interesting fact considering that African-Americans and other minorities outnumber Whites in prison. Nearly all parolees (94%) are felons, as opposed to probationers, half of whom committed a non-felony. Like probationers, not all parolees are under the same supervision level. Three-fourths are on active supervision; 1 in 10 is inactive.

Table 7.5 *(continued)*						
Adults on Parole, 1995						
Region and Jurisdiction	Parole population 1/1/95	1995 Entries	1995 Exits	Parole population 12/31/95	Percent change in parole population during 1995	Number on parole on 12/31/95 per 100,000 adult residents
Georgia[a]	17,505	10,862	9,479	19,434	11.0	368
Kentucky	4,380	3,256	3,379	4,257	−2.8	147
Louisiana	17,112	9,793	7,877	19,028	11.2	613
Maryland	14,795	11,921	10,968	15,748	6.4	418
Mississippi[a]	1,519	840	847	1,510	−0.6	78
North Carolina	20,159	11,530	13,188	18,501	−8.2	343
Oklahoma	2,604	661	909	2,356	−9.5	98
South Carolina	6,077	1,522	1,702	5,897	−3.0	216
Tennessee	9,353	3,357	3,859	8,851	−5.4	224
Texas[e]	108,563	24,425	29,899	103,089	−5.0	774
Virginia[e]	9,649	10,766	10,227	10,188	5.6	204
West Virginia[f]	1,380	645	917	1,108	−19.7	79
West	**118,850**	**140,550**	**133,225**	**126,243**	**6.2%**	**303**
Alaska[c,h]	412	439	392	459	11.4	111
Arizona	4,351	5,693	5,935	4,109	−5.6	136
California[f,g]	85,082	118,948	112,223	91,807	7.9	403
Colorado	2,463	3,021	2,460	3,024	22.8	109
Hawaii	1,650	668	629	1,689	2.4	192
Idaho[a,f]	931	539	676	862	−7.4	106
Montana	710	431	386	755	6.3	119
Nevada[e]	3,529	1,787	1,856	3,460	−2.0	306
New Mexico[g]	1,078	815	775	1,118	3.7	94
Oregon	14,264	6,160	5,405	15,019	5.3	641
Utah	2,417	1,818	1,504	2,731	13.0	214
Washington[e]	1,650	75	850	875	−47.0	22
Wyoming	313	156	134	335	7.0	97

Note:—Not calculated.
[a] Because of nonresponse or incomplete data, the population on December 31, 1995, does not equal the population on January 1, 1995, plus entries minus exits.
[b] Data do not include absconders.
[c] The December 31, 1995, count is estimated.
[d] The January 1, 1995, count is estimated.
[e] All data are estimated.
[f] Multiple agencies reporting.
[g] Data do not include absconders or out-of-State cases.
[h] Total entries are estimated.
Source: Department of Justice (1997,127).

The proportion of parolees who have absconded is about half that reported for absconded probationers. Out-of-state supervision for parolees, by contrast, is twice that of probationers.

Trends in Probation and Parole

Besides jurisdictional variations in the use of probation and parole, the trends for both yield interesting insights into our nation's punishment system. Figure 7.3 summarizes the federal and state probation trends between 1980 and 1995. The beginning point is critical because it was in the late 1970s and early 1980s that the nation's state and federal legislators adopted both a get-tough policy and just deserts philosophy toward criminals.

What are the trends? Between 1980 and 1995, the nation's probation population grew from 1,118,400 to 3,090,626.[6] These figures represent a 176% total increase, and a yearly rate of roughly 7%. This upward trend has begun

Table 7.6

Characteristics of Adults on Probation and Parole, 1995

	Percentage of Adult Parolees	Percentage of Adult Probationers
Number supervised	3,090,626	700,174
Sex		
Male	79%	90%
Female	21	10
Race		
White	64%	50%
African-American	34	49
All others	2	1
Offense		
Felony	54%	94%
Misdemeanor	26	6
DWI/DUI	17	N.A.
All others	3	N.A.
Current status		
Active supervision	78%	78%
Inactive supervision	8	11
Absconded	10	6
Supervised out-of-state	2	4
Other	2	*

Note: Percentages are based on reported data only; detail may not add to total because of rounding.

*Less than 0.05%.

Source: Department of Justice (1996d).

to slow: In the mid-1990s, the average yearly increase was between 2% and 3%. The per-capita or population-adjusted rate also increased at a proportionately similar rate over this period. Between 1980 and 1995 the per-capita rate (per 100,000 adult population) for state probation more than doubled, increasing from 695 to 1,573. The federal per-capita rates declined by one-third from 29 to 20.

Parole also experienced dramatic growth between 1980 and 1995. By 1995 that number had risen 218% to more than 700,000. The average annual growth rate for parole was 8%, higher than that observed for probation. Like probation, the annual rate of increase for parole dropped to 6% during the first five years of the 1990s. However, the 1% increase between 1994 and 1995 suggests even more dramatic declines may lie ahead. These trends could prove very troublesome for the nation's crowded prisons and jails.

The parole rate too increased 162% between 1980 and 1995. The change in the federal parolee rate, given the official policy that eliminated parole in 1987, was in the wrong direction: Whereas in 1980 the federal per-capita parole rate stood at 12, by 1995 this rate had risen to 30, an increase of 150%. We believe that this counter-intuitive trend is due to the enormous pressures on the federal prison system created by changes in sentencing that

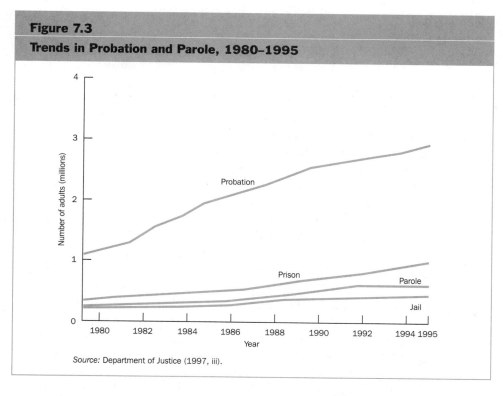

Figure 7.3

Trends in Probation and Parole, 1980–1995

Source: Department of Justice (1997, iii).

occurred in the 1980s and the use of mandatory release programs to relieve this pressure.

Three final observations about probation and parole trends merit our attention.[7] First, increases for the parolees slightly exceeded that for prisons between 1980 and 1995 (218% versus 212%). Probation increases trailed both, but by a slim margin. Second, the ratio of probationers to parolees to prisoners remained roughly the same throughout this period: 1 to 0.2 to 0.5. That is, for every 100 adults on probation, 20 were on parole and 50 were in prison or jail. What influences one part of the correctional system seems to have a proportionate impact on the others. Last, the proportion of the U.S. adult population under some form of supervision increased to nearly three times the 1980 rate. At any given time in 1995, 28 out of 1,000 adults in the U.S. were probationers, parolees, or prisoners.

Probation and Aftercare for Juvenile Offenders

Probation is probation, whether the probationer is an adult or a juvenile. In fact, in some jurisdictions probation services are provided to juveniles and adults by the same agencies. Unlike probation services for adults, probation for juveniles is not universal. Four states do not place juveniles on probation

(Nevada, Washington, West Virginia, and Wisconsin). In the remaining jurisdictions, courts with jurisdiction over juvenile matters have the option of placing youthful offenders on probation for nearly every crime.

In most jurisdictions, juvenile parole is called **aftercare.** This term derived from the Task Force on Corrections, which suggested that aftercare help to separate juvenile programs from "the legalistic language and concepts of adult parole" (1967, 149). The fact that most states continue to refer to juveniles in aftercare unofficially and officially as juvenile parole suggests that more than 30 years later the campaign has still not had much of an effect. When it comes to noninstitutional supervision of youthful offenders, the actions of the nation's juvenile courts and correctional systems are more than a little bewildering to outsiders.

Juvenile Probation and Aftercare

Juvenile probation was part of the original juvenile court concept initiated in Chicago late in the nineteenth century (Platt 1969). At the time, jurisdictions were more likely to institute probation for juveniles than to extend it to adults. Probation seemed to fit the idea that children in particular could benefit from being placed in the community rather than in jail or prison. The community can provide more opportunities and resources for the treatment of the youths' problems than total institutional settings.

Parole has its origins in the work of Brockway at the Elmira Reformatory. Brockway's ideas included both a strict institutional regimen and a closely supervised release. Parole from Elmira was tied to the indeterminate sentence. When a youth, by his (this was a school for boys) actions, had demonstrated sufficient good behavior, he was eligible for release. Without indeterminate sentences these correctional staff–based decisions would have been difficult if not impossible. Not surprisingly, then, unlike the criminal justice system, far fewer juvenile institutions release their inmates under terms of determinate sentencing and mandatory release: 45 states continue to use indeterminate sentences for juvenile offenders (Forst, Fisher, and Cates 1985, 1–12).

Today, two forms of probation serve juvenile clients. **Informal juvenile probation** is an agreement reached between the juvenile court (in the person of a juvenile probation officer), the child, his or her parents, and, in some jurisdictions, an attorney representing the state's interests. As in all forms of supervised release, the child agrees to behave according to a fixed set of guidelines. The period of supervision is usually fixed by statute as well. Informal probation is unique because the court has never made a determination that the child is under its jurisdiction. The child in question has not been adjudicated as a delinquent, status offender, or dependent/neglected child. Informal probation, like deferred prosecution for adults, requires an admission of some element of guilt. It is also unlikely to be used for serious acts of

A correctional officer interviews a juvenile detainee in the high security block of the California Youth Authority facility at Ventura. Inmates must complete a parole plan or similar pre-release program prior to receiving early release.

delinquency. Critics have attacked informal probation for its lack of accountability to any legal authority and susceptibility to coercive abuses (Institute of Judicial Administration–American Bar Association Juvenile Justice Standards Project 1980; Paulsen and Whitebread 1974). Nonetheless, juvenile court judges support its use (Binder and Binder 1982).

Formal juvenile probation closely parallels adult probation. Juvenile probation services emphasize investigation, selection, supervision, counseling, and surveillance. Juvenile probationers must abide by sets of rules and are subject to a revocation process not unlike that accorded adults. A key difference, however, is that juvenile probation work stresses counseling and social intervention more than law and rule enforcement. These different emphases have led some to speculate that juvenile probation officers—particularly when supervising informal probationers—are not, in the words of Arnold Binder and his associates (1988), "tough enough."

Most juvenile probationers are adjudicated delinquents. They are typically placed on one of three types of formal probation. **Nonpetitioned probation** is a form of preindictment (nonpetition) diversion. **Nonadjudicated probation** occurs after a juvenile petition but before a formal declaration of delinquency, the latter being the juvenile justice equivalent of a guilty verdict. As such, nonadjudicated probation is a traditional form of pretrial probation. Finally, juveniles pronounced delinquent by the juvenile court receive **adjudicated probation,** a form of probation.

Local juvenile courts or the state administrative office of courts administers juvenile probation services in 23 states (Torbet 1996, 3). A second model, found in 14 states, is a combination of structures, usually with services administered by the juvenile court in urban counties and by a state executive probation system in smaller counties. In a third group of 10 states, an executive branch department provides juvenile probation. Finally, a county executive administers probation in three states. Table 7.7 summarizes the various probation supervision methods found in the United States.

Aftercare is the method of release—parole—into the community for juveniles. Jurisdictions in the United States employ at least five different release mechanisms for institutionalized juveniles, including the following (Department of Justice 1978; American Correctional Association 1991a, 1997):

- Commitment court: The judge of the commitment court determines the point of release as one of the historical powers of the juvenile courts; the judge often relies for guidance on the recommendation of the superintendent of the youth facility.

- Board of pardons and paroles: A few states make no distinction between adults and juveniles, both being released by the same legal authority. Even fewer jurisdictions use a separate juvenile parole board.

- Youth correctional facility: In jurisdictions using this method, the superintendent, appointed staff members, or a committee or board of trustees at the institution decides to release inmates.

- State youth authority: A separate state-level bureaucracy, usually named Division of Youth Services, Youth Authority, Youth Development Center, or the Youth Conservation Committee, decides.

- Miscellaneous release mechanisms: Among the remaining methods are release under the authority of other specialized state agencies (including the Department of Health and Rehabilitative Services, the Department of Social Services, and state corrections departments, juvenile division) and direct probation after release from the institution.

Like juvenile probation, juvenile parole (aftercare) conditions and supervision are very similar to those for adults. Again, some states employ the same paroling authorities and agents to supervise juveniles, although a few states have special juvenile parole agents. Juvenile parolees encounter the same problems—and restrictions—as adults, and those added by the state-imposed requirement that they attend school. Even more than adults, the families of juvenile parolees play a critical role in the parole plan. Parole officers must often work far more closely with the families of juveniles than they do with adult parolees (Rogers and Mays 1987, 481). At times, as in the BARJ idea described in Box 7.8, specially trained PPOs may play a crucial role in restoring the balance between the offenders, their families, and the victims.

Table 7.7

Juvenile Probation Supervision in the U.S.

State Administration		Local Administration	
Judicial Branch	Executive Branch	Judicial Branch	Executive Branch
Connecticut	Alaska	Alabama	**California**
Hawaii	**Arkansas**	Arizona	**Idaho**
Iowa	Delaware	**Arkansas**	**Minnesota**
Kentucky	Florida	**California**	**Mississippi**
Nebraska	**Georgia**	Colorado	New York
North Carolina	**Idaho**	District of Columbia	Oregon
North Dakota	**Kentucky**	**Georgia**	**Washington**
South Dakota	**Louisiana**	Illinois	**Wisconsin**
Utah	Maine	Indiana	
West Virginia	Maryland	Kansas	
	Minnesota	**Kentucky**	
	Mississippi	**Louisiana**	
	New Hampshire	Massachusetts	
	New Mexico	Michigan	
	North Dakota	**Minnesota**	
	Oklahoma	Missouri	
	Rhode Island	Montana	
	South Carolina	Nevada	
	Tennessee	New Jersey	
	Vermont	Ohio	
	Virginia	**Oklahoma**	
	West Virginia	Pennsylvania	
	Wyoming	**Tennessee**	
		Texas	
		Virginia	
		Washington	
		Wisconsin	
		Wyoming	

Note: States in **boldface** indicate that probation is provided by a combination of agencies. Often larger, urban counties operate local probation departments, while the state administers probation in smaller counties.

Source: Hurst and Torbet (1993).

Trends in Juvenile Probation

We know a great deal about the extent of juvenile probation. Juvenile probation, the "workhorse" of the juvenile justice system, was the most severe disposition in more than 500,000 cases in 1994 out of roughly 1.6 million juvenile court cases (Sickmund 1997, 1; see also Butts 1997; Torbet 1996, 1). Between 1985 and 1994, the number of cases placed on probation grew 32%, while overall delinquency cases increased by 41%. Thus, other sanctions, including residential placement (that is, correctional institutions), have grown at a faster rate.

The average youthful probationer was a White male involved in a delinquent act involving a property offense. Most youths placed on probation in 1994 were White (68%), although the percentage of Black youths increased

Box 7.8

Balanced and Restorative Justice Project (BARJ)

Restorative justice (see Chapter 1) holds that some crimes upset a community's sense of well-being. The offender must restore this sense of well-being, starting with the victim. The idea of balance, as applied to restorative justice, is that the justice system should give equal weight to (1) ensuring community safety, (2) holding the offenders accountable to their victims, and (3) providing competency development for offenders in the system so that they can pursue legitimate endeavors after release.

Unlike treatment or punishment, the balanced and restorative justice (BARJ) model underscores the importance of the victims of crime, both the individual victim and the community as victim. BARJ, as applied to the juvenile justice system, accomplishes its goals in three ways. First, it improves the quality of life by engaging offenders in community improvement projects as part of the accountability and competency components. Second, BARJ restructures the role of staff from office-based functions to community involvement and supervision of offenders in the competency areas. Third, specially trained staff involve offenders in victim-offender mediation as part of the restoration process.

BARJ is part of the juvenile codes in 14 states, including Alabama, Connecticut, Florida, Idaho, Indiana, Maine, Maryland, Montana, Oklahoma, Pennsylvania, Tennessee, Texas, Utah, and Vermont. Another 10 states—Arizona, California, Hawaii, Minnesota, Nevada, New Hampshire, New Mexico, Oregon, Wisconsin, and Wyoming—are considering the inclusion of a BARJ provision in their juvenile codes.

Source: Freivalds (1996).

from 25% to 29% between 1985 and 1994 (Sickmund 1997, 1). The percentage of other races/ethnic groups stayed at 3% throughout this time. The proportion of males to females on juvenile probation did not change between 1985 and 1994: about 80 males for every 20 females.

Conclusion

Probation and parole share similar histories and, perhaps, will share similar fates in the twenty-first century. Yet keep in mind that they serve distinctly different populations and provide equally distinct relief to the criminal justice system. Probation gives the courts an administrative tool that serves as a less punitive and less costly alternative to prison or jail. The court, or its appointed agent, maintains some measure of control over the offender, while the community receives an equal measure of security. Similarly, the function of punishment is met. Probation gives the courts sentencing alternatives and reduces the number of people sent to prison and jail, if only temporarily.

Parole allows the executive branch to exercise a similar measure of control and provide a similar measure of security for what is acknowledged to be a more dangerous population. After all, parolees, for some reason, were deemed inappropriate for or failed probation. Parole, or supervised mandatory release, gives the convicted and imprisoned offender an opportunity to

Probation and Parole in the Twenty-First Century

The year is 2010. A guard rolls a 70+-year-old inmate—he looks 20 years older—down the hallway of a modern geriatric prison (a correctional facility for elderly inmates) in central California. Although he is in a wheelchair, manacles are visible on the old man's scrawny hands and legs. He is accompanied by a second guard who chats casually with his colleague. Other inmates, standing by the doors to their cells, look out at the defiant old man, his long, thin gray hair standing out from the crown of his head as if someone has just given him an electric shock. Visible on his forehead is a faint swastika, carved nearly five decades ago in an act of self-mutilation and group solidarity. "Shee-it," spits out one old inmate, "Old Charlie must hold the record for parole refusals. Do you think he really believes them people in Sacramento will ever let him out?" The cellmate, himself nearly 70, looks solemnly at the slowly disappearing wheelchair. Just as the entourage turns a corner headed for the maximum-security wing, the second old con speaks: "Well, it's like this. I figure Charlie thinks maybe someone will get soft in the head and let him out by mistake. Besides, he knows it pisses them off somethin' fierce just to have to review his butt for parole!"

Charles Manson has been incarcerated in California since his conviction in 1971 along with the other members of his "family." Manson continues to receive regularly scheduled parole hearings, although the likelihood of his release seems remote.

(continued on next page)

Probation and Parole in the Twenty-First Century (continued)

Release from the custody of the court or the correctional authorities has never been a very popular idea. In many ways, both probation and parole are unavoidable, from the perspective of the courts and prison authorities. The spectacle of Charles Manson, or another notorious and vicious criminal, being released into the community galvanizes public opinion against conditional release programs. As we noted at the beginning of this chapter, it just does not seem fair.

Part of the legacy of the 1970s research and political attacks on both the indeterminate sentence and parole was flat-time sentencing and determinate sentencing. Many observers of the nation's correctional system believed that this was the beginning of the end for parole. Maine abolished parole in 1976. By 1980 eight states, including indeterminate-sentence pioneer California, abolished traditional parole release. With the passage of the Crime Control Act of 1984, new federal sentencing guidelines spelled the end of parole in the federal prison system. The states were close behind the federal government. In 1977, 72% of all releases from prison were by parole. By 1988, this figure had dropped to 40%. The 1994 percentage for traditional paroles was 42%. However, those released on supervised mandatory release—the form of release favored in states that abandoned parole—stood at 43%. Combining parole and supervised mandatory release figures yields a total of 85% of those leaving prison in 1994 (Department of Justice 1996c).

Parole—and its more structured replacement, supervised mandatory early release—continues to play a critical role in the operation of the nation's prisons and jails. The crowded prison system needs a "back door" release mechanism. Parole has played this role for decades, as does supervised mandatory release now. Good time credits, critical to both parole and supervised mandatory release, are important to prison administrators for maintaining a modicum of control over inmates. For example, even in Maine, the state legislature enacted liberal "good time" provisions allowing early release. Despite inconclusive recidivism studies and political posturing, the future of parole—or some form of early supervised release—is safe and secure.

There is every reason to believe that probation's future is equally secure. In 1985, one of the nation's leading experts on prison control, Joan Petersilia (1985, 37), predicted a grim future for the nation's correctional system:

> Prison crowding dictates that probation populations will continue to grow. In California and 30 other states, prisons have become so crowded that courts have set limits on the number of inmates that may be housed. At the same time, shrinking budgets and political uncertainties preclude building enough new prisons to keep pace

Probation and Parole in the Twenty-First Century (continued)

with felony convictions. Consequently, the courts have had to seek other alternatives and, in many jurisdictions, probation is the only choice.

Petersilia was right more than she was wrong in her predictions. The number of prison bed spaces has grown, but has failed to keep pace with prison population growth. Moreover, what happens to one part of the corrections system affects the others. As prisons experienced dramatic increases in populations, the use of parole and probation necessarily and dramatically increased.

Technology, such as electronic monitoring, may lessen the burden on PPOs (Scott 1996, 174). Specialized forms of supervision, for example, treating drunk drivers and sex offenders apart from other law violators, will increasingly replace traditional probation. The use of intensive supervision for garden-variety criminals should increase the need for more PPOs with smaller caseloads. Courts are likely to turn increasingly to the types of intermediate sanctions discussed in the next chapter. Todd Clear (1995, 217) believes strongly in the movement from probation and parole to specialized nontraditional supervision service and intermediate sanctions. He predicts the next 20 years will see probation and parole account for a decreasing share of the offender population.

The fact remains that probation and parole are currently—and for the foreseeable future—the criminal justice system's workhorses. Without them, or some related form, the administration of justice would halt. The nation's prison system is not nearly large enough to hold the influx of offenders assigned to probation. Nor could it survive without some mechanism for reducing the inmate population short of natural causes.

show his or her ability to live again as a member of the free community. Parole also allows the prison and jail system to "let off steam" in the event they become too crowded to function (or, more likely, should some judge notice the prison has too many inmates crowded into too few bed spaces).

We must also bear in mind that both probation and parole populations, along with prisons and jails, are growing in size. Unless politicians change their law-enforcement priorities, for example, altering current strategies on the "War on Drugs," the volume of people entering the justice funnel is unlikely to decrease in the near future. Probation and parole remain the most cost-effective, widely accepted, and time-tested alternatives to incarceration. We turn to a detailed examination of the remaining alternatives in the next chapter.

Critical Review Questions

1. Each forerunner of probation "tested" criminals in different ways. Explain how each accomplished these tests.

2. What similarities do you see between the way the "neck verse" was originally practiced and the use of judicial reprieve in the *Killits* case?

3. How important to sentencing are the three questions answered by the PSI report? Do you see any problems with the fact that PSI reports include hearsay information? Describe the good and bad effects of their inclusion.

4. Are you bothered by the role that technical violations play in probation revocation? Does the fact that the proof required for revocation differs from that required for a criminal court conviction alter your response to the first question?

5. What is your opinion about which parole board model is better equipped to render the fairest, most equitable parole decisions?

6. What do you believe is the most difficult aspect of a PPO's job? Explain your response.

7. What most shocked you about the current statistics on probationers? Why were you shocked?

8. What most shocked you about the current statistics on parolees? Why were you shocked?

9. What legal, ethical, and moral dilemmas do you see in the common practice of informal juvenile probation? ("None" is not an appropriate answer.)

10. What law enforcement or general criminal justice changes would you support to reduce the supply of offenders into the probation and parole systems? (Remember that changes we make in the criminal justice system are likely to have an effect on other systems, such as mental health, social, and medical services.)

Recommended Readings

Abadinsky, Howard. 1997. *Probation and parole: Theory and practice.* 6th ed. Upper Saddle River, NJ: Prentice-Hall. Abadinsky wrote the first edition of this book while he was still a senior parole officer with the New York State Division of Parole. The current edition retains the gritty realism and no-nonsense approach to the work of supervising offenders in the free community found in the first edition.

Erickson, Rosemary J., Wayman J. Crow, Louis A. Zurcher, and Archie V. Connett. 1973. *Paroled but not free: Ex-offenders look at what they need to make it outside.* New York: Human Sciences Press. Roughly one-third of this small book consists of 14 short essays by offenders that detail, in their own words, the differences between succeeding and failing. The rest of the book analyzes the responses of 60 parolees to their experiences in the free community. It concludes with the recommendations of the researchers, parole officers, and ex-offenders. The comparisons among these sets of recommendations may surprise you.

Irwin, John. 1970. *The felon*. Englewood Cliffs, NJ: Prentice-Hall. A seminal work written by a convicted felon about convicted felons. Irwin captures the essence of the felon's life on parole and how they feel about the experience.

McCleary, Richard. 1978. *Dangerous men: The sociology of parole*. Beverly Hills, CA: Sage. The title of this research monograph is a bit misleading. McCleary focuses on the interactions between parole officers and parolees; between parole officers and their colleagues, including superiors; and on the organization of work in a parole agency. While 20 years old, this book is important for people considering parole work or those who want to know more about it.

Key Terms

absconded
actuarial risk assessment
    scale
adjudicated probation
aftercare
bail
benefit of clergy
case manager
caseload
citation
consolidated parole board
    model
discretionary release
expiration release
false negatives
false positives
formal juvenile probation
good time laws
hearing officer
independent parole board
    model

informal juvenile
    probation
intensive supervision
intensive supervision
    program (ISP)
judicial reprieve
mandatory release
medium supervision
minimum supervision
mixed caseload
National Probation
    Association
nonadjudicated probation
nonpetitioned probation
parole
parole eligibility date
Prayer of Repentance
pre-sentence investigation
    (PSI) report
preliminary hearing
probation

probation parole officer
    (PPO)
probation revocation
    process
recidivism
recognizance
revocation hearing
ROR (release on one's
    own recognizance)
special conditions of
    probation/parole
standard conditions of
    probation/parole
summary arrest
technical violation
victim impact statement
    (VIS)

Cases Cited

Booth v. Maryland, 482 U.S. 496 (1987)
Commonwealth v. Chase (1830)
Ex parte U.S., 242 U.S. 27-53 (1916) [the
    Killits case]
Gagnon v. Scarpelli, 411 U.S. 778 (1973)

Gardner v. Florida, 430 U.S. 349 (1977)
Mempa v. Rhay, 389 U.S. 128 (1967)
Morrisey v. Brewer, 408 U.S. 471 (1972)
U.S. v. Birnbaum, 349 U.S. 1044 (1970)

Notes

1. Probation is taken from the Latin noun *probatio,* meaning "a testing," which, in turn, is derived from a Latin verb *probare,* meaning "to prove."

2. In medieval chivalry, a defeated knight could give his word of honor to withdraw from the field of combat and walk away unscathed. By the eighteenth century, this custom had taken on the force of law. Section VII of the Lieber Code governed the use of parole by U.S. forces during the American Civil War: Captured soldiers received an offer of freedom in exchange for their word of honor (*parole d'honneur*) not to reenter the hostilities. Participation was voluntary (Friedman 1972; Catton 1960). Later in the nineteenth century, the Declaration of Brussels and the Hague Convention made parole conventions part of international law (Friedman 1972). These practices established the legal precedent that an imprisoned person could be freed in exchange for a promise to behave in accordance with a set of agreed-upon principles.

3. The averages came from several sources. First, the *ACA Directory* (American Correctional Association 1997) contained information on the number of probation and parole officers (PPOs). Second, a report from CEGA Publishing, summarized in the *Bureau of Justice Statistics Sourcebook of Criminal Justice Statistics* (Maguire and Pastore 1996, 81) added additional caseload information. In most cases, we simply summed adult probation and parole releasees in a state and divided that total by the reported number of PPOs. The former number we obtained from *Probation and Parole Populations in the U.S., 1995* (Department of Justice 1996d). The latter number we obtained from ACA (1997). In many cases, the numbers obtained from CEGA and our averages were identical. In other cases, the caseloads reported by CEGA were clearly estimates. Where the two numbers differed, we used the more conservative—and lower—figure, which in all cases was our own. Only in the case of Pennsylvania did we use the CEGA figure. Also, we do not report figures for Colorado, nor did CEGA. In both cases, the problem was nearly identical: Probation officers, parole officers, or both in these two states serve juveniles as well as adults. A meaningful average for adult caseloads alone is nearly impossible to calculate.

4. The information relative to probation and parole movements for the states and federal government is taken from Department of Justice (1997).

5. It is important to note that although we use the term *parole* without qualification in the discussion of the nation's parole population, these statistics include not only parolees but persons released from prison or jail as a result of mandatory release programs or other forms of conditional release. However, even the National Institute of Justice's Bureau of Justice Statistics calls these persons *parolees.*

6. The information relative to probation and parole trends is taken from Department of Justice (1996d).

7. This information is taken from Department of Justice (1996c), Bonczar and Beck (1997), and Gilliard and Beck (1997).

8

Community Corrections

Chapter Outline

- Introduction
- Defining Community Corrections and Intermediate Punishments
- Reentry Programs as "Community-Based Corrections"
- Diversion
- Fines, Forfeitures, and Restitution
- Community Service
- House Arrest and Electronic Monitoring
- Community Alternatives for Juveniles
- Issues in Community Corrections
- Conclusion
- Critical Review Questions
- Recommended Readings
- Key Terms
- Cases Cited
- Notes

 Introduction

John Goins, an "escapee" (really a walk-off) from a local halfway house, disappears while on a work assignment. Local law enforcement authorities are notified immediately after the 28-year-old man fails to report back in the evening. After three days of being missing, police detectives arrest Goins, not for being an escapee but on a new charge of sexual indecency with a minor child. As we would expect, this incident makes the front page of the morning newspaper, and the newspaper's editor, local politicians, and a large number of community residents all ask the same question: "How could this sexual predator be living in our neighborhood and be able to freely move around the community to offend again?"

This "case" is fictitious, but it is not totally unrealistic. We combined bits and pieces of true life stories to create this scenario, and above all else it illustrates the dilemmas that face us when we have offenders in nonsecure, community-based programs. In this chapter, we review why we should have community-based programs instead of relying on institutionalization. Moreover, we deal with the programs that constitute community corrections. Before getting into these issues, however, we must consider two points about community-based corrections.

First, community corrections has become an integral part of the corrections mission in the United States. With the creation of community-based alternatives to incarceration, the list of programs reaches from the least intrusive diversion efforts up to maximum security, fortress-like prisons. In fact, community corrections programming now occupies the niche frequently called **intermediate sanctions.**

Second, given the forces currently at work, community corrections is likely to expand, until these agencies and efforts come to dominate the corrections component of the U.S. criminal justice system, because of the following factors:

- Most correctional institutions in the United States presently are at or above their rated capacities. They can be expanded or replaced, but this is an expensive and time-consuming alternative to the current crowding crisis. If we have learned anything in the past decade it is that we cannot build our way out of the jail and prison crowding crisis (see, for example, Thompson and Mays 1991; Welch 1994; Welsh 1996).

- The general public, policy makers, and correctional administrators have been unhappy with the "lock them up or do nothing" alternative that seems to have been widely used in the past. Community-based programs can provide greater offender accountability and more "punishment" than typically might be a part of standard probation programs.

- Community corrections may provide more treatment options than traditionally have been available—and do it more humanely and effectively (Benekos 1990).

Why choose community corrections? Three factors provide at least primary justifications for their selection. In comparison to traditional community supervision (such as probation and parole, discussed in Chapter 7), intermediate sanctions can provide increased offender accountability, or what some have characterized as additional "risk control" (Rackmill 1993). Second, community corrections can result in cost-effective treatment alternatives to secure institutionalization (Sigler and Lamb 1995). Finally, intermediate sanctions allow agencies to continue to provide services to offenders while shifting program rhetoric from "treatment and therapy" to "punishment and control" (Benekos 1990).

Defining Community Corrections and Intermediate Punishments

In dealing with the definitions for this chapter, we would like to introduce a term that may be new to many of you: **extrainstitutional punishment.** Extrainstitutional sanctions involve punishing convicted offenders outside of locked and secure correctional facilities. In Chapters 4 and 5 we dealt with jails and prisons. These two types of facilities encompass most of what we normally consider institutional corrections. Therefore, any program operating outside of jail or prison would employ an extrainstitutional programming approach.

As we begin the definition process for community-based, or extrainstitutional, corrections, two points need to be acknowledged. First, we will not treat probation and parole as part of these efforts. These topics were covered in considerable depth in Chapter 7, and they each have a sufficient history and significant enough body of literature to be treated separately. Second, it is vital that we recognize that there are both supporters and detractors of this method of sanctioning offenders. Some of the points of contention between supporters and detractors are based on verified program outcomes. Others are merely philosophical differences in how convicted criminals should be treated.

Supporters

Community corrections proponents state their support in both negative and positive ways. For instance, from a negative perspective they might say something like: "Institutional programs largely have proven ineffective in changing criminal behavior and preventing recidivism, so why not try something different?" They are not saying that community-based programs work and produce specific results, they simply are saying that the community approach could work and that it would not do any worse than institutional programming.

On a more positive note, extrainstitutional punishment supporters find many appealing features to this method. For instance, community corrections provides a cost-effective option to institutionalization, and several of the programs currently being operated cost less per client per day to administer than institutional placements (Benekos 1990). Additionally, because they do not involve locking offenders behind jail or prison bars these programs appear to be much less stigmatizing. In fact, community corrections clients may go about their everyday routines without many community members knowing they are rubbing elbows with "convicts."

Proponents of extrainstitutional programming also believe that treatment efforts are more effective for some offenders than institutionalization (McCarthy 1992). There are several possible reasons for this perceived additional effectiveness. First, there may be some community-based treatment programs that are not available in an institution. Second, community-based treatment deals with the offender in his or her "natural" environment, rather than the artificial institutional environment. As a result, offenders must learn to deal with family problems and the temptations presented by peers and crime opportunities. In an institution they can talk about dealing with these issues, but in the community they will be confronted with the reality of these situations.

The final reason often given for supporting the community corrections approach is related to reducing the stigma associated with institutionalization: community-based programming eliminates the need to reintegrate the offender back into his or her family life and other aspects of the community. We know that institutionalization makes it difficult to return to a normal existence on the outside, particularly for long-term prison inmates (McShane and Krause 1993; Souryal 1997). To see an example of this, rent the movie *The Shawshank Redemption* and pay careful attention to the character named Brooks. The portrayal of his life paints a graphic picture of what it is like to become institutionalized, or what Donald Clemmer (1958) called prisonization. Obviously, not every offender is appropriate for extrainstitutional treatment, but those who are suffer fewer disruptions in their lives as a result of community-based treatment.

Detractors

Not everyone is enthusiastic about community corrections, and critics come from a variety of points along the political spectrum. It is not only conservatives who condemn such programs; liberals and even moderates may be equally critical (see Walker 1994). However, we can classify the main criticisms of community corrections in four categories: cost, net widening, public safety, and lack of effectiveness.

Community corrections opponents would say that comparisons of day-for-day costs between community-based and institutional programs do make the extrainstitutional efforts look less expensive. However, given that we continue to use institutional placements at the same or a greater pace, community corrections ventures serve as add-ons. Therefore, instead of reducing corrections costs, these programs actually contribute to the ever-upward budget spiral.

Related to costs is the issue of **net widening.** We often discuss net widening in the context of juvenile diversion (Austin and Krisberg 1981; Decker 1985). However, net widening can occur with adults as well (Balch, 1974). Net widening is a simple concept to define, but one that is difficult to fully understand. Net widening is said to occur when a treatment program brings more people under some form of social control than previously was the case. In many instances, we find that each new method employed brings increasing numbers of individuals into the corrections domain. When we take the issue of net widening and corrections costs together, we see that additional agencies and programming efforts mean not only that we are offering a broader menu of correctional techniques, but also we are increasing the cost we must pay as well. On the surface it might appear that widening the net is beneficial, in that more individuals receive services than would otherwise be the case. However, the other side of this issue is that some people will be brought under correctional control and authority who otherwise might not. There are clearly two sides to this issue.

The third critique leveled at community corrections is that these programs do not adequately provide for public safety. One of the keys to successful community-based programming is securing public support (Sigler and Lamb 1995). Unfortunately, program creators and managers often have not done a good job of informing the public of the program's purposes and the nature of the clients being served.

For some of the "high end" clients (that is, those who normally would qualify for institutional placement), critics believe that community programs are inappropriate; jail and prison placements are desirable, even at the cost of constructing additional bed space (McShane and Krause 1993, 5). In the past, a number of the clients sent to extrainstitutional programs would have been placed in correctional facilities. However, with institutional crowding being a part of everyday life in corrections, alternatives to incarceration increasingly are being pursued. Opponents believe that this is sacrificing community safety for cost savings or convenience.

The final criticism is one that must be taken very seriously by community corrections advocates: lack of program effectiveness (Latessa and Allen 1997, 376–405). If community-based programs do not reduce offenders' law-violating behavior—then it does not matter what else they do or what they cost. Therefore, these treatment efforts must stand or fall on the degree to which they impact criminal behavior.

What Is Reintegration?

Because we have mentioned **reintegration** several times in this chapter, it seems appropriate to consider what reintegration really means. To begin with, reintegration is necessary as a result of incarcerating offenders. When convicted criminals are ordered to spend time in jails or prisons, they begin to lose community contacts. One of the first breaks is with the place of employment. Those individuals who were employed prior to being charged with and convicted of a crime lose their jobs and contacts with fellow employees.

The loss of family contacts also negatively impacts offenders. Often the family strives valiantly to keep in touch with the member who has been imprisoned; however, regular visits may be difficult to arrange. If a husband is imprisoned, the wife may have to work outside of the home and take care of the children as well. At times, correctional facilities may be far from where the family lives. Even if the family members can get there, lodging may not be readily available or affordable. For most offenders, the longer they remain behind bars, the less frequent the contacts become and the more distant and strained the family relationships. The lack of freedom to contact people on the outside, and the lack of contact from friends and family members contribute to a growing isolation for many prisoners (McShane and Krause 1993; Snarr 1996).

In addition to personal isolation, inmates frequently suffer from the habits and experiences to which they are exposed during periods of incarceration. For instance, instead of teaching prisoners to be independent, incarceration frequently teaches them to be even more dependent. Instead of teaching them job skills, incarceration may diminish the skills they already possess, or it may result in reduced employment opportunities once they are released.

All of these factors contribute to the difficulty of reintegrating offenders into the community. Once they are released, they face the tasks of finding a place to live, obtaining a job, trying to reestablish broken family relationships, and generally trying to live down the reputation of being an ex-con.

Why are all of these things important? In the context of community-based programming, the offender is not removed from the community. This allows individuals to maintain their residences, places of employment, and interpersonal relations. Once again, all of this allows offenders to receive treatment and to work on their problems in the community context where they must confront those problems.

Government and Private Sponsorship

As we have discussed elsewhere in the text, some correctional institutions are privately funded and operated, but for the most part, contemporary correctional facilities are funded by governmental entities and are operated by government employees. This is not the case, to the same extent, with community-based programs. Many alternatives to incarceration were started as programs wholly or partially funded by the private sector. This is particularly true of diversion programs. Within contemporary community corrections we find a mix of local, state, and federal government moneys along with private sector program funding.

Governments join with the private sector for a number of reasons. For example, the community-based program may be a fairly small residential center focused on a particular offender group, such as those with drug and alcohol problems. This type of program might be too small for a governmental entity to operate efficiently, but if the service provider is a nonprofit community agency they may be able to make a go of it. This type of funding apparatus allows for innovative programming efforts. It places the programs in the community near where the clients are and where their problems can best be addressed. It also allows us to maximize the impact of the relatively small amounts of funding provided by any single organization.

There are, however, two major drawbacks to this funding procedure. First, one of the major struggles for community corrections is establishing a reasonable and reliable yearly budget. As a result, program administrators are constantly trying to cobble together next year's budget. Most alternatives to incarceration programs are only one year or even less away from financial extinction. It is very difficult to do long-range planning if you do not know whether your agency will survive the next budget cycle.

The second problem is that with multiple funding sources they are either accountable to everyone, or accountable to no one. It is usually the second of these two choices. Funding agencies may presume that someone else is looking over the shoulder of the community corrections program when, in reality, no one is holding the program's administrators accountable for their outcomes. If this is the case, we must rely on these programs to provide their own assessment of effectiveness—a risky proposition even under the best of circumstances.

The funding arrangements for community corrections may partially explain why these programs have expanded so widely in the past two decades. The methods of sponsorship, and unfortunate lack of program accountability, may also explain why there is so little in the way of evaluative research, and why the programs that have been evaluated have not demonstrated very positive results. For many community corrections programs it is difficult to tell who is paying the bills and who is really responsible for program outcomes and administration.

Administering Community-Based Programs

As with most aspects of contemporary corrections, community corrections administration has both pluses and minuses. One positive aspect is that community-based efforts will continue to grow and flourish. A negative is that we will constantly be relearning past lessons, including repeating past mistakes.

One of the best pieces of news about extrainstitutional programming is that it attracts many energetic and creative employees. These staff members often are fresh out of college with heads full of knowledge and hearts full of hope and enthusiasm. To the extent that community corrections works at all, a great deal of the success can be attributed to these individuals. A factor that makes many community approaches attractive, and one that contributes to their success, is that these programs have not developed firmly entrenched administrative bureaucracies. Unfortunately, in many correctional institutions, a philosophy that nothing is possible or that change is so difficult that it is not worth the effort has come to dominate the institution. Long-time institutional employees become infected with a cynicism and hopelessness that is difficult to defeat (Latessa and Allen 1997).

The other side of this coin is the bad news for community corrections. As a result of the intensive nature of client and staff relations, many staff members suffer burnout after one or two years on the job and they move on to other positions, either within or away from the criminal justice system. There is constant staff turnover, and a fairly steep learning curve for new employees entering the field. Jobs are always opening, but often these agencies have very little in the way of institutional memory. Nothing becomes set in stone but the staff foundation may never solidify for these organizations.

Measuring Success and Failure in Community Corrections

As we mentioned previously in this chapter, the true test of any corrections program is the degree to which it has an impact on law-violating behavior. We may never be able to change peoples' attitudes toward obeying or not obeying the law, but we do want to change their behaviors. That is why one of the most popular approaches to counseling in correctional settings is called "behavior modification." In this section we will explore the measures by which we judge program success or failure.

As we have discussed elsewhere in this text, perhaps the most common standard of success for contemporary corrections efforts is **recidivism.** To review briefly, recidivism means returning to law-violating behavior. Many people have noted over the years that recidivism is not a measure of success: It is a measure of failure or a lack of success. We measure recidivism by looking at those people who "fail" and return to their previous law-violating lifestyles. Unfortunately, many times we know more about our failures than we do about our successes. However, is recidivism the only way to measure program effectiveness? Are there other measures of success as well? What are these? How do we measure them?

Two areas of improvement seem particularly important for individuals participating in community corrections: those factors dealing with individual improvement and those factors related to improvements in the individual's circumstances. For instance, some treatment programs focus on improving the offender's self-esteem (Whitehead and Lab 1996). This is a worthy goal, but there is very little evidence that most criminals suffer from low self-esteem, and similarly there is little evidence to link varying levels of self-esteem to different levels or kinds of offenses.[1] However, some individual improvements (such as improved life skills or greater reliability) are observable and measurable.

One goal for community corrections is to avoid disrupting the offender's employment situation. Even though some offenders are employed at the time of their offense, most can benefit from job skills training and from job placement assistance. Although we cannot consistently link unemployment with criminality, we do know that quite a few offenders are unemployed or employed only on a part-time basis when they are arrested. A result of the movement into a post-industrial economy is a shift from blue collar, manufacturing jobs to service-oriented, minimum wage jobs, and a large number of inner city adults and juveniles find themselves with diminished employment prospects (Fagan 1996; Jackson 1991). Even fast food employment (not a very desirable choice for most of these individuals) may be limited. Therefore, community corrections may need to address job skills training, and staff members may need to pay particular attention to helping clients secure reasonably well-paying jobs.

Drug and alcohol treatment is another area where community corrections can help the individual change. We have noted that many of the offenders passing through the criminal justice system suffer from drug and alcohol dependency problems (Cordilia 1985; Gropper 1985; Mays, Fields, and Thompson 1991; Miller and Welte 1986; Nurco et al. 1986). Without some attention to these problems, the individual's behavior and circumstances may improve very little. Therefore, community corrections can be effective in targeting individuals who have chemical dependency problems, especially if these offenders are at a point in their lives where they want help. Extrainstitutional treatment may be able to call upon a variety of community resources that are not available in a secure correctional facility. As we have mentioned before, treatment in the community also forces the offender to face the source of the problems, and to overcome those problems. Additionally, community corrections may provide a more positive and supportive environment for drug and alcohol treatment than can be found in many jails and prisons. Locating treatment in the community allows the family to be involved in the treatment process. This takes us into the next feature peculiar to community corrections that can help offenders improve their situation.

Institutionalization removes the convicted offender from the home, and in some instances that might be welcomed by family members. In the long run, however, this will likely impede the reintegration process. Therefore, community corrections helps ensure more positive outcomes by treating the offender in the family context. In some situations family members may contribute to the offender's failures and the offender learns criminality in the context of the family. In other situations, family members—particularly parents and spouses—may not want the offender to get better, because this may decrease the offender's dependence on them. This is a process known in the treatment community as **codependency** (Enos and Southern 1996, 170–72). In situations such as this, community corrections treatment staff members must get at the source of the problems within the family and help the offender come to grips with how to effectively manage the situation. In this case locking the offenders up merely allows them to avoid some of their problems.

Prison Chaplain Roberto Rodriguez established a halfway house in a broken-down three story building in Bedford Stuyvesant, one of the poorest neighborhoods in Brooklyn. Rodriguez's philosophy is "No methadone. Counseling is based on God's word. When the word fills the heart, there is no more need for drugs."

Community-based treatment causes them to confront and deal with those problems.

While some might argue about the value of improving the individual and his or her circumstances, it is important to consider these factors when evaluating community corrections programming. Recidivism measures still may be the most important dimensions by which we determine success, but recidivism is by no means the only gauge of success available.

Reentry Programs as "Community-Based Corrections"

Halfway houses are, by definition, philosophy, and programming, halfway-in (or halfway-out) of correctional institutions. Such facilities may be operated by private for-profit or not-for-profit contractors or public agencies. Their primary purpose is to provide a transitional living arrangement between the environment found in typical state and federal correctional institutions and totally independent living in the community. Some provide room, board, and help with employment; others provide an even broader array of social services, including remedial education, individual or group counseling, and other types of life skills training. In this section we will explore halfway houses, and what they might contribute to correctional effectiveness.

Before we begin discussing halfway house programming, we need to consider three major obstacles faced by virtually every halfway house in the nation. The first major problem area is location. Many times halfway houses

Neighborhood residents are often concerned about the location of halfway houses or the release of convicted offenders back into the community. Here a group of residents protests the release of a convicted child molester.

are situated in large, older homes in well-established neighborhoods. The typical neighborhood response is "not in my back yard!" This set of circumstances gives rise to the **NIMBY syndrome.**

The difficulty of finding a suitable location is understandable. Often community input is not sought, and residents are simply informed that a halfway house is to be opened in their neighborhood. The residents reasonably express fears about having "criminals" living in their midst. They have images of convicted offenders preying upon the community's weak and defenseless. Therefore, halfway house staff members and managers have two options: (1) They can do a thorough job of informing community residents of their intentions (perhaps by including some of the neighborhood opinion leaders on an advisory board) in order to garner their support, or (2) they can choose another location, such as an old motel, in a commercial district away from residential neighborhoods. The second option often is chosen, not because of the suitability of the locale, but because there is less resistance to such a choice.

The second major obstacle facing halfway house operators is staffing. In some ways halfway houses are fortunate in that they can attract energetic young people for staff positions. Some are recent college graduates (sometimes married couples) who actually may live at the halfway house with the residents. The inducement is a place to live, a salary, and close contact with offenders who are in need of help. The drawback to these kinds of positions is that they require high emotional investments and, as a result, there is a tremendous amount of **staff burnout.** After a year or two of working in these positions, most staff members are ready to move on to other things. An additional problem with staffing is pay. The pay issue is related to the problem of budget considerations.

Halfway houses often depend on a number of public and private funding sources. This is a double-edged sword. On the one hand, the loss of one source of funding probably will not undermine operations. On the other hand, most halfway houses do not have reliable funding sources that they can count on year in and year out. Program managers are always scrambling to pull together bits and pieces from a number of funding sources in order to put together the annual budget. The "softer" the funding sources (for example, grant-funded positions), the more unsure about whether staff positions will be continued from one year to the next. This causes great uncertainly among staff members, and it works against the long-range planning process.

Now that we have addressed the impediments facing halfway houses, let us move to some of their specific programming efforts. In particular, we will focus on work release and educational release, as well as other reentry programs such as furloughs.

Work Release

Halfway houses can provide a transitional residential placement where offenders continue their jobs or reenter the work force. **Work release** programs can be operated out of both jails and prisons, but the halfway house's less restrictive environment makes this almost an ideal location for work release clients. Residents can work jobs, typically during the day, and return to the halfway house in the evening for treatment or additional job training or simply to eat and sleep. Clients have structure and support, while at the same time they experience a growing sense of freedom. They are not simply turned loose to fend for themselves.

In addition to providing an alternative to incarceration, the halfway house provides another benefit to the taxpayers and the criminal justice system. Most halfway house residents are required to pay part of their support from the money they earn. If they have families, they also may be required to support their families. Halfway house advocates see this as a win-win situation. The offenders are benefiting from not being incarcerated, and the public is benefiting from improved job and social skills, lower treatment costs, and hopefully reduced recidivism.

Educational Release

Educational release raises many of the same concerns that work release does. A problem for many offenders is their lack of education. In fact, a Bureau of Justice Statistics survey found in 1991 that 65% of state inmates did not graduate from high school (Beck et al. 1993). This was a decrease from 72% in 1986, but still represents a significant number.

In order to ensure their future employability and a smooth transition back into society (for parolees) education must be stressed. As we have mentioned previously, education and job training are offered in many correctional institutions. However, the programs may be limited in scope and size. In other words, not all inmates may be eligible, certain courses of study may not be large enough to meet inmate demand, and some educational programs simply may not be offered. Therefore, halfway house residents may be able to take advantage of certificate or degree programs offered at community colleges and universities. The goal is not simply to have a better educated ex-offender, but to have one whose education prepares him or her for a crime-free life.

Furloughs

Often we associate **furloughs** with short-term release from prison. However, furlough programs can operate with and through halfway houses as well. Furloughs typically involve short periods of release from custody without supervision. This allows the offender to return home for a few days in order to reestablish family ties. Again, the primary purpose is reintegration, and furloughs can be granted for individuals in secure custody (jail or prison) or residents of halfway houses.

Diversion

Diversion often is associated with juvenile offenders. However, diversion can be employed with adults as well. In fact, in the past two decades a process that some have called the "juvenilization" of the adult criminal justice system has occurred (Balch 1974). There are several justifications for diversion, and in the next section we will explore the origins of diversion and the purposes that we suppose will be served by diverting.

Origins of Diversion

Diversion is the process of removing individuals from the formal system of prosecution and adjudication and placing them in a less formal treatment setting. It is difficult to trace the history of diversion endeavors. It is possible that as long as there have been attempts to control and sanction law violators there have been diversion efforts. However, the modern concept of diversion frequently is traced to the work of Edwin Lemert. At the time of the president's Commission on Law Enforcement and the Administration of Justice, Lemert's notion of **labeling** was attracting particular attention (see Chapter 1). Labeling is the process whereby encounters with criminal justice agents results in a person's obtaining a "criminal," "delinquent," or some other negative status (label). Some have called labeling a theory, and others have called it a perspective or near-theory (Winfree and Abadinsky 1996).

However, whatever we call it, labeling influenced juvenile justice policy nationwide during the 1960s and 1970s.

Labeling is simple and intuitively appealing. To most people it "just makes sense," which explains why labeling has been so influential, even though researchers have had a difficult time empirically verifying it (Winfree and Abadinsky 1996, 262). Before we go further, there is one other definition issue that faces us: the distinction between "diversion" and "minimizing penetration." Many diversion proponents believe that true diversion can only occur in the criminal justice system prior to adjudication (Whitehead and Lab 1996, 264–65). Once we have taken an offender to trial and found that person guilty of some crime, efforts to remove the individual from the system really constitute **minimizing penetration.** At that point some stigma has already attached to the person, and our efforts to remove the offender from the system into a community corrections setting merely keeps the individual from moving into secure correctional institutions.

Can We Divert? Should We Divert?

One dilemma that faces us in regard to diversion programs involves the question of who should be considered for diversion. The "can we divert?" question is fairly easy to answer: yes, we can divert quite a few juveniles and adults as well. Should we divert? That seems to be a much more difficult question to answer, because this is the question that gets at the issue of who our target population for diversion should be. In order to answer this more difficult question, we need to look at two issues.

First, are candidates for diversion "appropriate?" In other words, are these individuals who will not pose a threat to public safety, irrespective of the stigma attached to them? For most diversion programs selection criteria are so stringent that only the "best of the best" get chosen. This means that very seldom will a diversion candidate be a public safety threat. In fact, most divertees will be first offenders and minor property offenders. The end result should be a noncontroversial program selection process that can show a high degree of success.

The second consideration for diversion is a little more problematic: the question of the services provided. There is a distinction between diverting from something (formal adjudication) and diverting to something (a community-based program). The first part typically is easy to achieve: we can divert lots of people from the criminal justice system. But to what will we divert them? Unfortunately, there are not always programs and services provided for offenders diverted from formal adjudication. Therefore, they do not obtain the services that they should receive. In order to assess the possible services that diversion programs can provide, the following section will examine different types of programs.

Types of Diversion Programs

Basically, we can say that there is an almost limitless number of diversion programs possible. However, for our purposes, it is easiest to group these programs into a small and manageable number of categories. Therefore, we will look at two "self-awareness" approaches: (1) educational or information programs and (2) counseling or self-help programs (Enos and Southern 1996).

Most diversion programs are structured as first offender projects, and some of them even carry that name. These efforts try to keep first offenders from becoming persistent offenders. In order to do this, the project must provide some assessment of the offender's problems and then help provide an appropriate treatment routine.

Educational or informational programs may have many goals. For instance, in the case of juvenile offenders the educational dimension might be expressed through tutoring or academic support for junior high school or high school courses. Similarly, educational support for adults might entail a course in English as a second language or help with obtaining a GED. By contrast, "education," or more properly information, might include classes on the consequences of further exposure to the criminal justice system. This approach is often used with first offenders who have been charged with crimes such as shoplifting or drunk driving. The program may include films showing the results of drunk driving accidents and guest speakers such as police officers and judges addressing the legal consequences of future law violations. These sessions may stress course content, but they frequently have a distinctively "scared straight" orientation.[2]

Counseling or self-help programs also may be informational. They frequently stress self-discovery and provision of skills aimed at dealing with one's problems (Enos and Southern, 1996; see also Lester and Braswell 1987). These programs may entail drug and alcohol counseling, group therapy sessions, parenting skills development, anger management, and problem solving. Some of these projects are particularly aimed at families, and they involve treating offenders in a family context with the assistance of family members in the treatment. Whatever the program emphasis, diversion efforts aim to help offenders identify and solve their personal problems.

Success and Failure

Diversion programs suffer from a problem common to virtually all community corrections approaches: lack of funding. Ventures may be funded by community groups such as the United Way, or they may have to ask businesses and other local organizations for donations. Typically volunteers staff these projects. This feature may make for a highly motivated staff, but such arrangements can create problems for long-term planning and programming efforts.

However, the two most persistent questions regarding these programs do not pertain to funding, they involve net widening and program effectiveness.

Net widening has been the one inescapable criticism of diversion programs (Austin and Krisberg 1981). Although there have been mixed results, there is a body of research that demonstrates that most diversion programs are net widening by their very nature (Decker 1985). The real dilemma we face is an increase in the offender population under social control in the diversion programs, and by diverting some people we free up space in the traditional formal control agencies and facilities as well. Thus, diversion programs may create a ratcheting effect by significantly increasing our capacity to punish.

The second criticism facing diversion programs deals with evaluation. Typically, diversion programs are praised for their client effectiveness. However, given that they deal with the least serious and, in some instances, the most motivated offenders, it is not surprising that these programs usually show high success rates (see, for example, Latessa and Allen 1997, 129). Unfortunately, many times they do not involve an evaluation component, so measures of success are based on anecdotal evidence.

Although a number of diversion programs have proven to be ineffective, they are likely to continue. Most program originators, managers, and staff members believe that they are doing some good. Therefore, based on their personal orientations these individuals are likely to try to keep diversion projects alive. We may never see rigorous evaluations of these programs, but they persist as a result of what Samuel Walker (1994, 16) calls crime control "theology."

Fines, Forfeitures, and Restitution

If we look back into the history of punishment we find that economic sanctions have been around for a long time (see Chapter 2). In fact, we find economic sanctions prescribed in both the Pentateuch, or the first five books of the Old Testament, and the Code of Hammurabi. Box 8.1 provides some specific examples.

During the past decade we seem to have rediscovered economic sanctions. For instance, fines have been provided for in criminal statutes for most of our nation's history; however, the passage of the federal Racketeering Influenced and Corrupt Organizations (RICO) statutes provided the means to use fines in a major way as criminal penalties.[3] In this section we will explore the use of fines, asset forfeiture, and other economic sanctions as alternatives to, or enhancements of, incarceration.

Objectives of Economic Sanctions

Why should we employ economic sanctions? First, economic sanctions are used for punishment. In that regard, fines like those we use with traffic offenders are a punishment for cases not requiring incarceration.

Box 8.1

Ancient Examples of Economic Sanctions

The following list, taken from the Old Testament book of Exodus, illustrates a very old and traditional form of economic sanctions:

Exodus 22:1
   "If a man shall steal an ox, or a sheep, and kill it or sell it, he shall restore five oxen for an ox, and four sheep for the sheep."

Exodus 22:5
   "If a man shall cause a field or vineyard to be eaten, and shall put his beast,

and shall feed in another man's field; of the best of his own field, and of the best of his own vineyard, shall he make restitution."

Exodus 22:6
   "If a fire break out and catch in thorns, so that the stacks of grain, or the standing grain, or the field, be consumed therewith, he that kindled the fire shall surely make restitution."

Source: The Holy Bible, King James Version.

Second, in addition to punishment we may want to hit economically motivated offenders where it hurts the most: in the wallet. It seems logical that if a crime was committed to make money, an appropriate punishment would be to try to retrieve some of that money. Therefore, the second justification for economic sanctions is to undermine the financial basis of certain major economic crimes.

We will now turn to the economic sanctions programs currently being employed. Remember, we present these programs in the context of community corrections; they may serve as alternatives to incarceration or merely additional punishments.

Types of Programs

We will examine three specific types of programs in this section: fines, asset forfeiture, and restitution. Each of these has been the focus of much attention over the past decade and we will try to examine each of these in terms of contemporary corrections.

As previously mentioned, fines have been used for traffic cases as long as there have been traffic cases. Most traffic cases are misdemeanors, and while incarceration might be appropriate for offenses such as drunk driving, many of these offenses are violations of municipal ordinances. Therefore, incarceration is not warranted based on the relative lack of seriousness of the violation, and incarceration might actually cost the jurisdiction more money than a fine would generate.

As we discussed in Chapter 3, a somewhat recent variation of the fine approach to sanctioning is the **day fine** (Winterfield and Hillsman 1993). Day fines can be used for misdemeanors more serious than traffic cases, and potentially even for some felonies. This method acknowledges that most fines are regressive. In other words, traditional fines exact a larger percentage toll on individuals with the lowest incomes.

To overcome the regressive nature of fines, some jurisdictions experimented with and eventually implemented day fines. Day fines do not stipulate a certain monetary amount for certain crimes. Instead the day fine is determined by the offender's earnings per day multiplied by a certain number of days. Thus a minor property crime might be "worth" three days. If person A earns $50 per day the total amount of the fine would be $150. However, if person B earns $200 per day the total fine for that individual would be $600. Each person still pays three days worth of fines, but the totals are different based on the ability to pay. Like federal and state income taxes, day fines are a progressive way of establishing penalties.

Perhaps no method of economic sanction has been any more praised, nor condemned in recent years, than **asset forfeitures.** Asset forfeitures came out of the Congressional passage of the RICO statutes. This legislation originally was designed to strike at traditional organized criminal entities such as La Cosa Nostra (the "Mafia"). However, during the past 10 to 15 years this legislation increasingly has been applied to cases involving major drug traffickers.

The thrust of the RICO statutes and the sanction of asset forfeiture is that criminals buy personal property with the profits they make from criminal enterprises. Therefore, any item that can be traced to money made from organized criminal activity is subject to seizure by the government and forfeiture upon the defendant's conviction. In those cases, the government will hold public auctions or they will turn over certain items (typically houses, cars, boats, and airplanes) to state and local law enforcement agencies. The fact that law enforcement agencies may benefit from property or cash seized as a result of criminal cases has caused some people to allege a conflict of interest on the part of these agencies.

Recently the use of asset forfeitures in federal cases has been challenged in the courts. The essence of these challenges is that this sanction imposes cruel and unusual punishment in violation of the Eighth Amendment of the U.S. Constitution, and the defendant is being punished twice—through incarceration and forfeiture of personal assets—for the same offense. While there probably will be additional legal challenges to this particular sanction, in all likelihood it will continue to be used in major criminal racketeering cases.

The final economic sanction we will consider is **restitution.** To make restitution an offender must pay back victims for losses suffered, especially when those losses involve property damages (see, for example, Department of Justice 1981, 185). Early restitution programs were touted as alternatives to incarceration. Within the past decade or so, restitution has become a fairly common sanction in U.S. courts, but not really as an alternative to incarceration. More than anything else, restitution has become a probation add-on. Judges now routinely order offenders to make restitution for stolen or damaged property, but sometimes there is little or no follow-up from the court.

In examining the status of restitution, particularly with probationers, Marilyn McShane and Wesley Krause (1993, 174–82) found that in one study involving 32 counties from around the United States the average amount of restitution ordered was $2,172. By contrast, the average amount paid was $972, or 45% of the total. A similar study in Chicago found that the average restitution amount actually paid over a three-year period was 34%. The Chicago study did find that warning letters sent by registered mail served as useful "reminders" to probationers who were delinquent in their restitution payments.

Success and Failure

Economic sanctions seem to be among the fastest growing segments of the contemporary community corrections movement in the United States. What is the appeal of economic sanctions and what seems to have been accomplished through the use of economic sanctions?

The appeal of this punishment seems to be reasonably clear. First, it can save money. If economic sanctions truly are alternatives to incarceration, they will save bed spaces and per diem costs for every inmate that otherwise would be locked up. The potential savings could run between $15,000 and $30,000 per year per inmate, and this could be a tremendous cost savings.

Furthermore, economic sanctions can be revenue generators. Although we usually do not talk about fines and forfeitures as governmental funding sources, in many jurisdictions seized drug money and assets are looked upon as revenues by state and local law enforcement agencies. Even if these moneys are not dedicated to additional law enforcement efforts, they go into government general funds and provide financial support that otherwise would not be available.

If fines and forfeitures are not alternatives to incarceration, but become probation and incarceration add-ons, then we have a different set of concerns. By aiming at crimes of an economic nature, economic sanctions are designed to take the profit motive out of crime. If these tactics do dissuade criminals from their illegal activities, then economic sanctions can be said to be successful, but participants in such activities, particularly organized crime activities, may ultimately view fines and forfeitures as simply another cost of doing business. In these latter cases, the economic sanctions are not deterrents but mere inconveniences.

Two observations can be made. First, economic sanctions can bring additional money into government coffers through fines and forfeitures. A policy of restitution passes these moneys on to the victims. However, these programs might actually lose money because of collection problems and their associated costs. Second, the jury still seems to be out on the degree to which economic sanctions deter individuals from criminal activity or provide rehabilitation or retribution.

Community Service

Community service is an area of community corrections that has seen enormous growth since the late 1970s. Like fines and restitution, community service has its roots in primitive legal codes and in notions such as restorative justice. In its modern form it has been seen as an alternative to incarceration. Community service programs seem especially appropriate for crimes such as spray painting graffiti or other forms of vandalism.

Objectives of Community Service

Community service is aimed at securing benefits for the community and for the offender as well. The offender provides a service to the community, helping to clean up graffiti, for example. But the offender gains something from community service as well. In fact, the offender seems to receive at least two major benefits. First, the offender is held accountable for the offense, which should help this person take responsibility for his or her actions in the future. Second, the offender benefits from not being incarcerated and from not incurring a financial cost—such as fines, forfeitures, or restitution payments—that may be difficult to repay.

Types of Programs

In the cases that do not seem to warrant incarceration, the judge may order the offender to participate in projects that should provide some community assistance. In some ways, like diversion programs, community service projects are only limited by our imagination. For instance, offenders may be ordered to clean up graffiti, to work in community parks and recreation programs, or to clean up government offices. On occasion offenders are ordered to wash government vehicles such as police cars or fire trucks as part of their obligation. Normally, this is done in conjunction with standard probation, and as one of the specific probation conditions. These efforts may be administered by a probation officer or some other governmental official, such as a parks and recreation supervisor.

Other community service programs may require offenders to work in hospital emergency rooms (especially for drunk driving cases), or facilities such as clinics, libraries, senior citizen centers, and schools. The objective is for the offender to develop a degree of accountability to the community and to see that the community has been harmed by his or her criminal action.

Issues in Community Service

Community service efforts would seem to be the least controversial community corrections programs imaginable, but this is not the case. In fact, there seem to be three issues that plague community service endeavors. First, ensuring offender accountability presents many problems. Although offenders

Courts sometimes order offenders to perform community service as a way of paying for their crimes. The Los Angeles Police Department supervises one such program where juvenile offenders are required to clean graffiti off of the walls of neighborhood businesses.

may appear for their assignments, this does not necessarily mean that the jobs are meaningful to them or that they learn any particular lesson as a result of having fulfilled the court order.

Second is the question of supervision of offenders involved in community service projects. Simply because a judge has ordered an offender to perform a certain number of hours does not mean that the person will complete the duties assigned or even show up when ordered to. Someone will have to assume the responsibility for holding the offender accountable, and often this falls to the lot of overworked probation officers.

Third, and perhaps the most severe community service criticism, deals with punishment ("Implementing Community Service" 1989; Maher and Dufour 1987). Many members of the general public do not believe that community service is "real" punishment. These projects may suffer from a lack of legitimacy because of this lack of credibility.

Success and Failure

The degree to which community service projects address these three issues will dictate how likely they are to be utilized. If they cannot deal adequately with these issues, community service may not be ordered by judges in the future.

Richard Maher and Henry Dufour (1987, 26) maintain that community service will continue to be part of the corrections continuum, if for no other reason than prison crowding and the lack of tax dollars to support ever-increasing institutional populations. However, they also contend that much of the existing enabling legislation keeps community service from being punitive. This undermines public confidence, and it keeps offenders from being sufficiently threatened with this sanction. Therefore, while community service will continue, the future nature and application of this intermediate sanction may have to be carefully reconsidered.

House Arrest and Electronic Monitoring

House arrest is a relatively old punishment concept, but it has been combined with a fairly new enforcement mechanism: electronic monitoring (Lilly and Ball 1987).[4] House arrest has been used worldwide with individuals not thought to be a risk for flight. More recently in the United States it has been used with offenders who might be candidates for jail or prison time.

Historically, house arrest had to be enforced with the presence of an armed guard at the offender's home, or through police or probation officers making frequent checks to ensure that the offender indeed was at home. However, with the advent of electronic monitoring a technology was in place to remotely monitor house arrest.

In April 1983, District Court Judge Jack Love, of Albuquerque, New Mexico, ordered use of an electronic anklet with a probation violator. About the same time other judges from around the country had decided that the traditional ways of dealing with drunk drivers, probation violators, and some other relatively minor offenders were ineffective. The typical choices for these offenders were jail time or nothing. Nothing really consisted of a fine and probation, but not a more punitive sanction such as incarceration. Judge Love stumbled upon the newly developing **electronic monitoring** technology, wherein offenders could be fitted with a tamper-resistant bracelet. These bracelets, coupled with telephone transmitter-receiver devices allow manual or computer-assisted dialers to check on the offender's whereabouts (Ford and Schmidt 1985). The normal procedure is to allow offenders to go to work or to have specified time periods when they would not be monitored, as long as prior approval was obtained. Thus, the monitoring officer might stipulate that the offender normally will not be monitored during the hours of 7:30 AM and 5:30 PM. From 5:30 PM until 7:30 AM, the offender is expected to be home, and when the dialer calls, the offender fits the device into the electronic receiver to send a verifying signal to the monitoring office. If no electronic reply is given (or in case of equipment malfunction) the offender is reported missing and surveillance officers are dispatched to the individual's home. In this way random checks, made possible by computerized dialing devices, can make certain that house arrest conditions are being observed.

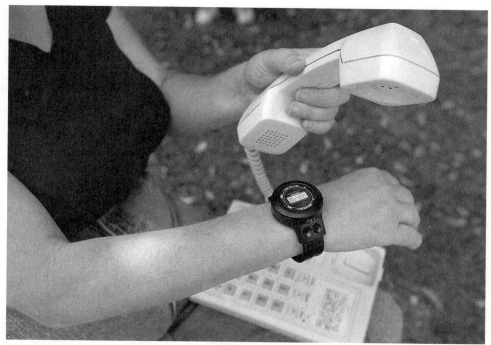

Nationwide offenders may be supervised under house arrest through the use of electronic monitoring. Here a female offender uses an electronic monitoring device that looks much like a digital watch to check in with her probation officer.

Objectives of House Arrest and Electronic Monitoring

As a community corrections program, what are we trying to achieve through the use of house arrest and electronic monitoring? First, as an alternative to incarceration, house arrest should save us jail and prison bed space. If the offenders assigned to house arrest are candidates for institutionalization, then every person we place under house arrest will save room in already crowded prisons and jails. Additionally, every inmate-day we can free up will save us money in the long run. Therefore, house arrest may be one way to reduce rapidly escalating correctional costs. However, how can we offset or justify electronic monitoring's additional costs? We need to remember that there are no "free" corrections programs. One answer to this has been that most jurisdictions utilizing electronic monitoring require program participants to pay a monthly monitoring fee. Thus, offenders pay for program costs themselves.

Second, not only should house arrest save institutional space, but it also should minimize the stigma and trauma faced by jail and prison inmates. One of the greatest dilemmas facing people who have served jail or prison sentences of any length is that reintegration back into the life of the community and their families is difficult. With house arrest the problem of reintegration does not exist. Associated with the issue of community placement is the consideration that some treatment programs are available in the community that are not available in an institution. Therefore, offenders under house arrest may have access to more and better types of programming to meet their specific needs and they may be required and able to pay all or part of the treatment costs because they have maintained gainful employment.

Success and Failure

One of the major problems with any new correctional program—and community corrections projects are no exception—is that they often appear on the scene and are proclaimed *the* solution to our problems. This clearly has been the case with house arrest enforced by electronic monitoring. At this point these programs have existed long enough for us to have a fairly clear picture of what they can and cannot do. House arrest with electronic monitoring can be a very useful community corrections program, but it is not without problems. In this section we will particularly focus on the failure of house arrest with electronic monitoring to live up to some of its early promises.

The cost-saving dimension of electronic monitoring seems to be one area where some promises have been delivered, however. Electronic monitoring often costs correctional systems little or nothing extra because the offenders must pay for the program. However, the cost-savings promised through additional free bed space is another matter. In most jurisdictions the majority of candidates for electronic monitoring are not really on their way to jail or prison. Because of the influence of public opinion against use of this technique with offenders who pose any significant risk, electronic monitoring typically is used with low-risk offenders who are not likely to reoffend or to commit a serious violation under this form of supervision.

In those instances where offenders have been diverted from a period of incarceration, the bed spaces saved frequently have been filled up with other offenders. Therefore, electronic monitoring simply may have expanded our capacity to punish. Another criticism of electronic monitoring is that it is not punitive enough. Many citizens and politicians feel that sending someone home to do time is not punishment, even if freedom of movement is restricted.

Electronic monitoring opponents also note that this technique monitors place, but not behavior. Monitoring the offender's place might be very important for crimes such as drunk driving, but for pedophiles or drug dealers place monitoring may not be sufficient. Another dimension of this criticism is highlighted by James Quinn and John Holman (1991b), who examined the incidents of family conflict in which offenders were under electronically monitored house arrest. While their conclusions were less than definitive, Quinn and Holman (1991b, 190) emphasize that "these findings suggest that greater attention be paid to offender household and related issues by professionals supervising offenders on EMHC [electronically monitored home confinement]."

Civil libertarians also might be opposed to electronic monitoring because of its intrusiveness. Although individuals supervised by means of an electronic bracelet are "volunteers," the reality is that there is a lot of coercion to get people to participate in the program. Some groups concerned about over-reach by the criminal justice system typically feel very uncomfortable about agents of government being free to "snoop" in offenders' homes at any time.

The most fundamental flaw facing electronic monitoring may be that it has no theoretical underpinnings. Todd Clear (1988) examines all of the different justifications for punishment from retribution to rehabilitation, and from deterrence to incapacitation, and on all points his assessment is that electronic monitoring is deficient. In the end, he finds electronic monitoring to be an add-on, net widening program in search of a purpose. Not everyone has been so critical, but the proof of effectiveness has yet to be established for electronic monitoring. If it cannot establish both economic and programmatic viability, electronic monitoring may not survive in its current form into the next century.

Community Alternatives for Juveniles

Part of the problem we have in discussing contemporary juvenile community programs is determining the actual status of juvenile offenders. The 1970s and 1980s substantially altered our concepts of juvenile justice. In this section we will examine some of the changes that have occurred in our orientation toward delinquents, and the types of community-based programs that seem most important for dealing with these youngsters, both now and in the future.

Changing Definitions of Juvenile Offenders

Our approaches to dealing with juvenile offenders have gone through several well-defined cycles over the past 200 years. In fact, historically there were only two categories of persons: adults and children (Bernard 1992; White-head and Lab 1996). There were few if any differences in the way adults and children were treated. When children violated the law they were incarcerated like, and often with, adults.

Because of the harsh realities of children's treatment for violating the law, the "child saving" movement of the nineteenth century advocated the creation of a separate justice system for children. The juvenile justice system really was based around the first juvenile court in Cook County (Chicago), Illinois, in 1899. The child saving movement and the founding of the first juvenile court solidified the notion of "juveniles" as offenders and created the concept of delinquency (Platt 1977; Schlossman 1977). From 1899 to 1966 juveniles existed in an entirely separate justice system, with different procedures than those of adult criminal courts (Champion and Mays 1991). See Chapters 4, 5, and 6 for additional treatment of juveniles and the corrections system.

In 1966 and 1967 things began to change for juvenile offenders in the United States. During this period the U.S. Supreme Court decided two cases—*Kent v. United States* (1966) and *In re Gault* (1967)—that established a due process basis for the nation's juvenile courts. From 1966 through the early 1970s the number of juvenile cases decided by the Supreme Court and other appellate courts increased, and, as a result of these decisions, extended a broad range of due process rights to juveniles (Whitehead and Lab 1996).

Beginning in the late-1970s through the 1980s a "get-tough" movement swept across the United States (Bernard 1992; Schwartz 1989). As a result of this movement and the additional due process guarantees extended to juveniles, the distinctions between juvenile and adult courts largely disappeared. Therefore, the contemporary scene consists of more punitive and adult-like sanctions for juvenile offenders. The most serious of these sanctions involves the transfer of juveniles to adult courts.

Transferring Juveniles to the Adult System

Throughout juvenile justice history in the United States there have been provisions for trying some youngsters as adults (Bernard 1992; Schwartz 1989). For much of the juvenile court's existence, this provision—also called waiver, remand, or certification—has been reserved for two groups of youngsters. One group typically thought of as most deserving of transfer included youngsters who committed very serious crimes involving personal violence. The good news about this group is that they have remained a fairly small percentage of the nation's juvenile offenders.

The second group considered for transfer is a little more problematic. This group includes adolescents who are deemed "not amenable to treatment" in the juvenile justice system. This group has passed through the juvenile justice system multiple times, and eventually the system gives up on them and sends them to the adult criminal justice system for disposition.

There are two very interesting features associated with the persistent juvenile offenders. First, these youngsters constitute most of the more than 12,000 youths transferred annually from juvenile to adult court (Butts 1996; DeFrances and Strom 1997). Second, overwhelmingly these are property offenders. Most of these juveniles are not threats to public safety, and any one of their violations taken alone would not justify a transfer, but when their delinquency histories are considered as a whole they warrant the youth's labeling as a "serious" offender.

What does the issue of transferring juveniles to adult courts have to do with community corrections? In many ways, quite a bit. When juveniles are tried as adults they face adult penalties, including incarceration in adult prisons. The vast majority of the youngsters tried as adults receive probation (Champion and Mays 1991). However, some need sanctions more serious than probation, but less serious than incarceration in an adult facility. Therefore, community-based programs hold a promise for appropriate sanctions for these offenders. The following sections will deal with the programs currently in use with juvenile offenders, both those processed within the juvenile system and those transferred to the adult system.

Diversion Programs

Diversion programs seem to have been motivated by action at the national level such as passage of the Juvenile Justice and Delinquency Prevention Act of 1974. A key provision of this legislation was the diversion of minor juvenile offenders from the formal adjudication system in order to minimize the stigma associated with formal processing.

Diversion programs can involve projects such as driving schools for traffic offenders, including individuals charged with drunk driving. They may also include first offender, or misdemeanor programs. In some communities, teen courts have been established as one mechanism to divert the least serious juvenile offenders away from the formal system into a community service oriented method of treatment. These programs may be able to provide some services to youngsters who need them, but who do not need incarceration in a secure confinement facility. They may provide a low visibility, nonstigmatizing treatment environment, but they may be the object of some criticism as well. Refer to the section "Diversion," earlier in this chapter, for a more complete discussion of diversion programs.

Restitution Programs

Restitution would seem to be a treatment method ideally suited to juvenile offenders. Because many juveniles have committed nonviolent property offenses such as burglary or larceny, they seem to be the most appropriate candidates for community-based dispositions involving restitution. Restitution is designed not only to pay back the victim for losses sustained, but also to hold the offender accountable for law-violating behavior. However, there are some fundamental problems with juvenile offenders and restitution.

A major problem with restitution programs is ensuring payment is made to the offender. Some enforcement mechanisms must be in place to collect the restitution amount included in the court order. A second problem relates to the young offender's ability to pay. Some youngsters work and in doing so help support themselves and their families. Many other juveniles do not have independent financial resources or jobs. Therefore, any requirement that they repay their victims becomes an additional burden on their parents. This does little to personalize the crime or to increase the offender's accountability for his or her actions. Nevertheless, a restitution order of even a very modest amount (say $5 per week) could serve as an ongoing reminder to youngsters about the consequences of their actions.

Wilderness, Survival, and Self-Reliance Programs

Wilderness and outdoor programs actually have been around for decades. For instance, Karl Holton established conservation and park development forestry camps for juvenile delinquents in Los Angeles County in the 1930s (Roberts 1988). This was followed by the creation of the first Outward Bound School in Wales during World War II. Originally this school was designed to "train merchant seamen to survive on the open sea, as well as to teach them self-discipline, physical preparedness, group pride and teamwork, and a shared trust as the group worked together to achieve strenuous goals" (Roberts 1988, 3). In 1960 the Outward Bound program was instituted in the United States, and it spawned a number of imitators, such as VisionQuest and similar programs sponsored by the Jack and Ruth Eckerd Foundation (see Castellano and Soderstrom 1992; Winterdyk and Griffiths 1984).

Wilderness programs have been used with juvenile delinquents and young adult criminals, as well as with drug offenders and individuals with mental or physical impairments. For delinquent youngsters, these programs assume that "juvenile offenders [are] the product of their environment and delinquent behavior [is] a consequence of their interaction with the environment" (Winterdyk and Griffiths 1984, 36). Albert Roberts (1988, 3) says that most outdoor programs have four elements in common:

- They provide an organized program that strives for mastering difficult physical challenges. These programs are designed to increase survival skills, perhaps including "urban survival" skills. This component teaches self-reliance, an element frequently missing in institutional placements.
- They provide participants with the opportunity to succeed. Many of the youngsters in these programs have been failures in school, in their relations with others, and within their own families. Most of the wilderness and survival efforts try to teach participants that they can cope with whatever situations confront them, both inside and outside of the program.
- They use the survival experience as a foundation to teach academic subjects.
- They provide the format for participants to learn how to work in cooperation with others in order to achieve specific goals.

To date there have been relatively few rigorous assessments of wilderness and outdoor programs, and most evaluations have focused on the psychological and attitudinal changes participants have undergone. By contrast, there has been very little analysis of the impact of these programs on recidivism (see Castellano and Soderstrom 1992; Winterdyk and Griffiths 1984). From the existing research, we know some things about program effectiveness. First, in most of these programs, individuals who completed the program (not just participated) showed an initial increase in law-abiding behavior. Second, this improvement typically was short-lived, and within two years the treatment effects largely had disappeared. Finally, wilderness and outdoor programs may not produce better results than institutional placements, but they may provide an alternative to traditional secure confinement (Castellano and Soderstrom 1992).

Success and Failure

Community-based corrections programs for juvenile offenders were not a part of this country's corrections system until the second half of the twentieth century. Beginning with passage of the Juvenile Justice and Delinquency Prevention Act of 1974 the federal government led the way in establishing diversion programs for first or minor offenders (Schwartz 1989). This time period also saw a special push to remove status offenders from secure correctional placements, a strategy that came to be known as the **deinstitutionalization of status offenders**—or DSO—movement (Schneider 1985).

Following the Juvenile Justice and Delinquency Prevention Act of 1974 a number of state and local jurisdictions created diversion programs. The results of such projects have been somewhat mixed. For instance, a number of juvenile offenders have benefited from services provided in the community that might not otherwise be available to them in an institution. They also have benefited from low-visibility, nonstigmatizing treatment. However, there seem to be two problems—net widening and program outcomes—that cannot be avoided.

As we stated previously, from their inception, diversion projects have been persistently criticized as net widening. To date, there is ample evidence that many juvenile diversion programs have indeed widened the net (Austin and Krisberg 1981; Decker 1985). Therefore, some youngsters have received useful and needed services, but others have been needlessly processed.

Beyond the net widening critique, the most fundamental question is, Are these programs effective? What has been the outcome of the community alternative programs for juvenile offenders? Unfortunately, it is this result that is the most disappointing. Many of these programs seem to have had very little long-term effect on the degree to which offenders repeat their law-violating behaviors. With or without these programs some offenders would have gone on to live law-abiding lives in the absence of these programs, and others would have continued violating the law. If the programs do no good, are they doing any harm to these youngsters? In the end, the programs simply may be irrelevant. Fortunately, most of the youngsters referred to community-based projects are not serious offenders to begin with.

Careers in Contemporary Corrections

Community Corrections

Aside from traditional probation and parole positions, there are numerous employment possibilities in **community-based corrections.** This is one of the most highly privatized parts of the corrections subsystem, and most of these programs are based in nonsecure residential settings such as group homes and halfway houses and other alternatives to incarceration programs.

Most community corrections employees have very positive feelings about the fact that these agencies are nonbureaucratic. In fact, community-based programs personify flexibility in corrections treatment. Additionally, these programs often demonstrate high levels of success with their clients. One reason for this is that they operate close to the clients, and the clients remain in the community. Therefore, concern over reintegration is eliminated. Additionally, offenders placed in community-based programs are the least serious public safety threats and are often the most amenable to treatment. As a result of client cooperation and a lack of compulsion, community-based programs are able to demonstrate high levels of success, and the people working in these agencies feel they are making major contributions to the program's direction and effectiveness. The end result is a high degree of job satisfaction among the people working in community corrections.

There are negative aspects to the community corrections work environment as well. One of these negatives is job burnout, a condition shared with other correctional careers. As we mentioned in regard to probation and parole and counseling positions, community corrections employees have close and often intense exposure to offenders and their problems. The result is a close attachment to some clients and this takes an emotional toll on community corrections personnel.

Another major negative feature of community corrections is lack of financial and program stability. Many community corrections programs are funded from year to year through a combination of private, lo-

cal, state, and federal moneys. This means that program administrators are always trying to piece together a budget for the following year, and this creates a sense of instability for the employees. For many of the people who have dedicated themselves to community-based programming, the lack of financial stability is a way of life to which they have become accustomed.

The expected pay for community corrections positions is somewhat tied to the issue of lack of financial and program stability. Jobs in community-based programs often pay less than those in state or federal institutional settings. They also may not provide the full range of benefits associated with working in a state or federal prison. While this is not universally true, most community corrections positions will be lower paying that their institutional counterparts.

Community corrections administrators often have an expanded view of the appropriate education and experience necessary to work in their programs. For instance, counselors and psychologists may be required to have the same levels of training as equivalent individuals working in prisons. However, in community corrections they may not be required to possess professional licenses. Many of the people working in counseling positions in community-based programs also will have either a bachelor's or master's degree in social work.

Experience is another place where community-based corrections and institutional corrections diverge. Some of the higher level positions in institutional corrections—case managers or classifications officers, for example—require applicants to have either graduate degrees, a certain number of years of related experience, or both. You may be thinking: How can I get experience if no one will hire me to begin with? One of the answers to that question is to look for jobs in community corrections. Some agencies, especially the small ones, look for availability and willingness even if experience is lacking. The community-based programs provide a front door to the

Careers in Contemporary Corrections *(continued)*

Community Corrections

work world of corrections for a number of recent college graduates.

There are many positive aspects to working in community corrections. Being employed in a nonbureaucratic environment in which successful treatment is very likely and one has close contact with clients is very appealing to many people. However, when it comes to the issue of promotion potential, these programs come up short. Because most of these agencies are small, there typically are few levels of supervisors or managers. Such an arrangement can mean almost instant access to decision makers, but it also means that there are not many promotional opportunities. Most community-based programs are local in their organization, funding, and orienta-

tion. This feature is appealing to some prospective employees, but stifling to others.

Community corrections organizations may have the fewest hiring restrictions of any of the correctional agencies. They seldom have physical restrictions, and virtually none of them requires a written entrance examination. There may be a cursory background check, but this usually consists of calling the candidate's references as would be done for any type of job. As a result of the existence of community-based agencies, some individuals will have the chance to work in corrections who otherwise might not qualify.

Sources: Cromwell and Killinger (1994); DeLucia and Doyle (1994); Henry (1994).

Issues in Community Corrections

Community corrections, like everything in corrections, is facing a number of issues as we approach the next century. In this section we will explore several of the issues that seem to be the most significant, and those that hold the greatest potential problems for the future of community corrections.

The Role of the Victim in Punishment

A major controversy surrounding sanctioning criminal offenders involves the victim's role in deciding the appropriate punishment. In this section we will examine the different dimensions of this issue.

From earliest periods of recorded history, victims have been a part of exacting retribution from offenders (Abadinsky and Winfree 1992). In fact, the Code of Hammurabi, the Law of Moses, and other ancient writings provide for a *lex talionis,* or law of retribution. We discussed the *lex talionis* in Chapter 2. But it is worth noting that the *lex talionis* is proscriptive, not prescriptive. In other words, it sets the outer limits of punishment, not the amount or type of punishment to be employed. Nevertheless, the ancient legal codes were written in such a way that they presume some involvement by the victim or the victim's family in assessing punishment. Gradually, over time we have gotten away from individual retribution or retaliation. Now crimes are prosecuted by the government, and the government is responsible for exacting punishment from the offender.

Where does this approach leave the victim? In most instances that question is very easy to answer: nowhere. To some extent victims are no more than witnesses in court. After they have testified, we consider their responsibilities to be over. However, many jurisdictions are taking the view that the victim's voice needs to be heard, especially when the disposition involves a community-based sanction.

Over the past decade several jurisdictions have adopted victim's "bills of rights" to articulate the legal protections that should be afforded crime victims (Walker 1994). Included as a part of many of these bills of rights is a provision allowing the victims to participate at sentencing. The idea is not to allow the victim some final act of revenge against the offender, but to more fully inform the court of the damage done to the crime victim. The provision for **allocution,** the opportunity to speak in court, has been available for a long period of time, some would say ever since there have been courts. However, with the passage of victims' bills of rights this allowance has been made even more explicit.

Victim input into the sentencing process seems critical in cases where the offender is going to be placed into a community corrections program. Under this arrangement, the offender is not incarcerated in a secure confinement facility and potentially could have access to the victim. Therefore, one of the chief concerns for everyone involved is protecting the victim from both harassment and actual physical harm. To the degree they are able to protect victims, community corrections programs will be accepted by the public and will be successful. If they cannot assure public safety, they will remain under a cloud of suspicion.

The Role of Community Stakeholders in Punishment

We already have made a number of references to public perceptions of community corrections programs. In this section we will address the problems of "selling" the general public on the acceptability of community-based programs in comparison to secure institutional placements (Sigler and Lamb 1995).

Corrections programs largely depend on public tax dollars for support, and politicians depend on the general public's support to hold their offices. Therefore, politicians are very sensitive to perceived changes in public opinion particularly in regard to issues of crime and punishment (see, for instance, Welsh et al. 1991). No politician wants to be thought of as "soft" on crime, and such an accusation may result in the individual losing an election. This means that one group of stakeholders who must be considered when designing and implementing a community corrections program is the state and local politicians.

Members of the general public also may get involved in the debate over the use of community-based programming. Community members typically become incensed about program costs and the apparent lack of public safety. Program costs become an issue when treatment is characterized as extravagant. If anything causes the public to become irate it is the perception that we are coddling criminals.

Related to the program cost issue is concern for public safety. Most members of the general public believe that when criminals are punished, they "really" should be punished, and for most people this means being locked up. Therefore, community-based programs already start with the disadvantage that they are perceived as being inherently unsafe, and if the public *feels* that the program is unsafe, to them it *is* unsafe.

Complaints about program safety typically manifest themselves at the time a new program is created. This especially is the case when the program is based around a residential group home or halfway house. Community residents may form neighborhood associations to protest the facility's location. Fear over public safety makes site selection one of the primary stumbling blocks to some community corrections programs, and one that requires a great deal of public relations work to effectively integrate these programs into the community.

Merging Treatment and Punishment

As Table 8.1 shows, many states are combining traditional sentences with intermediate sanctions.

Some hold that treatment and punishment are incompatible: Programs may punish or treat, but they cannot punish *and* treat at the same time. Community corrections is an attempt to blend a variety of correctional philosophies, with the result being less costly and more effective treatment. Is this possible, or are we simply being idealistic about community-based programming? The clear trend is to retain and even expand community corrections programs, with an increasing emphasis on their punitive aspects (see, for example, Maher and Dufour 1987). This may be a change in program orientation, or it may simply be a change in rhetoric. Only time will tell.

Gender and Community Corrections

As we have mentioned previously, one of the enduring criticisms of community corrections is the degree to which this approach widens the net. Simply by having these programs, are we bringing more people under some form of social control? The evidence to date is that many of these projects do indeed contribute to "wider, stronger, and different nets" (Austin and Krisberg 1981). In this section we will focus explicitly on the degree to which community corrections programs have a gender bias. We will deal with two questions: (1) To what extent do community-based programs target female offenders? and (2) Are females disproportionately placed in community corrections

Table 8.1

Felons Sentenced to an Additional Penalty by State Courts, by Offense, 1994

Most serious conviction offense	Percentage of felons with an additional penalty of				
	Fine	Restitution	Treatment	Community service	Other
All offenses	**21%**	**18%**	**7%**	**7%**	**8%**
Violent offenses	16%	17%	6%	4%	6%
Murder[a]	9	9	1	1	4
Rape	17	14	7	3	4
Robbery	12	13	2	2	4
Aggravated assault	19	20	8	5	6
Other violent[b]	23	20	12	8	12
Property offenses	19%	29%	5%	8%	7%
Burglary	17	27	5	6	6
Larceny[c]	20	26	5	8	9
Fraud[d]	21	38	5	10	7
Drug offenses	24%	11%	10%	6%	7%
Possession	23	8	12	8	10
Trafficking	25	14	9	5	6
Weapons offenses	16%	9%	4%	6%	6%
Other offenses[e]	28%	14%	9%	10%	14%

Note: Where the data indicated affirmatively that a particular additional penalty was imposed, the case was coded accordingly. Where the data did not indicate affirmatively or negatively, the case was treated as not having an additional penalty. These procedures provide a conservative estimate of the prevalence of additional penalties. Note also that a person receiving more than one kind of additional penalty appears under more than one table heading. Data on additional penalty were available for 872,217 cases.

[a] Includes nonnegligent manslaughter.
[b] Includes offenses such as negligent manslaughter, sexual assault, and kidnaping.
[c] Includes motor vehicle theft.
[d] Includes forgery and embezzlement.
[e] Composed of nonviolent offenses such as receiving stolen property and vandalism.

Source: Langan and Brown (1997).

programs in comparison to institutional programs? If there are affirmative answers to these questions, we also need to examine why this is so.

Most of the evidence we have on community programming and gender comes from the juvenile justice system (see, for example, Butts et al. 1996a, 1996b). Many of the community-based projects in the United States originally were developed to deal with youthful offenders, and some of these projects then were applied to adults. Based on the juvenile numbers, what do we know about gender and community corrections?

First, when the Juvenile Justice and Delinquency Prevention Act of 1974 was passed, there was a nationwide movement to divert offenders from the formal adjudication system and to deinstitutionalize status offenders. The DSO effort particularly had an impact on females who frequently were incarcerated for status offenses such as running away. Once this effort was in full swing, communities developed private placements and alternative programs for these formerly incarcerated status offenders. As a result of these alternative programs many of these youngsters disappeared from public juvenile correctional facilities and reappeared in private sector facilities and pro-

Community Corrections in the Twenty-First Century

While the future for parts of the corrections system is hard to forecast, this is not true for community corrections. In the twenty-first century we will be relying on community corrections to a greater extent than ever before. At least three things indicate that this is the trend for the future.

First, program costs on a client-for-client basis have proven to be lower for community corrections (Sigler and Lamb 1995). Although there is some concern about increasing overall corrections expenditures, as a result of net widening, these programs typically are much less costly than incarceration. Furthermore, when offenders are left in the community they can continue to work and support their families. They also can be required, as part of their sentences, to help defray part of their program costs. Although this is not an appropriate justification for a particular sanction, in some instances community-based corrections can generate revenue.

Second, we may be approaching the practical limit in terms of the number of correctional institutions we can support in the United States. Although there will be some prison space expansion, much of the new

building will be replacement space for old, worn-out facilities. As has often been noted, we cannot build our way out of the present crowding crisis, and we cannot afford to build and operate increasingly expensive secure institutions. Therefore, community-based alternatives will have to play a key role in our correctional programming. These projects may be alternatives to incarceration or alternative forms of incarceration, but they will not be the fortress-like prisons we have relied on for over a century in this country.

Finally, program effectiveness will be a factor in our choice of community corrections over institutionalization. Many of these programs have been criticized as ineffective for two reasons. In some instances these efforts truly have been ineffective. Such programs should be identified and eliminated. However, other programs have not been evaluated at all, or the evaluations have been methodologically inadequate. In these cases the projects are not at fault; the research is deficient. Therefore, as we approach the next century we need to be certain that every community corrections project has a rigorous evaluation component built into it.

grams (Schwartz 1989). We find that females and middle-class offenders especially are handled by the "low-end," less secure community corrections programs.

In some ways females are targeted by these projects (that is, certain programs are designed exclusively for female offenders or for certain types of offenders, such as runaways, who are mainly female). And in some ways they are simply the beneficiaries of changing treatment philosophies. Whichever factor is most influential, one thing is sure: Females appear in the community-based correctional programs in far greater numbers, and at a higher rate than they do in traditional public sector institutional placements.

Conclusion

In concluding our discussion of program effectiveness and community corrections, two elements need to be repeated. Community-based programs virtually always have been appealing because of the lack of stigma attached to them. This should not change. Many minor offenders can be treated most effectively if they are punished, and then can move on with their lives. Unfortunately, most institutional programs provide a lingering stigma that may undermine the long-term effectiveness of the treatment.

Additionally, the continuing battle with institutional crowding in local jails and state and federal prisons will result in growth of community-based alternatives. These programs can provide a cost-effective way to treat nondangerous offenders without the high costs of incarcerating them in a secure facility.

Finally, as we have mentioned frequently, community corrections projects eliminate the need to reintegrate offenders back into the community. Because they have not been removed from home, school, and work situations, the correctional program does not need to make provisions to move offenders back into society. If we can show that community corrections programs do not harm, but do some good, and that stigmatization and reintegration problems are minimized, this approach may not simply be the wave of the future, it may be the future.

Critical Review Questions

1. If you owned a home in an established residential neighborhood and there was an announcement that a halfway house would open one block from where you live, how would you react? What reasons would you have for supporting or opposing the location of the halfway house?

2. Imagine for a moment that you are the manager of the halfway house from which "John Goins" (the case at the beginning of the chapter) has escaped. How do you address the concerns of the press, politicians, and public *before* Goins is arrested? How do you address those concerns *after* his arrest?

3. Net widening is a concern raised with many diversion or alternative to incarceration programs. Briefly explain your understanding of net widening. Compare your answer with others in your class.

4. One of the major issues facing us in regard to incarceration is reintegration. What are some of the obstacles that hamper the reintegration of institutionalized offenders?

5. What do we hope to accomplish with programs such as work release, education release, and furloughs? Do such programs pose a risk to public safety? Why or why not?

6. We might say (in terms of the labeling perspective) that people will act in accord with our expectations of them. Are there social forces or personal characteristics that might neutralize the labeling process?

7. What kinds of cases seem most appropriate for fines and forfeitures? Would you be in favor of applying these sanctions to personal crimes such as aggravated assault, rape, robbery, and homicide? Why or why not?

8. Is restitution merely an idea that looks good on paper, but does not seem to work well in practice? What can make restitution effective? Are there impediments to its effectiveness?

9. Is house arrest punishment or not? What kinds of cases should be sentenced to home confinement, and what should be the maximum sentence length? Why?

10. Are outdoor programs a legitimate form of therapy, or are they, as Winterdyk and Griffiths said, "beating around the bush?"

Recommended Readings

Latessa, Edward J., and Harry E. Allen. 1997. *Corrections in the community.* Cincinnati: Anderson. This book takes a broad-ranging view of community corrections. The authors include treatment of the criminal justice system, sentencing, and jails and prisons. They also devote six chapters to a variety of topics dealing with probation and parole. Two chapters deal with intermediate sanctions (with one being a separate chapter on community residential—halfway house—programs). The final two chapters address the crucial issues of program effectiveness and the future of community-based corrections.

McCarthy, Belinda R., and Bernard J. McCarthy, Jr. 1991. *Community-based corrections.* 2nd ed. Pacific Grove, CA: Brooks/Cole. The authors provide a very thorough treatment of community-based corrections. They begin with discussions of reintegration and diversion. The chapters of special note in this text include those on female offenders, programs for juveniles, and one on drug and alcohol dependent offenders. Perhaps the most unique chapter in this book is the one dealing with volunteers, paraprofessionals, and ex-offenders in delivering treatment services.

McShane, Marilyn D., and Wesley Krause. 1993. *Community corrections.* New York: Macmillan. This text provides a comprehensive treatment of the field of community corrections. The first section of the book lays the foundation for the authors' examination. It attempts to answer many of the "why" questions that might be raised about the use of alternatives to incarceration. A very useful feature of the book is its detailed consideration of community corrections programs for adult and juvenile offenders. The final section deals with "people and process issues," which include legal considerations, community supervision officers' roles, and special needs populations (especially the mentally ill, sex offenders, and the chemically dependent). The book ends with a consideration of program evaluation.

Key Terms

allocution
asset forfeiture
codependency
community service
day fine
deinstitutionalization of
      status offenders
      (DSO)
diversion

educational release
electronic monitoring
extrainstitutional
      punishment
furloughs
halfway houses
house arrest
intermediate sanctions
labeling

minimizing penetration
net widening
NIMBY syndrome
reintegration
restitution
staff burnout
work release

Cases Cited

In re Gault, 387 U.S. 1 (1967)

Kent v. United States, 383 U.S. 541 (1966)

Notes

1. However, for a clear statement linking self-concept, self-esteem, and delinquent behavior see Yablonsky and Haskell (1988, 366–71).
2. For an extensive discussion of this approach to treatment see Finckenauer (1982).
3. The history, implementation, and impact of state and federal RICO statutes are dealt with in a number of places, but many of the issues raised by these statutes are covered in Brickey (1986), Bureau of Justice Assistance (1992), and North (1988).
4. Some other references you might consult include Charles (1989), on use with juveniles; Cooprider and Kerby (1990), on use at the pretrial stage; Lilly, Ball, and Wright (1987), on the evaluation of a project in Kenton County, Kentucky; and Quinn and Holman (1991a), with an examination of this approach as a case management technique.

9

Administration
of Corrections Programs

Chapter Outline

- Introduction
- Administration and Management
- An Overview of Bureaucracy
- Leadership Styles
- Issues Facing Corrections Managers
- Modern Management Tasks
- Inmate Management
- Conclusion
- Critical Review Questions
- Recommended Readings
- Key Terms
- Notes

Introduction

In criminal justice there are national and international associations to which administrators belong, and these groups include the International Association of Chiefs of Police (IACP) and the National District Attorneys' Association, among others. Within corrections, the preeminent associations include the American Correctional Association, American Jail Association, and their state and regional affiliates. At the local level, justice officials may meet regularly, either formally or informally. But to whom does a prison warden talk? As you read the following scenario ask yourself that question.

Jim Butler is a 51-year-old warden of a western state's medium-security men's prison. Jim's corrections career began after he served in the Army during the Vietnam War. His first job was as a corrections officer. Jim only had a high school diploma, but worked in military detention both in Vietnam and stateside. During his employment with the state corrections department he has worked his way up through the ranks, and along the way he earned an associate's degree in correctional science.

By his own admission, Jim is a "lifer." Short of dying on the job, he will serve the corrections department until his retirement in six years. In all likelihood he will never be promoted beyond his present position. The secretary of corrections expects to leave Jim at his present facility, since he seems to run a "tight ship."

Jim's problem is that he does not feel that he has either a personal or professional peer group with whom he can regularly talk. He belongs to the American Correctional Association and his state correctional association. He occasionally attends some national meetings, but never really has felt a part of these groups, many of which he characterizes as run by the "high fliers." Jim also attends the correction department's quarterly wardens' conferences, and he speaks by phone to other state prison wardens as the need arises. However, Jim's prison is located in a remote area of his state. The other state prisons are 200 to 400 miles away from him. The town in which he lives has 18,000 inhabitants, and the prison is the major "industry."

Warden Butler meets with his staff regularly, and he routinely participates in the life of the local community surrounding his prison. Nevertheless, he has the nagging feeling that on most occasions he makes decisions alone, that he really does not have someone with whom he can sit down over a cup of coffee and discuss the problems he and his institution are facing.

In this chapter we examine the work world of people like "Warden Butler" and others who work in corrections. Now that we have looked at the various programs and agencies that comprise the corrections subsystem, it is time to turn our attention to the administrative and legal environments found in contemporary corrections. In this chapter we focus on corrections administration; the next chapter explores the volatile legal environment.

Administration and Management

There are two points that we need to make at the outset of this chapter. First, the administrative environment is one of the most under-researched areas in contemporary corrections. Second, two terms that are central to all correctional organizations are *administration* and *management,* and though they will be used somewhat interchangeably, **administration** typically refers to the act of administering or managing "an office, employment, or organization." In criminal justice practice, administrators are the people at the top of the authority hierarchy, the organization's policy makers and chief executives. In community corrections, this includes chief probation and parole officers and community corrections managers. In institutional corrections, there are several facility managers including wardens and assistant wardens, institutional superintendents, and directors or administrators. At the state level the head of the department of corrections may be known as a director, commissioner, superintendent, or secretary (McShane and Williams 1993; 1996, 4). By virtue of their positions these individuals are likely to be more responsive to pressure from outside the organization than from within.

Alan Coffey (1975, 23–24) says that the administrative process within a correctional organization can be divided into three levels: administrative, managerial, and supervisory. At the *administrative level* we find concern for defining and integrating goals. The *managerial level* defines and integrates objectives and staffing concerns. The *supervisory managers* are the closest to the organization's line employees, and they are responsible for defining and directing program personnel.

In comparison to administration, **management** is defined as "the process by which the elements of a group are integrated, coordinated, and/or utilized so as to effectively and efficiently achieve organizational objectives" (Carlisle 1976, 1, 2). Klofas, Stojkovic, and Kalinich (1990, 7) observe that this definition says nothing about offices or office incumbents. Management is a process, not a person or an act. All personnel, from the highest to the lowest, engage in management. In sum, corrections employees of all ranks—line and staff as well—manage, but only a few administer. Corrections administrators receive their administrative authority from their organizational positions. Corrections managers, irrespective of rank, receive their professional authority from the breadth and depth of their knowledge about the positions they occupy and the personnel they supervise in the organization.

Why Study Administration or Management?

One of the unique features about the corrections field and corrections literature is the relative lack of attention paid to administration and management. Harry More (1977, 232) maintains that "The literature on correctional management is limited." Alvin Cohn (1991, 12) adds that "a review of several recent journals suggests that administration and management of correctional agencies are issues hardly examined—if studied at all."

If this is the case, why is it important to study corrections administration, particularly in an introductory corrections text? One reason is that while very few students taking this course will find themselves in administrative positions immediately after leaving college, every corrections agency operates in an administrative environment.

Alvin Cohn also provides us with another answer. He says that most corrections failure is not because of inadequate programming or underdeveloped philosophy, but is the result of "inadequate management and leadership of correctional programs" (Cohn 1977, 235). John DiIulio (1987, 6), in studying prison governance in three states, expands on this theme by adding that "the quality of prison life depends far more on management practices than on any other single variable." He concludes that "If most prisons have failed, it is because they have been ill-managed, under-managed, or not managed at all"

(DiIulio 1987, 7). Therefore, we need to turn our attention to the corrections administrative domain.

Managing Inmates and Managing Staff

Corrections management really has two distinct aspects. There is inmate management, in the form of institutions, programming efforts, and discipline. There is also organizational management, which is really concerned with keeping the various institutional and agency functions operating in an efficient manner. Cohn (1991, 13) recognizes this "organizational contradiction" when he notes that "Even the lowest status members of the hierarchy, such as probation, parole, and correctional officers, are also responsible for *managing* people as well as for the development of goals, albeit for clients." Here we focus on organizational management, but return to a brief discussion of inmate management before the end of the chapter.

When we consider the tasks performed by corrections administrators the most common ones fit into the categories of finances and personnel. Financial considerations include functions such as establishing annual budgets and purchasing of office supplies. Personnel concerns are the major consideration for any corrections administrator, however. That is, personnel issues that must be addressed include pre-service and in-service training and job assignments. Job assignments involve who does what within a given agency or office and who works particular shifts, if multiple shift assignments must be made. Personnel considerations also include scheduling leave time and covering for employees who have called in sick or who have been injured on the job.

Administration is much more than what a particular group of people does, however. It is probably much more useful to assess *how* things get done rather than *what* gets done. Therefore, we consider an assortment of administrative styles and related issues. The choice of focusing on how things get done, rather than on the specific functions performed, will allow students to apply the knowledge they gain in different contexts. That is, by taking this approach we avoid presenting you with agency-specific or component-specific information.

An Overview of Bureaucracy

Nearly every contemporary correctional organization could be described as a bureaucracy, and since some of you may end up working in corrections, it is important to understand some things about bureaucracies. Perhaps the easiest way to describe this approach is to say that historically the most common way of managing complex organizations has been from the top down. Bureaucratic management is often illustrated by a pyramid-shaped organizational chart with the different branches representing different organizational components. The more functionally specialized the organization becomes, the more branches there will be on the organizational chart, and the wider and higher the pyramid will become.

The bureaucratic management style has been associated with the military services, federal and state government agencies, and even the Roman Catholic church, the world's oldest continually operating bureaucracy. In corrections, prisons traditionally have been governed by a bureaucratic management style, particularly among custody staff members who hold military style ranks and wear uniforms (Bartollas and Miller 1978, 51, 59; Coffey 1974, 239; DiIulio 1987, 1994).

One of the organizational theorists most frequently associated with the bureaucratic management school is Max Weber. Several ideas associated with Weber's ideal type of bureaucracy are especially relevant to corrections. First, bureaucracies are based on controls established through the organization's rules. The stress is on **rationality,** the bureaucracy's members must assume the rules are correct, and follow them because they are correct.

Second, in Weber's ideal bureaucracy discretion is strictly limited by the rules and regulations. Some would say that the exercise of discretion is incompatible with the bureaucratic notion (Mouzelis 1967, 41). Third, although it may not seem so today, Weber saw bureaucracy as contributing to organizational efficiency.

Bureaucracies possess at least three strengths. The first is a stress on **efficiency.** For bureaucracies efficiency is assumed to be a byproduct of both task specialization and strict application of policies and procedures. In other words, efficiency *should* come from "going by the book." Another strength associated with bureaucracies is their emphasis on certain **standards of conduct.** These standards of conduct are expressed in policy statements designed to standardize organizational life (More 1977, 227). Therefore, predictability and stability are highly prized and closely associated with bureaucratic organizational patterns. Finally, bureaucracies develop and maintain a written record of their processes and accomplishments. In doing so, they define and control the organizational culture (Mouzelis 1967, 47). A useful but unintended consequence of this is that they provide a written record for students of organizational life, in general, and of correctional organizations, in particular.

While the bureaucratic organizational form is associated with efficiency, strength, and stability, we tend to associate certain weaknesses with bureaucracies. For example, bureaucracies provide an effective approach to dealing with routine tasks (Bartollas and Miller 1978, 53). In corrections, however, very few tasks can be described as "routine." Bureaucracies also strive to standardize the organizational conduct, but in so doing they often reduce employee initiative and create inflexible operations (Mouzelis 1967, 47).

Mouzelis (1967, 60) observes that when bureaucracies are faced with rules violations, the typical response is to enforce more fully the existing rules or to impose stricter rules.

Additionally, the stress on efficiency may be misplaced. More (1977, 229–30) maintains that efficiency may mean doing wrong or irrelevant tasks well. Given the emphasis on governmental accountability today, corrections agencies cannot afford to be doing a good job in accomplishing wrong or irrelevant activities.

Another bureaucratic weakness is an inherent inability to respond rapidly or to unexpected changes (More 1977, 228). The stability "strength" of bureaucracies becomes a "weakness" when the organization cannot respond to rapid changes or periods of political, social, or financial uncertainty. In these situations, employees quite often are told to work smarter not just harder, even though there may not be clear guidelines concerning what they should be working smarter or harder at doing.

Organizational growth, in size and complexity, also highlights bureaucratic weaknesses. One of the guiding principles of hierarchies is strong, centralized control of organizational goals and processes. However, as the organization begins to diversify, the need to delegate authority increases and this leads to a loss of centralized coordination and control (see More 1977, 228; Mouzelis 1967, 61).

Finally, bureaucracies often overlook the individual's significance. The ideal bureaucratic type may not account for the fact that employees may not follow the rules and that informal interactions may come into conflict with the idealized impersonal, formal bureaucratic relationships. The reality of organizational life is that individuals may pursue goals that are fundamentally in conflict with organizational goals (Mouzelis 1967, 59–60).

To understand the significance of bureaucratic notions to corrections, we next turn to an examination of leadership styles. As is obvious, some of these styles are consistent with bureaucratic organizations and some are not.

Leadership Styles

Until now, we have considered administration and management in somewhat abstract terms. However, from the standpoint of corrections organizations, the most important consideration is how these concepts translate into leadership styles. Initially we will consider three basic approaches to leadership: the authoritarian, the laissez faire, and the democratic or participatory (see Blau and Scott 1962; Etzioni 1964; Weber 1947).

First, the **authoritarian leader** is one who gives orders and is concerned with productivity. This person is the boss and expects subordinates to do as they are instructed. Authoritarian leaders communicate primarily by telling or commanding. In fact, communication is almost exclusively from the top to the bottom. Marilyn McShane and Frank Williams (1993, 9) characterize the authoritarian leader as an **autocrat.** Consistent with authoritarianism, the autocrat is task oriented rather than people oriented, dogmatic, and one who expects compliance with whatever orders are issued. This type of leader is found in many paramilitary organizations and may be particularly prevalent in prison administration (McShane and Williams 1993, 1996).

Second, the **laissez faire leader** is an administrator who provides little or no direction for subordinates. Employees are encouraged to do more or less as they think best and may be told to "use your own discretion." Far less autocratic than authoritarians, laissez faire leaders, in their zeal to let subordinates find their own way, may provide virtually no direction. This approach may work fine for some corrections organizations and employees, but it is not conducive to goal- or task-oriented activities.

A third leadership style stresses democratic ideals. The **democratic leader** communicates through explanation and elaboration rather than the authoritarian's ordering and commanding style. A democratic leader is often viewed as the first among equals; all of the people working under the leader's direction recognize their organizational roles and understand exactly what is expected of them. A difficulty associated with applying the democratic leadership style in corrections involves confusion over who is participating in decision making and to what degree (McShane and Williams 1993, 10). Does it mean that employees of all ranks and positions are involved in the organization's crucial decision-making processes? In prisons, would inmates have input into institutional operations? For the time being we should note that questions such as these remain largely unanswered.

While these leadership styles are useful for understanding many correctional leaders' administrative behaviors, they are not all-encompassing. In fact, the National Advisory Commission on Criminal Justice Standards and Goals (1973, 449–50) provides us with a list of four other leadership styles (see also Bartollas and Miller 1978, 60). The first of these leadership styles is characterized as the **bureaucratic leader.** Much like Weber's ideal bureaucracy, and the authoritarian or autocratic leader previously discussed, bureaucratic leaders are rule oriented and tend to lead from the top down. They frequently demand loyalty from their subordinates and expect obedience to policies without asking questions. The unfortunate thing about this style is that it is so status quo oriented that the bureaucratic leader may have difficulty responding quickly and appropriately in times of crisis.

A second style listed by the National Advisory Commission is the **technocratic leader.** These are managers who have achieved their positions based on some area of expertise. For example, in corrections, technocratic leaders might be psychologists or social workers who find themselves in management

---

Box 9.1

Joseph E. Ragen (1896–1971)

Joseph E. Ragen symbolizes what most correctional scholars would characterize as the "old school" of prison administration. Ragen had been a small town Illinois sheriff when he was appointed warden at Stateville Penitentiary, the state's largest maximum-security facility. He served in that capacity until 1961 when he became the state's public safety director.

In some ways Ragen typifies both the autocratic leader and the idiosyncratic leader in one person. James B. Jacobs (p. 29) says of Ragen:

> The "old boss" devoted his life to perfecting the world's most orderly prison regime. He exercised personal control over every detail no matter how insignificant. He tolerated challenges neither by inmates nor by employees nor by outside interest groups. He cultivated an image which made him seem invincible to his subordinates as well as to the prisoners.

Two features characterized Ragen's tenure as warden at Stateville and his personal management style. First, he was well respected in corrections circles in the United States and abroad as well. He was elected president of the American Correctional Association in 1951. Foreign visitors frequently came to Stateville for tours, and Ragen was called upon to serve as a consultant to a large number of prisons and correctional systems. Second, Ragen kept partisan politics out of personnel decisions and prison operations. As Jacobs (p. 31) notes: "Ragen established a patriarchal organization based upon his own charismatic authority," and an independence that is probably no longer possible in prison life in the United States.
Source: Jacobs (1977).

---

roles. Technocratic leaders are not as likely as generalists to be at the very top of an organization—a warden of a prison, for example—but they may be responsible for a particular division (such as programming, treatment, mental health services, etc.). Unlike the bureaucratic leader, the technocrat typically is not concerned about *how* the job gets accomplished. Therefore, the technocratic leader is likely to be guilty (from the bureaucrat's viewpoint) of ignoring the organization's policies, procedures, and the chain of command.

The **idiosyncratic leader** is the third style portrayed by the National Advisory Commission. This leader is a little bit laissez faire, but mostly autocratic. Idiosyncratic leaders are sometimes classified as "big daddy" managers. They work over, under, around, and through the hierarchy by exerting direct contact and control over decision making. Sometimes idiosyncratic leaders play employees off against one another. They create climates of fear and suspicion in the ranks. This practice places the leader in the position of having the fullest knowledge and, therefore, the greatest power.

Idiosyncratic leaders create two major problems within agencies and institutions. First, because they reserve most of the decision-making authority for themselves, decisions are made slowly or not at all. Second, idiosyncratic leaders suffer from blind spots that their employees do not warn them about (because of fear), or to which certain employees play. These leaders may

Box 9.2

Tom Murton (1928–1990)

Tom Murton was one of those individuals whose career crossed between the practitioner world and the world of academics. Murton was both an academic criminologist and a prison administrator and reformer. He held both master's and doctoral degrees in criminology from the University of California at Berkeley, and he served in a number of correctional positions including military and civilian. In 1982–83 Dr. Murton received the Paul Tappan Award from the Western Society of Criminology for "outstanding contributions to the field of criminology."

Perhaps Tom Murton is best known for his 1967–68 service in the Arkansas prison system, where he exposed the corruption and brutality at the Cummins State Prison Farm. The 1980 movie *Brubaker,* which starred Robert Redford, was based on Murton's experience in Arkansas. Tom Murton ended his career as a faculty member in the Sociology Department at Oklahoma State University.

Note: Materials for this biographical sketch were provided by Tara Gray, one of our colleagues at New Mexico State University and a student of Tom Murton's at Oklahoma State University.

Tom Murton served as superintendent of the Cummins Prison Farm in Arkansas. In this 1968 photograph, Murton stands in front of the superintendent's home, a stark contrast with the housing units for inmates, and holds a leather strap used as a disciplinary device by his predecessors to flog errant inmates.

have a difficult time discerning good ideas or decisions from bad ones, and no subordinate can or will tell them which ones are good and which ones are not. Some leaders exhibit qualities of two different types, as exemplified in Box 9.1.

Participative leaders are the final group in the National Advisory Commission's list. Participative leaders are much like democratic leaders. They are more group oriented than autocratic or bureaucratic leaders, and they frequently have informal contacts with employees under their direction. The chief weakness for many of these managers is they dislike conflict almost to the point of trying to avoid it at all costs. The problem is that in healthy organizations conflicts are bound to occur, and in the process of trying to avoid conflicts some decisions may not be made or less than optimal solutions may result from trying to reach a group consensus. Box 9.2 presents a brief biographical sketch of one man acknowledged to be a participative leader in corrections.

The National Advisory Commission's assessment of the four leadership styles made two important generalizations. First, they observed that seldom do any of the management styles appear in their purest form (National Advisory Commission 1973, 451). Second, the bureaucratic and idiosyncratic styles occur most often in correctional organizations (National Advisory Commission 1973, 450).

In his study of three state prison systems, John DiIulio (1987) characterizes the Texas Department of Criminal Justice (formerly the Texas Department of Corrections) as a system that was largely bureaucratic in nature, particularly prior to the 1983–84 time period. DiIulio (1987, 5, 105) describes the Texas prison system as operating under a "control model" for staff-inmate relations, but in which "the chain of command [is] followed rigorously" by employees. DiIulio (1987, 117) emphasizes that the Texas Department of Criminal Justice experienced some of its most difficult problems when it tried to run a largely bureaucratic system during rapidly changing and highly volatile political times.

Idiosyncratic leaders have shown up as prison wardens and state corrections directors in highly centralized systems. The National Advisory Commission (1973, 450) describes the idiosyncratic leader this way: "He likes to 'tour' the institution casually, not to make a grand inspection but to keep in close touch with operations. The general is sacrificed for the specific." Once again DiIulio gives us some insight into this leadership style. In his discussions of some of the wardens in the Texas Department of Criminal Justice, and particularly of its longtime director, George Beto, DiIulio (1987, 110–18), clearly illustrates the "walking around" management style associated with, and characteristic of, idiosyncratic leaders. Box 9.3 presents a brief look at the life of George Beto.

Two additional conclusions about corrections management remain. First, while the bureaucratic and idiosyncratic styles occur most frequently, "neither is ideally suited to the administration of large, complex systems under conditions of rapid change" (National Advisory Commission 1973, 450). The term *rapid change* certainly describes what has been happening in contemporary corrections, and, as a result of such change, the deficiencies of traditional administrative approaches have become more apparent. Second, most corrections administrators have a tendency to rely on what has worked in the past. Some administrators can change their leadership styles to fit the situation, but most will rely on familiar ways of managing, even if they are not especially effective (McShane and Williams 1993, 8). Box 9.4 reviews the career of one prison reformer and administrator who did not wait for the system to change for her.

Box 9.3

George Beto (1916–1991)

One of the most easily recognized names in twentieth-century corrections is that of George Beto, director of the Texas Department of Corrections (now the Texas Department of Criminal Justice) during the 1960s and early 1970s. Beto carefully cultivated the reputation of the TDC as "the best prison system in the nation," but he did not set out to be a correctional administrator.

George Beto originally was a Lutheran minister and trained in theology at Concordia Theological Seminary in Illinois. He began his professional life as a college professor and later as president of Concordia Lutheran College in Austin, Texas.

Beto's connection with corrections began in 1953 when he was appointed by the governor of Texas to the state prison board. As a member of the Texas Prison Board, Beto witnessed the transformation of the Texas prison system under the direction of O. B. Ellis.

For a few years Beto lived in Illinois and served as president of Concordia Theological Seminary. There, through his contact with Joseph E. Ragen, warden of the Stateville Penitentiary, Beto was appointed to the Illinois Parole Board.

When O. B. Ellis died in Texas in 1961 Beto was immediately contacted and offered the position of director of the Texas Department of Corrections. Although he did not take it immediately, Beto did accept the position.

The philosophy George Beto followed in managing the Texas prison system came to be known as the "control model." Charles Jeffords and Jan Lindsey (p. 59) note: "The control model involved the strict enforcement of discipline and the tight regulation of the inmate's daily routine, down to how he buttoned his prison uniform."

Two conclusions can be drawn about George Beto and his tenure as director of the Texas Department of Corrections. First, the value of the control model has been praised by some and seriously questioned by others. Second, during his lifetime George Beto earned a great deal of recognition and the "Texas prisons earned a national reputation based on an enviable record for order, efficiency, and inmate safety."

Sources: DiIulio (1987); Jeffords and Lindsey (1996); Gray and Meyer (1997).

Issues Facing Corrections Managers

Now that we have covered some of the foundational management concepts, we need to turn our attention to several issues facing contemporary corrections administrators. Some of these issues have been with us for most of this century, and as we will see in later sections some of these concerns will be with us into the next century.

Who Manages? The Characteristics of Corrections Managers

Both institutional and community-based corrections managers have not been especially well regarded for their qualifications, competence, or expertise. There are several factors that seem to have contributed to this state of affairs.[1] First, for much of our history, corrections agencies have been **closed systems.** This means that these agencies and institutions have not been open to close public scrutiny, and that promotions have come from within. By the

---

Box 9.4

Mary Belle Harris (1874–1957)

Mary Belle Harris was an early twentieth-century prison reformer, and one of the first female prison administrators in the United States. Harris, who earned a Ph.D. from the University of Chicago, became superintendent of the Women's Workhouse at Blackwell Island in New York City in 1913 at the age of 39. When she took over, the facility "was considered to be the worst among twelve institutions" under the direction of the New York Commissioner of Corrections (p. 225).

Harris's approach to dealing with inmates clearly was rehabilitative. She tried to maximize and humanize staff contacts (particularly her own) with the inmates. Under her leadership, Women's Workhouse inmates were provided with fresh air walks as well as the opportunity to engage in flower gardening. Drug-dependent inmates and those with venereal diseases were identified, classified, placed in separate units, and treated.

During the remainder of her career Mary Belle Harris served at the state reformatory in Clinton, New Jersey, as assistant director of the War Department's Section on Detention Houses and Reformatories for Women, and as superintendent of the State Home for Girls in Trenton, New Jersey. In 1925 Mary Belle Harris was chosen as the first superintendent of the new women's federal prison at Alderson, West Virginia. Harris held this post until her retirement in 1941. During her tenure at Alderson, the prison "was considered a model institution with relatively few serious disciplinary actions and no escapes" (p. 227).

Source: Rogers (1996).

---

time employees rise to management or administration positions, they are thoroughly indoctrinated with the way functions should be performed in their organization. The problem associated with having a closed system and promotion from within is that administrators at the level of warden, associate warden, or superintendent may not have a very broad worldview about how others across the nation or in the next state approach similar problems. We will expand upon this issue in the next section of this chapter.

A second factor influencing corrections' managers perceived status is the low level of qualifications that is required. In most institutional settings, entry-level employees are only required to possess a high school diploma or GED, and when promotions come from within, these are the people who eventually become supervisors, managers, and administrators. Francis Cullen and his colleagues (1993) found in a nationwide survey of 375 prison wardens that the average educational level was 16.6 years, or slightly more than two years of college. Generally speaking, prison administration has had a notorious record for not requiring college degrees for promotion.

By contrast, virtually all probation and parole administrators have at least bachelor's degrees, and many possess master's degrees. The same can be said for certain positions within institutional corrections, where technocrats become administrators. Nevertheless, though there have been improvements in the last decade or so in educational levels among corrections administrators, this is an area of continuing concern.

Warden Penny Lucero, seated to the left of the podium, presides over the GED graduating class at New Mexico Women's Correctional Facility. Warden Lucero follows in the tradition of Mary Belle Harris, the nation's first female warden.

Third, one of the most influential factors affecting corrections administrators' stature is the influence of **political patronage** over these positions. For most of the twentieth century, wardens and state corrections commissioners have been political appointees. Rather than receiving positions based on their qualifications and expertise, most were placed in office based on their work for—and loyalty to—some politician. This system has resulted in the common view that corrections administrators are no more than "political hacks" who depend on good fortune or the good nature of others for their jobs. An unintended consequence of political patronage is that there is frequent turnover of these positions. This results in a lack of long-term planning and in organizational instability. Only in the past 20 years or so have most states moved away from political appointments for corrections administrators such as wardens. The one exception, of course, is the position of state corrections commissioner, since this office typically is a member of the governor's cabinet.

Finally, the factors of promotion from within and political patronage have meant that most corrections administrators have been White males. In fact, a 1989 survey of U.S. prison wardens found that of the 375 respondents, 86.9% were White and the vast majority were male (Cullen et al. 1993, 77). As a result, women and minorities have had a difficult time breaking into the administrative ranks of some corrections systems. Tables 9.1 and 9.2 illustrate the gender and race or ethnicity of wardens or superintendents of U.S. adult and juvenile correctional facilities.

Table 9.1

Wardens and Superintendents of Adult Correctional Systems

By race, ethnicity, sex, and jurisdiction, as of June 30, 1994

Jurisdiction	Total	White Male	White Female	Black Male	Black Female	Hispanic/other Male	Hispanic/other Female	Female administrator/ male institution	Female administrator/ coed institution	Male administrator/ female institution	Male administrator/ coed institution
Total	**1,359**	**946**	**124**	**181**	**48**	**52**	**8**	**90**	**8**	**32**	**50**
Alabama	40[a]	29	1	8	1	1	0	1	0	1	0
Alaska	11[b]	9	1	1	0	0	0	0	1	0	1
Arizona	45[c]	33	4	3	0	5	0	0	0	0	0
Arkansas	24	13	2	8	1	0	0	2	0	1	0
California	28	10	2	5	3	4	4	0	0	0	0
Colorado	15	12	1	2	0	0	0	1	0	1	1
Connecticut	23	13	6	1	1	2	0	5	0	0	0
Delaware	7	6	0	0	2	0	0	1	2	1	2
District of Columbia	9	3	0	4	2	0	0	13	0	0	1
Florida	137	105	9	17	6	0	0	9	1	3	0
Georgia	76	52	7	12	5	0	0	9	0	3	4
Hawaii	8[d]	3	0	0	0	4	1	0	1	1	2
Idaho	10	6	4	0	0	0	0	2	0	0	0
Illinois	40	26	1	6	5	2	0	3	1	0	2
Indiana	29	20	5	4	0	0	0	3	0	2	1
Iowa	8	6	1	1	0	0	0	0	0	0	2
Kansas	9	7	1	1	0	0	0	0	1	0	0
Kentucky	11	8	1	2	0	0	0	0	0	1	1
Louisiana	14	11	0	2	1	0	0	0	0	1	2
Maine	6	6	0	0	0	0	0	0	0	0	0
Maryland	12	7	1	4	0	0	0	1	1	1	1
Massachusetts	22	14	6	2	3	0	0	6	0	0	0
Michigan	31	16	5	5	0	2	0	6	0	0	1
Minnesota	10	8	1	1	0	0	0	0	0	0	0
Mississippi	3	3	0	0	0	0	0	0	1	0	1
Missouri	17	15	1	0	1	0	0	0	1	1	3
Montana	3	3	0	0	0	0	0	0	0	1	0
Nebraska	11	9	2	0	0	0	0	2	0	2	2

Table 9.1 (continued)

Wardens and Superintendents of Adult Correctional Systems

By race, ethnicity, sex, and jurisdiction, as of June 30, 1994

Jurisdiction	Total	White		Black		Hispanic/other		Female administrator/male institution	Female administrator/coed institution	Male administrator/female institution	Male administrator/coed institution
		Male	Female	Male	Female	Male	Female				
Nevada	8	4	1	2	0	1	0	1	0	1	0
New Hampshire	3	2	1	0	0	0	0	0	0	0	1
New Jersey	14	8	1	5	0	0	0	0	0	0	0
New Mexico	6	4	1	0	0	1	0	1	0	0	0
New York	66	46	3	10	4	3	0	3	0	2	1
North Carolina	89	61	7	20	0	0	1	3	0	1	0
North Dakota	5	5	0	0	0	0	0	0	0	0	5
Ohio	26	13	5	5	3	0	0	6	0	1	1
Oklahoma	22	11	4	4	1	2	0	3	0	1	1
Oregon	8	6	1	1	0	0	0	0	0	0	1
Pennsylvania	22	19	0	2	1	0	0	0	0	1	1
Rhode Island	5	4	1	0	0	0	0	0	0	0	0
South Carolina	30	21	2	6	1	0	0	2	0	1	4
South Dakota	9	9	0	0	0	0	0	0	0	1	0
Tennessee	19	17	1	1	0	0	0	0	0	1	4
Texas	123	77	11	15	4	16	0	9	0	0	2
Utah	29	29e	NA	NA	NA	NA	NA	NA	NA	NA	NA
Vermont	8	7	1	0	0	0	0	1	0	0	1
Virginia	37	27	2	7	1	0	0	2	0	0	0
Washington	14	7	4	0	1	2	0	4	0	0	0
West Virginia	8	8	0	0	0	0	0	0	0	0	4
Wisconsin	24	17	6	1	0	0	0	5	0	1	0
Wyoming	5	4	1	0	0	0	0	0	0	1	0
Federal Bureau of Prisons	120	87	9	13	2	7	2	0	0	0	0

Note: a Includes wardens of work release facilities.
b Data as of June 30, 1992.
c Includes wardens, deputy wardens, and superintendents.

d Data as of June 30, 1993.
e Detailed breakdowns unavailable at time of publication.

Source: Maguire and Pastore (1996).

Table 9.2

Wardens and Superintendents of Juvenile Correctional Systems
By race, ethnicity, sex, and state, as of June 30, 1994

Jurisdiction	Total	Characteristics White Male	White Female	Black Male	Black Female	Hispanic/other Male	Hispanic/other Female	Female administrator/ male institution	Female administrator/ coed institution	Male administrator/ female institution	Male administrator/ coed institution
Total	**473**	**323**	**50**	**48**	**25**	**14**	**4**	**36**	**36**	**7**	**85**
Alabama	13	3	4	5	1	0	0	3	0	0	1
Alaska	5	4	1	0	0	0	0	0	1	0	4
Arizona	4	2	0	1	0	1	0	0	0	1	0
Arkansas	1	0	0	1	0	1	0	0	1	0	1
California	16	5	4	2	1	4	0	4	1	0	0
Colorado	9[a]	7	0	0	0	1	1	0	1	0	7
Connecticut	9	4	4	1	0	0	0	0	4	0	5
Delaware	3[a]	1	1	1	0	0	0	1	0	0	2
District of Columbia	6	0	0	1	5	0	0	0	3	0	0
Florida	148	148[b]	—	—	—	—	—	—	1	—	0
Georgia	4	0	0	2	2	0	0	1	1	0	0
Hawaii	1	0	0	0	0	1	0	0	0	0	1
Idaho	1	1	0	0	0	0	0	0	0	0	1
Illinois	[c]	X	X	X	X	X	X	X	X	X	X
Indiana	[c]	X	X	X	X	X	X	X	X	X	X
Iowa	1	1	0	0	0	0	0	0	0	0	0
Kansas	4[a]	3	1	0	0	0	0	1	0	1	1
Kentucky	47	24	18	5	0	0	0	7	6	0	13
Louisiana	[c]	X	X	X	X	X	X	X	X	X	X
Maine	[c]	X	X	X	X	X	X	X	X	X	X
Maryland	21	9	2	5	5	0	0	2	5	0	6
Massachusetts	5	5	0	0	0	0	0	0	0	0	0
Michigan	9	3	3	2	1	0	0	1	2	0	1
Minnesota	[c]	X	X	X	X	X	X	X	X	X	X
Mississippi	4	3	0	0	0	1	0	0	0	0	1
Missouri	20[a]	13	3	1	3	0	0	4	1	1	1
Montana	2	2	0	0	0	0	0	0	0	0	1
Nebraska	[c]	X	X	X	X	X	X	X	X	X	X

Table 9.2 (continued)

Wardens and Superintendents of Juvenile Correctional Systems

By race, ethnicity, sex, and state, as of June 30, 1994

Jurisdiction	Total	Characteristics						Female administrator/ male institution	Female administrator/ coed institution	Male administrator/ female institution	Male administrator/ coed institution
		White		Black		Hispanic/other					
		Male	Female	Male	Female	Male	Female				
Nebraska	c	X	X	X	X	X	X	X	X	X	X
Nevada	2ª	2	0	0	0	0	0	0	0	0	1
New Hampshire	3ª	3	0	0	0	0	0	0	0	0	3
New Jersey	c	X	X	X	X	X	X	X	X	X	X
New Mexico	4	0	1	0	0	3	0	0	1	1	1
New York	34	17	4	6	3	2	2	5	0	1	0
North Carolina	12	5	1	5	1	0	0	1	1	0	8
North Dakota	3	3	0	0	0	0	0	0	0	0	3
Ohio	8	4	0	2	2	0	0	1	0	0	0
Oklahoma	2	2	0	0	0	0	0	0	0	0	2
Oregon	6	5	1	0	0	0	0	0	1	0	0
Pennsylvania	9	6	0	3	0	0	0	0	0	0	1
Rhode Island	6	5	1	0	0	0	0	1	0	1	0
South Carolina	4	2	0	1	1	0	0	1	1	0	1
South Dakota	c	X	X	X	X	X	X	X	X	X	X
Tennessee	4	3	0	1	0	0	0	0	1	0	1
Texas	7	3	1	1	0	1	1	1	1	0	1
Utah	14ª	12	2	0	0	0	0	1	2	0	12
Vermont	5ª	2	3	0	0	0	0	0	3	0	3
Virginia	7	4	2	1	0	0	0	0	1	0	2
Washington	5	2	2	1	0	0	0	1	0	0	1
West Virginia	c	X	X	X	X	X	X	X	X	X	X
Wisconsin	3	3	0	0	0	0	0	0	0	0	1
Wyoming	2	2	0	0	0	0	0	0	0	1	0

Note: ª Data as of June 30, 1993.

ᵇ Detailed breakdowns unavailable at time of publication.

ᶜ Juvenile departments combined with adult departments.

Source: Maguire and Pastore (1996).

Careers in Contemporary Corrections

Wardens and Superintendents

Most of you taking this class will not finish your degrees and immediately enter the corrections field in an administrative position. However, we feel it is useful to at least mention where this career track might take you.

When we consider institutional correctional careers, we must give special attention to the positions of wardens or superintendents. The exact titles may vary from state to state, between more secure and less secure facilities, and between juvenile and adult institutions. However, these two designations are used to describe the highest institutional management positions, and they are commonly found throughout the United States.

Eventual promotion to a position such as warden or superintendent may be dependent on a certain number of moves throughout the system. In fact, for the U.S. Bureau of Prisons and most state prison systems, individuals can anticipate reassignment or relocation as they move up through the ranks.

Given the hundreds of thousands of line and support staff working in prisons, jails, and other correctional institutions, the level of competition for promotion to these positions is often quite high. Put another way, there are fewer wardens and superintendents than there are either Deputy U.S. Marshals or Alcohol, Tobacco, and Firearms agents (two of the smaller federal law enforcement agencies). Nationwide there are 1,359 state and 120 federal positions in adult corrections at the level of warden or superintendent. There also are 473 such positions in juvenile institutional corrections. These positions provide individuals the opportunities to exercise administrative skills and abilities.

As should be expected, along with increased responsibilities and expectations come increased compensation. In 1994 the starting pay for prison wardens in the United States began in the $25,000–35,000 range in Arkansas, Georgia, Indiana, Kentucky, Louisiana, Mississippi, Missouri, South Carolina, Tennessee, and West Vir-

ginia. The states of Alabama, Arizona, Delaware, Florida, Hawaii, Iowa, Kansas, Maine, Massachusetts, Nebraska, New Hampshire, New Mexico, North Carolina, North Dakota, Ohio, Oklahoma, Oregon, Utah, Wisconsin, and Wyoming start wardens in the salary range of $36,000–46,000. The remaining states had starting salaries for wardens above $46,000. The two states with the highest starting salaries in 1994 were California (at $62,640) and Rhode Island (at $62,844). The award for the top of the salary range for state wardens goes to Illinois, with a maximum pay of $87,550. The U.S. Bureau of Prisons had a salary range of $68,667 to $92,235 in 1994.

As we have mentioned in this chapter, the tradition has been to hire individuals as correctional officers (or case managers) and let them work their way up through the system until they achieve supervisory or management levels. The result has been that wardens have not always been well-educated individuals. This seems to be changing nationwide. It is not unusual to find that most wardens in a state have a bachelor's degree, and a number hold master's degrees. In fact in the federal system, and increasingly in state systems, the exceptional case is the warden who does not have a college degree.

Although most prison systems promote managers from within, some systems (including those in the private sector) are willing to look outside their particular agency or organization for administrative talent. As this happens, the opportunities for promotion open up to more people, but the competition becomes stiffer as well. Furthermore, as we continue to build and expand prisons nationwide, there will be an increasing demand for well-educated individuals who have corrections experience to fill vacancies for wardens and superintendents. The bottom line is that the road to an executive position can be navigated more quickly and by more people in the present expansive corrections environment.

Sources: American Correctional Association (1994); Maguire and Pastore (1995).

Corrections Administrators' Backgrounds

A lingering issue raised by the recruitment and promotion processes for corrections employees is what type of background corrections administrators should possess. Under the traditional approach of promotion from within the organization, all managers and administrators rose through the ranks from corrections officers until they achieved executive positions. Therefore, not only did they have corrections backgrounds, their experience had been with their particular agency. In the context of contemporary corrections we must ask ourselves whether a person from another state should be considered for appointment to a correctional administrative position. Also, we must consider whether an individual with public administration experience in a field other than corrections is a suitable candidate for appointment as a high-ranking corrections executive. These issues will be increasingly crucial as states expand their corrections systems, especially by building new prisons, and there will be a growing need for experienced and competent administrators. This demand will make it nearly impossible for most states to wait for individuals to work their way up through the ranks in preparation for administrative positions.

Centralization versus Decentralization

The final administrative issue we address is the degree to which operations should be **centralized.** Historically, many states operated a centralized main office for the corrections department. Although probation and parole offices typically have been **decentralized** in terms of their locations and administration, prisons have tended to be centrally controlled. Today, however, there are several forces at work that are moving corrections agencies in the direction of decentralization.

A major influence on decentralization is the movement away from the "mega-institutions" or very large prisons containing thousands of inmates (McShane and Williams 1993, 1996). Several states have established 500- to 800-bed prisons and have scattered them throughout the state. This approach makes it much more difficult to create and administer policies from a centralized headquarters.

A second influence is the trend toward **unit management** within prisons. In effect, unit management, pioneered by the U.S. Bureau of Prisons, creates prisons within prisons. It allows for more personalized inmate contact by the staff, and greater decentralization of decision making for most routine matters. Box 9.5 provides a brief overview of the unit management concept.

A third factor influencing the movement toward decentralization is the competition among state agencies for scarce resources. For instance, at budget time each prison in the state and the different probation and parole offices all may be vying for funding from the same finite pool of tax dollars. This fact

---

Box 9.5

Unit Management in the U.S. Bureau of Prisons

One form of participatory, nonhierarchical management is found in the institutions operated by the United States Bureau of Prisons (BOP) and the Michigan Department of Corrections. DiIulio describes unit management as one of many strategies designed to demilitarize prison operations. Unit management began as the "functional unit" concept described by Robert Levinson and Roy Gerard, who proposed that functional units present one way to decentralize prison management. Each unit is organized around the function it is designed to perform, and treatment is provided for the inmates within their assigned units.

The BOP implemented the unit management system in the early 1970s. In this approach prisons are divided into housing units of from 50 to 250 inmates. The offices of staff members assigned to each unit are located within the unit. Each housing unit has a unit manager—who is responsible for all of the programming and activities—and, depending on the unit's size, several case managers, correctional counselors, and correctional officers. In effect, each unit is a miniature prison unto itself.

Unit management is an example of one alternative to the traditional bureaucratic management of prisons. It is loosely based on a technocratic leadership style, but involves all members of the unit staff in a team-oriented decision-making process. A chief advantage of unit management, aside from its more democratic leadership style, is that it minimizes many of the traditional divisions between treatment and custody staffs found in most prisons.

Sources: Bartollas and Miller (1978); DiIulio (1987, 1994).

---

not only pits one agency against another, but also makes each institution and office build its best case for why it should be listed as a higher priority. The end result is greater organizational fragmentation rather than greater unity.

Modern Management Tasks

One of the most difficult aspects of the correctional administrator's job is that the policy agenda is often set by the governor, the state legislature, or the courts. As McShane and Williams (1996, 7) note in regard to prison wardens, "Many of the aspects of the job are simply out of one's control." Nevertheless, certain primary tasks seem to cut across all jurisdictions, agencies, and institutions.

Recruitment and Retention of Staff

One of the key functions performed by corrections administrators is recruitment of well-qualified staff members. As we have noted, many correctional positions suffer from poor public images. This poor reputation makes it difficult to recruit the best-qualified individuals on a consistent basis. In addition, as some of the workforce projections have indicated, in the coming decades there will be fewer people of any qualification from which to choose. Successful corrections administrators will have to be aggressive and proactive in locating highly qualified personnel. Obviously, colleges are one place to begin looking. As one component of future recruiting, corrections administrators will have to consciously diversify their staffs. The bottom line is that more women and minority group members will have to be located and recruited for a work world that traditionally has been male and White.

Retention is clearly related to the recruitment issue. Contemporary corrections administrators must pay attention to employee turnover and morale, especially given the investment in recruitment and training (McShane and Williams 1993). Turnover and excessive use of sick leave typically are indicators of some type of organizational ailment. In the past, administrators might be inclined simply to dismiss employees thought to be shirkers, but this defeats the purpose of recruiting and retaining employees who are increasingly difficult to find. Therefore, corrections managers must be adept at locating the sources of employee problems and correcting those problems.

Morale is another issue related to employee retention, job satisfaction, and ultimately to job performance. The difficulty facing public-sector managers is that they may not have a broad range of employee incentives at their disposal. Therefore, corrections managers now and in the future will have to be creative in designing incentive plans to build and maintain employee morale. Such strategies might include periodic pay bonuses, if they are allowed by union contracts and state personnel regulations; days off with pay; or plaques designating the employee of the month, quarter, and year. Interestingly enough, many of the most effective morale builders—simple recognition for achievement—may cost little or no money.

Dealing with Employee Unions

Now that we have mentioned employee unions, perhaps a further word on how these organizations fit into the administrative environment is in order. Over the past three decades public service employees have lobbied for legislation that allows them to unionize. This legislation was necessary in some states, because public employees were prohibited by state law from forming or joining labor unions.[2]

As a result of unionization, administrators have found that they do not enjoy the freedom to enact policy changes they might want to pursue. For example, most union contracts specify the number of hours employees can work in a certain pay period. They typically restrict reassignments or disciplinary actions unless a certain set of procedures is followed. Wardens may not be able to transfer employees within a prison, or from one prison to another without carefully consulting the union contract's restrictions. Although we cannot possibly explore all of the constraints on administrators that result from public employee unions, it is safe to say that in many states where these unions have grown powerful, administrators' discretionary powers are greatly restricted when dealing with union members.

Building Facilities

Administrators at the level of corrections secretary or commissioner are virtually all faced with the prospect of building new facilities or remodeling older ones. This task is primarily prison and jail construction, but even probation and parole agencies must have office space, and this space must be reviewed for suitability on an ongoing basis. Therefore, top-level corrections administrators must be concerned with site selection, building design, and construction (see Riveland 1991).

Managing Inmate Populations

Institutional crowding is a chronic problem plaguing corrections managers (Ford and Moore 1992). At first glance, this problem would seem to be confined to prison and jail administrators, but even community corrections managers are faced with controlling their "populations" or caseloads. Corrections agencies of all sizes and types are being asked to do more with the same resources—or to do the same with fewer resources. In the future corrections executives will continually have to deal with the problem of an ever-expanding number of individuals who are placed under some form of correctional supervision.

The traditional approach to inmate populations has been to receive whatever number of inmates are committed to corrections by the courts. Increasingly, corrections administrators are taking a proactive stance in advocating alternatives to traditional placements. This activity changes the role of the contemporary corrections manager from passive "victim" of the broader political and legal environment, to active player in policy creation and implementation.

Cost Containment

A somewhat unspoken, but nevertheless implicit concern in all of the areas addressed previously, is cost containment. Most corrections administrators today know that the public and their elected representatives are concerned about spiraling corrections costs, especially for institutional placements. They recognize that the supply of tax dollars is not infinite. This recognition, as hard as it is to come to, means that executives in corrections agencies at all levels must be concerned with cost containment. Of particular importance are the spiraling jail- and prison-based medical costs, for example, costs associated with inmates suffering from AIDS. As more individuals are incarcerated, and for longer sentences, prisons are likely to be faced with incredible medical costs and may come to resemble geriatric facilities.

Dealing with the Courts

As we mentioned briefly in a previous section, and as we will discuss more fully in the next chapter, much administrative time is spent dealing with legal issues. Virtually every corrections commissioner who comes into office today instantly becomes a party to one or more lawsuits. Thus, managers spend much initial time and energy dealing with "old court orders and consent decrees" (Riveland 1991, 10). Furthermore, given the litigation potential in all parts of the corrections subsystem, administrators also will have to be proactive in dealing with issues that potentially could result in lawsuits.

These administrative tasks illustrate the complex nature of contemporary corrections. They also show something of the volatile and challenging environment of administration. Many of these issues will continue with us into the next century, and we will explore the world of twenty-first century corrections administration later in the chapter. However, before we do, we want to turn our attention briefly to the second aspect of corrections management mentioned earlier in this chapter: inmate management.

Inmate Management

Most of what we have examined up until this point has dealt with the internal processes of corrections organizations: managers dealing with their employees. Practically all corrections employees are engaged in some form of inmate or client management (Ford and Moore 1992). As Greg Newbold (1992, 53) reminds us, in relation to prison administration, "[A] popular adage among prison employees holds that there are two ways of running a prison: with the inmates or without them." Based on this notion, it is possible to say that there are two views of dealing with inmates—or employees, for that matter—by corrections administrators.

The first view is that inmates are obstinate, uncooperative, and resistant to change. This is somewhat akin to Douglas McGregor's (1960) notion of Theory X management, the traditional approach to inmate and client management. By this approach, "A rigidly authoritarian relationship between inmates and keepers was maintained" (Newbold 1992, 53). Although this orientation can "keep the lid" on things for a while, it has the tendency to alienate and isolate the inmates from the staff (or from probation and parole officers in community supervision settings). In the end an authoritarian style of inmate management causes the inmates' commitment to the inmate subculture to deepen (Newbold 1992, 56).

The other approach to dealing with inmates takes the view that inmates are adults and that they will respond to the level of responsibility expected of them. This is much like McGregor's (1960) Theory Y style of management. The immediate response of most people to this attitude is likely that "you can't trust inmates, and you can't give them power over their own lives or the lives of others." Some prison administrators, notably Tom Murton when he was an Arkansas prison warden, have taken the opposite view, that inmates will act in accord to our expectations of them (see Gray and Meyer 1997).

Box 9.6

**A Comparison of McGregor's
Theory X and Theory Y Assumptions**

Theory X

1. The physical and mental aspects of work are as natural as rest or play.
2. Because people dislike work most of them must be "coerced, controlled, directed, [or] threatened with punishment" in order to get a sufficient amount of effort out of them.
3. The average person is not ambitious.
4. Most people avoid responsibility.
5. The average person wants to be directed and is security oriented.
6. In work environments most people do not use their intellectual capacities.

Theory Y

1. People dislike work and avoid it if they can.
2. People do not need external control if they are committed to the organization's goals.
3. The commitment to organizational goals is related to the rewards attached to achieving those goals.
4. Most people learn to accept and even seek responsibility.
5. Imagination, ingenuity, and creativity are widely distributed throughout an organization's personnel.
6. The work environment can release the intellectual capacities of most people.

Source: McGregor (1960).

This position is akin to the labeling theory we have discussed elsewhere. Box 9.6 presents the assumptions that underlie McGregor's X and Y theories.

As we end this brief discussion of inmate management, we need to turn to two conclusions from Greg Newbold, a criminologist who has served time in prison himself. First, Newbold maintains that as the level of threat from administration to inmates decreases, the tension among the inmate population also decreases. Second, he says that the "peaceful interface between management and inmates makes a prison a simpler place to operate and live in" (Newbold 1992, 56).

From inmate management we now turn to the future for corrections administrators. In the next section we will examine the forces with which executives, particularly those of the next generation, will have to deal. The future is not all gloom and doom, but it is one of great challenges nevertheless.

Conclusion

As we conclude this chapter, a lingering question is, Why be concerned with the corrections administrator's world in an introductory book? Although most of the students taking this course, and reading this book, will not step from the classroom into an administrative position, all who choose to work in

Corrections Management in the Twenty-First Century

Some of you taking this course will be corrections managers in the twenty-first century. What does the future hold in store for you? Although we cannot say with absolute certainty, several issues will undoubtedly carry over into the next century. Alvin Cohn (1995), who frequently comments on corrections management, gives us three such issues that will confront twenty-first century corrections managers.

The Development of Technology

Technology encompasses many different devices and applications. In terms of corrections, perhaps no technology has surpassed that of the computer. Historically, administrators had to consult with subordinates to gather information on agency operations. As Cohn (1995, 12) notes, now "managers have the ability to find out what is happening in institutions and in caseloads, as examples, without having to confer directly with staff." Technology clearly will shift power relationships in corrections organizations, and the most powerful will be those who know and can use the technology the best. The end result may be that "the traditional role of the correctional supervisor and, in fact, the need for such are about to be changed and, perhaps even eliminated!" (Cohn 1995, 12).

The Advent of Total Quality Management

Total quality management (TQM) is a concept that has been widely applied in U.S. businesses and elsewhere. From a correctional standpoint TQM demands that "clients" now be considered "consumers" and that agencies or organizations develop a strong consumer orientation. Cohn again gives us insights into how this will impact corrections: "Workers are being asked to reconsider their routines, to bring qualitative improvements to their services to consumers, and to ensure that the defined goals and objectives of the organization are met—and in ways that can be quantified."

Two dilemmas face corrections agencies in relation to the adoption of total quality management. First, correctional systems exhibit a tendency to do things the way they have always been done. Second, and perhaps even more problematic, is the definition of who the "customers" or "consumers" are. Does the corrections system serve the general public, the governor, the state legislature, inmates and probation and parole clients, or whom? Until this question can be answered with some degree of certainty, TQM may be a prospect, but not a reality in corrections management.

(continued on next page)

Corrections Management in the Twenty-First Century (continued)

Restructuring Government

Governments of all sizes, at all levels, and from all parts of the United States are faced with the prospect of being restructured or reinvented. In simplest terms, most agencies are being asked to do more with less. This tactic can result in **downsizing** or **rightsizing.** Whatever we call it, agencies are faced with the likelihood that budgets may not increase and that some positions may be lost or may have to be shifted from *desirable* to *essential* functions. Resources may be redirected toward those functions that are considered absolutely essential, and (nonessential) functions may be eliminated or placed in a much lower position of priority than they have traditionally held (see especially Cohn 1995). Of course, determining what is or is not essential is a hotly debated issue in the process of downsizing.

Before we end this consideration of corrections administration in the twenty-first century, let's look at some solutions to these problems. Marilyn McShane and Frank Williams (1993, 59–64) make 10 "recommendations for correctional managers" that should be given very serious consideration. We present them here in somewhat abbreviated form.

1. Unlike the traditional method of promotion from within, corrections agencies should select top administrators from different professional backgrounds as long as they have experience in human services management.

2. Rather than being prescriptive about the "right" leadership style, effective managers need to recognize that they should develop a "management style that is consistent with their personality and beliefs." McShane and Williams (1993, 60) add further: "Managers need to be both adaptable and adaptive."

3. Quite often corrections agency hiring is done through a central agency or location, either in the state personnel office or in the corrections department's headquarters. Institutional and community program managers need to provide feedback to the personnel offices on the desired qualifications for their employees. Managers should not simply resign themselves to taking those employees listed as "qualified" by the personnel office. Further, managers should monitor employee morale and track the reasons why employees resign from their positions. This gives some measure of the nature and quality of the work environment.

4. When shift work is utilized, especially in jail and prison settings, managers should make every effort to equalize the duties and responsibilities of each shift. That is, no one shift should be more or less desirable than any other. Al-

Corrections Management in the Twenty-First Century (continued)

though this is a difficult task, it is not impossible.

5. Management concepts such as "unit management" and "direct supervision" should be given very serious consideration. The literature on these topics, particularly direct supervision or the "new generation" model in jails, is becoming substantial, and future corrections managers would be well served by reviewing this research carefully.

6. Whenever changes in management style (for instance adoption of the TQM approach) or organizational arrangements are anticipated, managers must plan well in advance and solicit substantive input from all parts of the agency. Top-down management styles, in which orders are simply issued, are increasingly ineffective in most organizations.

7. Administrators should be actively looking for ways to enrich and enlarge the jobs of all corrections employees. Very few individuals working in corrections today are so tied to their jobs that they would not consider leaving for more rewarding opportunities. Unfortunately, several corrections positions, both within and outside of the institutional work world, are mind-numbingly routine. If we want to attract high-quality personnel and retain them for some length of time, we must

think seriously about career development strategies.

8. Corrections managers must recognize that they are part of a larger community and become involved in community activities. It is virtually impossible for corrections administrators to ignore the larger legal, political, and social environments in which they operate. Corrections agencies are becoming less and less closed systems.

9. Managers should become active consumers of management research. Very few agencies or managers can afford to learn by trial and error: the learning curve is simply too steep. One way to find out quickly what does and does not work is to review current management research both in the public and private sectors.

10. Corrections agencies, particularly jails and prisons, should move beyond the 9-to-5 mentality. A number of assignments can be accomplished throughout the day, and accommodations should be made for equalizing work assignments and duties (see also recommendation 4.)

Recommendations such as these, and the ones included in Box 9.7, should substantially improve corrections administration and in turn corrections effectiveness into the next century. Good luck to those of you who will take us there.

Box 9.7

Ten Ideas for Effective Managers

The following 10 ideas for effective managers come from Robert Wiggins, a criminal justice practitioner turned college professor:

1. Cultivate positive personal relationships. Organizations do not forget negative behaviors. Treat people as if they will have authority over you someday—some may very well be your bosses.
2. Remember that great leaders may be poor managers. Managers, in addition to leading, are also skilled at planning, organizing, and controlling.
3. Use personal power. Personal power is more effective than positional power because it is based upon the leader's personality, ability to inspire, or charisma.
4. Recognize that the purpose of organizational structure is to coordinate and communicate. There is no ideal span of control. The concept of chain of command is no longer sacred. Decentralization promotes faster, smarter decision making.
5. Recognize that organizational culture can be more effective than policy statements.
6. Use group activities to increase productivity and organizational intelligence. In brainstorming sessions the playing field must be level. High-level cohesive groups can do incredibly dumb things (avoid "groupthink").
7. Plan to succeed with strategic planning and program evaluation. Take time for strategic planning. Expand resources for ongoing evaluation research.
8. Enable organizational change by weakening restraining forces (such as rules or regulations that keep people from realizing their potential). Weakening restraining forces works better than strengthening driving forces because the dignity of the worker is respected and the personal power principle is used.
9. Focus on product rather than process. We need to recognize the importance of getting the job done with both effectiveness and efficiency. But if the standard rules and procedures don't accomplish this goal, they need to be changed.
10. Reward the right kind of behavior. Rewards, morale, ingenuity, and productivity go together in the workplace.

Source: Wiggins (1996).

corrections will work in an administrative environment. Those who come in contact with corrections (for example, police officers, prosecuting or defense attorneys, social workers, and the like) must also develop an appreciation for this complex work world. For instance, in the study of administration it is important to ask questions such as the following:

1. Do probation and parole offices have to be administered differently than prisons? If so, why?
2. Do probation and parole officers, almost like police officers, operate in a more autonomous atmosphere than do prison employees?
3. For prisons, to what extent does the management model chosen influence the entire institution's administrative style?

Even the casual student of administration should recognize, after reading this chapter, that corrections positions (especially those in prisons and jails) are much more interdependent than are many of the jobs in law enforcement. For example, many police departments could be described as loose confederations of jobs, some connected and some unconnected. In this way, probation and parole officers working in the field most closely resemble the police in their operations. By contrast, prisons and jails are institutions of more integrated functions that call for a more coordinated or team approach to accomplishing their goals.

Additionally, in an environment such as a jail or prison, in comparison with a police agency, the functions performed by the lowest-ranking employees are supervised more and more closely. Therefore, while corrections officers exercise some discretion, they do not exercise the same degrees of discretion as do uniformed police officers. Uniformed police officers in most agencies in the United States work alone or in pairs with little direct supervision. Virtually all prison and jail employees work in close proximity with fellow employees of the same rank, supervisors, and inmates. This condition makes the institutional environment emotionally intense and one in which most stressors cannot be escaped. Police officers can engage in numerous activities that serve as diversions from the frustrations of their jobs. Corrections officers may not enjoy such luxuries.

Finally, five points need to be reemphasized in regard to corrections management. First, we can improve correctional administration through greatly expanded education and training opportunities (Carter 1991). A sad fact of life in many corrections organizations is that administrators, even the relatively well-educated, often have risen through the ranks with little or no management training. In fact, much of their managerial knowledge is acquired during the process of learning their jobs (Cohn 1981). Therefore, we must devote additional time and resources to pre-service and in-service training, as well as what is often called "organizational development," in order to improve the quality of today's managers and to prepare tomorrow's corrections managers (Carter 1991). However, as Cohn (1981, 60) adds, simply providing more "education, training, and experience" will not solve the failures of corrections management. These factors must be combined with a basic commitment to improving correctional processes.

Second, although we have talked about "ideal types" of managers, we should not automatically assume that any type occurs in its purest form or that one management type is preferable to another (Bartollas and Miller 1978, 33; National Advisory Commission 1973, 451). Third, bureaucratic management and the bureaucratic leadership style are still very prevalent in corrections. Although the dominance of bureaucratic management may change over the next decade or so, we should not expect change to come quickly. This caution is important to remember because some people believe that the entrenched bureaucratic interests within corrections are fundamentally at odds with efforts to professionalize correctional services (Cohn 1981, 59).

Fourth, a variety of factors are bringing about corrections management changes, and most of the movement is in the direction of more flexible systems. We should increasingly expect to see more democratic and participatory management styles as the bureaucratic approach becomes less popular. Fifth, there is no "one best way" to manage that can be applied in, or transplanted to, every setting. Different agencies with different goals and different personnel will require different approaches to management (Bartollas and Miller 1978, 53).

Critical Review Questions

1. In the case of "Warden Jim Butler," what seems to be causing his sense of isolation? Who might be aware of how he is feeling? Can these feelings have any impact on his job performance? How?

2. When we think of a bureaucratic organization, which comes to mind: efficiency or inefficiency? Explain your answer.

3. What are the advantages associated with an authoritarian or autocratic leader? What are the disadvantages? Consider the advantages and disadvantages of the laissez faire and democratic leader as well.

4. After you have examined the basic leadership styles, which one would you prefer to work for? Why?

5. Which of the four leadership styles mentioned by the National Advisory Commission is most likely to occur in prisons? Would your answer be different if we considered probation and parole agencies? Why or why not?

6. Should corrections administrators reflect a cross-section of society in the United States? In other words, should more women and minority group members be administrators? Does it make any difference to operations? Why or why not?

7. Can corrections executives really "motivate" their employees? How? What motivates you to work harder or more effectively?

8. What approach makes the most sense in managing inmates, a "firm hand" or substantial inmate participation? Can all inmates (or prisons) be managed the same way?

9. What are Theory X and Theory Y? What factors shape the worldviews of those who employ the Theory X approach? the Theory Y approach? Are these attitudes something learned?

10. Total quality management has been embraced by businesses, particularly in Japan and now in the United States. Can this "business" orientation be applied to corrections? Why or why not?

Recommended Readings

Archambeault, William, and Betty Archambeault. 1982. *Correctional supervisory management: Principles of organization, policy and law.* Englewood Cliffs, NJ: Prentice-Hall. Although somewhat dated at this point, this book can be considered a classic in corrections management. Many of the issues are timeless, making this a must-have addition to any library on administration of correctional agencies and organizations.

DiIulio, John J., Jr. 1987. *Governing prisons: A comparative study of correctional management.* New York: Free Press. DiIulio's book has become a benchmark in the study of prison management. Some have praised it, and others have condemned it, but students and scholars of correctional administration all have to refer to it. The book is especially useful in that it gives a comparison of prison management styles and operations in Texas, California, and Michigan.

McShane, Marilyn D., and Frank P. Williams III. 1993. *The management of correctional institutions.* New York: Garland. This book focuses on institutional (mostly prison) management. The first section includes a brief treatment of the background and environment of institutional management. A unique feature of this book is a survey of corrections management practices. This gives us a look at how prison managers perceive their jobs. Probably the most important component of this book, and possibly its greatest contribution, is a very thorough bibliography of materials dealing with corrections management.

Phillips, Richard L., and Charles R. McConnell. 1996. *The effective corrections manager.* Gaithersburg, MD: Aspen. This book is intended for the corrections practitioner or would-be practitioner. Although it does provide some background and general context material, the book is, for the most part, a "how to" book. Different sections of the book deal with the qualities and characteristics of the effective corrections manager; relations between supervisors and employees; and supervisory tasks such as decision making, communicating, budgeting, and training. Two especially critical chapters deal with the supervisor's legal environment and unions. An annotated bibliography is also included.

Key Terms

administration	democratic leader	rationality
authoritarian leader	downsizing	rightsizing
autocrat	efficiency	standards of conduct
bureaucracy	idiosyncratic leader	technocratic leader
bureaucratic leader	laissez faire leader	total quality management
centralized operations	management	unit management
closed systems	participative leader	
decentralized operations	political patronage	

Notes

1. Much of the information utilized in this section is taken from McShane and Williams (1993, 1996).
2. For a thorough treatment of the history and development of public-sector employee unions see Ayres and Wheelen (1977), Stanley (1972), and Zagoria (1972).

10

Correctional Law and Inmate Litigation

Chapter Outline

- Introduction
- The History of Correctional Litigation
- Correctional Litigation and Post-Conviction Relief
- Laws and Litigation Dealing with Probation and Parole
- Issues Raised by Correctional Lawsuits

- Recent Trends in Litigation by Prison and Jail Inmates
- Capital Punishment and Prisoner Litigation
- Conclusion
- Critical Review Questions
- Recommended Readings
- Key Terms
- Cases Cited

Introduction

Marty Brown was almost indistinguishable from all of the other correctional officers at Central State Prison. He did not have a spotless employment record, but most of his coworkers and supervisors considered him a "good trooper." He showed up for work every day he was scheduled, on time, and with not a hint of drug or alcohol use on the job.

Marty had played football at the high school not far from the prison and now, as an adult, was large and physically intimidating. On a few occasions he had been warned by Pete Oliver, his sergeant, not to handle inmates roughly. No one on the staff thought Marty was brutal, and most of the COs agreed that if a disturbance broke out Marty was one of the people they wanted there. In fact, Marty was chosen to serve on the prison's special response team during his first year of service. Everyone agreed, and he basked in the adulation, that Marty Brown knew how to "jack-up" an inmate who needed it.

CO Brown had secrets. His personal life had grown increasingly chaotic and his wife complained about his shift work and the large number of overtime hours he volunteered for. To him he was simply being a "good breadwinner" for his family. In recent months, Marty's wife had called the police and even in one case the prison warden to complain about Marty's abusive behavior. However, nothing more serious than a verbal warning had ever been issued. But everyone knew about Marty's temper. In fact, it was legendary.

On February 3, Marty reported to the prison for the 2:00 PM to midnight shift. Sometime around 4:00 PM a dispute arose in one of the housing units between two inmates over alleged homosexual advances. Marty Brown was the first officer to respond to the report of a disturbance, and he separated the two inmates. However, before other officers arrived, and for reasons not completely clear, Marty exploded. He knocked one of the inmates unconscious by repeatedly slamming him against the wall. The second inmate suffered two broken teeth and facial lacerations. The first inmate would later die on the way from the prison infirmary to the local emergency room.

The second inmate and the first inmate's family filed a federal Section 1983 suit against Marty Brown alleging civil rights violations as a result of the brutal beating. Also named as defendants in the lawsuit were Warden Fred Parker and Sergeant Pete Oliver. The civil rights action claimed that both of these men should be held liable for failure to supervise. In other words, they should have seen this coming. Should they? Could they have known?

The 1970s were the decade of prisons in the U.S. criminal justice system. A variety of events—beginning with the 1969 U.S. Supreme Court case of *Johnson v. Avery* and including a series of well-publicized and brutal prison riots—made the public aware of the plight of U.S. prisons (Braswell, Dillingham, and Montgomery 1985; Champagne and Haas 1976; Singer 1980; Wicker 1975). Many of the nation's penal institutions were opened in the late nineteenth or early twentieth centuries, and some of their problems had been festering since the facilities first opened their doors.

Rhodes (1992, 215) notes that "prisons have traditionally been closed organizations, and it has been difficult for citizens in the outside world to learn about conditions inside them." Therefore, as long as prison problems were contained, they remained largely out of sight and out of mind for the general public. This relative lack of visibility often was reinforced by the isolated locations of most prisons.

When New York's Attica Correctional Facility erupted in 1971 and the Penitentiary of New Mexico followed in 1980, many policy makers and private citizens began to realize that something was wrong in many United States prisons (see, especially, Mahan 1982). The two most basic questions were (1) What is wrong? and (2) What can be done about it?

"What is wrong?" can be answered by referring to the problems endemic to all secure confinement correctional institutions. Rhodes (1992, 205–6) notes that at least three factors affected prison conditions and the increase in prison litigation during the 1970s: (1) rising inmate populations, (2) aging prison facilities, and (3) restrictive state budgets.

Responses to "What can be done about it?" likewise cover a wide range of issues, but since the 1970s one of the most common answers has been institutional reform litigation. Beginning with cases such as *Holt v. Sarver* (1970) and *Pugh v. Locke* (1976), a broad range of prison conditions were challenged in Arkansas, Alabama, and many other states. As an illustration of the prison litigation trend, on June 29, 1990, there were 323 state facilities under court order or consent decree in order to improve general conditions of confinement or to limit their populations (Department of Justice 1992a). In 1994, 39 states and the District of Columbia had all or part of their correctional systems under court order (*Correctional Law Reporter* 1994).

This chapter will primarily focus on litigation filed by prison and jail inmates and the rights asserted by inmates and inmate advocacy groups. Legal questions have also been raised about the rights of probationers and parolees and about the rights concerning individuals in the growing arena of intermediate sanctions as well. Therefore, our task in this chapter is to discuss inmate litigation at some length while also addressing the broader scope of correctional law.

The following sections will trace correctional litigation's history in the United States, especially the large body of cases relating to prisons and jails. Particularly of interest is the concept of inmates' access to the courts, and also the specific issues addressed in inmate lawsuits. Finally, perhaps the most important question in contemporary corrections is what has been the impact of more than two decades of prisoner lawsuits.

The History of Correctional Litigation

Correctional law has gone through several distinct periods of development. Call (1995, 36) asserts that case law addressing prisoners' rights can be divided into the "Hands-Off Period (before 1964) . . . the Rights Period (1964–78) and . . . the Deference Period (1979–present)." In this chapter we will consider all three of these periods, beginning with the hands-off era.

Any discussion of correctional litigation must begin with the case of *Ruffin v. Commonwealth* (1871). This Virginia case held that prisoners are slaves of the state (see Abadinsky and Winfree 1992; Allen and Simonsen 1986; Clear and Cole 1990), and as such they have no more rights than slaves. This ruling created the legal view that prisoners suffered a **civil death** when convicted of a crime and imprisoned (Alexander 1994; Palmer 1977, 125, 166). Under the notion of civil death, prisoners forfeited some of their citizenship rights and retained others but to a lesser degree (Harris and Spiller 1977).

When prisoners were considered slaves of the state, they held "nonperson" status. As such, the courts were free to ignore pleas based on allegations of deprivations of their rights, since prison inmates were presumed not to possess many (if any) constitutional rights. A result of the civil death view toward prison inmates was that the courts took a **hands-off approach** toward prison policies and practices (Bronstein 1985; Chilton 1991; DiIulio 1990; Nagel 1985; Robertson 1985–86).

The courts followed this tactic from the mid-nineteenth century until the 1960s, and justified it on three grounds (Coles 1987; Schuster and Widmer 1978; Thomas 1988). First, federal courts expressed some reluctance to intervene in the affairs of state executive agencies, such as corrections departments, because of questions of **federalism** and **separation of powers** (Alpert, Crouch, and Huff 1984; see also Collins 1993). Federalism means that there is a "division of responsibility between federal and state courts" (Mays 1983, 29). However, though each of our court systems has separate and unique responsibilities, it is clear that jurisdictions overlap as well. The separation of powers issue is related to the unique divisions of authority among the government's executive, legislative, and judicial branches. In this regard, some observers have felt it improper for a court—particularly a *federal* court—to tell a state correctional system how it should run its prisons (see, especially, Frug 1978; *Bounds v. Smith* 1977).

Second, many judges were hesitant to get involved in prison litigation cases because of their lack of correctional expertise. This gave prison administrators a great deal of discretion. As a result, when courts granted deference to prison officials, these officials were bound only by their own sense of appropriate conduct, since their actions effectively were shielded from public scrutiny or judicial review. Third, correctional administrators consistently maintained that court intervention would interfere with their authority and would reduce the ability of institutional personnel to operate safe prisons.

During the 1960s, the hands-off approach began to change. This period saw increasing claims to civil rights protections by racial minorities, aliens, the handicapped, the mentally ill, and women. In a sense, state prison inmates became another "minority" group seeking expanded civil rights. Additionally, the 1960s saw a number of individuals entering the practice of **public interest law.** Some of these attorneys had their own practices, but many worked for civil rights advocacy groups such as the American Civil Liberties Union or the Southern Poverty Law Center. Finally, both the federal district and appellate courts became more receptive to lawsuits from state prison inmates (Call 1995, 36–37).

The U.S. Supreme Court particularly seemed attentive to state prisoners' due process claims (see, for example, Smith 1986; Thomas 1988). Call (1995, 38) takes issue with the assertion by some that during this period the Supreme Court was engaged in a "prisoners' rights revolution." He says, instead, that the Court recognized that prisoners had constitutional rights and that these rights were equal to those of the prisons (Call 1995, 38).

Two Supreme Court cases of the early 1960s opened the prison litigation door. The first case, *Monroe v. Pape* (1961), made it procedurally easier to sue state officials in federal court for alleged constitutional rights violations (see Prigmore and Crow 1976). The other case—*Cooper v. Pate* (1964)—raised the issue of the free exercise of religion by Nation of Islam (Black Muslim) prisoners. In both of these cases, the Supreme Court held that the Civil Rights Act of 1871 (known in the statutes as 42 U.S.C. 1983) provided an appropriate mechanism by which to challenge state actions (Smith 1986).

As a result of such cases, the Supreme Court signaled the beginning of a **hands-on period** for state prison litigation (Nagel 1985). *Monroe* and *Cooper* provided state prisoners with a choice of options for filing federal lawsuits. They could follow the traditional path of **writs of habeas corpus,** or they could launch out on the relatively uncharted, but potentially more successful, path of **civil rights claims** (the so-called **Section 1983 suits**). Additionally, it is important to note that inmates may file **tort claims** to resolve some of their problems. Tort claims typically are filed in state courts seeking damages, and they allege negligence in the acts or failures to act by corrections personnel (Collins 1993, 22).

Correctional Litigation and Post-Conviction Relief

We must note here that not only are various legal mechanisms available to inmates in the litigation process, but so are various *litigation targets.* For instance, prisoners may challenge the actions of individual correctional officers or corrections officials such as a superintendent, warden, or commissioner of corrections (Collins 1993). Lawsuits can also be more broadly based and challenge the institutional conditions under which the inmate is confined.

Access to the Courts

In habeas corpus appeals, inmates allege that their confinement is unjust and that the state should demonstrate why continued incarceration should be allowed (see Flango 1994; Mays 1984). These actions challenge the legality of incarceration and, if the prisoner's allegations are substantiated, the inmate may be released (Department of Justice 1984; Collins 1993). During the United States Supreme Court's 1962–63 term, three cases—*Townsend v. Sain* (1963); *Fay v. Noia* (1963); and *Sanders v. United States* (1963)—were decided that gave expanded habeas corpus relief to state prisoners. As a result of these cases, writs of habeas corpus became the primary legal mechanism for most prisoners' appeals until the late 1970s. As Table 10.1 illustrates,

Table 10.1

Petitions Filed in Federal District Courts by State Inmates, 1966–1994

	Habeas corpus	Civil rights			Habeas corpus	Civil rights
1966	5,830	281		1982	8,059	16,741
1967	6,201	878		1983	8,532	17,687
1968	6,488	1,072		1984	8,349	18,034
1969	7,359	1,269		1985	8,534	18,491
1970	9,063	2,657		1986	9,045	20,072
1971	8,372	2,915		1987	9,542	22,972
1972	7,949	3,348		1988	9,880	23,559
1973	7,784	4,174		1989	10,545	25,039
1974	7,626	5,236		1990	10,817	24,843
1975	7,843	6,128		1991	10,331	25,046
1976	7,833	6,958		1992	11,299	29,646
1977	6,866	7,752		1993	11,587	33,018
1978	7,033	9,730		1994	11,918	37,925
1979	7,123	11,195		**Totals**	**246, 629**	**404,702**
1980	7,031	12,397				
1981	7,790	15,639				

Source: Maguire and Pastore (1995).

state prisoner habeas corpus petitions increased by roughly 85% between 1966 and 1990.

Flango (1994, 160) reports that habeas corpus petitions "are not used by the typical state prisoner." Most of these appeals are brought by inmates charged with serious offenses and most allege deficiencies in one of eight areas: ineffective assistance of counsel, due process concerns, trial court error, Fifth Amendment protections, detention and punishment concerns, prosecutor misconduct, police misconduct, and charges to the jury. Flango (1994, 168) notes that habeas corpus claims are filed by a small and declining number of prisoners, but those who do choose this route of appeal file multiple petitions in federal and state courts.

Beginning in 1966 civil rights actions were listed separately among prisoner litigation categories, and during this period they increased 875% (Department of Justice 1984; Flanagan and Jamieson 1988; Flanagan and Maguire 1992)! When inmates bring civil rights actions, several elements come into play. Collins (1993, 16) says that there are four key features of a Section 1983 action:

1. *The defendant must be a person.* The courts have held that states and state agencies, including corrections departments, are *not* persons and are immune from such suits; however, cities and counties, if they are incorporated, are "persons." Thus, an individual or a group of individuals must be identified as defendants in the suit.

2. *The defendant must be acting under color of state law.* The alleged violation occurred in the course of the defendant's employment with the governmental agency.

3. *The injury to the inmate-plaintiff must involve a violation of a protected right.* This may be a right protected by the U.S. Constitution or some federal statutory protection. Frequently, the allegations of injury or abuse are based on broad constitutional language such as the Eighth Amendment's prohibition against cruel and unusual punishment.

4. *The defendants must have been personally involved in the alleged injury.*

An exception to item four is what may be termed **vicarious** or **supervisory liability.** As Collins (1993 16–17) notes, supervisors are not automatically assumed to be liable for the injuries caused by their subordinates. However, under two sets of circumstances—failure to supervise and failure to train—supervisors also may become parties to Section 1983 suits. In these suits, the inmate-plaintiff must make a direct connection between the supervisor's action or failure to act and the injury that resulted.

As is readily apparent from Table 10.1, prisoner litigation increased dramatically from 1966 to 1990, and there are at least two prominent explanations for these increases. First, beginning in the 1970s, U.S. prison populations began expanding rapidly. Therefore, one reason for the increase in prisoners' lawsuits simply was the increasing number of prisoners. Second, prisoners began to file many more lawsuits—that is, there was an increase in inmate **litigiousness**—and the opportunities for litigation increased as well. This conclusion is buttressed by the fact that the growth of lawsuits has outpaced prison population growth.

These two points do not tell the whole story concerning litigation, however. Table 10.1 illustrates that while *both* habeas corpus and civil rights suits have demonstrated growth, by 1977 civil rights actions surpassed habeas corpus writs. Figure 10.1 shows the growth of Section 1983 suits relative to the growth in state prison inmate populations. Thomas (1988, 63) says that this change in prisoner litigation came about because state inmates were not interested in using the federal courts to secure their release—as would be the case with habeas corpus petitions—but they were much more interested in challenging their conditions of confinement. An equally plausible explanation seems to be that the federal courts were demonstrating a lack of receptivity toward state prisoner habeas corpus writs (Burger 1985; Powers 1987; Remington 1986).

One of the remaining unresolved issues is whether these individuals are government workers or whether they are employed by private contractors (Chaires and Lentz 1996). In one case, the federal district court for the Western District of Louisiana held that private corrections employees possess the same **qualified immunity** rights as do state government workers (*Citrano v.*

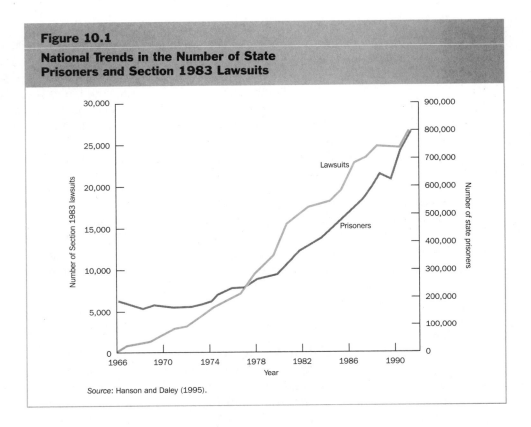

Figure 10.1

National Trends in the Number of State Prisoners and Section 1983 Lawsuits

Source: Hanson and Daley (1995).

Allen Correctional Center 1995). By contrast, in *Manis v. Corrections Corporation of America* (1994) a federal district judge in Tennessee ruled that private corrections officials were not entitled to qualified immunity. This position was reaffirmed by the United States Supreme Court in *Richardson et al. v. McKnight* (1997). Writing for a five member majority, Justice Breyer concluded: "Our examination of history and purpose thus reveals nothing special enough about the job or about its organizational structure that would warrant providing these private prison guards with a governmental immunity." Thus, private correctional employees do not enjoy the same protections from lawsuits as do public employees.

Legal Assistance and Legal Access

A critical issue involving prison litigation and access to the courts is inmate legal assistance. In simple terms: When must inmates be provided legal assistance, how, and under what constraints or guidelines? Two cases illustrate the dilemma correctional authorities have faced in providing inmates with legal assistance. A landmark Supreme Court case involving prison inmates' access to legal assistance was *Johnson v. Avery* (1969). This case dealt with whether Tennessee state corrections officials could prohibit one inmate from giving legal assistance to another (as mentioned in Chapter 3). The prison regulation provided that

> No inmate will advise, assist or otherwise contract to aid another, either with or without a fee, to prepare Writs or other legal matters. It is not intended that an innocent man be punished. When a man believes he is unlawfully held or illegally convicted, he should prepare a brief or state his complaint in letter form and address it to his lawyer or a judge. A formal Writ is not necessary to receive a hearing. False charges or untrue complaints may be punished. Inmates are forbidden to set themselves up as practitioners for the purpose of promoting a business of writing Writs.

The inmates who became informal legal assistants were called **writ writers** or **jailhouse lawyers** (Champagne and Haas 1976; Thomas 1988). Prison officials typically banned inmates from providing other inmates with legal help on the grounds that such skills and services placed jailhouse lawyers in powerful positions relative to other inmates.

The jailhouse lawyer's expertise could only reach so far. In *Bounds v. Smith* (1977), the Supreme Court said that *meaningful* legal access for prisoners could only come from adequate law libraries within correctional institutions in conjunction with jailhouse lawyers or through the use of trained legal assistants (that is, paralegals) or attorneys.

The standards developed in *Johnson v. Avery* and *Bounds v. Smith* have solidified the foundation for contemporary prison litigation. The Supreme Court has established in a long line of right-to-counsel cases that the effective assistance of counsel may be one of the Constitution's most fundamental due process rights, and for most state correctional systems these constitutional mandates have been fulfilled through providing law libraries and the use of jailhouse lawyers. Hiring attorneys to represent inmate-plaintiffs may be easier in the long run, because it would be more efficient and secure and less burdensome and expensive. The increased use of attorneys could actually save money through reduction in the costs associated with legal services, transportation, security, and a law library. Using licensed attorneys should also reduce the costs associated with frivolous suits filed by inmates in ***pro se* actions.** Attorneys are in a better position to understand the merits of cases and are more objective than inmates in trying to reach negotiated settlements with corrections officials (*Correctional Law Reporter* 1995, 67, 79).

Inmate Advocates and Advocacy Groups

As a number of scholars have noted, inmates are a relatively powerless social group (see, for example, Hanson 1987; Thomas, Wheeler, and Harris 1986). Not only are the inmates relatively powerless, but also their families typically do not come from the wealthy or politically influential segment of

Jailhouse lawyers or "writ writers" are very much a part of the inmate society in many prisons. These inmates file appeals on behalf of themselves and other inmates.

society. Therefore, what mechanisms are left for inmates to make their concerns heard by the public, politicians, and correctional administrators? Two answers come to mind: riots and lawsuits. Prison riots during the 1970s and 1980s brought national attention to the plight of U.S. prison inmates (Braswell, Dillingham, and Montgomery 1985; Useem and Kimball 1989).

By contrast, it has been through institutional reform litigation that some of the most far-reaching and long-lasting changes have been brought about in prison policies and practices. Litigation has given prisoners a forum in which they can air their grievances against state authorities. Thomas, Wheeler, and Harris (1986, 794) assert that litigation is one of the final "nonviolent and legitimate" mechanisms at the prison inmates' disposal.

Inmates seldom have the economic resources to undertake a wide-ranging and protracted class action lawsuit against a state corrections department. Therefore, prisoners' rights groups such as the American Civil Liberties Union's National Prison Project have come to inmates' aid (Bronstein 1985; Mays and Taggart 1985, 1988; Rhodes 1992). Changes in federal legislation concerning the bases for civil rights actions and expanded grants of lawyers' fees undoubtedly have contributed to an increase in inmate litigation and additional interest by potential prisoners' rights advocacy groups.

Laws and Litigation Dealing with Probation and Parole

Until the 1960s, probation officers enjoyed a great deal of freedom in discharging their duties. Probation officers frequently cooperated with police officers to incarcerate a suspected offender based on information that could not stand up to close legal scrutiny. The probation officer could take the "violator" into custody and request a re-sentencing, which normally resulted in a quick trip to prison. Rarely were either the formalities of due process or a hearing on the alleged charges part of this process.

Two cases defined the rights of probationers. In the 1967 ruling on *Mempa v. Rhay,* the Supreme Court ruled that the right of an accused to be represented by an attorney is not confined to the trial alone. The justices concluded that counsel is required at every stage when substantial rights of the accused may be affected. Sentencing, particularly upon probation revocation, qualifies as one of these critical stages.

Morrisey's appeal reached the Supreme Court in 1972. Iowa authorities maintained that parolees do not enjoy a basic right to a conditional release from prison. Instead, parole is a privilege extended by the executive branch of government to the convict. This position was rejected by the Court. During the past 60 years, the Court observed, parole has emerged as an integral part of correctional practices, and it occurs too regularly to be considered a privilege. Second, the Court noted that by whatever means freedom is obtained, "it must be seen within the protection of the Fourteenth Amendment. Its termination calls for some orderly process, however informal." Third, because revocations occur for between 35% and 40% of all paroles, protection of the parolee's rights is essential.

In *Morrisey,* the Court also addressed the nature of due process for parolees. In the majority opinion, the parole revocation hearing was considered a two-stage process: (1) arrest and preliminary hearing and (2) the revocation hearing. For these hearings, the Court extended parolees the following due process rights:

1. Written notice of the claimed violation of parole
2. Disclosure to the parolee of evidence against him
3. Opportunity to be heard in person and to present witnesses and documentary evidence
4. The right to confront and cross-examine adverse witnesses (unless the hearing officer specifically finds good cause for not allowing confrontation)

5. A "neutral and detached" hearing body such as a traditional parole board, members of which need not be judicial officers or lawyers

6. A written statement of the factfinders as to the evidence relied on and reasons for revoking parole

As it did with probation, the Court left unanswered the question of counsel. In practice parolees may have counsel present, but the government need not provide counsel.

The Court emphasized that the hearings should be kept informal. The justices noted that "it is a narrow inquiry; the process should be flexible enough to consider evidence, including letters, affidavits, and other material that would not be admissible in an adversary criminal trial." In short, like the probation hearing, the evidence heard and the standard of proof required for parole revocation is lower than that required in a trial court for conviction.

In *Gagnon v. Scarpelli* (1973), the Supreme Court, having ruled on a similar issue in a parole revocation case the year before, decided in Gerald Scarpelli's favor. The defendant, the Court decided, faced possible loss of liberty without benefit of a legal hearing on the charges. Therefore, at minimum, a probationer is entitled to

- A notice of the alleged violations.
- A preliminary hearing to decide if sufficient (probable) cause exists to believe that probation was violated.
- A revocation hearing, which is, in the words of the justices, "a somewhat more comprehensive hearing prior to the making of the final revocation decision." The revocation hearing should allow the accused the opportunity to appear to present witnesses and evidence on his or her own behalf. Concurrently, the probationer should be allowed to confront any accusatory witnesses or evidence.

The Court failed to clarify the right to counsel at these hearings. The justices suggested that the need for counsel be proved on a case-by-case basis. In practice, most jurisdictions provide the accused with counsel or allow private counsel at the preliminary hearings.

In the 1972 case *Morrisey v. Brewer,* the Supreme Court decided whether a parolee should enjoy basic due process rights during the revocation hearing. Before *Morrisey,* parole revocation hearings were not covered by *Mempa v. Rhay.* Parole authorities alleged that probation revocation hearings were decidedly judicial in nature, a characteristic not shared by the administrative parole revocation hearing. This position changed with *Morrisey.*

A final set of legal questions centers on the use of the pre-sentence investigation (PSI) report in the punishment phase of a criminal trial. As we learned in Chapter 7, this document is often prepared by the probation officer. It has the potential to determine the sentence, and, in death penalty cases, may play some role in the life-or-death decision confronting the court.

Table 10.2

Issues Arising from Inmate Lawsuits

Specific condition(s)	Number of facilities	Specific condition(s)	Number of facilities
Medical facilities	172	Administrative segregation	121
Staffing	155	Inmate classification	121
Education	139	Disciplinary policies	114
Food services/nutrition	136	Fire hazards	114
Visiting/mail policies	130	Grievance policies	113
Recreation	127	Counseling programs	106
Library services	122	Other	41

Note: Some prisons are sued to challenge a wide variety of conditions, thus the numbers cannot be summed to arrive at 323, the total number of prisons under court order.

Source: Department of Justice (1992a).

Issues Raised by Correctional Lawsuits

As noted previously, one of the fundamental prisoners' rights complaints alleges inadequate **access to the courts.** For almost three decades prison inmates have enjoyed relatively unimpeded access, especially to the federal district courts. Given the increasing volume of such suits, the day may be rapidly approaching when federal judges may place restrictions on state prison inmates' suits (Remington 1986).

Presently, however, inmates have the opportunity to challenge a wide range of prison conditions. For the 323 state prisons under court order or consent decree on June 29, 1990, there were two broad litigation categories: (1) general conditions of confinement and (2) crowding (Department of Justice 1992a). Although the courts have never held that crowding necessarily is an issue in and of itself, it affects many aspects of prison operations and is one of the most common factors cited in court orders.

Crowding has been a problem in state and federal prisons for 25 years. Many prisons are filled beyond operational capacity and some states, such as Texas, have their entire prison systems under court order as a result of persistent crowding (Alpert, Crouch, and Huff 1984; Crouch and Marquart 1989; DiIulio 1990). Therefore, it should come as no surprise to find that 186 of the 323 state prisons under court order in 1990 were crowded. Table 10.2 lists in order the other specific conditions challenged in these prison lawsuits (Department of Justice 1992a, 7).

Some of the key litigation points need to be discussed. For example, one important point of contention is **double-bunking** (sometimes referred to as **double-celling**) of inmates. In other words, are prisons and jails allowed to house two inmates in a cell originally designed to hold one?

The first definitive answer to this question was provided by the Supreme Court in *Bell v. Wolfish* (1979). This case has been characterized by some

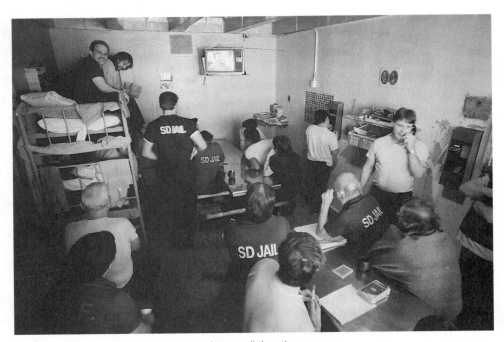

"Double-bunking" or placing more inmates into a cell than they were originally designed to hold has become a common practice in many crowded jails and prisons. Here, 16 inmates are housed in one cell at the San Diego County Jail. These living arrangements often increase the numbers of assaults among the inmates and custodial staff members.

observers as "probably the single most important corrections case the [Supreme Court] has ever decided" (Collins 1993, 11). This case was unique because it involved federal prisoners housed in the newly opened New York City Metropolitan Correctional Center (MCC).

The Court's opinion in *Bell v. Wolfish* was significant because it represented a return to the hands-off approach to prisoners' rights. Specifically, *Bell v. Wolfish* determined that double-bunking of inmates did not necessarily constitute cruel and unusual punishment and, therefore, was not unconstitutional (see also Collins 1993; *Correctional Law Reporter* 1994; Mays and Bernat 1988). The Supreme Court reinforced *Bell v. Wolfish* in *Rhodes v. Chapman* (1981). In this case from Ohio the Supreme Court once again held that placing two inmates in a cell designed for one is not constitutionally prohibited.

Another source of inmate litigation involves the area of health and safety issues (including medical care) in prisons and jails. Medical care standards, including dental and mental health provisions (that is, counseling and psychotropic drug therapy), often have been points of legal contention (Alpert, Crouch, and Huff 1984; Hopper 1985; Prigmore and Crow 1976; Selke 1985; Yarbrough 1984).

Health care apparently was an area in which corrections officials felt they could save money by cutting services. As a result, in some prisons physician's assistants serve as the primary health care providers (see *Corrections Digest* 1994, 7) and in others inmates have served as "medical technicians" and provided health care, even dispensing drugs (see Alpert et al., 1984). Various levels of health-care personnel, including registered nurses, certified nurse practitioners, certified nursing assistants, and medical technical assistants (correctional officers with some medical training), may be used in institutional medical facilities. In many cases, the federal courts have ordered prisons to implement or upgrade medical care to levels equal to those proposed by the American Correctional Association and the American Medical Association. The standard articulated in *Estelle v. Gamble* (1976) and typically employed by the courts in assessing blame is **deliberate indifference,** and at least one federal judge has ruled that county commissioners and the sheriff personally can be held liable when refusing to provide treatment to a jail inmate suffering from cancer (*Corrections Digest* 1993a, 10).

Additionally, food services and fire hazards can be considered inmate health and safety concerns. A variety of cases have mandated nutrition and fire safety standards for prisons (Mays and Taggart 1985). Food service is one of the perennial points of inmate dissatisfaction, and the courts have ruled that inmates must be provided nutritious, well-balanced meals. Also, some inmates may have special dietary needs. This is particularly true for certain religious groups such as Muslim inmates, who do not eat pork (*Cooper v. Pate* 1964), one of the most common meat items in prison diets.

Fire safety standards have mandated certain types of prison and jail construction or reconstruction and particularly have stressed the use of flame retardant materials in inmate clothing and bedding (American Correctional Association 1991b). Given the movement restrictions facing jail and prison inmates, fire safety is crucial.

Another condition, staffing, seems an unusual source of prisoners' lawsuits. However, inmates have petitioned for more custodial and treatment staff to increase prisoners' safety and service levels. In some instances lawsuits have even sought particular personnel deployment patterns (Bingaman 1980; Mays and Taggart 1985).

Education, recreation, and non-law library services can all be treated together. These three areas fall within what can be called inmate programs and services. Generally speaking, much prison and jail time is unproductive. Therefore, educational and recreation programs can benefit the inmates and assist in the facility's smooth operation. Library services provide inmates with recreational reading opportunities.

The final arena of concern addresses a broad area that can be called institutional governance; it includes issues relating to visiting and correspondence policies, administrative segregation, classification, and disciplinary and grievance policies. Concerns with governance, especially discipline and inmate grievances, seem to be a constant source of inmate litigation. It is important to remember that prisons have the authority to discipline inmates for infractions of institutional rules; however, there must be an orderly process of reviewing complaints, especially those that might result in administrative segregation, loss of privileges, and loss of good time credits (Cohen 1988, 338–42).

Recent Trends in Litigation by Prison and Jail Inmates

The previous sections have dealt with some of the history of correctional litigation. Nevertheless, there has been a great deal of litigation in recent years that has had a significant impact on the operation of contemporary correctional agencies and institutions.

Expanding Litigation to Jails

Many of the corrections lawsuits arising out of the 1960s and 1970s dealt with prisons. Although prison litigation has lead the way, suits involving jails and other local detention facilities have not been far behind. For example, many of the same items appearing in prison lawsuits are included in jail litigation (Champion 1991; Mays and Bernat 1988). These issues include crowding, recreation, medical care, staffing levels and staff training, food service, disciplinary practices, and treatment programs (see Guynes 1988; Kerle and Ford 1982). If jail administrators want to know the sources of potential litigation, all they have to do is read the major prison cases from the 1960s and 1970s.

New Areas of Litigation

We have already detailed some of the persistent sources of correctional litigation. However, corrections officials are now seeing new issues being raised by inmates. This section will discuss five of the newly emerging issues—inmates' right to privacy with respect to being guarded by members of the opposite sex, use of prison chain gangs, smoke-free environments, the Americans with Disabilities Act, and the use of excessive physical force by prison officials—and the impact each may have on correctional policy and practice.

One of the earliest cases addressing the issue of gender and correctional staff was *Lee v. Downs* (1981). This case dealt with the issue of whether a female inmate could be forced to remove her underclothing in the presence of male correctional officers when ordered by a physician. The court held that since the inmate was willing to remove her clothing if the male officers would withdraw, forcing her to remove it in their presence constituted an improper invasion of the inmate's privacy. In a related case, *Timm v. Gunter* (1990), a group of male inmates at the Nebraska State Penitentiary filed suit to prevent female corrections officers from performing pat searches and from seeing them in the nude. With an increasing number of female correctional officers working in all-male institutions, issues such as staff members of one sex guarding prisoners of the opposite sex are being raised. In *Timm v. Gunter* the inmates alleged that their privacy rights were violated when they were viewed in the nude while showering, using toilet facilities, dressing and undressing, and sleeping. In regard to observation by guards of the opposite sex, the appellate court held that they were "convinced that opposite-sex surveillance of male inmates, performed on the same basis as same-sex surveillance, is not 'unreasonable.'" Therefore, this practice "neither impermissibly violates[s] the inmates' privacy rights nor impermissibly violate[s] the guards' equal employment rights."

As part of the trend toward getting tough with offenders, some states have reinstituted **chain gangs.** Alabama and Arizona are using groups of inmates chained together to clean up along state highways. Florida has approved the idea and Iowa also has created a hard labor program, potentially involving chain gangs (*Criminal Justice Newsletter* 1995b, 1). Arizona prison officials have given four justifications for using chain gangs in their state:

1. State law requires prison inmates to work 40 hours per week.
2. Arizona's chain gang project (officially called the Hard Labor Program) is designed to promote self-discipline and a work ethic.
3. This project gets inmates out of their cells.
4. Chain gangs stigmatize inmates and send the message to others that incarceration is not going to be a pleasant experience (*Criminal Justice Newsletter* 1995b, 2).

Chain gangs seem popular with politicians and the general public. Inmates are less enthusiastic. The American Civil Liberties Union's National Prison Project has responded to this national trend toward harsher punishments. In fact, Alabama inmates, supported by the Southern Poverty Law Center, have filed suit to end the practice of chain gangs. The inmates complain that these work assignments expose them to traffic hazards and that they constitute cruel and unusual punishment, in violation of the Eighth Amendment. Male inmates also have alleged that they are unfairly discriminated against because initially chain gangs only involved males. Ironically, recent news reports indicate that Alabama's response has been to announce the creation of female chain gangs (*El Paso Times* 1996, 3A).

During the past few years prison and jail inmates have filed suit asserting their "right" to live in a smoke-free environment. Lawsuits have charged that environmental tobacco smoke (ETS) is a potential health risk. This issue is especially problematic for inmates because they cannot choose with whom they are housed. A federal district judge in Indiana ruled against an inmate who claimed to have a constitutional right to a smoke-free environment. In his decision, Judge Allen Sharp emphasized that if the corrections department desires to create smoke-free areas in its institutions it certainly may do so. However, nothing in the Constitution compels the state to provide inmates with smoke-free surroundings (*Substance Abuse Report* 1992, 7–8).

Inmates assigned to chain gang duty are commonly used in labor intensive, outdoor activities. Here a group of chain gang inmates break rocks outside of the Limestone prison in Capshaw, Alabama.

By contrast, when Nevada inmate William McKinney appealed to the U.S. Supreme Court, he argued that "involuntary exposure to cigarette smoke could be regarded as 'cruel and unusual' punishment and a violation" of his rights (*Helling v. McKinney* 1993; *Corrections Digest* 1993b, 4; *Criminal Law Reporter* 1993, 2229). This case is significant because the Supreme Court accepted the premise that involuntary exposure to secondhand smoke in a prison constitutes cruel and unusual punishment. In its ruling in this case, the Court recognized the potential harm that might result from exposure to environmental tobacco smoke and noted that actions should be taken to reduce or eliminate that harm.

Finally, the use of excessive physical force by prison personnel must be examined as an emerging area of prison litigation. The use of physical force certainly is not new in prisons, and inmates have long complained about the use of force to maintain order and discipline in prisons. However, del Carmen (1992, 44) says, "The question in prisons is not whether force can be used, but when and how."

The Supreme Court provided a partial answer in *Hudson v. McMillian* 1992, a Louisiana case. Inmate Hudson was restrained after arguing with CO McMillian. Hudson was taken from his cell in handcuffs and shackles and placed in lockdown. On the way to lockdown, McMillian and another correctional officer continued to punch Hudson while a supervisor watched but did not intercede.

Hudson brought a Section 1983 suit against the state prison officials and the case eventually reached the U.S. Supreme Court. The Court was asked to decide whether the excessive use of force constituted cruel and unusual punishment even though Hudson did not suffer serious physical injury. The Court decided that the correctional officers' actions were malicious and sadistic and constituted a violation of Hudson's Eighth Amendment protections against cruel and unusual punishment. Del Carmen (1992, 46) concludes that "the good news is that the *Hudson* decision has articulated a test for all excessive use of force cases in a prison setting; the bad news is that it fails to lay the issue to rest."

The Impact of Litigation

Collins (1993, 4) says that "since about 1970, litigation—or the threat of litigation—has probably had a greater effect on changing the way corrections does business than any other factor." The number of habeas corpus writs and civil rights actions filed by state prisoners between 1966 and 1994—a total of 651,331—indicates that prisoner litigation indeed is big business. What evidence exists of changes resulting from such litigation? Schuster and Widmer (1978, 11) say that the essential question is, "Has court intervention made an appreciable difference in prisoners' daily lives?"

One way to measure the impact of litigation is to look at occasions when lawsuits may have changed the conditions of confinement or prison operation. In an early assessment of prison litigation impact, Harris and Spiller (1977, 21) concluded that there were four outcomes from the broad-based prison lawsuits. First, they believe that there have been qualitative improvements in the particular prisons against which suits have been filed and generally in the state corrections departments. Second, contrary to the fears of the hands-off period, state authority has not been undermined. Third, lawsuits have not created "country club" prisons. Fourth, federal judges have not taken over the day-to-day administration of the prisons under litigation.

However, these conclusions may not apply when it comes to some of the more recent cases. For example, in Texas, *Estelle v. Gamble* (1976) and *Ruiz v. Estelle* (1980) brought about improvements in "personal living space, medical care, access to the courts, and working conditions" (Alpert, Crouch, and Huff 1984; see also Crouch and Marquart 1989; Martin and Ekland-Olson 1987; Rhodes 1992). Alpert and his colleagues (1984, 298) add that an unintended consequence of the *Ruiz* case has been a rising expectation by prisoners that has "set in motion a chain of events that has undermined the traditional stability, safety, and regularity" within the Texas Department of Corrections.

Mississippi is another state that has experienced a significant amount of prison inmate litigation. The positive impacts of litigation in that state included an end to racial segregation and improvements in prison conditions relating to mail censorship, disciplinary procedures, access to legal materials,

Agricultural pursuits such as the one pictured here in Parchman, Mississippi, have been a part of many prison facilities around the United States. Prison litigation has caused some of these programs to be eliminated.

religious freedom, improved medical care, and additional cell space. However, as Hopper (1985, 61) notes, the improvements changed the state prison at Parchman from a "feudal system to a fortress," that is, it changed from an essentially farm-based, plantation-style prison to a high-security, walled institution.

In Indiana litigation resulted in "hiring more personnel, upgrading prison programs, and repairing the physical facilities" (Selke 1985, 34). Much to the disappointment of some prison reform advocates, in order to make some of these changes, Indiana was forced to build new facilities and to expand existing ones.

In the end, assessment of the outcome of prison inmate litigation can be classified as optimistic or reserved. Characteristic of optimistic assessments is that provided by Thomas (1988, 250). He says that litigation has had a profound impact on corrections. Litigation has expanded the base of prison reformers, created inmate grievance mechanisms, granted additional mail privileges, eliminated some of the outrageous administrative practices, decreased staff arbitrariness, and widened prisoners' legal access (Thomas 1988, 252).

A more cautious appraisal is provided by Mays and Taggart (1988, 194), who say that court-ordered prison reform "will be a labored process even under the best of circumstances." They add that "the formulation and implementation of court-ordered reforms [resulting from prison litigation] is most likely to be measured in decades instead of years" (Mays and Taggart 1988, 194). Perhaps Collins (1993) gives us the best summary of correctional litigation. He notes that in as many as 98 out of every 100 suits filed, the defendants (that is, the state corrections officials) win. Inmate-plaintiffs are only victorious in about 2% of the suits filed. Hanson and Daley (1995, 39) support this contention by saying that "Prisoners do win Section 1983 lawsuits, though this is statistically rare." Nevertheless, these lawsuits "have had a tremendous effect on the administration of corrections in America since the late 1960s" (Collins 1993, 23).

Whatever the substantive changes may be, one inescapable conclusion is clear: as a result of state inmates' civil rights actions, now more than 1 out of every 10 civil suits filed in the federal district courts involves a prisoner's claim (Dilworth 1995, 98; Hanson and Daley 1995, 38). However, not all of these cases go all the way through to trial or settlement. For instance, about 75% of these actions are dismissed by the federal courts themselves and another 20% are terminated on motions to dismiss from the states. Because inmates are not guaranteed the right to counsel in Section 1983 (civil) suits, many of these cases are dismissed outright as lacking merit or on procedural grounds (Dilworth 1995, 98, 100).

Capital Punishment and Prisoner Litigation

Some people might debate whether capital punishment is a correctional issue, since most of the factors surrounding it arise out of legislative actions or judicial decisions. Some of these issues are addressed in Chapter 3 on sentencing. Nevertheless, capital punishment is a question to which we must turn our attention, and inmate litigation concerning the death penalty needs to be addressed because (1) the appeals of death row inmates are filed during their imprisonment and (2) correctional authorities ultimately are responsible for carrying out any death sentence.

For the more than 3,000 prisoners currently on death rows, capital punishment is a very real concern and an issue over which they file much litigation (Lemov 1996). Perhaps the place to start with litigation and the death penalty is the 1972 Supreme Court case *Furman v. Georgia* 1972. In *Furman* the Supreme Court, by a 5-to-4 vote, struck down as unconstitutional the death penalties of Georgia and most other states. In simplest terms, the Supreme Court held that the death penalty was unconstitutional because of broad jury discretion in most states. Therefore, although the Court did not say that the death penalty was unconstitutional in and of itself, it was unconstitutional when its application was arbitrary and capricious (see Felkenes 1988, 394).

Inmates have received increasing amounts of services as a result of prison litigation. Lawsuits filed by inmates challenging their conditions of confinement have resulted in improved medical care, food services, education, and recreation.

This interpretation allowed the states and the federal government to redraw death penalty statutes that would meet the Supreme Court's criticisms, and in 1976 the Court heard the case of *Gregg v. Georgia* (1976). In a 7 to 2 decision, the Supreme Court upheld the revised Georgia statute. Only Justices Brennan and Marshall, both ardent opponents of the death penalty, opposed the newly imposed death penalty statutes.

Under the revised law, Georgia and a number of states established a **bifurcated system** of adjudication for death penalty cases. In the first phase the jury decides the question of guilt. If the defendant is found to be guilty beyond a reasonable doubt the jury begins the sentencing phase and deliberation on the appropriate disposition. A number of factors about the dispositional hearing are worthy of note.

- Juries now must take into consideration **mitigating** or **aggravating circumstances.** These involve any factors that would diminish (mitigating) or enhance (aggravating) the seriousness of the crime.
- In most states only murder is considered worthy of punishment by death. Although the actual statutory definitions vary from state to

state, for instance, the definitions of first-degree murder, aggravated murder, and felony murder may vary, the death penalty is generally reserved for the most serious type of murder (Department of Justice 1994a).

- A sentencing jury must return a unanimous verdict for the death penalty. In the absence of a unanimous verdict, life or a similar prison term becomes the default sentence. This means that both the decision relating to guilt and innocence and the sentence must be supported by the 12 members of the jury.

- In 36 of the 37 states providing for capital punishment there is an automatic review of death sentences, no matter whether the defendant wishes such a review or not (Department of Justice 1996a, 4). Most of these appeals go directly to the state supreme court. This practice ensures that no errors of law were made in the original trial or in the judge's jury instructions before either of its deliberations.

As Box 10.1 shows, several recent cases have been decided regarding the legality of, and the parameters for, the death penalty. However, the basic fact remains, 37 states and the federal government provide for capital punishment under carefully defined circumstances. Additionally, from January 1, 1977, to December 31, 1993, 21 states carried out 226 executions. This certainly implies several things in terms of the death penalty's future.

There is no rush to execute prisoners in this country. Yet a steady number of executions occur annually. For prison authorities, the problem is that the number of death row inmates continues to grow every year by more than the number of executions. For instance, the U.S. death row population has increased by about 280 inmates per year during the 1990s (Lemov 1996, 30). Executions reached a contemporary high of 56 in 1995 (about twice the 1994 total).

Additionally, several death row inmates appeal their convictions to the U.S. Supreme Court, and every term of the Court sees a variety of death penalty issues. However, given the Court's current composition, it seems unlikely that the death penalty will be struck down in its entirety any time in the near future. Therefore, prisons will have to accommodate growing death row populations, and this means expensive housing in what amounts to segregation units. In California, Texas, and Florida—with more than 300 death row inmates each and nearly 1,000 total among the three states—this is a substantial correctional expenditure.

The bottom line for capital punishment is that public opinion polls show overwhelming support for the death penalty. The topic is also a source of political capital and popularity among politicians. Capital punishment will continue to be on the statute books in most states, a few states every year will execute inmates, and, as a result, the death penalty will continue to be a source of litigation.

Box 10.1

Recent Supreme Court Death Penalty Cases

Dobbs v. Zant (1993)

The Supreme Court heard a habeas corpus appeal from a criminal defendant who alleged ineffective assistance by court-appointed counsel. The Court held that there was an error when the Court of Appeals for the Eleventh Circuit refused to consider a newly discovered transcript that was not available during the original sentencing.

Graham v. Collins (1993)

The substance of this case involved the requirement under Texas law that to impose the death penalty three questions had to be answered affirmatively by the jury: (1) Was the conduct of the defendant committed deliberately and with the reasonable expectation that death would result? (2) Is there a probability that the defendant would commit criminal acts of violence that would constitute a continuing threat to society? (3) Was the conduct of the defendant unreasonable in response to the provocation, if any, by the deceased? The trial jury in this case answered all three questions in the affirmative. The defendant based his claim on the grounds that answering these three questions did not sufficiently allow the jury to consider mitigating circumstances. The Supreme Court ruled against the criminal defendant on procedural grounds. The ruling held that the route of appeal—collateral review—would require the Court to develop a new rule under constitutional law where one did not already exist.

Herrera v. Collins (1993)

The defendant in this case was convicted of killing one police officer and subsequently pleaded guilty to killing a second officer. Ten years after his conviction he filed a federal habeas corpus petition alleging that his brother (who was now dead) actually had been the murderer. The U.S. Supreme Court upheld the constitutionality of the Texas statute that provided that a motion for a new trial based on newly discovered evidence must be filed within 60 days of

judgment. Therefore, the Court, in a 5-to-3 decision, refused to overturn Herrera's conviction, plea, and sentences.

Lockhart v. Fretwell (1993)

The Supreme Court was asked to decide whether a defense attorney's failure to object during sentencing, on a matter that would have precluded the death penalty, deprived the defendant of a fair trial. The defendant was convicted of capital felony murder and sentenced to die by an Arkansas trial jury. The defendant's attorney did not raise the issue of unconstitutionality of the death penalty at the sentencing hearing. The Supreme Court in a 7-to-2 ruling, held that the defendant did not suffer prejudice from his attorney's deficient performance and, therefore, the sentencing proceeding was neither unfair nor unreliable.

Delo v. Lashley (1993)

The defendant appealed on the basis of a lack of instruction by the trial court that mitigating circumstances existed since there was "no significant history of prior criminal activity" and lack of instruction to the jury that they should remember that the defendant is presumed innocent. The Supreme Court ruled against the defendant on the basis that (1) there is no constitutional obligation to give mitigating circumstance instructions if there is no evidence offered to support mitigating circumstances during the trial and (2) the defendant appeared to be fairly convicted and there was no automatic requirement that the judge issue a presumption of innocence instruction.

Arave v. Creech (1993)

The accused in this case was an Idaho state prison inmate who was incarcerated for killing at least 26 people (the bodies of 11 of whom were found in seven states). While in prison he killed another inmate whom he bludgeoned with a sock full of batteries and repeatedly kicked in the head and throat. The appeal was based on the allega-

Box 10.1 (continued)

Recent Supreme Court Death Penalty Cases

tion that Idaho's aggravating circumstance of "utter disregard for human life" was unconstitutionally vague. The United States Supreme Court, by a 7-to-2 vote, held the Idaho standard for aggravating circumstances was not unconstitutionally vague and, in fact, it provided for a clear and objective standard.

Sullivan v. Louisiana (1993)

A Louisiana criminal defendant was convicted of first-degree murder during the commission of an armed robbery, but the judge gave the jury instructions concerning the definition of "reasonable doubt" that previously had been held to be unconstitutional. The U.S. Supreme Court unanimously held that relying on an unconstitutional definition of reasonable doubt violates a defendant's right to a fair trial.

Godinez v. Moran (1993)

Prior to trial for the murders of three individuals, two psychiatrists examined the defendant and determined that he was competent to stand trial. After the evaluations the defendant dismissed his attorneys and entered a plea of guilty. The trial court reviewed the defendant's mental condition,

accepted the waiver of counsel and the guilty pleas, and sentenced the defendant to death. When the appeal eventually reached the Supreme Court, the question was whether the decision to waive the right to counsel requires a higher level of mental functioning than other rights (after sentencing this defendant had alleged that he was incompetent to represent himself). The Supreme Court ruled that the standard for competency to waive the right to counsel or to plead guilty is not higher than the standard for mental competency to stand trial.

Johnson v. Texas (1993)

The defendant in this case was convicted, while still a minor, of the robbery and murder of a convenience store clerk. The appeal was based on the contention that the Texas trial court erred in not instructing the jury to consider the defendant's age as a mitigating factor. The Supreme Court rejected the argument that this was an error of constitutional magnitude and held instead that the jury properly considered the extent to which this defendant would be a continuing threat to the community (irrespective of age).

Source: Department of Justice (1994a).

Conclusion

There seems to be no end to the increasing numbers and expanding issues arising from inmate litigation. While the rush to file **class action lawsuits** against jails, prisons, and entire prison systems seems to have slowed down, many states still find themselves in court over conditions of confinement, particularly crowding.

Where prisons have lead, jails have followed. Contemporary jail administrators, county executives, and boards of commissioners frequently find themselves parties to lawsuits. The problem in many jails and prisons is that the government could lose a suit, be ordered to pay damages, and still be faced with the condition (crowding, for instance) that was the basis for the suit to begin with.

With inmate populations continuing to rise, prisons and jails will struggle to provide adequate space. In the meantime, inmates will continue to file suits

Inmate Litigation in the Twenty-First Century

With the number of jail and prison inmates throughout the United States increasing every year, the future would seem to hold inmate litigation. Several features indicate the likelihood of more and more diverse litigation arising from jail and prison inmate suits. However, the federal courts, and particularly the U.S. Supreme Court, have become less receptive to inmate lawsuits, signaling a slowdown for this type of litigation. For example, the general shift to conservatism was made concrete in the 1987 Supreme Court case *Turner v. Safley*. This case dealt with Missouri's prohibition against inmate romances and inmates corresponding with one another. The Supreme Court established the "reasonableness test" in determining the constitutionality of prison officials' actions. The reasonableness test measures inmates' rights against the prison's security. Alexander (1994, 104) says that this test, in contrast to the "strict scrutiny test," is "highly deferential to prison officials and has the potential for a significant erosion in prisoners' rights."

As a result of this trend, some people have characterized the contemporary era as "one-hand-on, one-hand-off" (Collins 1993, 10–12) or "hands semi-off" (Alexander 1994). In the Supreme Court cases decided since 1979 inmates seldom have been the winners. Furthermore, many of these decisions have made it unlikely that inmates will be successful in future cases (Call 1995, 41).

On the side of expansion would seem to be the continuing increase

in inmate populations compared to the available prison and jail space. As populations have increased nationwide, some correctional systems have found themselves curtailing or totally eliminating some programs. Expensive resources must be diverted to providing the basic food, shelter, and security needs of inmates. More inmates, with more idle time, will use some of that time to bring suits against their keepers. Furthermore, not only will inmates turn to the courts for redress of their grievances, but new issues (such as living in smoke-free environments) will continue to arise.

The U.S. Supreme Court's conservative mood seems typified by cases such as *Bell v. Wolfish* (1979) when it found that there was no constitutional mandate for single-celling and marked the beginning of the **one-hand-on era.** Collins (1993, 12) says that the Court's message in *Bell v. Wolfish* was that prisoners have constitutional rights but that those rights are not unrestricted. He speculates that correctional litigation in the future will focus on five areas. First, conditions of confinement—particularly crowding—cases will continue to dominate correctional litigation. Therefore, state and federal governments will have to devote increasingly larger segments of their budgets to building and operating facilities. Second, inmates will continue to litigate in areas involving previously articulated rights, such as medical care. In fact, medical care may be an intensely important issue as we put more people in prison and keep them there for longer periods

Inmate Litigation in the Twenty-First Century (continued)

of time. The next decade may see the practice of geriatric medicine a common feature in the nation's correctional facilities (see Chapter 11).

Third, if inmates feel that the federal courts have become unreceptive to their claims, they will turn instead to state courts. Fourth, inmates will not be the only group asserting "corrections" issues. Staff members will enter the fray, raising concerns over pay and other working conditions such as safety. Finally, newly created statutory rights, such as those mandated by the Americans with Disabilities Act, will provide a fertile ground for inmate and staff litigation (see, especially, Collins 1993, 12–14).

There are a variety of alternative mechanisms for dealing with the increasing number of inmate lawsuits, particularly civil rights actions. In fact, the procedures are already in place to provide for federally certified internal dispute resolution: namely, the Civil Rights of Institu-tionalized Persons Act (CRIPA). This 1980 federal legislation authorizes the U.S. attorney general and the federal courts to certify state administrative grievance mechanisms for handling routine inmate complaints. For those states with certified plans, all administrative mechanisms must be exhausted before inmates are allowed to file suit in federal court (Collins 1993; Hanson and Daley 1995). This procedure is designed to handle most problems as close to the source as possible and to keep many cases off of federal court dockets. Unfortunately, most states have not sought certification of their grievance procedures and there has been little prompting from the federal courts to do so. The result is that CRIPA remains a largely unused, but potentially very significant, vehicle for settling inmate complaints (Collins 1993; *Criminal Justice Newsletter* 1995b, 6–7; Hanson and Daley 1995, 40).

alleging their conditions of confinement constitute cruel and unusual punishment. Just so you do not think we have left out probation and parole, this too will be a fertile area for litigation. With more offenders, and more serious offenders, being placed in community supervision programs, lawsuits will escalate here too. Offenders will sue because they have not received adequate treatment services. The public will sue because they are not being adequately protected. And the employees will sue because they are being overworked in a dangerous and stressful environment. The end is not in sight.

Critical Review Questions

1. List some of the reasons inmate lawsuits increased so dramatically during the 1970s. Which of these reasons had the greatest impact?

2. What is your reaction to a federal judge telling a state prison how many prisoners it should house? Would you feel differently if you were a prison warden?

3. Should inmates' rights groups, such as the ACLU's National Prison Project, be filing lawsuits on behalf of inmates? Why don't inmates take care of their own litigation interests?

4. Aside from minimizing the number of lawsuits that result, why would prisons want to limit or prohibit the practice of inmates helping other inmates file appeals?

5. When comparing parolees and probationers, what differences do you see in their legal status and protection under the Constitution?

6. Should offenders be represented by an attorney during parole revocation proceedings? If they cannot afford attorneys should the state appoint counsel?

7. Should prisons and jails be smoke-free environments for inmates and staff members? What would you do to change an institution from a smoking facility to a smoke-free facility?

8. Do inmates have a "right to privacy?" What does this mean in terms of correctional officers of one gender guarding prisoners of another gender?

9. What evidence do we have that litigation is improving the lives of jail and prison inmates? Are there two or three areas where we see the greatest improvement?

10. Much has been written and said about the impact of capital punishment on crime in the United States. What evidence can you point to on the impact of capital punishment?

Recommended Readings

Collins, William C. 1993. *Correctional law for the correctional officer.* Laurel, MD: American Correctional Association. This book is one of the many training materials produced by the American Correctional Association. The materials present a very useful how-to look at the general environment of correctional litigation, some of the sources of litigation, and what corrections personnel generally (not just corrections officers) can do to anticipate and avoid litigation.

Crouch, Ben M., and James W. Marquart. 1989. *An appeal to justice: Litigated reform of Texas prisons.* Austin: University of Texas Press. The title of this book offers a play on words: Judge William Wayne Justice was the federal judge who oversaw the Texas prison litigation case, hence the "appeal to Justice." Crouch and Marquart carefully detail the history of Texas prisons, some of the key players in Texas prison history, and the events that lead the state into federal court. For students of correctional law this book (along with the one by Martin and Ekland-Olson, on page 371) provides fascinating and insightful reading.

DiIulio, John J., Jr., ed. 1990. *Courts, corrections, and the Constitution: The impact of judicial intervention on prisons and jails.* New York: Oxford University Press. DiIulio's book is an edited volume on prison and jail litigation. It includes articles by some of the best-known researchers in the area, and it covers some of the specific cases (states and institutions) that have resulted in judicial intervention. Several of the pieces in this volume cover the litigation arising in Texas, but there are also articles on litigation in Georgia, West Virginia, and New York City. This volume is very useful when studying the general political and legal contexts in which institutional reform litigation arises.

Martin, Steven J., and Sheldon Ekland-Olson. 1987. *Texas prisons: The walls came tumbling down.* Austin: Texas Monthly Press. Like the book by Crouch and Marquart, this volume also contains a word play in the title (the "Walls" was one of the main units in the Texas prison system). Martin, a journalist, is joined by Ekland-Olson, an academic, in chronicling the process of litigation in Texas.

While much of the same information is covered in this book as in the text by Crouch and Marquart, this volume tends to focus more on some of the less well-known, but still important, actors in the litigation process. Martin and Ekland-Olson make the Texas prison litigation case a much more human process.

Thomas, Jim. 1988. *Prison litigation: The paradox of the jailhouse lawyer.* Totowa, NJ: Rowman & Littlefield. Thomas does the world of corrections research a great favor with this book. He explores in great detail the inmate world, and particularly the place the jailhouse lawyer plays in it. He provides information on the processes and bases for inmate litigation, but takes a more sociological and less legalistic look at the reasons for inmate lawsuits.

Key Terms

access to the courts	double-bunking (double-celling)	*pro se* actions
aggravating circumstances	federalism	public interest law
bifurcated system	habeas corpus, writ of	qualified immunity
chain gangs	hands-off approach	separation of powers
civil death	hands-on period	tort claims
civil rights claims (Section 1983 suits)	jailhouse lawyers	vicarious (supervisory) liability
class action lawsuits	litigiousness	writ writers
deliberate indifference	mitigating circumstances	
	one-hand-on era	

Cases Cited

Arave v. Creech, 113 S. Ct. 1534 (1993)
Bell v. Wolfish, 441 U.S. 520 (1979)
Bounds v. Smith, 430 U.S. 817 (1977)
Citrano v. Allen Correctional Center, DC WLa, No. CV94-1076 (1995)
Cooper v. Pate, 378 U.S. 546 (1964)
Delo v. Lashley, 113 S. Ct. 1222 (1993)
Dobbs v. Zant, 113 S.Ct. 835 (1993)
Estelle v. Gamble, 429 U.S. 97 (1976)
Fay v. Noia, 372 U.S. 391 (1963)
Furman v. Georgia, 408 U.S. 238 (1972)
Gagnon v. Scarpelli, 411 U.S. 778 (1973)
Godinez v. Moran, 113 S.Ct. 2680 (1993)
Graham v. Collins, 113 S. Ct. 892 (1993)
Gregg v. Georgia, 428 U.S. 153 (1976)
Helling v. McKinney, 113 S.Ct. 2475 (1993)
Herrera v. Collins, 113 S. Ct. 853 (1993)
Holt v. Sarver, 309 F. Supp. 362 (E.D. Ark., 1970)
Hudson v. McMillian, 501 U.S. 1279 (1992)

Johnson v. Avery, 393 U.S. 483 (1969)
Johnson v. Texas, 113 S.Ct. 2658 (1993)
Lee v. Downs, 641 F. 2d 1117 (4th Cir., 1981)
Lockhart v. Fretwell, 113 S.Ct. 838 (1993)
Manis v. Corrections Corporation of America, 859 F. Supp. 302 (D.C. M.Tenn., 1994)
Mempa v. Rhay, 389 U.S. 128 (1967)
Monroe v. Pape, 365 U.S. 167 (1961)
Morrisey v. Brewer, 408 U.S. 471 (1972)
Pugh v. Locke, 406 F. Supp. 318 (M.D. Ala., 1976)

Rhodes v. Chapman, 452 U.S. 337 (1981)
Richardson et al. v. McKnight (case no. 96-318, decided June 23, 1997)
Ruffin v. Commonwealth, 62 Va. 790 (1871)
Ruiz v. Estelle, 503 F. Supp. 1265 (S.D. Tex. 1980)
Sanders v. United States, 373 U.S. 1 (1963)
Sullivan v. Louisiana, 113 S. Ct. 2078 (1993)
Timm v. Gunter, 917 F. 2d 1093 (8th Cir., 1990)
Townsend v. Sain, 372 U.S. 293 (1963)
Turner v. Safley, 107 S. Ct. 2254 (1987)

11

Unresolved Issues and the Future of Corrections

Chapter Outline

- Introduction
- Future Correctional Philosophies
- Future Correctional Practices
- Future Correctional Populations
- Future Correctional Problems

- Conclusion
- Critical Review Questions
- Recommended Readings
- Key Terms
- Notes

Introduction

One of the exciting things about studying the subject of corrections, or being a practitioner in the field, is that there always seem to be more questions than there are answers. For some people this is extremely frustrating, but for others it presents the challenge of being the person who discovers the answer to life's long-term crime and punishment dilemmas.

In this chapter we will examine several issues that have been with us for some time. For many of these issues there are no easy answers, and most of them do not seem to point to future solutions. These concerns are both persistent and critical, and they remain issues that we as a society and those who work in the criminal justice system seem destined to deal with well into the next century. Therefore, let us move on to identifying some of the unresolved issues, and how they may affect the future of corrections. We should warn the reader that the list we will treat through the remainder of the chapter is by no means exhaustive. Each of you may feel that there are troublesome problems that have not been included in our final treatment. We concede that many more concerns could have been addressed, but we chose to focus on four main areas, with some subcategories.

As you read this final chapter, you will no doubt recognize previously reviewed material. Occasionally, we present entirely new content, speculations, observations, or, more rarely, offender statistics. Our goal here is to suggest that the future problems and answers for corrections are firmly rooted in the present and the past. We begin this "review" where we began the book, with the philosophical basis of corrections.

Future Correctional Philosophies

One of the most basic unresolved issues in contemporary corrections, and one likely to plague us for some time, is the correctional philosophy we choose to follow. We could call this the choice of a model or paradigm. However, whatever label we choose, the basic question is, What underlying social values will guide our approach to correcting criminal behavior into the twenty-first century? For most people today, the clear guiding principle in U.S. corrections is *punishment.* The interrelated philosophies of retribution (revenge), deterrence, and incapacitation seem to drive our public policy choices in terms of crime and punishment issues. The public seems to have an unquenchable thirst for even more severe criminal sanctions, and policy-makers appear to share it. When we examine the statements relating to the "get-tough" approach to crime and criminals, do we find that the public truly wants these specific policies or are these strategies really a quick fix proposed to exploit public fears about crime? To ask it another way: Does the issue of increased punishment surface frequently because of the mileage politicians can get from it?

In the short term, we seem destined to live with a retributionist approach to corrections. When dealing with jail and prison population predictions, one word says it all: more. Following the adoption of sentencing guidelines by Congress in 1987, social scientists predicted massive growth in federal prison populations (Block and Rhodes 1987; Mays 1989). This increase has largely come to pass. Furthermore, changes in sentencing practices (from indeterminate to determinate, presumptive, and mandatory sentences), combined with the adoption of more criminal sanctions, a general lengthening of sentences, and reduced mechanisms for early release all contribute to the growth in inmate populations and attest to a more punitive approach to dealing with offenders.

This discussion does not tell us where the future will take us in terms of the paradigm we will employ. What should we expect after the turn of the century? We must consider two factors in answering that question. First, there is probably a natural "break point" in terms of prison and jail prisoner populations in the United States. The deciding factor is likely to be how much incarceration we can afford. Recently, taxpayers have been willing to pay for ever-increasing levels, but at some point supporting additional numbers of prisoners, and other correctional clients, will become burdensome. If state and federal budgets cannot tap unlimited pools of money, then taxpayers soon will realize that dollars expended for incarceration are dollars that are not available for schools, roads, health care, recreation facilities, and the like for all citizens, and general entitlement programs for the community's disadvantaged citizens. A taxpayer revolt may halt the size of the corrections piece of the budget pie. Voters also could refuse to approve capital bond referendums for prison and jail renovation or construction. The ultimate signal of a taxpayer revolt might be the election of legislators who promise to bring a halt to the policies of increasing punitiveness and seemingly endless additional incarceration.

The second factor influencing the future of corrections is the historical cycles we have moved through in our attitudes toward punitiveness. Thomas Bernard (1992) notes that over the past century we have experienced periods of lenient treatment for juvenile offenders. At some point, however, comes a public perception that leniency is not working and that permissive treatment is causing additional delinquency. The response to the perceived crime wave projected by Bernard's model is a call for much harsher penalties for juvenile offenders, in order to "solve" the problem of delinquency.

Many people see elements comparable to Bernard's juvenile cycle in the criminal justice system. If harsh treatment seems justified for juvenile offenders, then it certainly is justified for adults. At some point it becomes apparent—at least to many criminal justice researchers and practitioners—that getting tougher and tougher does not seem to be working either. (See Box 11.1 for one cartoonist's take on "tough on crime" rhetoric.) Therefore, criminal justice system personnel begin to engage in adaptive responses to the harsher penalties. Samuel Walker (1994, 51–52) calls this the **law of criminal justice thermodynamics.** By this term he means that the harsher criminal penalties become, the less likely they are to be applied in full force. The result is a much less severe approach to dealing with offenders than policymakers had originally envisioned. In the end the crime is made to fit the punishment rather than the punishment to fit the crime (Walker 1994, 52).

A perfect contemporary example of the law of criminal justice thermodynamics in action is the use of mandatory minimum sentences for certain crimes. The most frequently cited example are laws covering the use of firearms in the commission of a crime in some states. For states with firearms enhancements, individuals charged with and convicted of crimes in which a firearm is involved should receive some mandatory minimum prison sentence, or some additional period of imprisonment added to the basic sentence. Researchers have shown that in many instances the police or prosecutor may simply ignore the presence of the firearm as part of a plea bargain, or if a "good citizen" (for example, a local convenience store owner or family-practice dentist) is charged with illegally carrying a concealed

Box 11.1

"Get-Tough" Cartoon

Source: Mike Thompson / Copley News Service. ©1997 State Journal-Register. Used by permission.

weapon (Pierce and Bowers 1981). Thus, a more punitive response to offenders is negated by the behaviors of criminal justice system actors. This means that the law has little to no effect because participants in the process do not apply it in many circumstances, and the less it is applied the more arbitrary the applications become (Walker 1994, 51, 197–99).

This example illustrates adaptive behaviors by the so-called courtroom work group (Eisenstein and Jacob 1977; Neubauer 1992). However, corrections officials may engage in adaptive responses as well. One of the most obvious cases involves the use of determinate sentencing. Beginning with Maine in 1976, a total of 10 states—California, Connecticut, Florida, Illinois, Indiana, Maine, Minnesota, New Mexico, North Carolina, and Washington—moved to sentencing systems that were exclusively or primarily determinate in nature (Department of Justice 1988, 91). This change came about for numerous reasons (Department of Justice 1988, 90–91; Walker 1994, 90, 94). For example, many liberals believed that the parole system associated with indeterminate sentences allowed far too much discretion to be exercised by parole boards. By contrast, conservatives believed that indeterminate sentences were dishonest in that the sentence imposed was not the sentence actually served. Under this system, a one- to ten-year sentence might translate into less than one year of incarceration. By the mid-1980s, several state legislatures, followed by the U.S. Congress, changed sentencing laws to provide for flat-time or determinate sentences. This change in sentencing philosophy has been a hallmark of the get-tough movement and the more punitive orientation toward criminal offenders.

After only a few years of determinate sentences, corrections officials recognized the impact such changes can have on prison populations. In most states, new laws were being created and longer sentences were being imposed for existing violations. These factors, and determinate sentencing, dramatically increased the average sentence length for most state, and eventually federal, prisoners. Therefore, to cope with having more offenders for longer periods of time—and the concomitant significant rise in prison populations—corrections officials began to develop adaptive responses. One of the most conspicuous adaptive responses has been the use of good time credits. In some states, the good time credit **discount rate** is as much as one-half of the original sentence imposed (Mays 1989). For instance, in New Mexico prison inmates can earn one day of good time credit for every day they serve, thus the 50% discount. This type of adaptive response illustrates Walker's law of criminal justice thermodynamics.

If some of the current trends continue, we may see a less punitive correctional philosophy come to dominate the beginning of the twenty-first century. Will we return to the "golden age" of rehabilitation? Probably not, but we may see an increasing emphasis on treatment programs of some sort and a greater stress on behavioral changes and offender accountability. Only the passage of the next few years will tell.

Future Correctional Practices

In this section we will address a number of programmatic or institutional practices that present unresolved issues for the near future. These areas may not provide a common theme, but they do represent the kinds of practices with which correctional personnel will be faced into the next century.

Intermediate Sanctions

In the final section of this chapter we will deal with institutional crowding, but at this point we need to recognize that one response to crowding has been the development of intermediate sanctions. As institutional crowding and questions of correctional effectiveness became major issues in the 1980s, intermediate sanctions became very appealing. As we noted in Chapter 8, intermediate sanctions include any type of correctional approach that falls on the continuum between traditional probation and incarceration. The development and rapid expansion of intermediate sanctions came about for several reasons.

One of the chief motivations behind many of the intermediate sanctions programs was institutional crowding. Because there was little or no room available in many prisons and jails, correctional administrators looked for alternatives to incarceration or alternative forms of incarceration. A second reason behind developing intermediate sanctions was the dissatisfaction surrounding traditional probation. For many people, traditional probation was not effective and more punitive programs were called for. The reality of the situation has been that the conditions surrounding probation administration have changed so much in the past two decades that probation was almost destined to fail. More offenders and more serious offenders have been placed on probation, often because of institutional crowding, and probation resources have been stretched to the limit. Probation officers have had so many clients on their caseloads that they could go weeks without ever leaving the office to make client contacts in the field. As a result, probation has been meaningless for many probationers. A third factor promoting intermediate sanctions was operational costs. The presumption behind all of these programs was that anything short of prison or jail time was less costly, and perhaps preferable on that basis alone.

Whatever the motivations for intermediate sanctions, research efforts during the 1990s have shown that most of these programs have not been able to deliver on their promises (Clear 1988; Sechrest 1989; Irwin and Austin 1993; MacKenzie 1997). For instance, programs such as electronically monitored home confinement have been reasonably useful in supervising the location of probationers and parolees in intensive supervision programs. However, as we mentioned, electronic monitoring fails on at least two counts: (1) it monitors location, but it does not monitor behavior and (2) instead of being an alternative to incarceration that would free up additional bed space, most of these programs are used with individuals who would not be incarcerated at all (Clear 1988). If that is the case, house arrest—with or without electronic monitoring—becomes a probation add-on (MacKenzie 1997; Walker 1994).

Intensive supervision for both probationers and parolees has come under close scrutiny also. These programs have been criticized on two bases. First, as some observers have suggested, for anyone who needs intensive supervision, jail or prison provide us with the level of supervision public safety would demand. Second, clients on intensive supervision caseloads have high rates of "failure" simply because increased surveillance is more likely to detect technical violations.

Therefore, the major questions facing us in this area are these:

1. If they can be evaluated properly, will intermediate sanctions programs prove to be effective?

2. In the long run, will these programs turn out to be more cost effective than standard incarceration facilities?

3. Will the public and politicians grow weary of these programs and demand something else either more or less punitive?

4. If the answer to Question 3 is yes, will we completely scrap these programs and reinvent the wheel?

The answers to these questions can give us a good idea about the role intermediate sanctions will play in the future of corrections.

Parole Supervision

Related to the issue of intermediate sanctions is the question of parole supervision. At one point it seemed that the movement toward determinate sentencing and away from indeterminate sentencing had spelled the end of parole. However, before we bury it, two factors must be taken into account. First, some states (for example, New York and Texas) have continued the practice of parole, although with procedural changes. Second, even states that have moved from discretionary parole decision making have **mandatory supervised release** (Ringel, Cowles, and Castellano 1994). Therefore, states are still dealing with offenders—under whatever label we may want to apply—who will receive some type of early, conditional release from prison. The question becomes, then, what do we do with these people?

Parole supervision practices will be impacted in at least two ways. First, parole supervision will be increasingly assessed in terms of accountability as opposed to treatment (Ringel, Cowles, and Castellano 1994). Parole officers will worry less about providing their clients with services, and will concentrate instead on preventing them from reoffending. This may not be true for all parolees, as the second future parole practice illustrates.

A second future parole practice will be the development of **specialized caseloads.** Parole officers will be assigned groups of clients with very specific problems and concerns, for example, sex offenders. (See Box 11.2.) Parole (and probation) officers will be able to develop specialized expertise in dealing with these clients (Clear 1994; English, Pullen and Jones 1996). Special-needs parolees (or probationers) will get not only additional attention but will be likely to receive the highest levels of services as well. Some treatment will be provided by the officers, and some will be provided by community-based treatment facilities.

Boot Camps

Shock incarceration programs, such as boot camps, have become the "hot-button" response of policy makers and correctional administrators alike (MacKenzie 1990, 1997). Early, nonsystematic evaluations suggested that boot camps could be effective, if effectiveness means a reduction in subsequent criminal activity. Programs that include education, social skills training,

Box 11.2

Case-in-Point: The Impact of Sex Offenders on Correctional Philosophies, Practices, Populations and Problems

Sex offenders represent an interesting example that cuts across all four of the concerns addressed in this chapter. Nearly 250,000 correctional clients (that is, prisoners, parolees, and probationers) are sex offenders, a significant number. Between 1980 and 1994, the general prison population grew by 206%, whereas the number of sex offenders grew by 330%. Sex offenders are clearly a large and growing segment of the correctional population.

In the mid-1990s a new strategy developed, based on the preventive detention philosophy. The image of convicted pedophiles at large in the community so traumatized the nation in the early 1990s that **sex-offender notification laws** passed in state after state. In their wake, sex offenders were required to notify the police that they had moved into a particular neighborhood and, in some jurisdictions, the police notified local residents.

An extension of these preventive measures is the **civil detention of sex offenders.** This tactic, ruled constitutional by the Supreme Court in 1997, allows states to transfer convicted sex offenders to hospitals for the criminally insane after they have served their sentences if they are judged to be likely to commit another sexual offense. Civil libertarians argue that such practices amount to punishment for crimes not yet committed. Writing for the majority, Justice Clarence Thomas observed that these people clearly are different from other members of the community and, to protect society, can be further incarcerated as mental patients with periodic review of their status.

The presence of sex offenders, both in the free community and those institutionalized, impacts correctional practice. As discussed in Chapter 6, the volume of sex offenders in the nation's prison system has required many states to create separate facilities for their incarceration or special units within larger correctional facilities.

Managing these populations under community supervision also poses unique problems, sometimes requiring new approaches. For example, English and her associates suggest a **containment model** for managing sex offenders in the community. This approach, heavily dependent upon agency coordination, multidisciplinary partnerships, and specialized personnel, seeks to hold sex offenders accountable through internal personal and external criminal justice control measures. Client monitoring by skilled professionals and even surveillance by officers are essential parts of this approach; moreover, sex offenders in the community must submit to periodic polygraph testing to gauge internal control compliance. A "bad" polygraph may not be considered a violation by the offender, but it will cause increased surveillance, heightened supervision and a reassessment of the treatment program.

Legal challenges of these approaches may constitute a key future correctional problem associated with the treatment of sex offenders. For example, the Supreme Court has placed a great deal of faith in the correctional system to monitor the status of civil commitments. However, it is not unusual for jail inmates to be held beyond their release dates and sue the jail systems. How egregious will the noncompliance by state correctional agencies have to be before the appellate courts order the release of a civilly committed pedophile? Also, what happens when a sex offender is able to "beat" the lie detector and remain free in the community after violating the conditions of probation or parole? Can we place too much faith in technology? Can the victims of such offenders sue the state for failing to protect them against sexual predators? Once again, only time will tell. What do you think?

Sources: English, Pullen, and Jones (1996); Greenfield (1997, 17).

substance abuse counseling, and some mechanism for aiding the transition back into the community do appear to make a difference. The model employed by New York State is one that particularly seems worth copying (New York Department of Correctional Services, Division of Parole 1995; New York Department of Correctional Services 1992, 1993). By contrast, boot camps that simply emphasize military drill and discipline and physical training do not seem to influence recidivism rates. In fact, in the 1990s, numerous researchers reported that recidivism rates for boot camp participants, probationers, and those individuals who have done traditional prison time are virtually identical (Flowers, Carr, and Ruback 1991; MacKenzie and Shaw 1993; MacKenzie, Shaw, and Gowdy 1993; Wright 1996).

Three reasons have been offered in support of boot camps:

1. Inmates are incarcerated for less time; thus, there are cost savings.
2. Inmates may improve self-esteem, although the value of this in-and-of itself is questionable.
3. These programs are politically popular.

Boot camps have major hidden costs. If the participants truly were prison bound, and they were diverted to a boot camp program, their shorter sentence would be less costly. In reality, some boot camp participants have not been prison bound. As a result, total correctional programming costs actually increase. Furthermore, most boot camp programs have lower inmate-to-staff ratios than prisons, so they are relatively more expensive to run than a prison would be.

New Kinds of Institutions and Architecture

Although institutional corrections has evolved slowly over the past century, new types of facilities have come on the scene periodically. Throughout our history, facilities such as houses of refuge, penitentiaries, reformatories, and juvenile detention centers have been touted as institutional innovations. Three such facilities emerged during the last half of the 1990s. The first is the state-run jail. For some time six states (Alaska, Connecticut, Delaware, Hawaii, Rhode Island, and Vermont) have operated combined jail and prison systems (Thompson and Mays 1988b). A quick look at this list indicates that geography has a great deal to do with these combined systems. However, in recent years the Texas legislature passed a bill allowing for the creation of state-run jails. These jails are designed to hold inmates sentenced but not ready for transportation to one of the state's prisons. They also can hold prisoners for counties with jail crowding problems. In effect, these "new" jails are designed largely to hold overflow populations.

A second type of "new" institution is the correctional facility designed to hold youthful offenders. These inmates may be older teenagers, or they may

Los Angeles County built a futuristic looking, high-tech jail known as the "Twin Towers." Unfortunately, there is a lack of funding to open the facility.

be young adults in their early 20s. They may have been convicted of serious juvenile offenses, or they may be serving adult time. Some states have had such facilities for decades. Other states are having to play catchup, especially because of the number of juvenile offenders now being tried as adults. Youthful offender facilities typically house young criminals convicted of serious crimes. The chief advantage is that they will not prey upon other youths convicted of less serious offenses or be preyed upon by the older adult offenders.

In addition to different "types" of facilities, we are likely to see more interest in the architectural design of the facilities that are built. Three factors are of concern: cost, safety for inmates and staff, and an environment conducive to treatment. For all three of these factors we see some promising solutions. As we have noted, some states have experimented with innovative construction techniques that can increase the speed with which we can build, while decreasing the costs. Additionally, inmate management techniques such as the direct supervision approach being utilized in jails and prisons across the nation are likely to make these institutions safer while at the same time reducing the "pains of imprisonment."

Prison (and Jail) Industries

Within the world of institutional corrections, industries programs will increasingly be a focus of attention and resources (Dwyer and McNally 1994; Lammay 1996). There are numerous reasons for this developing trend (Gray and Meyer 1996). For example, inmate idleness is one of the greatest concerns for correctional administrators nationwide. Industries programs help provide a productive way for inmates to spend their time. Prisons have pioneered this effort, but jails will begin to examine such programs as well, especially for inmates who are serving misdemeanor sentences of three months or more.

Another reason for promoting industries programs is the development of job skills and a work ethic among the inmates. We have relatively good evidence that one of the best ways to assure reintegration and to forestall recidivism is to provide strong employment prospects.

Finally, with corrections agencies more and more strapped for funding, industries programs provide one way to offset some operational costs. Today the general public and politicians alike want to hear that inmates are helping pay their own way, and that they are not simply another weight on overburdened taxpayers.

Banishment

In corrections, everything old is new again. If you do not believe this, look at the move to reinstitute chain gangs in Alabama and Arizona. Periodically, legislative or administrative bodies put a new face on an abandoned practice. A likely candidate is **banishment,** a correctional practice that ended when the French quit sending prisoners to Devil's Island in the 1940s. However, the time may be rapidly approaching when banishment could be practiced again. Banishment would be politically popular, and palatable to the public as well. The two questions that would have to be resolved are (1) Where would we banish offenders to? and (2) How much would it cost?

The "where" question raises a number of interesting prospects. For instance, there are still many sufficiently remote places around the United States that could serve as penal colonies. There are large tracts of land owned by the federal government in some of the less populous Western states, and they might provide sites for banishment still within the limits of the continental United States. Imagine, for example, Federal Penal Colony-Arizona or Federal Penal Colony-Utah. Before you reject this idea as pure speculation, recall that the Federal Bureau of Prisons has a huge correctional complex near Florence, Colorado, that includes the entire range of prisoner classifications. Is this Federal Penal Colony-Colorado?

Locating penal colonies within the U.S. borders does not really seem that creative. What about penal colonies in outer space? One of the occasional story lines on the original *Star Trek* television show—and in several science fiction movies—involved sentences to **prison planets.** Is it possible? Is it practical? It is probably neither possible nor practical, at least for the foreseeable future, and the same could be said for penal colonies located under our planet's oceans. Nevertheless, though such discussion today seems extremely speculative, at some point serious discussions may occur about using physical locations never considered before to house convicted criminals.

The problem with most of these localities is infrastructure or support systems. Because these sites are remote and unpopulated, they have no roads, utilities, or places for staff members to live, except on the prison compound itself. Remote locations currently would be costly to support in terms of supplies and personnel. Staff would be prisoners of such facilities even more than they are today. In effect, the keepers would have more in common with the kept than the rest of society. If these barriers could be overcome, banishment might become a more realistic correctional option in the not-too-distant future. One could argue that with "three strikes and you're out" laws (or "two strikes and you're out" for sex offenders), along with existing habitual offender laws, our system of punishments already practices banishment—life in prison without the hope of parole. After all, the idea behind banishment is that the convicted criminal is not permitted to rejoin the community he or she offended. Where these people live from sentencing to death is what will be negotiated in the future.

Technological Applications

Beginning with correctional programs such as electronic monitoring, we have caught a glimpse of what technology might hold for the future of corrections. And, although this section clearly is the most speculative of any in the book, most of the technology mentioned already exists, or the capacity exists to create or implement such innovations. A few brief illustrations should be enough to spark your imagination about what the future may hold for us. However, before going further, it is important to note that technological applications can be considered in two distinct categories: *mechanical* technologies (such as electronic monitoring) and *biological* technologies (eugenics, or genetic engineering).

As discussed previously, most current forms of electronic monitoring employ **passive electronic monitoring devices.** Monitoring is done in one place (normally the offender's home) on a periodic basis by a computer-based dial up system. The systems in place today around the country can tell the computer operator or surveillance officer if the offender is at home or not. However, if the offender is not at home or the electronic receiver is not sending the appropriate response signal, the offender's location is not known. To take this technology to the next level, **active monitoring devices** could track offenders continuously throughout the day. Wherever they might go, their locations could be pinpointed in fractions of seconds. This would allow the person monitoring the offenders to follow them much like air traffic controllers track airplanes, and to send a surveillance officer to check on the offender if a prohibited location (or activity) is suspected.

An extension of house arrest potentially could be based on the concept of **invisible fences** used to keep dogs in their own yards. With the invisible fence, an electronic collar is placed on the dog (or offender, in this case) and an electric wire is buried around the perimeter within which we wish to contain the subject. When the pet tries to cross the invisible boundary, the collar first vibrates then shocks the animal to warn that the boundary is about to be crossed. While these approaches with human beings would have to be made tamper proof, and although it does not sound terribly humane, it could be applied. Furthermore, when considering the alternative of incarceration in a secure facility, maybe it is *more* humane.

The science fiction concept of the force field is an extension of the invisible fence. In many science fiction television shows and movies, individuals are restrained by an invisible shield surrounding their living quarters. With a force field, inmates could be held without using steel doors in jails and prisons, and house arrest really could be enforced. Electronic monitoring would be unnecessary, because the offender would not have any way to leave the premises without the lowering of the "force field." Of course, in the absence of physical barriers or restraints, such a system would have to be free from electrical brown-outs or black-outs. If the current dies, so does the containment system. Such a force field exists today in the **acoustic fence** (Pasternak 1997, 41). Unlike the electronic "pet fence," the acoustic fence does not require a device be worn by the prisoner. An array of high frequency sounds surround the protected area. As one approaches the "sonic speakers," the discomfort level increases, internal organs resonate, the inner ear vibrates causing nausea, and even death can ensue.

While we are on the subject of electronics to track or contain offenders, what about other possibilities of offender control through electronic means? For instance, we could take the concept of acupuncture and apply it electronically. If certain nerves control corresponding body functions and responses, then perhaps we might utilize **electronic brain implants** to control certain types of thoughts or behaviors. Does this sound too far-fetched? Do not be so sure! All we need for this approach to work—besides the technology—is to learn which centers in the brain correspond to what forms of behavior, a task currently underway as part of the National Institute of Mental Health's Human Brain Project (Winfree and Abadinsky 1996, 331). However, such a crime control strategy removes any shred of free will from consideration. For example, the anti-hero in Anthony Burgess's *A Clockwork Orange* refrains from violent sexual acts not because he understands that they are bad but because his body has been conditioned to respond negatively to the mere thought of such behavior.

The arena of **eugenics,** or genetic engineering, is a fascinating and rapidly expanding field of research and practice (Fishbein 1990). If we find that certain criminogenic factors are biological (and a great debate is raging over this issue) we might be able to genetically re-engineer people so that these factors are removed or controlled. The specter of scientists doing genetic experiments on people causes much concern for very legitimate reasons. Both the Germans and the Japanese conducted biological experiments on human subjects during World War II. The latter used them as human guinea pigs for biological and chemical weapons; the former extended the use of human subjects to attempts at perfecting a superior biological being.

Even if we could effect the changes sought by the Nazis and whispered about by some academics today, should we do it? To really see where this could take us, pick up a copy of Aldous Huxley's *Brave New World*. More than 50 years ago Huxley explored the concept of test tube babies in a society where an individual's fate was determined chemically and genetically at the point of conception. Having said all of this, however, we must acknowledge that while our research into DNA, the blueprint for human beings, is proceeding at a bewildering pace, our ability to effect changes—particularly behavioral changes—in individuals may be a long way off (Nelkin and Lindee 1995).

Although genetic engineering seems to be the most unlikely response to crime that we have proposed, think about the following two factors. First, very frequently scientists and medical researchers demonstrate to us that our technological capacities often outrace our ethics. Second, if society became sufficiently chaotic, to the point of anarchy, what price would people be willing to pay for peace and safety? Now, after considering these two factors, do the notions presented above seem so outrageous?

The Future of the Death Penalty

For most of the general public, and for many of the criminal justice system's personnel, the death penalty is a settled issue. The U.S. Supreme Court in the case of *Gregg v. Georgia* (1976) upheld the death penalty's constitutionality, and a number of states (with Texas in the lead) have gone forward with executions. Recent Supreme Court cases could be characterized as "fine tuning," but there seems little chance that the death penalty will be eliminated in the foreseeable future. Nevertheless, there are at least five issues facing the corrections subsystem, as its employees carry out executions.

First, will the death penalty continue to be employed at the current rate? Further, is there any likelihood that the pace of executions will quicken? It seems that we can provide the answers to these questions based on at least two factors. In the first instance, since the death penalty was reinstituted in 1976, we have averaged between 10 and 20 executions per year (Department of Justice 1994a, 1996). During the 1990s, the numbers stabilized to about 35 per year, and given current conditions it does not seem likely that the pace will increase. However, it is critical to note that as of midyear 1997 the State of Texas had surpassed its record for having the most executions in one year (in the twentieth century).

Second, there has been much talk about eliminating some of the "excessive" appeals employed by death row inmates. If this does indeed happen, we may be faced with the prospect of much shorter time frames from conviction to execution in this country. This could mean that the net gains we currently are experiencing in our death row populations will slow down as the pace of executions nears the number of newly convicted death row inmates. Discontent over lengthy execution delays has resulted in federal legislation to limit the appeals by death row inmates. The Anti-Terrorism and Effective Death Penalty Act passed by Congress is one such piece of legislation.

The second capital punishment issue facing us is the method of execution. As we discussed in Chapter 3, states employ a variety of methods for executing inmates, including electrocution, firing squads, hanging, and the gas chamber. However, with states such as Texas leading the way, the use of lethal injection as an execution method seems to have gained acceptance from the public, corrections officials, and the courts. Until a more "humane" way is devised, lethal injection will most likely be the preferred method of execution for some time to come.

A third unresolved dilemma in the area of capital punishment involves the intrusion of the private sector into corrections. Will private corrections corporations find themselves confronting the possibility of having to carry out an execution? Legally, is it possible for a private corporation to serve as the state's executioner? The answer in all likelihood is yes (Chaires and Lentz 1996; Mays 1996). In the past, the U.S. Supreme Court and other appellate courts have looked at the functions being performed and not at whether the actor was public or private to determine the applicable legal standards. More than likely, private corporations will not rush to become executioners, but unless specifically prohibited by state law (or by some provision of their contracts) they could do so if the need arose.

The fourth unresolved issue in the realm of the death penalty relates to the concern addressed in the previous section: juvenile offenders. Under current laws and court opinions, juveniles tried as adults can be executed for crimes that were committed when they were 16 or 17 years old. To date, we have not had a great controversy over these executions because of the lengthy appeals process. As things now stand, a 16-year-old murderer probably would be in his or her mid-20s before an execution would take place. Under these circumstances, the public does not seem terribly outraged. If the appeals process is substantially limited, however, and teenagers face execution in this country, the public mood may change. This issue awaits further resolution.

The fifth and final question relating to capital punishment is straightforward: does the death penalty have any impact on the crime rate? Unfortunately, the answer is not so simple. Several considerations are worthy of mention, however. For one thing, it is important to remember that relatively few crimes committed in this country are eligible for the death penalty. In most states only first-degree murder, including several variations on that offense, qualifies as a capital crime. Thus, by definition the death penalty cannot have much of an effect on the overall U.S. crime rate.

What about the effect of the death penalty on the murder rate? Does the death penalty deter killers? The answer to these questions is that we simply do not know for certain (Walker 1994). The death penalty *might* be a deterrent, but we do not have a record of the murders that did not occur. However, if executions did lower the murder rate, we would expect Texas to have the nation's lowest per-capita murder rate. To date there is little evidence that the number of executions carried out by Texas has had an appreciable effect on the number of murders there.

Finally, it is important to remember that all convictions for first-degree murder do not result in capital sentences, even in the death-penalty states. And because each year between 200 and 300 inmates enter death row nationwide, but between 30 and 40 inmates are executed each year it may be that for most murderers execution seems a remote possibility. Although this may not eliminate the death penalty's deterrent effect, it certainly may diminish it.

Future Correctional Populations

Inmates of the next century's prisons and jails will most likely face all of the problems found in the correctional institutions of the past 200 years and then some. Several key characteristics of inmates, including race, gender, and age, will raise many issues in correctional practices. In addition, the crowded conditions found in many of the nation's prisons and jails have made infectious diseases nearly inescapable. Although these aspects of future correctional populations are not the only ones that will challenge those charged with correcting criminals in the twenty-first century, they cut across all critical demographic dimensions. In order to appreciate this fact, review the figures for the nation's prison guard force—those charged with maintaining order in an increasingly minority community—contained in Table 11.1, and then consider the next four subsections.

Race and Prisoners

In the 1950s and before, the racial composition of the nation's prisons was less skewed toward racial minorities. Before the 1960s, actual racial segregation in the South and de facto segregation in the rest of the nation's prisons kept prisoners of different races physically apart. In 1923, the first year for which such statistics exist, Blacks accounted for 31% of the nation's prison population, but only 10% of the national population. During the mid-1990s, Hispanics accounted for about 10% of the national population, and Blacks constituted about 12%. In 1993, the Black prison population stood at 51%, with Hispanics adding another 16% (Beck and Gilliard 1997). Blacks accounted for 41% of the 1996 jail population; another 15% were Hispanic (Gilliard and Beck 1997). Among Black males, the lifetime likelihood of going to a state or federal prison is greater than one in four (Bonczar and Beck 1997, 1). This rate is twice that for non-Black Hispanics and six times that for White males. What's wrong with the vision of U.S. society revealed by these statistics?

Criminologists provide more than one answer for the disturbing racial imbalance in incarceration rates. For example, one group of criminologists suggests that much of the fault lies with the decay of inner cities in the United States. In the nation as a whole, one Black male in four between the ages of 20 and 29 is under the control of the nation's prison system (Clear 1994, 174). In some U.S. cities, however, correctional authorities manage the lives of more than one-half of all young Black males (Miller 1992). In New York State the situation is even worse: three-fourths of the prison inmates come from seven Black and Hispanic neighborhoods in New York City (Clines 1992). What these high crime metropolitan centers share in common, note some criminologists, is an inner city that is best—and perhaps charitably—described as socially disorganized (Bursik 1986; Sampson and Groves 1989). According to the **social disorganization theory,** the inner cities' increased levels of physical deterioration and lack of a cohesive community find expression in high crime rates (Esbensen and Huizinga 1990; Sampson and Groves 1989). An important distinction contained in this theory is that the race or ethnicity of the neighborhood's inhabitants is unimportant: High crime areas exist, but not high crime groups.

Still others believe that inner-city violence is part of a **subculture of violence.** In the 1950s Marvin Wolfgang observed that most criminal homicides occurred among the members of certain social groups. He speculated that for these people, certain types of derogatory remarks or even gestures take on great social significance (Wolfgang 1958, 189). Later, Wolfgang and Franco Ferracuti (1967) suggested that those who committed much of the unpremeditated homicide in Philadelphia were psychologically normal but belonged to a subculture of violence based on conduct norms that valued pride, self-respect, and status more highly than human life. Most adherents to these subcultural tenets were young African-American males.

Rather than look to biology, ecology, or psychology for their explanations, some criminologists offer less scientific explanations. They contend that minority group members cannot simply make full use of the resources provided by the system for their defense. Other critics believe that these individuals have inferior personal resources compared with nonminorities (Mann 1993; Nelson 1991; Wilbanks 1987). From this perspective, the culprit is **institutionalized racism,** supported by educational and social support systems that perpetuate minority group membership in the underclass. Still others suggest that the high levels of discretion found in the criminal justice system create a climate in which significant racial biases can flourish. For example, a recent

Table 11.1

The Nation's Prison Guards: Race and Gender Breakdowns

Jurisdiction	Number of correctional officers				
		Sex		Race	
	Total	Male	Female	White	Nonwhite
Total	**213,370**	**174,206**	**38,345**	**145,149**	**64,865**
Alabama	2,519	1,956	563	995	1,524
Alaska	765	NA	NA	NA	NA
Arizona	4,597	3,692	905	3,268	1,329
Arkansas	1,815	1,429	385	914	901
California	18,587	15,121	3,466	10,228	8,359
Colorado	1,923	1,557	366	1,413	510
Connecticut	4,379	3,712	667	2,799	1,580
Delaware	910	785	125	533	377
District of Columbia	2,537	1,788	749	NA	NA
Florida	13,907	10,498	3,409	9,811	4,096
Georgia	8,233	6,553	1,680	4,277	3,956
Hawaii[a]	889	779	110	165	724
Idaho	511	430	81	468	43
Illinois	7,490	6,551	939	6,357	1,133
Indiana[b]	3,709	2,860	795	2,864	791
Iowa	1,220	1,042	178	1,150	70
Kansas	1,782	1,510	272	1,577	205
Kentucky	1,736	1,450	286	1,623	113
Louisiana[c]	4,199	3,274	925	2,376	1,823
Maine	854	589	65	641	13
Maryland	4,528	3,481	1,047	2,311	2,217
Massachusetts	3,321	2,971	350	2,934	387
Michigan	9,658	7,657	2,001	7,709	1,949
Minnesota	1,534	1,158	376	1,398	136
Mississippi	1,921	1,129	792	347	1,574
Missouri	3,029	2,560	469	2,855	174
Montana	303	291	12	271	32
Nebraska	605	499	106	534	71

sentencing study found that African-Americans were twice as likely as Whites to receive habitual offender sentences even after controlling for the offender's offense and prior criminal record (Irwin and Austin 1993, 54). Sentences for possession of or dealing in crack cocaine, a drug of choice among Black youths, are typically much longer than for drug crimes involving the powder variety of cocaine (Inciardi 1992), more commonly used by Whites. The result is often far longer prison sentences for Black drug offenders than for Whites (Snyder 1990).

Whatever the source, this process of racial concentration in U.S. prisons and jails has many consequences, none of which are pleasant. Two consequences are particularly important to any study of punishments in the United States. The first concern, erosion of laws as a moral force, reaches far beyond the prison system into the fabric of society. Todd Clear (1995, 174, 175) states the issue in plain terms:

Table 11.1 (continued)

The Nation's Prison Guards: Race and Gender Breakdowns

| Jurisdiction | Total | Number of correctional officers | | | |
| | | Sex | | Race | |
		Male	Female	White	Nonwhite
Nevada	1,106	928	180	929	179
New Hampshire	493	453	40	485	8
New Jersey	5,470	4,765	705	3,002	2,468
New Mexico	1,185	1,094	91	342	843
New York	20,756	19,226	1,530	17,836	2,920
North Carolina	8,619	7,259	1,360	5,251	3,368
North Dakota	135	120	15	130	5
Ohio	6,926	5,552	1,374	5,415	1,511
Oklahoma	1,826	1,587	239	1,454	372
Oregon	1,095	917	178	941	154
Pennsylvania	5,756	5,278	478	5,151	605
Rhode Island	956	883	73	855	101
South Carolina	3,589	2,554	1,035	1,272	2,317
South Dakota	310	250	60	293	17
Tennessee	3,057	2,424	633	2,416	641
Texas	21,101	15,973	5,128	13,513	7,688
Utah	700	486	214	668	32
Vermont[d]	465	420	45	460	5
Virginia	5,848	4,259	1,589	2,911	2,937
Washington	2,546	2,063	463	2,052	494
West Virginia	650	555	95	628	22
Wisconsin	2,348	1,938	410	2,173	175
Wyoming	238	189	49	195	43
Federal Bureau of Prisons	10,932	9,691	1,241	6,959	3,973

[a] As of Jan. 1, 1994.

[b] Total excludes 53 employees whose race and sex were unknown.

[c] Excludes probation and parole employees; includes employees in secure juvenile residential facilities.

[d] Data for race and sex were estimated.

Source: Camp and Camp (1995, 70, 71).

No moral problem haunts the United States' sense of identity more intractably than race relations. We are a society that has never successfully overcome its history of slaves and slave owners; this is true despite the heroic efforts of citizens of all races and ethnic backgrounds to make social justice a reality. . . . The penal system is a part of the problem, because penal harms are inequitably distributed among our racial and ethnic populations. . . . We have argued that the credibility of the criminal law lies in its ability to serve as the community's moral instrument; we have also argued that problems of race are this culture's main moral failing. It follows that the penal system cannot serve its moral function when it intensifies this country's moral failing.

The "race question" also has important implications for the daily operation of the nation's prisons and jails. As U.S. prisons desegregated in the 1960s and became increasingly "majority-minority" institutions,[1] the base of inmate power shifted. Whites reluctantly shared power with Blacks. Moreover, as reflected in Table 11.1, the ratio of White to non-White guards certainly does not reflect the ratio among inmates. In some prison systems, clashes between the races in prison were violent, including outright riots involving White, Black, and Hispanic inmates (Irwin 1980). Prisons also became far more hostile social environments, since life there became far less predictable. In many ways, prison problems simply reflect the problems of the larger society, especially when it comes to questions of race and ethnicity. As Clear suggests, until the larger society resolves its racial problems, we can expect no improvement in our prisons.

Women in the Correctional System

Incarcerated women present gender-specific problems for correctional authorities. Most have been recognized by appellate courts as legitimate reasons for providing special services and engaging in correctional practices not normally found in facilities for men. Included among these special needs are the following:

- *Medical services needs:* Few jails or prisons have gynecologists or obstetricians on call, let alone on the facility's staff. Few jails have even a general practitioner physician on staff. Nevertheless, a recent survey of female prison inmates reported that 9 in 10 received a gynecological examination sometime after admission. About 6% of all female prison inmates are pregnant upon admission (Snell 1994, 10). Nearly 20% of these women receive no prenatal care. Conditions of specialized medical care for women in jails are far worse (Gray, Mays, and Stohr 1995; Zupan 1991). The female inmate who needs to see a medical specialist or requires a preventive procedure such as a mammogram may have to wait many months for a referral. Besides the problems associated with gynecological and obstetrical needs, women also have higher rates of drug abuse upon entry into the correctional system. Their rates of testing positive for **HIV** are nearly twice that of male inmates (4.2% versus 2.5%).[2] Women prisoners also show a slightly higher incidence of tuberculosis than men (11% versus 10%).[3] Consequently, long- and short-term facilities must address the additional medical needs that set women apart from men.

- *Opposite-sex supervision:* This concern is just as real for men as women. However, the percentage of female jail guards is low. The courts have upheld objections to opposite-sex supervision in areas of "protected privacy" such as toilets and showers. However, many jails simply do not have the female guards to guarantee both supervision (and protection) of inmates and privacy.

- *Exploitation and degradation by guards:* The potential for sexual exploitation of female inmates by guards certainly exists. Women are more vulnerable than men in this regard, as revealed by the differences in their social systems. Women inmates looking for protective, nurturing, affective relationships are typically more susceptible to exploitation. Many correctional officers continue to treat female inmates as "errant children" (Pollock-Byrne 1990, 122), which contributes to the already high frustration levels felt by female inmates (Fox 1984).

- *Problems associated with motherhood:* In jail, a female inmate may find that her minor children cannot visit her. In prison, she may encounter severe restrictions on the number and length of family visitations. A woman who gives birth to a child in prison may lose her child to state authorities or have her parental rights severely restricted. In nearly every case, the child is removed from the mother shortly after birth. A few states operate cottages within the prison compound for either short-term or long-term care of inmate babies or allow the mother to reside temporarily in community-based centers (Chapman 1980).

- *Training, counseling, and rehabilitation program needs:* Since their inception, training and rehabilitation programs at women's prisons have emphasized feminine gender stereotypes. The only widely available programs are those geared to "traditional" feminine occupations, including cosmetology, food preparation and service, sewing, housekeeping, and the like. Real-world job training programs exist in women's prisons, although the few that exist have little variety (American Correctional Association 1990). Few jails offer job-training or vocational education. Nonvocational programs, including drug rehabilitation, general counseling, and the like, even in women-only jails, which should be among the best institutions of this type for women, exhibit significant shortcomings (Gray, Mays, and Stohr 1995).

Throughout the 1980s, the number of women in prison grew. In spite of the fact that their incarceration rate is currently growing faster than men, we suspect that the number of women confined will not achieve numerical parity with men even in the next century (Gilliard and Beck 1997, 3). These trends suggest that worse times for women prisoners and prison administrators may be ahead. Because women inmates are few in number, their needs receive less attention and money. Should their numbers double—from 7% to 14%—over the next 20 years, the resources allocated to women inmates' unique needs will fail to keep pace, if the past is a guide to the future. Women in prison and jails are a bereft group, largely forgotten by the public and policy makers, and even largely ignored by researchers (Fletcher and Moon 1993, 6–7).

The Young and the Restless, the Old and the Infirm

Two parallel trends could spell disaster for correctional populations. The first is the tendency to incarcerate younger, more violent offenders, an offshoot of the "get-tough" movement throughout the nation. Unlike the young offenders described earlier in this chapter, these are chronic-offending, state-raised, streetwise youth. They are unlikely to find themselves sent to special youthful offender units or facilities. Rather, they will be mainstreamed with offenders exhibiting similar criminal records.

The second trend is the "graying" of the nation's prison population, which owes much to changes in sentencing laws, including "three-strikes-and-you're-out" initiatives and federal and state "truth in sentencing" mandates. Three-time losers, sentenced to life in prison and other offenders serving 75% and more of their sentences will grow old in prison.

As the new generation of "state-raised" youths enter prison, they may face an increasingly divisive correctional population, one divided not just along lines of race and ethnicity, but on age lines as well. Young, violent offenders will enter the corrections pipeline, but fewer than in the past will leave the nation's prisons, stacking up those at the "senior-prisoner" end of the age continuum.

These trends have at least two implications for corrections: we will be filling prisons with people who know no life other than juvenile and adult correctional facilities and we will be creating an extremely disaffiliated class of people. Cut off from noncriminal society for extended periods of time and given little hope of altering their lives, these inmates—with their lengthy sentences—are a prison administrator's worst nightmare. Rehabilitation aside, they must be managed in correctional settings for decades not years. They also constitute a threat to older, more vulnerable inmates, the likely targets of opportunity for these violent, young offenders (Vito and Wilson 1985).[4] Prison classification can reduce the contact between these two groups of inmates. However, these strategies have their limits. Consequently, mixing very young and very old populations together has the potential to create a new prison and jail problem that has roots in a problem in the free community: mistreatment of the elderly (Douglas 1995).

The costs of incarcerating an elderly prison population is a second age-related problem. Prison gerontologists report that imprisonment, especially extended periods of repeated incarceration, ages humans at an accelerated rate. The lack of proactive medical care, poor life habits, inadequate nutrition, and the like, translate into lost years. A prisoner who is 50 years of age may have the physiology and medical history of a 70 year old (Adams and Vedder 1961).[5] The mental problems associated with growing old, particularly clinical psychiatric disorders including hypochondria and depression, are believed to be higher in elderly prisoners than in the elderly residing outside of prisons and jails (Goetting 1984; Golden 1984; Lynch 1988). Providing for the medical, dental, and mental needs of elder offenders may be second only to providing care for **AIDS-HIV** sufferers, in terms of per-inmate costs.

We suspect, however, that executive clemency may assert itself as the only discretionary release mechanism for such expensive prisoners—short of new legislation targeting the release of elder, infirm, and low-threat inmates. As

Older and medically disabled inmates increasingly are becoming a part of the nation's prision population. This group of inmates at the Hamilton A & I Prison in Alabama illustrate something of the nature of "special needs" inmates.

penalties become harsher, they are less likely to be employed or applied in full force (according to the law of criminal justice thermodynamics, discussed earlier). A related hypothesis involves restricting discretion, as is often the case for mandatory sentencing. According to the **hydraulic displacement of discretion thesis,** as discretion is suppressed or eliminated at one part of the criminal justice system, it emerges at some other point not covered by legislation or reform (Alschuler 1980; McCoy 1984; Meithe 1987; Winfree et al. 1990a, 1990b). In short, when there is pressure on the corrections system, the pressure causes a leak at the weakest point, the point with greatest discretion. Clearly, the humane release of elder inmates either by statute or executive clemency is such a case.

Infectious Diseases and Crowded Facilities

Besides aging, the crowding found in most U.S. prisons and jails creates situations ripe for the spread of infectious diseases. Two diseases stand out above all others, AIDS and tuberculosis.

All 50 states, the District of Columbia and the Federal Bureau of Prisons have the authority to test inmates for HIV. Most (43) jurisdictions test if there are HIV-related symptoms or at the inmate's request. Another 20 test "high risk" inmates, while 23 test inmates upon involvement in "an incident,"

Table 11.2

Inmates in Custody of State or Federal Authorities and Known to Be Positive for HIV, 1991–94

Jurisdiction	Total known to be HIV positive				HIV/AIDS cases as a percentage of total custody population[a]			
	1991	1992	1993	1994	1991	1992	1993	1994
U.S. total[b]	17,551	20,651	21,538	22,713	2.2%	2.5%	2.4%	2.3%
Federal	630	867	959	964	1.0%	1.2%	1.2%	1.1%
State	16,921	19,784	20,579	21,749	2.3	2.6	2.6	2.5
Northeast	**10,247**	**11,422**	**10,690**	**11,001**	**8.1%**	**8.3%**	**7.4%**	**7.4%**
Connecticut	574	621	886	940	5.4	5.6	6.5	6.6
Maine	1	21	8	8	.1	1.4	.6	.5
Massachusetts	484	322	394	388	5.3	3.2	3.9	3.4
New Hampshire	18	26	17	26	1.2	1.4	.9	1.3
New Jersey	756	1,326	881	770	4.0	5.9	3.7	3.6
New York	8,000	8,645	8,000	8,295	13.8	14.0	12.4	12.4
Pennsylvania	313	338	409	461	1.3	1.4	1.6	1.6
Rhode Island	96	120	89	113	3.5	4.4	3.4	3.8
Vermont	3	3	6	0	.3	.2	.5	0
Midwest	**1,128**	**1,392**	**1,671**	**1,750**	**.7%**	**.9%**	**1.1%**	**1.0%**
Illinois	299	403	591	600	1.0	1.3	1.7	1.6
Indiana	62	—	—	—	.5	—	—	—
Iowa	19	18	11	25	.5	.4	.2	.5
Kansas	13	20	39	20	.2	.3	.7	.3
Michigan	390	454	434	384	1.1	1.2	1.1	.9
Minnesota	14	26	30	35	.4	.7	.7	.8
Missouri	127	164	136	146	.8	1.0	.8	.8
Nebraska	11	26	17	16	.4	1.0	.7	.6
North Dakota	1	1	2	3	.2	.2	.3	.5
Ohio	152	232	355	454	.4	.6	.9	1.1
South Dakota	—	—	—	2	—	—	—	.1
Wisconsin	40	48	56	65	.5	.6	.6	.6
South	**4,314**	**5,659**	**6,657**	**7,410**	**1.5%**	**2.0%**	**2.1%**	**2.0%**
Alabama	178	183	194	210	1.1	1.1	1.1	1.1
Arkansas	68	70	80	81	.9	.9	1.0	1.0
Delaware	85	104	113	34	2.6	2.6	2.7	.8
District of Columbia	—	—	—	—	—	—	—	—

including an alleged rape, exposure to another individual's blood, and an assault involving someone suspected of being HIV-positive.

As summarized Table 11.2, the percentage of HIV/AIDS cases increased between 1991 and 1994, but the percentage of inmates remained relatively flat at between 2.2% and 2.5%. About 5,000 of the HIV-positive inmates showed signs of AIDS or related infections (Brien and Beck 1996, 3). The states with the largest number of HIV-positive inmates are New York, Florida, Texas, and California, which together account for about 6 in 10 HIV-positive inmates. Only about 1% of federal prisoners tested positive for HIV. By 1994, AIDS was the second most frequent cause of death for prison inmates, after other illnesses and natural causes; it accounted for over one-third of all inmate deaths in 1994 (Brien and Beck 1996, 1).

Table 11.2 (continued)

Inmates in Custody of State or Federal Authorities and Known to Be Positive for HIV, 1991–94

| Jurisdiction | Total known to be HIV positive | | | | HIV/AIDS cases as a percentage of total custody population[a] | | | |
	1991	1992	1993	1994	1991	1992	1993	1994
Florida	1,105	1,616	1,780	1,986	2.4	3.3	3.4	3.5
Georgia	807	733	745	854	3.4	2.9	2.7	2.6
Kentucky	27	35	42	44	.3	.4	.5	.5
Louisiana	100	425	262	285	.7	2.6	1.6	1.2
Maryland	478	666	769	774	2.5	3.4	3.8	3.7
Mississippi	106	—	115	119	1.3	—	1.4	1.2
North Carolina	170	364	485	521	.9	1.8	2.2	2.2
Oklahoma	74	94	102	102	.7	.8	.8	.8
South Carolina	316	350	452	434	2.0	2.1	2.7	2.5
Tennessee	28	53	88	89	.3	.5	.8	.7
Texas	615	846	1,212	1,584	1.2	1.4	1.7	1.6
Virginia	152	112	207	285	.9	.7	1.1	1.4
West Virginia	5	8	8	8	.3	.5	.4	.4
West	**1,232**	**1,311**	**1,561**	**1,588**	**.8%**	**.8%**	**.8%**	**.8%**
Alaska	9	13	—	—	.4	.5	—	—
Arizona	84	78	89	143	.5	.5	.5	.7
California	786	899	1,048	1,055	.8	.8	.9	.8
Colorado	82	52	74	79	1.0	.6	.8	.9
Hawaii	19	24	21	14	.8	.9	.7	.5
Idaho	10	20	26	20	.5	.9	1.0	.8
Montana	7	4	5	7	.5	.3	.3	.4
Nevada	117	106	163	118	2.0	1.8	2.6	1.7
New Mexico	10	5	11	19	.3	.2	.3	.5
Oregon	24	21	29	24	.4	.3	.4	.3
Utah	35	30	26	48	1.3	1.0	.9	1.5
Washington	42	54	63	65	.5	.5	.6	.5
Wyoming	7	6	6	6	.6	.6	.5	.6

[a] The custody population includes only those inmates housed in a jurisdiction's facilities.
[b] Totals exclude those inmates in jurisdictions that did not report data on HIV/AIDS.

[c] Reported only confirmed AIDS cases in 1994.
Source: Brien and Beck (1996).

We lack an accurate picture of the AIDS-testing policies of the nation's 3,000-plus jails. Among the nation's 50 largest jail jurisdictions, the practices concerning HIV testing varied greatly: 42 tested if an inmate asked. Another 36 tested inmates if staff observed clinical indications of the disease. Finally, another 21 tested if an inmate was involved in an incident with another inmate or staff member that involved possible contact with bodily fluids. We do know that in 1993, only about 2% of the nation's jail inmates tested positive. However, in the nation's 50 largest jail jurisdictions, the proportion of infected inmates was 50% higher. In jail systems with fewer than 250 inmates, the rate was one-half the national average. Fewer than 100 inmates died of AIDS or AIDS-related infections while in custody, a number no doubt largely due to the greater number of options to release infected inmates jails have than do prisons.

Tuberculosis (TB) is potentially a greater threat to U.S. prisons and jails than HIV/AIDS for four important reasons.[6] First, TB can become airborne, spread by tiny water droplets from infected patients. Most older prisons and jails have inadequate ventilation systems. They often recycle the same air continuously throughout the facility. This practice increases the ability of the TB bacterium (*Mycobacterium tuberculosis*) to spread throughout the facility. Second, TB-infected individuals may, like HIV-positive inmates, remain symptom-free for long periods. Third, over the past decade disease epidemiologists have recorded the appearance of a multidrug-resistant form of tuberculosis (**MDR-TB**), one that does not respond to traditional treatment strategies. Finally, those who are dually infected with HIV and MDR-TB have twice the risk of developing active TB as those who test positive for TB alone.

Tuberculosis in prison and jail settings poses a risk to more than the health of inmates. These facilities provide hosts for MDR-TB, which could be spread throughout the population and can certainly affect correctional staff. Also, treatment of HIV-positive and active AIDS inmates increases correctional costs exponentially. For example, in 1992–93 New York State spent approximately $4 million on drug treatment for 1,900 HIV-positive inmates (Hammett et al. 1994, 69). Jail and prison administrators of the future will have to become increasingly sensitive in their training, policies, and practices to the nonviolent, disease-related threats posed by inmates to staff and other inmates.

Whether the issue is age, disease, or other infirmities, inmates with disabilities are covered under the **Americans with Disabilities Act (ADA).** (See Box 11.3.) Criminal justice agencies are not exempt from this 1990 federal legislation (Rubin 1993; Rubin and McCampbell 1994). Although the law may be clear on this issue, the exact nature and extent of the problem for corrections remains somewhat elusive. Those with mental and physical disabilities constitute about 5% of the prison population and 10% to 15% of the jail population (Hodgins 1993; Rubin and McCampbell 1995).[7] The simple truth is that we have no substantive information about mental illness in correctional institutions, and until legal claims under the ADA enter the judicial system, the nation's correctional agencies, prisons, jails, community corrections, and so forth, are unlikely to be proactive.

Correcting Juvenile Offenders

Another issue of some concern and persistence is the future of juvenile offenders in the corrections system. If the rehabilitative philosophy is alive and well anywhere today, it is in juvenile corrections. But even with juveniles, the opinion of the public and policymakers seems to be "if you're old enough to do the crime, you're old enough to do the time." This frequently quoted

---

Box 11.3

What is ADA?

On July 26, 1990, Congress passed the Americans with Disabilities Act, considered the most sweeping piece of civil rights legislation since the Civil Rights Act of 1964. The law contains several key provisions, including the following:

- It requires that employers provide access to employment and makes discrimination based upon disabilities illegal.
- It requires that employers provide reasonable accommodation to persons with disabilities, meaning that public entities could be required to modify existing facilities to make them accessible, restructure jobs, establish part-time or modified work schedules, acquire or modify equipment, and change policies, as long as these alterations do not provide an undue hardship.
- It requires that government entities deliver services to disabled persons and ensure that its facilities are accessible to persons with disabilities.

All three of these provisions are potentially troublesome for corrections, particularly in the delivery of services to clients and in the hiring of employees.

Who is disabled? The ADA defines a disabled person as someone who

- Has a physical or mental impairment.
- Has a record of such an impairment.
- Is regarded as having an impairment.

As a rule, the person claiming protection under ADA must provide documentation. Most public agencies in the late 1990s have ADA compliance officers who monitor complaints and establish a grievance procedure.

Source: Rubin (1993).

---

phrase is indicative of the get-tough mood toward juvenile offenders. However, though we will continue to wrangle with the issue of correctional philosophy for some time to come, practical problems of an immediate nature remain unresolved.

The detention of accused offenders in adult jails is a major problem for juvenile corrections and has been since the passage of the Juvenile Justice and Delinquency Prevention Act of 1974 (Schwartz 1989). For instance, in order to lawfully detain a juvenile in a jail he or she must be separated by sight and sound from adult inmates. This arrangement is especially difficult in some of the small, rural counties where juveniles are housed in adult jails (Kimme et al. 1986). When a local detention facility only has cell space for 10 to 20 detainees at a time, there may be very little flexibility in separating males from females, adults from juveniles, and pretrial detainees from those serving sentences.

Among the other problems associated with housing juveniles in adult jails, two are especially troubling for jail managers. First, in order to provide sight and sound separation from adults, some juveniles will have to be housed in remote parts of the jail, which can result in a lack of direct visual contact with detainees and an increased suicide potential. Second, though juvenile detainees may be physically separated from most inmates, they may still come in contact with jail staff members and trustees. Both groups have been known

Table 11.3

Juveniles in Adult Jails, 1983–94

	One-day count	Average daily population		One-day count	Average daily population
1983	1,736	1,760	1989	2,250	1,891
1984	1,482	1,697	1990	2,301	2,140
1985	1,629	1,467	1991	2,350	2,333
1986	1,708	1,404	1992	2,804	2,527
1987	1,781	1,575	1993	4,300	3,400*
1988	1,676	1,451	1994	6,725	—

* Beginning with 1993 the numbers include juveniles tried or awaiting trial as adults.

Source: Snell (1995, 533).

to abuse teenage detainees physically, especially sexually. We must acknowledge that this could happen in separate juvenile detention centers as well, especially with staff members, but the presence of adult inmates compounds this problem.

The number of juveniles housed in adult jails has fluctuated during the last two decades. Beginning with the passage of the Juvenile Justice and Delinquency Prevention Act the numbers of juveniles in adult jails fell from around 3,000 in the mid-1970s to between 1,500 and 1,700 in the 1980s. The numbers stabilized around 1988 because of counties that did not provide for separate detention centers for accused delinquents. In relative terms, though, the decrease in numbers did represent an improvement.

Unfortunately, the most recent bad news is that during the 1990s the numbers have started to increase again, and as Table 11.3 shows for the one-day count in 1994 there were more than 6,000 juveniles in adult jails. However, the largest growth in juvenile detainees is not among those held for delinquent offenses, but for those held to be tried as adults. This means that the housing of juveniles in adult jails presents a mixed picture, at best, and it is likely to continue to be troubling for sheriffs and jail administrators well into the next century.

Another issue that has yet to be resolved is the presence of juveniles who have been tried for and convicted of adult offenses, and who are to be housed in adult prisons. We will explore the issue of new kinds of institutions later in this chapter, but it is very important to note that some states have only adult facilities and juvenile facilities with nothing in between. For those states, juveniles tried as adults typically will be housed in adult prisons. Given the general trend toward a much more punitive orientation for juvenile offenders, there is every likelihood that we will see more youngsters appearing in our adult prison populations. Most prison reform organizations and even many prison wardens find this situation unacceptable. If the current trend of merging the juvenile and adult systems continues through the end of the decade, the ultimate outcome could be the complete elimination of the juvenile court. This would leave us pondering the fate of juvenile corrections as well.

Dealing with Institutional Violence and Inmate Uprisings

It is an unfortunate fact of life that violence is very much a part of prisons and jails in the U.S. Prison and jail experts speculate that the nature of current institutional life creates conditions rife for violence (Irwin and Austin 1993). Whatever its origins, this violence can take several different forms, and we will explore the three most common.

Inmate-on-Inmate Violence. Perhaps the most frequently occurring incidents of institutional violence involve inmate-against-inmate assaults. Several factors may precipitate these occurrences (see Sechrest 1989; Welch 1996a). For instance, a number of states—particularly California and Texas—have had to deal with the presence of gangs in their prison systems (see, for example, Fong 1990; Fong and Vogel 1996). At times inter-gang conflicts result in assaults and even "hits" by one gang against members of a rival gang.

More frequently, inmate assaults result from simple interpersonal conflicts. Disputes arise about lost or stolen property, personal insults or challenges, refusals of sexual advances, and a host of other possible factors. Often these individual conflicts are compounded by the necessity of placing more inmates in housing units than they were designed to hold.

Inmate-on-Staff Violence. Every year inmates will assault and even kill a few correctional staff members. Although such cases are rare, assaults on staff members come about in one of two ways. First, some personnel are injured accidentally while trying to break up inmate fights or other disturbances. Second, and even more troubling, are the injuries and deaths that result from direct inmate-on-staff attacks. Many result from retaliations against staff members who have disciplined an inmate. Sometimes they also happen because a staff member has manipulated or lied to an inmate. Such cases of not "playing straight" are considered great personal insults and inmates may harbor anger and hatred for long periods of time until they see the opportunity to retaliate.

Collective Violence—Prison Riots. The most extreme form of institutional violence is the collective violence of a riot. Over the past decades the United States has experienced a number of notorious riots in both state and federal institutions (Braswell, Montgomery, and Lombardo 1994; Saenz 1986; Useem et al. 1995; Wicker 1975).

Box 11.4

**Strategies for Responding to the Threat
of Prison Riots and Related Disturbances**

Useem and associates say attention to several factors related to staff vigilance and physical control can prevent prisoner uprisings and disturbances. These include the following:

1. *Experienced staff and supervision:* High-security units that house violent or potentially violent inmates must have an experienced complement of correctional officers and supervisors.
2. *Post orders:* The orders "for posts in restricted units should anticipate the possibility" of riots or other inmate disturbances.
3. *Physical plant and equipment:* Prisons need to pay particular attention to reinforced glass, blind spots both inside and outside of the facility, and other structural or security weaknesses.

4. *Escalation of conflict:* Many full-scale riots are preceded by an escalation of inmate-on-inmate or inmate-on-staff conflicts. Line staff and correctional administrators need to pay particular attention to an increase in the number and seriousness of such incidents.
5. *Riots with warning:* Staff members may be advised formally or informally through the institution's rumor channels ("grapevine") that an inmate disturbance is impending. Although not every rumor is grounded in facts, staff members must weigh and assess the likelihood of such events and not discount them without attempting to verify the information.

Source: Useem et al. (1995, 6–7).

Welch (1996a, 329–32) offers six models to explain the causes of prison riots:

1. *Environmental conditions* include institutional food, staff brutality, lack of treatment programs, and the nature of the inmates themselves.

2. *Spontaneity* combines preexisting environmental conditions with some "spark" or spontaneous event that sets off the collective violence.

3. *Conflict* suggests that inmates respond to an environment of official repression through the use of collective violence.

4. *Collective behavior/social control* proposes that correctional institutions maintain a very delicate balance between staff control and inmate cooperation; any failure of formal or informal control mechanisms can precipitate collective violence.

5. *Power vacuum* recognizes that some group, either the inmates or the staff, "runs the joint"; if there is instability resulting from lack of decisiveness or staff turnover, collective violence may result as inmates try to assert their power.

6. *Rising expectations* recognizes that as prisons and jails have gone through periods of reform, inmates have come to expect improvements in confinement conditions; when these conditions are not met or when the fulfillment of promises is delayed (for example, after a "successful" lawsuit), inmates may express their frustration through collective violence.

As with most correctional problems, the best way to deal with violence is to prevent it in the first place. This may not be possible with some types of interpersonal violence, but well-trained and vigilant staff members may be able to prevent or to intercede quickly in many cases. Box 11.4 presents some strategies for coping with the threat of a prison riot.

If recent history is any indicator, as long as we have prisons, and as long as some of these prisons are crowded, we are likely to have inmate disturbances and riots. The challenge for all correctional personnel will be to prevent, contain, and respond effectively to such incidents.

Future Correctional Problems

There is no limit to the number of problems that we could have chosen to address in a representation of the future of corrections. In fact, almost daily the people who are managing the correctional enterprise in the United States recognize that the problems just keep coming. However, we have chosen the following issues because we believe they represent some of the most difficult concerns facing us, and ones that will carry us into the twenty-first century.

Women in the Correctional Workplace

Women have entered the correctional workforce in increasing numbers over the past 10 years. However, this entry has not been without problems. Much like women employed in policing, female correctional employees have been used in exclusively female facilities for much of their employment history. The trend since the 1970s has been to use women as frontline correctional officers as well as in other staff positions in all-male institutions. This entrance into an exclusively male work world has raised two concerns.

First, correctional administrators initially questioned the women's ability to handle the dangerous and stressful part of working in male prisons. The concern seemed to be primarily the women's safety. Second, administrators also recognized the potential for workplace disruption caused by incidents of **sexual harassment** (see, for example, Stohr et al. 1997).

The results of both of these concerns have been somewhat surprising to all of the parties involved. In regard to safety, females serving as officers and other frontline personnel do not seem to be in any greater danger than male staff members. In fact, because of their size and strength relative to most male prisoners, female corrections officers seem to get into fewer confrontations and physical altercations with inmates. Therefore, safety has proved to be a nonissue. Relative to sexual harassment, early findings indicate that sexual harassment does occur, not only from male staff members, but also from inmates. However, the rates that are reported—given the unique environment in which female employees work in corrections—do not seem to be substantially higher than in any other traditionally male-dominated workplace.

For the future, female employees will play a critical role for one reason: the dynamics of the workforce in the U.S. are changing dramatically (Gido 1996). Therefore, if correctional agencies are going to meet their quotas of educated, qualified employees they will have to turn to females with a growing frequency. In the end, we can say that women in the correctional workplace represent a significant part of the future of corrections in the United States.

Legislative Trends

It is important to remember that the corrections agenda in the United States often is set by legislative bodies. We need to be aware of four specific issues. First, legislatures nationwide are continuing to expand the definition of criminality. We are faced with more and more actions that are now defined as crimes. Second, legislatures are continuing to exhibit punitiveness toward juvenile and adult offenders. Not only are we incarcerating more people, on average we are holding them for longer periods of time.

Third, much has been made of the movement toward correctional privatization. In some states leadership in this direction has come from the governor, but in virtually every state the legislature has been a key player in the process. Now that we have more than a decade of experience with privatization, what can we say about the results? As of the mid-1990s less than 3% of the nation's correctional population was housed in a private facility. Therefore, though we will continue to see private correctional facilities, it seems unlikely that these groups will dominate institutional corrections.

Fourth, legislatures are having an impact in the area called "reinventing government." We are seeing calls for agencies to do more with less, and generally to scale back on the size of government in order to save money and to provide only the essential services. This means that correctional agencies may face tighter budgets, including budget and hiring freezes. The extent to which this happens will determine something of the fate of corrections, particularly with swelling inmate populations.

Reform Movements

The next few decades are likely to see additional calls for correctional reform in the United States. Some of the reform initiatives will come from legislatures and executives, as we have indicated. However, there are at least two additional sources of reform. Certainly, one of the ongoing players in correctional reform will be the courts. We have witnessed something of a slow-down in regard to sweeping reforms being ordered for entire correctional systems (as happened in Texas), but we are nowhere near a return to the hands-off period. Judges seem somewhat more restrained in their dealings with correctional agencies, but the notion of prisoners' rights is fairly well established now.

The second major influence on correctional reform will be internal. Professional organizations such as the American Correctional Association and the American Jail Association have developed training materials and seminars as well as standards for jails, prisons, and juvenile detention centers. The movement toward **accreditation** seems to be gaining momentum, and there is increasing professional pressure from peers and professional organizations to operate an accredited facility, which is another way to prevent successful inmate lawsuits.

Controlling Correctional Costs

The corrections philosophy we choose and the populations we are facing inevitably bring us to the issue of controlling correctional costs. Although we cannot address this issue extensively here, a few of the most important numbers can be presented. For example, construction costs are a major factor in prison and jail expansion and renovation. Many of these facilities must be built to high security standards, and it is not unusual to find that each new bed space constructed costs around $50,000. New construction methods may save some in terms of the costs of construction materials and time, but most correctional facilities still entail very large capital outlays.

Although construction costs are astounding because of the large initial investments they involve, over the life span of most correctional facilities 90% of the expenditures will be operational costs. These include personnel salaries and fringe benefits, utility and maintenance expenses, programming costs, and a host of other day-to-day obligations.

When these two budget categories are considered together, we must ask: What, if anything, can be done to contain correctional expenditures? Fortunately, there are a few promising responses.

First, the biggest cost-saving measure is to keep people out of correctional facilities. Therefore, alternatives to incarceration can substantially contain corrections costs, if

- Alternatives to incarceration do not shift "costs" to the public by increasing the amount of crime committed by those diverted into alternative programs.
- Alternatives to incarceration truly are alternatives and not just net expansions that bring more offenders under some form of social control.

Second, construction costs may be reduced by speedier methods, such as the use of standardized or prefabricated materials. Using lower cost commercial grades of construction materials (as opposed to the high-security materials) also will save costs. This already has been demonstrated in many of the podular-design, direct supervision jails (Nelson 1988).

Third, some degree of privatization may result in cost savings (Mays and Gray 1996). This could include financing, construction, programming, or total operations. For most states a public/private partnership mix will provide the most cost-effective solution (Cox and Osterhoff 1991).

Finally, even in those prisons operated exclusively by government agencies, we need to recognize that things can be done better. Most public bureaucracies have never been held to high standards of efficiency, and we may see that change. Furthermore, many state agencies (not just corrections) are saddled with regulations that make them inherently inefficient. Where we can identify these impediments, we should eliminate them.

Dealing with Crowding

The final future problem involves institutional crowding. In fact, it is perhaps *the* future (and current) correctional dilemma. In medicine we talk about two kinds of conditions: acute (severe, immediate and potentially life-threatening) and chronic (long-term or persistent). When we apply these terms to corrections, it becomes apparent that institutional crowding has moved from being an acute to being a chronic problem. Practically every jail and prison system in the United States has been involved in the crowding problem. The Department of Justice (1988, 108) reports that between 1980 and 1985 U.S. prison populations grew by more than 150,000 inmates (52%). The BOP and 34 state prison systems grew by more than 50% during this period, and five states (Alaska, Hawaii, Nevada, New Hampshire, and California) grew by more than 100%. The solution for handling part of the population growth has been to "back up" inmates into local jails (Allinson 1982; Taft 1979). In fact, in 1992 over 18,000 inmates were being held in local jails as a result of prison crowding (Snell 1995, 68).

As indicated previously, part of the problem has been an increase in the number of offenses we have made punishable (what some have called the **crisis of over-criminalization**), and part of the problem has been the result of more punitive legislative policies. Typical of these policies are longer sentences, mandatory sentences, and some form of determinate sentences, including presumptive sentencing and the use of sentencing guidelines.

The end result has been that much of the crowding crisis in which we find ourselves is of legislative making. Legislatures have added to the potential pool of prison inmates, on the one hand, and they have underfunded correctional budgets, on the other. This has left prison and jail administrators, who have inadequate facilities to begin with, trying to house burgeoning inmate populations. The results have been fairly predictable. In some state and federal facilities we have seen inmate uprisings, including full-scale riots (Braswell, Montgomery, and Lombardo 1994). In nearly all states, we have seen significant increases in inmate lawsuits. This latter mechanism has been employed to such an extent that inmate suits account for over 10% of the civil cases on federal court dockets (Dilworth 1995; Hanson and Daley 1995). Although litigation may not be as successful as we might initially imagine, it illustrates one way inmates can utilize symbolic resistance to their conditions of confinement (Mays and Olszta 1989; Thomas 1988).

To deal with the persistent problem of institutional crowding, state and local governments have been engaged in a decade-long period of building and renovation. Sometimes this has come as a result of litigation. At other times, construction has been advocated by corrections officials themselves to replace deteriorating physical plants. However we got into it, we find ourselves in the midst of a corrections building boom in the United States (Coughlin 1996; DeWitt 1986; Lemov 1995). A decade of building has not left us relatively better off in terms of crowding in many jurisdictions. In fact, we have come to realize what many prophets predicted as early as the 1970s: We cannot build ourselves out of a crowding crisis.

Conclusion

As we come to the end of this text, it is important to make a point that we have not dealt with explicitly: although corrections in the United States is something of a loose confederation of agencies, organizations, and institutions, all of these entities are interconnected. This association means that changes in the number and size of prisons, and the number of inmates sentenced to prison, has an impact on jail populations as well. As we have painfully learned during the 1990s, when prisons become crowded inmates back up in local jails that are not equipped to deal with serious, long-term populations. By the same token, incarceration rates and policies affecting those rates have an impact on probation, parole, and community-based programming efforts. If we have learned anything about corrections in the past 20 years, it is that we cannot tinker with one part of the system without throwing the rest of the system out of balance as well.

Two final issues must be noted as we close out this book. First, in any society, no matter how primitive or sophisticated, there will always be people who will violate the law. Second, when violations occur, some attempt will be made to punish or correct those who offend the society's laws or sense of decency and good order. Society will always need, therefore, some mechanism to deal with criminal offenders, a mechanism that we call in contemporary terminology "corrections."

Critical Review Questions

1. After examining the nature of intermediate sanctions, what are the two factors you see as influencing their expansion the most? What two factors might be most likely to limit their expansion?

2. Is parole on its last legs in the United States, or has something caused its revitalization? If you were projecting to the year 2010, where would you say we are going with parole and why?

3. Some people have said that boot camps are an idea whose time never came. Are more states jumping on the boot camp bandwagon? Why or why not?

4. How do you react to the notion of banishment? Is this really "punishment?" Take a map of the U.S. and identify three or four likely areas for a penal colony. Would these be impacted by the NIMBY syndrome?

5. Do you think genetic engineering is a real solution? What about this as a method of crime control or treatment? What ethical issues would this raise?

6. In this chapter, we explored a series of questions about the racial composition of the nation's correctional system. Which argument about the reasons for the racial disparities in prison and jail populations did you find most persuasive? Why were you persuaded? (If you feel that none of the arguments helped you understand this problem, where do you think we should look for answers?)

7. Women in prison must face problems unique to their sex. Assume that you are the assistant director of a state department of corrections. You have been given the assignment of prioritizing the needs of the female inmates under your division of the DOC. Where do you start and why?

8. Which infectious disease, HIV/AIDS or TB, poses the greatest threat to the nation's prisons? Support your selection from the text.

9. Do you sense a quickening of the pace of executions in the U.S.? Watch the daily papers for stories on the death penalty in your own and other states.

10. Think of recent bills in your state through which the legislature has created new categories of crimes and where criminal penalties have been made more severe. Can you list two or three examples?

Recommended Readings

Cromwell, Paul F., and Roger G. Dunham, eds. 1997. *Crime & justice in America: Present realities and future prospects.* Upper Saddle River, NJ: Prentice-Hall. This reader represents some of the best of contemporary thought on the state of affairs and the future of the criminal justice system in the United States. Though it covers the broad spectrum of the criminal justice system, the section on corrections deals with a number of issues that we have covered throughout this book. The final section "Looking Toward the 21st Century" has three readings that are especially intriguing.

Klofas, John, and Stan Stojkovic, eds. 1995. *Crime and justice in the year 2010.* Belmont, CA: Wadsworth. This fun and intriguing book includes 15 creative essays by some of the best-known experts—criminologists, penologists, and others—in criminal justice. The chapters on corrections, authored by David Kalinich, Paul Embert, Lucien X. Lombardo, Todd R. Clear, and Gennaro Vito, are excellent.

Muraskin, Roslyn, and Albert R. Roberts, eds. 1996. *Visions for change: Crime and justice in the twenty-first century.* Upper Saddle River, NJ: Prentice-Hall. This intriguing companion piece to the previous two books, includes five chapters specifically on correctional issues of the future. The authors address the respective futures of sentencing, prisons, jails, and correctional health. Several other chapters, on the death penalty, technology and the criminal justice system, and gender issues, are also worth reviewing. The authors represent an interesting mix of practitioners and academics. In general, this book is a bit more scholarly and less speculative than the one edited by Klofas and Stojkovic.

Roberts, Albert R., ed. 1994. *Critical issues in crime and justice.* Thousand Oaks, CA: Sage. This reader is interesting and useful because each of the 17 entries was prepared especially for this volume and not reprinted from other sources. It provides a broad overview of "critical issues" facing the criminal justice system, but it includes three selections specifically on corrections. These entries detail jail crowding, prison industries, and parole supervision. Therefore, while this book is not focused exclusively on corrections, it can help fill out our understanding of some present and future dilemmas in a number of arenas of criminal justice, including corrections.

Key Terms

accreditation
acoustic fence
active monitoring devices
AIDS
Americans with
    Disabilities Act
    (ADA)
banishment
civil detention of sex
    offenders
constitutional-learning
    theory
containment model
crisis of over-
    criminalization

discount rate
electronic brain implants
electronic monitoring
    devices
eugenics
force field
HIV
hydraulic displacement of
    discretion thesis
institutionalized racism
invisible fences
law of criminal justice
    thermodynamics
mandated supervised
    release

MDR-TB
passive monitoring
    devices
prison planets
sex-offender notification
    laws
sexual harassment
social disorganization
    theory
specialized caseloads
subculture of violence

Notes

1. A "majority-minority" institution is one in which minority group members numerically account for most of the participants.
2. Interestingly, the AIDS-related prison death rate per 100,000 inmates for men is twice that reported for women [98 versus 54] (Brien and Harlow 1995, 7).

Either women are receiving better medical care than men, which is doubtful, or the prison system provides early releases for HIV-positive women who develop AIDS-related complexes, or, owing to their shorter sentences, they are leaving prison before they develop AIDS and die. At any rate, despite their higher incidence of HIV, female inmates are not dying at a rate anywhere near equivalent to that for males in prison.

3. This statistic, although taken from a national sample, should be interpreted with caution as several jurisdictions could not provide gender-based distinctions (Hammett and Harrold 1994, xii). Other sources, however, verify the observation that women have a higher incidence of TB than men (Bershad 1985).

4. Not everyone believes that old inmates are necessarily "victims-in-waiting." Depending upon what age-breaks one employs, older inmates may not be as infirm as previously believed. For example, a study of disciplinary reports for elderly prisoners suggests that they may be old and ornery, but not necessarily old and infirm, as their records are indistinguishable from other inmates (McShane and Williams 1989).

5. Age-breaks are critical. Studies employ at least three or four different breaks, ranging from 40 and above to 60 and above. Using the former break, for example, about 16% of the nation's prisoners were elderly in 1991, though only 1% were 60 or older (Lynch et al. 1994). However, these figures are likely to change in the early part of the next century. Even using these conservative figures, the nation's prisons hold more than 10,000 inmates who are over 59 years of age.

6. Unless otherwise noted, Hammett and Harrold (1994) are the source for the information about tuberculosis in correctional settings.

7. Whereas about 2% of the U.S. population are mentally or developmentally disabled, at least 5% of the prison population falls into this category (Hodgins 1993).

Glossary

Numbers in parentheses indicate the chapter(s) in which the term is primarily discussed.

absconded (7): To depart one's place of residence in a sudden or secretive manner, usually in order to avoid legal proceedings.

access to the courts (10): Inmates have a variety of legal mechanisms they may use in the process of litigation.

accessories (3): Persons who help, aid, or otherwise assist a criminal either before or after a crime is committed, but are not present during the crime.

accreditation (11): The process of reviewing operating procedures and policies against a set of standards published by a professional organization such as the American Correctional Association.

accusatorial system (3): A legal system associated with the administration of criminal justice in which the fact-finding efforts involve a contest between opposing parties: the accused, or the defendant, and the accuser, or plaintiff. See also *adversarial system.*

actuarial risk assessment scale (7): A device used to assist in the determination of the risk posed by an offender, often employed in the decision to grant parole.

actus reus (3): (Latin: guilty act) The legal requirement that, for an act to be considered criminal, the individual must have committed an overt act that created some harm.

adjudicated probation (7): In juvenile justice, when a youth is awarded a conditional release from the court following an actual judicial decision.

administration (9): The act of administering or managing an office, employment, or organization.

administrative segregation (6): A term in correctional jargon that means solitary confinement.

adversarial system (3): In the Anglo-American legal system, for both civil and criminal disputes, two parties must confront each other in a court of law. In civil matter, the initiating party is called the plaintiff; in criminal matters the prosecutor, as the state's representative, initiates the charges; in both proceedings, the responding party is called the defendant. In a bench trial, the judge decides both matters of law and matters of fact (that is, renders a decision); in jury trials, the judge decides matters of law, but the jury is the trier of facts.

affirmative defenses (3): Under the terms of this defense, the accused does not deny the facts. Instead, the defense raises matters, not covered in the plaintiff's complaint, that will defeat the plaintiff's claim even if the plaintiff is able to prove all allegations. For example, the defendant may claim self-defense or defense of another when charged with murder.

aftercare (7): The status or program membership of a juvenile who has been committed to a treatment or confinement facility, conditionally released from the facility, and placed in a supervisory and/or treatment program.

Age of Enlightenment (2): A historical period of the late seventeenth and eighteenth centuries; the writers who best represent this period, also called the Age of Reason, applied reason to politics, religion, morality, and social life and believed that the state was the logical instrument for societal change. Enlightenment philosophers such as Locke and Rousseau laid the intellectual foundations for the American and French revolutions. See also *natural law.*

aggravating circumstances (3, 10): Circumstances relating to the commission of a crime that cause its gravity to be greater than that of the average instance of the given type of offense. For example, a person may have used a firearm in the commission of a robbery or demonstrated extreme callous disregard for human life by driving when severely impaired by alcohol. See also *mitigating circumstances*.

alibi (3): A type of defense in a criminal prosecution that proves the accused could not have committed the crime with which he or she is charged, because the evidence shows the accused was in another place at the time the crime was committed.

allocution (8): A prisoner's answer (which is recorded in the trial proceedings) to the court's query as to whether or not judgment should be pronounced against the prisoner if he or she is convicted. Often used as a condition of a plea bargain in which the accused admits to the *actus reus*.

anomic trap (1): According to Merton, a situation said to exist when people are faced with goals that are unattainable because of the absence of the requisite means, for example, when a person aspires to be a doctor but cannot gain admission to medical school.

anomie (1): (French: normlessness) A term attributed to Durkheim and a succession of sociologists that study crime and deviance. At the societal level: a condition in which the old ways of doing things no longer seem to apply; for example, when suicide, crime, and general misconduct increase among individuals as a result of the nation's defeat in war. At the individual level: a breakdown between the institutionally approved means of achieving goals and the culturally defined success goals; for example, when a person wants a fancy car and a big house but does not want to obtain them by traditional, legal means but by selling drugs.

archon (2): Chief magistrate, or judge, in ancient Greece. In ancient Athens nine chief magistrates, each one chosen from the city's most illustrious families, watched over all civil and religious matters.

arousal theory (1): A theory used in psychopathology. Because the brain functioning of psychopaths is quickly habituated to incoming stimuli they seek maximal sensory stimulation, perhaps through risk taking or criminal activity. People with this type of brain functioning disorder may be immune to traditional behavior-altering therapies.

Ashurst-Sumners Act (5): Legislation passed by Congress in 1935 that restricted the movement across state borders of prison-manufactured goods. See also *Hawes-Cooper Act*.

asset forfeiture (8): The governmental seizure of personal assets obtained from or used in a criminal enterprise; for example, forfeiture of an airplane to the government if the craft was used to facilitate a crime, such as distributing narcotics, or was purchased with proceeds from an illegal enterprise, such as drug trafficking.

atavistic (2): In an organism or in any of its parts: recurrence of a form typical of ancestors more remote than the parents, usually as the result of genetic recombination. In an individual: recurrence of behavior characteristic of an earlier form of the species; a "throwback." The term was popularized by Italian criminologist Cesare Lombroso.

attachment (1): Hirschi's term for the affective (emotional) bonds between a youth and members of various social groups. See also *social bonding*.

attempts (3): An act done with intent to commit a crime and tending to, but falling short of, its commission. All attempts to commit a crime, whether the crime be a felony or a misdemeanor, in common law or by statute, are misdemeanors in common law.

Attica prison riot (6): Four-day revolt in 1971 of 1,200 inmates of the Attica Correctional Facility in New York. Inmates held 38 guards hostage; an assault on the prison staged by more than 1,000 police and state troopers killed one hostage and 28 inmates.

Auburn system (2): Method of imprisonment practiced at the Auburn (New York) prison in the nineteenth century. System characterized by enforced silence at all times and by night confinement in small solitary cells. Inmates allowed to congregate with other prisoners during meals and while at work. See also *silent system*.

authoritarian leader (9): An individual who approaches administration from the top down; they believe in a system in which their orders will be carried out without question or hesitation.

autocrat (9): One who employs an authoritarian management system.

bail (7): The process for securing an individual's release after arrest and booking and prior to adjudication; a guarantee to appear for future court hearings, secured by money or property on deposit with or pledged to the court.

banishment (1): Punishment by exile, typically practiced in pre-legal societies.

Battle of Alcatraz (6): In 1946 several inmates at the nation's most notorious federal prison, Alcatraz, turned an aborted escape attempt into a riot of sorts. A full-scale military assault of "the Rock" returned the prison to government control, but at considerable loss of life.

behavior modification (1): A psychological approach to altering human conduct, based on a form of conditioning, whereby the subjects are rewarded for proper conduct and punished for improper conduct.

belief (1): Hirschi's term for the idea that the laws or other rules have moral force. See also *social bond.*

benefit of clergy (7): A twelfth-century compromise between England's Henry II and the Roman Catholic church. The practice allowed members of the clergy to escape capital punishment and other severe sentences by transferring their cases from secular courts and the king's law to church courts and canon law, where they were routinely acquitted or subjected to far less severe penalties such as penitence.

bifurcated hearings (310): A special two-part trial proceeding. The question of guilt is determined in the first step. Should a conviction result, the appropriate sentence or applicable sentencing statute is determined in the second step. The two steps of a bifurcated trial generally take place in separate hearings but use the same jury. This procedure is an integral part of capital-murder cases.

big-house prison (2): Traditional Auburn-style prison that emphasizes severe methods of social control: stacked one- and two-person cells surrounded by high stone walls and guard towers. One of the last big-house prisons was New York State's Attica prison.

biological determinism (1): As applied to crime and justice, the theory that social or psychological phenomena are causally determined by biological factors, including genetics. See also *atavistic.*

blood revenge (2): Under tribal law, a system in which the victim's family could extract a punishment in kind from the perpetrator or the perpetrator's family. Practice often led to long-standing feuds between family groups or clans.

body cavity search (5): Anal, oral, or vaginal search for contraband such as weapons, communications, or drugs; employed as a security weapon against prison/jail inmates and others taken into custody when probable cause exists that contraband may be present.

boot camp (5): Military-style correctional programs designed for short-time and generally first-time offenders operated by more than one-half of the states and the federal government. The concept was first introduced in Georgia during the early 1980s and represents a rebirth of the early days of the Elmira reformatory, in which military training and discipline was employed for youthful offenders.

BOP (5): United States Bureau of Prisons, founded in 1930 (although federal prisons existed since the founding of the nation).

BOP drug treatment programs (5): A series of institutional treatment programs implemented by the federal government as a result of the influx of large numbers of drug-related inmates (one-half or more of all federal prisoners).

botes (2): A series of specific compensations described in the *lex salica* of the Middle Ages; for example, the family of a person who killed another could be ordered to pay a wergild, or man payment, where a member of the offending family became the slave of the victim's family to replace the murdered individual. In some instances, a specific loss could result in a fixed monetary payment. See also *lex salica.*

Bridewell (2) English prison established in 1557, also known as St. Bridget's Well. Became the model for British prisons in 1576 when Parliament ordered each county in England and Wales to create a Bridewell.

broker model (7): A probation or parole officer work-role orientation in which the officer functions as a referral service and supplies offender-clients with contacts to agencies who provide needed services.

building tenders (6): A system of inmate-guards used extensively in Texas and Arkansas, among other states. This system became the basis of litigation against the operation of cruel and unusual penal systems.

bureaucracy (9): Organizational approach that vests individuals with authority and spheres of competence in a predetermined hierarchy with abstract rules and selection by test; also includes a strictly defined chain of command.

campers (5): A low-security level inmate in the Federal Bureau of Prisons classification scheme; also, residents of BOP camps, most of whom are "white-collar" or other nonviolent criminals.

career criminal (2): An individual who makes crime a way of life and whose level of involvement in crime remains relatively constant throughout his or her life, until "retirement" or death.

case law (2): An outgrowth of Roman law whereby judges, as they decide cases and render decisions, create new law; also called judge-made law.

case manager (7): A prison official who works with inmates on such matters as classification, prison-work assignment, staff-inmate and inmate-inmate complaints, and the like. The case manager approach to unit management has been employed by the BOP since the 1970s.

caseload (7): The total number of clients registered with a correctional agency or probation or parole officer on a given date or during a specified period, often divided into active supervisory cases and inactive cases. Even within active supervisory cases, some may require more resources than others. See also *intensive supervision*.

centralized operation (9): An approach to correctional organization in which the vast majority of authority is held in one location or position.

chain gangs (10): A group of jail or prison inmates forced to work outdoors, often outside of the institution, on public works projects; they may be shackled together to prevent escape.

citation (7): An order, issued by the police, to appear before a magistrate or judge on a specific date, usually used for minor violations; the suspect does not have to be taken into immediate physical custody by the police officer or probation or parole officer.

civil death (10): The legal idea that offenders lose most if not all of their rights of citizenship once they have been convicted and incarcerated.

civil rights claims (Section 1983 suits) (10): Suits filed under a part of the United States Code that permits prison and jail inmates, as well as probationers and parolees, to sue those responsible for their care and custody

under the "due process" and "equal protection" clauses of the Fourteenth Amendment; such suits may also be filed by correctional personnel against their employers when discrimination is alleged.

class action lawsuit (10): Litigation involving not only a single petitioner but a group of similarly situated petitioners such as jail or prison inmates.

classification officers (5): Prison (and less often jail) personnel whose job it is to determine the appropriate level of security for a given prisoner; decisions are based on such factors as offense charged, prior criminal or institutional record, and psychometric testing results. Classification officers may be found in jails large enough to segregate inmates.

clinical psychologist (6): A person who treats individuals with mental and behavioral problems; in corrections, a person who is responsible for supervising counselors and for approving treatment plans.

closed systems (9): The view of organizations that they are internally governed and self-sufficient, that no forces outside the organization impact or control what the organism does or how it reacts.

Code of Hammurabi (2): Eighteenth-century B.C.E. Babylonian legal code compiled during the reign of Hammurabi; represents perhaps the oldest codified system of crime and punishment; emphasized the *lex talionis*. See also *lex salica*.

codependency (8): A term derived from psychotherapy in which two or more people develop a complex symbiotic relationship, each fulfilling the other's need for support or power. One person in the relationship has, in the present context, a legal problem. The other party or parties may not want the "troubled" individual to "get better." The offender's trouble means that the offender must rely on the codependent for aid and assistance, thus maintaining the codependent's power over the offender.

commitment (1): Admission of an adjudicated and sentenced adult, delinquent, or status offender into a short-term or long-term correctional facility.

common law (3): Unwritten law developed in England primarily from judicial decisions based on custom and precedent that constituted the basis of the English legal system and the legal system of the U.S. except for Louisiana.

community service (8): A form of community corrections, usually recommended in cases of vandalism and minor property offenses. The intent is to secure some benefits for the public from the offender, increase offender accountability, and reduce the need for incarceration.

con-politician (6): One of Schrag's prison role-types: the inmate who attempts to influence guards and other inmates by money and influence; tends to be pseudosocial, that is, he pretends to be prosocial but in reality is antisocial. See also *outlaw, right guy, square John.*

concurrent sentences (3): Two or more terms of imprisonment, all or a part of each to be served simultaneously. Normally, the prisoner is eligible for discharge at the end of the longest term specified. For example, a convicted criminal sentenced to terms of 10 and 15 years, to be served concurrently, would be eligible for release at the parole eligibility date for the 15-year sentence. See also *consecutive sentences.*

consecutive sentences (3): A sentence consisting of two or more individual sentences imposed simultaneously after conviction for more than one offense, all of which are to be served in sequence; or, a new sentence for a new conviction, imposed upon a person already under sentence for a previous offense. In either case, the offender must serve all but the final sentence before being considered for release, thus increasing the maximum time the offender may be confined or under supervision. For example, a convicted criminal sentenced to 10 years, followed by an additional 15 years, to be served consecutively, would be eligible for release at the parole eligibility date for the 15-year sentence only after first serving the 10-year sentence. See also *concurrent sentences.*

consensus models (5): Contemporary prisoner classifications schemes that base predictions on correctional officer views of what constitutes risky inmate characteristics; based on the observations and insights of serving correctional officers.

consolidated parole board model (7): A type of parole board that consists of an autonomous (independent) panel within a state-level corrections department or division; makes all decisions about conditional release from prison, but delegates supervision to another part of the system. See also *independent parole board model.*

conspiracy (3): An agreement between two or more persons to commit an unlawful act; it is essentially unimportant whether the illegal act is committed or simply planned.

corpus delicti (3): (Latin: body of the crime) The facts that prove a crime, composed of the illegal act and the criminal agent (actor or perpetrator) that produces it.

Corpus Juris Civilis (2): A legal code created by 12 Roman scholars in 535 at the order of Justinian I of Constantinople; became the criminal (and civil) code of most of the old Roman Empire until the end of the Middle Ages; also known as the Code of Justinian or the Institutes of Justinian.

Correctional Classification Profile (5): An inmate classification system created by Correctional Services Group; assesses inmate and institutional needs on eight dimensions.

correctional counselor (6): A professional staff member who provides individual or group treatment to correctional clients. This could take place in institutional (prison or jail) settings or extrainstitutional (community corrections, probation and parole) settings.

correctional officer (9): Prison guard; custody officer, sometimes uniformed, in jails and prisons.

criminal intent (3): The intent to commit an act, the results of which are a crime or violation of the law. Offenders either intended the exact harm to befall the victim of an illegal act (specific intent) or understood that harm to someone was possible (general intent). See also *mens rea.*

cultural importation hypothesis (6): Clemmer's idea that convicted offenders bring key elements of the inmate code, along with most inmate role adaptations, into the prison community. See also *deprivation perspective.*

cultural transmission thesis (1): A key explanatory element of the Chicago School of sociology's social disorganization theory; states that there are no criminal groups, only criminal areas of neighborhoods that pass the criminality from one generation to the next as part of the area's culture. Important idea in the development of Sutherland's differential association theory.

custody (5): In correctional practice, the legal, supervisory, and physical responsibility and control over a person.

custody determination model (5): A classification scheme created by the National Institute of Corrections; bases assignments on such factors as the offender's expression of violence before and since incarceration, alcohol and drug abuse, and severity of current offense.

day fines (3): A modern and equitable version of an old form of punishment—monetary sanctions geared to the average daily income of convicted offenders; an effort to bring equity to the sentencing process, or to compensate victims or the state (for court costs and supervisory fees). For example, Mr. Johnson and Ms. Jones are each fined 10 days income for a Class B misdemeanor. Mr. Johnson, a dishwasher earning $25 per day, pays $250. Ms. Jones, an executive with a major corporation earning $10,000 per day, pays $100,000. See also *means-based penalties*.

decentralized system (9): A system that invests administrative authority in officials at different institutions and agencies; authority is not confined to one location, office, or agency. Compare *centralized system*.

dehumanization (5): A process, described by Goffman, whereby prisoners and others in total institutions are stripped of their humanity. They are treated as nonpersons, creatures without worth. See also *rites of passage*.

deinstitutionalization of status offenders (DSO) (8): The federal initiative to remove status (noncriminal) offenders from secure juvenile corrections facilities.

deliberate indifference (10): The legal test employed by the courts to determine whether correctional officials ignored the physical (medical) conditions of an inmate, to that inmate's long-term detriment or harm.

democratic leader (9): Person in a position of trust, power, and authority over others who relies upon explanation and elaboration as means of communicating.

deprivation perspective (6) The view, derived from the work of Clemmer, that prison culture, including its code and inmate role types, results directly from the act of incarceration and the pains of imprisonment. See also *cultural importation hypothesis*.

determinate sentence (3): A sentence to confinement for a fixed period as specified by statute. Compare *indeterminate sentence*.

deterrence (1): One of seven philosophical responses to crime; asserts that an impending, swift, certain, and appropriately severe punishment will deflect individuals from committing an initial or repeated criminal offense (specific

deterrence) or keep others from following in the footsteps of those so sanctioned (general deterrence). The death penalty is often viewed as the ultimate specific deterrent. See also *incapacitation, isolation, rehabilitation, reintegration, restitution, restoration, retribution*.

differential association theory (1): Sutherland's perspective on why people commit crimes: Criminals learn motives, ideas, and rationalizations from others. See also *duration, frequency, intensity, priority*.

differential opportunity theory (1): A form of anomie theory advocated by Lloyd Ohlin, among others.

differential reinforcement (1): The key operant conditioning part of Akers's social learning theory; causes the illegal behavior to continue, often by neutralizing or negating punishments. See also *discriminative stimuli*.

direct supervision (4): Utilized in both temporary confinement facilities, such as jails, and prisons, this approach to CO-maintained custody and security eliminates many of the traditional barriers between inmates and staff; affords staff members greater interaction with and control over institutional residents. See also *intermittent supervision, remote supervision*.

disciplinary/punitive segregation (6): Formerly called solitary confinement, this method of isolating and punishing troublesome inmates is closely regulated by court decisions and penal policies.

discretionary release (7): Release of inmates from incarceration at the discretion of parole boards within limits set by the sentence and penal law.

discriminative stimuli (1): Akers's idea that definitions that advocate the violation of laws motivate offenders to violate the law; these definitions and other stimuli cause the offender to view the illegal behavior as acceptable and even desirable. See also *differential reinforcement*.

diversion (8): The official suspension of criminal or juvenile proceedings against an alleged offender at any point after intake into the system but before involvement in other increasingly criminalizing steps. For example, a substance abuser accused of drug dealing may be placed in treatment prior to a trial, on the condition of zero tolerance for a return to drug use. Another person convicted of child molestation may be allowed to participate in a noninstitutional treatment program at his or her own expense.

doing time (6): A term, attributed to Irwin, describing the outlook expressed by some inmates in which prison is viewed as a temporary break in their criminal career. See also *gleaning, jailing.*

dooms (2): British royal proclamations issued prior to the Norman invasion of 1066; the content of the Domesday Book, the source of all English common law.

double-bunking (double-celling) (10): Placing two or more inmates in a jail or prison cell that is intended to accommodate one inmate.

downsizing (9): A policy in which budgets are reduced or do not increase proportionally per year and jobs are cut as employment shifts from desirable and essential functions to essential functions only. Also called rightsizing.

drakon (2): (Greek: serpent or dragon). The root of the name Draco, a severe lawgiver in ancient Greece, whose name is the basis of the word *draconian,* describing an especially harsh or severe penal system.

duration (1): A key part of Sutherland's differential association theory; the amount of time a person has been exposed to the sources of various definitions; also a part of Akers's social learning theory. See also *frequency, intensity, priority.*

economic victimization (6): The idea that inmates are taken advantage of within prisons and jails, owing to the monopolistic prices they must pay for goods and services on the inmate sub rosa economy.

education release (8): Temporary, unescorted leaves from prison or jail accorded inmates so that they may attend courses at schools, colleges, and universities.

efficiency (9): One of three strengths associated with bureaucracies: the ability to accomplish a task with a minimum of effort and expenditure of resources.

ego (1): According to Freud, the part of the individual influenced by parental training and the like.

electronic monitoring (8): A method for keeping track of the whereabouts of suspects and even convicted offenders released into the community. Radio-tracking devices and other electronic equipment transmits information from the offender to a monitoring agency.

Enlightenment. See *Age of Enlightenment.*

entrapment (3): When a legal authority induces an individual to commit a crime he or she did not contemplate—the intent on the part of the government is to institute a criminal action against the offender. Entrapment is an affirmative defense used to negate criminal responsibility that arises from improper acts committed against an accused by an agent of the state, usually an undercover officer or informant.

equity (3): Natural justice system developed and administered by the English court of chancery.

equity-based models (5): Contemporary prisoner classification schemes that attempt to treat all inmates the same way and that bases classification on only those factors related to the current offense, for example, legal classification and extent of violence.

expiration release (7): The termination of an offender's sentence—minus any good time credits—that results in an unconditional release from custody or supervision.

extrainstitutional punishment (8): The idea that offenders may be adequately punished for their crimes by means other than prison or jail.

facility-design models (4, 5): Four main facility designs, include radial-design, telephone-pole design, courtyard-design, and campus-design prisons and jails.

fag (6): Although also used as a derogatory term for a homosexual, Sykes and Messinger report that the term has special meaning in prisons and jails: homosexual inmates who play the passive or submissive role in a sexual relationship. See also *wolf, punk.*

false negative (7): An offender who is predicted to be nonviolent and to pose no serious public threat, but who in fact is dangerous and does pose a serious public risk. See also *false positive, actuarial risk assessment scale.*

false positive (7): An offender who is predicted to be dangerous or to pose serious public threat, but who in fact is not dangerous and does not pose a risk to the public. See also *false negative, actuarial risk assessment scale.*

FCI (5): BOP's federal correctional institution, a less-than-high-security facility between the *USP* and the *FPC.*

federalism (10): A division of responsibility between federal and state courts in which the power of the former is paramount.

felony (3): A criminal offense punishable by death or incarceration in a state or federal prison facility. Compare *misdemeanor.*

feudalism (2): The social, economic, and political system of Medieval Europe, in which serfs (essentially slaves) worked the land held by vassals, or minor nobility, who, in turn, owed allegiance to the overlords.

fish (6): An inmate term for new inmates; signifies their low status in the prison social system.

focal concerns (1): An essential element in Miller's subcultural thesis about crime and delinquency: a series of values and behaviors, including getting into trouble and other thrill-seeking behavior, that sometimes places the practitioner in conflict with the law.

formal juvenile probation (7): A form of supervised release from a juvenile court authority that is virtually indistinguishable from adult probation.

FPC (5): BOP's federal prison camp, the lowest security facility widely available in the federal system.

free will (1): The power or right to act according to the dictates of one's own judgment and conscience.

frequency (1): A key part of Sutherland's differential association theory: the rate of recurrence of exposure to people espousing criminogenic definitions; also a part of Akers's social learning theory. See also *duration, intensity, priority.*

FTC (5): BOP's federal transfer center, the facility that coordinates the movement of all federal prisoners, located in Oklahoma City.

furloughs (8): Temporary releases—leaves—from incarceration granted to an inmate, usually lasting only overnight or for a few days.

general deterrence (1): See *deterrence.*

gleaning (6): Term attributed to Irwin that describes the practices of some inmates to gain as much personal improvement from their incarceration as they can. Compare *doing time* and *jailing.*

going rate (3): The current, local view of the appropriate sentence or punishment for a particular offense considering the defendant's prior record and other factors.

good time credits (3): The amount of time deducted from time to be served in prison on a given sentence, awarded at some point after a

prisoner's admission to prison and contingent upon good behavior.

good time laws (7): Laws, originating in New York in 1817, that allow a reduction of a portion of a prisoner's sentence for "good behavior' while in prison.

gorilla (6): A classification of inmate according to Schrag; an extremely predatory inmate bent on exploiting other prisoners.

guilt beyond a reasonable doubt (3): The legal element required for a trier-of-fact to return a guilty verdict against a person accused of a criminal-law violation; the judge or any member of the jury, defined as a reasonable person, must not entertain any doubt that the accused committed the crime as charged.

habeas corpus, writ of (10): (Latin: (that) you have the body) An order requiring that the named prisoner be brought before a court at a stated time and place to decide the legality of his or her incarceration. Formalized by the British Parliament in the Habeas Corpus Act of 1679, this important concept was written into the U.S. Constitution as Article III, Section 9: "The privilege of the writ of habeas corpus shall not be suspended, unless when in a case of rebellion or invasion the public safety may require it."

habitual offender statutes (2, 3): A statutory designation for criminals convicted of a third felony; depending on the wording of the statute, they may be sentenced to life without parole upon the third conviction ("three strikes and you're out" laws).

habitual offenders (2): See *habitual offender statutes.*

halfway house (8): Originally described as a residential center for paroled offenders who were halfway out of prisons. The use of the term has been expanded to include any residential program for offenders existing between incarceration and total freedom in the community.

hands-off approach (10): Judicial doctrine followed by state and federal judges until the 1960s whereby matters pertaining to inmate rights—that is, internal matters of prison or jail management—were the domain of correctional administrators alone.

hands-on period (10): Initiated by the Supreme Court as a result of a series of prison litigation cases involving serious constitutional issues and egregious human rights violations; the courts, both state and federal, took a greater interest in jailhouse and prison life during this time.

Hawes-Cooper Act (5): A law, enacted by Congress and approved by the president on January 19, 1929, to became operative after five years, that subjected all prison-made goods entering interstate commerce to the laws of any state or territory of the U.S. through which they passed. See also *Ashurst-Sumners Act.*

hearing officer (7): An officer within an administrative agency; someone who presides over administrative hearings pursuant to an agency's quasi-judicial power, including parole revocation prehearing.

high-use jails (4): Klofas's term for jails that both book and hold high numbers of inmates.

holding jails (4): Klofas's term for jails that book inmates at a low rate and hold them for some time.

horizontal overcharging (3): A prosecutorial practice whereby the state charges the defendant with every possible criminal charge related to the event; an essential incentive element in the plea-bargaining process.

house arrest (8): An accused or convicted offender is subject to monitored restriction at his or her residence. St. Paul the Apostle was placed under house arrest, as was Galileo. Under apartheid, the Republic of South Africa practiced a form of house arrest for political prisoners.

house of refuge (5): A workhouse, the first of which was established in 1824 as a means of separating juveniles from the adult correctional process; widely accepted as the beginning of the juvenile corrections movement in the United States.

id (1): According to Freud, the part of the individual that responds to primitive, hedonistic urges.

idiosyncratic leader (9): Leaders that work over, under, around, and through the hierarchy by exerting direct contact and control over decision making.

imitation (1): Akers's idea that observing and copying the behavior of those with whom we interact is part of the learning process, including the learning of criminal actions, motives, intents, rationalizations, and the like.

imprisonment binge (2, 6): A term used by Irwin and Austin to describe the trend in the mid- to late-1990s of using incarceration as the primary—if not sole—method for combating crime; results in an ever-increasing re-

liance upon prisons and more prison construction, consuming ever-increasing proportions of the state and federal budgets.

incapacitation (2): One of seven philosophical responses to crime; strategy for limiting an adjudicated criminal's ability to commit new crimes. That is, if a convicted criminal is in prison or jail, they lack the opportunity to reoffend. See also *deterrence, isolation, rehabilitation, reintegration, restitution, restoration, retribution, selective incapacitation.*

inchoate offenses (3): Also called anticipatory offense, a violation consisting of an action or conduct that is a step toward the intended commission of another offense.

independent parole board model (7): An entity that controls the release of inmates from prison and makes revocation decisions; in this model the entity is not under the control of any other state agency. Compare *consolidated parole board model.*

indeterminate sentence (3): A type of sentence to imprisonment in which the commitment term, rather than being for a specific time, such as three years, is for a range of time. In its most extreme cases, the sentence is one year to life; more common are such sentence as two to five years or ten years maximum and zero minimum. Compare *determinate sentence.*

infancy (3): In criminal law, the statutorily defined age below which a human being is not able to distinguish between right and wrong, normally between 8 and 10 years of age.

informal juvenile probation (7): A conditional release agreement reached between the juvenile court, the child, his or her parents, and, in some jurisdictions, an attorney representing the interests of the state. Often the juvenile probation officer represents juvenile court and may be empowered to make all release decisions in the name of the court.

informal probation (3): A criminal court requirement that a defendant or offender fulfill specified conditions of behavior in lieu of a sentence to confinement, but without assignment to a probation agency's supervisory caseload.

infraction (3): (1) In general, a violation of state statute or local ordinance punishable by a fine or other penalty but not by incarceration, unless it is a specified, unusually limited term; (2) in corrections, a statutory offense or a violation of prison or jail administrative regulations committed by an incarcerated offender or one in a temporary-release program such as work release.

inmate classification (5): The method by which correctional organizations make residential and programmatic placement decisions about convicted offenders; usually includes some form of psychometric testing, such as the MMPI, Custody Determination Model, or Correctional Classification Profile.

inmate classification models (5): The basis of most correctional classification systems. See also *consensus models, equity-based models, prediction models.*

inmate code (6): Informal set of rules reflecting values of the prison society. Often harsh and unforgiving, the code constitutes the normative content of the inmate social system.

inmate count (5): A security practice in which COs physically account for each inmate in their area of responsibility. Some counts are regularly scheduled, such as meal, work, and evening counts; others are unscheduled and random.

insanity (3): An affirmative criminal defense in which the accused contends that he or she should not be held accountable for the criminal act because he or she was incapable of knowing right from wrong at the time of the act or was incapable of acting upon that difference because of a defect of reason.

institutional racism (11): An endemic or society-wide problem in which racial stereotypes, discrimination, and prejudices shape the way most people view members of racial and ethnic minority groups.

intake (2): The information gathering and personal interviews that occur when an inmate is first brought to a corrections facility.

intensity (1): A pivotal part of Sutherland's differential association theory; the affective part of the theory, that is, the part that related to the depth of the emotional connection between the individual and the source of his or her legal and illegal definitions; also a part of Akers's social learning theory. See also *duration, frequency, priority.*

intensive supervision (7): A supervisory system in which probation officers have lighter caseloads, perhaps as few as 10 clients per month, institute regular drug tests, and carry out other intensive measures, such as work and home visits.

intermediate sanctions (3): Punishments involving sanctions existing somewhere between incarceration and probation on a continuum of criminal penalties; may include home confinement and electronic monitoring.

intermittent supervision (4, 5): A custodial surveillance practice whereby COs observe prisoners at irregular and unpredictable time intervals; observation takes place when COs look into individual cells or cell blocks. Compare *direct supervision, remote supervision.*

involvement (1): A variable used by Travis Hirschi to describe an individual's participation in conventional activities.

Irish ticket-of-leave system (2): See *ticket-of-leave.*

irresistible impulse test (3): A test to determine whether an urge to do certain acts could not be overcome by willpower or reasoning; irresistible impulse is sometimes used in insanity pleas.

isolation (1): One of seven philosophical responses to crime in which it is believed that the offender should be separated from the rest of the community. See *banishment, deterrence, incapacitation, rehabilitation, reintegration, restitution, restoration, retribution, transportation.*

jail annex (4): A special facility built to house the overflow from the main jail; may be constructed specifically for this purpose, or may be a converted school, warehouse, barge, or similar structure.

jailhouse lawyer (10): An inmate in a prison or jail who becomes skilled in the law and assists other prisoners in filing suits largely against prison or jail administration; sometimes called "writ writer."

jailhouse suicide (6): Death of an inmate by his or her own hand while incarcerated; frequently occurs within the first few hours of incarceration and often by hanging.

jailing (6): Term coined by Irwin to refer to the inmate practice of seeking positions of power and authority within the prison; prison or jail is, for these inmates, home.

jails (4): The more than 3,000 facilities for confinement generally operated by local (county) governments. These facilities may be operated by the sheriff or other law enforcement (or non–law enforcement) officials, and they house pretrial detainees, convicted misdemeanants serving sentences, convicted felons awaiting transportation to prison, and others who have been incarcerated for a short time.

joint venture program (5): An association of persons (and companies or corporations) who together undertake a commercial enterprise. Typically, inmate-employees earn, by prison standards, high pay; policies and practices for the operation of the commercial enterprise are determined by both the correctional agency and the external participants; however, control and security issues remain the primary benchmarks for developing both.

judicial reprieve (7): An action by a judge that suspends imposition of a sentence until a convicted offender can appeal to the monarch (for example, the king) for a pardon.

jury nullification (3): An action by a jury that runs contrary to the evidence presented in the trial. In effect, the jury may find a defendant not guilty, even in the face of overwhelming evidence, if they do not agree with the law under which the person is charged.

jus civile (2): (Latin: civil law) The law created by Roman jurists for resolving issues between Roman citizens.

jus gentium (2): (Latin: the law of nations) The law, originally developed by Roman jurists, for trying aliens or non-Roman citizens, invoked by Hugo Gaotius, a Dutch jurist, as the basis of international law.

jus honorarium (2): (Latin: supplemental law) A method of magisterial law meant to supplement, aid, and correct existing law.

just deserts (2): The idea that individuals exhibit free will in the violation of laws and, therefore, the government is justified in punishing them; the idea that "criminals get what they deserve" or "you reap what you sow."

justice model (2): Often attributed to Fogel and Von Hirsch, among others; the goals of the justice model are to confine as punishment, to provide a safe and humane system of offender control, to offer treatment programs (but not require them), and to provide public safety.

juvenile correctional institution (5): Any one of a variety of facilities for confining youngsters found to have committed delinquent acts. These facilities may be known as state industrial or training schools and may range from essentially open campuses to very secure prison-like institutions.

Juvenile Justice and Delinquency Prevention Act (5): Major piece of federal legislation enacted in 1974 and subsequently amended on a number of different occasions; emphasized the deinstitutionalization of status offenders, removal of juveniles from adult jails, and the development of a number of different types of diversion programs.

king's peace (2): Any crime committed in the king's presence or against one of his officers. Originally intended to protect the king from assassins and other malcontents, the king's peace provided the king's officers, many of whom were disliked tax collectors, some small measure of protection.

labeling (8): A theoretical approach to deviant behavior attributed to Schur, Lemert, and Becker in which formal and informal "naming" of a person (e.g., as a pervert, weirdo, freak, deviant, or criminal) has the potential to change that individual's life dramatically. A theory that asserts that the formal designation of an individual as a criminal (as in a convicted offender) can result in a negative self-concept that will push the person deeper into crime.

laissez faire leader (9): An administrator who adopts a style that provides little or no direction for subordinates.

Law of Moses (2): The Ten Commandments that Moses brought down from Mount Sinai.

legal system stage (2): The last of Gargarin's three stages of legal development, consisting of written codes specifying all necessary procedures, punishments, and enforcement methods for "civilized" social relations. See also *pre-legal stage, proto-legal stage.*

lex salica (2): (Latin: law of the Salian Franks, or Germans) Germanic tribal law.

lex talionis (1, 2): (Latin: law of the claw) Law of retaliation, such as "an eye for an eye, a tooth for a tooth."

linear design (4): Second-generation jails that frequently employ the use of closed-circuit television cameras or other types of devices to enhance officers' observations of inmate activity.

litigiousness (10): The inclination of individuals to file lawsuits.

living unit design models (5): Among the oldest designs for incarceration facilities currently in use today; living units have a hallway leading to individual cells, two-person (or more) cells or dormitories. A central control area at one end of the hallway controls movement in and out of the cell area.

lockstep shuffle (2): A method of controlling groups of prisoners as they walk, "invented" by the Auburn prison in which an inmate stands in line with his right foot slightly behind the left and his right arm outstretched with his hand on the right shoulder of the man in front of him.

longitudinal study (2): Research that employs multiple data collection efforts over an extended period of time, usually measured in years.

low-use jails (4): Klofas's term for jails that both book and hold inmates at very low rates.

M'Naughton rule (3): An 1843 English legal precedent that established the first clear basis for acquittal based on the defense of insanity: the offender, at the time of the act's commission, did not appreciate or understand the illegal nature of the act and therefore could not formulate guilty intent.

management (9): There are two kinds of management in corrections; inmate management and organizational management, which is concerned with keeping the various functions of institutions and agencies operating in a relatively efficient manner.

mandatory minimums (3): Legislative requirement that established the least or lowest sentence, or other penalty, that must be imposed upon conviction of a specific offense.

mandatory release (7): A conditional release from prison required by statute when an inmate has been confined for a period equal to his or her full sentence minus statutory good time, if any.

mandatory sentences (3): Legislative requirement that a conviction for certain offenses requires a certain amount of incarceration or other appropriate penalty.

MCC/MDC (5): Metropolitan Correctional Center/Metropolitan Detention Center: short-term detention or incarceration facilities operated by the federal government in a number of major metropolitan areas in the United States. These facilities typically hold federal prisoners awaiting trial, or those serving short sentences.

MDR-TB (6): Multidrug-resistant form of tuberculosis.

means-based penalties (3): Financial punishments that take into account the ability of a given defendant to pay. See also *day fines*.

medical model (2): The notion popular in criminology from the 1940s to the 1970s that crime is a societal illness that can be cured by scientifically studying the problem; can be applied to the individual as well, as in the devis-

ing of a treatment plan to rehabilitate an offender.

medium supervision (7): Term applied to prisons where some direct supervision of inmates is maintained; prisoners are eligible for recreational activities and visitation privileges are more relaxed than in a maximum-security prison.

mens rea (3): (Latin: guilty mind) See *criminal intent*.

merchant/peddler (6): Similar to the conpolitician classification of inmate personalities; an inmate with money and influence over guards and other inmates.

minimizing penetration (8): Efforts to remove the individual from the system once an offender is taken to trial and found guilty of some crime; at that point some stigma has already attached to the person, and the efforts to remove the offender from the system into a community-based correctional setting merely keeps the individual from moving into what are characterized as "deep-end" placements, or secure correctional institutions.

minimum supervision (7): The lowest custody level employed in most correctional systems; inmates have the maximum amount of freedom or movement throughout the institution.

misdemeanor (3): The least serious type of crime; in most states, a misdemeanor is punishable by fines or a combination of fines and incarceration for less than one year, typically in a county jail or similar facility. Compare *felony*.

mitigating circumstances (10): Those factors or situations surrounding the commission of a crime that would cause a jury to consider a lesser penalty once a person has been found guilty of a law violation.

mixed caseload (7): The assignment of both felony and misdemeanor offenders to supervision by a given probation and parole officer.

MMPI (5): Minnesota Multiphasic Personality Inventory. See *classification models*, *inmate classification*.

National Probation Association (7): An organization that lobbied Congress to pass a probation law in on March 4, 1925, creating the federal probation system.

natural law (2): A system of rules and principles (not created by human authority or enacted law) that can be discovered by the rational intelligence of a person as growing out of and conforming to the nature of human beings. See also *Age of Enlightenment.*

net widening (8): The more options a correctional program—or any criminal justice agency—has, the more people will be brought under some form of social control.

new generation jails (4): Third generation jails; also called podular or direct supervision jails, in design it confines inmates in housing pods with relatively few inmates, perhaps as few as 15 or as many as 100.

Newgate Prison, Connecticut (2): Often confused with New York City's Newgate Prison, this facility is considered by some penologists to be the first state prison; however, it was little more than a former tin mine in which inmates lived under especially harsh conditions.

Newgate Prison, New York (2): Opened in 1797; soon became overcrowded and experienced a series of riots and uprisings.

nexus (3): In criminal law, the intersection of two factors; in corpus delicti, the merging of *mens rea* (guilty mind) and *actus rea* (guilty act or deed).

NIMBY (4, 8): Not In My Back Yard; sentiment shared by neighboring landowners of prospective sites for jail or halfway house construction.

nonadjudicated probation (7): Occurs after a juvenile petition but before a formal declaration of delinquency, the latter being the juvenile justice equivalent of a guilty verdict.

nonperson status (5): Goffman's idea that people can be treated as if they were not human, beings of no consequence; normally associated with the treatment of total institution inmates.

nonpetitioned probation (7): A form of pre-indictment diversion.

one-hand-on era (10): The period of moderate court involvement, especially by the federal courts, in inmates' conditions of confinement and the procedures for operating jails and prisons. In this era, judges were not as activist in their orientations as they had been in the hands-on era. See also *hands-on era, hands-off era.*

outlaw (6): Schrag's role type of inmate that relies on force and physical violence to obtain what he wants from other, more easily exploited inmates.

pains of imprisonment (1, 6): According to McCorkle and Korn, the deprivations associated with imprisonment, including loss of freedom, autonomy, goods and services, security, and heterosexual relationships.

parens patriae (5): (Latin: father of the country, or, state as parent) An English chancery legal concept in which the king is viewed as father of the country, the king's chancellor could intervene in cases where children needed legal assistance, such as when they were orphaned or needed to have their inheritances protected; applied to juvenile courts in the United States, with the judge acting as the father figure.

parole (7): An administrative function where convicted offenders are conditionally released, under community supervision, prior to completion of their sentences.

parole eligibility date (7): The earliest possible point at which an inmate can leave prison.

participative leader (9): A group-oriented leader that frequently has informal contacts with employees under his or her direction.

penal colony (2, 11): An isolated place used for the confinement of convicted offenders; in most penal colonies, geography or topography provide the means of confinement and control, e.g., Australia, Devil's Island, and Siberia.

penal harm (1): The idea that the promotion of overcrowding has extended the punishment of incarceration to include degradation, provocation, and deprivation.

Penal Servitude Act (2): An 1853 act of the English Parliament allowing prisoners to be released, that is, paroled, on a ticket-of-leave system and supervised by local officials in the community.

Pennsylvania system (2): Method of imprisonment designed to isolate inmates from other criminals and to provide a prolonged opportunity for reflection and self-reform.

penology (1): The formal and systematic study of reformation and rehabilitation, punishments and prisoners; includes an appreciation for the operation and management of places designed for punishment..

petty misdemeanor (3): The most minor of criminal offense; sometimes called infraction; may call for fines or very brief periods of incarceration.

physical violence (6): Assault; violent acts that typically result in death or injuries.

play families (6): An abiding characteristic of women's prisons, in which inmates role play family members, including spouses, children, parents, siblings and grandparents, to provide emotional support for one another.

podular design jails (4): Pods consist of individual cell or living areas, often arranged in a triangle, which share a central commons or day area.

point of convergence (3): The point at which the guilty mind and the guilty act come together to result in a crime.

police lockup (4): Incarceration facility, generally located in a police building, for the temporary detention of suspects until they can be interrogated or fully processed by the police prior to being transferred to the county jail. There are somewhere between 13,000 and 15,000 facilities in the country.

political patronage (9): The appointment of individuals to an office based on who they know, not what they know.

positivists (1): A major trend in criminological theory popular from the mid–nineteenth century through the early twentieth century, the proponents of which believe that human behavior was determined by factors beyond the individual's control; also stressed science as a way of knowing more about crime and criminals.

post (4): Any position, fixed or mobile, that must be staffed in a correctional facility on a 24-hour basis.

PPO (7): Parole and probation officer.

prayer of repentance (7): Proof of literacy to seek protection under the benefit of clergy.

pre-legal stage (2): One of Gargarin's three evolutionary stages where a community has no formal and public ways to settle disputes among members. See also *legal system, proto-legal system.*

pre-sentence investigation report (1, 7): The document prepared by the probation officer, case worker, or other court officer detailing the life history of the criminal defendant and suggesting the appropriate method for disposing of the case.

prediction models (5): Contemporary prisoner classification scheme based on a variety of legal, psychological, social, and medical information about the offender. They predict the likelihood of intrainstitutional violence with the "client" as either perpetrator or victim.

preliminary hearing (1): An initial or show-cause hearing in which the government is required to establish that probable cause exists for further judicial action.

preponderance of the evidence (3): The civil standard of proof; establishes that one party to a suit is more liable than the other; less rigorous than the criminal standard of "beyond a reasonable doubt."

presumptive sentences (3): A legislatively prescribed method for determining the appropriate sentence; a determinate sentencing approach that identifies the "normal" or presumptive sentence to be imposed absent mitigating or aggravating circumstances.

principal (3): Individual accused of actually committing a crime; the person most directly involved in the criminal act.

priority (1): A key part of Sutherland's differential association theory; those sources of definitions one comes into contact with early in life. Also a part of Akers's social learning theory. See also *duration, frequency, intensity.*

prison (5): A correctional facility operated by a state or the federal government for the confinement of convicted felons serving sentences in excess of one year.

prison gang (6): A clique or informal group found in U.S. prisons today such as the Mexican Mafia, La Nuestra Familia, the Aryan Brotherhood, the Black Guerrilla Family, and the Texas Syndicate. See also *security threat group.*

prison labor model (5): A model in which participation in prison industries prevents inmate idleness as well as provides economic value.

prison riot (6): A collective attempt by inmates to take over part or all of the prison.

prison subculture (6): According to Clemmer and others, the inmate social community, governed by the inmate code; traditionally aligned against staff and legitimate society, may exhibit less solidarity today than in the 1950s and before.

prisonization (1, 6): According to Clemmer, the taking on to greater or lesser extent, the folkways, mores, customs, and general culture of the penitentiary; a form of institutionalization whereby the prison is home and other inmates are fellow citizens of the prison community.

privatization (4): The movement toward having jails and prisons or specific functions within a facility constructed and/or operated by private contractors.

pro se action (10): (Latin: for one's self; as in acting for one's self) Acting as one's own defense attorney in criminal proceedings.

probation (3, 7): The conditional freedom granted by a judicial officer to an alleged or adjudged adult or juvenile offender, as long as the person meets certain conditions of behavior.

probation revocation process (7): The procedure initiated by a probation officer whereby the court will convene a hearing to determine whether the conditions of probation have been violated and, if so, whether the probation should be withdrawn and the offender incarcerated or placed on stricter conditions.

procedural law (3): The "rules of the game"; the legal procedures under which the criminal law will be enforced and applied to those accused of crimes.

processing jail (4): Klofas's term for a jail that books persons at a high rate, but holds them for relatively short periods of time.

property offense (6): A crime that involves items with some monetary value, including larceny-theft, burglary, and auto theft.

proportionality (3): Being in proportion; adjusted to something else according to a certain rate of comparative relation.

protective custody unit (PCU) (6): The housing unit within a prison or jail where inmates may be held for their own protection.

proto-legal stage (2): According to Gargarin, societies that have dispute-resolution procedures but lack formalized procedural or enforcement rules. Compare *pre-legal stage, legal system.*

PS/PIEC (5): Prison Industries Enhancement Certification; enacted into law in 1979 by Congress, removed many of the interstate restrictions on prisoner-made goods created by Hawes-Cooper and Ashurst-Sumners.

psychological determinism (1): A form of positivism in which psychological or mental factors are believed to cause most human behavior, including crime.

psychological diagnostician (6): See *psychological technician.*

psychological technician (6): An individual who holds the entry-level psychologist position; is not certified as a counselor or clinician, but can conduct certain types of screening tests and other preliminary psychometric testing.

psychological victimization (6): The threat of physical harm.

psychopath (1): (sociopath) A person who is not truly mentally ill, but who has a severe personality disorder; is deficient in the capacity to feel guilt, shame, or remorse; may engage in criminal behavior.

public interest law (10): An approach to litigation where activist groups use the courts and litigation to change certain social conditions, such as civil rights, school desegregation, and prison and jail conditions.

public-order offenses (6): State-level crimes that include weapons violations, sex crimes (except rape, prostitution, and commercialized vice), liquor law crimes, disorderly conduct, public drunkenness, and vagrancy.

punk (6): An inmate personality type according to Sykes and Messinger; an otherwise heterosexual inmate coerced into a submissive homosexual role. Compare *wolf, fag.*

qualified immunity (10): A defense to civil rights claim that asserts that the violations were unintentional (not deliberate) and that the offending official should not be held liable.

rapo/innocent (6): Included among Sykes and Messinger's low-status inmate role types: an irritating inmate who maintains his innocence to whomever will listen. Compare *weakling/ weak sister, rat/squealer.*

rat/squealer (6): Included among Sykes and Messinger's low-status inmate role types: an inmate who betrays his peers to staff and, in so doing, violates one of the most sacred tenets of the inmate code; if he is known to other inmates, he will likely seek refuge in protective custody; information about rats, also called snitches, is prized by inmates, who often seek revenge during prison uprisings. See also *rapo/innocent, weakling/weak sister;* also *snitching.*

rationality (9): The notion that organizations (particularly bureaucracies) act in predictable ways; operations are governed by tightly defined and well-understood rules.

reality therapy (1): A therapy with roots in behaviorism, in which the moral standards of the therapist must become the moral standards of the client; uses praise and concern as the reinforcers and punishers to achieve accountability from the offender.

recidivism (3, 7, 8): Relapsing into criminal behavior after a period of correctional treatment.

recognizance (ROR) (7): Release on one's personal word, unsecured by money or property, to return to court at a scheduled time.

rehabilitation (1): One of seven philosophical responses to crime; a sometimes acknowledged goal of penal systems, generally relying on (a) individualized treatment that emphasizes the offender, not the violation, (b) flexible sentences and indeterminacy, so that release is based on the "social health" of the offender rather than the amount of time served, and (c) high levels of staff discretion, allowing those doing the rehabilitation to determine when the treatment is complete. See also *deterrence, incapacitation, isolation, reintegration, restitution, restoration, retribution;* also *medical model, treatment.*

reintegration (1): One of seven philosophical responses to crime; stresses that the most positive method of corrections is a phased-in and controlled reentry of the offender into the community, based on the observation that 90% of all prison inmates leave confinement and reenter the free world. See also *deterrence, incapacitation, isolation, rehabilitation, restitution, restoration, retribution.*

remote supervision (4): A custodial surveillance practice whereby COs observe prisoners using closed-circuit television cameras and other electronic means to enhance officers' observation of inmate activity. Often found in jails and prisons that employ high staff-to-inmate ratios. A few COs are expected to supervise a large number of inmates. Compare *direct supervision, intermittent supervision.*

restitution (1): One of seven philosophical responses to crime; a court requirement that an alleged or convicted offender pay money or provide services to the victim of the crime or provide services to the community. See also *deterrence, incapacitation, isolation, rehabilitation, reintegration, restoration, retribution.*

restoration (1): One of seven philosophical responses to crime. The idea that crime creates an imbalance in society; moreover, the combined efforts of the state, the victim, and the offender have the potential to reestablish a much needed sense of fairness and justice. See also *deterrence, incapacitation, isolation, rehabilitation, reintegration, restitution, retribution.*

retribution (1): One of seven philosophical responses to crime; the exact payment of a debt to society and thus the expiation of one's offense. Its essence was codified in the biblical injunction, "an eye for an eye, a tooth for a tooth." See also *deterrence, incapacitation, isolation, rehabilitation, reintegration, restitution, restoration.*

revocation hearing (7): For parolees and probationers, a judicial hearing to determine whether the releasee's behavior warrants withdrawal of the privileges of either status. In both cases, a body of case law has developed that defines the constitutional rights the probationer or parolee retains in revocation proceedings.

right guy (6): According to Schrag, an inmate who follows all of the precepts of the inmate code. Compare *con-politician, outlaw, square John.*

rightsizing (9): A policy in which budgets are reduced or do not increase proportionally per year and jobs are cut as employment shifts from desirable and essential functions to essential functions only. Also called downsizing.

rites of passage (5): Rituals, often highly orchestrated and formal, through which an initiate to a formal or informal group must pass prior to gaining full membership; for prison and jail inmates, many of these rites are dehumanizing.

Santa Fe prison riot (6): A 36-hour period, in which the Penitentiary of New Mexico became a "killing ground" as inmates rampaged through the facility killing 33 fellow inmates, many of them snitches.

satellite jail (4): A structure such as a school, warehouse, or similar existing structure that is converted for use as a jail.

security levels (5): The range from maximum-security facilities, which typically imprison the most dangerous prisoners, to minimum-security facilities, which house far less dangerous individuals.

security threat group (6): American Correctional Associations' term for prison gang. See also *prison gang.*

selective incapacitation (1): Process of incarcerating certain offenders who are defined by various criteria as having a strong propensity to repeat serious crimes; based on research by Wolfgang and associates that showed that a very busy 6% of all offenders accounted for 50% of all crime. Thus, offenders who are recidivists or who have prior criminality should be incapacitated with relatively long prison sentences.

separation of powers (10): The principle that governmental power is distributed among three branches—the judicial, legislative, and executive—to ensure that no one person or entity will make the law (legislative), interpret the law (judicial), and apply the law (executive).

sex-offender notification laws (11): Statutory requirement that when convicted sex offenders move into a neighborhood they must register with local law enforcement, who, in turn, notify his or her neighbors about the presence of a sex offender in their midst.

sexual harassment (11): Unsolicited and unwanted sexually based acts, ranging from lewd remarks to groping and touching.

shakedown (5): A search of jail or prison inmate cells, by force if necessary, in order to discover contraband or evidence of crimes or rule infractions.

shock incarceration (6): Military-style boot camps designed for short-term and generally first-time offenders; operated by the federal government and more than one-half of the states. The concept was first introduced in Georgia during the early 1980s and has become a response to overcrowding in existing prisons.

silent system (2): Method of imprisonment characterized by enforced silence at all times and by night confinement in small solitary cells; during the day at meals and work, inmates are allowed to congregate with other prisoners. See also *Auburn system.*

silentium (5): (Latin: silence) A correctional facility for youthful offenders operated by the Vatican in the eighteenth century.

snitching (6): Within the inmate social system, the informing on one inmate by another inmate; at times considered the ultimate form of betrayal. See also *inmate code, rat/squealer.*

social bond (1): The sum of forces in a person's social and physical environment that connect him or her to society and its moral constituents.

social debt (3): The notion that a sentence should incorporate some recognition of the offender's criminal history.

social disorganization (6): Perspective in which the inner cities' increased levels of physical deterioration and lack of a cohesive community find expression in high crime rates.

social learning theory (1): Akers's theory that stresses the importance of acquiring definitions, motivations, methods supportive of

criminal conduct (and, conversely, noncriminal conduct). See also *imitation, differential association theory, discriminative stimuli.*

solidary opposition (6): Inmates, banded together by common rules, norms, expectations, and deprivations, form a group with very similar concerns and interests; they express uniform hostility and criticism of prison/jail administration and staff.

special conditions of probation/parole (7): Taking into account the unique characteristics of each offender and each offense, it provides a set of tailor-made conditions for each offender.

specific deterrence (1): See *deterrence.*

square John (6): Schrag's role type played by inmates who are noncriminal types and considered situational offenders. This type of inmate does not adjust well to prison life and does not conform to the inmate code. Compare *con-politician, outlaw, right guy.*

staff burnout (8): An experience of individuals in positions, such as operators of halfway houses, that require high emotional investments, in which the individual loses interest in the work because of the emotional and sometimes physical cost.

standard conditions of probation/parole (7): A set of broad and identical conditions for all releases.

standards of conduct (9): One of three strengths associated with bureaucracies, expressed in policy statements designed to standardize and stabilize organizational life.

state-raised youth (6): Individuals who went from "the youth prison" to the adult prison.

state-run jail (4): Six states currently operate jails; this arrangement departs from the tradicional city or county administration of jails.

sub rosa inmate economy (6): The illegal means by which inmates acquire and distribute valued goods and services in prisons and jails (the "black market").

subcultural hypothesis (1): The aggregate of symbols, beliefs, and values shared by members of a subgroup within the larger society; a sociological theory based on the idea that much crime emerges from such aggregates of delinquent youth or deviant persons.

subculture of violence (6): Wolfgang observed that most acts of criminal homicide occurred among the members of certain social groups.

substantive law (3): The statutes enacted by legislative bodies that define the elements of crimes; substantive law defines what is "against the law."

summary arrest (7): An arrest undertaken without formality or done spontaneously or in haste without legal formalities.

super-max security (5): A prison management strategy whereby high-risk inmates, or those who pose an unusual threat of escape or physical harm to others, are locked up for 23 hours per day in extremely secure housing units. The inmates are allowed an hour of exercise per day under close supervision.

superego (1): Freud's label for that part of personality concerned with moral values.

supervision models (5): An approach of building design for prison to focus on inmate management.

technical violation (7): In both probation and parole, infractions of the rules or conditions of release that are unrelated to commission of new offenses.

technocratic leader (9): Managers who have achieved their positions based on some area of expertise.

ticket-of-leave (2): System of graduated punishment that provided for progressive stages in a prison term and for release under supervision before final termination of sentence, used in the 1840s by Alexander Maconochie in England and Sir William Crofton in Ireland.

Times Square (5): The centralized control zone in a maximum-security prison, through which all inmates moving about the prison must pass.

tort claim (10): Violation of a legal duty; a private or civil wrong. Normally, a successful claim results in the award of monetary damages.

total institution (5): Erving Goffman's term describing a facility that completely controls the lives of those who work and live within it. See also *rites of passage, nonperson status.*

total quality management (9): The approach to operations that defines success in terms of customer orientation, maximum worker input, and a concern over the quality of the product that is produced.

tough (6): Sykes and Messinger's term for the highly volatile and aggressive inmate who fights for any reason. Compare *gorilla, merchant, rapo/innocent, rat/squealer, weakling/weak sister.*

transportation (1): A method of punishment originally devised in England for the most hardened criminals; legislatively sanctioned during the colonization of North America. When the American Revolution ended the practice there, England began transporting convicts to Australia and Van Diemen's Land (Tasmania).

treatment (5): All the steps taken to effect a cure for criminal tendencies; an essential element in the medical model of corrections.

Twelve Tables (2): Rome's first major civil and criminal code.

underclass (6): According to Julius Wilson, the permanent lower class that becomes institutionalized in a welfare state.

UNICOR (5): An acronym for the prison industries program operated by the BOP.

unit management (6, 9): Pioneered by the U.S. Bureau of Prisons, it creates prisons within prisons: the inmates in a given unit, all of whom have similar classifications and release dates, are supervised by the same team of correctional specialists.

USP (5): United States Penitentiary; one of the categories of facilities operated by the federal BOP

vertical overcharging (3): The practice of charging a suspect with more serious charges than can be proven in court.

vicarious (supervisory) liability (10): Liability for the actions of another in the absence of fault, where the persons did not know of, did not encourage, and did not assist in the criminal act(s) ; usually imposed because of the person's supervisory position over the offender.

victim impact statement (7): A statement, provided at sentencing to the sentencing authority, by the victims or victims' next of kin to personalize and explain the crime's short-term and long-term effects.

video arraignment (4): Arraignment in which the judge and lawyers can be in one place while the prisoners are in another.

Walnut Street Jail (2): Erected in Philadelphia in 1773, it was later called a penitentiary. Unlike previous prisons, it received convicted felons from a statewide area and kept its prisoners at hard labor in solitary confinement. It was expected that prisoners in solitary confinement would meditate on their evil ways and become penitent, which lead to the term *penitentiary.* This institution served as a model of humane penal reform and was widely adopted by European penologists. Among the characteristics that were most impressive were the facts that prisoners were paid for their work, men and women prisoners were separated, corporal punishment was forbidden, and religious instruction was required.

weakling/weak sister (6): In the Sykes and Messinger typology, an inmate who is not tough and is unable to withstand the rigors of prison life. Compare *gorilla, merchant/peddler, rapo/innocent, rat/squealer, tough.*

wergild (2): A medieval term for the worth of a person injured by another according to the victim's status in society. The wergild was the amount of compensation the offender was compelled to pay either the victim or a representative in order to resolve the difficulty. If the wergild was not paid, private retaliation could then be exercised against the offender and kin by the victim and kin. See also *wites.*

wites (2): Portion of the wergild that went to the victim's family.

wolf (6): One of three role types created by Sykes and Messinger's based on sex roles; a predatory inmate who provides protection for weak inmates in return for sexual favors.

work release (8): A program whereby jail or prison inmates work at jobs in the community while being held in a facility for incarceration (either secure or community-based residential) during the evening hours and on weekends.

writ writer (10): Jailhouse lawyer.

References

Abadinsky, Howard. 1995. *Law and justice: An introduction to the American legal system.* 3rd ed. Chicago: Nelson-Hall.

————. 1997. *Probation and parole: Theory and practice.* 6th ed. Upper Saddle River, NJ: Prentice-Hall.

Abadinsky, Howard, and L. Thomas Winfree, Jr. 1992. *Crime & justice: An introduction.* 2nd ed. Chicago: Nelson-Hall.

Abbott, Jack Henry. 1982. *In the belly of the beast: Letters from prison.* New York: Vintage.

Adams, Mark E., and Clyde B. Vedder. 1961. "Age and crime: Medical and sociologic characteristics of prisoners over 50." *Geriatrics* 18: 177–81.

Advisory Commission on Intergovernmental Relations. 1984. *Jails: Intergovernmental dimensions of a local problem.* Washington, DC: Advisory Commission on Intergovernmental Relations.

Aichhorn, August. 1925 (1973). *Wayward youth.* New York: Viking.

Akers, Ronald. 1985. *Deviant behavior: A social learning approach.* 3rd ed. Belmont, CA: Wadsworth.

————. 1992. *Drugs, alcohol and society: Social structure, process and policy.* Belmont, CA: Wadsworth.

————. 1996. *Criminological theories: Introduction and evaluation.* 2nd ed. Los Angeles: Roxbury.

Alexander, Rudolph, Jr. 1994. "Hands-off, hands-on, hands-semi-off: A discussion of the current legal test used by the United States Supreme Court to decide inmates' rights." *Journal of Crime and Justice* 17 (1): 103–28.

Allen, Harry E., and Clifford E. Simonsen. 1986. *Corrections in America.* 4th ed. New York: Macmillan.

Allinson, Richard. 1982. "Crisis in the jails: Overcrowding is now a national epidemic." *Corrections Magazine* (April): 18–24.

Alpert, Geoffrey P., Ben M. Crouch, and C. Ronald Huff. 1984. "Prison reform by judicial decree: The unintended consequences of Ruiz v. Estelle." *Justice System Journal* 9 (3): 291–305.

Alschuler, A. W. 1980. "Sentencing reform and parole release guidelines." *University of Denver Law Review* 51: 237–45.

American Bar Association. 1970. *Standards relating to probation.* Chicago: American Bar Association.

American Correctional Association. 1986. *A study of prison industry: History, components, and goals.* Washington, DC: U.S. Government Printing Office.

————. 1990. *The female offender: What does the future hold?* Alexandria, VA: Kirby Lithographic.

————. 1991a. *ACA directory: Juvenile and adult correctional departments, institutions, agencies, and paroling authorities.* College Park, MD: American Correctional Association.

————. 1991b. *Standards for adult local detention facilities.* 3rd ed. Laurel, MD: American Correctional Association.

————. 1994. *Gangs in correctional facilities: A national assessment.* Laurel, MD: American Correctional Association.

————. 1997. *ACA directory: Juvenile and adult correctional departments, institutions, agencies, and paroling authorities.*

College Park, MD: American Correctional Association.

American Friends Service Committee. 1971. *Struggle for justice.* New York: Hill & Wang.

American Jail Association. 1994. *Who's who in jail management.* 2nd ed. Hagerstown, MD:

Anderson, Elijah. 1994. "The code of the streets." *Atlantic Monthly* (May): 80–94.

Armstrong, T. L., D. Maloney, and R. Romig. 1990. "The balanced approach in juvenile probation: Principles, issues, and application." *Perspectives* 14 (1): 8–38

Augustus, John. 1972. *John Augustus, first probation officer.* Montclair, NJ: Patterson-Smith.

Austin, James, Michael Jones, and Melissa Bolyard. 1993. "The growing use of jail boot camps: The current state of the art." Washington, DC: U.S. Government Printing Office.

Austin, James, Charles Jones, John Kramer, and Phil Renninger. 1996. *National assessment of structured sentencing.* Washington, DC: U.S. Government Printing Office.

Austin, James F., and Barry Krisberg. 1981. "Wider, stronger and different nets: The dialectics of criminal justice reform." *Journal of Research in Crime and Delinquency* 18: 165–96.

Austin, James F., Barry Krisberg, Robert DeComo, Sonya Rudenstine, and Domine Del Rosario. 1995. *Juveniles taken into custody: Fiscal year 1993.* Washington, DC: U.S. Government Printing Office.

Ayres, Richard M., and Thomas L. Wheelen. 1977. *Collective bargaining in the public sector.* Gaithersburg, MD: International Association of Chiefs of Police.

Badillo, Herman, and Milton Haynes. 1972. *A bill of no rights: Attica and the American prison system.* New York: Outerbridge & Lazard.

Bain, William E. 1988a. "I'm in the jailhouse now, part I." *American Jails* (Summer): 8–14.

———. 1988b. "I'm in the jailhouse now, part II." *American Jails* (Fall): 15–22.

Balch, Robert W. 1974. "Deferred prosecution: The juvenilization of the criminal justice system." *Federal Probation* 38 (2): 46–50.

Barak, Gregg. 1995. "Media, society, and criminology." In *Media processes and the social construction of crime,* ed. Gregg Barak. New York: Garland.

Barnes, Harry Elmer, and N. K. Teeters. 1959. *New horizons in criminology.* Englewood Cliffs, NJ: Prentice-Hall.

Barry, John Vincent. 1958. *Alexander Maconochie of Norfolk Island.* Melbourne: Oxford University Press.

Bartol, Curt R. 1991. *Criminal behavior: A psychological approach.* 3rd. ed. Englewood Cliffs, NJ: Prentice-Hall.

Bartollas, Clemens, and John P. Conrad. 1992. *Introduction to corrections.* 2nd ed. New York: HarperCollins.

Bartollas, Clemens, and Simon Dinitz. 1989. *Introduction to criminology.* 2nd ed. New York: HarperCollins.

Bartollas, Clemens, and Stuart J. Miller. 1978. *Correctional administration: Theory and practice.* New York: McGraw-Hill.

Baunach, P. 1985. *Mothers in prison.* NJ: Transaction Books.

Bazemore, Gordon. 1992. "On mission statements and reform in juvenile justice: The case of the 'balanced approach.'" *Federal Probation* 56 (3): 64–70.

Beccaria, Cesare. 1764 (1963). *On crimes and punishments.* Trans. Henry Paolucci. Indianapolis: Bobbs-Merrill.

Beck, Allen, Darrell Gilliard, Lawrence Greenfield, Caroline Harlow, Thomas Hester, Louis Jankowski, Tracy Snell, James Stephan, and Danielle Morton. 1993. *Survey of state prison inmates, 1991.* Washington, DC: U.S. Government Printing Office.

Beck, Allen, and Darrell K. Gilliard. 1995. *Prisoners in 1994.* Washington, DC: U.S. Government Printing Office.

Becker, Howard. 1963. *Outsiders: Studies in the sociology of deviance.* New York: Free Press.

Bedau, Hugo Adam. 1967. *The death penalty in America.* Chicago: Aldine.

Benekos, Peter J. 1990. "Beyond reintegration: Community corrections in a retributive era." *Federal Probation* 54 (1): 52–56.

Benekos, Peter J., and Alida V. Merlo. 1995. "Three strikes and you're out!: The political sentencing game." *Federal Probation* 59 (1): 3–9.

Berman, Louis. 1938. *The glands regulating personality.* New York: Macmillan.

Bernard, Thomas J. 1992. *The cycle of juvenile justice.* New York: Oxford University Press.

Bersani, Carl A. 1989. Reality therapy: Issues and a review of research." In *Correctional counseling and treatment,* 2d. ed., P.C. Kratcoski, ed. Prospect Heights, IL: Waveland.

Bershad, Lawrence. 1985. "Discriminatory treatment of the female offender in the criminal justice system." *Boston College Law Review* 26: 389–438.

Binder, Arnold, and Virginia L. Binder. 1982. "Juvenile diversion and the Constitution." *Journal of Criminal Justice* 10: 1–24.

Binder, Arnold, Gilbert Geis, and Dickson Bruce. 1988. *Juvenile delinquency: Historical, cultural, legal perspective.* New York: Macmillan.

Bingaman, Jeff. 1980. *Report of the attorney general on the February 2 and 3, 1980, riot of the Penitentiary of New Mexico.* Vols. 1 & 2. Santa Fe: Office of the Attorney General.

Blau, Peter M., and W. Richard Scott. 1962. *Formal organizations.* San Francisco: Chandler.

Block, Michael K., and William M. Rhodes. 1987. *The impact of the federal sentencing guidelines.* Washington, DC: U.S. Government Printing Office.

Blumstein, Alfred, Jacqueline Cohen, Somnath Das, and Soumyo D. Moitra. 1988. "Specialization and seriousness during adult criminal careers." *Journal of Quantitative Criminology* 4: 303–45.

Bonczar, Thomas P., and Allen J. Beck. 1997. *Lifetime likelihood of going to state or federal prison.* Washington, DC: U.S. Government Printing Office.

Bourque, Blair R., Mei Han, and Sarah M. Hill. 1996. *A national survey of aftercare provisions for boot camp graduates.* Washington, DC: U.S. Government Printing Office.

Bowen, Bruce, and Dierdre Kelly. 1987. "Lease-purchase financing for jails." *American Jails* 1 (1): 57.

Bowker, Lee M. 1980. *Prison victimization.* New York: Elsevier.

———. 1981. "Gender differences in prisoner subcultures." In *Women and crime in America,* ed. Lee M. Bowker. New York: Macmillan.

Braswell, Michael, Steven Dillingham, and Reid Montgomery, eds. 1985. *Prison violence in America.* Cincinnati: Anderson.

Braswell, Michael C., Reid H. Montgomery, and Lucien X. Lombardo, eds. 1994. *Prison violence in America.* 2nd ed. Cincinnati: Anderson.

Brickey, Kathleen F. 1986. "Forfeiture of attorneys' fees: The impact of RICO and CCE forfeitures on the right to counsel." *Virginia Law Review* 72 (3): 493–542.

Brien, Peter M., and Allen J. Beck. 1996. *HIV in prisons 1994.* Washington, DC: U.S. Government Printing Office.

Brien, Peter M., and Caroline Wolf Harlow. 1995. *HIV in prisons and jails.* Washington, DC: U.S. Government Printing Office.

Brockway, Zebulon Reed. 1912 (1969). *Fifty years of prison service.* Montclair, NJ: Patterson-Smith.

Bronstein, Alvin J. 1985. "Prisoners and their endangered rights." *The Prison Journal* 65 (1): 3–17.

Buchanan, R. A., and K. L. Whitlow. 1987. "National evaluation of objective prison classification systems: The current state of the art." *Crime and Delinquency* 32: 272–90.

Bureau of Justice Assistance. 1992. *State civil RICO programs.* Washington, DC: U.S. Government Printing Office.

Bureau of Prisons. 1994. *The state of the Bureau: 1993.* Washington, DC: U.S. Government Printing Office.

———. 1997a. *Bureau of Prisons facilities.* Washington, DC: U.S. Government Printing Office.

———. 1997b. *Quick facts.* Washington, DC: U.S. Government Printing Office.

Burger, Warren E. 1985. "The need for change in prisons and the correctional system." *Arkansas Law Review* 38 (4): 711–26.

Burgess, Robert, and Ronald L. Akers. 1966. "A differential-association-reinforcement theory of criminal behavior. *Social Problems* 14: 128–47.

Bursik, Robert J. 1986. "Ecological stability and the dynamics of delinquency." In *Communities and crime,* ed. Albert J. Reiss and Michael J. Tonry. Chicago: University of Chicago Press.

Burton, Velmer S., James W. Marquart, Steven J. Cuvelier, Leanne Fiftal Alarid, and Robert J. Hunter. 1993. "A study of attitudinal change among boot camp participants." *Federal Probation* 57: 46–52.

Butts, Jeffrey A. 1996. *Offenders in the juvenile court, 1994.* Washington, DC: U.S. Government Printing Office.

———. 1997. *Juvenile court processing of delinquency cases, 1985–1994.* Washington, DC: U.S. Government Printing Office.

Butts, Jeffrey A., Howard N. Snyder, Terrence A. Finnegan, Anne L. Aughenbaugh, Rowen S. Poole. 1996a. *Juvenile court statistics 1993.* Washington, DC: U.S. Government Printing Office.

Butts, Jeffrey A., Howard N. Snyder, Terrence A. Finnegan, Anne L. Aughenbaugh, and Rowen S. Poole. 1996b. *Juvenile court statistics 1994.* Washington, DC: U.S. Government Printing Office.

Cahalan, Margaret W. 1986. *Historical corrections statistics in the United States, 1850–1984.* Washington, DC: U.S. Government Printing Office.

Call, Jack E. 1995. "The Supreme Court and prisoners' rights." *Federal Probation* 59 (1): 36–46.

Camp, Camille Graham, and George M. Camp. 1995. *The corrections yearbook 1995: Adult corrections.* South Salem, NY: Criminal Justice Institute.

Carlisle, H. M. 1976. *Management: Concepts and situations.* Chicago: SRA.

Carroll, Leo. 1974. *Hacks, blacks and cons.* Lexington, MA: Lexington Books.

Carter, Dianne. 1991. "The status of education and training in corrections." *Federal Probation* June: 17–23.

Cary, M., and H. H. Scullard. 1975. *A history of Rome: Down to the reign of Constantine.* 3rd ed. New York: St. Martin's Press.

"Cashier killer marks Texas' 100th execution." 1995. *El Paso [TX] Times,* Oct. 5, p. 5B.

Castellano, Thomas C., and Irina R. Soderstrom. 1992. "Therapeutic wilderness programs and juvenile recidivism: A program evaluation." *Journal of Offender Rehabilitation* 17 (3/4): 19–46.

Castle, Michael N. 1991. *Alternative sentencing: Selling it to the public.* Washington, DC: U.S. Government Printing Office.

Catton, Bruce. 1960. *The American Heritage picture history of the Civil War.* New York: Outlook.

Chaires, Robert, and Susan Lentz. 1996. "Some legal considerations in prison privatization." In *Privatization and the provision of correctional services,* ed. G. Larry Mays and Tara Gray. Cincinnati: Academy of Criminal Justice Sciences and Anderson.

Chambliss, William J., and Robert Seidman. 1982. *Law, order and power.* Reading, MA: Addison-Wesley.

Champagne, Anthony, and Kenneth C. Haas. 1976. "The impact of Johnson v. Avery on prison administration." *Tennessee Law Review* 43: 275–303.

Champion, Dean. 1988. *Felony probation: Problems and prospects.* New York: Praeger.

———. 1990a. *Corrections in the United States: A contemporary perspective.* Englewood Cliffs, NJ: Prentice-Hall.

———. 1990b. *Probation and parole in the United States.* Columbus, OH: Merrill.

———. 1991. "Jail inmate litigation in the 1990s." In *American jails: Public policy issues,* ed. Joel A. Thompson and G. Larry Mays. Chicago: Nelson-Hall.

———. 1992. *The juvenile justice system.* New York: Macmillan.

Champion, Dean, and G. Larry Mays. 1991. *Transferring juveniles to criminal courts: Trends and implications for criminal justice.* New York: Praeger.

Chapman, Jane Roberts. 1980. *Economic realities and the female offender.* Lexington, MA: D. C. Heath.

Charle, S. 1981. "Suicides in the cellblocks." *Corrections Magazine* 7: 7–16.

Charles, Michael T. 1989. "The development of a juvenile electronic monitoring program." *Federal Probation* 53 (2): 3–12.

Chermak, Steven. 1995. "Crime in the news media: A refined understanding of how crimes become news." In *Media processes and the social construction of crime,* ed. Gregg Barak. New York: Garland.

Chesno, Frank A., and Peter R. Kilmann. 1975. "Effects of stimulation intensity on sociopathic avoidance learning." *Journal of Abnormal Psychology* 84: 144–50.

Chilton, Bradley. 1991. *Prisons under the gavel: The federal court takeover of Georgia prisons.* Columbus: Ohio State University Press.

Clear, Todd R. 1988. "A critical assessment of electronic monitoring in corrections." *Policy Studies Review* 7 (3): 671–81.

———. 1994. *Harm in American penology: Offenders, victims, and their communities.* Albany: State University Press of New York.

———. 1995. "Ophelia the C.C.W.: May 10, 2010." In *Crime and justice in the year*

2010, ed. John Klofas and Stan Stojkovic. Belmont, CA: Wadsworth.

Clear, Todd R.,and George F. Cole. 1986. *American corrections.* Pacific Grove, CA: Brooks/Cole.

———. 1990. *American corrections.* 2nd ed. Pacific Grove, CA: Brooks/Cole.

———. 1997. *American corrections.* 4th ed. Pacific Grove, CA: Brooks/Cole.

Clear, Todd R., and K. W. Gallagher. 1985. "Probation and parole supervision: A review of current classification practices." *Crime and Delinquency* 31: 423–43.

Clemmer, Donald. 1951. "Observations on imprisonment as a source of criminality." *Journal of Criminal Law and Criminology* 41: 311–19.

———. 1958. *The prison community.* New York: Holt, Rinehart & Winston.

Cline, Hugh F. 1968. "The determinants of normative patterns in correctional institutions." *Scandinavian Studies in Criminology* 2 (April): 189–93.

Clines, Frances X. 1992. "Ex-inmates urge return to areas of crime to help." *New York Times,* December 23, 1ff.

Cloward, Richard, and Lloyd Ohlin. 1960. *Delinquency and opportunity: A theory of delinquent gangs.* Glencoe, IL: Free Press.

Coffey, Alan R. 1974. *Administration of justice: A management systems approach.* Englewood Cliffs, NJ: Prentice-Hall.

Coffey, Alan R. 1975. *Correctional administration.* Englewood Cliffs, NJ: Prentice-Hall.

Cohen, Albert K. 1955. *Delinquent boys: The culture of the gang.* New York: Free Press.

Cohen, Fred. 1988. "The law of prisoners' rights: An overview." *Criminal Law Bulletin* 24 (4): 321–49.

Cohen, Robyn. 1995. *Probation and parole violators in state prison, 1991.* Washington, DC: U.S. Government Printing Office.

Cohn, Alvin W. 1977. *Criminal justice planning and development.* Beverly Hills, CA: Sage.

———. 1981. "The failure of correctional management–reconsidered." *Criminal Justice Review* 6 (2): 55–61.

———. 1991. "The failure of correctional management–reviewed: Present and future dimensions." *Federal Probation* (June): 12–16.

———. 1995. "The failure of correctional management: Recycling the middle manager." *Federal Probation* 59 (2): 10–16.

Cole, George F. 1993. "The decision to prosecute." In *Criminal justice: Law & politics,* 6th ed., George F. Cole, ed. Belmont, CA: Wadsworth.

Cole, George F., Stanislaw J. Frankowski, and Marc G. Gertz. 1987. *Major criminal justice systems: A comparative survey.* Beverly Hills, CA: Sage.

Coles, Frances S. 1987. "The impact of Bell v. Wolfish upon prisoners' rights." *Journal of Crime and Justice* 10 (1): 47–69.

Collins, William C. 1987a. "Privatization: Some legal considerations from a neutral perspective, part I." *American Jails* 1 (1): 40–45.

———. 1987b. "Privatization: Some legal considerations from a neutral perspective, part II." *American Jails* 1 (2): 28–34.

———. 1993. *Correctional law for the correctional officer.* Laurel, MD: American Correctional Association.

Colvin, Mark. 1982. "The 1980 New Mexico prison riot." *Social Problems* 29: 449–63.

Comptroller General of the United States. 1976. *Correctional institutions can do more to improve the employability of offenders.* Washington, DC: U.S. Government Printing Office.

Connecticut State Department of Corrections. n.d. *Close custody phase program manual.* Newtown, CT: Garner Correctional Institution.

Conroy, Robert, Wantland J. Smith, and Linda L. Zupan. 1991. "Officer stress in direct supervision jail." *American Jails* 5 (5): 34–36.

Cooprider, Keith W., and Judith Kerby. 1990. "A practical application of electronic monitoring at the pretrial stage." *Federal Probation* 54 (1): 28–35.

Cordilia, A. 1985. "Alcohol and property crime: Exploring the causal nexus." *Journal of Studies on Alcohol* 46 (2): 161–71.

Correctional Law Reporter. 1994. "Corrections court cases with greatest impact identified by CLR Poll." (June): 1–15.

———. 1995. "Access to a law library and inmates assisting inmates may not be the best ways of guaranteeing prisoners' right to court access." (Feb.): 67–69.

Corrections Digest. 1993a. "Federal court ruling holds official personally liable for inmate's medical help." (Aug. 25): 10.

———. 1993b. "Nevada not obligated to provide nonsmoking facilities, state argues." (Jan. 27): 4–5.

———. 1994. "ACLU joins inmates in federal suit over prison conditions." (Jan. 12): 7–8.

———. 1995. (Feb. 10): 3.

Coughlin, Ellen K. 1996. "Throwing away the key." *The Chronicle of Higher Education* (April 26): A8.

Cowles, Ernest L., Thomas C. Castellano, and Laura A. Gransky. 1995. *"Boot camp" drug treatment and aftercare interventions: An evaluation review.* Washington, DC: U.S. Government Printing Office.

Cox, Norman R., Jr., and William E. Osterhoff. 1991. "Managing the crisis in local corrections: A public-private partnership approach." In *American jails: Public policy issues,* ed. Joel A. Thompson and G. Larry Mays. Chicago: Nelson-Hall.

Craddock, Amy. 1996. "Classification systems." In *Encyclopedia of American prisons,* ed. Marilyn D. McShane and Frank P. Williams III, pp. 87–96. New York: Garland.

Crawford, William. 1834 (1969). *Report on the penitentiaries of the United States.* Montclair, NJ: Patterson Smith.

Cressey, Donald R. 1955. "Changing criminals: The application of the theory of differential association." *American Journal of Sociology* 61: 116–20.

Criminal Justice Newsletter. 1995a. "Chain gangs return to prisons in Alabama and Arizona." (May 15): 1–3.

———. 1995b. "Inmate suits a growing burden on federal courts, study finds." (Feb. 15): 6–7.

Criminal Law Reporter. 1993. "Opinion of the U.S. Supreme Court." (June 16): 2229.

———. 1994a. "Prisons and jails." (June 8): 2135.

———. 1994b. "Prison TB case shows effect of recent decision defining 'deliberate indifference.'" (Sept. 14): 1517–18.

———. 1995. "Guards at privatized prison entitled to qualified immunity from civil rights suit." (July 19): 1349–50.

Cromwell, Paul F., and George G. Killinger. 1994. *Community-based corrections: Probation, parole, and intermediate sanctions.* 3rd ed. St. Paul, MN: West.

Crouch, Ben M., and James W. Marquart. 1989. *An appeal to justice: Litigated reform of Texas prisons.* Austin: University of Texas Press.

Cullen, Francis T., and Karen E. Gilbert. 1982. *Reaffirming rehabilitation.* Cincinnati: Anderson.

Cullen, Francis T., Edward J. Latessa, Velmer S. Burton, Jr., and Lucien X. Lombardo. 1993. "The correctional orientation of prison wardens: Is the rehabilitative ideal supported?" *Criminology* 31 (1): 69–92.

Cuniff, Mark, and Mary K. Shilton. 1991. "Variations in felony probation: Persons under supervision in thirty-two urban and suburban counties." Washington, DC: Criminal Justice Planers Association.

Curran, Daniel J., and Claire M. Renzetti. 1994. *Theories of crime.* Boston: Allyn & Bacon.

Czajkoski, Eugene H. 1973. "Exposing the quasi-judicial role of the probation officer." *Federal Probation* 37 (2): 9–13.

Dale, Michael J. 1988. "Detaining juveniles in adult jails and lockups: An analysis of rights and liabilities." *American Jails* 2 (1): 467, 50.

Darwin, Charles. 1936. *The origin of the species by means of natural selection, or, The preservation of favored races in the struggle for life and the descent of man and selection in relation to sex.* New York: Modern Library.

Davis, Mark, and Joshua E. Muscat. 1993. "An epidemiological study of alcohol and suicide risk in Ohio jails and lockups, 1975–1984." *Journal of Criminal Justice* 21: 177–283.

Davis, Russell M. 1987. "Direct supervision as an organizational management system." *American Jails* 1 (1): 50–53.

De Beaumont, Gustave, and Alexis de Tocqueville. 1832 (1964). *On the penitentiary system in the United States and its application to France.* Carbondale, IL: Southern Illinois University Press.

Decker, Scott H. 1985. "A systematic analysis of diversion: Net widening and beyond." *Journal of Criminal Justice* 13 (3): 207–16.

De Frances, Carol J., and Kevin J. Strom. 1997. *Juveniles prosecuted in state criminal courts.* Washington, DC: U.S. Government Printing Office.

del Carmen, Rolando. 1992. "The Supreme Court and prison excessive use of force cases: Does one test fit all?" *Federal Probation* 56 (2): 44–47.

De Lucia, Robert C., and Thomas J. Doyle. 1994. *Career planning in criminal justice,* 2nd ed. Cincinnati: Anderson.

Department of Justice. 1978. *State and local probation and parole systems.* Washington, DC: U.S. Government Printing Office.

———. 1981. *Dictionary of criminal justice data terminology.* Washington, DC: U.S. Government Printing Office.

———. 1983. *Report to the nation on crime and justice.* Washington, DC: U.S. Government Printing Office.

———. 1984. *Habeas corpus.* Washington, DC: U.S. Government Printing Office.

———. 1988. *Report to the nation on crime and justice.* 2nd ed. Washington, DC: U.S. Government Printing Office.

———. 1991a. *Census of local jails, 1988.* Vol. 1. Washington, DC: U.S. Government Printing Office.

———. 1991b. *Profile of jail inmates, 1989.* Washington, DC: U.S. Government Printing Office.

———. 1992a. *Census of state and federal correctional facilities, 1990.* Washington, DC: U.S. Government Printing Office.

———. 1992b. *Correctional populations in the United States, 1990.* Washington, DC: U.S. Government Printing Office.

———. 1992c. *Women in jail, 1989.* Washington, DC: U.S. Government Printing Office.

———. 1994a. *Capital punishment 1993.* Washington, DC: U.S. Government Printing Office.

———. 1994b. *Comparing federal and state prison inmates, 1991.* Washington, DC: U.S. Government Printing Office.

———. 1994c. *Prisoners 1993.* Washington, DC: U.S. Government Printing Office.

———. 1995. *HIV in prisons and jails, 1993.* Washington, DC: U.S. Government Printing Office.

———. 1996a. *Capital punishment 1994.* Washington, DC: U.S. Government Printing Office.

———. 1996b. *Correctional population in the U.S., 1994.* Washington, DC: U.S. Government Printing Office.

———. 1996c. *Probation and parole population reaches almost 3.8 million.* Bureau of Justice Statistics press release, June 30, 1996.

———. 1996d. *Probation and parole populations in the U.S., 1995.* Washington, DC: U.S. Government Printing Office.

———. 1997. *Correctional populations in the United States, 1995.* Washington, DC: U.S. Government Printing Office.

De Witt, Charles. 1986a. *California tests new construction concepts.* Washington, DC: U.S. Government Printing Office.

———. 1986b. *Florida sets example with use of concrete modules.* Washington, DC: U.S. Government Printing Office.

———. 1986c. *New construction methods for correctional facilities.* Washington, DC: U.S. Government Printing Office.

———. 1986d. *Ohio's new approach to prison and jail financing.* Washington, DC: U.S. Government Printing Office.

DiIulio, John J., Jr. 1987. *Governing prisons: A comparative study of correctional management.* New York: Free Press.

———. ed. 1990. *Courts, corrections, and the Constitution: The impact of judicial intervention on prisons and jails.* New York: Oxford University Press.

———. 1994. "The evolution of executive management in the Federal Bureau of Prisons." In *Escaping prison myths,* ed. John W. Roberts. Washington, DC: American University Press.

Dickens, Charles. 1838. *Oliver Twist.* Philadelphia: Carey, Lea and Blanchard.

———. 1839. *Nicholas Nickleby: The life and adventures of Nicholas Nickleby.* New York: Turney.

———. 1842. *American notes.* London: Chapman and Hall.

———. 1859. *A tale of two cities.* Philadelphia: Peterson.

Dilworth, Donald. 1995. "Prisoners' lawsuits burden federal civil courts." *Trial* 31 (5): 98, 100.

Dopsch, Alfons. 1969. *The economic and social foundation of European civilizations.* New York: Fertig.

Douglas, Richard L. 1995. *Domestic mistreatment of the elderly: Towards prevention.* Washington, DC: American Association of Retired Persons.

Dressler, David. 1962. *The theory and practice of probation and parole.* New York: Columbia University Press.

Duffee, David E. 1989. *Corrections: Practice and policy.* New York: Random House.

Durham, Alexis M. 1989. "Origins of interest in the privatization of punishment: The nineteenth and twentieth century American experience." *Criminology* 27: 107–39.

Durkheim, Emile. 1897 (1951). *Suicide.* Trans. J. A. Spaulding and G. Simpson. New York: Free Press.

Dwyer, Diane C., and Roger B. McNally. 1994. "Public policy and prison industries for the 1990s." In *Critical issues in crime and justice,* ed. Albert R. Roberts. Thousand Oaks, CA: Sage.

Eaglin, J. and P. Lombard. 1982. A *validation and comparative evaluation of four predictive devices for classifying federal probation caseloads.* Washington, DC: Federal Judicial Center.

Edgerton, Robert. 1976. *Deviance: A cross-cultural perspective.* Menlo Park, CA: Cummings.

Eisenstein, James, and Herbert Jacob. 1977. *Felony justice: An organizational analysis of criminal courts.* Boston: Little, Brown.

El Paso Times. 1996. "Alabama to create female chain gangs." (April 26): 3A.

Ellis, Lee. 1990. "Conceptualizing criminal and related behavior from a biosocial perspective." In *Crime in biological, social, and moral contexts,* ed. L. Ellis and H. Hoffman. Westport, CT: Praeger.

Ellis, Lee. 1991. "Monoamine oxidase and criminality: Identifying an apparent biological marker for antisocial behavior." *Journal of Research in Crime and Delinquency* 28: 227–51.

English, Kim, Suzanne Pullen, and Linda Jones. 1996. *Managing adult sex offenders: A containment approach.* Lexington, KY: American Probation and Parole Association.

Enos, Richard, and Stephen Southern. 1996. *Correctional case management.* Cincinnati: Anderson.

Esbensen, Finn-Aage and David Huizinga. 1990. "Community structure and drug use from a social disorganization perspective: A research note." *Justice Quarterly* 7: 691–709.

Etzioni, Amatai. 1964. *Modern organizations.* Englewood Cliffs, NJ: Prentice-Hall.

Fagan, Jeffrey. 1996. "Gangs, drugs, and neighborhood change." In *Gangs in America,* 2nd ed., C. Ronald Huff, ed. Thousand Oaks, CA: Sage.

Farmer, Richard E. 1977. "Cynicism: A factor in corrections work." *Journal of Criminal Justice* 5: 237–46.

Feeley, Malcolm. 1979. *The process is the punishment: Handling cases in a lower criminal court.* New York: Russell Sage Foundation.

———. 1991. "The privatization of prison in historical perspective." *Criminal Justice Research Bulletin* 6 (2): 1–10.

Feld, Barry. 1981. "Legislative policies toward the serious juvenile offender." *Crime and Delinquency* 27 (4): 497–521.

Felkenes, George T. 1988. *Constitutional law for criminal justice.* 2nd ed. Englewood Cliffs, NJ: Prentice-Hall.

"Felons may get microchip implants." 1995. *Las Cruces [NM] Sun-News,* Sept. 2, p. A6.

Fields, Charles B. 1996. "Protective custody." In *Encyclopedia of American prisons,* ed. Marilyn D. McShane and Frank P. Williams III, p. 373. New York: Garland.

Finckenauer, James O. 1982. *Scared straight! and the panacea phenomenon.* Englewood Cliffs, NJ: Prentice-Hall.

Fishbein, Diana. 1990. "Biological perspectives in criminology." *Criminology* 28: 27–72.

Fishman, Joseph F. 1934. *Sex in prison.* New York: National Liberty Press.

Flanagan, Timothy J., and Katherine M. Jamieson, eds. 1988. *Bureau of Justice Statistics sourcebook of criminal justice statistics 1987.* Washington, DC: U.S. Government Printing Office.

Flanagan, Timothy J., and Kathleen Maguire, eds. 1990. *Bureau of Justice Statistics sourcebook of criminal justice statistics 1989.* Washington, DC: U.S. Government Printing Office.

———. 1992. *Bureau of Justice Statistics sourcebook of criminal justice statistics 1991.* Washington, DC: U.S. Government Printing Office.

———. 1993. "A full employment policy for prison in the United States: Some arguments, estimates, and implications." *Journal of Criminal Justice* 21: 117–30.

Flango, Victor E. 1994. "Federal court review of state court convictions in noncapital cases." *Justice System Journal* 17 (2): 153–70.

Fletcher, Beverly R., and Dreama G. Moon. 1993. Introduction to *Women prisoners: A forgotten population,* ed. B. R. Fletcher, L. D. Shaver, and D. G. Moon, pp. 5–13. Westport, CT: Praeger.

Flowers, G. T., T. S. Carr, and R. B. Ruback. 1991. *Special alternative incarceration evaluation.* Atlanta, GA: Georgia Department of Corrections.

Fogel, David. 1975. *". . . We are the living proof . . . " The justice model for corrections.* Cincinnati: Anderson.

———. 1981. Preface to *Justice as fairness,* ed. David Fogel and Joe Hudson, pp. v–xi. Cincinnati: Anderson.

Fong, Robert S. 1990. "The organizational structure of prison gangs." *Federal Probation* 54 (4): 36–43.

Fong, Robert S., and Ronald E. Vogel. 1996. "A comparative analysis of prison gang members, security threat groups, and general population prisoners in the Texas Department of Corrections." In *Gangs and gang behavior,* ed. G. Larry Mays. Chicago: Nelson-Hall.

Ford, Daniel, and Annesley K. Schmidt. 1985. *Electronically monitored home confinement.* Washington, DC: U.S. Government Printing Office.

Ford, Francis R. 1993. "Politics and jails, part II." *American Jails* 7 (1): 11–16.

Ford, Marilyn Chandler, and Francis T. Moore. 1992. "Fiscal challenges facing local correctional facilities." In *Corrections: Dilemmas and directions,* ed. Peter J. Benekos and Alida V. Merlo. Cincinnati: Anderson and Academy of Criminal Justice Sciences.

Forst, Martin L., Bruce A. Fisher, and Robert B. Cates. 1985. "Indeterminate and determinate sentencing of juvenile delinquents: National survey of approaches to commitment and release decision-making." *Juvenile and Family Court Journal* 36: 1–12.

Fox, James. 1984. "Women's prison policy, prisoner activism, and the impact of the contemporary feminist movement: A case study." *The Prison Journal* 64: 15–36.

Freedman, Estelle B. 1981. *Their sisters' keepers: Women's prison reform in America, 1830–1930.* Ann Arbor: University of Michigan Press.

Freivalds, Peter. 1996. *Balanced and restorative justice project (BARJ).* Washington, DC: U.S. Government Printing Office.

Friedman, Lawrence M. 1977. *Law and society: An introduction.* Englewood Cliffs, NJ: Prentice-Hall.

Friedman, Leon. 1972. *The law of war: A documentary history.* Vol. 1. New York: Random House.

Frug, Gerald E. 1978. "The judicial power of the purse." *University of Pennsylvania Law Review* 126 (4): 715–94.

Gaes, Gerald, and William J. McGuire. 1985. "Prison violence: The contributions of crowding versus other determinants of prison assault rates." *Journal of Research on Crime and Delinquency* 22: 41–65.

Gargarin, Michael. 1986. *Early Greek law.* Berkeley, CA: University of California Press.

Garson, G. David. 1972. "Force versus restraint in prison riots." *Crime and Delinquency* 18: 411–21.

Gershman, Bennett L. 1995. "Why prosecutors misbehave." In *Courts and justice,* ed. G. Larry Mays and Peter R. Gregware. Prospect Heights, IL: Waveland Press.

Giallambardo, Rose. 1966. *Society of women: A study of women's prison.* New York: Wiley.

Gibbon, Edward. 1932. *The decline and fall of the Roman empire.* New York: Modern Library.

Gibbons, Don C. 1996. "Pennsylvania system." In *Encyclopedia of American prisons,* ed. Marilyn D. McShane and Frank P. Williams III, pp. 351–52. New York: Garland.

Gibson, Helen C. 1976. "Women's prisons: Laboratories for penal reform." In *The female offender,* ed. Laura Crites, pp. 93–119. Lexington, MA: D. C. Heath.

Gido, Rosemary. 1996. "Organizational change and workforce planning: Dilemmas for criminal justice in the year 2000." In *Visions for change: Crime and justice in the twenty-first century,* ed. Roslyn Muraskin and Albert R. Roberts. Upper Saddle River, NJ: Prentice-Hall.

Gilbert, Michael J. 1996. "Private confinement and the role of government in a civil society." In *Privatization and the Provision of*

Correctional Services, ed. G. Larry Mays and Tara Gray. Cincinnati: Anderson and Academy of Criminal Justice Sciences.

Gilliard, Darrell K., and Allen J. Beck. 1996. *Prisoners in 1995.* Washington, DC: U.S. Government Printing Office.

———. 1997a. *Prison and jail inmates, 1995.* Washington, DC: U. S. Government Printing Office.

———. 1997b. *Prison and jail inmates at midyear, 1996.* Washington, DC: U.S. Government Printing Office.

Glueck, Sheldon, ed. 1933. *Probation and criminal justice.* New York: Macmillan.

Goetting, Ann. 1984. "Prison programs and facilities for elderly inmates." In *Elderly criminals,* ed. Evelyn S. Newman, Donald J. Newman, Mindy L. Gewirtz, and associates. Cambridge, MA: Oelgeschlager, Gunn and Hain.

Goffman, Erving. 1961. *Asylums.* Garden City, NY: Anchor.

Gold, Mark S., Arnold M. Washton, and Charles A. Dackis. 1985. "Cocaine abuse: Neurochemistry, phenomenology, and treatment." In *Cocaine use in America: Epidemiology and clinical perspectives,* ed. N. J. Kozel and E. H. Adams. Rockville, MD: National Institute of Drug Abuse.

Golden, Delores. 1984. "Elderly offenders in jail." In *Elderly criminals,* ed. Evelyn S. Newman, Donald J. Newman, Mindy L. Gewirtz, and associates. Cambridge, MA: Oelgeschlager, Gunn and Hain.

Goleman, Daniel. 1990. "Scientists pinpoint brain irregularities in drug addicts." *New York Times* (June 26): B5.

———. 1992. "New storm brews on whether crime has roots in genes." *New York Times* (Sept. 15): B5, B7.

Gordon, Robert A. 1987. "SES versus IQ in the race-IQ-delinquency model." *International Journal of Sociology and Social Policy* 7: 30–70.

Gottfredson, Stephen D., and Sean McConville. 1987. *America's correctional crisis: Prison population and public policy.* New York: Greenwood.

Gowdy, Voncile B. 1993. *Intermediate sanctions.* Washington, DC: U.S. Government Printing Office.

Gray, Tara, and Jon'a F. Meyer. 1996. "Expanding prison industries through privatiza-

tion." In *Privatization and the provision of correctional services,* ed. G. Larry Mays and Tara Gray. Cincinnati: Anderson and Academy of Criminal Justice Sciences.

———. 1997. "Prison administration: Inmate participation versus the control model." In *Correctional contexts,* ed. James W. Marquart and Jonathan R. Sorensen. Los Angeles: Roxbury.

Gray, Tara, G. Larry Mays, and Mary K. Stohr. 1995. "Inmate needs and programming in exclusively women's jails." *The Prison Journal* 75: 186–202.

Greenberg, Reuben. 1988. Interview on "probation," *Crime File II Series.* Washington, DC: U.S. Government Printing Office.

Greenfield, Lawrence A. 1991. *Women in prison.* Washington, DC: U.S. Government Printing Office.

———. 1997. *Sex offenses and offenders: An analysis of data on rape and sexual assault.* Washington, DC: U.S. Government Printing Office.

Greenwood, Peter, with Allan Abramse. 1982. *Selective incapacitation.* Santa Monica, CA: Rand Corp.

Grizzi, Lisa. 1994. "Helling v. McKinney and smoking in the cell block: Cruel and unusual punishment?" *American University Law Review* 43: 1091–134.

Gropper, B. A. 1985. "Probing the links between drugs and crime." Washington, DC: U.S. Government Printing Office.

Guynes, Randall. 1988. *Nation's jail managers assess their problems.* Washington, DC: U.S. Government Printing Office.

Hackett, Judith C., Harry P. Hatry, Robert B. Levinson, Joan Allen, Keon Chi, and Edward D. Feigenbaum. 1987. "Contracting for the operation of prisons and jails." Washington, DC: U.S. Government Printing Office.

Haddad, Jane. 1993. "Managing the special needs of mentally ill inmates." *American Jails* 7 (1): 62–65.

Hall, David B. 1987. "Jail facility renovation and expansion." *American Jails* 1 (1): 38–39.

Hammett, Theodore, and Lynne Harrold. 1994. *Tuberculosis in correctional facilities.* Washington, DC: U.S. Government Printing Office.

Hammett, Theodore, Lynne Harrold, Michael Gross, and Joel Epstein. 1994. *1992 update:*

HIV/AIDS in correctional facilities: Issues and options. Washington, DC: U.S. Government Printing Office.

Hammett, Theodore, and Saira Mioni. 1990. *Update on AIDS in prisons and jails.* Washington, DC: U.S. Government Printing Office.

Hanson, Richard A. 1987. "What should be done when prisoners want to take the state to court?" *Judicature* 70 (4): 223–27.

Hanson, Roger A., and Henry W. K. Daley. 1995. *Challenging the conditions of prisons and jails: A report on Section 1983 litigation.* Washington, DC: U.S. Government Printing Office.

Haque, Ekram U. 1989. "New York City Department of Correction: The successes and challenges of a giant system." *American Jails* 2 (4): 51, 55.

Harlow, Caroline Wolf. 1994. *Comparing federal and state prison inmates.* Washington, DC: U.S. Government Printing Office.

Harris, M. Kay, and Dudley P. Spiller, Jr. 1977. *After decision: Implementations of judicial decrees in correctional settings.* Washington, DC: National Institute of Law Enforcement and Criminal Justice.

Harris-George, Becky, Herbert H. Jarrett, and Richard T. Shigley. 1994. "State jails: Texas' answer to overcrowding!" *American Jails* 8 (5): 17–20.

Hassine, Victor. 1996. *Life without parole: Living in prison today.* Los Angeles: Roxbury.

Hatrack, Robert. 1987. "Electronic monitoring throughout the U.S." *American Jails* 1 (3): 39–40.

Hawke, D. F. 1971. *Benjamin Rush: Revolutionary gadfly.* Indianapolis: Bobbs-Merrill.

Hawkins, Richard, and Geoffrey P. Alpert. 1989. *American prison systems: Punishment and justice.* Englewood Cliffs, NJ: Prentice-Hall.

Hecht, Frank R., and Ramon Smithhart. 1987. "Management of the acute and chronically mentally ill inmate: A new experience." *American Jails* 1 (3): 10–12.

Heffernan, Elizabeth. 1972. *Making it in prison: The square, the cool and the life.* New York: Wiley.

Henry, Stuart, ed. 1994. *Inside jobs.* Salem, WI: Sheffield.

Herrnstein, Richard J., and Charles Murray. 1994. *The bell curve: Intelligence and class structure in American life.* New York: Free Press.

Hippchen, Leonard. 1982. *Holistic approaches to offender rehabilitation.* Springfield, IL: Charles C. Thomas.

Hindelang, Michael J. 1973. "Causes of delinquency: A partial replication and extension." *Social Problems* 20: 471–87.

Hipschman, D. C. 1987. "Electronic monitoring now makes house arrest a viable way to alleviate overcrowding." *American Jails* 1 (1): 63–64.

Hirschi, Travis. 1969. *Causes of delinquency.* Berkeley: University of California.

Hodgins, Sheilagh. 1993. "The criminality of mentally disordered persons." In *Mental disorder and crime,* ed. Sheilagh Hodgins. Newbury Park, CA: Sage.

Holten, N. Gary, and Lawson L. Lamar. 1991. *The criminal courts: Structures, personnel, and processes.* New York: McGraw-Hill.

Hopper, Columbus B. 1985. "The impact of litigation on Mississippi's prison system." *The Prison Journal* 65 (1): 54–63.

Howard, John. 1973. *The state of prisons in England and Wales.* Montclair, NJ: Patterson Smith.

Hughes, Robert. 1987. *The fatal shore.* New York: Knopf.

Hunt, Chester L., and Lewis Walker. 1974. *Ethnic dynamics: Patterns of intergroup relations in various societies.* Homewood, IL: Dorsey.

Hurst, H., and Patricia Torbet. 1993. *Organization and administration of juvenile services: Probation, aftercare, and state institutions for delinquent youth.* Washington, DC: U.S. Government Printing Office.

"Implementing community service: The referral process." 1989. *Federal Probation* 53 (1): 3–9.

Inciardi, James. 1992. *The war on drugs II.* Mountain View, CA: Mayfield.

Institute of Judicial Administration–American Bar Association Juvenile Justice Standards Project. 1980. *Standards relating to the juvenile probation function.* Washington, DC: U.S. Government Printing Office.

Irwin, John. 1970. *The felon.* Englewood Cliffs, NJ: Prentice-Hall.

———. 1980. *Prisons in turmoil.* Boston: Little, Brown.

———. 1985. *The jail: Managing the underclass in American society.* Berkeley: University of California Press.

Irwin, John, and James Austin. 1993. *It's about time: America's imprisonment binge.* Belmont, CA: Wadsworth.

Irwin, John, and Donald Cressey. 1962. "Thieves, convicts and the inmate culture." *Social Problems* 10: 142–55.

Jackson, Pamela Irving. 1991. "Crime, youth gangs, and urban transition: The social dislocations of postindustrial economic development." *Justice Quarterly* 8 (3): 379–97.

Jackson, Patrick G. 1988. "The uses of jail confinement in three counties." *Policy Studies Review* 7 (3): 592–605.

———. 1991. "Competing ideologies of jail confinement." In *American jails: Public policy issues,* ed. Joel A. Thompson and G. Larry Mays. Chicago: Nelson-Hall.

Jacobs, James B. 1977. *Stateville: The penitentiary in mass society.* Chicago: University of Chicago Press.

———. 1979. "Race relations and the prison subculture." In *Crime and justice: Volume I,* ed. Norval Morris and Michael Tonry. Chicago: University of Chicago Press.

Jeffords, Charles, and Jan Lindsey. 1996. "George Beto (1916–1991)." In *Encyclopedia of American prisons,* ed. Marilyn D. McShane and Frank P. Williams III. New York: Garland.

Jerrell, Jeanette M., and Richard Komisaruk. 1991. "Public policy issues in the delivery of mental health services in a jail setting." In *American jails: Public policy issues,* ed. Joel A. Thompson and G. Larry Mays. Chicago: Nelson-Hall.

Johnson, Elmer H. 1996. "Auburn system." In *Encyclopedia of American prisons,* ed. Marilyn D. McShane and Frank P. Williams III. New York: Garland.

Johnson, F. R. 1928. *Probation for juveniles and adults.* New York: Century.

Johnson, Herbert A., and Nancy Travis Wolfe. 1996. *History of criminal justice.* 2nd ed. Cincinnati: Anderson.

Johnston, James. 1949. *Alcatraz: Island prison and the men who live there.* New York: Scribner's.

Johnston, Norman. 1969. Introduction to *Report on the penitentiaries of the United States,* ed. William Crawford. Montclair, NJ: Patterson Smith.

Jolowicz, H. F. 1954. *Historical introduction to the study of Roman law.* Cambridge: Cambridge University Press.

Judiscak, Daniel. 1995. "Why are the mentally ill in jail?" *American Jails* 9 (5): 9–15.

Kalinich, David. 1980. *Power, stability, and contraband: The inmate economy.* Prospect Heights, IL: Waveland Press.

———. 1996. "Contraband." In *Encyclopedia of American prisons,* ed. Marilyn D. McShane and Frank P. Williams III, pp. 111–15. New York: Garland.

Kalinich, David, Paul Embert, and Jeffrey D. Senese. 1988. "Integrating community mental health services into local jails: A policy perspective." *Policy Studies Review* 7 (3): 660–70.

———. 1991. "Mental health services for jail inmates: Imprecise standards, traditional philosophies, and the need for change." In *American jails: Public policy issues,* ed. Joel A. Thompson and G. Larry Mays. Chicago: Nelson-Hall.

Kassin, Saul M. 1995. "The American jury: Handicapped in the pursuit of justice." In *Courts and justice,* ed. G. Larry Mays and Peter R. Gregware. Prospect Heights, IL: Waveland Press.

Kennedy, D. B., and R. J. Homant. 1988. "Predicting custodial suicides: Problems with the use of profiles." *Justice Quarterly* 5 (3): 441–56.

Kerle, Kenneth E., and Francis R. Ford. 1982. *The state of our nation's jails.* Washington, DC: National Sheriffs' Association.

Kimme, Dennis A., Gary M. Bowker, Bruce R. Bounds, Robert G. Deichman, Harry L. Baxter. 1986. *Small jail special issues.* Washington, DC: National Institute of Corrections.

Klein, Philip. 1920. *Prison methods in New York State.* New York: Columbia University Press.

Klofas, John M. 1987. "Patterns of jail use." *Journal of Criminal Justice* 15: 403–11.

———. 1988. "Measuring jail use: A comparative analysis of local corrections." Paper presented at the annual meeting of the American Society of Criminology, Chicago, IL.

———. 1991a. "Disaggregating jail use: Variety and change in local corrections over a ten-year period." In *American jails: Public policy issues,* ed. Joel A. Thompson and G. Larry Mays. Chicago: Nelson-Hall.

———. 1991b. "Jail crowding." In *Setting the jail research agenda for the 1990s,* ed. G. Larry Mays. Washington, DC: National Institute of Corrections.

Klofas, John, Stan Stojkovic, and David Kalinich. 1990. *Criminal justice organizations: Administration and management.* Pacific Grove, CA: Brooks/Cole.

Knapp, Kay. 1982. "The impact of the Minnesota sentencing guidelines on sentencing practices." *Hamline Law Review* 5: 237–56.

———. 1984. "What sentencing reform in Minnesota has and has not accomplished." *Judicature* 68: 181–89.

———. 1986. "Proactive policy analysis of Minnesota's prison populations." *Criminal Justice Policy Review* 1: 37–57.

Krisberg, Barry, and James Austin. 1993. *Reinventing juvenile justice.* Newbury Park, CA: Sage.

Krisberg, Barry, Robert DeComo, and Norma C. Herrera. 1992. *National juvenile custody trends 1978–1989.* Washington, DC: U.S. Government Printing Office.

Lagoy, Stephen P., Frederick A. Hussey, and John H. Kramer. 1978. "A comparative assessment of determinate sentencing in the four pioneer states." *Crime and Delinquency* 24: 385–400.

Lammay, Rich. 1996. "The role of corporate America in prison industries: A practitioner's view." In *Privatization and the provision of correctional services,* ed. G. Larry Mays and Tara Gray. Cincinnati: Anderson and Academy of Criminal Justice Sciences.

Lammers, Norma Phillips, and Mark O. Morris. 1990. *Jail construction in California.* Washington, DC: U.S. Government Printing Office.

Langan, Patrick A., and Jodi M. Brown. 1997. *Felony sentences in state courts, 1994.* Washington, DC: U.S. Government Printing Office.

Lanier, Mark M., and Cloud Miller. 1995. "Attitudes and practices of federal probation officers toward pre-plea/trial investigative report policy." *Crime and Delinquency* 43: 364–77.

Latessa, Edward J., and Harry E. Allen. 1997. *Corrections in the community.* Cincinnati: Anderson.

Lawrence, James E., and Van Zwisohn. 1991. "AIDS in jail." In *American jails: Public policy issues,* ed. Joel A. Thompson and G. Larry Mays. Chicago: Nelson-Hall.

Le Goff, Jacques. 1989. *Medieval civilization, 400–1500.* Trans. Julia Barrow. New York: Blackwell.

Lemert, Edwin M. 1967. *Human deviance, social problems, and social control.* Englewood Cliffs, NJ: Prentice-Hall.

Lemov, Penelope. 1995. "Corrections: Is anything working?" *Governing* (Oct.): 53–54.

———. 1996. "Long life on death row." *Governing* 9 (6): 30–34.

Lester, David, and Michael Braswell. 1987. *Correctional counseling.* Cincinnati: Anderson.

Levinson, Robert B., and Roy E. Gerard. 1973. "Functional units: A different correctional approach." *Federal Probation* 37: 8–16.

Lewis, Naphtali, and Meyer Reinhold, eds. 1990. *Roman civilization: Selected readings; Volume 1: The republic and the Augustan age.* New York: Columbia University Press.

Liebowitz, Morton J. 1991. "Regionalization in Virginia jails." *American Jails* 5 (5): 42–45.

Lillis, J. 1994. "Prison escapes and violence remain down." *Corrections Compendium* 19: 6–21.

Lilly, J. Robert, and Richard A. Ball. 1987. "A brief history of house arrest and electronic monitoring." *Northern Kentucky Law Review* 13 (3): 343–74.

Lilly, J. Robert, Richard A. Ball, and Jennifer Wright. 1987. "Home incarceration with electronic monitoring in Kenton County, Kentucky: An evaluation." In *Intermediate punishments,* ed. Belinda R. McCarthy. Monsey, NY: Willow Tree Press.

Lipton, Douglas, Robert Martinson, and Judith Wilks. 1975. *The effectiveness of correctional treatment.* New York: Praeger.

Lockwood, Daniel. 1980. *Prison sexual victimization.* New York: Elsevier.

Logan, Charles H. 1987. "The propriety of proprietary prisons." *Federal Probation* 51: 35–40.

———. 1990. *Private prisons: Cons and pros.* New York: Oxford University Press.

Lombardo, Lucien X. 1984. "Group dynamics and the prison guard subculture: Is the subculture an impediment to helping inmates?"

International Journal of Offender Therapy and Comparative Criminology 29: 70–90.

Lombroso, Cesare. 1876. *L'uomo delinquente [The Criminal Man]*. Milan: Hoepli.

Lozano, Antoinette, G. Larry Mays, and L. Thomas Winfree, Jr. 1990. "Diagnosing delinquents: The purpose of a youth diagnostic center." *Juvenile and Family Court Journal* 41: 25–39.

Lynch, James P., Steven K. Smith, Helen A. Graziadei, Tanutda Pittyathilchun. 1994. *Profile of inmates for the U.S. and England and Wales, 1991*. Washington, DC: U.S. Government Printing Office.

Lynch, P. J. 1988. "Criminality in the elderly and psychiatric disorder: A review of the literature." *Medical Science and the Law* 28: 65–74.

———. 1993. "Boot camp prisons in 1993." *National Institute of Justice Journal* (Nov.): 21–28.

———. 1997. "Criminal justice and crime prevention." In *Preventing crime: What works, what doesn't, what's promising?* ed. Lawrence W. Sherman. Washington, DC: U.S. Government Printing Office.

MacKenzie, Doris L., and James W. Shaw. 1990. "Inmate adjustment and change during shock incarceration: The impact of correctional boot camp programs." *Justice Quarterly* 7 (1): 125–50.

———. 1993. "The impact of shock incarceration on technical violations and new criminal activities." *Justice Quarterly* 10: 463–87.

MacKenzie, Doris L., James W. Shaw, and Voncile Gowdy. 1993. "An evaluation of shock incarceration in Louisiana." Washington, DC: U.S. Government Printing Office.

Maguire, Kathleen, and Ann C. Pastore, eds. 1995. *Bureau of Justice Statistics sourcebook of criminal justice statistics 1994*. Washington, DC: U.S. Government Printing Office.

———. 1996. *Bureau of Justice Statistics sourcebook of criminal justice statistics 1995*. Washington, DC: U.S. Government Printing Office.

Mahan, Sue. 1982. "An 'orgy of brutality' at Attica and the 'killing ground' at Santa Fe: A comparison of prison riots." In *Coping with imprisonment,* ed. N. Parisi, pp. 65–78. Beverly Hills, CA: Sage.

———. 1984. "Imposition of despair: An ethnography of women in prison." *Justice Quarterly* 1: 357–83.

Maher, Richard J., and Henry E. Dufour. 1987. "Experimenting with community service: A punitive alternative to imprisonment." *Federal Probation* 51 (3): 22–27.

Maloney, D., D. Romig, and T. L. Armstrong. 1988. "Juvenile probation: The balanced approach." *Juvenile and Family Court Journal* 39 (3): 1–63.

Mann, Coramae Richey. 1993. *Unequal justice: The question of color.* Bloomington: Indiana University Press.

Marchese, Joe. 1989. "AIDS training for jail personnel." *American Jails* 3 (1): 27–28.

Martin, Steven J., and Sheldon Ekland-Olson. 1987. *Texas prisons: The walls came tumbling down.* Austin: Texas Monthly Press.

Martinson, Robert. 1974. "What works? Questions and answers about prison reform." *Public Interest* 35: 22–54.

Maurer, Marc. 1985. *The lessons of Marion: The failure of a maximum security prison: A history and analysis, with voices of prisoners.* Philadelphia: American Friends Service Committee.

———. 1992. *Americans behind bars: One year later.* Washington, DC: The Sentencing Project.

May, Edgar. 1978. "Weekend jail: Doing time on the installment plan." *Corrections Magazine* (March): 28–38.

Mays, G. Larry. 1981. "Supreme Court disengagement from the exclusionary rule: The impact of Stone v. Powell." *Criminal Justice Review* 6 (2): 43–46.

———. 1983. "Stone v. Powell: The impact on state supreme court judges' perceptions." *Journal of Criminal Justice* 11 (1): 27–34.

———. 1984. "The Supreme Court and development of federal habeas corpus doctrine." In *Legal issues in criminal justice: The courts,* ed. Sloan Letman, Dan Edwards, and Daniel Bell. Cincinnati: Anderson.

———. 1989. "The impact of federal sentencing guidelines on jail and prison overcrowding and early release." In *The U.S. sentencing guidelines: Implications for criminal justice,* ed. Dean J. Champion. New York: Praeger.

———. 1996. "Correctional privatization: Defining the issues and searching for answers." In *Privatization and the provision of correctional services: Context and consequences,* ed. G. Larry Mays and Tara Gray. Cincinnati: Anderson and Academy of Criminal Justice Sciences.

Mays, G. Larry, and Frances P. Bernat. 1988. "Jail reform litigation: The issue of rights and remedies." *American Journal of Criminal Justice* 12 (2): 254–73.

Mays, G. Larry, and Robert Czerniak. 1992/93. "The political problems of planning for a new jail: Dona Ana County, New Mexico's experience." *Texas Journal of Political Studies* 15 (1): 31–45.

Mays, G. Larry, Charles B. Fields, and Joel A. Thompson. 1991. "Preincarceration patterns of drug and alcohol use by jail inmates." *Criminal Justice Policy Review* 5 (1): 40–52.

Mays, G. Larry, and Tara Gray, eds. 1996. *Privatization and the provision of correctional services.* Cincinnati: Anderson and Academy of Criminal Justice Sciences.

Mays, G. Larry, and Michelle Olszta. 1989. "Prison litigation: From the 1960s to the 1990s." *Criminal Justice Policy Review* 3 (3): 279–98.

Mays, G. Larry, and William A. Taggart. 1985. "The impact of litigation on changing New Mexico's prison conditions." *The Prison Journal* 65 (1): 38–53.

Mays, G. Larry, and William A. Taggart. 1988. "The implementation of court-ordered prison reform." In *Research in law and policy studies,* vol. 2, ed. Stuart S. Nagel. Greenwich, CT: JAI Press.

Mays, G. Larry, and Joel A. Thompson. 1988. "Mayberry revisited: The characteristics and operations of America's small jails." *Justice Quarterly* 5 (3): 421–40.

———. 1991. "The political and organizational context of American jails." In *American jails: Public policy issues,* ed. Joel A. Thompson and G. Larry Mays. Chicago: Nelson-Hall.

McCampbell, Susan W. 1990. "Direct supervision: Looking for the right people." *American Jails* 4 (4): 68–69.

McCarthy, Bernard J. 1992. "Community residential centers: An intermediate sanction for the 1990s." In *Corrections: Dilemmas and directions,* ed. Peter J. Benekos and Alida V. Merlo. Cincinnati: Anderson and the Academy of Criminal Justice Sciences.

McCleery, Richard H. 1968. "Correctional administration and political change." In *Prison within society: A reader in penology,* ed. Lawrence Hazelrigg, pp. 113–49. New York: Doubleday-Anchor.

McCorkle, Lloyd, and Richard Korn. 1954. "Resocialization within walls." *The Annals of the American Academy of Political and Social Sciences* 293: 5–19.

McCoy, Candace. 1984. "Determinate sentencing, plea-bargaining bans, and hydraulic discretion in California." *Justice System Journal* 9: 256–75.

McCullough, H. Laws, and Timothy S. Maguigan. 1990. "PRICOR: Proving privatization works." *American Jails* 4 (4): 46–49.

McCurdy, Howard E. 1979. *Public administration: A synthesis.* Menlo Park, CA: Cummings.

McGregor, Douglas. 1960. *The human side of enterprise.* New York: McGraw-Hill.

McKelvey, Blake. 1936. *American prisons: A study in American social history prior to 1915.* Chicago: University of Chicago Press.

McShane, Marilyn D., and Wesley Krause. 1993. *Community corrections.* New York: Macmillan.

McShane, Marilyn D., and Frank P. Williams III. 1989. "Old and ornery: The disciplinary experiences of elderly prisoners." Paper presented at the annual meeting of the American Society of Criminology (Nov.).

———. 1993. *The management of correctional institutions.* New York: Garland.

———. 1996. "Administration." In *Encyclopedia of American prisons,* ed. Marilyn D. McShane and Frank P. Williams III. New York: Garland.

Meithe, T. D. 1987. "Charging and plea bargaining practices under determinate sentencing: An investigation of the hydraulic displacement of discretion." *Journal of Criminal Law* 78: 155–76.

Merton, Robert K. 1957. *Social theory and social structure.* New York: Free Press.

Messing, Howard. 1993. "AIDS in jail." *American Jails* 7 (1): 40–46.

Miller, B. A., and J. W. Welte. 1986. "Comparisons of incarcerated offenders according to use of alcohol and/or drugs prior to offense." *Criminal Justice and Behavior* 13 (4): 366–92.

Miller, Jerome. 1992. "56 percent of young black males in Baltimore under justice control." *Overcrowded Times* 3 (Dec.): 1–10.

Miller, Walter B. 1958. "Lower-class culture as a generating milieu of gang delinquency." *Journal of Social Issues* 14: 5–19.

Moone, Joseph. 1997. *Juveniles in private facilities, 1991–1995.* Washington, DC: U.S. Government Printing Office.

More, Harry W., Jr. 1977. *Criminal justice management: Text and readings.* St. Paul, MN: West Publishing.

Morris, Norval. 1974. *The future of imprisonment.* Chicago: University of Chicago Press.

Morris, Norval, and Michael Tonry. 1990. *Between prison and probation: Intermediate punishments in a rational sentencing system.* New York: Oxford University Press.

Moses, Marilyn C. 1995. *Keeping incarcerated mothers and their daughters together: Girl Scouts behind bars.* Washington, DC: U.S. Government Printing Office.

Mouzelis, Nicos P. 1967. *Organisation and bureaucracy: An analysis of modern theories.* Chicago: Aldine.

Moynahan, J. M., and Earle K. Stewart. 1980. *The American jail: Its development and growth.* Chicago: Nelson-Hall.

Mullen, Joan. 1984. *Corrections in the private sector.* Washington, DC: U.S. Government Printing Office.

Mumola, Christopher, and Allen J. Beck. 1997. *Prisoners in 1996.* Washington, DC: U.S. Government Printing Office.

Nagel, William G. 1985. "Hands off, hands on, hands off." *The Prison Journal* 65 (1): i–iii.

National Advisory Commission on Criminal Justice Standards and Goals. 1973. *Corrections.* Washington, DC: U.S. Government Printing Office.

National Advisory Committee for Juvenile Justice and Delinquency Prevention. 1980. *Standards for the administration of juvenile justice.* Washington, DC: U.S. Government Printing Office.

National Task Force on Correctional Substance Abuse Strategies. 1991. *Intervening with substance abusing offenders: A framework for action.* Washington, DC: U.S. Government Printing Office.

Nelkin, Dorothy, and M. Susan Lindee. 1995. *The DNA mystique: The gene as a cultural icon.* New York: Freeman.

Nelson, James F. 1991. *The incarceration of minority defendants: An identification of disparity in New York State, 1985–86.* Albany: New York State Division of Criminal Justice Statistics.

Nelson, W. Raymond. 1988. *Cost savings in new generation jails: The direct supervision approach.* Washington, DC: U.S. Government Printing Office.

Neubauer, David W. 1992. *America's courts and the criminal justice system.* 4th ed. Pacific Grove, CA: Brooks/Cole.

New York Department of Correctional Services. 1992. *The fourth annual report to the legislature on shock incarceration and shock parole supervision.* Albany: Department of Correctional Services and Division of Parole.

———. 1993. *The fifth annual report to the legislature on shock incarceration and shock parole supervision.* Albany: Department of Correctional Services and Division of Parole.

New York Special Commission on Attica. 1972. *Attica.* New York: Bantam.

New York State, Department of Correctional Services, Division of Parole. 1995. *Annual shock legislative report.* Albany: New York State, Department of Correctional Services, Division of Parole.

Newbold, Greg. 1982. *The big huey.* Auckland: William Collins.

———. 1992. "What works in prison management: Effects of administrative change in New Zealand." *Federal Probation* 56 (4): 53–7.

Newman, Graeme. 1958. *Sourcebook on probation, parole and pardons.* Springfield, IL: Charles C. Thomas.

———. 1978. *The punishment response.* New York: Pantheon.

———. 1983. *Just and painful: A case for the corporal punishment of criminals.* New York: Macmillan.

North, Donald V. 1988. "RICO: A theory of investigation." *The Police Chief* (Jan.): 44–47.

Norwich, John Julius. 1988. *Byzantium: The early centuries.* New York: Viking.

Nugent, Thomas, trans. 1977. *Montesquieu, On the spirit of laws.* Book 6, chap. 9. Berkeley: University of California Press.

Nurco, D. N., J. W. Shaffer, J. C. Ball, T. W. Kilock, and J. Langrod. (1986). "A comparison by ethnic group and city of the criminal activities of narcotic addicts." *Journal of Nervous and Mental Disease* 174 (2): 112–16.

Ohlin, Lloyd. 1956. *Sociology and the field of corrections.* New York: Russell Sage.

Orrick, David. 1989. "New construction as a solution to jail overcrowding: Some policy and funding implications." *American Journal of Criminal Justice* 14 (1): 71–86.

Oswald, Russell G. 1972. *Attica: My story.* Garden City, NY: Doubleday.

Palmer, John W. 1977. *Constitutional rights of prisoners.* 2nd ed. Cincinnati: Anderson.

Parent, Dale G., Valerie Leiter, Stephen Kennedy, Lisa Livens, Daniel Wentworth, and Sarah Wilcox. 1994. *Conditions of confinement: Juvenile detention and corrections facilities.* Washington, DC: U.S. Government Printing Office.

Pasternak, Douglas. 1997. "Special report: Wonder weapons." *U.S. News and World Report* 123 (1): 38–41, 45–46.

Patzman, John, and Kim English. 1994. *Parole guidelines handbook.* Denver: Division of Criminal Justice.

Paulsen, Conrad G., and Charles H. Whitebread. 1974. *Juvenile law and procedure.* Reno, NV: Institute of Court Management.

Pelz, Mary E. 1996. "Gangs." In *Encyclopedia of American prisons,* ed. Marilyn D. McShane and Frank P. Williams III, pp. 213–18. New York: Garland.

Perkins, Craig. 1994. *National corrections reporting programs, 1991.* Washington, DC: U.S. Government Printing Office.

Perkins, Craig, James J. Stephan, and Allen J. Beck. 1995. *Jails and jail inmates 1993–1994.* Washington, DC: U.S. Government Printing Office.

Petersilia, Joan. 1985. "Rand's research: A closer look." *Corrections Today* 47: 37, 40.

———. 1993. *Evaluating intensive supervision probation/parole: Results of a nationwide experiment.* Washington, DC: U.S. Government Printing Office.

Petersilia, Joan, and Susan Turner. 1990. *Intensive supervision for high-risk probationers: Findings from three California experiments.* Santa Monica, CA: RAND Corp.

Peterson, Eric. 1996. *Juvenile boot camps: Lessons learned.* Washington, DC: U.S. Government Printing Office.

Pfohl, Stephen J. 1981. "Labeling criminals." In *Law and Deviance,* ed. H. L. Ross, pp. 65–97. Beverly Hills, CA: Sage.

Pierce, Glenn L., and William J. Bowers. 1981. "The Bartley-Fox gun law's short-term impact on crime." *Annals of the American Academy of Political and Social Science* 455 (May): 120–37.

Platt, Anthony. 1969. *The child savers.* Chicago: University of Chicago Press.

Pollock-Byrne, Joycelyn M. 1990. *Women, prison and crime.* Pacific Grove, CA: Brooks/Cole.

Poole, Eric D., and Robert M. Regoli. 1983. "Violence in juvenile institutions: A comparative study." *Criminology* 21: 213–32.

Powers, Richard A., III. 1987. "Comment: Restrictions on state prisoner habeas corpus review by federal courts." *Criminal Law Bulletin* 23 (1): 30–35.

Prigmore, Charles S., and Richard T. Crow. 1976. "Is the Court remaking the American prison system?" *Federal Probation* 40: 3–10.

Propper, Alice M. 1981. *Prison homosexuality: Myth and reality.* Lexington, MA: Lexington Books.

Quinn, James F., and John E. Holman. 1991a. "The efficacy of electronically monitored home confinement as a case management device." *Journal of Contemporary Criminal Justice* 7 (2): 128–34.

———. 1991b. "Intrafamilial conflict among felons under community supervision: An examination of the co-habitants of electronically monitored offenders." *Journal of Offender Rehabilitation* 16 (3/4): 177–92.

Quinney, Richard. 1970. *The social reality of crime.* Boston: Little, Brown.

Rackmill, Stephen J. 1993. "Community correction and the Fourth Amendment." *Federal Probation* 57 (3): 40–45.

Rafter, Nicole Hahn. 1985. *Partial justice: Women in state prison, 1800–1935.* Boston: Northeastern University Press.

Reid, Sue Titus. 1981. *The correctional system.* New York: Holt, Rinehart & Winston.

Remington, Frank J. 1986. "Change in the availability of federal habeas corpus: Its significance for state prisoners and state correctional programs." *Michigan Law Review* 85 (3): 570–91.

Renzema, Marc, and David T. Skelton. 1990. *Use of electronic monitoring in the United States: 1989 update.* Washington, DC: U.S. Government Printing Office.

Rhodes, Susan L. 1992. "Prison reform and prison life: Four books on the process of court-ordered change." *Law & Society Review* 26 (1): 189–218.

Ricci, Kenneth. 1986. "What can county commissioners do about their jails?" *The Prison Journal* 61: 14–18.

Ringel, Cheryl L., Ernest L. Cowles, and Thomas C. Castellano. 1994. "Changing patterns and trends in parole supervision." In *Critical issues in crime and justice,* ed. Albert R. Roberts. Thousand Oaks, CA: Sage.

Riveland, Chase. 1991. "Being a director of corrections in the 1990s." *Federal Probations* 55 (2): 10–11.

Robbins, Ira P. 1988. *Legal dimensions of private incarceration.* Washington, DC: American Bar Association.

Roberts, Albert R. 1988. "Wilderness programs for juvenile offenders: A challenging alternative." *Juvenile & Family Court Journal* 39 (1): 1–12.

Robertson, James E. (1985–86). "Surviving incarceration: Constitutional protection from inmate violence." *Drake Law Review* 35 (1): 101–60.

Rogers, Joseph W. (1996). "Mary Belle Harris (1874–1957)." In *Encyclopedia of American prisons,* ed. Marilyn D. McShane and Frank P. Williams III. New York: Garland.

Rogers, Joseph W., and G. Larry Mays. 1987. *Juvenile delinquency and juvenile justice.* New York: John Wiley.

Rowan, Joseph R. 1993. "Politics in jail operations–Some good, some bad." *American Jails* 6 (6): 58–60.

Rowe, David. 1990. "Inherited dispositions toward learning delinquent and criminal behavior: New evidence." In *Crime in biological, social and moral contexts,* ed. L. Ellis and H. Hoffman. Westport, CT: Praeger.

Ruanda, J., E. Rhine, and R. Wetter. 1994. *The practice of parole boards.* Lexington, KY: Council of State Governments.

Rubin, H. Ted. 1984. *The courts: Fulcrum of the justice system.* 2nd ed. New York: Random House.

Rubin, Paula N. 1993. *The Americans with Disabilities Act and criminal justice: An overview.* Washington, DC: U.S. Government Printing Office.

———. 1994. *The Americans with Disabilities Act and criminal justice: Hiring new employees.* Washington, DC: U.S. Government Printing Office.

———. 1995. *The Americans with Disabilities Act and criminal justice: Mental disabilities and corrections.* Washington, DC: U.S. Government Printing Office.

Rubin, Paula N., and Susan W. McCampbell. 1994. *The Americans with Disabilities Act and criminal justice: Providing inmate services.* Washington, DC: U.S. Government Printing Office.

Ruggles-Brise, Sir Evelyn. 1921. *The English prison system.* London: Macmillan.

Rush, George E. 1994. *The dictionary of criminal justice.* 4th ed. Guilford, CT: Dushkin.

Saenz, Adolph. 1986. *Politics of a riot.* Washington, DC: American Correctional Association.

Sagatun, Inger, Loretta L. McCollum, and Leonard P. Edwards. 1985. "The effect of transfers from juvenile court to criminal court: A loglinear analysis." *Journal of Crime and Justice* 8: 65–92.

Sampson, Robert J., and W. Byron Groves. 1989. "Community structure and crime: Testing social disorganization theory." *American Journal of Sociology* 94: 774–802.

Santos, Michael G. 1996. "Commissaries." In *Encyclopedia of American prisons,* ed. Marilyn D. McShane and Frank P. Williams III, pp. 100–102. New York: Garland.

Saxton, Samuel F. 1991. "Reintegration: A strategy for success." In *Setting the jail research agenda for the 1990s,* ed. G. Larry Mays. Washington, DC: National Institute of Corrections.

Scacco, Anthony M. 1982. *Male rape: A casebook of sexual aggression.* New York: AMS Press.

Schafer, Stephen. 1969. *Theories in criminology.* New York: Random House.

Schaller, Jack. 1982. "Work and imprisonment: The overview of the changing role of prison labor in American prisons." *The Prison Journal* 62: 3–11.

Scheb, John M., and John M. Scheb II. 1989. *Criminal law and procedure.* St. Paul, MN: West.

Scheflin, Alan W., and Jon M. Van Dyke. 1995. "Merciful juries." In *Courts and justice,* ed. G. Larry Mays and Peter R. Gregware. Prospect Heights, IL: Waveland Press.

Schlossman, S. L. 1977. *Love and the American delinquent: The theory and practice of "progressive" juvenile justice, 1825–1920.* Chicago: University of Chicago Press.

Schneider, Anne L. 1985. *The impact of deinstitutionalization on recidivism and secure confinement of status offenders.* Washington, DC: U.S. Government Printing Office.

Schrag, Clarence. 1944. "Social role types in a prison community." Master's thesis, University of Washington, Seattle.

Schur, Edwin. 1971. *Labeling deviant behavior: Its sociological implications.* New York: Harper & Row.

———. 1973. *Radical nonintervention: Rethinking the delinquency problem.* Englewood Cliffs, NJ: Prentice-Hall.

Schuster, Richard L., and Sherry Widmer. 1978. "Judicial intervention in corrections: A case study." *Federal Probation* 42 (3): 10–17.

Schwartz, Ira M. 1989. *(In)Justice for juveniles: Rethinking the best interest of the child.* Lexington, MA: Lexington Books.

———. 1991. "Removing juveniles from adult jails: The unfinished agenda." In *American jails: Public policy issues,* ed. Joel A. Thompson and G. Larry Mays. Chicago: Nelson-Hall.

Scott, Lori. 1996. "Probation: Heading in new directions." In *Visions for change: Crime and justice in the twenty-first century.* Upper Saddle River, NJ: Prentice-Hall.

Sechrest, Dale K. 1989a. "Population density and assaults in jails for men and women." *American Journal of Criminal Justice* 14 (1): 87–103.

———. 1989b. "Prison 'boot camps' do not measure up." *Federal Probation* 53 (3): 19–24.

———. (1991). "The effects of density on jail assaults." *Journal of Criminal Justice* 19: 211–23.

Selke, William L. 1985. "Judicial management of prisons? Responses to prison litigation." *The Prison Journal* 65 (1): 26–37.

Sellin, Thorsten J. 1976. *Slavery and the penal system.* New York: Elsevier.

Senese, Jeffrey D., David B. Kalinich, and Paul S. Embert. 1989. "Jails in the United States: The phenomenon of mental illness in local correctional facilities." *American Journal of Criminal Justice* 14 (1): 104–21.

Sexton, George E. 1995. *Work in American prisons: Joint ventures with the private sector.* Washington, DC: U.S. Government Printing Office.

Shaw, Clifford R., and Henry D. McKay. 1942. *Juvenile delinquency and urban areas: A study of rates of delinquency in relation to different characteristics of local communities in American cities.* Chicago: University of Chicago Press.

Sickmund, Melissa. 1997. *The juvenile delinquency probation caseload, 1985–1994.* Washington, DC: U.S. Government Printing Office.

Siegler, M., and Humphry Osmond. 1974. *Models of madness, models of medicine.* New York: Macmillan.

Sigler, Robert, and Jimmie J. Williams. 1994. "A study of the outcomes of probation officers and risk-screening instruments classifications." *Journal of Criminal Justice* 22 (6): 495–502.

Sigler, Robert T., and David Lamb. 1995. "Community-based alternatives to prison: How the public and court personnel view them." *Federal Probation* 59 (2): 3–9.

Simmons, I. 1975. *Interaction and leadership among female prisoners.* Ph.D. diss. University of Missouri, Columbia, MO.

Singer, Richard. 1980. "The *Wolfish* case: Has the *Bell* tolled for prisoner litigation in the federal courts?" In *Legal rights of prisoners,* ed. Geoffrey P. Alpert. Beverly Hills, CA: Sage.

Skinner, B. F. 1974. *About behaviorism.* New York: Knopf.

Smart, Carol. 1976a. "Criminological theory: Its ideology and implications concerning women." *British Journal of Sociology* 28: 89–100.

———. 1976b. *Women, Crime and Criminology.* Boston: Routledge and Kegan Paul.

Smialek, J. E., and W. U. Spitz. 1978. "Death behind bars." *Journal of the American Medical Association* 240: 2563–64.

Smith, Christopher E. 1986. "Federal judges' role in prison litigation: What's necessary? what's proper?" *Judicature* 70 (3): 144–50.

Snarr, Richard W. 1996. *Introduction to corrections.* 3rd ed. Dubuque, IA: Brown & Benchmark.

Snell, Tracy L. 1992. *Women in jail, 1989.* Washington, DC: U.S. Government Printing Office.

———. 1994. *Women in prison: Survey of state prison inmates, 1991.* Washington, DC: U.S. Government Printing Office.

———. 1995. *Correctional populations in the United States, 1992.* Washington, DC: U.S. Government Printing Office.

———. 1996. *Capital punishment, 1995.* Washington, DC: U.S. Government Printing Office.

Snyder, Howard. 1990. *Growth in minority detentions attributed to drug law violations.* Washington, DC: U.S. Government Printing Office.

Souryal, Sam S. 1997. "Romancing the stone or stoning the romance?" In *Crime & justice in America,* ed. Paul F. Cromwell and Roger G. Dunham. Upper Saddle River, NJ: Prentice-Hall.

Spencer, Herbert. 1864 (1961). *The study of sociology.* Ann Arbor: University of Michigan Press.

Stanley, David T. 1972. *Managing local government under union pressure.* Washington, DC: The Brookings Institution.

Stinchcomb, James. 1992. *Opportunities in law enforcement and criminal justice careers.* Lincolnwood, IL: NTC.

Stohr, Mary K., and G. Larry Mays. 1993. *Women's jails: An investigation of offenders, staff, administration and programming.* Washington, DC: National Institute of Corrections.

Stohr, Mary K., Ruth L. Self, and Nicholas P. Lovrich. 1992. "Staff turnover in new generation jails: An investigation of its causes and prevention." *Journal of Criminal Justice* 20 (5): 455–78.

Stohr, Mary, G. Larry Mays, Ann C. Beck, and Tammy Kelley. 1997. "Sexual harassment in women's jails." *Journal of Contemporary Criminal Justice* (in press).

Stojkovic, Stan. 1996. "Building tenders." In *Encyclopedia of American prisons,* ed. Marilyn D. McShane and Frank P. Williams III, pp. 66–69. New York: Garland.

Street, David, R. D. Vinter, and Charles Perrow. 1966. *Organization for treatment.* New York: The Free Press.

Struckhoff, David. 1989. "Deputies or correctional officers in jails: Is there a controversy?" *American Jails* 2 (4): 32–34.

Substance abuse report. 1992. "Federal court says inmate has no right to smoke-free prison." (Dec. 15): 7–8.

Sutherland, Edwin H., and Donald R. Cressey. 1974. *Criminology.* 9th ed. Philadelphia: Lippincott.

Sykes, Gresham M. 1958. *The society of captives: A study of a maximum security prison.* Princeton, NJ: Princeton University Press.

Sykes, Gresham M., and Sheldon L. Messinger. 1960. "Inmate social system." In *Theoretical studies in social organization of the prison,* ed. Richard A. Cloward, Donald R. Cressey, George H. Grosser, Richard McCleery, Lloyd E. Ohlin, Gresham M. Sykes, and Sheldon L. Messinger, pp. 5–19. New York: Social Science Research Council.

Taft, Philip B., Jr. 1979. "Backed up in jail." *Corrections Magazine* (June): 26–33.

Takas, Marianne, and Theodore M. Hammett. 1989. *AIDS bulletin: Legal issues affecting offenders and staff.* Washington, DC: U.S. Government Printing Office.

Task Force on Corrections. 1967. *Task force report: Corrections.* Washington, DC: U.S. Government Printing Office.

Taylor, Ian, Paul Walton, and Jock Young. 1973. *The new criminology: For a social theory of deviance.* New York: Harper & Row.

Thomas, Charles W. 1970. "Toward a more inclusive model of the inmate contraculture." *Criminology* 8: 251–62.

Thomas, Charles W., Jeffrey Hyman, and L. Thomas Winfree, Jr. 1983. "The impact of confinement on juveniles." *Youth and Society* 14: 301–19.

Thomas, Charles W., and David M. Petersen. 1977. *Prison organization and inmate subcultures.* Indianapolis: Bobbs-Merrill.

Thomas, George C., III, and David Edelman. 1988. "An evaluation of conservative crime control theology." *Notre Dame Law Review* 63 (2): 123–60.

Thomas, Jim. 1988. *Prison litigation: The paradox of the jailhouse lawyer.* Totowa, NJ: Rowman & Littlefield.

Thomas, Jim, Harry Mika, Jerome Blakemore, and Anmarie Aylward. 1991. "Exacting control through disciplinary hearings: 'Making do' with prison rules." *Justice Quarterly* 8 (1): 37–57.

Thomas, Jim, Devin Wheeler, and Kathy Harris. 1986. "Issues and misconceptions in prisoner litigation: A critical view." *Criminology* 24 (4): 54–63.

Thompson, Joel A. 1986. "The American jail: Problems, politics, prospects." *American Journal of Criminal Justice* 10: 205–21.

Thompson, Joel A., and G. Larry Mays. (1988a). "The impact of state standards and enforcement procedures on local jail performance." *Policy Studies Review* 8 (1): 55–71.

———. 1988b. "State-local relations and the American jail crisis: An assessment of state jail mandates." *Policy Studies Review* 7 (3): 567–80.

———. 1991. "Paying the piper but changing the tune: Policy changes and initiatives for the American jail." In *American jails: Public policy issues,* ed. Joel A. Thompson and G. Larry Mays. Chicago: Nelson-Hall.

Thompson, Joel A., and G. Larry Mays, eds. 1991. *American jails: Public policy issues.* Chicago: Nelson-Hall.

Toch, Hans. 1976. "A psychological view of prison violence." In *Prison violence,* ed. Albert K. Cohen, George Cole, and Robert G. Bailey, pp. 43–58. Lexington, MA: D. C. Heath.

———. 1985. "Warehouses for people." *The Annals of the American Academy of Political and Social Sciences* 478: 58–72.

Tonry, Michael. 1995. "Intermediate sanctions." In *Crime and justice: An annual review,* ed. Norval Morris and Michael Tonry. Chicago: University of Chicago Press.

Topp, D. O. 1979. "Suicide in prison." *British Journal of Psychiatry* 134: 24–27.

Torbet, Patricia. 1996. *Juvenile probation: The workhorse of the juvenile justice system.* Washington, DC: U.S. Government Printing Office.

Turner, Michael G., Jody L. Sundt, Brandon K. Applegate, and Francis T. Cullen. 1995. "'Three strikes and you're out' legislation: A national assessment." *Federal Probation* 59 (3): 16–35.

Useem, Bert, Camille Graham Camp, George M. Camp, and Renie Dugan. 1995. *Resolution of prison riots.* Washington, DC: U.S. Government Printing Office.

Useem, Bert, and Peter Kimball. 1989. *States of siege: U.S. prison riots, 1971–1986.* New York: Oxford University Press.

Van den Haag, Ernest. 1975. *Punishing criminals: Concerning a very old and painful question.* New York: Basic Books.

Van den Haag, Ernest, and John Conrad. 1983. *The death penalty: A debate.* New York: Plenum Press.

Vinogradoff, Paul. 1920a. *Outlines of historical jurisprudence. Volume One: Introduction and tribal law.* Oxford: Oxford University Press.

———. 1920b. *Outlines of historical jurisprudence. Volume two: Jurisprudence of the Greek city.* Oxford: Oxford University Press.

Vito, Gennaro F., and Deborah G. Wilson. 1985. "Forgotten people: Elderly inmates." *Federal Probation* (March): 18–24.

Von Hirsch, Andrew. 1976. *Doing justice.* New York: Hill & Wang.

Walker, Samuel. 1994. *Sense and nonsense about crime and drugs: A policy guide.* 3rd ed. Belmont, CA: Wadsworth.

Wallenstein, Arthur M. 1987. "New generation/direct supervision correctional operations in Bucks County, Pennsylvania." *American Jails* 1 (1): 34–36.

Ward, David, and Gene Kassebaum. 1965. *Women's prison: Sex and social structure.* Chicago: Aldine-Atherton.

Ward, Julia. 1990. "Bay County Jail and Jail Annex: A case for private enterprise in corrections." *American Jails* 4 (4): 38–42.

Weber, Max. 1947. *The theory of social and economic organization.* Trans. A. M. Henderson and Talcott Parsons. New York: Oxford University Press.

Welch, Michael. 1989. "Social junk, social dynamite and the rabble: Persons with AIDS in jail." *American Journal of Criminal Justice* 14 (1): 135–47.

———. 1991. "The expansion of jail capacity: Makeshift jails and public policy." In *American jails: Public policy issues,* ed. Joel A. Thompson and G. Larry Mays. Chicago: Nelson-Hall.

———. 1994. "Jail crowding." In *Critical issues in crime and justice,* ed. Albert R. Roberts. Thousand Oaks, CA: Sage.

———. 1996a. *Corrections: A critical approach.* New York: McGraw-Hill.

———. 1996b. "Prisonization." In *Encyclopedia of American prisons,* ed. Marilyn D. McShane and Frank P. Williams III, pp. 357–63. New York: Garland.

Wellford, Charles. 1967. "Factors associated with adoption of the inmate code." *Journal of Criminal Law, Criminology and Police Science* 58: 197–203.

Wells, James B. 1987. "Direct supervision: Panacea or fad." *American Jails* 1 (1): 46–49.

Welsh, Wayne N. 1996. "Jail overcrowding and court-ordered reform: Critical issues." In *Visions for change: Crime and justice in the twenty-first century,* ed. Roslyn Muraskin and Albert R. Roberts. Upper Saddle River, NJ: Prentice-Hall.

Welsh, Wayne N., Matthew C. Leone, Patrick T. Kinkade, and Henry N. Pontell. 1991. "The politics of jail overcrowding: Public attitudes and official policies." In *American jails: Public policy issues,* ed. Joel A. Thompson and G. Larry Mays. Chicago: Nelson-Hall.

Wexler, David B. 1975. "Behavior modification and other behavior change procedures: The emerging law and the proposed Florida guidelines." *Criminal Law Bulletin* 11: 600–616.

Wexler, Harry K., Douglas S. Lipton, and Bruce D. Johnson. 1988. *A criminal justice strategy for treating cocaine-heroin abusing offenders in custody.* Washington, DC: U.S. Government Printing Office.

Whitehead, John T., and Steven P. Lab. 1996. *Juvenile justice: An introduction.* 2nd ed. Cincinnati: Anderson.

Wicker, Tom. 1975. *A time to die.* New York: Quadrangle.

Wiggins, R. R. 1996. "Ten ideas for effective managers." *Federal Probation* 60: 43–49.

Wilbanks, William. 1987. *The myth of a racist criminal justice system.* Pacific Grove, CA: Brooks/Cole.

Williamson, Harold E. 1990. *The corrections profession.* Newbury Park, CA: Sage.

Wilson, James Q., and Richard Herrnstein. 1985. *Crime and human nature.* New York: Simon & Schuster.

Wilson, William Julius. 1987. *The truly disadvantaged: The inner city, the underclass and public policy.* Chicago: University of Chicago Press.

Wines, Enoch Cobb. 1864. *The true penitent portrayed: A doctrine of repentance.* Philadelphia: Presbyterian Board of Publication.

Winfree, L. Thomas, Jr. 1987. "Toward understanding state-level jail mortality: Correlates of death by suicide and by natural causes." *Justice Quarterly* 4: 51–71.

———. 1988. "Rethinking American jail death rates: A comparison of national mortality and jail mortality, 1978, 1983." *Policy Studies Review* 7 (3): 641–59.

Winfree, L. Thomas, and Howard Abadinsky. 1996. *Understanding crime: Theory and practice.* Chicago: Nelson-Hall.

Winfree, L. Thomas, Christine S. Sellers, Veronica Smith Ballard, and Roy R. Roberg. 1990. "Responding to a legislated change in correctional practices: A quasi-experimental study of revocation hearings and parole board actions." *Journal of Criminal Justice* 18: 195–215.

Winfree, L. Thomas, Jr., and John Wooldredge. 1991. "Exploring suicides and deaths by natural causes in America's largest jails: A panel study of institutional change, 1978 and 1983." In *American jails: Public policy issues,* ed. Joel A. Thompson and G. Larry Mays. Chicago: Nelson-Hall.

Winfree, L. Thomas, John Wooldredge, Christine S. Sellers, and Veronica Smith Ballard. 1990. "Parole survival and legislated change: A before/after study of parole revocation decision making." *Justice Quarterly* 7: 151–73.

Winfree, L. Thomas, Jr., and Matthew T. Zingraff. 1973. "The intake process and institutional goal orientations: A question of priority for juvenile corrections." *Proceedings of the Montana Academy of Science* 33: 110–17.

Winterdyk, John, and Curt Griffiths. 1984. "Wilderness experience programs: Reforming delinquents or beating around the bush?" *Juvenile & Family Court Journal* 35 (3): 35–44.

Winterfield, Laura A., and Sally T. Hillsman. 1993. *The Staten Island Day-Fine Project.* Washington, DC: U.S. Government Printing Office.

Wolfgang, Marvin E. 1958. *Patterns of criminal homicide.* Philadelphia: University of Pennsylvania Press.

———. 1973. "Cesare Lombroso." In *Pioneers of criminology,* ed. Herman Mannheim. Montclair NJ: Patterson-Smith.

Wolfgang, Marvin E., and Franco Ferracuti. 1967. *The subculture of violence.* London: Tavistock.

Wolfgang, Marvin, Robert M. Figlio, and Thorsten Sellin. 1972. *Delinquency in a birth cohort.* Chicago: University of Chicago Press.

Wooden, Kenneth Tom. 1976. *Weeping in the playtime of others: America's incarcerated children.* New York: McGraw-Hill.

Wooldredge, John D., and L. Thomas Winfree. 1992. "An aggregate-level study of inmate suicides and deaths due to natural causes in U.S. jails." *Journal of Research in Crime and Delinquency* 29 (4): 466–79.

Wright, Dionne T. 1996. *Effectiveness of correctional boot camps on improving attitudes and reducing recidivism.* Master's thesis, New Mexico State University–Las Cruces, Department of Criminal Justice.

Wright, Richard. 1996. Afterword to *Life without parole: Living in prison today,* by Victor Hassine, 129–39. Los Angeles: Roxbury.

Yablonsky, Lewis. 1989. *The therapeutic community.* New York: Garden.

Yablonsky, Lewis, and Martin R. Haskell. 1988. *Juvenile delinquency.* 4th ed. New York: Harper & Row.

Yarbrough, Tinsley E. 1984. "The Alabama prison litigation." *Justice System Journal* 9 (3): 276–90.

Zagoria, Sam, ed. 1972. *Public workers and public unions.* Englewood Cliffs, NJ: Prentice-Hall.

Zald, M. N. 1968. "The correctional institution for juvenile offenders: An analysis of organizational 'character.'" In *Prison within society,* ed. L. Hazelrigg, pp. 229–46. New York: Doubleday-Anchor.

Zausner, Stuart. 1985. *Unusual incident reports 1984 calendar year.* Albany: New York State Department of Correctional Services.

Zingraff, Matthew T. 1975. "Prisonization as an inhibitor of effective personalization." *Criminology* 13: 366–88.

Zupan, Linda L. (1991). *Jails: Reform and the new generation philosophy.* Cincinnati: Anderson.

Zupan, Linda L., and Ben Menke. 1988. "Implementing organizational change: From traditional to new generation jail operations." *Policy Studies Review* 7: 615–25.

———. 1991. "The new generation jail: An overview." In *American jails: Public policy issues,* ed. Joel A. Thompson and G. Larry Mays. Chicago: Nelson-Hall.

Zupan, Linda L., and Mary K. Stohr-Gillmore. 1988. "Doing time in the new generation jail: Inmate perceptions of gains and losses." *Policy Studies Review* 7 (3): 626–40.

Photo Credits

Page 2 Castle Rock Ent./Shooting Star
Page 3 © A. Lichtenstein/Sygma
Page 4 Photo by Joseph P. Manguno–UPI/Corbis-Bettmann
Page 8 Los Angeles Times photo/Julie Markes
Page 19 © Joseph Rodriguez/Black Star
Page 24 Corbis-Bettmann
Page 33 Alinari/Art Resource, NY
Page 36 The Granger Collection
Page 39 Corbis-Bettmann
Page 41 Corbis-Bettmann
Page 49 The Granger Collection
Page 54 Courtesy of the American Correctional Association
Page 60 © A. Ramey/Photo Edit
Page 66 © MacDonald Photography/The Picture Cube
Page 71 © Frank Fournier/Woodfin Camp & Associates
Page 78 (left) © Dennis Brack/Black Star
Page 78 (right) © P. Forden/Sygma
Page 78 (bottom) © Dennis Brack/Black Star
Page 79 © Bob Daemmrich/Sygma
Page 109 © Mike Yamshita/Woodfin Camp & Associates
Page 110 © Michael L. Abramson/Woodfin Camp & Associates

Page 112 © Alain McLaughlin/Impact Visuals
Page 114 © 1997 Phillip Roullard
Page 119 © David Woo/Stock, Boston
Page 134 © Bob Riha/Gamma Liaison Network
Page 152 UPI/Corbis-Bettmann
Page 156 © Stephen Ferry/Gamma Liaison Network
Page 163 © A. Ramey/Photo Edit
Page 194 © Joseph Rodriguez/Black Star
Page 201 © Stephen Ferry/Gamma Liaison Network
Page 208 © A. Ramey/Photo Edit
Page 217 © Andrew Lichtenstein/Sygma
Page 248 © Cathy Cheney/Stock, Boston
Page 263 © A. Ramey/Photo Edit
Page 267 UPI/Corbis-Bettmann
Page 282 © George Cohen/Impact Visuals
Page 283 © A. Ramey/Photo Edit
Page 293 © A. Ramey/Woodfin Camp & Associates
Page 295 © A. Ramey/Woodfin Camp & Associates
Page 319 UPI/Corbis-Bettmann
Page 323 Courtesy of Penny Lucero, Warden of New Mexico Women's Correctional Facility
Page 352 © Anne Dowie/The Picture Cube
Page 356 © Alon Reininger/Contact Press Images
Page 360 © Les Stone/Sygma
Page 362 © A. Keler/Sygma
Page 364 © Michael McGovern/The Picture Cube
Page 382 © Alon Reininger/Contact Press Images
Page 395 © Alon Reininger/Contact Press Images

Index

Note: Page references to figures and tables are printed in italic type.

Acoustic fence, 385
Administration of corrections programs, 311–342
  bureaucracies and, 314–316
  centralized vs. decentralized, 329–330
  characteristics of wardens, superintendents, 321–329
  educational qualifications and, 322
  future issues of, 335–337
  inmate management, 333–334
  leadership styles and, 316–321
  management tasks of, 330–333
  political patronage and, 323
  solutions for future managers, 336–340
  staff recruitment and retention, 330–331
  versus management of, 312–313
Administrative security units, 165
Advisory Commission on Intergovernmental Relations (ACIR), 103
Advocacy groups for inmates, 346, 351–353
African Americans. *See also* Race and ethnicity
  in federal prisons, 188, *189*
  female prisoners, 193
  imbalances in incarceration rates and, 388–392
  in jails (local and federal), *195, 197,* 389
  in juvenile facilities, 213–214
  percentage of death row population, 83
  probability of incarceration and, 1, 187–188, 389
  in state prisons, 192, *193*
  street gangs and, 205
  wardens and superintendents, *324–327*
Age factors. *See also* Juvenile offenders
  capital punishment and, *83*
  of future inmates, 223, 267, 393–395
  probability of incarceration and, 187–188
  segregation of inmates by, 43

AIDS (acquired immunodeficiency syndrome)
  inmate deaths due to, 207
  jail inmates with, 126–127
  number of HIV-positive inmates, *396–397*
Alaskan Natives, in jails, 196, 197
Alcatraz riot, 210
Alcohol use. *See* Drug and alcohol use
American Bar Association (ABA), guidelines for probation/parole, 236–238
American Civil Liberties Union's National Prison Project, 352, 359
American Correctional Association (ACA), 53, 311
  jail/detention facility standards of, 122–123
American Jail Association, 311
Americans with Disabilities Act (ADA), 358, 369, 398–399
Anti-Terrorism and Effective Death Penalty Act, 387
Appeals, 92–96. *See also* Inmate litigation
Arave v. Creech, 366–367
Arizona chain gang project, 359
Arpaio, Sheriff Joseph, 119, 120
Arraignments by video, 118
Aryan Brotherhood (AB), 220–221
Asian Americans
  in federal prisons, 188, *189*
  in jails, 196, 197
  in juvenile facilities, 213–214
Assaults
  inmate-on-inmate, 205, 207–210, 401
  inmate-on-staff, 207–208, 401
Attica (New York) Prison, 152, 210–212
Auburn System, 44, 47–50
  inmate labor in, 160
  layout of, *48,* 150, *151*
  living units in, 153
Augustus, John, 232–233

Balanced and restorative justice (BARJ) project, 266
Banishment, 34, 39
  future uses of, 383–384
  to penal colonies, 41–42, 50–52
Barker v. Wingo, 94–95
Batson v. Kentucky, 94

Beccaria, Cesare, 5, 13, 43
Bell v. Wolfish, 355–356, 368
Bentham, Jeremy, 5, 45
Beto, George, 320, 321
Black Guerrilla Family (BGF), 220–221
Black Muslims (Nation of Islam), 211, 347
Blood feuds, 33–34, 38
  of gangs, 220–221
Boot camps, 127–130, 176, 194
  future issues of, 379, 381
Booth v. Maryland, 235
Borstal System, 55
Bounds v. Smith, 93, 346, 351
Brittin, William, 47
Brockway, Zebulon Reed, 54–56, 158, 160
Bruscino v. Carlson, 220
Bureau of Prisons (BOP)
  classification system for inmates, 149
  early goals of, 163–164
  unit management strategies of, 330
Burnout. *See* Staff burnout

Camps
  boot. *See* Boot camps
  federal, 164, 165
  forestry, 182, 300–301
Campus-design prison, 151–152
Caning, public, 97, 98
Capital punishment. *See also* Death penalty
  inmate litigation and, 363–367
  issues in, 77–83
Careers in corrections
  case manager, 206, 245
  classification officer, 148, 206
  clinical psychologist, 206
  community-based counselor/manager, 302–303
  correctional counselor, 206–207
  correctional officer, 145–147
  probation/parole officers, 250–255
  psychological diagnostician, 206
  psychological technician, 206
  superintendent, 328
  warden, 328
Caseloads, 251–254
  specialized, 379
Chain gangs, 359, 360
Cherry Hill Prison, 45–47
Children. *See also* Juvenile offenders

child saver movement,
178–179, 297
colonial jails and, 103
infancy defense and, 68–69
Chimel v. California, 94
*Citrano v. Allen Correctional
Center,* 349–350
Civil Rights Act (1871), 347
Civil Rights of Institutionalized
Persons Act (CRIPA), 369
Civil rights litigation
basis for, 94, 347, 355
key features of, 348–350
trends in numbers of, *350,
361*
Classification of inmates, 49,
92, 147–149, 253–255
Clemmer, Donald, 197, 201
Code of Hammurabi, 5, 34–35,
288, 289, 303
Colorado Actuarial Risk Assessment Scale, 245, 246
Commonwealth v. Chase, 232
Community corrections,
273–310
administration of, 279–280
community service, 26, 73,
133, 292–294, *306*
costs of, 275, 276
definition of, 25–26, 275
detractors of, 276–277
diversion and, 285–288
educational release, 284–285
effectiveness of, 301
electronic monitoring. *See*
Electronic monitoring
fines, forfeitures, restitution,
288–291
funding of, 278–279
furloughs, 285
gender and, 305–308
halfway houses, 282–284
house arrest. *See* House
arrest
as intermediate sanction, 274
for juvenile offenders,
297–301
probation/parole in relation
to, 274, 275
recidivism and, 280–282
reentry programs of,
282–285
supporters of, 275–276
token economies and, 17
victims' role in, 303–304
work release, 284
Community service, 26, 73,
133, 292–294, *306*
Containment model, 380
Control model, 320, 321
Convictions, inmate appeals of,
92–96
Cooper v. Pate, 347, 357
Corporal punishment
in colonial prisons, 49–50
in Middle Ages, 39–40

public caning, 97, 98
Correctional litigation. *See*
Inmate litigation
Correctional officers (CO),
145–147
women as, 403–404
Correctional Services Group,
149
Corrections. *See also* Jails;
Prisons
adults under custody of, 255
attitudes toward, 10–12
careers in. *See* Careers
community-based. *See* Community corrections
components of, 25–27
definitions of, 1–2, 27
future issues of, 377–388,
403–407
as a growth industry, 11–12
history of, 31–63
parole. *See* Parole
philosophies of, 2–10,
374–376
private companies in, 11,
120–122, 177, 212–213
probation. *See* Probation
Corrections Corporation of
America, 121, 177, 350
Costs
of boot camps, 381
of community vs. institutional
placements, 275, 276
of electronic monitoring,
295–296
of future corrections,
405–406
of incarcerating elderly
prisoners, 394
of inmate maintenance, per
year, 11
of jail construction, 117,
134–135
of prison construction, per
bed, 11
Cottage-design correctional
facilities, 158
Courts Regimented Intensive
Probation Program (Texas),
130
Courtyard-design prison, 150,
151
Crawford, William, 52
Cressey, Donald, 19
Crime rate. *See also* Incarceration
perceptions of, 10–11, 98
prison population rate and,
59
Crime-related news media coverage, 11
Crime theories, 12–25
corrections, and relationship
to, 22–25
cultural transmission, 18, 20
deterministic forces, 14–16

free will, 13–14
learned responses, 16–18
power-based, 23
social forces, 18–22
Crime waves, perceptions of,
10, 11, 98
Criminal behavior
as biologically determined,
14–16
as culturally transmitted, 18,
20
as genetically determined,
56–57
as learned response, 16–18
as psychologically deter-
mined, 16–18
Criminal law
degree of involvement, 68
misdemeanors vs. felonies,
66–67
proof, standards of, 67, 96
substantive vs. procedural,
67
Criminological theories. *See*
Crime theories
Crofton, Walter, 51–52, 53
Crowding. *See* Overcrowding
Cryogenics, as criminal
sanction, 98
Culture of jails and prisons,
197–205
juvenile facilities and, 216
for men vs. women, 203–204
prisonization process in, 197
Custody officer, 146. *See also*
Correctional officers
in jails, 114–116
treatment staff vs., 145, 147

Day fines, 74–76, 289–290
Death penalty
appeals directed at, 80
execution methods, 35,
39–40, 78, *82,* 387
future of, 386–388
historical aspects of, 32–42
impact on crime rate,
387–388
inmate litigation and,
363–367
jurisdictions without, *81*
jury's role in, 70, 80, 364
number of executions, *81,*
365, 386
sentencing issues of, 77–83
statistics on, 80, *81, 82, 83*
Supreme Court decisions on,
80, 364, 366–367, 386
Death row inmates
age of, 82–83
number of, 78, *81,* 365
de Beaumont, Gustave, 52
Deinstitutionalization, 23
of status offenders (DSO),
301, 306–307

Deliquency. *See also* Juvenile offenders
  rates, and IQ scores, 15
  subculture of, 20–21
Delo v. Lashley, 366
Design and architecture
  of future facilities, 381–382
  of jails, 109–113, 133–134
  of prisons, 149–158
Detention facilities, 127–131, 138
  for juvenile offenders, 180, 212
  privately operated, *121*
Determinate sentencing, 86–87, 376–377
Determinism
  biological, 14–16
  psychological, 16–18
Deterrence, 4, 5, 65, 374–376
de Tocqueville, Alexis, 52
Detroit House of Shelter for Women, 158
Deviant subcultures, 20–21
Devil's Island, 32, 52
Diagnostic units, 180, 212–213
Direct supervision, 154
  in jails, 111–113, 134–135
Discount rate, for good time credit, 377
Disease model of crime, 25, 57
Diversion, 285–288
  of juvenile offenders, 6, 299
Dobbs v. Zant, 366
Domesday Book, 39
Drug and alcohol use
  alcohol screening in jails, 123
  as a cause of crime, 15
  community corrections and, 281–282
  jail inmates and, 125–126, 196
  sentencing guidelines and, 88
Drug offenses
  average time served, 190
  by women, 194
  of federal prisoners, 188, *190*
  of state prisoners, *192*
  trafficking, fines for, 76
Drug treatment programs
  in community corrections, 281
  in federal facilities, 167
  in state prisons, 177–178
Durkheim, Emile, 21

Early release, 268–269
Eastern State Penitentiary (Pennsylvania), 45–47, 52–53, 150
Economic sanctions, 288–291.
  See also Fines and forfeitures
Economies, inmate, 209–210, 221

Education
  backgrounds of inmates, 125, 284–285
  as correctional philosophy, 5, 21–22, 57
Educational training programs
  at federal facilities, 167
  at state facilities, 176
  as diversion programs, 287
Electric chair, 78
Electrocution, states that execute with, *82*
Electronic monitoring
  brain implants, 385
  drawbacks of, 378
  for felons, 76
  future uses of, 384–386
  goals of, 26, 132–133, 269, 294–297
  for inmate surveillance, 153, 154
  microchip implants, 99
  for probationers, 72–73
Elmira (New York) Reformatory, 54–56, 160
Emotional support, prison subculture and, 204
Estelle v. Gamble, 357, 361
Ethnicity. *See* Race and ethnicity
Eugenics, 385–386
Exclusionary punishment, 32–34, 60–61
Ex-cons, attitudes toward, 9, 23, 278
Execution methods
  in antiquity, 35
  contemporary, 78
  of the future, 387
  in Middle Ages, 39–40
  most common, by state, *82*
Executions
  number of, *81,* 365, 386
  privatization and, 387
Exile. *See* Banishment
Ex parte U.S. (*Killits* case), 233

Family relationships
  community corrections and, 281
  in female prisons, 204
  reintegration and, 277–278
Farms, penal, 131, 182, 212–213
Fay v. Noia, 347
Federal Correctional Complex, at Florence (Colorado), 157, 166
Federal Correctional Institutions (FCIs), 158, 164, 165, 212
Federal Detention Center (FDC), at Oakdale (Louisiana), 212
Federal jails, 114, 196–197
Federal prison camps (FPCs), 164, 165

Federal Prison Industries, Inc. (UNICOR), 162, 164, 166
Federal prison system, 163–168
  boot camps, 176, 194
  characteristics of inmates in, 188–190
  facility types in, 164–166
  gender/race/ethnicity in, 188, *189*
  non-U.S. citizens in, 188–189
  number of facilities, *171*
  number of persons held in, *13,* 164, *168–169, 172–173*
  offense types in, 188, *190*
  programs of, 166–167
  security levels for, 164
Federal Probation and Pretrial Services System, 233
Federal transfer center (FTC), 164
Felonies, 66–67
  classification schemes for, 88–90
  intermediate sanctions for, 305, *306*
  probation for, 76, 238, 258
  sentencing and, 76–77
Female inmates. *See also* Gender; Women
  building design for, 158–159
  chain gangs and, 359
  characteristics of, 193–194
  federal prison camps for, 165
  federal prisoners, 188, *189*
  first U.S. prison for, 158
  in jails, 107, *108,* 127
  MCC/MDC facilities for, 165
  medical service needs of, 392–393
  motherhood issues and, 393
  prison subculture and, 203–204
  separate prisons for, 158–159
Financial status. *See* Socioeconomic status
Fines
  as additional penalty for felonies, *306*
  day, 74–75, 289–290
  history of, 35–36, 39
  for infractions, 66
Firing squad, states that execute with, *82*
Florida State Prison at Starke, 78
Folsom (California) Prison, 211–212, 221
Force fields, 385
Forestry camps, 182, 300–301
Forfeitures, 35–36, 39, 290
Fox-Bartley handgun law, 90
Free Ventures Project, 161
Freudian theory, 16
Frustration riots, 211, *212*
Furman v. Georgia, 80, 363

Gagnon v. Scarpelli, 239, 354
Gangs, prison, 220–222, 401
Gardner v. Florida, 236
Gas chamber, 78, *82*
Gender
  building design and, 157–158
  colonial jails and, 103
  community-based programs
    and, 305–308
  of correctional staff, inmate
    litigation on, 358–359
  federal jail inmates and,
    196–197
  federal prisoners and, 188,
    189
  incarceration rates by,
    168–170
  jail prisoners and, 104, 107,
    196
  juvenile facilities and,
    213–214
  juvenile probationers and,
    266
  of prison guards, *390–391*
  probationers and, 257–260
  segregation of inmates by, 43,
    158
  sentencing disparities and,
    193–194
  state prisoners and, 190, *191*
Genetic engineering, 98,
  385–386
Genetics, psychopathic behavior and, 17–18
Geriatric prisons of the future,
  267, 368
Godinez v. Moran, 367
Goffman, Erving, 144
Graduated release systems,
  51–56
Graham v. Collins, 366
Gregg v. Georgia, 80, 364
Group homes, 25, 212–213
Gypsy Jokers Motorcycle Club,
  221

Habeas corpus appeals, 94,
  347–350
  numbers of, *350,* 361
Habitual offender statutes, 59,
  85, 90–91, 384, 390
Halfway houses, 25–26,
  282–284
  for juvenile offenders,
    212–213
Hammurabi Code. *See* Code of
  Hammurabi
Hanging, states that execute
  with, *82*
Hard Labor Program (Arizona),
  359
Harris, Mary Belle, 322
Hayes, Rutherford B., 53
Helling v. McKinney, 360
Heredity, as cause of crime,
  56–57
Herrera v. Collins, 366

Hirschi, Travis, 22
Hispanics. *See also* Race and
  ethnicity
  on death row, 83
  jail incarceration rates for,
    195
  in juvenile facilities, 213–214
  in prison, 188, *189,* 192, *193,*
    388–389
  probability of incarceration
    and, 1, 187–188
  wardens and superinten-
    dents, *324–327*
HIV infection
  among female inmates, 392
  among jail inmates, 126–127
  number of inmates positive
    for, *396–397*
  testing for, 395–396
Holt v. Sarver, 345
Home confinement. *See* House
  arrest
Homicide
  in antiquity, 35–38
  insanity defense and, 69
  plea bargaining and, 85
  in pre-legal societies, 34
House arrest
  as alternative to incarcera-
    tion, 132–133
  definition/purposes of,
    294–297
  drawbacks of, 132–133, 378
  for felons, 76
  as intermediate sanction, 26
  as probation add-on, 72–73,
    378
Howard, John, 43–44
Hudson v. McMillian, 360–361
Human Brain Project, 385
Human immunodeficiency
  virus. *See* HIV infection
Hydraulic displacement of discretion thesis, 395

Imprisonment binge, 59, 60,
  98, 225
Incapacitation, 7–8, 59, 65,
  374–376
Incarceration
  alternatives to, 127–131,
    136–138
  rates of, 11–13, *168–169,*
    193, 195
Indeterminate sentencing, 55,
  86, 241, 376–377
Indirect/remote supervision,
  153, 154
  in jails, 110–111
Infectious diseases, overcrowding and, 395–398
Inmate code, 198, 199, 203,
  205
Inmate litigation, 343–355
  advocacy groups for, 351–353
  assistance/legal access and,
    350–351

  of the future, 368–369
  history of, 345–347
  impact of, 361–363
  issues raised by, 355–358
  jails and, 122, 123
  legal mechanisms used in,
    347–350
  percentage of all civil cases,
    406–407
  recent trends in, 358–361
  targets of, 347
  to overthrow convictions,
    92–96
  who wins, 363, 368
Inmates, 187–229
  advocates for, 351–353
  civil death of, 345–346
  classification of, 49, 92,
    147–149, 253–255
  deaths of, 123, 124, 131, 205,
    207
  dress codes for, 49
  educational backgrounds of,
    125, 284
  elderly, 223, 267, 393–395
  federal prison, characteris-
    tics of, 188–190
  fee system for, 115
  future populations, charac-
    teristics of, 223, 388–403
  gangs (prison or street) and,
    220–222
  gender/race/ethnicity of, *189,*
    388–392
  issues concerning, 218–224
  as labor source, 41–42, 47,
    50, 159–163
  living units for problem
    and/or violent, 218–220
  number of HIV positive,
    126
  roles adopted by, 198–201
  safety issues for, 158, 205,
    207–210, 218–224, 401
  state prison, characteristics
    of, 190–192
  subculture of, 197–205, 216
  sub rosa economies of,
    209–210
  suicide, 222–224
  violence initiated by, 205,
    207–210
  wages of, 166–167, 176–177
Innocents/rapos, 200
In re Gault, 96, 298
In re Winship, 96
Intelligence, and crime-
  proneness, 14–15
Intensive Confinement Centers
  (ICCs), 176, 194
Intensive supervision, 26, 73,
  76, 252–254, 378
Intermediate sanctions, 26,
  76–77, 274. *See also* Community corrections
  factors promoting, 377–378

Intermittent supervision, 26, 153, 154
  in jails, 110, *111*
Invisible fences, 385

Jackson, George, 221
Jails
  administration of, 105, 113–115
  annexes to, 119–120, 128
  architecture of, 133–134
  boot camps as alternatives to, 127–130
  capacities of, 106
  definition of, 104–105
  expansion issues of, 117–118, 136
  floor plans/layouts of, 109–113
  functions served by, 105
  funding issues of, 117
  of the future, 132–136
  gender distribution in, 107, *108*
  growth rates for populations of, *12*, 106
  high-use, 109
  history of, 40–44, 103
  as holding facilities, 109
  inmate characteristics, 194–197
  inmate as labor source, 383
  inmate litigation and, 358
  juvenile offenders in, 123–124, 197
  legal liability and, 122
  location issues of, 105, 117–118, 135
  low-use, 109
  makeshift structures as, 118–120
  number of inmates held in, *13*, 105–107
  number of juveniles housed in, *108*
  per-capita incarceration rates by race and ethnicity, *195*
  personnel of, 114–116
  physical plant of, 109–113
  political issues of, 116–117
  privately operated, by facility/contractor, *121*
  as processing facilities, 109
  programs and services in, 124–127
  regional, 131
  satellite, 119–120, 128
  security levels in, 109–113
  standards for, 122–123
  state-run, 131, 138
  suicides in, 123, 207, 222–224
  to house misdemeanants, 76
  types of inmates housed in, 103, 194–195
  unique characteristics of, 104–105

uses of, 107–109
  women-only, 107, *108*, 127, 136
Job training, 21–22
  for jail custody officers, 116
Johnson v. Avery, 93, 344, 350–351
Johnson v. Texas, 367
Judges' role
  in Roman law, 36–37
  in sentencing, 70–71
  in supervising probation, 72
Juries, death penalty and, 70, 80, 364–365
Just deserts, 4, 57–59, 64
Justinian Code, 33, 37–38
Juvenile correctional systems
  attitudes toward, 10–12
  community-based programs in, 297–301
  correctional facilities in, 178–180, 182, 381–382
  diversion programs, 299
  first juvenile court, 297
  gender and, 306–308
  restitution programs, 299–300
  sentencing considerations in, 96–99
  state facilities in, 180, 182
  trying juveniles as adults, 298–299
  wardens and superintendents of, *326–327*
  wilderness/self-reliance programs, 300–301
Juvenile offenders, 54–56
  in adult jails, 123–124, 399–400
  aftercare and, 261–266
  Borstal System for, 55
  characteristics of, 212–218
  conditions of confinement for, 216–218
  future issues of, 398–401
  offenses of, 215–216
  probation and, 261–266
  restitution orders and, 73

Kent v. United States, 97, 298
Killits case, 233
Klass, Polly, 91
Klopfer v. North Carolina, 94–95

Labeling, 23, 285–286, 334
Labor, prison, 159–163
Labor unions
  inmate labor and, 160–162
  of prison staff, 331
La Nuestra Familia (NF), 220–221
Law of criminal justice thermo-dynamics, 375–377
Law libraries for inmates, 351, 357

Law of retaliation. *See lex talionis*
Leadership styles, 316–321
  authoritarian, 316–317
  "big daddy," 318–319
  bureaucratic, 317, 320
  democratic, 317
  idiosyncratic, 318–319, 320
  laissez faire, 317
  "old school," 318
  participative, 319–320
  technocratic, 317–318
Leavenworth Penitentiary, 150, 163
Lee v. Downs, 358–359
Legal assistance for inmates, 350–351
Legal systems, early history of, 32–42
Lemert, Edwin, 285
Lethal gas, states that execute with, *82*
Lethal injection, 78, 387
  states that execute with, *82*
lex talionis, 3–5, 34–35, 303
Liability issues
  for correctional staff, 122, 177, 349–350
  jails and, 122, 356–357, 358
  for probation/parole officers, 353–354
  supervisory or vicarious, 349
Linear design
  of jails, 110, *111*
  of living units, 152–153
Literacy programs, 167
Litigation
  by inmates. *See* Inmate litigation
  history of correctional, 345–347
Lockdown, 220
Lockhart v. Fretwell, 366
Lockups
  police, 130–131
  suicides in, 224
Lombroso, Cesare, 14, 56–57
Low-security federal prisons, 164–165
Lynds, Captain Elam, 52

McGregor's X and Y theories, 333–334
Maconochie, Alexander, 50–51, 53
McVeigh, Timothy, 79
Management of corrections programs. *See also* Admin-istration of corrections programs
  by unit, 222, 329, 330
  characteristics of wardens, superintendents, 321–329
  future issues of, 335–337
  inmate management styles, 333–334
  leadership styles, 316–321

recommendations for future managers, 336–340
tasks involved in, 330–333
total quality management concept and, 335
versus administration of, 312–313
Mandatory sentencing, 88–91, 375–376
Manis v. Corrections Corporation of America, 350
Manson, Charles, 267, 268
Mapp v. Ohio, 94
Maricopa County (Arizona) jail, 119, 120
Maximum-security prisons, 26, 155–156
Maximum-security units, 218–220
Maximum terms of imprisonment, 86
Media coverage of crime-related news, 11
Medical care, 164, 356–357
for female prison inmates, 392
in future correctional facilities, 368–369
in jails, 123, 125
Medical Center for Federal Prisoners, at Springfield (Missouri), 164
Medical model
of crime, 25, 57
of prison treatment programs, 148–149
Medium-security prisons, 26, 156–157
Mempa v. Rhay, 239, 353, 354
Mental age of offenders, 69
Merton, Robert K., 21–22
Metropolitan Correctional Centers/Detention Centers (MCC/MDC), 164, 165
at New York City, 356
at San Diego, 114
gender/race/ethnicity in, 196–197
Mexican Mafia (EME), 220–221
Minimum-security prisons, 26, 157–158
Minimum terms of imprisonment, 86
Minnesota Multiphasic Personality Inventory (MMPI), 149
Minnesota sentencing guidelines, 87–88
Minority groups. *See specific groups*
Misdemeanors, 66, 75–76, 238, 258
Mitigating circumstances, 80, 235, 364–365
Modified linear-design living units, 153
Monitoring devices. *See* Electronic monitoring

Monoamine oxidase (MAO) blood levels, crime-proneness and, 15
Monroe County (New York) Penitentiary, 54–55
Monroe v. Pape, 347
Montesquieu, 42–43
Morales v. Turman, 179
Morrisey v. Brewer, 248, 353–354
Murder
first-degree, 77
juvenile offenders and, 97–98
number of death-row inmates convicted of, 82
plea bargaining and, 85
Murton, Tom, 32, 43, 319, 333

National Institute of Corrections Model Probation Client Classification and Case Management System, 253
National Institute of Corrections (NIC), 149
National Institute of Drug Abuse (NIDA), 167
National Prison Association, 53–54, 56
National Probation Association, 233
Nation of Islam (Black Muslim), 211, 347
Native Americans
in federal prisons, 188, *189*
in jails, 197
in juvenile facilities, 213–214
Neck verse, 232
Nelson v. Heyne, 179
Net widening, 276–277
diversion programs and, 288
electronic monitoring and, 297
New generation jails, 111–113, 132, 135, *137*
New York City Metropolitan Correctional Center, 356
New York House of Refuge, 178
New York System. *See* Auburn System
NIMBY (Not In My Back Yard), 118, 135, 283
Nuestra Familia (NF), 220–221

Oakdale Federal Detention Center (Louisiana), 212
Open-campus correctional institutions, 157
Operant conditioning, 19
Organized crime, 74, 76
Ossining Prison (Sing Sing), 49, 50
Outward Bound, 182, 300–301
Overcrowding, 4, 11, 132
administrators approach to, 332
causes of crisis in, 406–407

community corrections as alternative to, 274
infectious diseases and, 395–398
inmate litigation on, 355
intermediate sanctions resulting from, 377–379
jail boot camps to reduce, 128
in jails, 106–107, 118–120
in juvenile facilities, 216
physical violence and, 209
statistics on, 172–173, *174–175,* 406

Pacific Islanders, in jails, 196, 197
Pains of imprisonment, 20–21, 202, 203, 224
Panopticon (inspection house), 45
Parchman State Prison (Mississippi), 362
Parole, 241–249
ABA recommendations on, 237
administration of, 242–247
chemical therapies and, 16
as community-based program, 25
conditions of, 245
definition of, 241
eligibility date, 243
of the future, 267–269
future issues of, 379
gender/race/ethnicity and, 257–258, *260*
good-time credits instead of, 87
intensive supervision of, 252–254, 378
for juvenile offenders, 261–266
length of supervision, 245, 247
litigation regarding, 353–354
medium supervision for, 254
minimum supervision for, 254
number of adults on, 1, 242, 255–256, *258–259*
origins of, 241–242
parole boards and, 243–245
release categories for, 243
return to prison and, 247–249
risk assessment scales for, 245, 246, 253–255
trends in, 259–261
violation of, 247–249
Parole boards, 243–245
Parole officers
career of, 249–255
caseloads of, 251–254, 379
Penal colonies, 41–42, 50–52
of the future, 98, 383–384

Penal farms, 131, 182, 212–213
Penitentiaries, 43–44, 50–56. *See also* Prisons; United States Penitentiaries
Pennsylvania System, 44–47, 52–53
  layout of, *46*, 150, *151*
  living units of, 153
Personnel issues
  in jail staffing, 114–116
  of prison staffing, 330–331
Philadelphia Birth Cohort Study, 7, 59
Physical force, excessive, 360–361
Plea bargaining, 84–85
  PSI reports and, 236
Podular design
  of jails, 111–113, 136
  of living units, 153–154
Police lockups, 130–131
  suicides in, 224
Political criminals, 40
Political riots, 211, 212
Power-based crime theories, 23
Preliminary hearing
  parole, 248
  probation, 239–240
Pre-sentence investigation (PSI) report, 70–71, 91–92, 234–236, 354
Prisoner lawsuits. *See* Inmate litigation
Prison industries. *See* Prison labor
Prison Industry Enhancement Certification Program (PIEC), 161–162
Prisonization, 20, 197–205, 276
  of juvenile offenders, 216
Prison labor, 55–56, 159–163
  future issues of, 382–383
  wages and, 166–167
Prison riots, 57, 210–212, 392, 401–403
Prisons, 143. *See also* Penitentiaries
  alternatives to, in nineteenth century, 50–52
  architecture/design of, 149–158
  Auburn System, 44, 47–50, *48*
  definition of, 143
  early release from, 268–269
  foreign critics of colonial, 52–53
  inmate classification in, 147–149
  inmate management in, 144–149
  living units in, 152–155
  Pennsylvania System, 44–47, 52–53, 150, 151, 153
  population rates for, various years, 59, 242

private, 177
reformation movements and, 50–56
security levels of, 26–27, 155–158
as total institutions, 143–145
for women, 158–159
Prison systems, 142–186
  federal, 163–168
  of the future, 181, 377–388, 403–407
  institutional goals of, 144–146
  juvenile, 178–180, 182
  state, 168–178
Privacy issues, 155, 358–359, 392
Private funding, 278–279
Private jails and prisons. *See* Privatization
Private Sector/Prison Industry Enhancement Certification Program (PS/PIEC), 161–162
Privatization
  of corrections facilities, 11
  of executions, 387
  of jails, 120–122
  of juvenile facilities, 180, 212–213
  liability issues and, 122, 177, 349–350
  of prisons, 177, 181
Probation, 230–270
  ABA recommendations on, 237, 238
  absconded, 240
  add-ons, 9, 73, 132, 378
  administration of, 234–238
  authority for, by state, *234, 265*
  chemical therapies as part of, 16
  as community-based corrections program, 25
  conditions of, 72–73, 236–237
  definition of, 71–73, 234
  eligibility for, 234
  for felony offenders, 76, 238, 258
  of the future, 267–269
  gender/race/ethnicity of adults on, 257–258, 260
  history of, 230–233
  informal, 72
  intensive supervision of, 26, 73, 76, 252–254, 378
  as judicial function, 72
  laws and litigation regarding, 353–354
  medium supervision for, 254
  minimum supervision for, 254
  for misdemeanors, 76, 238, 258
  number of adults on, 1, 71, 255, *256–257*

outcomes for, 239
preliminary hearings and, 238–240
revocation process, 238–241
risk classification instruments for, 253–255
shock, 26, 76, 127, 176
trends in, 259–261
violation of, 238–241
Probation officers
  career of, 249–255
  caseloads of, 251–254, 379
  collection of restitution orders and, 73
  combined with parolee supervision, *249*
  PSI report and, 234
Probation parole officers (PPOs), 249–255
Proof, standards of, 67, 68, 70, 96
Property offenses
  by women, 194
  of federal prisoners, 188, *190*
  of state prisoners, *192*
Protective custody unit (PCU), 219–220
Public attitudes, 8, 10–12, 98
Public-order offenses
  of federal prisoners, 188, *190*
  of state prisoners, *192*
Public-private partnership, 120–122
Public safety, community corrections and, 277, 304–305
Pugh v. Locke, 345
Punishment
  community service as, 293
  for crimes not yet committed, 380
  economic sanctions as, 288–291
  extrainstitutional, 275
  history of, 31–63
  imprisonment binge and, 59, 60, 98, 225
  philosophies of, 2–10, 374–376
  treatment combined with, 305–306

Quay Adult Internal Management System, 149

Race and ethnicity
  in capital punishment debate, 83
  crime-proneness and, 15
  of federal prisoners, 188, *189*
  inmate subculture and, 205
  IQ scores and, 15
  of jail inmates, 124, *195*
  juvenile facilities and, 213–214
  juvenile probationers and, 265–266

per-capita incarceration rates by, *193*
prison gangs and, 220–222
of prison guards, *390–391*
in prison riots, 211–212, 392, 401–403
in prisons of the future, 223, 388–392
probability of incarceration and, 1, 187–188, 389
probationers and, 257–260
in sentencing guidelines, 88
of state prisoners, 190, *191*
Race riots, 211–212, 392
Racism, institutionalized, 389–390
Racketeering Influenced Corrupt Organizations (RICO) statutes, 74, 290
Radial-design prison, 150, *151*
Ragen, Joseph E., 318
Rage riots, 211–212
Rapos/innocents, 200
Reception and diagnostic units, 180, 212–213
Recidivism, 9, 77, 236
  community corrections and, 280–282
Reconciliation rituals, 32–34
Reentry programs, 282–285
Reformation, as correctional philosophy, 6
Reformatories, early, 54–56
Reform movements, 404–405
Rehabilitation, 4–7, 57, 65
Reintegration, 8–9, 57, 277–278, 308
Release on one's own recognizance (ROR), 231–232
Remote/indirect supervision, 153, 154
in jails, 110–111
Repeat offenders, 9, 59, 77, 90–91
Reprieve, judicial, 231–232
Restitution, 290–291
  as additional penalty for felonies, *306*
  as condition of probation, 9, 73
  as correctional philosophy, 9
  juvenile offenders and, 299
  in prehistoric context, 32–34
  as sentencing goal, 65
Restorative justice, 9–10, 32–34
  juvenile offenders and, 266
Retribution, 3–5, 64, 374–376
  victims and, 303–304
Revenge, blood, 33–34
Revised Oregon probation screening instrument, 255
Revocation hearing
  parole, 248–249, 354
  probation, 240–241, 353
Rhodes v. Chapman, 356
Richardson et al. v. McKnight, 350

Riker's Island (New York City), 109
Riots and prison uprisings, 57, 210–212, 392, 401–403
Risk-screening instruments, 245–246, 253–255
Role adaptations
  in prisons and jails, 198–201
  in women's prisons, 203–204
Rotten apple sentiment, 7
Ruffin v. Commonwealth, 345
Ruiz v. Estelle, 222, 361
Rush, Benjamin, 44

Safety
  inmate, 158, 205, 207–210, 218–224, 401
  of the public, 277, 304–305
St. Bridget's Well, 41
Salaries and wages
  in community-based corrections, 302
  of correctional counselors, 206
  of correctional officers, 146–147
  of inmates, 166–167, 176–177
  of probation and parole officers, 250
  of wardens and superintendents, 328
Salient Factor Score, 255
Sanders v. United States, 347
Santa Fe prison riot, 210–212, 221
Satellite jails, 119–120, 128
Satellite prison camps, 164, 165
Screening instruments, 245–246, 253–255
Section 1983 lawsuits, 347. *See also* Civil rights litigation
Security levels, 157
  in jails, 109–113, 134–135
  in prisons, 155–158, 165
Segregation
  by age or gender, 43, 158
  punitive/disciplinary, 219–220
Selective incapacitation, 7–8, 59
Self-help programs, as diversion, 287
Self-reliance programs, 300–301
Sentencing, 64–101
  available options in, 71–83
  concurrent, 84
  consecutive, 84
  date setting for, 70
  death penalty, 77–83
  determinate, 86–87
  discretionary powers in, 87, 88
  enhancements, 90
  for felonies, 76–77, 88–90

fines and forfeitures, 66, 74–75, 289–290, *306*
genetic engineering, 98
goals of, 64–65
guidelines, 87–89, 374
indeterminate, 86
judge and jury's role in, 70–71
for juvenile offenders, 96–99
legislative role in, 65–70
mandatory, 88–91
microchip implants, 99
for misdemeanors, 75–76
plea bargaining and, 84–85
pre-sentence investigation report, 70–71, 91–92, 234–236, 354
probation, 71–73
probation revocation hearing and, 241
race and ethnicity in, 88
strategies for, 86–91
three-strikes, 90–91, 384
time and time served, 83–85
truth in sentencing law, 86, 189
weekend, 118
Sentencing Reform Act of 1984 (truth in sentencing), 86, 189
Sex offenders
  castration proposals for, 98
  hormonal treatments for, 16
  impact on corrections, 380
  notification laws, 380
  state prison treatment programs, 177–178
Sex and prison life, 200, 204
Shock incarceration, 26, 76, 127, 176
Sindicato Nuevo Mexico, 221
Smoke-free environments, inmate litigation on, 359–360
Social control theorists, 21, 22
Social disorganization, 18–19, 389
Social forces, as cause of crime, 18–22
Social learning theory, 19–20
Social organization of prisons and jails, 201–204
Social sanitation, 7
Socioeconomic status
  crime-proneness and, 14–15
  jail inmates and, 105, 124
  in sentencing guidelines, 88
  underclass, 105, 124, 223
Solitary confinement, 157, 219–220
  in Pennsylvania System, 44–45, 47
Southern Poverty Law Center, 346, 359
Speedy trials, 94–95
Spencer, Herbert, 14
Split sentences, 26

Staff burnout, 146, 250, 280, 283–284, 302
Stanford v. Kentucky, 99
Staten Island Day-Fine Project, 74–75
State prison systems, 168–178
design and rates capacities of, *174–175*
facilities profile of, 170–173
growth of, 168–169
non-U.S. citizens in, 191
number of facilities, *171*
number of persons held in, *13, 168–169, 172–173*
offense types in, 191–192
programs of, 173, 176–178
State-raised youths, 216, 394
State-run jails, 131, 138, 381
Stateville (Illinois) Penitentiary, 205, 318
Stigmatization, 9, 275–276, 278, 286
Street gangs, prison gangs and, 205, 220–222
Subculture, 20–21
of jails and prisons, 197–205
of juvenile facilities, 216
of violence, 389
Sub rosa inmate economy, 209–210, 221
Suicide
by juvenile offenders, 124, 217, 399
in jails, 123, 207, 222–224
to avoid banishment, 34
Sullivan v. Louisiana, 367
Supervisory liability, 349
Survival programs, 300–301
Sutherland, Edwin H., 18–19

Technical violation, 238–239, 378
Technology and corrections, 384–386. *See also* Electronic monitoring
Tennessee
anti-jailhouse lawyer regulations of, 93
Class X Felony Act of, 88
public caning legislation and, 97
Texas Department of Criminal Justice, 320, 321
Texas Syndicate (TS), 220–221
Theory X and Y management styles, 333–334
Three strikes legislation, 90–91, 384
Timm v. Gunter, 358–359
Token economies, 17
Torts, 37, 347
Townsend v. Sain, 347

Training schools, 182, 212
Treatment, 145, 147, *306*
Truth in sentencing law, 86, 189
Tuberculosis, 392, 398
Turner v. Safley, 368

Underclass, 105, 124, 223
UNICOR, 162, 164, 166
United States Penitentiaries (USPs), 164, 166
at Atlanta (Georgia), 163, 166, 212
at Florence (Colorado), 156, 166
at Leavenworth (Kansas), 150, 163, 166
at Marion (Illinois), 157
United States v. Birnbaum, 234
United States v. Marion, 94–95
United States v. Russell, 70
Unit management, 222, 329, 330
U.S. Corrections Corp., 177
U.S. Parole Commission's Salient Factor Score, 255

Victimization
economic, 209–210
inmate initiated, 205, 207–210, 401
psychological, 208–208
Victim-offender confrontation programs, 20, 26
Victims
assistance programs, 75
role in punishment, 20, 26, 303–304
victim impact statement (VIS), 235
Violation
of parole, 247–249
of probation, 238–241
Violence
inmate-on-inmate, 205, 207–210, 401
inmate-on-staff, 207–208, 401
news media coverage of, 11
riots and disturbances, 210–212
subcultures of, 20–21
Violent offenses
by women, 194
of federal prisoners, 188, *190*
of state prisoners, *192*
VisionQuest, 182, 300–301
Vocational training programs
at federal facilities, 167
at state facilities, 176
Volstead Act, 163
Volunteers, prison, 145

Wackenhut Corrections Corp., 177
Wages. *See* Salaries and wages
Wardens and superintendents. *See also* Administration of corrections programs
Captain Elam Lynds, 52
as a career, 328
first, 47
gender/race/ethnicity of, 323, *324–327*
George Beto, 320, 321
Joseph E. Ragen, 318
Mary Belle Harris, 322
Tom Murton, 32, 43, 319, 333
Zebulon Reed Brockway, 54–56
War on Drugs, impact of, 188–189
War on Poverty, 21–22
Weber, Max, 315
Weekend sentences, 118, 128
Western State Penitentiary (Pittsburgh), 45
Whites. *See also* Race and ethnicity
on death row, 83
jail incarceration rates for, *195*
in juvenile facilities, 213–214
odds of going to prison, 1
on parole, 258
in prisons, 188, *189,* 388–389
on probation, 257
White supremacist groups, 220–221
Wilderness programs, 182, 300–301
Wines, Enoch Cobb, 53–54
Wisconsin System (risk-management instrument), 253
Wolfgang, Marvin, 7, 59
Women. *See also* Female inmates; Gender
in the correctional workplace, 403–404
incarceration rates for, 168–170
as prison administrators, 322, 323, *324–327*
in prisons of the future, 223
probability of incarceration and, 187–188
special needs of, 392–393
Wong Sun v. United States, 94
Workhouses, 41, 131
Writ of habeas corpus, 94, 347–350, 355
Writ writers, 92, 351, 352